DATE DUE

OC 13 '95			
JY 10 '97			
MY 10 '99			
OC 13 04			
NO 8 04			
MY 9 '06			

DEMCO 38-296

AIDS Law Today

AIDS Law Today
A New Guide for the Public

Edited by   Scott Burris

Harlon L. Dalton

Judith Leonie Miller

and the

Yale AIDS

Law Project

Yale University Press
New Haven & London

The Yale AIDS Law Project is composed of members of the Yale Law School community who joined together to produce this book. The Project is not a formal part of the university and has not been endorsed by it. Opinions expressed by the authors of the various chapters are their own and do not necessarily reflect the opinions of members of the Project.

Chapter 8, "Drug Dependency and HIV," is adapted from an article entitled "The Interconnected Epidemics of Drug Dependency and AIDS," that appeared in volume 26 of the *Harvard Civil Rights-Civil Liberties Law Review,* and is published here with permission.

Designed by Deborah Dutton.
Set in Times Roman type by Rainsford Type, Danbury, Connecticut.
Printed in the United States of America by Vail-Ballou Press, Binghamton, New York.

Library of Congress Cataloging-in-Publication Data
AIDS law today : a new guide for the public / edited by Scott Burris . . . [et al.].—[2nd ed.]
   p. cm.
  Includes index.
   ISBN 0-300-05505-6 (cloth : alk. paper). — ISBN 0-300-05512-9 (paper : alk. paper)
   1. AIDS (Disease)—Law and legislation—United States. 2. AIDS (Disease)—United States. I. Burris, Scott.
KF3803.A54A943 1992
344.73′04369792—dc20
[347.3044369792]
                        92-35572
                        CIP

A catalogue record for this book is available from the British Library.

The paper in this book meets the guidelines for permanence and durability of the Committee on Production Guidelines for Book Longevity of the Council on Library Resources.
10 9 8 7 6 5 4 3 2 1

Contents

Preface

The Editors

Five years ago, as *AIDS and the Law: A Guide for the Public* went to press, there were only a handful of judicial decisions involving HIV. Harlon Dalton, looking ahead in his preface, expressed a guarded optimism for the legal system's ability to do justice in the rush of cases inevitably to come. In the intervening years, HIV has become the most litigated of diseases. The system's response has been complex, sometimes heartening and more than sometimes disappointing.

We had hoped that the development of HIV law would be guided by (the exercise of) humane imagination, a necessary empathy on the part of the lawmaking elite for the very different experiences of people living with HIV, in poverty, and without power. More than a few judges have heard the voices of difference and have used the law to tie the experiences of the marginalized to our national aspirations for justice and equality. Others, unsurprisingly, have not. In the last few years, we have seen how some judges seem to have learned their trade from Dickens, if not Kafka.

We had hoped that the law would aspire to lead the public past our fears. Sometimes it has, but too often a "tabloid imagination" has overtaken both judicial humanity and common sense.

We aspire to be a nation of laws, not men [*sic*], but in the legal system, as the Rodney King verdict shows again, it does matter who you are. Some jurists are blind to race, caste, and sexual preference, but not all of them are.

We had hoped that the law could serve to unravel complicated issues and help us face hard choices straightforwardly. We find that it has—again, *sometimes*—but we find also that the law's focus on individual claims, necessarily defined to fit preexisting legal niches, can orphan the larger issues for which no niches yet exist in the law. Access to health care, for example, is a fundamental social issue, and not just for people with HIV. Yet our legal system, for arbitrary reasons rooted deep in our legal history, has no niche called "right to health care," and consequently addresses access-to-care issues in the most strained, indirect, and incomplete way. In the conversation about ourselves that is the law, people with the "wrong" legal needs are silenced, and all of us are the poorer for the loss of their voices.

Taking into account the inherent deficiencies of the law, the impact of an increasingly diffident judiciary, the torpor of a hobbled Congress, and the malign neglect of two presidents, we still retain the shreds of our optimism, at least insofar as we feel that change is our responsibility, and even within our power as citizens. Warren Rudman, retiring from the Senate, recently reminded us that, however fashionable it may be to blame the system, we get the laws we deserve. In this narrow sense we stand ready to blame the victim, so long as it is recognized that every one of us is the victim of our collective failure to push our leaders to do more and better. We begin to hope that citizen apathy itself may be growing tired and that communities will grasp the changes that are within their reach.

At the same time, we recognize that lots of people in America do not get the laws they deserve. For many of us, the ability to effect change is more real in theory than in practice. We are disabled from the start from active participation in the legal management of our lives and are more likely to view the law as a source of oppression than a font of protection. Long before HIV entered the scene, we were disdained, marginalized, shunted aside. The system cannot be working until all of us have change within our reach.

In *AIDS and the Law: A Guide for the Public*, we included several chapters that focused on especially marginalized groups for whom HIV is yet another burden. Now, some five years later, it has become apparent that the margin has become the center. One cannot talk meaningfully about AIDS without confronting issues of race, class, gender, and sexual orientation. These concerns are not exceptions, add-ons, or additional considerations. They are, in the truest sense, the thing itself. For that reason, we have sought to treat them as integral aspects of everything we address.

In fact, what began as a second edition has become a new book. Chapters have been added on privacy, reproduction and parenting issues, and criminal law. Most of the other chapters have been completely rethought and rewritten to address changes in the structure of the legal issues. The chapter on the military has grown, with a new author, to cover the response of the federal government as a whole. Two chapters on health care issues have been combined into a comprehensive treatment of HIV in the provider-patient relationship. Chapters on prisons and employ-ment discrimination have grown to accommodate new statutes and the flood of cases.

If we sound like "proud parents," then at least one thing hasn't changed.

Preface to *AIDS and the Law: A Guide for the Public* (1987)

Harlon L. Dalton

This book is about *law*. It is not, however, aimed exclusively (or even primarily) at those who are steeped in the law. Rather, it is meant for whoever has a professional need to come to grips with the legal issues spawned by the HIV epidemic—for educators, counselors, legislators, policymakers, law enforcement and corrections officials, public health officials, health care providers, social service providers, research scientists, employers, employee representatives, insurers, providers of goods and services, social workers, social scientists, social activists, representatives of interest groups, the staffs of drug treatment programs, members of AIDS support groups, and, of course, lawyers for any and all of the above.

Ever since its spontaneous generation eighteen months ago when several law students and faculty expressed to each other the desire to do something about AIDS, the Yale AIDS Law Project has had one overriding goal: to sift through the law as it relates to AIDS and to communicate what we find to the people who most need to understand the law's sweep. To that end, we have abandoned, in large measure, the private language that serves to separate us legal types from the great unwashed. Figuring out how to speak plain English, without sacrificing precision or sophistication, has not, however, been easy. It is therefore not surprising that talking about how to talk about law quickly became a major focus of the semester-long AIDS law seminar that sprang up as an adjunct to the project. (We also focused on the difficulties inherent in writing about issues that are contemporaneous, ever-changing, and deeply political.) To ease our "translation" burden, we intentionally solicited authors who, in addition to expertise, had demonstrated the ability to communicate effectively with non-lawyers. Even so, throughout the editorial process the student editors engaged the authors in a continuing dialogue regarding whether the contours of the law, and its shadings as well, had been conveyed in a way that was accessible to our target audience.

Taken as a whole, *AIDS and the Law* reflects the unique challenge the AIDS epidemic poses for our legal system. In general, the law presupposes that we are rational, self-regarding beings. Its frequent invocation of the "reasonable person" standard suggests, at a minimum, a reluctance to reward or accommodate irrationality. Efforts to regulate conduct through incentives presuppose that people and organizations rationally calculate their self-interest. And even though the law occasionally recognizes (in, for example, statutes permitting consumers to rescind door-to-door sales transactions within a set number of days) that in some circumstances our rational will can be overborne, such enactments look rather like the exceptions that prove the rule.

AIDS stands all that on its head; or, if not AIDS, then the secondary epidemic of fear sometimes labeled AFRAIDS. Increasingly, the law is asked to mediate or resolve conflicts in which at least some of the parties are so consumed by fear as to be incapable of exercising rational judgment. Not infrequently, those tormented by fear disavow any obligation to be rational. "I don't care if the odds are a million to one, I don't want to take the chance." "I know it's crazy, but . . . " Equally unreachable are people who dispose of that which is fearful by simply denying its existence. "If I'm gonna get it I'm gonna get it and there is nothing I can do about it."

Not only do the fears engendered by AIDS strip people of their capacity to be rational; the fears themselves have a deeply irrational element. No matter how rooted they are in common sense and informed opinion, they inevitably tap into other fears that are deep-seated and largely pre-rational: fear of sex; fear of the unclean; fear of the uncontrollable; and fear of death. In the first category, I would include both the scariness of our own sexuality and the equally scary fact that we are surrounded by sexual beings, whichever way we turn. In thinking about the second, I am struck by our particular culture's discomfort with disease and, more broadly, with physical abnormality. And of course, for many, attitudes toward sex and toward the unclean overlap.

Third, AIDS anxiety taps into our previously stilled suspicions that, despite our fervent wishes, science cannot save us from random and arbitrary pain and dissolution. In a sense, AIDS stands as a surrogate for all the risks and uncertainties that attend living in a technologically advanced and spiritually desolate society. We can remove asbestos, ignore acid rain or radon, and keep switching from one artificial sweetener to another. But we can't seem to make AIDS go away, either through mental gymnastics or the magic of science. And then there is death.

Given this psychic assault, the AIDS epidemic challenges the law to face up to our irrational as well as our rational selves; to structure procedures and fashion rules that, simultaneously, give vent to our fears and life to our aspirations. If the law is to be effective in dealing with the conflicts and turmoil generated by this dread disease, we must learn to console the inconsolate and convince the incredulous. We cannot pretend that we are any less complicated or any more Mr. Spock-like than we truly are.

Now for the good news. In putting together this book, I have become convinced (much to my surprise) that our legal system is uniquely suited to the task at hand. My optimism springs from two rather curious, and somewhat contradictory, features of the system: its tendency to reduce to a formula the most passionate of concerns and its tendency to promote confrontation. The first feature is familiar to anyone who has turned to the courts for vindication on a matter of some importance and been forced to transmogrify her concerns into a stylized "cause of action" with preset "elements" that may resemble only faintly the precipitating real-world event. The second is familiar to anyone who has experienced the adversarial side of the adversary system. Despite their drawbacks when viewed from any number of perspectives, these features in tandem hold out the promise of a sane and sensitive response to the fallout from AIDS.

The law's formulaic quality means, among other things, that we need not reinvent the wheel to deal with AIDS-related legal issues. As chapter after chapter makes clear, the institutional and conceptual framework for dealing with such issues already exists; the principles and procedures that will guide decision-making are, for the most part, already in place. Analogous situations abound, from cases involving sexual transmission of genital herpes to attempts to quarantine persons with bubonic plague; from cases involving schoolchildren infected with the hepatitis B virus to efforts to round up prostitutes to stem the spread of syphilis. Perhaps the most important guiding light is the explosion of statutes and cases addressing discrimination against the disabled and against people who are perceived as disabled. The tools are there.

Despite its enormous benefits, reasoning from the old to the new has a major downside, especially as respects AIDS issues. For no matter what the analogy, AIDS is viewed by most people as significantly different. The practical differences—difficulty of transmission, prospects for treatment and cure, available safeguards, for example—can be apprehended and taken account of by the law with relative ease. The *emotional* differences are much trickier. In rounding off the edges, in rendering the unique ordinary so as to achieve predictability and order, our legal system can sometimes be deaf to the true anguish that propels people to turn to it in the first place. We cannot let that happen.

Deafness, silence, and denial, by people and by institutions, can lead only to greater pain for all concerned. In other areas, we can count on anger dissipating and fear subsiding as people get drawn along through the legal process. That simply won't happen with AIDS. Fears left unattended will erupt eventually, in settings we can't control and with a fury beyond any we anticipate. We must therefore use the law to promote recognition rather than denial; to encourage people to air their fears and to defend them if possible; to give the fearful the courtesy of responding to their fears, if only by laying out what we find compelling on the other side.

This is where the second peculiar feature of our legal system comes into play—the centrality of confrontation. So long as one "combatant" desires to engage, the silence will be broken. Whether we envision a seropositive employee suing an employer bent on dismissal or a fearful co-worker suing to protect the workplace, the law provides a mechanism for all voices to be heard. Confrontation can be and often is wounding; it can also be healing. Our task is clear. We must think creatively about ways of using confrontation to promote reconciliation.

Finally, we should remember that just as the law frames society's response to the AIDS epidemic, the society as a whole shapes the law. Like it or not, we must decide what kind of society we will be: mean-spirited, shortsighted, and judgmental or compassionate, clearheaded, and accepting. In the end, society will determine where the burdens of AIDS—social, financial, and emotional—will fall. We can make the choice consciously and purposely, or we can make it by indirection or default, but make it we will. We can refashion our legal rules—reporting requirements, antibody-screening provisions, confidentiality laws, antidiscrimination laws, definitions of terms such as *handicap,* insurance regulations, quarantine measures, and the like—to isolate and segregate the people most likely to contract and spread AIDS. Or we can work to ensure that they remain among us, for as long as they are able, free of the weight of our anxieties and fears.

If instead of choosing we simply let matters drift, we will trend, inevitably, in the direction of isolation, segregation, and repression. After all, the pressure to contain AIDS is enormous, and though we can't quite get at the disease, we *can* get at the people we think are most likely to spread it. Gay and bisexual men and intravenous drug users are the targets of massive societal disapproval quite apart from AIDS and are thus in a uniquely poor position to hold off the fearful majority. Moreover, homophobia, racism, and the current climate of antidrug mindlessness put those who speak on behalf of such persons at considerable political and social risk. Without a massive, purposeful, and broadly supported effort by the larger society to rein in its worst impulses, the law will surely come to rest heavily upon those who already suffer most.

Such an effort requires healthy doses of what my former colleague Charles

Black has labeled "humane imagination," the ability to comprehend, however dimly, how life is lived by people very different from ourselves. We must struggle to see through the eyes and feel with the hearts of those whom AIDS is most likely to fell. We must strive to appreciate how dreadful it is to wait for the disease to make its awful appearance, thinking constantly of the disintegration it promises; and how more dreadful still when the nightmare becomes a waking reality. If only we could imagine how crushing it is to the spirit to be held at arm's length when what it desires most is society's embrace.

Connecting up with the experiences of others is never easy, especially when they engender fear or loathing in us. I sometimes despair when I realize that many of his neighbors have not been able to bridge the gap to Ryan White, a sweet-faced Midwestern boy with a ready smile and a winning way. What hope is there, then, that the fearful majority will empathize with Ryan's black and brown big-city counterparts, with adults who stick needles in their arms, or with men who engage in sodomy with other men? The prospects are grim, until and unless we, as a people, take fear and loathing seriously, lance it where possible, and where not, express openly our reasons for siding with those who are dreaded. Admittedly, this is a prescription for short-term pain, but if we want the society that emerges from the AIDS epidemic to be one we can be proud of, we have little choice in the matter.

At a meeting of the Yale AIDS Law Project, called to recruit new blood for the final push toward publication of this book, I rather proudly began to tick off the incredible array of areas the book would cover. One newcomer interjected, quite innocently, "Do you have a chapter on the licensing of new drugs?" It was an excellent question, one that should have gladdened the Mr. Chips in me. In truth, my initial reaction was mild embarrassment that in soliciting manuscripts fifteen months earlier, we had not anticipated how important the issue would become, with the advent of potentially ameliorative drugs such as AZT and DDC. Such are the trials of trying to produce a book about an epidemic when its collateral consequences continue to multiply.

Quite apart from the difficulties of foresight, we doubtless have failed to address issues that even we, upon reflection, may agree are as important as the ones we covered. I am particularly chagrined at not having included a chapter on the impact of AIDS on this nation's Latino communities. I suspect that it, like the chapter we did include on Blacks and AIDS, would have significantly enriched the overall enterprise. As time goes on, I know that I will experience other regrets.

Even so, I think you will agree that the scope and reach of this book is remarkable. Some of the topics we cover ("Traditional Public Health Strategies," "AIDS in the Workplace," and "Insurance," for example) are addressed elsewhere, but usually in less depth and with a specialized audience in mind. Other chapters ("Prostitution as a Public Health Issue," "The Military," "Prisons," and "Intravenous Drug Abusers," for example) stand alone in the field and would by themselves justify this book. Some chapters ("Schoolchildren with AIDS," "Housing Issues," and "Torts," for example) grapple directly with legal issues—with cases, statutes, and administrative regulations. Other chapters provide much-needed context: historical ("A Historical Perspective"), cultural ("Physicians versus Lawyers: A Conflict of Cultures") and social ("The Black Community," "The Lesbian and Gay Community"). Finally, some who have previewed the book report that the opening two chapters, taken together, are among the most comprehensive, and comprehensible, treatments of medical issues available anywhere. If I sound like a "proud papa," at least it is with good reason.

Acknowledgments

We are grateful to the many people and institutions that have provided intellectual, financial, spiritual, and physical support through two books. We are greatly indebted to Yale Law School and its dean, Guido Calabresi, and to Temple Law School and Dean Robert Reinstein. Scott Burris' work on this volume was generously supported by a research grant from Temple Law School.

Many individuals deserve special mention. Ruth Harlow worked on *AIDS and the Law: A Guide for the Public* as a Yale law student and, now as staff attorney at the ACLU's AIDS and Civil Liberties Project, helped edit chapter 9 for this book. Several students at Temple Law School helped with research, cite-checking, and proofreading. Our thanks go to Ann Butchart, Robin Chodak, William F. Kullman, Dino Privitera, Matthew Roazen, and Magdalena Schardt. Walter Bross, a volunteer at the ACLU in Philadelphia, did extensive background research on state HIV statutes.

Jill Tobey once again coordinated the production of the manuscript and once again did so with intelligence, dedication, and an attitude. Geraldine Perillo saved us several times. Gladys Washington at Temple entered thousands of corrections without complaint.

We thank all the members of the first Yale AIDS Law Project whose work on *AIDS and the Law* continues to bear fruit. They include Paul Bird, Rosann Bocciarelli, Rhonda Brown, Sabina Bruckner, Mark Emerson Collins, Geoffrey B. Dryvynsyde, David Huebner, Alexander Kaplan, Elizabeth A. Leiman, Sandra E. Lundy, Julia Mahoney, Louise Melling, Andrea M. Mercado, Nina Morais, Tanina Rostain, John Steiner, Malcolm Stewart, Anthony Thomas, Lee Weinberg, Catherine Weiss, and Judith B. White. The high standards set in *AIDS and the Law* by our commanding copy editor Catherine Iino continued to daunt us.

Finally, we are extremely grateful to Haesun Burris-Lee, Sung-Hey Lee, Barbara Safriet, and Jill Strawn.

I Background

1 A Little Law for Non-Lawyers

Scott Burris

We, the People, are the source of law in this democracy. In the Constitution, we have organized our form of government. Through our elected representatives, we make the law. We elect the judges (or elect the people who select the judges) who interpret the law. But when this theory becomes practice, law can seem just as unfamiliar as our sick bodies or our nonstarting cars. If the legal system embodies many fine ideas about how we should live together—ideas we can all understand—it is also a Byzantine tangle of rules giving other people power over our lives.

This book is an attempt to explain how the law deals with the many social conflicts generated by Acquired Immune Deficiency Syndrome (AIDS). The epidemic poses challenges to our ideals of fairness, challenges that are being played out according to legal rules most of us don't know, in a legal system most of us don't understand. The legal system cannot be made simple, but we have the right to demand of lawyers, just as we demand of mechanics or doctors or anyone else in whom we place our trust, that they apply their special knowledge in conformity with our values and desires. This book will not teach you how to be the mechanic; we commend it to you rather as a kind of consumer report, a guide to the right questions.

Within the first day or two of law school, the new student is introduced to the *hypothetical,* a teaching tool best analogized to the medical student's cadaver. A hypothetical is a story (or, as lawyers say, *fact pattern*) under whose flaccid skin the legal novice is challenged to discover a world of elaborate legal relations. I will adopt that device here, to illustrate several of the most important rules and practices of our legal system.

The hypothetical: Sally is ten years old. Three years ago, she was injured in a car accident. Through an emergency blood transfusion, she was infected with Human

3

Immunodeficiency Virus (HIV), the virus associated with AIDS, and last year she was diagnosed as having AIDS. First because of her injuries, and then because of various illnesses related to her AIDS, she has not attended school since the accident. Recently, however, she has been doing better, and her doctors found her healthy enough to enroll. Following guidelines developed by the federal Centers for Disease Control (CDC) and adopted by the state department of health, the principal of Sally's public school appointed a panel of local doctors and educators to assess her placement.

The guidelines were premised on the medical judgment that AIDS may be spread only by intimate transmission of infected bodily fluid, especially blood and semen, into a healthy person's bloodstream—something exceedingly unlikely to occur in the casual interaction of school children. The panel's job was to make sure that Sally had no physical or behavioral problems—such as open sores or a tendency to biting or incontinence—that would create an unusual risk that her fluids would infect another child. The panel found Sally to be well adjusted and well behaved, with an understanding of her disease and the precautions necessary to avoid its transmission. Because she presented no meaningful danger to other children according to the guidelines, it approved her placement in a regular fifth-grade class. The principal ordered her enrolled.

The guidelines stressed the need for confidentiality, recommending that only the principal and the child's teacher be informed of her AIDS. Unfortunately, Sally's teacher did not take the news well, and immediately called his union representative and several friends. Word spread, and within a few days, the entire community was upset and divided. A large minority of parents claimed Sally had no right to be in school and threatened a boycott if she attended. After a painful public meeting, the school board voted to overrule the principal. It ordered Sally to be taught, by telephone, at home.

At this point, Sally and her parents have several choices, only one of which is to get involved in a legal battle. Besides simply accepting the school board's decision and devoting their energies to finding other ways to make Sally happy, they might seek to enroll her in private school, or a special school for handicapped children, or a public school in a district following a different policy. They might play the system—call their senator, tell their story to sympathetic reporters, try to enlist the support of local organizations. People are often prepared to give up quite a bit to avoid getting involved in the expense and publicity of a controversial lawsuit.

GETTING A LAWYER

Sally's parents decide to fight the decision head-on, which they probably cannot do without a lawyer. Unless the board quickly changes its mind, the legal bills in a case like Sally's could quickly run into thousands of dollars. In this hypothetical, Sally's parents are of modest means. Sometimes, especially in personal injury cases where high money damages may be awarded, attorneys will work on a contingency basis—that is, for a percentage of whatever the plaintiff eventually wins in lieu of an hourly fee. But Sally's victory would be getting into school, not getting money, so a contingency arrangement is out. Fortunately, Congress has recognized that inability to pay for counsel may prevent people who have a valid reason to sue from doing so, and some federal laws allow courts to award attorney's fees to the plaintiff if she prevails. (The Education for All Handicapped Children Act, a law that may cover Sally's problem, has such a fee provision.)

If Sally cannot pay for a lawyer or find a private attorney willing to bet on her prevailing, she may seek the help of a public interest legal organization. Groups such as the American Civil Liberties Union (ACLU) and the Lambda Legal Defense and Education Fund provide legal services in cases that fall within their areas of concern. Such groups are generally underwritten by foundations and private donors, although they also may receive attorney's fee awards authorized by statute. Because they have only limited resources for achieving their legal goals, they usually take only cases with the potential to make major legal points.

Finally, if Sally is unable to afford or find any other help, she might qualify for legal services for the poor provided by government-funded agencies, bar associations, and even a few law schools. (Some private law firms also commit a certain percentage of their time to cases taken, at no charge, *pro bono publico*—for the public's benefit.) In recent years, however, legal aid has suffered serious budget cutbacks, and demand outstrips supply. To a legal aid office without the staff to handle every case that comes in, Sally's problem might seem less compelling than the problem of a poor family about to be evicted from its home or a social security recipient about to lose his benefits. On the other hand, Sally's case may be quite attractive to a pro bono lawyer: at least it will be exciting and rewarding, and it may even be good advertising.

Sally is lucky: because of its importance, Lee, a local attorney, is willing to take on her case without pay. The ACLU volunteers to help. This does not necessarily mean that Sally will sue the board. Most legal disputes never go that far. For better or for worse, the mere prospect of protracted and expensive litigation is often sufficient to put even a person confident of the justice of her position into a mood for compromise. (Even after a suit is filed, settlement remains high on the agenda; much of the legal maneuvering before trial is aimed as much at bolstering a negotiating position as preparing to win a trial, and two parties can settle a case at any time up until, and sometimes even after, the moment the jury renders its verdict.) The school board, however, lets Lee know that it is dead-set against allowing Sally into school at any time, under any circumstances. It appears that a lawsuit may be needed to get Sally past the schoolhouse door, and her attorney sets about exploring how it should look.

GETTING INTO COURT

Case or Controversy

Courts in this country do not give advice. The board could not simply send a note over to the courthouse asking whether children with AIDS must be allowed into schools. To get before a court, a dispute must present a "case or controversy," a concrete disagreement between two parties who can present it in an adversarial fashion. Sally's case certainly qualifies. But the case must also be *ripe* and it cannot be *moot*. Ripeness and mootness are both concepts having to do with the practical necessity of deciding a case. If Sally's parents were to enroll her in a private school, a court might see no reason to decide the now-theoretical question of whether she should be allowed into a public school she no longer wishes to attend and might dismiss her case as moot. Conversely, if the board were attempting to formulate a policy that, upon its completion, might result in Sally's admission, a court could deem her case unripe, refusing to hear it unless and until the board had finally barred Sally.

Standing

A real case or controversy is not enough. The person who brings the case to court must herself have a concrete stake in the outcome, providing her a powerful incentive to bring strong, pertinent arguments before the court. A local law professor might be interested in Sally's case for the precedent it would create, but neither mere interest nor even profound concern is enough to confer standing. In this case, Sally (and her parents acting on her behalf) are the only people who have standing to bring her claim.

Cause of Action

Sally and the board clearly have a case or controversy, and Sally has standing to bring it to court. This doesn't mean that Sally has a lawsuit. The law protects us from some things—such as breaking of contracts, the reckless behavior of others, and monopolistic practices by our competitors—and it guarantees us some things— such as freedom of speech or fair trials. But not every right we believe we have is a legal right, and not every wrong done us is a legal wrong. To get into court, Lee must be able to place Sally's problem into a *cause of action*—a legal wrong or right.

Sally's parents believe she has a right to go to school, but that is not strictly true in law. Sally has a right to receive the same educational benefits as other children, *unless* the board has an important reason for treating her differently. Similarly, a classmate's father feels strongly that it is wrong of Sally's parents to expose other children to AIDS by sending her to school, but he has no legal grounds for suing them for damages. Often a lawyer can translate a client's view of right or wrong into a cause of action, but not always. (Indeed, the frequent gap between what large segments of the population perceive to be their rights or protections and what the law decides they are is one of the most troubling features of our legal system. Why, one may well ask, doesn't a child have a right to education?) In looking for a suitable cause of action, Sally's lawyer considers constitutions, statutes, and the common law.

State and Federal Constitutions. In addition to the U.S. Constitution, each state has its own constitution. These documents set forth the fundamental rights of citizens and lay out the powers and structure of government. The U.S. Constitution is the supreme law of the land, and any law in conflict with it (including a state constitutional provision) is invalid. State constitutions enjoy a similar preeminence vis-à-vis state laws. People whose constitutional rights have been violated often have a cause of action. In Sally's case, Lee believes that her right to equal protection of laws (guaranteed in the Fourteenth Amendment to the U.S. Constitution as well as in her state's constitution) has been abridged because she has been arbitrarily singled out for special treatment. But Lee does not stop here; for reasons that will become clear, constitutional causes of action can be problematic, and it is quite normal in any case for there to be more than one cause of action.

State and Federal Statutes. A *statute* is a law passed by a legislative body (local statutes are commonly referred to as *ordinances*). The term is used to distinguish this legislative law from "the common law," legal rules created by courts in the absence of statutes. As with constitutions, there are also distinctions of rank within the realm of statutes. In general, federal statutes trump conflicting state statutes, just as state statutes trump conflicting city and county ordinances.

There are some statutes whose primary purpose is to create a cause of action. For example, an important federal statute granting jurisdiction (see below) over civil rights cases to the federal district courts establishes a cause of action for people whose constitutional rights have been deprived "under color of any State law, statute, ordinance, regulation, custom or usage." More typical statutes, those that themselves confer rights or create obligations, often explicitly provide the right to sue to enforce their provisions. On occasion, the right to sue is reserved to the government, which does so on behalf of aggrieved individuals. And some statutes say nothing at all about how they are to be enforced, which may leave a party with an unprotected right. Courts, observing the legal maxim that there is no right without a remedy if the right is abridged, will sometimes provide one by interpreting the statute to include an "implied cause of action."

The implied cause of action is just one illustration of why a lawyer who reads only the statute is leaving half the job undone. To understand what a statute really means, one must see how it has been interpreted by judges in lawsuits. Statutes and constitutions typically are written in general terms; it is hardly possible to imagine in advance all the situations in which a law will be applied. It is up to the judge to decide whether a statute's general terms apply to a case's specific facts; whether a situation that is not covered, but is like those that are, would have been covered had the legislature thought about it; or how social or technological changes since the statute's passage should affect its application.

Sally's case provides an example (and allows one more digression, onto the subject of how lawyers think through a problem by analogy). Lee is considering a cause of action under the Education for All Handicapped Children Act (EHA), a federal law requiring schools receiving federal funds (virtually all public schools) to place handicapped children into regular classroom settings whenever possible. The law defines "handicap" broadly, but the judge in Sally's case will have to decide whether the definition encompasses AIDS, a disease that was unknown when the EHA was passed. In addition to this question of interpretation, the judge might also be asked by the board to fill a perceived gap in the law: the EHA does not distinguish between handicaps that are the result of contagious diseases and those that are not. Since Congress could hardly have intended to require local schools to enroll dangerous students, should the law be read to include some kind of exception to its presumption of admission where the handicap is a contagious disease?

Lee turns to an *annotated code*, a collection of statutes that includes summaries of court decisions interpreting each provision. He finds that there has been no definitive court decision that AIDS is a handicap according to the definition in the EHA. But he also finds a very important case in which hepatitis B, a disease more readily transmitted than AIDS, was found to be covered. Arguing, as lawyers do, by analogy, Lee will say that the judge is bound by the previous decision to treat AIDS as a handicap; the board will argue that any similarity in transmission is outweighed by the differences in effect—AIDS, unlike hepatitis, is always fatal—and therefore the analogy is flawed. Whichever way Sally's court eventually rules, however, she can at least credibly *argue* that the law protects her, and therefore she may take advantage of the cause of action the EHA provides.

The Common Law. The common law of England preceded the advent of the modern legislature; judges, not Parliament, provided most of the basic rules of social and economic organization. Gradually, legislatures asserted themselves. Today, they not only make most laws, but also have the power to repeal or replace the laws made by judges. Even torts and contracts,* the legal realms traditionally governed exclusively by the common law, are now substantially run according to statutory rules. The shift in power from courts to legislatures is not, however, quite as great as might appear: the power courts lose to make the rules is offset by that which they retain to interpret the rules made by the legislatures. Furthermore, they retain the authority to make rules where the legislature has not acted.

There are many practical differences between statutory and judge-made law. Unlike statutes, which apply to the future behavior of everybody, judicial decisions apply first and foremost to the past acts of the parties who fought the case. Future impact comes in part from the weight the decision will have with other judges deciding similar cases and in part from a general moral imperative to respect judicial pronouncements of law. Whereas a statute is passed all at once, judicial rules are fashioned incrementally, emerging from lines of cases dealing with similar issues. The incremental and case-specific nature of the common law is often said to make it more responsive than statutory law to social and technological changes; it is often

---

* The law of contract sets forth the rules for making binding agreements. The common, and not very helpful, definition of a tort is a legal wrong, other than a breach of contract, for which money damages are appropriate. In general, a tort involves an injury of some kind caused by the defendant or which the defendant had a legal duty to prevent. There are many kinds of tort, ranging from battery, an injury to the body, to products liability, the responsibility of a manufacturer for injuries caused by a product it has introduced into the marketplace.

easier, for example, to get a judge to update a common law rule than it is to get a legislature to amend a dated statute.

Lee is considering a tort claim against the school board as part of Sally's suit. The teacher who spread the news of Sally's disease told his friends that Sally was involved in a Communist germ-warfare conspiracy. Lee believes that this may constitute slander (an injurious and untrue statement) and that the board can be sued under the doctrine that the employer is responsible for the torts of its employee (*respondeat superior*). Lawyers sometimes find themselves with more causes of action than they can use, however, and Lee makes the strategic decision that a slander action would be difficult to win and would divert the court's attention from Sally's more important claims to a normal education.

CHOOSING A COURT

Armed with his causes of action, Lee must select a court in which to bring them. The United States has a dual system of national (federal) and state courts, which may hear many, but not all, of the same causes of action.

Jurisdiction

Jurisdiction is the authority of a court to hear a case. State courts have what is known as general jurisdiction—authority over virtually all cases pertaining to people, property, or events in their territory. Sally could have sued the loquacious teacher for slander even if the slander had taken place in a neighboring state or if the teacher were a resident of another state. Further, Sally could bring her case to a state court even if her cause of action were based solely on the U.S. Constitution or federal law (except in the rare instances—antitrust cases, for example—where Congress has reserved jurisdiction for federal courts alone).

Federal courts, by contrast, are courts of limited jurisdiction: they may hear cases only if the authority to do so has been conferred by the Constitution or a federal statute. Principally, federal courts deal with two categories of cases: those involving causes of action based on federal laws or the Constitution (*federal question* jurisdiction) and those in which all the parties reside in different states (*diversity* jurisdiction). Sally's EHA cause of action brings her within the subject matter jurisdiction of the federal courts. However, since her slander action would have been based on state tort law, she could not have brought it in federal court unless she and the teacher lived in different states.

Tactics

Lee also weighs important qualitative differences between the two court systems. Experienced attorneys know the judges in their area and will choose a court for a particular case with judges' preferences and predilections in mind. In Sally's case, Lee wants a judge who is sympathetic to civil rights claims in general and disabled people in particular. He does not want a judge known to believe that the federal government should stay out of local affairs. He is particularly concerned to find a judge who will not be swayed by the politicized status of the case. Most of the state judges to which his case might be assigned were politicians before going on the bench—they are still politicians in the sense that, like judges in most other states, they are elected (or periodically put before the voters in a yes-or-no reelection). Federal judges, on the other hand, are appointed for life, insulating them, in theory, from political pressure. In this case, Lee decides he has a better chance for a calm trial in federal court.

THE TRIAL

Sally's case begins, like all cases, in a trial court. In the federal system, the *district court* tries cases. Each of the fifty states has at least one federal court district.

Causes of Action and Preliminary Injunction

Sally claims, first, that she is entitled to regular school placement under the EHA and, second, that her constitutional right to equal protection of law was violated by the school's action. She also seeks a *preliminary injunction* ordering the school to admit her while the case is proceeding. Normally, courts do not give plaintiffs what they are suing for until after a case has been tried and won, but in the ordinary course of events Sally's trial might not take place for months and even if she wins, the judge may postpone (*stay*) his decision to admit her while the board appeals. Lee's argument to the court is that such delay will make Sally the loser even if she wins, because her goal is to be admitted to school during the brief time she has left to lead a normal life. Sally's request for a preliminary injunction marks the case as an emergency. The clerk of the court immediately transmits the papers to the judge, who sets a hearing in a matter of days instead of months.

Situations analogous to Sally's are common, and the preliminary injunction was designed to deal with them. The standard for granting an injunction turns on whether either party will be irreparably harmed if the status quo is not disturbed. (Often, an injunction is used to prevent a case from becoming moot, as, for example, where preservationists sue to prevent a developer from demolishing a landmark building; once the building is gone, there is nothing to sue about.) If money damages at the end of the trial will sufficiently compensate the victim, a preliminary injunction will not be granted even if harm will continue to occur while the suit goes on. Another important factor is whether the party seeking the injunction appears to have a strong case.

Issues of Law and Issues of Fact

The district court hearing on Sally's request for a preliminary injunction is, by agreement of the two sides, converted into a full trial of the merits of the case. The two sides present their legal arguments, their witnesses, and their physical evidence. There is, of course, a judge, but because of the nature of the claim no jury (there is no general right to a jury in noncriminal cases). Sally's case, like any other case, is said to present two kinds of issues: issues of fact and issues of law. Roughly, issues of law have to do with which laws apply and how they are to be interpreted. Whether Congress intended to protect children with contagious diseases when it passed the EHA is an issue of law. Issues of fact have to do with the events disputed in the particular case, such as whether, if admitted to school, Sally would really pose a threat to other children.

The distinction is not perfect—some questions are mixed—and can be difficult to apply, but it largely determines who in the system will make which decisions. Questions of law are decided by the judge; questions of fact are decided by the jury (if there is one). If the verdict is appealed, the focus in the court of appeal will be on whether the judge correctly interpreted the law: there will be no witness testimony or other evidence, only lawyers arguing the legal points in written briefs and short oral presentations. The findings of fact of the jury at trial (or judge in the absence of a jury) will be presumed complete and correct and will not be overturned unless they are, on their face, "clearly erroneous."

In Sally's case, the board does not dispute her account of the events leading up to her expulsion; the only real issue of fact disputed by the board is whether Sally would endanger other children in a regular classroom. In law, the board challenges Sally's claim that AIDS is a handicap under the EHA and argues that her removal did not violate the Constitution because it served an important state interest.

Burden of Proof

Both sides call several medical experts to testify concerning Sally's dangerousness. As the plaintiff, Sally bears the burden of proof (sometimes called the risk of nonpersuasion). Most people are familiar with the prosecutor's burden in a criminal trial to prove the defendant's guilt "beyond a reasonable doubt." In Sally's case, as is the norm in civil cases, she must show that "it is more likely than not" that she will not present a danger to other children. In this hypothetical, the judge finds that Sally has satisfied this burden. The overwhelming weight of the testimony and the evidence of the policy of the CDC show that Sally would not pose a danger in the classroom.

Interpreting the Law

The legal decision is more complicated. To begin with, the judge has to decide which legal issues to decide. Judges, for reasons of principle and practicality, try to decide cases on the narrowest possible grounds. Because every case makes rules for later cases, there is reluctance to make a sweeping decision when a narrow and conservative one is possible (though, of course, for the same reason, judges sometimes decide broadly in order to increase the impact of an important case). A broad decision in Sally's case might conclude that the Constitution's equal protection clause prohibits a school from keeping any nondangerous sick child home unless it is prepared to exclude every child with any illness. In this case, the judge finds instead that all the issues in Sally's case can and should be decided under the EHA and that there is no need to reach the constitutional issue. (This does not mean that Sally could not have won on the constitutional issue; only that the case can be resolved without deciding that.)

To determine whether the EHA applies, the judge first looks to the language of the statute. AIDS had not yet been identified when the law was passed, but it probably would not have been mentioned anyway. In the EHA, Congress sought to secure as normal a public education as possible for every handicapped child; this is clear from both the broad language of the statute and statements the judge finds in the legislative history (speeches by members of Congress or reports or declarations of committees that worked on the bill). But it left the details to the Department of Health, Education and Welfare (now the Department of Health and Human Services), which was charged with promulgating regulations to implement the general principles set forth in the EHA. Looking at the "regs," the judge notes a broad definition of handicap that seems to encompass AIDS.

The judge next consults other court decisions. In the classic view of courts, judges do little more than identify the past rule that covers the case at hand—the "precedent"—and apply it. This is a little too simple. To begin with, Sally's judge is formally bound to follow only the rulings of the Supreme Court, the U.S. court of appeals for her circuit, and other federal courts in her district. She may follow the decisions of other courts as well, but that is discretionary. (The same holds true for state court systems, where decisions of federal or other states' courts are not binding on matters of state law.)

In practice, the nature of legal argument itself weakens the bonds of precedent. Looking over the prior cases, the judge finds one case in her circuit applying the EHA to a contagious disease, the hepatitis B case relied on by Lee; one case in a neighboring state's court ruling that AIDS is not covered; and one in another federal district saying that it is. She is not bound to follow either of the cases directly dealing with Sally's disease; and, while the decision of the circuit seems to suggest strongly that the EHA covers AIDS, there is an out. The judge can read the case narrowly—it deals only with hepatitis B and has no implications for AIDS; or distinguish it on the facts—AIDS, unlike hepatitis B, is uniformly fatal; or distinguish it on the law—the case was actually decided under the Constitution, not the EHA. In practice, a judge so inclined can nearly always find a way to avoid applying an unwanted precedent, though many try hard to figure out what rules emerge from previous cases and to apply them properly in the cases before them.

Of course, judges do not work in a vacuum. Even federal judges, free from direct political pressure, are aware of the broader implications of individual rulings, and most make their decisions with an eye to something like the greatest good for the greatest number. Lee and the attorney for the board have both larded their legal positions with arguments designed to focus the judge's attention on the larger "policy issues." (How should a humane society deal with sick children? What is the most economically efficient way to distribute the costs of education for the handicapped? What do they do in Sweden?) Many of these considerations naturally arise as part of the process of interpreting the statute, but the personal values and interests of the judge are inevitably an important factor in a decision. Finally, even a judge who does not need to worry about reelection may be concerned about the well-being of the court as an institution. Judges tend to be rather careful about using their power to go against the strongly held views of the community.

The Judge's Decision

There is often quite a bit more than meets the eye in a judicial decision, which, after all, is essentially a political document. Some decisions are painfully honest, revealing how difficult it can be to decide a hard case justly. Other opinions are devoted to obfuscating the issues and hiding the traces of whatever reasoning process the judge used. It never hurts to be skeptical, and this is true in Sally's case.

The judge begins by proclaiming the importance of fair treatment and a normal education for handicapped children. She claims to be "compelled" to follow the precedent of the hepatitis case and rules that the EHA does apply to AIDS. She does not, however, order Sally into school. Instead, Sally must start over. Under the law and regulations, the judge says, children with a school placement dispute under EHA are not allowed to sue in federal court until they have appealed the school's decision administratively. Although a federal district court can eventually decide the case, Sally must first go through a four-tiered process of administrative hearings set up by the state department of education. Lee is a little put out about this, because the hepatitis case that "compelled" this decision also ruled that the district court could short-circuit the administrative hearing process and immediately order the child into school.

APPEALING A VERDICT

If no one is entirely happy with the decision, no one is unhappy enough to exercise their right to appeal. Sally's parents would rather not go softly into that good night of bureaucracy, but, on balance, it is her fastest and least expensive chance of getting into school. For its part, the board is satisfied that her entrance will at least be delayed; the hepatitis case suggests to its lawyer that the court of appeals might reverse the district judge and order her admitted. A brief description of the appellate process is nevertheless in order.

Decisions of the district court may be appealed to the *circuit court of appeals*. The nation is geographically divided into twelve circuits, each of which takes appeals from several district courts. Appeals from the circuit court of appeals, when permitted, are taken to the Supreme Court of the United States. About half the states have similar three-tiered systems; a few have an extra intermediate appellate court; and the rest have a two-tiered system composed of trial courts and a single appellate court. The state supreme court has the final say on matters of state law, but its decisions on federal constitutional or statutory issues may be appealed to the U.S. Supreme Court.*

---

* A warning on wording: state systems do not necessarily adopt federal nomenclature.

In the United States, there is virtually a universal right to one appeal. Although states with three tiers of courts give litigants the right to appeal unsatisfactory decisions of the intermediate court to the highest court, this right is limited (in most states, severely limited) to particular types of cases. Cases not falling into the right categories may be appealed to the supreme court only with its permission. The federal system is similar: an appeal may be taken "as of right" from the district court to the court of appeal, but most can go on to the Supreme Court only if it gives its permission in the form of a *writ of certiorari*. A denial of "cert" (the most frequent outcome) means that the decision in the next lowest court stands.

THE ADMINISTRATIVE HEARING PROCESS

The EHA's provision of an administrative procedure for deciding placement is not unusual, nor is the fact that the statute left most of the detailed law-making to a cabinet-level department. Since the New Deal, large government bureaucracies have played a growing role in the day-to-day making and adjudicating of rules. Not surprisingly, as the job of the federal government has become more complicated and the amount of money expended has grown, Congress has delegated increasing responsibility to the executive branch of the government. What is perhaps more interesting is the way statutes like the EHA allow the federal government—both Congress and the executive branch—to regulate the behavior of states.

In theory, ours is a federal system, with the national government designated to perform certain national tasks (such as providing for the common defense and regulating interstate commerce) and local affairs (such as public education) left to the states. But the federal government has learned to use its wealth to indirectly regulate affairs nominally outside its authority, principally by attaching strings to the money it gives. Congress, for example, probably could not order states to enforce a speed limit of fifty-five miles per hour. Instead, it simply says that any state that wants federal highway funds (and that is every state) must agree to that speed limit.

The EHA was a similar gambit. Congress felt that education for the handicapped was a national problem and was prepared to spend money to solve it. But it could not act directly: schools are run by the states. So it passed the EHA, with instructions to the Department of Health, Education and Welfare to design a model program in

New York, for example, calls its trial court the *Supreme Court,* and its supreme court the *Court of Appeals.* The intermediate appellate court—the court of appeals in the federal system—is a happy medium in New York: *Supreme Court, Appellate Division.*

its regulations. In order to get the money offered under the act, each state had to pass a law adopting the federal government's program, which explains why Sally, having been told her disease was covered by a *federal* law, is compelled to comply with a *state* administrative procedure.

About two months after the federal judge's verdict, Sally had her first state hearing. The "judge" was an administrator in the state department of education. Several doctors testified. Both sides were represented by counsel. The hearing officer ruled in favor of the board. The decision was appealed to a similarly constituted tribunal, and, after a few more months, it was overturned. The board appealed to yet another department official and lost again. At that point, more than a year after she first sought admission, Sally was allowed to start school. Immediately, several other parents went to a state court, seeking to have Sally quarantined. That is another story.

Sally is a hypothetical child, but her story is based on the experience of real children. Legal rules and analogies are ultimately imperfect reflections of complicated problems as they exist in the world. It is a very good idea for all of us to have some acquaintance with the jargon of law, but it is an even better idea to nurse our sense of simple justice. We ought not allow the complexity and formality of law to be the excuse for denying the jurisdiction of humanity and compassion.

2 Transmission and Treatment

Helena Brett-Smith, M.D., and
Gerald H. Friedland, M.D.

HISTORY AND TRENDS

The first recognition of AIDS as a unique medical entity came in June 1981 with a brief mention in the Centers for Disease Control (CDC) publication Morbidity and Mortality Weekly Report (MMWR).[1] Within the next six months several articles followed in which physicians from Los Angeles and New York City described a series of young, gay men who were dying from "opportunistic" infections or malignancy and in whom laboratory studies revealed a profound suppression of the immune system ("immunosuppression") that was both unexpected and unexplained.[2] Early epidemiologic studies of these men noted their multiple sexual partners, which suggested that a new sexually transmitted infectious agent might account for the disease. The nature of the illness in these men was so radically new to medical experience, however, that alternative explanations based on other behavioral observations were also entertained.[3] As the number of AIDS cases rapidly increased, initially doubling every six months, several other so-called risk groups were identified: in the United States and Western Europe, these included intravenous drug users and hemophiliacs, both suggesting a blood-borne route of transmission.[4] Simultaneously, numerous cases of a virtually identical disease were noted among Haitians, and soon thereafter among central Africans, where no obvious risk behavior emerged except nonmonogamous heterosexuality.[5]

Over the ensuing years, and within what is historically a remarkably short period of time, the cause of this disease has been identified as a retrovirus known by the acronym HIV (for Human Immunodeficiency Virus). Its life cycle and molecular-genetic structure are now surprisingly well understood, and it can be studied effectively in the laboratory thanks to the development of practical culture systems. Most important, simple blood tests using modern microbiologic techniques can identify the presence of the virus in asymptomatic people. This capacity to identify

18

carriers of disease maximizes the opportunity for early treatment of infected individuals and for education to interrupt the cycle of transmission. It also prevents transfusion-related spread of the disease by providing a reliable and practical mechanism for screening the blood supply.

Despite this series of very real accomplishments, HIV is an increasingly important cause of illness and death. Statistics reveal a number of important trends in the ten-year evolution of the epidemic. The most important is the rapid growth in the absolute number of people infected with HIV. Current estimates by the World Health Organization conclude that between 8 and 10 million adults and 1 million children worldwide are infected, and the numbers may quadruple by the year 2000.[6] From a global perspective, it will be the developing countries of Africa, the Caribbean, Latin America, and Southeast Asia that will bear the greatest burden of this disease. In the United States, over 200,000 cases of full-blown AIDS were reported to the CDC by the end of 1991, and over half of these people had died. The first 100,000 cases were reported over an eight-year period (1981–89); the second 100,000 cases accumulated in only two years.[7] In addition, the AIDS category represents only the tip of the iceberg, or the sickest of those with HIV infection. Public health authorities estimate that there are about 1 million people currently infected in the United States, many of them unrecognized carriers. Thus, even if all HIV transmission were to cease, the greatest impact of the epidemic would lie ahead. It is sometimes argued that rates of transmission have stabilized or even peaked in certain behavioral risk groups; this assessment may be premature, but even if it is accurate most symptomatic disease will manifest itself in the future. As a society we have yet to experience the full magnitude of this epidemic, whether it is measured in terms of total person-years of illness and disability, in terms of the economic and social costs of medical care and social service systems, or in terms of the absolute number of deaths.

The second observation that emerges from the past ten years' experience is that the global pandemic remains volatile and represents a multitude of even more intense and focused epidemics within specific communities of risk. It is essential to recognize that these groups reflect population prevalence and *not* some more basic biologic affinity of the virus. Communities at increased risk are defined not just by a single, clearly identifiable risk behavior—for example, men having sex with men or intravenous drug users sharing needles—but by much broader social and economic structures within which these behaviors occur, such as geography, race, social institutions (such as prostitution), and economic class. (It is interesting to note, for example, that the dispersion of HIV in Africa has been traced along trucking routes; among inner-city communities of the Northeastern United States, prevalence spreads outward from New York City along highway and railroad routes and diminishes in direct proportion to distance from New York.)[8] The boundaries of these at risk communities are poorly understood because of incomplete knowledge about their social dynamics. As a consequence of these undefined connections between HIV and social and economic structures, the epidemic may appear to spread erratically. Different communities affected by HIV may be separated by geography, or by class and income, yet connected by behavior. If behavior conducive to transmission is prevalent in a newly infected community, the epidemic can spread rapidly in this one area, while its overall growth may be much more moderate. Recent seroprevalence data for Thailand, for instance, mimic those of the early years in San Francisco or New York, whereas figures for the United States show a moderation in the rate of transmission. At the same time, of course, even in the United States large numbers of currently uninfected people remain at risk because of their ongoing patterns of behavior. Unless we understand these social network patterns, our well-intended attempts to halt the spread of HIV may have unanticipated outcomes.

Moreover, the course of the epidemic in this country has been characterized by an increasing inequality of vulnerability and exposure. As AIDS has become endemic in pockets of urban poverty, this inequality has come increasingly to mirror the larger socioeconomic inequalities in America. In addition to gay men, people of color have experienced a disproportionate amount of disease: of the second 100,000 cases reported to the CDC, 31 percent were among African Americans and 17 percent were among Hispanics, figures representing, respectively, two and one-half and two times the expected proportions based on the population distribution of these groups in the United States.[9] Further, death rates per 100,000 population are far higher for African Americans and Hispanics (29 and 22, respectively) than for non-Hispanic Whites (9).[10]

One final but very important aspect of the epidemic's changing demographics is its increasing impact on women. Although HIV has always been evenly distributed between the sexes in areas of heterosexual spread such as Haiti and Africa, its rising impact on women in the United States—and its close link, for women, with heterosexual sex—warrants attention. Women account for 12 percent of the second 100,000 AIDS cases, but 61 percent of all cases attributed to heterosexual contact. As early as 1988, in certain geographic areas of the United States (for example, New York and New Jersey), AIDS had become the leading cause of death for African American women between the ages of fifteen and forty-four. It is estimated that in 1992 AIDS will surpass cancer as the single leading cause of death for all women in this age group.[11] Despite its increasing impact on women, however, most of the medical and social research on HIV disease in Western societies has been based on overwhelmingly male study populations. One of the most important tasks facing current HIV programs, both those providing care and those generating research information, is to reach out to women.

BASIC BIOLOGY

AIDS is caused by a virus first identified in 1983 and now internationally recognized as the Human Immunodeficiency Virus or HIV.[12] (Previously used acronyms are HTLV-III, or human T cell leukemia virus, type 3, and LAV, or lymphodenopathy associated virus. There is also a related but distinct virus, HIV–2, that has been identified as the cause for a significant proportion of AIDS cases in West Africa.) HIV belongs to a particular family of viruses (the retroviruses) whose members share a specific mechanism of reproduction and are characterized by two distinctive features. First, the genetic information for the virus is stored in molecules or building blocks of RNA, rather than in the usual DNA of human genes. Second, the virus possesses a unique enzyme or protein not otherwise present in human cells, called "reverse transcriptase," that enables it to translate its RNA into an equivalent DNA sequence. These features are basic to the reproductive strength of the virus and its capacity to survive in human cells. They also represent the Achilles' heel toward which we direct our pharmacologic attack, discussed later in this chapter.

The life cycle of the virus can be summarized briefly. Each viral particle is composed of the viral genome (RNA) protected by a coating of structural proteins. These proteins enable the virus to attach to a specific receptor protein (referred to as "CD_4") on the outside of certain human cells that are crucial to the normal functioning of the human immune system. Once attached, the virus enters these cells and activates its own reverse transcriptase to copy viral RNA into its analogous DNA sequence. The resulting fragment of DNA then inserts itself into the DNA strands of the host cell's genes, ensuring lifelong infection of that cell and its descendants. At this point, the virus may either turn off and become latent or remain active. In the first case the infected cell continues to function normally but carries the more-or-less quiescent virus. In the second, the viral genes remain turned on, taking over the normal machinery of the cell and forcing it to produce huge numbers of new viral particles. These new viruses move on to infect other tissue, and eventually the host cell dies. In certain types of body tissue, direct cell-to-cell transfer of the virus may also occur, usually resulting in larger conglomerates of infected cells.[13]

Aside from the part played by reverse transcriptase and the consequent role-reversal between DNA and RNA, there is nothing very unusual in this life-cycle. Its broad outline applies to a wide variety of DNA viruses that insert themselves into human genes and persist over many years, often without causing active disease. For instance, after the acute illness from hepatitis B has passed, most people suffer few further consequences despite the fact that viral DNA can be found in the liver for the rest of their lives. HIV is different for two reasons. First, its "latency" seems to be relative and not absolute, in that there is always some low background level of viral growth and reproduction. Second, and more important, its target cells are those that direct and coordinate the normal immune response. As the virus destroys these cells, the body's ability to respond to other secondary infections is profoundly changed.

In order to appreciate both the subtleties of transmission and the consequences of this particular viral infection, one must understand some simple medical terminology. The human immune system comprises many cells and tissues, each of which plays a unique role. Many of the most important immune cells move freely back and forth between blood and solid tissues such as muscle and brain. When found in the blood these cells are called "white blood cells," a term that developed long before their biologic function was understood. White blood cells form a large family comprising many different subtypes—the major subsets include lymphocytes, monocytes, and neutrophils—each of which performs a different function in protecting the body from infection.

When not in the bloodstream, lymphocytes concentrate in the lymph nodes, where they form two main subsets named after the tissues in which they originate: "B" cells from the bone marrow and "T" cells from the thymus. Further subcategories have been identified through the observation that some lymphocytes carry specific proteins or markers on their surfaces. For instance, T_4 lymphocytes carry the CD_4 protein, whereas T_8 cells carry the CD_8 protein. These proteins have particular biologic functions that determine the cell's role in immunity. The CD_4 protein receives and recognizes foreign material. Thus CD_4 lymphocytes, also referred to as T_4 or T helper cells, perform the extremely important function of initiating or stimulating immune system activities. CD_8 lymphocytes, also called T_8 or T suppressor cells, control an overenthusiastic immune response and thereby prevent the body from attacking itself. A healthy immune system requires a sophisticated interaction and balance between T_4 and T_8 cells. HIV infection disrupts this normal balance. In fact, the virus enters and infects a new organism precisely by attaching to the CD_4 protein. It then reproduces inside the T_4 cells and destroys them. In short, HIV disease's primary target is the human immune system itself.

AIDS has become renowned for so-called opportunistic infections that take advantage of the compromised immune system. Normally these particular micro-organisms are well controlled: they may enter and infect human tissue, but they do not usually cause significant disease. In an immunosuppressed person (whether the immunosuppression is due to HIV, chemotherapy, or drugs taken to prevent the rejection of transplanted organs), these dormant infections may reactivate and cause clinical illness. Because T_4 cells coordinate so many different facets of immunity, the list of potential secondary problems extends beyond the specific AIDS-defining opportunistic infections described later in this chapter. For instance, HIV-infected people may be more vulnerable to common bacterial infections and to certain types of cancers. In the final analysis, their medical care must include two distinct components: primary treatment directed at the virus itself, and new preventative and treatment strategies directed at the secondary complications of immunosuppression.

TRANSMISSION

Because we cannot eradicate HIV from the human body once it is established there, prevention is still the most powerful intervention available. In order to interrupt the cycle of transmission, one must understand its mechanism. Despite all the public fear and misunderstanding surrounding this epidemic, a few simple facts have been clear for some years now, and they continue to be confirmed by more recent data. For infection to occur, an infected person's blood, semen, or vaginal secretions (hereinafter "body fluids") must come into intimate contact with the blood or mucous membranes (such as the mouth, eyes, urethra, vagina, or anus) of an uninfected person. Only in this way can the virus find its way into a new cell. Sweat, tears, and saliva are not considered to be infectious body fluids because the virus, if present at all, occurs in such low numbers that it is medically insignificant. No case of transmission has been shown to have resulted from contact with any of these fluids.

The concept that only certain types of body tissues or cells are susceptible is important. What seems to make a cell susceptible is primarily the presence of the CD_4 protein on its surface. Blood itself contains the richest supply of vulnerable CD_4 cells; conversely, an infected person's blood also has the highest concentration of infectious virus, as compared to semen or vaginal secretions. Blood-to-blood contact therefore carries the highest risk of transmission. However, any contact between an infected body fluid and mucous membranes—especially in sexual intercourse—must be considered potentially infectious. Concern has also been raised that HIV may be able to enter certain cells of the intestines and rectum directly, without involving CD_4 cells.[14] This possibility may play a role in transmission through anal intercourse, which is already a high-risk activity because of the likelihood of mucosal tears.

It is equally important to recognize that intact skin does *not* permit the virus to enter the body and is not a route for transmission. Even direct contact between intact skin and infected blood is not a risky exposure. Moreover, HIV does not survive well outside human tissue and is easily inactivated by many household cleaning agents, including bleach, rubbing alcohol, hydrogen peroxide, and lysol.[15] Therefore HIV, unlike those diseases associated in the public mind with other historic epidemics, is not transmitted by air, food, or water, or by the shared use of household objects. Casual contact cannot spread it, nor can the communal activities of daily living. Instead, there is only one mechanism of transmission—intimate contact with infected body fluids—which translates into a limited repertoire of risk behaviors or situations: sex, use of shared needles (intentionally or accidentally), transfusion of blood or blood products, and pregnancy. We will discuss each of these in turn. (The risks of transmission between patients and health care workers, although they also involve contact with infected body fluids, are discussed separately in chapter 17.)

Sexual Transmission

On a worldwide scale, sex is responsible for the largest number of HIV infections. Given the mechanism described above, it should be clear that all sexual activity involving genital contact carries some risk of transmission if engaged in with an infected partner. People's individual lifetime risk increases with the number of their sexual partners and with the prevalence of infection in the population of those with whom they have sex. Both of these factors indirectly measure the likelihood of encountering an infected partner.

The risk to an HIV-positive person's uninfected partner has been shown to increase if the partner has other sexually transmitted diseases, particularly those that cause genital ulcers. The risk also increases as the infected person progresses to more advanced stages of disease. Particularly high-risk periods for sexual contact with an infected person *probably* include the time of his or her initial seroconversion and the period just before the onset of AIDS; at these times, large amounts of free virus circulate in the bloodstream. Some people also argue that the number of sexual encounters and the duration of the sexual relationship are additional risk factors, but quantitative studies to date have not supported these conclusions. This fact, together with the unpredictability of individual outcomes (some partners become infected after a single sexual contact, whereas others remain negative after years of exposure) suggest that there are biologic determinants of transmission that we do not fully understand. Differences between viral strains may be important, with some being more infective than others; some carriers may be more efficient transmitters; and some individuals may be less susceptible recipients.[16]

Although these remain important questions for future investigation, the basic elements of sexual transmission are well understood. Studies have demonstrated repeatedly that the receptive partners in gay male anal sex have the highest risk, as do women—the receptive partners—in heterosexual vaginal sex.[17] The unifying theme is that the receiving partner is relatively more exposed, since the penetrating partner's body fluids remain deposited in the vagina or rectum. Similarly, anal intercourse itself—whether heterosexual or homosexual—is thought to be riskier than vaginal sex, presumably because the mechanics of penetration generate more frequent tears of the mucous membranes. Sex during menstruation is also thought to increase the risk for both partners, though this has not been demonstrated unequivocally. The woman's normal mucosal barriers may be compromised during menstruation, putting her at greater risk if her partner is infected; conversely, if she is infected her menstrual blood poses a greater risk to her partner than do normal vaginal secretions. Finally, several epidemiologic studies have suggested that people with sexually transmitted diseases that cause ulcers or open breaks in the skin (such as syphilis, chancroid, and herpes) face a greater risk of infection. In this context the current epidemic of syphilis in many United States cities is a cause for concern; not only does it reflect ongoing unsafe sexual behavior with multiple partners, but the syphilitic skin lesions themselves facilitate the transfer of HIV.[18]

The risk of transmission through oral sex and deep kissing is an area of significant public anxiety. The question is difficult to study in part because this behavior usually occurs in association with other, higher-risk behavior, particularly intercourse. Early studies of gay men found that neither insertive nor receptive oral sex was an independent risk factor.[19] These studies, however, may have been inadequate to evaluate this question in a population whose baseline rate of positivity was already so high. Subsequently, several published cases have been attributed to lesbian sex,[20] and oral sex has been implicated as the route of transmission for the receptive partners of infected men.[21] Since two mucous membranes are involved in these activities, there may be some finite risk, though it seems to be much less than for anal or vaginal intercourse. There has been no documented case of transmission by kissing. Although HIV has been detected in human saliva in vanishingly small amounts, experts in the field do not consider saliva to be a source of infection.[22]

Needle Sharing

The second major route for transmission is needle sharing by drug users. While the sharing includes syringes and other paraphernalia as well as needles, it is difficult to research the specific risks for each because of the clandestine context within which drug use takes place. It is noteworthy, however, that an established technique for "shooting up" involves withdrawing blood into the drug-containing syringe before reinfusing this mixture into the vein. The sight of blood verifies that the needle is in place in the vein and that the drug will reach the bloodstream. Such techniques mean that anyone who shares any part of another person's "works" (either needle or syringe) may risk significant exposure. The social setting in which such shared use takes place can magnify the risk by increasing the number and anonymity of needle-sharing partners. The evolution of "shooting galleries" as a social phenomenon is enormously important in the spread of HIV among inner-city users. Shooting galleries are places where people may buy drugs and rent injection equipment for one-time, on-site use; the customers then return the needles and syringes to the proprietor of the gallery, who recycles them to new clients. Over the course of a single day a contaminated needle or syringe may be used by multiple individuals, creating an ideal setting for blood-borne HIV transmission.

Whereas the risk of patronizing a shooting gallery is self-evident, several researchers have begun to quantify the statistical associations between specific patterns of drug use and the degree of risk for seroconversion. Of the drugs whose use involves needles, cocaine is associated with a higher rate of transmission than is heroin,[23] probably because the "high" from cocaine is much shorter, leading to more frequent injections and therefore to more frequent exposure. Users also report that cocaine craving is more intense than the equivalent desire for heroin, suggesting that the behavior surrounding injection may therefore be less planned. Other factors that have been closely linked with the risk of infection include the total number of injections per month; the percentage of injections using needles shared with strangers or acquaintances, as opposed to friends or relatives; the percentage of injections in shooting galleries; and the ethnic background and socioeconomic status of the drug user (presumably because the social milieu in which drug use takes place varies with race and economic status).[24]

Finally, in the drug-using community as a whole, there are now new patterns of spread that are independent of needle use. Specifically, "crack" or smokeable cocaine has recently been recognized as a risk factor, primarily because of the sexual behavior that accompanies its use.[25] So-called crack houses serve as hubs of sexual activity, since many users combine their peak "high" with sex or exchange sex for money in order to continue their drug use. The frequency and anonymity of such sexual encounters mirror the behavioral patterns associated with gay men's bath houses in the late 1970s and early 1980s. Yet the crack user's subjective perception of risk may well lag behind the reality, in part because the public still believes that HIV is associated exclusively with needles or gay male sex. The interconnection between sex and drugs, particularly for inner-city communities, needs to be emphasized. Researchers have documented that sexual contact is an independent risk factor among recovering addicts enrolled in a New York City methadone program. This correlation was most notable for women and for those who had stopped using drugs before 1982,[26] demonstrating that drug users remain members of a high-risk social network even after they have entered treatment and that sexual activity within such a community constitutes a real and independent risk.

Mother-to-Infant Transmission

As more women become infected with HIV, through either shared needles or heterosexual activity, the problem of mother-to-infant transmission escalates proportionately. Again, the most acutely affected groups in the United States have been the poor residents of inner cities. Hospital surveys in inner-city areas have shown that as many as one in thirty-three African American infants are born to HIV-infected mothers. These children all carry the HIV antibody in their blood at birth, although this reflects the transfer of maternal antibody across the placenta rather than the infants' own response to the virus.[27] Thus, in newborns, the antibody test for HIV (see next section) actually reflects *potential* exposure, whereas in all other children and adults it reflects actual infection. In order to determine true infection status, it is necessary to follow the newborn's clinical course and to continue testing until the child is fifteen or eighteen months of age. In the near future, new technologies such as polymerase chain reaction (PCR), described later in this chapter, may allow for more rapid and precise diagnosis.

Longitudinal studies demonstrate that between 12 and 30 percent of the infants of positive mothers will end up truly HIV-infected.[28] Because we understand only poorly the biological mechanism of transmission in this setting, we are unable to predict which infants are at particularly high risk or to intervene appropriately during pregnancy. Given what we know about the virus, there are three routes for infection that are conceptually possible.

First, and probably most important, is direct HIV transfer into the fetal circulation and tissues in utero, as occurs with other viral infections. Whether there is a particular "window of vulnerability"[29] during fetal development and how the activity of the mother's disease during pregnancy plays into this transfer are factors that are still not entirely clear. It is reasonable to presume that the risk for the fetus may increase with the level of free or active virus in the mother's bloodstream. Based on this presumption, current studies are investigating whether the use of antiviral drugs such as aziothymidine (AZT) during pregnancy will decrease transmission.

Second, exposure to maternal blood and secretions during the trauma of a spontaneous vaginal delivery may be an independent risk for those infants who escape transplacental infection. One study of twins has shown that the first-born babies have a higher rate of infection, suggesting that the trauma of the first birth leads to increased infection. This study also suggested that delivery by cesarean section may decrease the risk, though most previous investigators had been unable to document such an advantage.[30]

Third, viral particles have been isolated from breast milk, and case reports have documented the reality of this route of infection, although breastfeeding is generally felt to account for a small percentage of perinatal transmissions and to be of relatively low inherent risk. The one exception is when the mother's primary infection occurs during the period of breastfeeding, because there is a large amount of free virus circulating in the mother's blood. In this setting, the rate of transmission may be as high as 50 percent.[31]

Blood Product Transfusion

People who received blood or blood product transfusions in the years between 1979 and 1985, before the availability of the HIV antibody test, are the fourth group experiencing a high rate of infection. Not surprisingly, direct infusion of a large quantity of infected blood provides an efficient mechanism for transmission, and more than 90 percent of such cases resulted in the recipient's infection.[32] Hemophiliacs were at particularly high risk during this period; they require frequent transfusions, and the clotting factors or processed blood products that they require were traditionally prepared by pooling extracts from thousands of donors. Currently, in the United States, up to 90 percent of severe, clotting factor-dependent hemophiliacs are known to be infected. The exact rate of infection depends on two variables: the severity of the hemophilia, which determines the frequency of transfusions and the total amount of blood product received, and the type of hemophilia (type A hemophiliacs, who require factor VIII, have a higher rate of positivity than do type B hemophiliacs, who require factor IX).[33] For all hemophiliacs, technical improvements in the preparation of clotting factors (especially heat treatment) have made this therapy much safer.

The risk of transfusion-associated transmission has been markedly reduced since March 1985, when nationwide antibody screening of the blood supply was introduced. Other preventive measures include reliance on voluntary donations (rather than paid exchange); voluntary self-exclusion of high-risk donors regardless of known HIV status; and the increasing use of autologous blood products for elective surgery (in other words, patients donate blood for their own later use). Although these precautions do not guarantee that the blood supply is 100 percent safe, the real risks of transfusion-related transmission have dropped dramatically. It is now estimated that the risk of transmission per unit of blood falls between 1 in 35,000 and 1 in 150,000.[34] The remaining risk reflects the presence of a "window" of seronegativity, during which donors are infected but do not yet carry antibodies in their bloodstreams.

Nontransmission of HIV

Just as it is important to recognize which behaviors involve a high risk of transmission, it is equally important to recognize those that do not. Public intolerance has been strongly associated with ignorance of the fact that casual contact does not transmit HIV.[35]

At least fourteen different studies have followed well over 700 people who have had close, but nonsexual, family contact with an AIDS patient. Not one instance of HIV transmission has been detected that could not be explained by a more traditional route of exposure. One study obtained detailed information about sharing razors, toothbrushes, bath towels, and toilets; sharing unwashed utensils and drinking glasses; and hugging, kissing, or sleeping in the same bed with an infected person. None of these activities resulted in a single case of viral transmission, although many of them involved sharing objects that were soiled with saliva, feces, and urine. Similarly, spitting, biting, and exposure to urine or feces are not routes of transmission, because in most such situations the skin remains intact, and the amount of virus present in these fluids is in any case insignificant. It is important to recognize that simply because the virus can be isolated from these body fluids in the laboratory does not mean that they play any significant role in the real-world transmission of the virus.[36]

Finally, less intimate contact in the workplace—for example, shaking hands and sharing objects such as water fountains and telephones—does not constitute a risk for transmission. Indeed, the fear that surrounds HIV has at times been so extreme that even the specter of insect-related transmission has been raised. One Florida community became the subject of careful epidemiologic investigation because of wide publicity attributing its high incidence of infection to insects. The study confirmed that the well-established routes of sex and needle-sharing explained all observed disease and that mosquitoes played no role in transmission.[37]

THE NATURAL HISTORY OF HIV DISEASE

Questions about transmission and prevention remain some of the hottest medical-legal issues surrounding HIV, but the disease has also profoundly challenged scientific, medical, legal, and ethical thinking on many other fronts. In order to appreciate these challenges—such as drug evaluation and approval, access to care, and suicide for the terminally ill—one must develop a factual framework about the natural history and treatment of HIV disease. Although we know how the virus is transmitted from person to person, our understanding of how to treat those already infected continues to evolve rapidly. What is now the accepted standard of treatment may soon become obsolete or assume a different significance in light of new knowledge.

In 1992, HIV infection is viewed as a single spectrum of disease, with manifestations that evolve over time in infected individuals. It is recognized as AIDS when certain specific, severe complications develop. The terms "ARC" ("AIDS-related complex," now often referred to as "HIV positive, symptomatic") and "AIDS" were developed before the virus was discovered, at a time when it was possible to hope that the disease might have only limited manifestations in certain people. It was thought that the asymptomatic carrier state might be life-long in some subset of individuals, or that in others the damage might be limited to a less severe form of immunosuppression with only ARC-like symptoms that could be indefinitely controlled. In the early 1980s "ARC" and "AIDS" could still be thought of as independent but parallel responses to an unknown stimulus, though many people suspected a sequential temporal relationship even then. The ARC-AIDS nomenclature has persisted, although its conceptual context has changed, and the appropriateness of "ARC" in particular is strongly debated. Now the different syndromes related to HIV infection—asymptomatic carriage, symptomatic disease or "ARC," and AIDS—are viewed as sequential stages that evolve in a predictable pattern, albeit over an unpredictable time frame, in each infected individual. Once infection occurs, an irreversible course of progressive illness has been set in motion, and the goal of medical intervention is to slow viral activity and delay the next step in immune deterioration. HIV disease is not now reversible, and periods of stability are seen as temporary halts rather than permanent arrests. This current understanding is based on the experience of the vast majority of patients; there may in fact be a small minority who tolerate the virus well and seem to be long-term survivors. In a San Francisco cohort of gay men, 19 percent were asymptomatic ten years after seroconversion, though some of them had T cell abnormalities.[38] AIDS is still an evolving epidemic whose natural history is not yet completely described and whose patterns are constantly being changed through medical and social interventions. Although a framework based on stages of disease seems to be the best way of understanding this illness at present, such thinking is itself subject to evolution.

Seroconversion and HIV Tests

The first recognizable event in HIV disease is the period of acute infection associated with seroconversion. Within weeks to a few months after exposure, a newly infected person may experience a syndrome of fever, malaise, and swollen lymph glands, with or without a rash and a sore throat.[39] These symptoms may vary greatly in severity, behaving on the one hand like a mild episode of flu lasting a few days, or on the other hand like a severe case of mononucleosis lasting several weeks. Most patients, even in retrospect, may have had no such identifiable illness.

During this period the virus reproduces rapidly, becomes highly concentrated in the bloodstream (between 10 and 10,000 infectious particles per milliliter of blood), and disseminates to the entire body. A newly infected person is probably especially infectious during this period of high-level "viremia," or free virus in the blood, though only through the established routes of sex and blood contact. Interestingly, this period of high viral activity seems to be very short-lived, in the range of ten to twenty days.[40] The immune system responds rapidly and effectively to the initial burst of infection, and it is part of this response that produces the first signs of swollen or activated lymph glands. As the normal immune defenses are activated, they produce antibodies against HIV; these antibodies are protein molecules that circulate in the blood, recognize and attach onto virus or virally infected cells, and help either to inactivate them or to mark them as targets for further attack. We can test blood for the presence of these proteins, and this provides an *indirect* test for HIV infection. "Seroconversion" literally means that the blood (serum) changes (converts) from negative to positive for the antibody test.

Seroconversion is an important event on two levels. First, it constitutes an important part of the body's natural defenses against HIV. As the amount of antibody in the blood increases, the amount of virus decreases. In fact, viremia usually diminishes to such a degree that we cannot find free virus in the blood anymore but must look for it inside the white blood cells where it remains partly protected. Once the virus has moved into this latent phase, infected people recover from their flu-like illness and may feel perfectly healthy. Thus, antibodies seem to play a significant role in the natural defenses that keep HIV under control. Physicians and scientists have tried to exploit this mechanism in several of the treatment strategies discussed later in this chapter.

Seroconversion is also important because the presence of antibodies provides the current "gold standard" for assessing whether a person is infected. There are two ways to test for antibodies in the laboratory: the first is referred to as the ELISA or enzyme-linked immunosorbent assay; the second is called a Western Blot. The ELISA can be completed in a matter of hours. It is extremely sensitive (that is, it picks up the overwhelming majority of positive blood samples), but it is not as specific as the Western Blot (that is, it can falsely identify samples as positive). The usual laboratory protocol is therefore to take a single test tube of blood but perform two sequential tests. The ELISA is done first, and if it is positive the remaining blood is checked by Western Blot. If the ELISA is negative, most test centers will not routinely run a follow-up Western Blot because of the expense and technician time it requires.

Reliability is one of the important problems presented by HIV testing. HIV is an emotional issue, and a fearful public unrealistically demands absolute answers and guarantees. It is therefore important to understand the limits of the HIV tests. Most important, the time frame within which seroconversion takes place may vary from one individual to another. In all prospectively studied cases, when the specific time of first exposure—such as sexual contact or needle-sharing—is known, this event occurs within six months. Blood tests usually become positive much earlier (often within four to six weeks), and it is estimated that at least 95 percent of those who eventually develop true infection test positive within the first six months.[41]

Whereas the ELISA and Western Blot are indirect tests, several other techniques exist for detecting the presence of HIV itself. These include viral culture of blood samples, in which the plasma, or free fluid, and the white cells are each cultured to see if HIV can be grown from them; PCR, or polymerase chain reaction, which is a relatively new and sophisticated way to probe samples of tissue or blood genetically for specific patterns of DNA that are unique to HIV; and the so-called p24 Antigen assay, which tests for the presence of a core viral protein (p24) in the blood.

Each of these tests has certain drawbacks. Although the technology for p24 testing is simple and widely available, the biology of HIV infection makes it unreliable as a measure of exposure. Only a small subset of infected people have sufficient quantities of free virus in their blood to be detected by the p24 assay; most viral particles are hidden within cells and cannot be detected by this test. The people who usually test positive are those in the midst of acute seroconversion and those with severe end-stage AIDS, in whom the virus is out of control.[42] Both of these groups have a high level of viral reproduction and free virus in the blood, but the vast majority of HIV carriers, both symptomatic and asymptomatic, have amounts of free virus that are too small to be picked up by the p24 test. The other two tests, viral culture and PCR, use very sophisticated and expensive laboratory techniques that are still difficult to perform accurately in a high-volume, clinical setting, although they have been available for a number of years. They remain important research tools, but their results have not been validated in such a way as to make them useful in the care of individual patients.

Unfortunately, rare discrepancies have been reported between these research techniques and more conventional antibody testing. Some experts have become concerned that the antibody test may remain negative in rare individuals for up to one to three years after the virus can be detected by viral culture or PCR. These data, however, have not been reproducible and have been reinterpreted by the original laboratory investigators.[43] In addition, several prospective studies comparing antibody testing to viral culture and PCR techniques reveal a close temporal relationship (well within the predicted six-month window) between antibody seroconversion and positivity measured by PCR and viral culture.[44] Thus, relying on ELISA and Western Blot techniques to determine HIV infection appears to be increasingly justified.

Stages after Seroconversion

Following seroconversion, most infected people completely recover their sense of health and well-being and become virtually asymptomatic. The current understanding is that the virus remains more or less quiescent within cells during this phase. As mentioned earlier, however, this asymptomatic stage does not represent true biologic latency. HIV, unlike other viruses, continues to produce low levels of new virus throughout its lifetime in the cell, and it seems to possess special genetic and molecular techniques of avoiding the normal mechanisms for viral suppression. In other words, at a cellular level, HIV is never biologically latent or inactive, even though infected people may remain entirely asymptomatic for long periods.

This ongoing production of low levels of new virus is an important part of the disease process. First, it provides a reservoir for infecting previously healthy host cells that somehow escaped infection during the initial seroconversion period. Second, viral reproduction destroys the T_4 lymphocytes that constitute a key component of the immune system. As these cells die, the body's natural defense system is silently undermined. Thus, although they may feel perfectly well, asymptomatic infected people should be concerned for two reasons: first, they continue to be infectious through sex and blood contact; second, the ongoing viral activity results in a slow and often hidden deterioration of the immune system. Early medical intervention has been shown to delay this deterioration, and this is the most significant argument for early HIV testing of otherwise healthy people who know themselves to be at risk.

Once people have tested positive, it is important to monitor the status of their immune systems. The most useful current measure of immune status is the T_4 or CD_4 cell count, which may be obtained through a simple blood test. Even during the asymptomatic phase of disease, when a person feels perfectly well, the number of T_4 cells may be drastically reduced; often, even when the absolute number itself is acceptable, an abnormal ratio between T_4 and T_8 cells may result in more subtle immune deficits. These changes themselves do not make a person feel ill, and it is often not until the immune system fails and some secondary infection occurs that the person feels sick. For these reasons, monitoring asymptomatic HIV carriers with special blood tests to measure the T_4 cell count has become standard practice.

The next stage in HIV progression is that of symptomatic disease, whose more severe forms have been referred to as ARC. (As noted earlier, this usage is currently debated.) This stage covers a broad spectrum of clinical illness, from the very mild to the most severe. Problems can include oral and vaginal thrush (a yeast infection); oral ulcers; swollen lymph glands; low platelets (blood cells that are important for clotting); anemia; kidney failure; certain bacterial infections such as pneumonia and, in women, pelvic inflammatory disease; nerve pain in the feet and hands; mild changes in memory and concentration; nonspecific muscle and joint pains; fevers and night sweats without a specific infectious cause; loss of appetite with mild weight loss; shingles; and a multitude of different skin problems and rashes including psoriasis, oral and genital herpes, and fungal infections of the finger and toe nails, among others.

Other infectious diseases that may be related to a high-risk lifestyle (such as syphilis, hepatitis, and tuberculosis) may also become active and may be more difficult to treat than they would otherwise have been in a non-HIV infected person. The connection between TB and HIV disease, in particular, is rapidly becoming a major public health issue. There are both demographic and biological connections between the two diseases that help to explain why they are increasingly seen together. Many HIV-infected people come from poor, inner-city backgrounds where housing is crowded and tuberculosis remained a problem even in the pre-HIV era. This means that they have a much higher statistical risk of exposure to TB.

The biological connection between the two diseases is more complicated. It centers on the fact that HIV-related immune suppression makes a person more vulnerable to TB. HIV-positive people are more likely to become seriously ill with TB at the time of first exposure, and those who already carry the TB organism in a quiescent form are more likely to become sick from reactivation. TB is a serious illness requiring prolonged treatment (six to eighteen months, depending on the individual situation). Preventing exposure has therefore always been a cornerstone of public health policy. Since HIV-positive people are especially vulnerable to TB, preventing exposure is a particularly important aspect of their care. Special precautions must be taken to ensure a safe environment in clinics and hospitals where they come into contact with other sick people who may have TB.

The fact that HIV and TB travel together raises several other issues. TB is a serious public health problem for everyone, not just for people who are HIV-positive. In recent years resistant strains of TB have emerged that do not respond to antibiotics. Several such outbreaks have occurred in hospitals where HIV-positive patients receive care. Multidrug-resistant TB presents the same kind of problems we used to face in the pre-antibiotic era. TB is a life-threatening disease which, unlike HIV, is transmitted through airborne contact (that is, by sharing an enclosed space and breathing the same air as someone who is actively infectious). Isolation of actively infectious TB patients, whether or not they are HIV-positive, is therefore appropriate and necessary.

It is important to recognize that the need for isolation is based upon the presence of TB and has nothing to do with a patient's HIV status. Medical staff must become increasingly alert and proactive about the risk for TB in all patients. It is also important to note that the isolation required for TB is of limited duration: patients are considered non-infectious after two weeks of effective treatment, even though they must continue taking medications for much longer. In any case, there is no medical justification for isolation based on HIV status alone.

The final stage in the clinical progression of HIV disease is AIDS itself. In order to make the distinction clear in lay terms, this stage is often referred to as "full-blown" AIDS. The best current estimate is that approximately 50 percent of infected people will have developed an AIDS-defining complication within ten years after seroconversion.[45] Biologically, this stage is characterized by a very low level of intact T_4 cells, and the patient is permanently at risk for truly opportunistic infections that simply do not develop when healthy immune defenses are functioning properly.

Unlike the term "ARC," "AIDS" has a very specific definition determined by the CDC. Although it has changed over time, this definition is rooted primarily in observations of gay male cohorts. Only recently has anyone questioned whether the disease is manifested differently in women and intravenous drug injectors, and the answer is not yet clear.

In the early 1980s, when very little about this bizarre disease was understood, the CDC definition was designed to select and group together a small cluster of dissimilar but abnormal medical conditions that were believed to be connected manifestations of a single disease process. They included pneumocystis carinii pneumonia (PCP), Kaposi's sarcoma (a blood vessel tumor), toxoplasmosis of the brain, cryptococcal meningitis, and certain types of lymphoma, among other problems. The CDC's short-term goal was to facilitate epidemiologic tracking of this new phenomenon in order to better assess different theories about its underlying cause and mode of transmission. As the facts of viral infection have been established, and as antibody testing has permitted researchers to identify infected cohorts of patients in whom the natural history of disease can be observed over time, the case definition of AIDS has been rewritten.

In 1987, the CDC added HIV-related dementia and HIV-related wasting as conditions warranting the "AIDS" designation.[46] AIDS dementia is generally considered to be one of the later manifestations of the HIV disease process. Although significant numbers of AIDS patients have obvious evidence of impaired thought processes in the few months preceding death, it has been estimated that under 5 percent of CDC-defined AIDS cases have presented with this syndrome as their initial problem. When used rigorously, the term "AIDS dementia" refers to a specific clinical symptom of severely crippling dementia resembling Alzheimer's disease in the degree of impairment and care required. This pattern of illness must be clearly distinguished from the more minor cognitive changes that do occur in significant numbers of patients in earlier stages of the disease. These changes are often not detectable without sophisticated neuropsychological testing. Though they may cause great distress to the patients who experience them, they do not usually impair the ability to work or to participate fully in society.

Given the fact that HIV disease appears to be a progressive process, the CDC AIDS designation clearly marks an arbitrary boundary along a spectrum of illness. In a rather crude fashion it draws a distinction between the sick and the very sick. Nevertheless, like all black-and-white distinctions, it is limited by its own arbitrariness. It cannot, for instance, accommodate the real-world overlap between those who have had one episode of PCP, have recovered, and are fully functioning (although they have CDC-defined AIDS), and those whose health is radically compromised by chronic fevers, fatigue, and disabling skin problems, although they have not suffered from an opportunistic infection.

These contradictions help to explain why the CDC has expanded its most recent proposed revision of the AIDS definition to include people with persistent T_4 count below 200. However, by adding a purely laboratory-defined criterion rather than relying solely on the occurrence of a well-defined clinical event, the newest definition includes a much more heterogeneous HIV population, extending from those who are severely immunocompromised but clinically well to those who are dying. A second epidemiologic and political issue that this raises is the method of national reporting for HIV. Currently, reporting to the CDC is mandatory for all AIDS cases, and it occurs through the individual physician's office at the time that the AIDS-defining opportunistic infection occurs. The proposed change in the CDC definition means that, in the future, laboratory facilities may automatically report anyone with T cells less than 200. Advocacy groups for people with HIV are concerned that this change from individual physician to laboratory-based reporting may lead to greater breaches of confidentiality.

The concept that AIDS is the final stage in the natural history of HIV disease raises one further point. The public in general, and patients in particular, tend to understand "final stage" to mean that death is imminent once one crosses the threshold into AIDS. There is some basis in historical reality for this fear, since the life expectancy of people with AIDS was very limited in the early 1980s (median survival was eleven months).[47] Since then, however, the effectiveness and variety of treatment options have so increased that survival can be measured in terms of years rather than months. In addition, there is growing recognition that some AIDS-defining illnesses are more severe than others. For instance, disseminated mycobacterium avium complex (MAC) and cytomegalovirus (CMV) retinitis occur at lower T cell levels (less than fifty), and carry a shorter life-expectancy, than the first episode of uncomplicated PCP or toxoplasmosis.[48]

In sum, the AIDS designation is becoming less and less medically significant for two reasons. First, the definition itself has been broadened; second, improved treatment and prevention measures have changed the natural history of the disease and have prolonged survival. The net effect is that, for practicing physicians concerned with individual treatment and prognosis, the distinction between AIDS and non-AIDS HIV disease is becoming less and less significant. Nevertheless, it is important to distinguish between medical and social realities. The term "AIDS" still has a powerful psychological impact on individuals and a very real financial impact on disability determinations and publicly funded benefits.

The preceding discussion has treated the spectrum of HIV disease as an orderly progression in which people are healthy but infected, then fall mildly ill, and finally become severely ill with terminal complications. Though it is helpful as a framework within which to understand the disease, this time-line concept can be misleading. It is easy to assume that there is some standard time-frame, and that the disease progresses at an orderly and even predictable rate. Although many cohort studies have now delineated the average rates of T_4 cell decline, progression to AIDS over specified time intervals, and survival after particular complications have developed, these population-based statistics are of limited use in predicting any single individual's experience with the disease. Many patients do not experience a steady decline in their overall health; often the disease exacerbates in fits and starts. An asymptomatic person may have a moderate T_4 cell count that is rock-stable for years (four to six, perhaps more) then suddenly drops to severely immunocompromised levels. Some patients develop multiple AIDS-qualifying complications within a matter of months and then stabilize on treatment for the next two years. Some newly infected people do not have the expected prolonged asymptomatic period but rapidly progress to full-blown AIDS within one to three years. (This may be related to the particular strain of the virus, or their body's particular response, or both.) Some patients remain problem-free for several years despite extremely low T_4 cell counts (sometimes less than fifty).

For patient and caregiver alike, this wide range of possibilities presents a problem of unpredictability. It is impossible to give a definite and specific prognosis during most of the disease process, and this uncertainty is one of the most stressful things about the disease. "Living with HIV" means tolerating a high level of anxiety, which takes a tremendous toll at every stage. For these who are well, it means the uncertainty of waiting for the other shoe to drop, sometimes for years. For those who are already sick, it means worrying about what the next complication will bring, how their bodies will betray them next, whether they will lose some crucial faculty such as sight, or how much pain they may be asked to tolerate. The unanswerability of these questions may well be one of the major factors contributing to the increased rate of suicidality that has been documented among at least some HIV subpopulations.[49] Medical caregivers alone cannot meet these needs, and the complementary expertise of psychosocial staff members is an integral part of HIV care.

TREATMENT

Treatment for patients with HIV can be divided into two major categories: primary antiviral therapy and secondary therapy to treat and prevent specific opportunistic infections. Although details of clinical practice rapidly become outdated, the general principles behind therapy remain relatively constant.

Antiviral Therapies

There are several very different theoretical approaches to the problem of preventing HIV reproduction in human tissue. In terms of practical, widely available clinical treatments, however, one group of drugs has become pre-eminent. Referred to as "nucleoside analogues," they include the first recognized anti-HIV drug, AZT, as well as the related compounds ddI and ddC. *Nucleoside analogue* is a pharmacologic term meaning that these drugs are fake building blocks for the virus. The viral protein called reverse transcriptase assembles the appropriate building blocks to create new virus, thereby serving as the Achilles' heel that makes treatment with nucleoside analogues possible.

The simplest analogy for explaining how these drugs interfere with reverse transcriptase and viral reproduction is as follows. Each unit of virus can be thought of as a brick wall of certain specified dimensions. The goal of each virus is to make as many copies of itself as possible, as many new brick walls as it can. It does this by using a mechanical arm (reverse transcriptase), which picks up individual bricks and drops them into place in a new brick wall running parallel to the old established wall. AZT, ddI, and ddC masquerade as building blocks; each appears neat and square on one side, though each has a large lump on the other. These fake bricks disrupt the wall-building process in two ways. First, they may be picked up by the mechanical arm and then, because they are not perfectly square and do not fit exactly right, they may jam the machinery. That particular wall-building unit, or reverse transcriptase, is permanently inactivated. Second, some bricks do get cemented, squareside down, into the developing wall or virus. But the lumpy part remains face-up, and no new bricks can be laid on top. The wall cannot be finished; the new virus is incomplete and therefore biologically inactive.

Once this imagery is understood, an important difference emerges between the pharmacologic approach to HIV (and viral disease in general) and traditional antibiotic therapy for bacterial infections. In the latter case, drugs are designed to kill the bacteria. Viruses, however, cannot be "killed" once they have gained entry to human tissue because of their extreme simplicity and their insinuation into normal cellular processes. (On the other hand, they can easily be killed or inactivated outside the body through the use of bleach, alcohol, heat or other simple chemical disinfectants.) Thus, a biologic cure—eliminating the virus from the infected person's body—is virtually impossible, given our current level of biochemical and pharmacologic technology. Instead we have to settle for second-best, containing the damage of infection over time by limiting the reproductive activity of the virus and reducing the total burden of HIV in the body.

In addition to nucleoside analogues, several other antiviral approaches are being investigated and developed. These include entirely different categories of nonnucleoside analogue drugs that also interfere with reverse transcriptase and viral reproduction (for example, BI-RG587 and the TIBO family); immunomodulators, which are naturally occurring biologic compounds that are produced in small quantities by a healthy immune system and which can now be synthesized and administered in very high doses (for example, alpha inteferon); and a number of substances whose mechanism of activity is still poorly understood (for example, compound Q and hypericin or Saint-John's-wort). Yet another approach relies on the observation, mentioned previously, that anti-HIV antibody, which develops spontaneously during the initial period of seroconversion, seems to play a role in the suppression and control of early viral infection. Researchers hope that maintaining extremely high levels of antibody may prolong the quiescent period and prevent the progression of disease. Two techniques have been tried: first, HIV vaccines may slow early disease by stimulating spontaneous synthesis of antibody;[50] second, passive transfer therapy has been tried by taking blood from a healthy infected donor, purifying the antibody-containing plasma, and infusing it into a sicker patient who presumably has lower levels of effective antibody. These various therapies are truly experimental and are of unproven efficacy, though they certainly provide hope for the future.

HIV treatment presents many practical issues that can only be briefly touched on in this chapter. Over the last five years, early intervention—meaning the initiation of AZT therapy as soon as the T_4 cell count drops below 500—has become the standard of care in the United States. The decision about when to change from AZT to one of the alternate nucleoside analogues (ddI or ddC) remains a question of clinical judgment. Matching the different toxicities of each drug to the individual patient's clinical situation will become increasingly important. Problems of viral resistance to these drugs, and AZT in particular, are becoming increasingly important as more and more patients remain on long-term therapy for several years. Finally, the potential for combination therapy—the simultaneous or sequential use of drugs with different toxicities and different mechanisms of antiviral activity—is rapidly becoming a practical reality as we develop a broader spectrum of anti-HIV drugs, though the efficacy of this approach still needs to be carefully evaluated.

Opportunistic Infections

Opportunistic infections and the secondary complications of HIV infection still cause most HIV-related illness and death. The rapid progress of the last ten years has radically changed the natural history of the disease. As we become more practiced in controlling familiar problems like PCP, others emerge with greater frequency, such as CMV and MAC. Before the AIDS epidemic we had had only limited experience with many of these diseases, and much current research focuses on developing new drugs to treat them. For example, in certain settings an oral drug called fluconazole has replaced our prior reliance on a more toxic intravenous therapy called Amphotericin B for fungal infections; when the latter is still needed, new formulations may have fewer side effects than the traditional preparation. In addition, there is a great deal of work being done to develop prophylactic regimens that prevent such problems in the first place. The successful use of inhaled pentamidine or low-dose oral trimethoprim-sulfamethoxazole (commonly known as Septra or Bactrim) to prevent PCP has stimulated questions about analogous approaches to toxoplasmosis and CMV.

While this progress is encouraging, and these therapies have undoubtedly extended the life expectancy of people with AIDS, there is a steep psychosocial cost (let alone the economic one). The brunt of this burden is carried by the individual patient and his or her intimate family. HIV treatment can take over most of a sick person's waking time, especially as one complication builds on another in the end-stages of this disease.

Imagine a forty-year-old woman. She is the single head of her household, with three children (ages eight to thirteen) at home, and she has sight-threatening CMV retinitis and MAC, which causes fever and diarrhea. Her treatment for these two problems alone may require daily intravenous therapy, which she will often have to self-administer at home, and a complicated dosing schedule of three to five oral medications. She also needs PCP prevention, which means either another set of pills each week or a monthly clinic visit for a breathing treatment. Of course, her treatment for HIV itself requires several daily doses of something, whether it be AZT, ddI, or ddC. Then there is her anemia, a complication of her illnesses exacerbated by the toxicities of the drugs she must take; for this, she injects a hormone under her skin three times a week. (The alternative would be another set of monthly visits to a clinic for transfusions.) Meanwhile, she must see a gynecologist every few months to monitor the abnormal Pap smears she has had for some time. There is the eye doctor to be seen monthly. And then there are the visits to her primary doctor, perhaps only once a month if she is going through a "good" period; sometimes every two weeks or every week, if she is not. The litany is overwhelming. Survival in such circumstances is an exercise in courage and determination, yet this is how many people with HIV disease live the last months and years of their lives.

Moreover, while the ill person struggles to maintain her own fragile existence, she must also face the reality of her imminent death and its practical consequences—legal, social, financial—for her immediate family. In the midst of her physical and psychological battle to survive, she must be able to step back and ask herself the difficult questions: When have I fought enough? Are the treatments worth it? Has the moment arrived when the daily routine of discomfort and fatigue is more daunting than death? She and her physician must plan for this, at the bare minimum with some kind of advance directive regarding resuscitation should her heart or breathing stop (often referred to as a "living will"). She may choose to do more than this;

perhaps seeing a comfortable death as part of her treatment plan, she may choose to stop some or all of her therapies and to seek hospice care either at home or in an institution. Finally, she may seek even greater control over her death and may actively pursue plans for suicide, perhaps with the knowledge of her physician or the assistance of a lay organization such as the Hemlock Society. In addition, she must attend to the practical details of a will, of planning the funeral service, of establishing with her family who will take care of the children when she is gone (her husband died years ago) and who their legal guardian will be. For many months now, every ounce of her energy has been spent on staying alive; these difficult decisions raise questions that challenge her will to live. Perhaps she is not strong enough physically, let alone emotionally, to face that challenge. Perhaps her family—and the courts—will be left to deal with these issues. If she is to cope with all of this, she needs many different resources far beyond the purely medical: she needs psychosocial support, legal advice, pastoral counseling, and someone to help with public assistance or insurance paperwork. Moreover, this help must be provided as a coordinated team effort focusing on her needs and her priorities. Yet such services are often inadequate, or inaccessible geographically or financially, or scattered among different organizations.

AIDS is a resource-intensive disease that not only strains the individual's capacity to cope, but also challenges our systems of medical, social, and legal support. Even the imagery of natural disaster is inadequate, for unlike tornadoes or floods, which happen once and pass on, AIDS is a self-perpetuating phenomenon. There has been no "afterwards" in this epidemic. Communities, like individuals, do not recover from AIDS but rather learn to live with it. The meanings of HIV disease are diverse and profound. How we as a society choose to respond will reflect upon and deeply mark the development of our national character for years to come.

NOTES

1 Gottlieb, et al., Pneumocystis Pneumonia— Los Angeles, 30 MMWR 250 (1981).

2 See, e.g., Kaposi's Sarcoma and Pneumocystis Pneumonia Among Homosexual Men— New York City and California, 30 MMWR 305 (1981); Follow-up on Kaposi's Sarcoma and Pneumocystis Pneumonia, 30 MMWR 409–10 (1981); Siegal, et al., Severe Acquired Immunodeficiency in Male Homosexuals, Manifested by Chronic Perianal Ulcerative Herpes Simplex Lesions, 305 New Eng. J. Med. 1439 (1981).

3 For a full history of the early debates about etiology, including theories about cytomegalovirus, exposure to amyl nitrate, and cumulative damage from multiple infections, see R. Shilts, And the Band Played On 80–92 (1987); Centers for Disease Control, Task Force on Kaposi's Sarcoma and Opportunistic Infections, Epidemiologic Aspects of the Cur-

rent *Outbreak of Kaposi's Sarcoma and Opportunistic Infection*, 306 New Eng. J. Med. 248 (1982).

4 *Update on Kaposi's Sarcoma and Opportunistic Infections in Previously Healthy Persons—United States*, 31 MMWR 294, 300–01 (1982); Ehrenkranz, *et al.*, *Pneumocystis Carinii Pneumonia among Persons with Hemophilia A*, 31 MMWR 365 (1982).

5 Hensley, *et al.*, *Opportunistic Infections and Kaposi's Sarcoma among Haitians in the United States*, 31 MMWR 353 (1982); Clumeck, *et al.*, *Acquired Immune Deficiency Syndrome in Black Africans*, 1 Lancet 642 (1983).

6 *The HIV/AIDS Epidemic: The First 10 Years*, 40 MMWR 357, 369 (1991).

7 *The Second 100,000 Cases of Acquired Immunodeficiency Syndrome—United States, June 1981-December 1991*, 41 MMWR 28 (1992) [hereinafter *The Second 100,000 Cases*].

8 D'Aquila, *et al.*, *The Association of Race/Ethnicity and HIV Infection among Connecticut Intravenous Drug Users*, 2 J. A.I.D.S. 503 (1989).

9 *The Second 100,000 Cases*, note 7 above.

10 *Mortality Attributable to HIV Infection/AIDS—United States, 1981–1990*, 40 MMWR 41 (1991).

11 *The Second 100,000 Cases*, note 7 above; *Mortality Attributable to HIV Infection/AIDS*, note 10 above; *see also* Chu, *et al.*, *Impact of the Human Immunodeficiency Virus Epidemic on Mortality in Women of Reproductive Age, United States*, 264 J.A.M.A. 225 (1990). It should also be noted that by 1989 AIDS had already become the second leading cause of death for all men between the ages of twenty-five and forty-four.

12 The exact sequence of discovery has been a topic of great controversy, but recognition has been given both to Luc Montagnier and Robert Gallo for near-simultaneous discovery. For the original descriptions of the virus see

Gallo, *et al.*, *Isolation of Human T-Cell Leukemia Virus in Acquired Immune Deficiency (AIDS)*, 220 Science 865 (1983); Barrie-Sinoussi, *et al.*, *Isolation of a T-Lymphotropic Retrovirus from a Patient at Risk for Acquired Immune Deficiency Syndrome (AIDS)*, 220 Science 868 (1983).

13 For an excellent but medically sophisticated summary of the basic mechanisms by which HIV causes disease, *see* Fauci, *et al.*, *Immunopathogenic Mechanisms in Human Immunodeficiency Virus (HIV) Infection*, 114 Annals Internal Med. 678 (1991).

14 Nelson, *et al.*, *Human Immunodeficiency Virus Detected in Bowel Epithelium from Patients with Gastrointestinal Symptoms*, 1 Lancet 259 (1988).

15 *See, e.g.*, Martin, *et al.*, *Disinfection and Inactivation of the Human T Lymphotropic Virus Type III/Lymphadenopathy-Associated Virus*, 152 J. Inf. Dis. 400 (1985).

16 Friedland & Klein, *Transmission of the Human Immunodeficiency Virus*, 317 N. Eng. J. Med. 1129 (1987); *see also* Holmberg, *et al.*, *Biologic Factors in the Sexual Transmission of Human Immunodeficiency Virus*, 60 J. Inf. Dis. 116, 117–18 (1989).

17 *See, e.g.*, Goedert, *et al.*, *Determinants of Retrovirus (HTLV-III) Antibody and Immunodeficiency Conditions in Homosexual Men*, 2 Lancet 711 (1984); Padian, *et al.*, *Female-to-Male Transmission of Human Immunodeficiency Virus*, 266 J.A.M.A. 1664 (1991).

18 For an excellent summary of the data regarding factors in transmission such as menstruation, circumcision, ulcerative diseases, tampon use, and birth control use, *see* Friedland & Klein, note 17 above.

19 Winkelstein, *et al.*, *Sexual Practices and Risk of Infection by the Human Immunodeficiency Virus*, 257 J.A.M.A. 321 (1987); Kingsley, *et al.*, *Risk Factors for Seroconversion to Human Immunodeficiency Virus among Male Homosexuals*, 1 Lancet 345 (1987).

20 See Perry, et al., Orogenital Transmission of Human Immunodeficiency Virus (HIV), 111 Annals Internal Med. 951 (1989).

21 Fischl, et al., Evaluation of Heterosexual Partners, Children and Household Contacts of Adults with AIDS, 257 J.A.M.A. 640, 641 (1987).

22 Friedland & Klein, note 16 above, at 1132–33 ("The isolation of virus from a body fluid does not necessarily mean that the fluid is important in transmission.").

23 Chaisson, et al., Cocaine Use and HIV Infection in Intravenous Drug Users in San Francisco, 261 J.A.M.A. 561 (1989).

24 Schoenbaum, et al., Risk Factors for Human Immunodeficiency Virus Infection in Intravenous Drug Users, 321 New Eng. J. Med. 874 (1989).

25 See, e.g., Des Jarlais, et al., Crack Use and Multiple AIDS Risk Behaviors, 4 J. A.I.D.S. 446 (1991).

26 See Schoenbaum, et al., note 24 above.

27 Checko, et al., HIV Seroprevalence among Childbearing Women in Connecticut, 55 Conn. Med. 9 (1991).

28 See, e.g., The European Collaborative Study, Mother-to-Child Transmission of HIV Infection, 1 Lancet 1039 (1988). The lower number comes from more recent follow-up. The European Collaborative Study, Children Born to Women with HIV-I Infection: Natural History and Risk of Transmission, 337 Lancet 253 (1991).

29 See Friedland & Klein, note 16 above, at 1131.

30 Goedart, et al., High Risk of HIV-I Infection for First-born Twins, 338 Lancet 1471 (1991). At least two previous studies have noted as incidental findings that route of delivery does not affect rate of transmission. See note 28 above; Blanche, et al., A Prospective Study of Infants Born to Women Seropositive for Human Immunodeficiency Virus Type I, 320 New Eng. J. Med. 1643 (1989).

31 Van de Perre, et al., Postnatal Transmission of Human Immunodeficiency Virus Type I from Mother to Infant, 325 New Eng. J. Med. 593 (1991).

32 Donegan, et al., Infection with Human Immunodeficiency Virus Type I (HIV-I) among Recipients of Antibody-Positive Donations, 113 Annals Internal Med. 733 (1990).

33 Goedart, et al., Antibodies Reactive with Human T Cell Leukemia Viruses in the Serum of Hemophiliacs Receiving Factor VIII Concentrate, 65 Blood 492 (1985). More recent evaluations confirm similar findings. See, e.g., Gjerset, et al., Treatment Type and Amount Influenced Human Immunodeficiency Virus Seroprevalence of Patients with Congenital Bleeding Disorders, 78 Blood 1623 (1991). The purification process for Factor IX is more extensive and probably eliminates most of the cellular debris that remains present in Factor VIII.

34 Cumming, et al., Exposure of Patients to Human Immunodeficiency Virus through the Transfusion of Blood Components that Test Antibody-Negative, 321 New Eng. J. Med. 941 (1989); see also, e.g., Busch, et al., 322 New Eng. J. Med. 850 (1990) (letter responding to Cumming, et al.).

35 Dab, et al., Misconceptions about Transmission of AIDS and Attitudes toward Prevention in the French General Public, 3 AIDS 433 (1989).

36 Friedland, et al., Lack of Transmission of HTLV-III/LAV Infection to Household Contacts of Patients with AIDS or AIDS-Related Complex with Oral Candidiasis, 314 New Eng. J. Med. 344 (1986); Friedland, et al., Additional Evidence for Lack of Transmission of HIV Infection by Close Interpersonal (Casual) Contact, 4 AIDS 639 (1990); Gershon, et al., The Risk of Transmission of HIV-I through Non-Percutaneous, Non-Sexual Modes—A Review, 4 AIDS 645 (1990).

37 Acquired Immunodeficiency Syndrome (AIDS) in Western Palm Beach County, Florida, 35 MMWR 609 (1986).

38 Lifson, *et al.*, *Long-term Human Immunodeficiency Virus Infection in Asymptomatic Homosexual and Bisexual Men with Normal CD4+ Lymphocyte Counts: Immunologic and Virologic Characteristics*, 163 J. Inf. Dis. 959 (1991); Rutherford, *et al.*, *Course of HIV-I Infection in a Cohort of Homosexual and Bisexual Men: An 11-year Follow Up Study*, 301 British Med. J. 1183 (1990).

39 Tindall & Cooper, *Primary HIV Infection: Host Responses and Intervention Strategies*, 5 AIDS 1 (1991).

40 Daar, *et al.*, *Transient High Levels of Viremia in Patients with Primary Human Immunodeficiency Virus Type I Infection*, 324 New Eng. J. Med. 961 (1991); Clark, *et al.*, *High Titers of Cytopathic Virus in Plasma of Patients with Symptomatic Primary HIV-I Infection*, 324 New Eng. J. Med. 954 (1991).

41 Horsburgh, *Duration of Human Immunodeficiency Virus Infection before Detection of Antibody*, 2 Lancet 637 (1989).

42 *See* Daar, *et al.*, note 40 above; *see also* Goudsmit, *et al.*, *Expression of Human Immunodeficiency Virus Antigen (HIV-Ag) in Serum and Cerebrospinal Fluid during Acute and Chronic Infection*, 2 Lancet 177 (1986); Paul, *et al.*, *Correlation of Serum HIV Antigen and Antibody with Clinical Status in HIV-Infected Patients*, 22 J. Med. Virol. 357 (1987); Coombs, *et al.*, *Plasma Viremia in Human Immunodeficiency Virus Infection*, 321 New Eng. J. Med. 1626 (1989).

43 Imagawa, *et al.*, *Human Immunodeficiency Virus Type I Infection in Homosexual Men Who Remain Seronegative for Prolonged Periods*, 320 New Eng. J. Med. 1458 (1989); Imagawa & Detelo, *HIV-I in Seronegative Homosexual Men*, 325 New Eng. J. Med. 1250 (1991).

44 Pan, *et al.*, *Lack of Detection of Human Immunodeficiency Virus in Persistently Sero-negative Homosexual Men with High or Medium Risks for Infection*, 164 J. Inf. Dis. 962 (1991); Yerly, *et al.*, *Absence of Chronic Human Immunodeficiency Virus Infection without Seroconversion in Intravenous Drug Users: A Prospective and Retrospective Study*, 164 J. Inf. Dis. 965 (1991).

45 *See* Rutherford, *et al.*, note 39 above.

46 Council of State and Territorial Epidemiologists, *Revision of the CDC Surveillance Case Definition for Acquired Immunodeficiency Syndrome*, 36 MMWR 1S (Supp. 1987).

47 Bacchetti, *et al.*, *Survival Patterns of the First 500 Patients with AIDS in San Francisco*, 157 J. Inf. Dis. 1044 (1988).

48 *See, e.g.*, Horsburgh, *et al.*, *Survival of Patients with Acquired Immune Deficiency Syndrome and Disseminated Mycobacterium Avium Complex Infection with and without Antimycobacterial Chemotherapy*, 144 Am. Rev. Respir. Dis. 557 (1991); Holland, *et al.*, *Survival of Patients with the Acquired Immune Deficiency Syndrome after Development of Cytomegalovirus Retinopathy*, 97 Ophthalmology 204 (1990).

49 Marzuk, *et al.*, *Increased Risk of Suicide in Persons with AIDS*, 259 J.A.M.A. 1333 (1988).

50 Redfield, *et al.*, *A Phase-I Evaluation of the Safety and Immunogenicity of Vaccination with Recombinant gp160 in Patients with Early Human Immunodeficiency Virus Infection*, 324 New Eng. J. Med. 1677 (1991). Though we continue to use the word "vaccine," this approach to treatment is quite new. In the past, a vaccine was regarded as a strictly preventive measure. In HIV disease, however, we have experimented with the use of vaccinations both to protect the uninfected and to treat the infected by boosting the immune response and slowing the progression of disease.

3 A Historical Perspective

Allan M. Brandt

Despite philosopher George Santayana's famous injunction that those who do not remember the past are condemned to repeat it, history is not a fable with the moral spelled out at the end. Even if we could agree on a particular construction of past events, it would not necessarily lead to consensus on what is to be done. And yet history provides us with one means of understanding hidden influences and possible courses of action in the present.

The history of medicine and public health can tell us much about contemporary approaches to the very difficult dilemmas raised by HIV disease. The way a society responds to problems of disease reveals its deepest cultural, social, and moral values. These core values—patterns of judgment about what is good or bad—shape and guide human perception and action. The HIV epidemic has been shaped not only by powerful biological forces but by behavioral, social, and cultural factors as well. This essay briefly analyzes the process by which social and cultural forces affect our understanding of disease by examining a telling analogue to the current health crisis.[1]

THE PROGRESSIVE ERA AND THE SOCIAL HYGIENE MOVEMENT

The first two decades of the twentieth century witnessed a general hysteria about venereal infections that parallels today's concern about AIDS.[2] This period, often referred to as the Progressive Era, combined two powerful strains in American social thought: the search for new technical, scientific answers to social problems and the search for a set of unified moral ideals. Both branches of thought were reflected in the "social hygiene" movement, the Progressives' campaign against venereal infection. The social hygiene movement was predicated on a series of major scientific breakthroughs. The specific organism that causes gonorrhea, the gonococcus, and

46

the causative agent for syphilis, the spirochete, were both identified. By the end of the first decade of the twentieth century, diagnostic exams had been established. In 1911, the first major drug effective against the spirochete—Salvarsan—was discovered. These advances reframed the perception of venereal disease in the scientific community: the availability of effective means of diagnosis and treatment led to a more open discussion of the enormous social, cultural, and economic costs of the disease.

Physicians who had been reluctant to discuss and often to treat venereal diseases began to trace the repercussions of syphilis within the family. Doctors came to define what they called *venereal insontium,* or venereal disease of the "innocent." Perhaps the best known example of *venereal insontium* was *opthalmia neonatorum,* gonorrheal blindness of the newborn. As late as 1910, up to 25 percent of all the blind in the United States had lost their sight in this way, despite the earlier discovery that silver nitrate solution could prevent infection. Increased public discussion of this form of blindness led many states to require prophylactic treatment.[3]

Doctors stressed the disease's impact on women even more than that on children. In 1906, for example, an American Medical Association symposium on the duty of the profession to womanhood examined the physician's duty to report venereal infection to wives and fiancées.[4] The distinction between venereal disease and *venereal insontium,* of course, had the effect of dividing victims; some deserved attention, sympathy, and medical support, others did not. By determining how infection was obtained, doctors separated victims into the "innocent" and the "guilty."

The train of family tragedy was a frequent cultural theme in these years. In 1913, a hit Broadway play by French playwright Eugene Brieux, *Damaged Goods,* told the story of young George Dupont who is warned by his physician not to marry because he has syphilis but disregards the advice, only to spread the infection to his wife and, ultimately, to their child. This story was told and retold; it revealed evolving social attitudes about science, social responsibility, and the limits of medicine to cure the moral ailments of humankind.[5]

Intrafamily transmission was not the only fear of Progressive Era physicians. The last years of the nineteenth century and the first of the twentieth were the most intensive periods of immigration to the United States in its entire history; more than 650,000 immigrants came to these shores each year between 1885 and 1910. Many doctors and social critics suggested that these outsiders were bringing venereal disease into the country. Howard Kelly, a leading gynecologist at Johns Hopkins, explained, "think of these countless currents flowing daily from the houses of the poorest into those of the richest, and forming a sort of civic circulatory system expressive of the body politic, a circulation which continually tends to equalize the distribution of morality and disease."[6] In fact, examinations at the ports of entry failed to reveal a high incidence of disease. Nevertheless, nativists called for the restriction of immigration.

And how were these immigrants spreading sexually transmitted diseases to native, middle-class, Anglo-Saxon Americans? It was suggested that immigrants constituted the great bulk of prostitutes who inhabited American cities, although data indicated that most prostitutes were native-born.[7]

More important, physicians now asserted that syphilis and gonorrhea could be transmitted in any number of ways. Doctors catalogued the various modes of transmission: pens, pencils, toothbrushes, towels, bedding, and medical procedures were all identified as potential means of communication.[8] One woman explained in an anonymous essay in 1912:

> At first it was unbelievable. I knew of the disease only through newspaper advertisements [for patent medicines]. I had understood that it was the result of sin and that it originated and was contracted only in the underworld of the city. I felt sure that my friend was mistaken in diagnosis when he exclaimed, "Another tragedy of the common drinking cup!" I eagerly met his remark with the assurance that I did not use public drinking cups, that I had used my own cup for years. He led me to review my summer. After recalling a number of times when my thirst had forced me to go to the public fountain, I came at last to realize that what he had told me was true.[9]

The diagnosis, of course, had been syphilis. One indication of how seriously these casual modes of transmission were taken is the fact that the Navy removed doorknobs from its battleships during the First World War, claiming—in a remarkable act of denial—that this had been a source of infection for many of its sailors.

We now know, of course, that syphilis and gonorrhea cannot be contracted in these ways. Why, then, did physicians believe they could be? Theories of casual transmission reflected deep cultural fears about disease and sexuality in the early twentieth century. Venereal disease was viewed as a threat to the entire late Victorian social and sexual system, which placed great value on discipline, restraint, and homogeneity. The sexual code of the era sanctioned only sex-in-marriage. But the concerns about venereal disease also reflected a pervasive fear of the urban masses, the growth of the cities, and the changing nature of familial relationships.

In short, venereal disease became a metaphor for the anxieties of the time. Such metaphors are not simply innocuous linguistic constructions; they have powerful sociopolitical implications. And they have been remarkably persistent during the twentieth century.

Beginning in the early 1900s, concerns about sexually transmitted diseases led to a major public health campaign to stop their spread. Many of the public health approaches applied to communicable infections today were developed in these years.

Educational programs formed a major component of the campaign, though, to be sure, when schools instituted sex education programs in the first decade of the twentieth century, their basic goal was to inculcate fear of sex in order to encourage premarital continence. Indeed, it would be more accurate to call these programs antisexual education.

The new ability to diagnose syphilis and gonorrhea led to other important public health interventions. American cities began to require the reporting of venereal diseases around 1915. Some states used reports to follow contacts and bring individuals in for treatment. By the 1930s, many states had come to require premarital and prenatal screening. Some municipalities mandated compulsory screening of food handlers and barbers, even though it was by then understood that syphilis and gonorrhea could not be spread through casual contact. The rationale offered was that individuals in these professions were at risk for infection anyway and that screening might reveal new cases for treatment.

Perhaps the most dramatic public health intervention devised to combat sexually transmitted diseases was the campaign to close red-light districts. In the first two decades of the twentieth century, vice commissions in almost all American cities had identified prostitutes as a major risk for American health and morals and decided the time had come to remove the sources of infection. During the First World War, more than one hundred red-light districts were closed in an attempt to "drain the swamps" that harbored infection. The crackdown on prostitutes constituted the most concerted attack on civil liberties in the name of public health in American history.

Not surprisingly, in the atmosphere of crisis that the war engendered, public health officials employed radical techniques in their battle against venereal disease. State laws held that anyone "reasonably suspected" of harboring a venereal infection could be tested on a compulsory basis. Prostitutes were also subjected to quarantine, detention, and internment.[10] Attorney General T. W. Gregory explained: "The constitutional right of the community, in the interest of the public health, to ascertain the existence of infections and communicable diseases in its midst and to isolate and quarantine such cases or take steps necessary to prevent the spread of disease is clear."[11]

In July of 1918, Congress allocated more than $1 million for the detention and isolation of venereal disease carriers. During the war, more than 30,000 prostitutes were incarcerated in institutions supported by the federal government. One federal official noted:

Conditions required the immediate isolation of as many venereally infected persons acting as spreaders of disease as could be quickly apprehended and quarantined. It was not a measure instituted for the punishment of prostitutes on account of infraction of the civil or moral law, but was strictly a public health measure to prevent the spread of dangerous, communicable diseases.[12]

Although many of these interventions were challenged in the courts, most were upheld; the police powers of the state were deemed sufficient to override any constitutional concerns. The program of detention and isolation, it should be noted, had no impact on rates of venereal disease, which increased dramatically during the period. Many of the prostitutes were later found to be free of infection; nevertheless, their incarceration—often in barbed wire-enclosed camps—was justified on the grounds that they were likely, if released, to become infected.

The prostitute had been anathema to generations of American reformers; the exigencies of war effected her banishment from the urban landscape. Issues previously seen to be of a moral nature now achieved the powerful legitimacy of scientific and health concerns. The "cult of the expert" made possible far-ranging policies that conflicted with basic civil liberties.

SOCIAL VALUES AND HIV

The analogies between reactions to HIV disease and reactions, in the early 1900s, to venereal disease are striking: the pervasive fear of contagion, concerns about casual transmission, the stigmatization of victims, the conflicts between protecting public health and ensuring civil liberties. Of course, HIV disease is not syphilis, and 1992 is not 1918. Certainly, however, the response to HIV disease is no more strictly determined by its biological character than was the Progressive Era response to venereal disease; rather, social policies are powerfully affected by social and cultural understandings of disease and its victims.

How will social and cultural values concerning HIV influence public policies toward the disease? We face a series of difficult dilemmas. How can the impact of this disease be mitigated? Can we protect the rights of individuals living with the disease while protecting the public—and vice versa? What types of policies should be employed? And how will these policies reflect our cultural notions of the disease?

Already, traditional public health policies—screening, testing, reporting, contact tracing, isolation, and, to a lesser degree, quarantine—have been invoked. Will these measures be effective in the case of HIV, which is complicated by the large number of apparently healthy carriers perhaps infectious for life? How do we construct a just, humane, and effective policy? How do we protect civil liberties while protecting the public good?

As in the early 1900s, the fear and uncertainty surrounding the epidemic could make us less, rather than more, cautious in seeking solutions. Although we know much about HIV, much lies outside current scientific understanding. Scientists and physicians have experience tolerating such ambiguities, but this level of uncertainty is often avoided or denied by the larger society. Policies relating to HIV will, of course, be created in this atmosphere of uncertainty. Moreover, a series of dramatic human-made disasters, from Three Mile Island, to Love Canal, to the space shuttle Challenger, to Chernobyl has dramatically lessened the public's faith in experts.

As a society, we have not had to address any epidemics of major infectious diseases since polio. This good fortune means that we lack recent social and political experience in dealing with such problems. And, indeed, we would probably have to go back to the influenza pandemic of 1918 to identify a pathogen as dangerous as HIV. Thus, we have few models for dealing with public health issues of this magnitude and complexity.

And as a society, we are not good at comparing risks. How does the danger of HIV compare to other risks? How will the courts, for example, determine the relative risk posed by individuals who carry the virus? We need to develop better measures for making more sophisticated assessments of the risks we face.

All social policies carry costs, but in our political culture, we tend to reject policies when the costs become explicit, even if they promise significant benefits. For example, as in the early twentieth century, education has been put forward as one of the few positive activities that might slow the spread of HIV. But some see explicit sexual education as encouraging homosexuality or promiscuity, and many policymakers, from television executives to elected officials, have been unwilling to risk offending them. Similarly, the idea of providing sterile needles to intravenous drug abusers to prevent the further spread of the disease has been rejected by many because it is seen as contributing to the drug problem.

On the other hand, policies that have little or no potential for slowing the epidemic could have considerable legal, social, and cultural appeal. What can be done to separate realistic concerns from irrational fears? How can victim-blaming and stigmatization of groups who are already socially disvalued be avoided?

In many respects, the process of dividing people into the "innocent" and the "guilty"—analogous to the early twentieth-century approach to venereal disease— has been activated once again. Take, for example, the following assessment offered by a journalist in the *New York Times Magazine* in 1984:

The groups most recently found to be at risk for AIDS present a particularly poignant problem. Innocent by-standers caught in the path of a new disease, they can make no behavioral decisions to minimize their risk: hemophiliacs cannot stop taking bloodclotting medication; surgery patients cannot stop getting transfusions; women cannot control the drug habits of their mates; babies cannot choose their mothers.[13]

In some quarters the misapprehension persists: AIDS is caused by homosexuality rather than by a retrovirus. In this confused logic, the answer to the problem is simple: repress these behaviors. Implicit in this approach to the problem are powerful notions of guilt.

The high mortality associated with HIV could yet become the justification for drastic measures. "Better safe than sorry" could become a catch phrase to justify dramatic abuses of basic human rights in the context of an uncertain science. Moreover, the social construction of this disease—its close association in much of the public's eye with violations of the moral code—could contribute to mounting hysteria and anger, producing a double jeopardy of lethal disease and social and legal oppression.

The social costs of ineffective draconian public health measures would only augment the crisis. But we will avoid such measures only if we are sophisticated in our medical and cultural understanding of this disease and if we are able to create an atmosphere of social tolerance. Only when we recognize the ways in which social and cultural values shape our responses to this disease will we be able to sustain effective and humane public health policy.

NOTES

1 One model has already been proposed in Susan Sontag's brilliant polemic, *Illness as Metaphor* (1978). In this work, Sontag assessed the important ways in which tuberculosis and cancer have been used as metaphors. Using techniques of literary analysis, she demonstrated prevailing cultural views of these diseases and their victims. But disease is more than a metaphor. These "social constructions" have very real sociopolitical implications.

2 The following discussion is abbreviated from A. Brandt, No Magic Bullet: A Social History of Venereal Disease in the United States since 1880 (1985).

3 On the problem of *opthalmia neonatorum,* see Wolbarst, *On the Occurrence of Syphilis and Gonorrhea in Children by Direct Infection,* 7 Am. Med. 494 (1912); Von Blarcum, *The Harm Done in Ascribing All Babies' Sore Eyes to Gonorrhea,* Am. J. Pub. Health, 926–31 (1916); Kerr, *Opthalmia Neonatorum: An Analysis of the Laws and Regulations in Relation Thereto in Force in the United States,* Pub. Health Service Bull. No. 49 (1914).

4 *See* Burr, *The Guarantee of Safety in the Marriage Contract,* 47 J.A.M.A. 1887–88 (1906).

5 *See* E. Brieux, Damaged Goods (J. Pollack trans. 1913). On the critical reception of the play, see *Demoralizing Plays,* Outlook, Sept. 20, 1913, at 110; Rockefeller, *The Awakening of a New Social Conscience,* 19 Med. Reviews of Reviews 281 (1913); *Damaged Goods,* Hearst's Mag., May 1913, at 806; *Brieux's New Sociological Sermon in Three Acts,* Current Opinion, Apr. 1913, at 296–97; *see also* Rosenkrantz, *Damaged Goods: Dilemmas of Responsibility for Risk,* 57 Health and Soc'y. 1 (1979).

6 Kelly, *Social Diseases and their Prevention,* Soc. Diseases, July 1910, at 17; Kelly, *The Protection of the Innocent,* Am. J. Obstetrics, Apr. 1907, at 477–81.

7 On prostitution in Progressive America, see Boyer, *Urban Masses and Moral Order* (1978); R. Rosen, *The Lost Sisterhood: Prostitution in America, 1900–1918* (1982); M. Connely, *The Response to Prostitution in the Progressive Era* (1980).

8 On nonvenereal transmission, see especially L. Bulkey, Syphilis of the Innocent (1894).

9 *What One Woman Has Had to Bear,* 68 Forum (1912); *see also, New Laws about Drinking Cups,* 58 Life 1152 (1911).

10 The wartime policy for the attack on the red-light districts and the testing and incarceration of prostitutes is described in greater detail in A. Brandt, note 2 above, at 80–95.

11 T. W. Gregory, Memorandum on Legal Aspects of the Proposed System of Medical Examination of Women Convicted under Section 13, Selective Service Act, National Archives, Record Group 90, Box 223; *see also,* Dietzler, Detention Houses and Reformatories as Protective Social Agencies in the Campaign of the United States Government Against Venereal Diseases (United States Interdepartmental Social Hygiene Board, 1922).

12 Pierce, *The Value of Detention as a Reconstruction Measure,* Am. J. Obstetrics, Dec. 1919, at 629.

13 Henig, *AIDS: A New Disease's Deadly Odyssey,* N.Y. Times Magazine, Feb. 6, 1983, at 36.

4 A Seat on the Merry-Go-Round: A Consumer's View

Belinda Ann Mason

Because my HIV infection came from tainted blood and the hospital responsible for transfusing me with a whole new identity, as well as a political and social agenda, freely admits that its blood bank did not screen that unit for the presence of antibody, I am involved in litigation. By not testing for HIV, the hospital, I contend, fell shamelessly below acceptable standards of care.

The case, my high-priced Eastern-bred lawyers tell me, "looks good."

If they're right, then sometime in the next year my family and I stand to come into an obscene sum of money. I hate to seem coy, but I'd rather have won the lottery. For me, the lawyer is just an extra seat on the AIDS merry-go-round. Another reminder of what I resent most about this disease, not that it might kill me, but that it's stolen away the "normal" life I had forever.

My father-in-law, a Kentucky farmer and breeder, who never wore a suit to work a day in his life, says this: "You've come to a bad out when you get tied up with doctors and lawyers."

My husband and I were country mice in the legal world. In our innocence and with a concept of justice honed in Sunday school and cowboy movies, we originally believed the young doctor who told us how "bad" everyone at the hospital felt about what had happened and how "eager" the administration was to make restitution.

Now, as the months crawl by and we're bothered repeatedly by this system, I've been tempted more than once to call off the whole thing—which is, my lawyer points out, exactly what the hospital's insurance carrier wishes me to do.

Our initial faith in the inevitability of justice and the power of right to prevail was the first casualty in this battle. Right and wrong, we've learned, have no place in the world of medical malpractice, which measures itself by such fabricated concepts as "comparative negligence" and failure to meet acceptable "standards of care."

In what is surely the demonstration of an inborn sense of order, my five-year-old daughter asked "Why did the hospital give you the AIDS virus if they were trying to cure you?" But the system is not designed to respond to the obvious question. It's not "pertinent to the case." Any hope of a hasty resolution was abandoned long ago. We've become accustomed to the delays in court dates, the hocus-pocus of motion filing and all the postponing, by both sides, as we live on borrowed money. (My husband left his job to care for our children and me. I'm not well enough to hold down a regular job—even if someone should be bold enough to hire me.)

The frustration of the endless delays and disappointment was overshadowed this week, though, when I came face to face with the nastiest aspect of the whole affair.

I was evaluated by a vocational rehab expert who'll determine a "life-worth profile" for me. His assistant, still new to her job, asked an exhausting list of questions and took an extensive work history, which encompassed the first dollar I ever earned (as a waitress and fry cook when I was fourteen).

I went across the hall, then, to the expert's office, and took a seat in a stylish leather chair across from him. The carpet was plush, the walls were neutral and the windows generous. The room was, I noted, half as large as my grandmother's house. Above the desk were professionally framed pictures of his sons. He looked over my papers and asked half a dozen questions. "My job," he said, "is to provide an economic assessment for the case. You know future earnings, that sort of thing."

"You want to know what I'm worth dead so the insurance company can buy me," I said.

He tittered nervously and looked away. "What is it worth," I asked him, "that I'm a good friend? What is it worth if I have a big heart, I like country music, or that I'm good to old people? Is there a place on the form for that?"

In retrospect, I feel a little foolish, but not sorry, about what I said. The immorality, or rather the amorality of this process is too large to comprehend. But again, my daughter's clear eye and razor-sharp instincts cut to the core of the matter. She asked: "What does money have to do with a mistake?" Indeed.

On the way home, I thought about Max Navarre, who was known to me only by his writings in "Surviving and Thriving." When I received my copy last summer, it became a good luck charm. People could live with AIDS. I had pictures to prove it and words to tell me how. I never knew Max Navarre, but I borrowed some of his courage. My copy of "Surviving and Thriving" is tattered and worn. Although part of the advice was useless to me—an article about subway fares by David Summers was as remote from my life in Indiana as space travel—the important thing was that the authors were people who were *living* with, as opposed to dying from, AIDS. I soon knew the faces in S&T by heart. When I heard Max Navarre had died, a little of my hope died with him. "In the media," he wrote, "everyone is a victim."

My lawyer once told me that his case would be easier had I lost a body part. "I can tell you what an eye goes for in Kentucky. I can tell you what insurance companies will pay for a leg, but this I don't know."

Human beings, though, are more than the sum of their parts. We know part of what the loss of the Max Navarres, the hundreds of them, is costing our society. The economic loss to the fashion and art world, only two of the communities, touched by AIDS, is being documented every day. But that's too easy. As Michael Callen has written, we must be able to experience each death as an individually painful and unique loss. Perhaps we are numbed to inaction by the thousands of losses precisely because we've never truly appreciated the vastness of the one.

II Primary Public Health Measures against HIV

5 Traditional Public Health Strategies

Larry Gostin

Human immunodeficiency virus (HIV) infection is the most serious communicable disease epidemic in contemporary times. HIV disease is uniquely problematic: infection cannot currently be prevented or cured; the virus changes easily, making the future development of vaccines difficult; there is no finite incubation period, so carriers of the virus are chronically infectious; and many of those at greatest risk are vulnerable to social prejudice and private discrimination because of their race, class, or sexual orientation, posing special problems for public health officials seeking to identify people carrying the virus and capable of transmitting it. The fact that the burden of the epidemic is shifting markedly toward the poor, ethnic minorities, and drug users only heightens the emotional undertone of the debate. HIV poses an incomparable challenge for health policymakers who must seek methods of reducing its spread and of helping to ensure the public safety consistent with the protection of individual dignity and autonomy.

In the face of these charged medical and social conditions, the law regulating public health actions is complicated and uncertain, rooted in turn-of-the-century court decisions about very different diseases. Many of our public health responses to epidemic disease are decades or even centuries old, yet the medical basis and appropriate uses of measures like quarantine have changed considerably as twentieth-century medicine has developed a better understanding of the cause and transmission of disease. In this century, too, American society and its judiciary have become more sophisticated about individual liberties: more rights have been recognized—ranging from privacy in reproductive decisions to nondiscrimination on the basis of disability—and protection of all rights has been enhanced.

The HIV epidemic is an invitation to the legal system to fully incorporate these legal and medical developments into public health law. Although this is an ongoing process, the general trend is toward a more searching judicial evaluation of the medical bases of health actions. Traditionally, judges have deferred to the decisions

59

of legislators and health officials, upholding health measures as long as they were reasonably necessary and not unreasonably oppressive. Citing such legal maxims as "the health of the people is the supreme law," judges were reluctant to second-guess government officials in times of health crisis.[1] At the same time, however, courts have a special duty to protect individuals from unreasonable or discriminatory government actions, and courts frequently overturned or modified health measures that appeared to lack a solid medical basis, or that arose out of hysteria or prejudice. Deference to elected officials remains a basic judicial value, but the enhancement of individual rights means that more health actions will be seen as infringing rights in a way that requires court intervention and close scrutiny, while advances in medicine and public health practice allow courts to compare individual health actions against established, national norms.

This chapter evaluates the application to the HIV epidemic of classic public health responses to infectious disease. I begin with an introduction to the law governing public health measures. I then examine two measures commonly used to determine the prevalence and distribution of disease and to provide information to the people most directly affected by it: case finding (the use of testing, screening, and partner notification), and case reporting of infectious individuals to public health officials. These practices raise serious practical and policy problems, but, if properly designed and tailored, are likely to withstand legal challenge, both because they are justified by current medical knowledge and because they can be accomplished with minimal detrimental impact on individual rights. In the third part of this chapter, I examine the use of public health powers to isolate those believed capable of transmitting the infection, particularly those who are believed to be persisting in dangerous conduct. Isolation measures are very intrusive and will have little impact on the course of the epidemic, and many isolation laws are open to serious legal challenge. The final part of the chapter summarizes my conclusions.

THE LAW GOVERNING PUBLIC HEALTH ACTIONS

The day-to-day protection and promotion of public health has traditionally been a state function.[2] The federal government's role, especially in policy coordination, research, and funding, has grown steadily, but it is the states, through health departments and school districts, that administer such primary public health measures as school inoculation and disease reporting.[3] States have the authority to carry out health measures under what is traditionally, if confusingly, referred to as their "police power"—the power reserved to the states in the federal Constitution to take necessary action to promote the public health and welfare, to foster prosperity, and to maintain public order.[4] But while the state's power to enact and administer health laws is unquestionable,[5] the *exercise* of this power in any particular case is subject to limitations arising from the constitutional and statutory protection of individual rights.[6]

Basic individual rights are guaranteed by both the federal Constitution and the constitutions of the several states, and, until the 1970s, most challenges to health measures were brought on constitutional grounds. (Even though this chapter focuses on the U.S. Constitution, it is well to remember that state constitutions may offer the same or even broader protection.) The Bill of Rights (the first ten amendments of the Constitution) established basic rights that cannot be infringed by the federal government. These include freedom of speech and religion, freedom from unreasonable searches and seizures, and, most significant for our purposes, the insistence that life, liberty, and property cannot be abridged without due process of law.[7] The Fourteenth Amendment, enacted after the Civil War, extended many of these protections to the actions of state governments.[8] The Fourteenth Amendment also expressly provides, via its equal protection clause, that laws may not treat in an unequal fashion people who are in relevant respects the same.[9]

Whenever individuals (or classes of people) assert in litigation that their rights have been abridged by the act of a local, state, or federal government, they are implicitly asking the court to undo the will of the majority as expressed through the elected executive or legislature. Forcing state officials to show up in court to justify their decisions, much less overturning those decisions, takes judges to the limit of their authority. Given this reality, it is not surprising that rights are rarely regarded as absolute. Some constitutional provisions, by their very terms, invite the exercise of judicial judgment in deciding when the government has overstepped. The Fourth Amendment, for example, prohibits only "unreasonable" searches and seizures, leaving to courts the task of defining the parameters of reasonableness. Even rights that are phrased in absolute terms—the First Amendment's command that "Congress shall make no law" abridging freedom of speech and religion is a good example[10]— are treated as if they were, of necessity, qualified.[11] Thus, courts necessarily engage in a legal balancing act, with the constitutional rights of the disfavored in one pan and the state's interest in the other. No matter how reluctant a judge is to get involved in deciding whether a challenged health measure is a good idea, he or she can hardly weigh its value against its harm to individual rights without taking a serious look at the measure's propriety, utility, and necessity.[12] The principal response of courts to this tension between majority rule and individual rights has been the development of formal tests that purport to tell judges how deeply, and under what circumstances, they must scrutinize a challenged measure.

Most of the important public health cases were decided around the turn of the century. Their hallmark is the deference consistently shown by courts to the will of the legislature. Legislatures were given substantial latitude in determining which health measures were necessary, and their handiwork was regarded as presumptively valid.[13] The courts generally took the view that they would not substitute their own judgment for that of the legislature, and that the "manner and mode" of regulatory efforts was wholly within the ambit of states' police powers.[14]

The major impetus for judicial activity in the public health field was the sporadic occurrence of epidemics of venereal disease,[15] tuberculosis,[16] smallpox,[17] scarlet fever,[18] leprosy,[19] cholera,[20] and bubonic plague.[21] In this context, private rights were subordinated to the public interest, and individuals were seen as bound to conform their conduct for society's good.[22] As one court put it, quarantine does not frustrate constitutional rights because there is no liberty to harm others.[23] Even when courts recognized that personal control measures cut deeply into private rights, they would not allow the assertion of those rights to thwart public policy.[24] This preference for social control over individual autonomy emerged as a major characteristic of judicial rulings of the period.[25]

The conceptual underpinning for this deferential approach was what is now known as the rational basis or means-ends test: a health measure would be upheld if there was a "real or substantial" connection between the measure and the end it was meant to secure.[26] Although this test was used in a notoriously intrusive fashion by the United States Supreme Court in striking down economic regulations at the start of the New Deal,[27] in general, courts used it to justify a hands-off policy with respect to measures aimed at combating disease. Courts tended to uphold public health statutes as long as the state did not act in "an arbitrary, unreasonable manner" or go "beyond what was reasonably required for the safety of the public." In practice, this standard left basic questions unanswered, the most important of which was how "rationality" was to be judged. The "rationality" of a measure was normally analyzed in terms of whether it was necessary for the protection of public health, but this only raised a more basic question: by what standard was "necessity" itself to be judged?

Many early cases viewed necessity as a general determination to be made by the legislature under such criteria as it judged useful. A New York opinion left the question of necessity to "the people": "While we do not decide, and cannot decide, that vaccination is a preventative of smallpox, we take judicial notice of the fact that this is the common belief of the people of the State, and with this fact as a foundation, we hold that the statute in question is a health law, enacted in a reasonable and proper exercise of the police power.''[28] Neither did the Connecticut court in *State v. Rackowski* require any more stringent evidence than ''common knowledge'' in deciding that a person exposed to scarlet fever may communicate the disease.[29]

The harm to individual interests that can occur from imposing control measures not clearly supported by scientific evidence is illustrated by *Kirk v. Wyman*, a 1909 South Carolina case. An elderly woman with anaesthetic leprosy was quarantined even though there was ''hardly any danger of contagion.'' She had lived in the community for many years, attended church services, taught in school, and mingled in social life without ever communicating the disease. The South Carolina Supreme Court thought it ''manifest that the board [of health] were well within their duty in requiring the victim of it to be isolated'' when the ''distressing nature of the malady is regarded.''[30]

In the absence of scientific criteria, social prejudice often provided the principal basis for action. The Ohio Supreme Court upheld a quarantine regulation including a provision that ''all known prostitutes and people associated with them shall be considered as reasonably suspected of having a venereal disease.'' ''Suspect conduct and association'' were deemed sufficient to justify imposition of control measures, and the court did not appear concerned with whether the person before the court actually had venereal disease.[31] In *People v. Strautz*, the Illinois court accepted similarly unfounded assumptions. ''Suspected'' prostitutes were considered ''natural subjects and carriers of venereal disease,'' making it ''logical and natural that suspicion be cast upon them [necessitating] a physical examination of their persons.''[32] The court was unclear as to the evidence required to establish a reasonable belief that a person engaged in prostitution.

From the earliest days of major public health litigation, however, some courts recognized the need for more objective and reliable criteria. Several early cases were much stricter in requiring a demonstration of public health necessity and medical proof that individuals were in fact infectious.[33] *Ex parte Shepard*, a California decision, specifically rejected the proposition that mere suspicion of venereal infection is sufficient to uphold a quarantine order.[34] Similarly, in *Ex parte Arata*, the California court required that reasonable grounds exist to support the claim that a person is afflicted with venereal disease: ''Mere suspicion unsupported by facts giving rise to reasonable or probable cause will afford no justification at all for depriving people of their liberty.''[35]

Smith v. Emery, an 1896 New York decision, presents one of the earliest and clearest statements by a court on the need for *medical* evidence to support control measures: "The mere possibility that persons might have been exposed to [smallpox] is not sufficient" to justify a control measure. They must *in fact* have been exposed to it, the conditions must "actually exist for a communication of the contagion," and all such issues must be determined by "medical science and skill," not "common knowledge."[36]

The highwater mark of the early cases (from the perspective of judicial oversight of public health measures) is *Jew Ho v. Williamson*. There, a federal district court refused to uphold the quarantine for bubonic plague of an entire district of San Francisco containing a population of more than fifteen thousand Chinese people. Because bubonic plague is most easily communicated in conditions of overcrowding and poor sanitation, "it must necessarily follow that, if a large territory is quarantined, intercommunication of the people within that territory will rather tend to spread the disease than to restrict it." The court noted that the form of quarantine applied would therefore enlarge the sphere of the disease and increase its danger and destructive force; that the evidence to show the existence of plague and the circumstances of its transmission was slight; and that the quarantine demonstrated an "evil eye and an unequal hand" because it was made to operate exclusively against the Chinese community.[37] The court's unabashedly close scrutiny of the means adopted by the municipal health officials was uncharacteristic of early public health cases but foreshadowed contemporary judicial analysis, particularly in the implicit recognition of the potential for prejudice to play itself out in the form of unnecessary health measures.

As epidemic disease receded as a feature of American life, challenges to health measures receded as a feature of American law. Water fluoridation programs and school vaccination laws each inspired a flurry of cases, but court decisions did little to resolve the old tension between deference and close medical scrutiny.[38] In other areas, however, law was changing in ways that would have a profound impact on how courts would treat public health measures in the time of AIDS.

Constitutional law as a whole has changed substantially since the turn of the century. The Supreme Court has recognized new rights—for example, the right to privacy[39]—and has developed new ways of balancing them against governmental interests. The unitary rational basis test, applied without formal regard to the importance of the particular right compromised, has given way to three different tests, with the choice of which one to employ dependent on the nature of the rights infringed or the groups affected by the challenged measure.[40] Most cases continue to be judged under the deferential rational relationship test: a state may justify a measure merely by showing that it has some plausible connection to a legitimate state goal.[41] At the other extreme is the "strict scrutiny test": measures that infringe upon a fundamental right, or which appear to discriminate against minority groups historically subject to discrimination ("suspect classes") must be proven vital to a compelling state interest; further, even a measure that passes this test may fall if another less restrictive means to the same end is available.[42]

In some cases, the Court has explicitly or in effect applied "intermediate scrutiny," requiring a challenged measure to have a "substantial" (as distinct from merely rational) relationship to an important goal and to be the least restrictive means available. These cases have involved either important rights that have not (or not yet) achieved full-fledged constitutional status (such as the right to education), or "quasi-suspect" classifications (notably those based on gender).[43]

The reader who finds this structure confusing is not alone. It has been criticized even from within the Supreme Court;[44] it has been called artificial, mechanical, and even dishonest.[45] One of the most frequent complaints is that the selection of the test determines the outcome: virtually no laws survive strict scrutiny, and virtually none are overturned for lack of a rational relationship.[46] Then, too, the reverse may be true, namely that courts select the test that justifies the desired outcome. Be that as it may, there is no indication that this structure will be abandoned in the near future. Fortunately, the realities of public health law force courts to deal with concrete facts rather than slippery abstractions. In practice, it is only through an examination of medical facts that judges evaluating a particular health measure can decide, for example, how "compelling" a state's interest in the measure is, how "substantially" it is related to the health problem, and whether it is the "least restrictive" alternative.

Health actions against HIV have been subject to numerous challenges under modern constitutional doctrines. Closing bathhouses has been opposed as an infringement on the rights of free association and privacy;[47] compulsory HIV testing has been opposed as an unreasonable search,[48] and a denial of equal protection;[49] and isolating HIV-infected prisoners in an "AIDS dormitory" has been opposed as a violation of the right of privacy.[50] Both the analyses and the results have been decidedly mixed. The future of constitutional law in HIV cases looks far from promising, particularly given the Supreme Court's perceptible trend toward narrowing individual rights. The health measures least likely to pass constitutional muster are those involving a clear restriction of a well-established right without significant evidence of benefits to the public health. Challenges to health measures that rely on the right to privacy may become more difficult as the Court increasingly restricts the right in the abortion context.[51] Likewise, challenges resting on the Fourth Amendment are also becoming more difficult, given Supreme Court drug testing decisions that relax the standard for involuntary testing outside the law enforcement setting.[52] (For more on privacy and testing, see chapter 7.)

The changes in constitutional law are arguably not as significant for public health cases as the 1973 passage of the federal Rehabilitation Act. With this law, Congress prohibited discrimination against people with disabilities by any entity receiving federal funds—including most state and local government agencies. As it became clear that the law's definition of "handicap" included people with such communicable diseases as hepatitis and HIV, there was a basic change in the legal analysis of many health actions. Instead of asking whether the health action has a reasonable relationship to protecting the public health, the question a court asks in a Rehabilitation Act case is whether the health action unnecessarily discriminates against a person with a disability.

From the start, courts applying the Rehabilitation Act did not readily defer to government health decisions infringing upon the rights of the disabled, requiring proof of a solid medical basis for any measures. In *New York State Ass'n for Retarded Children v. Carey,* a United States court of appeals determined that mentally retarded children who were carriers of serum hepatitis could not be excluded from attending regular public school classes. Although it recognized that the decision to exclude the children "involve[d] the very essence of the state's police power to protect the health, welfare, and safety of its citizens," the court refused to defer to the school board's decision because its duty to ensure that constitutional and statutory rights were protected could be discharged only through an independent review of the facts and the board's reasoning. In the end, the court found that "the School Board was unable to demonstrate that the health hazard . . . was anything more than a remote possibility." This remote possibility did not justify the action taken, considering "the detrimental effects of isolating the carrier children." The court was sensitive to the fact that segregation of mentally retarded children would "reinforce the stigma to which these children have already been subjected."[53]

Then, in 1987, the Supreme Court decided a case widely seen as a test of how public health law would apply to HIV. *School Board v. Arline* was a challenge by a teacher with tuberculosis to her dismissal by school officials. After confirming the view of the lower courts that communicable diseases could be handicaps under the Rehabilitation Act, the Court read the Act to require a close, individualized examination of the facts justifying the dismissal in order "to replace such reflexive reactions to actual or perceived handicaps with actions based on reasoned and medically sound judgements."[54] A health action against a disabled person, the Court explained, is not allowed under the Act unless the person poses a "significant risk" of harm, as assessed by medical standards. Such an assessment should be made with deference to the judgments of health officials, but only if those judgments appear, after careful judicial inquiry, to be reasonable in light of the medical facts.

Furthermore, the person with a communicable disease does not have to prove she is safe; the government must prove she is dangerous and must look for reasonable ways to reduce the threat before taking discriminatory action.

After *Arline*, courts applying the Act have tested the medical value of health actions ranging from the exclusion of children with HIV from school to the involuntary testing of health care workers.[55] In nearly all cases, the discriminatory measure was invalidated based on a medical evaluation of the risk. In 1990, Congress extended the scope of disability law to private employment, public accommodations, public services, and telecommunications by passing the Americans with Disabilities Act (ADA). Congress endorsed the *Arline* approach by explicitly adopting its medical standard for judging discrimination against people with communicable diseases. Under the ADA, a person with a communicable disease cannot be discriminated against unless he or she poses a "direct threat" to others.[56] People challenging health actions can be expected to rely on the Rehabilitation Act and the ADA as their best protection against irrational health measures, and, with the evident support of Congress, the courts can be expected to overturn measures that do not find support in national public health practice and the particular facts of the case.[57] (For more on disability discrimination law, see chapter 13.)

CASE IDENTIFICATION

Epidemiologists require accurate data about the prevalence, distribution (geographic and demographic), and transmission modes of diseases. Consequently, public health authorities traditionally engage in broad-scale data collection. To that end, they may screen segments of the population considered to be at risk, trace the "contacts" of people found to be infected, and collect information on people diagnosed as having the relevant disease.

Screening

"Screening" is the systematic use of a medical test on population groups.[58] No one proposes that screening be employed to locate and identify people who have full-blown AIDS. Given the debilitating nature of the disease, they are likely to seek medical help well before an official AIDS diagnosis could be made. Instead, proposed screening measures focus on identifying people who are infected with HIV and may, or may not, be symptomatic.

If administered properly, with appropriate confirmatory tests, HIV antibody screening has a degree of reliability comparable to, or better than, that of other widely used medical tests. (For more on the reliability and methodology of HIV testing, see chapter 7.) At the same time, the psychological costs of an erroneous result are high. The test was developed to screen blood, for which purpose it has been successful and largely uncontroversial. It is also employed, again uncontroversially, in *voluntary* testing programs, through which people who fear they have been exposed to the virus can obtain counseling and, if appropriate, take the test under conditions of assured confidentiality. More controversial and problematic is the use of testing on a compulsory basis. In the United States, compulsory screening has been used by the Department of Defense, the State Department, the Job Corps and the Immigration and Naturalization Service. (See chapter 9.) Compulsory testing is also increasingly being used in the criminal justice system. (See chapters 7 and 11.)

Properly understood, screening is a means, not an end. It provides information, the value of which depends on the use to which it is put.[59] In both the legal and medical arenas, proposals for screening can be sensibly evaluated only in terms of how well they accomplish some desirable public health goal. In theory, HIV antibody screening can help provide a clearer statistical picture of the prevalence of the virus; identify infected individuals who may benefit from clinical intervention; and identify candidates for counseling and education to help prevent the spread of HIV to sexual or needle-sharing partners.

Screening that is offered on a truly voluntary and confidential basis can help achieve these purposes. The national Centers for Disease Control (CDC) is undertaking seroprevalence surveys across a wide section of the community—for example, universities, hospitals, and pregnant women. The hallmark of this screening is that it is "blind." A positive HIV result, that is, cannot be linked to any person's identity. The purpose of the survey is to trace the course of the epidemic and to enable public health officials to target resources and programs toward populations in greatest need. The benefits of this kind of screening are substantial, but blinded testing can pose two potential ethical dilemmas that need to be carefully considered in evaluating any particular screening program.

First, if a person is HIV positive, there is no way the information can be brought to the person's attention. Some cultures, such as Great Britain and the Netherlands, initially objected to blind seroprevalence screening for just this reason. The World Health Organization and most public health commentators have not seen this problem as sufficiently strong to counteract the good that comes from such studies. This is particularly so when voluntary counseling and testing are readily available to members of the population being screened.

The second potential problem with seroprevalence screening is that the statistics are often presented in ways that can stigmatize populations. In the United States, for example, statistics are consistently broken down on racial lines. This gives the false impression that race is a risk factor, rather than a risk marker. African Americans, for example, do not make up a disproportionate number of AIDS cases because Black people are more susceptible than White people to HIV, but because people of color make up a disproportionate number of intravenous drug users in the communities where HIV is most common. The practice of classifying by race has become so well established that few people, outside of minority communities, stop to ask what purpose is served by presenting the information in this way, and whether there are more efficient ways of analyzing the data.

Testing programs in which the subject's identity can be *linked* to the test result can be used to find individuals in need of public health interventions. Linked testing may also be justified under prevailing ethical standards, if it will be to the *tested person's* benefit—medical, psychological, and social. Several critical points must be borne in mind in assessing the benefits of testing from an ethical standpoint. First, the testing must be truly voluntary in the sense that each individual must give a fully informed consent *prior* to the test's being performed. Second, the test must be performed by qualified professionals and confirmatory tests used to minimize the possibility of a false positive result. Third, the test results must be kept strictly confidential and should be disclosed only with the tested person's express consent. (In many states, these standards are mandated by law as well as ethics. See chapter 7.) Finally, and perhaps most important, an appropriate range of services must be actually available to the individual including pre- and post-test counseling, T$_4$ cell count monitoring, and full access to state-of-the-art treatment.

Unfortunately, many see screening as an end in itself, often without any careful examination as to whether the person will receive the services he or she needs and desires. Public health service proposals for routine screening of large-scale populations such as hospital patients sometimes justify the program based on the need for counseling, T$_4$ cell monitoring, and early treatment with PCP prophylaxis and AZT. No clear plan or sufficient resources, however, are put in place to ensure that the people screened will actually receive any of these services.[60]

Careful thought needs to be given to the efficiency of any wide-scale population screening. A program aimed at the general population, such as pre-marital screening, can be an inefficient way to reach those who need counseling and treatment. At present, many people in need of testing are readily identified and can be reached by voluntary programs and public education. Although concern about the spread of HIV into the White, middle-class heterosexual population is quite prudent, the scope of the problem is much smaller than the attention being paid to it would suggest.

Since most heterosexual cases involve intravenous drug users or their sexual partners, it makes sense to focus our resources on drug users in particular rather than on heterosexuals in general. (For more on the epidemiology of HIV, see chapter 2.) To be sure, any public health program that aims beyond groups at high risk will reach some people—notably the heterosexual contacts of bisexual men—who might not otherwise know they are at risk.

With other diseases, health authorities have made limited use of mandatory screening in connection with marriage license applications, blood donation, or treatment at drug dependency and venereal disease clinics. The "mandatory" label, however, is inaccurate. These programs might better be thought of as "conditional." They impose upon those who give blood, or wish to marry, or seek medical treatment, the requirement of being tested. But all these activities can, to some degree, be avoided. As long as the perceived social costs of being tested are very high, at least some people will, for example, forego marriage, or obtain medical treatment from private doctors, and the people most likely to make this decision are those who know themselves to be at risk. Mandatory screening, therefore, creates incentives for those most in need of the test not only to avoid screening, but also to avoid medical intervention—like venereal disease treatment and prenatal counseling—that is independently beneficial to both the individual and society. Moreover, massive screening of low-risk groups requires the investment of considerable time and money to find a relatively small number of cases. It is exactly this needle-in-a-haystack aspect of massive screening that has produced the recent trend among the state legislatures to repeal pre-marital testing for venereal disease.[61]

Screening may also be utilized to take coercive measures, such as isolation or criminal prosecution, against infected people. This, too, is an ill-conceived use of medical casefinding. All testing can realistically do is identify people who are infected. Testing provides no information at all about whether the person will engage in dangerous behaviors. Thus, while testing on a purely voluntary basis in conjunction with the providing of services may be highly beneficent to individuals, massive population screening and screening without informed consent provides no clear benefit either to the individual or to the public health.

Contact Tracing, Partner Notification

Contact tracing—also known as partner notification—is a form of medical surveillance by which public health officials seek to discover people with whom an infected person has had dangerous contact (with HIV, sex or needle-sharing partners) and then inform and, if possible, treat them. Like screening, its utility depends in large part on what positive action public officials can take once they have found a potentially infected person.

There is much to be said for partner notification—for counseling people at risk and encouraging them either to inform their sex partners themselves or to give public health officials permission to do so. In particular, notification of heterosexual partners of people exposed to HIV may be an efficient way of reaching a relatively small, discrete class of people—such as the heterosexual partners of covert drug users— who do not know they are at risk. San Francisco, New York, and other cities, as well as states such as Colorado and South Carolina, have set up such programs.

There are, however, several reasons to view contact tracing as a very limited tool. First, even more than screening, contact tracing depends on cooperation: there is little a health official can do to force a person to identify truthfully all his or her sexual contacts. The problems are only aggravated if the informant doubts the confidentiality of any disclosure. Second, as in the screening context, counseling and services must be made available to provide a benefit to the person. Finally, contact tracing requires sensitive, trained investigators, and a fair investment of time; it is ill-suited for use on a large scale.[62] In light of these limitations, public health officials have generally not been aggressive in promoting large-scale partner notification programs as a primary tool against HIV.

Reporting

Every state requires that specific "listed" or "notifiable" diseases be reported by physicians, laboratories, hospitals and other health practitioners to its public health department. The rules for reporting HIV vary, but AIDS qualifies as a notifiable disease throughout the country.

State reporting requirements can be divided into three categories: rules specifying the reporting of all cases that meet the CDC definition of AIDS; rules specifying that positive test results for HIV antibodies be reported; and general provisions that do not specify HIV infection as notifiable but require the reporting of any "case," "condition," or "carrier state" relating to listed diseases, including AIDS. In some states that require the reporting of HIV test results, only the result itself, and not the identity of the subject, is required to be reported. (This sort of reporting serves primarily statistical purposes.)[63]

In 1977, in *Whalen v. Roe*, the Supreme Court concluded that "limited reporting requirements in the medical field are familiar, and are not generally regarded as an invasion of privacy." The Court was strongly influenced in its decision by the high level of legal protection generally afforded to the privacy of health department records, and the good track record of health officials in maintaining privacy.[64] Thus, current requirements to report AIDS or HIV infection are likely to withstand constitutional challenge so long as the information sought is reasonably related to a valid public health purpose and is limited to public health departments, and so long as statutory confidentiality protections are in place.

Without doubt, the states have a valid public health interest in collecting information about the epidemiological distribution of AIDS within the general population. Reporting of CDC-defined AIDS, if carefully regulated, is a narrowly tailored (and thus constitutional) means of collecting vitally important data: it minimizes the privacy problems associated with other case identification measures, such as mass screening, and is unlikely to deter its targets from seeking medical help, given their advanced stage of illness.

Reporting of HIV antibody status was originally seen as more problematic. Statutory requirements to report every positive test result were seen as likely to provide a disincentive to voluntary testing by people who are well but worried. Today, a majority of states require HIV reporting, and the controversy has quieted. States that do require named reporting, however, will harm the public health if they do not provide alternative test sites that are anonymous (that is, do not require a name). Studies confirm that voluntary test rates drop off if there is no alternative anonymous testing made available.

PERSONAL CONTROL MEASURES

Traditionally, public health authorities seek not only to identify individuals capable of transmitting infection, but also to take positive action to prevent them from doing so. At present, the U.S. Public Health Service and most state health departments rely solely on voluntary measures, such as encouraging testing and providing individual counseling and public education. These measures clearly have altered behavior, as evidenced by the substantial reduction in the number of cases of rectal gonorrhea, a disease associated with the same sexual practices that spread HIV.[65] The perception nevertheless persists that HIV could be controlled if health authorities made greater use of their authority to confine or otherwise control the behavior of HIV-infected people.

Types of Personal Control Measures

Infection control measures have traditionally rested on the assumption that disease carriers must be physically separated from the rest of the population to prevent transmission of the infectious agent. This approach to disease control has declined substantially in importance as medical science has produced a much more sophisticated understanding of individual diseases and their modes of transmission. Although the terms *isolation* and *quarantine* are often used interchangeably to describe this kind of physical separation, both in public health statutes and in common parlance, there is a useful technical distinction between them. "Isolation" is the separation of infected people from others during the period of communicability so as to prevent transmission of the infectious agent; "quarantine" is the detention of people who are healthy but have been exposed to a communicable disease for a period of time equal to the longest usual incubation period of the disease, to prevent effective contact with people not exposed.[66] Since proposals for confining people with HIV tend to apply to people who already exhibit symptoms of the disease or who have tested positive for the virus, the term *isolation* is more appropriate in the HIV context.

The power to isolate is given to state health departments by state legislatures, and varies in its breadth from state to state. In some places, the legislature identifies the diseases subject to isolation; in others, that determination is left to the health department as a matter of professional judgment. Where the legislature has authorized measures like isolation for "communicable diseases" or "sexually transmitted diseases," there has been controversy over whether or not HIV meets the definition. In most states, however, there is little doubt that health authorities have the power to order isolation.[67]

General Isolation. From the earliest days of the HIV epidemic, there were calls for health departments to identify and isolate everyone infected with HIV. Among public health authorities, however, general isolation of large numbers of infected people purely on the basis of their infection was always a nonstarter. The number of people capable of transmitting the virus is currently at least one million, making general isolation unmanageable. Since there is no finite period of infectiousness and no known cure, isolation would be permanent, and those whose liberty is infringed would have no way to restore themselves to a "normal" condition in order to rejoin the community. Furthermore, because casual contact does not spread the virus, segregation from society is unnecessary and thus, by definition, overly restrictive. Taken together, these factors set HIV apart from other communicable diseases that have been the subject of traditional personal control measures and make isolation a singularly inappropriate policy.[68]

General isolation would also be put to a strict legal test, which it would certainly fail. Isolation is a uniquely serious form of deprivation of liberty, which would withstand judicial challenge only if there were a tight fit between the measure and the attainment of a compelling public health benefit. Such a close relationship between legislative (or administrative) means and ends could not be established in relation to the general isolation of all who are seropositive or even all who have AIDS. General isolation would carry in its sweep people who are not engaging in high-risk behavior that makes transmission possible, and people who are so debilitated or demoralized as to be unable to engage in high-risk behavior. Isolation based on HIV status alone, with no individualized evidence of dangerous behavior, could very well be invalidated as discrimination against the disabled.

Modified Isolation Based upon Behavior, Not Disease Status. Public health authorities have occasionally used their powers of isolation to restrict the activities of HIV-infected people who are unable or unwilling to abstain from behavior capable of spreading the virus. Isolation based on dangerous behavior, the purpose of which is ultimately to alter the behavior, avoids many of the problems of general isolation. In theory, at least, individuals are isolated only when they can be proven to be engaging in dangerous activities, so only the truly dangerous are affected. Moreover, isolation can be used to force people to confront problems of addiction or mental health, and to get dangerous people into the treatment they need to change their behavior. Once "cured" of the drug dependency or depression or desperation that was causing the dangerous behavior, people can be released from isolation. A number of states have passed new isolation laws that embody this philosophy and explicitly link isolation to demonstrable dangerous behavior, the provision of social services, and the failure of less drastic measures.[69]

As a public health practice, however, even modified isolation has serious drawbacks. In the real world, the promised services may rarely be provided, and even if they are, isolation is a wrongheaded way to get people to accept behavioral change assistance. People who are addicted to drugs, or are poor, or are psychologically unable to cope with HIV in a responsible manner, often find voluntary treatment impossible to obtain. "Forcing" a few of them into treatment will not change that, or alter the course of the HIV epidemic. Many people who are addicted to drugs, for example, continue to take, and pose, HIV risks; the social challenge is not to isolate those who reject drug treatment, but to provide access to the many who would accept treatment were it available. Indeed, the threat of coercive measures may discourage members of risk groups from seeking testing or treatment and from speaking honestly to counselors about their future behavior.

A program of isolation would be difficult to conduct in a fair way. Objective statutory criteria and psychological tests could not readily be framed to determine accurately enough who was "recalcitrant" or to predict future dangerous behavior. Errors would probably arise from social and racial prejudice, as those who come to the attention of public health officials as candidates for isolation are likely to be the poorest and least articulate of those harboring the virus. Finally, isolation to prevent sexual activity or drug use would be extremely difficult to monitor and enforce and could be viewed as a license for public health and law enforcement officials to intrude into the most private areas of the lives of people in high-risk groups.

Despite its defects, modified isolation is likely to escape judicial censure for the following reasons. First, unlike general isolation, it does not focus on a person's health *status* but rather upon his or her *behavior*. Second, it is targeted at a small number of individuals rather than at a sizeable class of people united by a common characteristic unrelated to a specific threat of harm. Third, the most likely targets of modified isolation would be people engaged in activities that in and of themselves are *criminal*—prostitutes and intravenous drug users. The courts have not been particularly sympathetic to the civil rights of such people in the past.

Even a well-tailored modified isolation statute would not survive constitutional challenge if it did not create a mechanism for determining, with full due process, that the target of isolation will not or cannot refrain from engaging in conduct likely to spread the AIDS virus. The due process clause in the Fourteenth Amendment guarantees that no one can be deprived of basic rights without a fair and proper hearing. Even when the courts accede to the power of state legislatures to protect the public health, they may require procedural safeguards prior to or immediately after the use of control measures. The West Virginia Supreme Court, for example, has held that the same procedural safeguards required in contemplation of civil commitment to mental hospitals are applicable in cases of involuntary confinement of infectious patients. The procedures include written notice, representation by counsel, the right to present evidence, cross examination, commitment only if the proof of commitability is "clear and convincing," and a verbatim transcript in the event of an appeal.[70] Strict observance of due process in deciding to isolate is necessary because fundamental freedoms are at stake. There is a distinct risk of erroneous fact-finding, and there is no state interest in confining nondangerous individuals. (Although there are no recent cases on the issue, it is also very likely that courts would require that the isolation quarters be clean, healthy and safe; isolation in a prison or jail, which has often occurred in the past, might well be deemed unacceptably punitive even if the living conditions themselves were otherwise adequate.[71])

Isolation and Tuberculosis Control

Tuberculosis, after decades of decline, has been increasing since the mid–1980s. The disease, which can remain silent and non-infectious for years, spreads through the air when the carrier develops "active" TB. More worrisome still is the serious increase in TB that is not treatable with the standard medications (multidrug-resistant tuberculosis, or MDR-TB). MDR-TB requires eighteen to twenty-four months of treatment, compared to six months for nonresistant strains. The cure rate decreases from nearly 100 percent to 60 percent or less. Treating a case of MDR-TB can cost as much as $200,000. Major outbreaks of MDR-TB have resulted in clusters of illness and death in such congregate living places as correctional institutions, homeless shelters, and hospitals.[72]

TB raises particular problems in relation to HIV. People with HIV disease are at greater risk of developing and dying from TB. A person with an intact immune system has only a 10 percent lifetime chance of developing active TB after infection. For a person with a compromised immune system, such as a person living with AIDS, the risk of active TB is 10 percent *each year*. A person with AIDS who is infected with TB, and who lives long enough, will almost certainly develop active disease and may well die from it within weeks. Moreover, latent TB is harder to detect in people with seriously compromised immune systems because they may not be able to mount a sufficient immune response to test positive on standard TB skin tests. Their TB may even be hard to diagnose through chest X rays.

Because it is spread through the air, TB raises again the question of the role of personal control measures. It should be standard hospital practice to isolate people with active TB until treatment renders them non-infectious. This requires as little as two weeks in the case of nonresistant TB. Assuming the conditions and medical care are adequate, short-term isolation of infectious patients is not likely to be legally challenged or, if challenged, invalidated. More problematic are personal control measures aimed at non-infectious people to assure that they complete the entire course of their medication.

Within a short time after beginning treatment for active disease, a person will feel better and will no longer be infectious. At that point, isolation and hospitalization will no longer be necessary, but treatment to eliminate the disease and prevent relapse must continue for months or years. Extended preventive treatment is also sometimes appropriate for patients who have not developed active disease. A significant number of patients in both groups stop taking their medication too soon, which not only compromises their own health but fosters the development of drug-resistant strains of TB. The reasons people stop treatment are many and often have as much to do with the challenges of homelessness, poverty, access to health care, and drug addiction as with disinterest. We must be especially sensitive to such factors, for the course of TB policy in this country is likely to be determined by whether incomplete treatment is attributed primarily to "recalcitrant" or "noncompliant" patients or to defects in our social and health care delivery systems.

With visions of TB sanitoria apparently fresh in their minds, some have called for isolating any TB patient who seems unwilling or unable to pursue a full course of treatment. Such measures, however, are likely to founder on economic grounds alone. The personal control measure preferred by public health authorities it to enroll all patients being treated for active disease in programs for "directly observed therapy" (DOT). Such programs ensure compliance by requiring a health worker to monitor patients as they take medication. A proper respect for the dismal history of coercive health measures suggests that patients be given positive incentives to voluntarily enter and continue treatment. Some public health departments have instituted incentives in connection with DOT, including cash payments, free food, health care, or other services.

Any use of personal control measures must be considered in light of the broader social causes of TB. the reemergence of the disease is neither inexplicable nor unexpected but the predictable outcome of health care and social policy decisions over the past decade.[73] These include a decrease in resources devoted to surveillance and control of the disease; cost-cutting in health care, leading to patients with TB getting less or no treatment and facilities failing to acquire or maintain adequate ventilation systems; cuts in the safety net contributing to poverty and homelessness; and the congregation of more people in prisons, shelters, and nursing homes.[74] Unless we deal with these broad causes of TB, individual interventions are doomed to failure.

CONCLUSION

By the foregoing, I do not mean to place a greater emphasis on liberty, autonomy, and privacy than on public health, but public health intervention must focus on modifying the behaviors that transmit HIV. Compulsory measures are ill-suited to modify the intimate personal behaviors that are at issue. If anything, compulsory legal intervention will deter people vulnerable to HIV infection from being tested, seeking advice and treatment, and cooperating with public health programs.

Public health officials can effectively encourage voluntary behavior modification by disseminating accurate information and offering services such as free counseling and treatment. Thus, substantially greater resources should be devoted to providing highly specific information and counseling to those most vulnerable to HIV, including information about modes of transmission, safer sexual practices, and safer use of intravenous drugs. Health officials should encourage people to take the HIV antibody test on a confidential basis if they believe it relevant to future behavioral choices, and to notify their sex partners of their antibody status.

Public officials must allocate greater resources to treatment programs for sexually transmitted diseases and intravenous drug abuse. The current patient capacity of such programs is drastically insufficient. Clinics dealing with sexually transmitted disease could teach individuals about safer forms of sexual behavior; drug treatment programs could couple their efforts to wean clients from illicit drugs with realistic advice about how to reduce the risk of infection along the way.

A comprehensive public health program that provides education, counseling, treatment, and other health services to vulnerable groups would have a substantial impact on the continued spread of AIDS. Efforts to encourage voluntary risk reduction are both more respectful of civil liberties and more beneficial to the public health than the imposition of compulsory control policies.

NOTES

1 *See, e.g.*, Haverty v. Bass, 66 Me. 71 (1876) ("salus populi suprema lex").

2 Several excellent articles have been written in recent years that explicate the law governing public health actions. *See* Burris, *Rationality Review and the Politics of Public Health*, 34 Vill. L. Rev. 933 (1989); Parmet, *Legal Rights and Communicable Disease*, 14 J. Health Politics, Pol'y & L. 933 (1989).

3 *See generally* Morgenstern, *The Role of the Federal Government in Protecting Citizens From Communicable Disease*, 47 U. Cin. L. Rev. 537 (1978).

4 16A Corpus Juris Secundum § 432–433 (1979). The federal government's health authority is derived from its power to regulate commerce and its taxing and spending powers. Morgenstern, note 3 above, at 545.

5 Jacobson v. Massachusetts, 197 U.S. 11, 37–38 (1905); *see, e.g.*, McCarthy v. Austin,

296 N.Y.S.2d 26, 27 (N.Y. App. Div. 1969) ("That statutes of this nature . . . are within the police power and thus constitutional generally is too well established to require discussion.").

6 *See generally* Parmet, *AIDS and Quarantine: The Revival of an Archaic Doctrine*, 14 Hofstra L. Rev. 53 (1985).

7 U.S. Const. amends. I, IV, VI, V; *see, e.g.*, L. Tribe, American Constitutional Law § 10–15 (2d ed. 1988).

8 *See, e.g.*, L. Tribe, note 7 above, § 11–2.

9 *See, e.g.*, L. Tribe, note 7 above, § 16–1.

10 U.S. Const. amend. I, states: "Congress shall make no law respecting an establishment of religion, or prohibiting the free exercise thereof; or abridging the freedom of speech, or of the press, or the right of the people peaceably to assemble, and to petition the Government for a redress of grievances."

11 *See, e.g.,* L. Tribe, note 7 above, § 12–2, at p. 583 (discussing First Amendment).

12 *See id.* § 16–2.

13 *See, e.g.,* Varholy v. Sweat, 15 So.2d 267, 269–70 (Fla. 1943); State v. Rackowski, 86 A. 606, 608 (Conn. 1913) (and cases cited therein); Allison v. Cash, 137 S.W. 245 (Ky. 1911); Highland v. Schulte, 82 N.W. 62, 64 (Mich. 1900).

14 Jacobson v. Massachusetts, 197 U.S. 11, 25 (1905) (and cases cited therein).

15 *Ex parte* Martin, 188 P.2d 287 (Cal. Ct. App. 1948); State *ex rel.* Kennedy v. Head, 185 S.W.2d 530 (Tenn. 1945); *Varholy,* 15 So.2d 267 (Fla. 1943); City of Little Rock v. Smith, 204 P. 364 (Ark. 1922); *Ex parte* Company, 139 N.E. 204 (Ohio 1922); *Ex parte* Arata, 198 P. 814 (Cal. Ct. App. 1921); *Ex parte* Shepard, 195 P. 1077 (Cal. Ct. App. 1921); *Ex parte* McGee, 184 P. 14 (Kan. 1919); State *ex rel.* McBride v. Superior Court, 174 P. 973 (Wash. 1918).

16 Greene v. Edwards, 265 S.E.2d 662 (W. Va. 1980); *In re* Halko, 54 Cal. Rptr. 661 (Cal. Ct. App. 1966); Jones v. Czapkay, 6 Cal. Rptr. 182 (Cal. Ct. App. 1960); White v. Seattle Local Union No. 81, 337 P.2d 289 (Wash. 1959).

17 Crayton v. Larrabee, 116 N.E. 355 (N.Y. 1917), *aff'g* 147 N.Y.S. 1105 (N.Y. App. Div. 1914); *Allison,* 137 S.W. 245 (Ky. 1911); Hengehold v. City of Covington, 57 S.W. 495 (Ky. 1900); Henderson County Bd. of Health v. Ward, 54 S.W. 725 (Ky. 1900); *Highland,* 82 N.W. 62 (Mich. 1900); Smith v. Emery, 42 N.Y.S. 258 (N.Y. App. Div. 1896); *In re* Smith, 40 N.E. 497 (N.Y. 1895); City of Richmond v. Henrico County Supervisors, 2 S.E. 26 (Va. 1887); Spring v. Inhabitants of Hyde Park, 137 Mass. 554 (1884); Beckwith v. Sturdevant, 42 Conn. 158 (1875); Harrison v. Mayor & City Council of Baltimore, 1 Gill. 264 (Md. 1843).

18 People v. Tait, 102 N.E. 750 (Ill. 1913); State v. Rackowski, 86 A. 606 (Conn. 1913).

19 Kirk v. Wyman, 65 S.E. 387 (S.C. 1909).

20 Rudolphe v. City of New Orleans, 11 La. Ann. 242 (1854).

21 Jew Ho v. Williamson, 103 F. 10 (N.D. Cal. 1900).

22 *See, e.g.,* State *ex rel.* McBride v. Superior Court, 174 P. 973 (Wash. 1918).

23 *Kirk,* 65 S.E. at 392.

24 *See, e.g., Ex parte* McGee, 185 P. 14 (Kan. 1919).

25 *See, e.g.,* Mugler v. Kansas, 123 U.S. 623 (1887) (power to quarantine "so as to bind us all must exist somewhere; else, society will be at the mercy of the few, who, regarding only their appetites or passions, may be willing to imperil the security of the many, provided only they are permitted to do as they please"); Irwin v. Arrendale, 159 S.E.2d 441 (Ga. Ct. App. 1967) (individuals must submit to reasonable public health measures for the common good); City of Little Rock v. Smith, 162 S.W. 2d 705 (Ark. 1942) ("'private rights . . . must yield in the interest of security"; venereal disease "affects the public health so intimately and so insidiously that considerations of delicacy and privacy may not be permitted to thwart measures necessary to avert the public peril").

26 *See* Jacobson v. Massachusetts, 197 U.S. 11, 31 (1905); L. Tribe, note 7 above, § 8–3.

27 *See* Parmet, note 6 above, at 76–77; L. Tribe, note 7 above, § 8–4.

28 Viehmeister v. White, 72 N.E. 97 (N.Y. 1904) (quoted in *Jacobson,* 197 U.S. at 34–35).

29 State v. Rackowski, 86 A. 606, 608 (Conn. 1913).

30 *Kirk,* 65 S.E. 387, 390 (S.C. 1909).

31 *Ex parte* Company, 139 N.E. 204, 205–06 (Ohio 1922); *see also Ex parte* Johnson, 180 P. 644 (Cal. Ct. App. 1919).

32 People v. Strautz, 54 N.E.2d 441, 444 (Ill. 1944); *see also* State *ex rel.* Kennedy v.

Head, 185 S.W.2d 530 (Tenn. 1945); State v. Hutchinson, 18 So.2d 723 (Ala. 1944); *In re* Caselli, 204 P. 364 (Mont. 1922).

33 Railroad Company v. Husen, 95 U.S. 465, 471–73 (1877); *see also Ex parte* Martin, 188 P.2d 287 (Cal. Ct. App. 1948): People v. Tait, 30 N.E. 750 (Ill. 1913).

34 *Ex parte* Shepard, 195 P. 1077 (Cal. Ct. App. 1921).

35 *Ex parte* Arata, 198 P. 814, 816 (Cal. Ct. App. 1921); *see also In re* Smith, 40 N.E. 497 (N.Y. 1895).

36 Smith v. Emery, 42 N.Y.S. 258, 260 (N.Y. App. Div. 1896).

37 *Jew Ho*, 103 F. 10, 22 (N.D. Cal. 1900).

38 *See, e.g.,* Beck v. City Council of Beverly Hills, 106 Cal. Rptr. 163 (Cal. Ct. App. 1973); Davis v. State, 451 A.2d 107 (Md. 1982).

39 Roe v. Wade, 410 U.S. 113 (1973); Eisenstadt v. Baird, 405 U.S. 438 (1972); Griswold v. Connecticut, 381 U.S. 479 (1965).

40 *See generally* G. Gunther, Constitutional Law 586–92 (11th ed. 1985).

41 City of New Orleans v. Dukes, 427 U.S. 297 (1976).

42 Dunn v. Blumstein, 405 U.S. 330 (1972); Korematsu v. United States, 323 U.S. 214 (1944).

43 *See, e.g.,* Craig v. Boren, 429 U.S. 190, 197 (1976) (gender classification); Bell v. Burson, 402 U.S. 533 (1971) (right to driver's license); L. Tribe, note 7 above §§ 16–33..

44 *See, e.g.,* San Antonio Ind. Sch. Dist. v. Rodriguez, 411 U.S. 1, 98 (1973) (Marshall, J., dissenting).

45 G. Gunther, note 40 above, at 589–92.

46 L. Tribe, note 7 above, §§ 16–2, 16–6. *But see* City of Cleburne v. Cleburne Living Ctr., 105 S. Ct. 3249, 3258–3260 (1985).

47 *See, e.g.,* City of New York v. New St. Mark's Baths, 497 N.Y.S.2d 979 (N.Y. Sup. Ct. 1986).

48 Glover v. Eastern Nebraska Community Office of Retardation, 686 F. Supp. 243 (D. Neb. 1988), *aff'd,* 867 F.2d 461 (8th Cir. 1989), *cert. denied,* 493 U.S. 932 (1989).

49 *See, e.g.,* People v. Madison, No. 88–123613 (Ill. Cir. Ct. Aug. 3, 1989).

50 Doe v. Coughlin, 697 F. Supp. 1234 (S.D.N.Y. 1988).

51 *See, e.g.,* Rust v. Sullivan, 111 S. Ct. 1759 (1991); Webster v. Reproductive Health Servs., 492 U.S. 490 (1989).

52 *See* National Treasury Employee's Union v. Von Raab, 489 U.S. 656 (1989); Skinner v. Railway Labor Exec. Ass'n., 489 U.S. 602 (1989).

53 New York State Ass'n for Retarded Children v. Carey, 672 F.2d 644, 648–50 (2d Cir. 1979).

54 *See* School Bd. v Arline, 480 U.S. 273 (1987).

55 *See, e.g.,* Leckelt v. Board of Commissioners, 909 F.2d 820 (5th Cir. 1990); Martinez v. School Board, 861 F.2d 1502 (11th Cir. 1988); Chalk v. United States Dist. Ct., 840 F.2d 701 (9th Cir. 1988). *See generally,* Gostin, *The AIDS Litigation Project: Part II, Discrimination,* 262 J.A.M.A. 2086 (1990).

56 42 U.S.C.A. § 12101 *et seq.* (West Supp. 1991). For a comprehensive discussion of the Americans with Disabilities Act, see *The Americans with Disabilities Act Symposium: A View from the Inside,* 64 Temp. L. Rev. 371 (1991).

57 For a discussion of the need for a scientific foundation for public health measures, see Burris, *Fear Itself: AIDS, Herpes, and Public Health Decisions,* 3 Yale L. & Pol'y Rev. 479 (1984).

58 Bayer, Levine & Wolf, *HIV Antibody Screening: An Ethical Framework for Evaluating Proposed Programs,* 256 J.A.M.A. 1768, 1768 (1986).

59 For thorough discussion of the ethics of testing, *see id.*

60 *See, e.g.,* Centers of Disease Control, Guidelines for HIV Testing Services for Inpatients and Outpatients in Acute-Care Hospital Settings (draft Sept. 20, 1991).

61 *MacNeil Lehrer News Hour* (PBS television broadcast, interview with Kristine Gebbie, chair of Association of State and Territorial Health Officials, AIDS Task Force, Feb. 4, 1987); *see, e.g.,* Alaska Statutes § 25.05.101 (Michie. Supp., 1986), *repealed by* 1984 Alaska Sess. Laws ch. 134 § 4; N.Y. Dom. Rel. Law § 13-a (McKinney 1977 and Supp. 1986), *repealed by* 1985 N.Y. Laws 674 § 1; Wis. Stat. Ann. § 765.06 (West 1981 and Supp. 1986), *repealed by* 1981 Wis. Laws ch. 20, § 1777r.

62 *Requiring Physicians to Warn Contacts Seen as Misguided,* 1 AIDS Policy & Law (BNA), Nov. 5, 1986, at 8.

63 W. Curran, L. Gostin & M. Clark, Acquired Immunodeficiency Syndrome: Legal, Regulatory and Policy Analyses (U.S. Dep't H.H.S. No. 282–86–0032, 1986).

64 Whalen v. Roe, 429 U.S. 589, 606 (1977) (Brennan, J., concurring); *see also, e.g.,* Schulman v. NYC Health and Hospitals Corp., 342 N.E.2d 501 (N.Y. 1974) (abortion reporting).

65 *Self-Reported Behavior Change Among Gay and Bisexual Men—San Francisco,* 34 MMWR 613 (1985); Schecter, Jeffries & Constance, *Changes in Sexual Behavior and Fear of AIDS,* 1 Lancet 1293 (1984); *Declining Rates of Rectal and Pharyngeal Gonorrhea Among Males—NYC,* 33 MMWR 295 (1984). *See generally* chapters 6 and 7 in this volume.

66 Cal. Health & Safety Code §§ 2520, 2525 (Communicable Disease Control) (West 1976).

67 *See, e.g., In re* Stilinovich, 479 N.W.2d 731 (Minn. Ct. App. 1992); *see also* New York Soc'y of Surgeons v. Axelrod, 572 N.E.2d 605 (N.Y. 1991) (upholding health commissioner's decision not to list HIV as a communicable or sexually transmitted disease against challenge from doctor's organization).

68 *See generally* R. Bayer, Private Acts, Social Consequences: AIDS and the Politics of Public Health 169–206 (1989).

69 *See* Wash. Rev. Code Ann. § 70.24.105(6) (West. Supp. 1991); Minn. Stat. §§144.4171 *et seq.* (1990) (discussed in *Stilinovich,* 479 N.W.2d at 735–36).

70 Greene v. Edward, 263 S.E.2d 661 (W. Va. 1980).

71 *See Ex parte* Martin, 188 P. 2d 287, 291 (Cal. Ct. App. 1948); *Kirk,* 65 S.E. 387, 391 (S.C. 1909).

72 *See* U.S. Dep't of Health & Human Services, Advisory Counsel for the Elimination of Tuberculosis, Strategic Plan for the Elimination of Tuberculosis in the United States (1989); U.S. Dep't of Health & Human Services, National MDR-TB Task Force, National Action Plan to Combat Multidrug-Resistant Tuberculosis (1992); Braun, *et. al., Increasing Incidence of Tuberculosis in a Prison Inmate Population: Association with HIV Infection,* 261 J.A.M.A. 393 (1989); Snider, *et. al., Tuberculosis in Correctional Institutions,* 261 J.A.M.A. 436 (1989); *Nosocomial Transmission of Multidrug-Resistant TB to Health-Care Workers and HIV-infected Patients in an Urban Hospital-Florida,* 39 MMWR 718 (1990); *Nosocomial Transmission of Multidrug-Resistant Tuberculosis among HIV-infected Persons: Florida and New York, 1988–1991,* 40 MMWR 585(1991); Goldsmith, *Forgotten (Almost) But Not Gone: Tuberculosis Suddenly Looms Large on Domestic Scene,* 264 J.A.M.A. 165 (1990).

73 Cowley, *A Deadly Return,* Newsweek, Mar. 16, 1992, at 53.

74 Goldsmith, *Medical Exorcism Required as Revitalized Revenant of Tuberculosis Haunts and Harries the Land,* 268 J.A.M.A. 174 (1992).

6 Education to Reduce the Spread of HIV

Scott Burris

Education to induce people to stop doing things that put them at risk of acquiring HIV infection has been all but universally acknowledged as the primary means of controlling the epidemic. Yet in the United States, official education efforts have been halfhearted. A substantial share of federal prevention money has been invested in individual testing and counseling, while other forms of prevention education have been largely left to private organizations whose effective use of federal education grants has been hampered by blue-nosed content restrictions. Despite the unimpeachably good intentions of many individual officials, the government has never thrown its full leadership and organizational weight behind education; on the contrary, its policies of censorship and shame have sounded sympathetically with the AIDS-phobia of leaders in the national media, who for ten years have resisted so slight a step as accepting paid condom advertising. On several occasions, crucial studies of Americans' sexual behavior have been cancelled under conservative pressure, and only in the past couple of years has the government begun assessing the success of such education as has been conducted.

The ambivalence this record reflects is commonly attributed to the moral issues raised by explicit talk of drug use and sex. There is, however, much more at stake than a breach of national decorum. Education challenges the status quo. In a culture steeped in the sort of naughty, teasing sexiness of MTV and fashion ads, explicit public health education becomes impolite by omitting the obligatory bow to shame that even pornography makes. Education's premise that risk arises from behavior challenges the comforting delusion that infection must be linked to some innate characteristic of the infected—something "they" have and "we" don't. It is a remedy that does nothing to satisfy the urge to identify and isolate, if only in our own minds, the infected. Education in safer sex and drug use implicitly requires us to comprehend homosexuals and drug users as more than the sum of their disfavored acts. Education forces people to take responsibility for their own choices, but it also forces society to look at the meager options we are providing. Its message of change cannot properly be confined to the individual consumer.

So far, the law has been used as much to limit as to encourage effective HIV education. In this chapter, I will discuss the few bases upon which people can argue that the law requires the government to provide HIV education, and then discuss how the law addresses censorship of educational messages and the suppression of efforts to promote behavior change. By way of introduction, I will review current approaches to HIV education, and the education efforts of the first decade of the epidemic. I will conclude with a discussion of the role of courts and legislatures as health educators.

CURRENT APPROACHES TO HIV EDUCATION

"HIV education" actually describes several different tasks, including providing basic HIV information to millions of people who are at little or no risk of acquiring the disease, but whose fear of the disease can exacerbate its impact; training health care providers in diagnosing and treating the disease; teaching health and public safety workers to be at once less afraid of transmission and more careful about the use of barrier precautions; and educating private and public employers about the illegality and irrationality of discrimination against the infected. In its primary public health sense, however, "HIV education" refers to activities aimed at reducing risky behavior among those in danger of becoming infected. This has been the area of most dispute, and is the major focus of this chapter.

Education suffers in policy debate as much when its goals are overstated as when its accomplishments are undervalued. The goal of HIV prevention education is to reduce the occurrence of behavior that spreads HIV. Unlike such health measures as screening and contact tracing, education does not indulge social fantasies of stopping all HIV transmission; it cannot even be guaranteed to stop any one particular instance. Education is successful if it reduces HIV-transmitting behavior to the greatest degree possible, given the limits of funding and human nature. To anyone who judges a health measure by the number of identifiable infected individuals who are rendered harmless, education inevitably seems like pie in the sky. To everyone whose psychological defenses against HIV depend upon stigmatizing the infected, education's suggestion that "we" all need to be careful is discomfiting.

The core messages of HIV risk-reduction education are simple and direct: don't have unprotected sex involving the exchange of semen or blood; don't share syringes and needles, or, if these "works" are shared, disinfect them thoroughly with bleach between users. Data from the first decade of the epidemic suggest that people can be taught to avoid infection, but the same data show that education is no simple program. Education must be diverse and sensitive enough to communicate with the many different sorts of people at risk, but such individually tailored messages must be coordinated with consistent messages to the population as a whole. Simply presenting information is important, but ultimately norms of safer behavior have to be adopted, enforced, and supported by communities and leaders.[1]

Successful education begins with an acceptance of the worth and uniqueness of the consumer, whether the education is aimed at an individual or a community. Sex and drug use are highly personal, sensitive behaviors, and will not be altered unless treated as such. From this reality flow several specific prerequisites for successful education.

Educators have found that the educational message must be linguistically and culturally appropriate and responsive to the people receiving it. If the consumer uses the word "cum," the educator should, too, not simply because the consumer might not understand "semen" (a concern often based on the faulty assumption that people who use colloquialisms don't know any better), but because speaking the same language is a way of expressing respect and cultural acceptance. The need for clarity is equally great in the language of pictures. There is no room for a fig leaf in a picture intended to illustrate how to properly put on a condom.

In a larger sense, appropriateness is a matter of being responsive to the special needs of each consumer. Drug users come from every class, cultural, educational and linguistic group. Men who have sex with other men may live as openly gay, or may, happily married, believe that active anal sex is not even a homosexual act. Women at risk from their bisexual or drug-using partners may be yuppies, or working class, or entirely shut out of the economy. Sexually active teenagers may be earning A's in high school or be on the streets of Des Moines turning tricks. For each, HIV is linked to other life issues, which the educator must recognize and address. How do these particular people feel about sex? About talking about sex? What choices do they have?

Encouraging people to face the way in which HIV and dangerous behavior come into their lives requires a trusted and credible educator. That credibility may come from being a member of the community with a bond of common background and life experience, or simply from empathy and trustworthiness. One positive aspect of the government's retiring role in HIV education has been the growth of a network of community-based organizations with the ability, if not always the resources, to provide education from a grass-roots perspective.

To a considerable extent, the structure of the educational presentation influences the quality of interaction between the educator and the consumer. Education in small, homogeneous peer groups has been very effective in creating an atmosphere in which those at risk can talk about intimate behaviors and the barriers to change in their own lives. Surveys of a variety of educational formats indicate that the ability of the audience to participate and ask questions is strongly linked to successful learning. A smaller group also affords the educator a better opportunity to learn about and respond to the particular needs of the audience. One corollary is that mass forms of education—large lectures, videotapes, public service announcements—are of limited value in getting people to deal seriously with their risky behaviors, although they may be effective in getting across basic concepts and supporting more focused efforts.[2]

Educators must reach people where they live. To reach drug users, educators go to shooting galleries; to reach sexually active gay men, they go to the bars and baths. One judge in New York City set up counseling for prostitutes in the back of his courtroom. Educators can use things that people do want—like free condoms or clean needles—to draw an audience for information, and they can package information in an enticing way: education aimed at risky sex, for example, may be presented in erotic safer sex workshops.[3]

Effective education accepts that people desire, and are entitled to, pleasure. Understandable language, clear pictures and a positive attitude help make the safer behavior attractive as well as accessible. Indeed, what upsets people about safer-sex education is not that it is pornographic, but that it is pedagogic: it teaches people to pleasure themselves. We tolerate a great deal of sexual expression in our popular culture—pornography is easier to find than safer sex brochures—but pop sexuality is safely traditional, defined by notions of sin, of guilty pleasure, of rebellion, all of which inherently pay homage to the power of the traditional rules. Safe-sex education, by contrast, is interested in the sex of sex, not the gloss on sex. It tells the consumer how to get the greatest amount of pleasure at the lowest possible risk, using techniques and with an attitude that would probably work just as well for cooking school.[4]

Education does not, in intention or in fact, encourage homosexuality, teen-age sexuality, or drug use, in the sense of moving someone who would not otherwise engage in the behavior to begin doing so. Yet while educators will sometimes claim that they are neutral about the behavior, promoting only safety, successful HIV education requires an acceptance of homosexuality and drug use that goes beyond mere toleration. Safer-sex education facilitates the expression of one's sexuality; it helps people be gay in a dangerous time. Simultaneously, safer-sex education for gay people challenges the ingrained identification of homosexuality with particular sex acts, recognizing that people can be gay in ways that transcend what they do in bed. HIV education, like HIV disease, is taking place within a social context: education's supportive openness about gay sexuality complements in fact, if not by conscious design, a larger movement for gay civil rights. (As I will discuss in a moment, the ''acceptance'' of drug use entailed in safer injection education and needle exchange is more problematic.)

The notion that people's HIV-transmitting behaviors take place in a social and cultural context is crucial to successful education. Not just the specific work product of HIV educators, but the millions of daily clues sent by peers and the videos they peer at should, ideally, be consistent with safety. Safer behavior must be supported, and reinforced, throughout the community. As the long campaign against smoking has radically changed social attitudes about the habit, HIV education must aim for a larger change in sexual mores.[5]

Dealing with the social context requires a recognition, by both the educator and the consumer, that HIV issues are inextricably tied to other life and health issues. Many people at risk need specialized assistance to deal with underlying conditions influencing behavioral choices, and HIV education needs to serve as a bridge to that assistance. Promoting safe behavior among young people often requires training in cognitive decision-making and assertiveness. A conversation that begins with HIV as its subject may well end up focused on self-esteem.[6] A drug user may be taught that his risk of HIV is high and that he should stop using drugs, but if he cannot get into a treatment program or get a vial of bleach, or, indeed, if he is subject to arrest for possessing a clean needle, the education is little better than a tease.[7] A woman may want very badly for her partner to use a condom, yet be involved in an abusive relationship. HIV education that merely tells her she's in even more trouble than she suspected is not helpful to her or the public health; she needs assistance in getting out of or changing the relationship.[8] Unless education also equips the consumer with the tools to change—whether drug treatment, ongoing counseling, or simply some hope of building a better life—there will be more knowledge in the world, but no less AIDS.

The inextricability of HIV from other social issues is nowhere more apparent than in communities of color. Seventy-four percent of the 18,602 women diagnosed with AIDS as of April 1991 were non-White, primarily Black and Latina. The statistics on prevalence per 100,000 people show an even more striking imbalance: by 1988, the cumulative number of cases per 100,000 was nearly three and one-half times higher among Black men, two and one-half times higher among Latino men, fourteen times higher among Black women, and seven times higher among Latina women than among their White counterparts. Prevalence per 100,000 was four times higher among Black children and two times higher among Latino children than among White children.[9]

The communities where poor people of color live are already suffering epidemic levels of public health threats, including violence, tuberculosis, syphilis, infant mortality and measles.[10] To a considerable extent, these health and social problems are the result not of nature but of social decisions to remove or withhold resources from these communities and distribute them elsewhere. Here the battle over the morality of HIV education merges with the struggle between those who control the money and those who need it. It is a matter of whether or not outside public health workers deserve the trust of communities whose dismal states testify to the value of previous "help" from the dominant social factions.

Under these circumstances, the notion that the answer to HIV is to make sex and drug use safer meets with considerable skepticism. Education's implicit acceptance of HIV-transmitting behavior as a fact of life—a liberating force for gay people—has oppressive overtones for poor people of color, particularly as applied to drug abuse. In a community beset with crime, drug use, violence and crumbling social structures, passing out clean needles and condoms may strike many people not as a solution but as a non sequitur. It might make sense to those who have decided that half measures are better than none, but who exactly decided that? Health authorities supporting education cannot ignore the reality that behavioral change cannot be separated from empowerment, nor imposed from above. Nor can they change the fact that serious resources are not likely to be directed to those communities to improve health and safety any time soon.[11]

At every level and in every setting, AIDS and HIV education confronts us with the fact that changing behavior is no less political than the behavior itself. HIV may be spread by deliberate acts, but society defines the range and much of the meaning of individual choices. HIV is not spread simply by ignorance or carelessness or bad luck, but also by powerlessness, shame, racism and mistrust. Change demands introspection and taking responsibility, but also a critical examination of external forces and their impact on one's life. When one New Yorker decides to use drugs it is a tragedy; when 200,000 New Yorkers decide to use drugs, it is a social failure to create alternative choices. HIV education necessarily points the finger at that failure, and so is ultimately subversive, if not revolutionary. As Nicholas Freudenberg wrote:

> The reality is that a world without AIDS, or a world with this epidemic under control,
> will look very different. AIDS educators need to help people visualize this world
> and connect their daily lives to making it happen. It will be a world where every one
> is entitled to comprehensive education about sexuality, drugs, and health; a world

where those who need treatment for drug addiction can get it on demand; a world
where basic health care is a right, not a privilege; a world where gay men and
lesbians, women and people of color, are not discriminated against; a world where
alternatives to drug use exist for the young people of this country; a world where
no one has to die on the streets because there is no home for them.[12]

In short, education may well be the primary means of preventing HIV transmission, but it is not a quick fix. Effective education is part of a web of services
that is neither cheap nor easy to provide, and which, indeed, will require changes
not just in those at risk, but in society.

HIV EDUCATION EFFORTS SO FAR

In his 1986 report on AIDS, Surgeon General Koop wrote that universal HIV education
to the earliest grade levels was "the only way we can stop the spread of AIDS." He
estimated that a program could save twelve to fourteen thousand lives in five years.
Koop's views were (and continue to be) widely shared.[13] Between 1982 and 1991,
the Public Health Service (which includes the Centers for Disease Control [CDC],
the national epidemiological agency, as well as such research-oriented agencies as
the National Institutes of Health [NIH] and the Alcohol, Drug Abuse and Mental
Health Agency) spent over $1.6 billion on prevention efforts.[14] This is in addition
to any state or local funding and to the uncounted sums raised and spent by private
organizations. It is not at all clear how well the money has been spent.

The CDC's three-pronged strategy includes general messages for the public,
chiefly through a national media campaign ("America Responds to AIDS"); somewhat more detailed curricula for school-aged people; and focused, risk-reduction
education for those at high risk. The centerpiece of the federal prevention program,
particularly for those at highest risk, is HIV testing, which includes individualized
counseling as well as voluntary partner notification and referral to local service
providers. In 1990, a representative year, the CDC entered into funding agreements
for HIV prevention with sixty-five state and local health departments. The contracts
included $23.8 million for risk-reduction education, $16.8 million for initiatives in
minority communities, $12.3 million for public information—and $117.6 million
for counseling and testing. Overall, 69 percent of government prevention dollars
were spent on counseling and testing. (All prevention activities, in turn, comprised
15 percent of total HIV-related expenditures.)[15]

The testing program rests on the theory that the offer of HIV testing is an
effective way to reach those who believe themselves to be at risk. Even if an

individual's test is negative, the program has succeeded in providing intensive education to a particularly likely candidate. Between 1985 and 1990, CDC-funded operations had performed over 3.85 million tests, at an approximate cost of $66 per person counseled, or $1,767 per infected person identified.[16]

It seems reasonable to believe that individual testing has substantial benefits to those who are tested (particularly now that early medical intervention is helpful), and that it may result in a reduction of risky behavior and an increase in knowledge. But despite the massive amounts spent on the program, the CDC has not undertaken to assess whether any of these beliefs about testing are true as well as reasonable. HIV testing probably helps reduce risky behavior to some degree, but is it effective enough, compared to other interventions, to justify the fiscal priority it has received? The research so far raises serious doubts.[17]

Why has so much been invested in an untested testing strategy? In addition to the educated hunches of CDC policymakers, I suggest there are two more troubling reasons that should give us pause about testing. First, the program of confidential, voluntary testing arose in the mid–1980s out of a bitter political dispute about how the newly developed antibody test should be used. Voluntary, confidential testing was a compromise between those who sought widespread screening and those who opposed any use of the test at all beyond the blood banking system.[18] Voluntary testing and counseling to some degree satisfied those who saw the primary task of public health as marking the sick, but also those who argued that identification was largely irrelevant to prevention through education. It seems too telling to be coincidental that private, one-on-one education allows the government to avoid the problem of publicly promoting explicit risk-reduction messages. The confidentiality of the counseling relationship protects the funding government as much as the patient, allowing explicit education that would never appear in a pamphlet.

The job of actually delivering basic risk-reduction education to people in danger has been left largely to private, community-based organizations and state and local health departments. Since 1985, all states, most territories and many hard-hit cities have received CDC funding. Directly or through state and local agencies, the CDC funds more than 700 community-based organizations providing educational services.[19] The CDC's program for youth, initiated in 1987, funds the training of educators, the development of school-based programs, surveys to monitor risky behaviors among students, and program evaluation. The program budget in 1990 was $45.6 million.[20] All this federal money has been conditioned on regulations severely restricting the explicitness—and effectiveness—of the message.

The general public information effort, called the National AIDS Information and Education Program, serves the goal of informing the population about HIV and fostering social attitudes supportive of low-risk behavior. In addition to a national hotline and information clearinghouse, its principal activity is marketing the message in the mass media, posters, and brochures, and in the activities of cooperating local governments and agencies like the Red Cross. CDC officials can muster impressive statistics: between 1987 and 1990, "80 television, 61 radio, and 75 print ads [were] produced and marketed to national, regional and local public media service directors . . . receiv[ing] 52,454 airings worth $58,500,000 of donated time."[21]

The program is, however, entirely dependent on media largesse in the form of donated air time and ad placements. Fewer than 10 percent of the television spots in one study ran in prime time; 65 percent appeared after 11 P.M. The CDC has also been largely unsuccessful in overcoming media resistance to some of the messages, particularly about drug use. Not until 1988 did the networks agree to run public service announcements that promoted the use of condoms. To this day, only one of the major networks, Fox, will accept paid advertising from condom manufacturers, despite polls indicating that 70 percent of Americans think condoms should be advertised on television. Switzerland's experience suggests how significant this censorship may be: beginning in 1986, the Swiss allowed paid condom advertising in conjunction with a public health media campaign. In the next four years, the number of seventeen- to thirty-year-olds who had never used condoms fell more than five-fold, while the number who reported always using them increased by more than three hundred percent.[22] Critics of the CDC's campaign remain concerned about the appropriateness of the messages, their cost-effectiveness given their usual placement off prime-time, and whether they are actually conveying the necessary information.[23]

THE IMPACT OF HIV EDUCATION

It is very difficult to prove that education, to the extent that it has been tried, is working. For one thing, little was done in the first decade of the epidemic to properly evaluate which programs were effective and which ones were not, a difficult but not impossible task in a society that has no trouble measuring how people respond to different detergent ads or presidential campaign themes.[24] We also lack "baseline" data about people's sexual behavior against which to compare behavior after education is delivered. One need say no more than that in 1992, the Kinsey reports of 1948 and 1954 remain the basic source of data about America's sexual practices.

We know that general knowledge about HIV has reached deep into the population. Surveys indicate that, by 1991, most Americans were familiar with the fundamentals of AIDS: how the disease is transmitted and what people need to do to protect themselves.[25] For most people, this information has come from television and newspapers, and is neither complete nor accurate in all its details. Misinformation about transmission through casual contact and insect bites, and about techniques for risk reduction, remains common.[26] Moreover, people of color, particularly poor people of color and those whose primary language is not English, are generally less well informed.[27]

A more important and elusive question is whether information has translated into behavioral change. Here the results are decidedly mixed. According to some polls, the fear of AIDS has caused a sea change in the sexual habits of single Americans; a New York Times–CBS News Poll in 1991 reported that half of American adults under the age of forty-five say they have changed their behavior.[28] Other studies, however, come to more guarded conclusions, noting that most Americans still do not perceive themselves to be at risk. One study found that college undergraduates actually increased their levels of unsafe sexual behavior between 1986 and 1988, despite an increase in their general knowledge about HIV.[29] A 1988 survey of adolescent males found that the number of respondents who had used a condom during their most recent intercourse had more than doubled since 1979, but that condom use was significantly below average among those engaging in behaviors at high risk for HIV.[30]

Gay men have shown significant changes, reducing the number of sexual partners, increasing use of condoms, and reducing the incidence of anal intercourse. One study characterized the changes as perhaps "the most rapid and profound response to a health threat which has ever been documented."[31] On the other hand, there is growing concern about "relapses" into risky behavior, and fear that a new generation of gay men will not recognize themselves as being at risk. For example, the San Francisco Health Department has found that gay men under thirty are three times as likely as gay men over forty to have anal sex without a condom.[32]

There is some evidence that women at higher risk are changing their behavior. A survey conducted by the National Center for Health Statistics indicates that women with ten or more lifetime sexual partners are most likely to have made changes to reduce their risk of contracting HIV. It found, too, that poor Black women, for whom AIDS is becoming a major killer, are more likely than the average woman to recognize that they are at risk and to change sexual behavior.[33]

Venereal disease rates have also been used as an indicator of behavior change, and here, too, the picture is not entirely positive. The mid-1980s saw a decrease in such sexually transmitted diseases as rectal gonorrhea among gay men, indicating a reduction in unprotected anal intercourse. Similarly, hepatitis B (HBV) transmission among gay men dropped by more than 50 percent between 1982 and 1987. Unfortunately, the overall rate of sexually transmitted HBV remained about the same because of an increase in heterosexual transmission. Optimism about behavioral change among poor women of color is dampened by the soaring rates of venereal diseases in inner cities.[34]

Intravenous drug users have also shown signs of adopting HIV-avoidance behaviors. Increased use of clean needles, reduced needle sharing, and a lower incidence of unprotected sex have all been reported among supposedly uneducable drug users, although these behavioral changes have been most marked in individuals already in drug treatment or whose previous incidence of high-risk behavior was low. It also appears that maintaining lower-risk drug use behavior is easier than maintaining safer sex behavior, and that unsafe sex remains a major risk factor among drug users and their sexual partners. Moreover, the overall success of efforts to decrease unsafe drug use is strongly dependent upon the availability of drug treatment, clean needles, and bleach.[35]

Recent statistics support the view that needle-exchange programs can have a direct impact on the spread of HIV. Health officials in Toronto and Vancouver credit needle distribution with stabilizing seroprevalance among drug users and significantly reducing the spread of the epidemic. In San Francisco, there has been no discernible change in seroprevalence among drug users during the two years of the country's largest needle-distribution program. An influential Yale study of a New Haven needle-exchange program reported a 33 percent reduction in new infections among participants over an eight-month period.[36]

For the future, the National Commission on AIDS has urged more support for behavioral, social science and medical research to improve knowledge about risky behavior and how to change it; broad public and private support for community-based organizations; more and better drug abuse treatment; and the development of a true national HIV prevention initiative. Other commentators have also warned of persistent bias against gay men and insensitivity to the needs of women and people of color, leading to mistrust, misassessment of the problem, and misdirection of resources.[37]

IS THE GOVERNMENT OBLIGED TO EDUCATE?

Given the importance of education, one may well ask whether a recalcitrant government can be forced, through legal action, to provide it. The short answer is "no." There is no support in prevailing constitutional theory for a "right" to receive

HIV education, nor even for a right to have the government act efficiently to protect public health. Courts hesitate to cast themselves as policymakers in health matters, and have consistently ruled that decisions about how to protect public health should be left to legislatures and health departments. (For more on traditional public health law, see chapter 5.)

There are ways that a creative lawyer can try to force the government to educate, but only in limited circumstances at the margins of the epidemic. In several cases involving bathhouse closure, opponents tried to turn the tables by arguing that health departments could not take the drastic step of limiting First Amendment rights of association if there was a more effective, less restrictive alternative. Courts accepted the value of education, but uniformly rejected the claim that health officials had to choose education over closure.[38]

If a specific state or federal law can be read to require education (if, that is, the legislature has positively mandated some government agency to educate), individuals may sue the officials who have failed to provide it. In the only such suit so far, however, AIDS advocates in Los Angeles argued in vain that a provision of the California Health and Safety Code prescribing that health officers "shall take such measures as may be necessary" to prevent the spread of disease required the Health Department and Board of Supervisors to begin a serious HIV education program.[39]

While government bears no general duty to provide education to people at risk, the Constitution has been read to require a municipality to train its police officers in the basic facts of HIV and the importance of nondiscrimination and confidentiality. In a notable New Jersey case, a federal district judge derived an obligation to educate from "section 1983," a federal statute that allows an individual to sue state and local government officials, or others acting in the name of the law, who deprive that individual of any civil right.[40] (The Supreme Court has applied section 1983 to punish civil rights violations resulting from a local government's "failure to train" its employees for some obvious contingency, such as a police officer's use of deadly force, if the failure reflects "deliberate indifference" to the rights of the citizenry.[41]) By 1987, the boroughs of Runnemede and Barrington, New Jersey, had made no effort to provide their police officers with basic information about the transmission of HIV, universal precautions, and the need to treat HIV-infected people with respect and discretion. Thus, when some of their officers learned that a man recently arrested was infected with HIV, they felt the need to warn the man's neighbors, who in turn contacted the media and several parents whose children attended school with the infected man's children. The man's family brought suit, and the district court found not only that the individual officers had violated the family's privacy rights, but that the boroughs, too, were liable by virtue of their failure to train their employees: "City policy makers must know to a moral certainty that their police officers will come into contact with those known or suspected to have AIDS and that transmission of the disease will cause death. The need to train officers about AIDS and its transmission and about the constitutional limitations on the disclosure of the identity of AIDS carriers is so obvious that failure to do so is properly characterized as deliberate indifference to constitutional rights."[42]

This is a single decision in a damages case that, strictly speaking, does not require any other city to do anything. In practice, however, the case will have a powerful impact nationally. Any police department in an area where HIV is prevalent should be advised by its attorneys to develop and implement basic HIV education and training for police and public safety workers. (For a discussion of similar efforts to force HIV education for incarcerated people, see chapter 12.)

MAY THE GOVERNMENT COMPEL PRIVATE PARTIES TO PROVIDE OR RECEIVE EDUCATION?

Although government is under no obligation to educate, it may take up the burden voluntarily or, as is more common, selflessly place it on someone else's shoulders. Federal, state and local governments have moved in the last ten years to require education to be delivered in a variety of settings, from the classroom to the workplace, usually at the educator's own expense.

About a third of the states have passed laws that require or encourage the addition of HIV prevention education to the public school curriculum. Elsewhere, education has been implemented by state or local school authorities under existing law. Many states grant parents a right to review curricula in advance and remove their children if they choose.[43]

Several states require information about HIV and HIV testing to be distributed to marriage license applicants. Michigan goes the farthest, requiring actual counseling by a physician or local health officer as a prerequisite for marriage, although the law exempts anyone who has a religious objection. Rhode Island not only requires an offer of the test, but will pay for it if the offer is accepted.[44] A number of states have required education to be provided, with or without mandatory testing, to people charged with or convicted of crimes involving prostitution or drug abuse.[45]

An ambitious Philadelphia city ordinance, passed in 1990, requires any employer of three or more people to provide education, conducted orally "by a senior management official, regarding the ways HIV can and cannot be transmitted, and the rights of affected employees, accompanied by personal distribution to each employee of printed materials'' produced by the health department. The law even includes a penalty of up to three hundred dollars per employee for failure to provide the education, though it provides no funds to allow the city health department to prepare the materials or monitor compliance.[46]

Governments have long regulated workplace safety, and have moved in recent years to address the risk of HIV transmission in various settings through prevention education. About half the states have "Right-to-Know" laws, requiring employees and the public to be provided with some information by manufacturers or suppliers about hazardous substances in the workplace. In a case under the New York Right-to-Know law, the New York attorney general won an agreement with the New York City Transit Authority to train all its workers in the proper handling of waste, such as used needles, that could transmit HIV or other infectious diseases.[47]

More significant has been federal action in the health care area to require education and preventive measures focused on occupational transmission. In 1988, Congress directed the CDC to develop risk-reduction guidelines for all health and public safety workers. The CDC subsequently worked with the Occupational Safety and Health Administration (OSHA), which regulates workplace safety, to produce binding requirements including training and education. OSHA released final regulations in 1991. The agency monitors compliance with its regulations, and workers may file complaints and, in instances of imminent danger, go to court to force OSHA to take immediate action.[48]

Laws requiring someone to offer, or receive an offer of, education, are normally uncontroversial. The burden they impose is usually minimal, even if the effectiveness of the education is, too. Such laws are so well within the zone of legislative discretion that they are unlikely even to be challenged in court. The exception that proves the rule is school-based HIV education for children. In this area, the political debate over explicitness and the fear of outraged parents has led most states to forbid explicit materials and to stress abstinence as the primary means of prevention. In spite of these limitations, there has already been one case in which parents went to court to keep their children from being exposed to any HIV education whatsoever.

New York's HIV education curriculum—including instruction on the nature of the disease as well as modes of transmission and methods of prevention—is compulsory for all students. Unlike many states, New York declined to allow a total exemption for objecting families, authorizing children to be excused only from the portion of the curriculum dealing with prevention (five lessons on abstinence), and then only if the parents agreed to provide alternative education on the topic at home. A suit was brought by members of the Plymouth Brethren, a 170-year-old separatist

Christian sect.[49] The Brethren work and send their children to school in the larger community but otherwise associate only with one another. They shun some modern products and subscribe to a strict moral code, including a prohibition on extramarital sex and drug use. They claimed that the mandatory HIV education violated their First Amendment right of freedom of religion and their privacy right to bring up their children as they see fit. For its part, the state argued that exempting Brethren children from HIV education would undermine the state's prevention efforts.

School boards and legislatures have broad authority to prescribe the curriculum. Although the Supreme Court has in the past shown sensitivity to parents' rights and to religious communities whose traditions place them at odds with rules inoffensive to the general public, it has recently ruled that even a strongly held religious belief does not entitle one to an exemption from a generally applicable law whose purpose is not to interfere with religion.[50] Two lower New York courts dismissed the Brethren's claim based on the state's compelling interest in preventing HIV. The state's highest court, however, found that both the Brethren's claim of harm to religion and the state's claims of harm to public health were unsupported by the evidence, and sent the case back for trial.[51] The case reminds us that mandated HIV education may not triumph over all opposition, but that only the most sincerely held (and solidly proven) parental objections will be accepted by courts as the basis of an exemption.

CAN THE GOVERNMENT CENSOR EDUCATION?

Efforts by officials to control the education conducted by private citizens have inspired some of the most pointlessly tragic battles of the HIV education effort. Free expression, a category into which most forms of HIV education fall, is a basic right protected by the Constitution, but the Supreme Court has drawn a crucial, and controversial, distinction between expressive activities in private settings paid for by private funds, and speech on the government's nickel or the government's turf.

Limits on Subsidized Speech

The federal government, through the CDC, is a major funder of HIV education by state and local governments and private agencies. In 1986, already feeling the ire of those determined to limit open discussion of sexuality and drug use, the CDC for the first time issued content guidelines for the education it funded. The guidelines, which the CDC characterized as a compromise between fostering useful HIV education and maintaining the "broad support . . . vital to its public health mission," were superficially altered several times in the succeeding years, but their essence remained unchanged, and controversial: educators using federal funds for written materials were required to "use terms or descriptors . . . which a reasonable person would conclude should be understood by a broad cross-section of educated adults in society." As to audiovisual and pictorial materials, the CDC required the presentation of safe-sex messages by "inference" rather than the "overt depiction of the performance of 'safer sex' or 'unsafe sex' practices" or any display of the "anogenital area of the body." If the education was addressed to a specific community, materials could employ colloquial language more accessible to consumers in that community— but only if the material "would [not] be judged by a reasonable person to be [ ]offensive to most educated adults *beyond that group.*" (In 1990, guidelines were revised to authorize a review panel to approve material that would offend a majority of adults outside the intended audience *if* the panel believed that the material's effectiveness outweighed its potential offensiveness.[52])

In 1987, Senator Jesse Helms weighed in with a law forbidding the use of federal funds to "promote or encourage, directly, homosexual sexual activities," and requiring instead that all materials "emphasize" sexual abstinence outside of heterosexual marriage and complete abstinence from drug use.[53] The Helms Amendment was replaced, after one year in effect, by a compromise engineered by Senators Kennedy and Cranston. The Kennedy-Cranston Amendment forbade use of federal funds only for materials "*designed* to promote or encourage, directly" IV drug abuse or homosexual or heterosexual activity. This satisfied proponents of HIV education, who took the position that even the most explicit messages were "designed to promote" risk reduction. The CDC, however, did not change its guidelines.[54]

To enforce all these restrictions, the guidelines mandated local project review panels, to be established by recipients, which would screen out any proposed material that crossed the "bounds of explicitness." At first, members of these panels were *not* to be predominantly drawn from the communities to which the materials were directed. In later versions of the guidelines, this requirement was waived for ethnic and racial minorities, but not for gay or IV-drug using consumers. All materials proposed to be created with federal funds had to be approved in advance by the panels.[55]

From the first, HIV educators reacted to the guidelines with hostility and dismay. It went without saying that educational materials should not offend the intended consumers, but the CDC never satisfactorily explained why materials should not be offensive to people who were never intended to see them. The Helms Amendment, and even Kennedy-Cranston, injected what was at best an irrelevant consideration into the evaluation of educational materials. The project review panels added a burdensome layer of regulation, made more onerous by their dedication to enforcing rules that had only a harmful effect on HIV education.

Over the years, panels compiled a record of arbitrary denials of approval. A North Carolina panel rejected a poster that showed two men holding condoms and draped in an American flag over the motto "Life, Liberty and the Pursuit of Happiness." The CDC approved a major campaign by Black and White Men Together, including posters advertising "Hot, Horny, and Healthy Playshops." A San Francisco review panel approved as well a poster showing Black and White men sitting together. The same materials were disapproved by panels in Los Angeles and the District of Columbia. Worse than outright denial was the chilling effect of the rules. Educators, with little time or money to waste, learned to censor themselves to avoid disapproval by review panels. Some educators, unable to reconcile the needs of effective education with the demands of the CDC, simply gave up applying for federal money altogether.[56]

In what became the test case on the government's power to censor publicly funded HIV education, Gay Men's Health Crisis (GMHC), the New York State Department of Health, and several other organizations providing HIV education across the country brought a lawsuit in 1988 against the Department of Health and Human Services (HHS) and the CDC. The plaintiffs sued in the belief that the guidelines "impede[d] their ability to provide the most medically accurate and effective education about AIDS."[57] Given that there is no right to medically accurate and effective education as such, the plaintiffs' lawyers had to translate these very urgent, practical objections to the content restrictions into more or less abstract legal claims. The lawyers came up with three principal arguments.

The GMHC's lawyers led with an administrative law claim, contending that the CDC's guidelines were contrary to the intent of Congress. Congress commonly passes very general laws, leaving it up to agencies in the executive branch to draft detailed regulations to flesh them out. It is a basic principle of administrative law that a federal agency has only that authority that has been delegated by Congress and must always act in a way that carries out the Congressional will. Agency regulations that clearly go beyond or against the will of Congress may be invalidated in court.[58]

The GMHC argued that the CDC's guidelines blatantly ignored Congressional instructions. When it passed the Kennedy-Cranston Amendment in 1988, Congress also stipulated that federally funded HIV education "contain material, and be presented in a manner, that is specifically directed toward the group for which such materials are intended." It ordered that the prohibition on promoting or encouraging homosexuality and drug abuse "may not be construed to restrict . . . accurate information about various means to reduce an individual's risk . . ., provided that any informational materials used are not *obscene*."[59]

In a detailed 1992 decision, the federal trial court agreed with the plaintiffs. Congress, the court found, had been concerned about the suppression of culturally sensitive, explicit materials under the guidelines, and had made it clear that it intended to ban only "obscene" materials. Obscenity is a very limited concept in the law, and does not encompass HIV education designed to save lives, even if many people would find it offensive. The CDC had no authority to go beyond the will of Congress and impose the much broader "offensiveness" restriction, and that, the court said, "is the end of the matter."[60]

The court also agreed with the plaintiffs that the education restrictions violated the Fifth Amendment's guarantee of due process, which requires that a law clearly indicate what conduct it prohibits. Statutes that fail to do so may be "void for vagueness."[61] "Offensiveness," the court found, was a hopelessly elastic term, with no "core meaning" in any of its applications in the guidelines:

> The CDC has made no affirmative statement as to what constitutes "offensive" materials, nor has it set forth a method by which to determine what materials will be deemed "offensive." . . . Can educational material be offensive simply because it mentions homosexuality? Because it depicts an interracial couple? Can a proposed AIDS education project be offensive because it traps a captive audience, such as subway riders, and forces them to look at a condom? Does offensiveness apply to all descriptions of sexual behavior, graphic depictions of sexual behavior, or descriptions of unusual sexual behavior?[62]

The vagueness was only compounded by instructions that panels measure offensiveness against the values of "a majority of adults outside the intended audience," or "a majority of the intended audience." Neither, once "offensiveness" was found, was there any predictable way to "weigh" that against the material's potential effectiveness. Any group seeking or getting CDC education money was forced to take the chance that its interpretation of the guidelines would match that of the local Project Review Panel. A bad guess meant the denial of funding and the wasted expenditure of time and energy.[63]

The GMHC decision looks like a ringing vindication of citizens' right to speak freely on a matter of considerable importance, but, strictly speaking, nothing in the decision challenges the authority of the government to place misguided restrictions on the speech it funds, so long as the rules are clear. When the case was originally filed, the plaintiffs had been able to rely on a long line of cases suggesting that government could not attach to its funding any conditions that placed a burden on constitutional rights, particularly speech rights.[64] In 1991, however, the Supreme Court drastically increased the authority of the government to control the speech of people who accept its money. In *Rust v. Sullivan,* the Court upheld restrictions under Title X of the Public Health Service Act that, among other things, forbid physicians in federally funded family planning projects to discuss abortion with their patients, even if such discussion is medically appropriate. The decision, which left one dissenting justice asking "what force the First Amendment retains if it is read to countenance the deliberate manipulation by the government of the dialogue between a woman and her physician,"[65] made this the weakest of the GMHC plaintiff's claims, and the court, having already found two reasons to invalidate the guidelines, elected not to reach it.

Censorship of Privately Funded Education

The GMHC case highlights the practical difficulty of using federal funds for effective HIV education, but even organizations that have money of their own run into censorship problems. Access to television, radio, and newspapers is essential for wide dissemination of any message in this society. The private media, however, are not covered by the Constitution's prohibition of censorship. Indeed, their right to refuse advertising on virtually any basis is itself protected by the First Amendment. The Supreme Court has upheld the Federal Communications Commission's "fairness doctrine," which requires some modicum of balance in broadcast coverage of public issues, but that fading remnant of another regulatory era does not seriously limit broadcasters' editorial discretion today.[66] Thus, private media are free to refuse messages on the grounds of offensiveness, disagreement with the message, or pure commercial caution—a freedom the media have exercised with gusto in the age of AIDS.

There remains one area, however, where the command of the First Amendment still rings clearly and with force. The government cannot censor HIV educators who take to the public streets, with their own money, on their own time. The police may not, for example, confiscate condoms or prohibit the distribution of explicit safe-sex flyers. Nor may the government discriminate against HIV educational messages in any media of public communication it controls, as the following case illustrates.

Advertising on buses and subways, often provided free or at cost for public service announcements, is an attractive, cost-effective way to reach some communities at risk. There have been anecdotal reports of disputes between educators and transit systems over HIV campaigns for several years, but only in Chicago did the issue reach the level of a lawsuit. In 1987, the Kupona Network, an organization based in the African American community, won a grant from the Illinois Department of Health to do a broad-based AIDS awareness campaign. Kupona developed a bus poster for selected Chicago Transit Authority (CTA) routes. The placard depicted, in a stylized manner, several figures shooting drugs and an androgynous couple holding a packaged condom. The placard included Kupona's phone number and the slogan: "SEX WITHOUT CONDOMS + DRUG ABUSE = AIDS. AIDS IN THE BLACK COMMUNITY IS VERY REAL." CTA officials rejected the ad as not "appropriate for public vehicles." Kupona said it was also told the CTA considered the ad to be "too black oriented." In September 1989, after months of fruitless negotiation, Kupona Network was forced to go to court.[67]

At first blush, this would seem, like GMHC, to be an open-and-shut case of government censoring speech because it disagreed with the message. But here, too, the Supreme Court has spun a rule to constrict the First Amendment. The "forum doctrine" draws a distinction, strained and much criticized, between public property opened up by tradition or deliberate designation for free-speech activities and public property reserved for the particular proprietary purposes of the government. (Here, as in the cases about government-funded speech, we see a split between jurists who focus on protecting the rights of citizens and those more protective of the prerogatives of the government.) In "traditional public forums"—places like parks and sidewalks that the Court believes have always been sites of public debate—the government has little authority to regulate speech. The government is also barred from censoring speakers in places it has designated to be public forums—like university classrooms and municipal auditoriums—although the government can place neutral limits on the forms of expression that the forum will accommodate. A city could, for example, refuse to rent its auditorium for any theatrical productions, but it could not pick and choose among plays based on their political slant. Finally, in "non-public forums," like military bases, the government can impose just about whatever limits it likes so long as they are "reasonable"; that is, not arbitrary, capricious, or invidious.[68]

The Supreme Court ruled in 1974 that advertising space in a city bus system was not a traditional public forum, but part of a government business venture. Thus a transit system, as a designated public forum, may refuse broad categories of ads— such as campaign messages—as long as it has clear guidelines that are uniformly applied.[69] The CTA tried to drive its buses through this loophole by claiming to have a neutral policy against controversial ads, but, like many government agencies, it was a sporadic censor. What it had was a record of shying away from ads that, for whatever reason, made its decisionmakers nervous—exactly the sort of arbitrary, content-based censorship the First Amendment forbids. Kupona's lawyers must have been surprised that the mere threat of a lawsuit was not enough to back the transit agency down, because just a few years before the CTA had lost an almost identical case arising from its refusal to run a series of abortion-related ads offered by Planned Parenthood.[70] Once Kupona's case reached court, the CTA saw the writing on the wall and, early in 1990, finally began running the posters.

Censorship as a System

Both the *Kupona* and GMHC cases were victories for HIV education. In *Kupona*, the legal invalidity of censorship was reinforced, and the posters ran. (Moreover, later that year the CTA ran an even more controversial poster portraying three kissing couples of various genders and races, over the slogan "Kissing Doesn't Kill; Greed and Indifference Do."[71]) In GMHC, the CDC's onerous content restrictions were struck down. But these cases also illustrate how censorship can work despite its illegality, at least in the absence of vigorous support for free expression in the courts.

Litigation is slow. For more than seven years, federally funded education was crippled by the various forms of the CDC's obscenity restriction, and having won in the trial court, GMHC might have to defend its victory through a long process of appeals. Kupona had to spend more than a year fighting while its posters sat in their wrappings.

Victory, moreover, does not come cheap. Even if a plaintiff can get free legal services, litigation is a serious drain on the energy of an agency that already has enough to cope with in fulfilling its primary purpose of preventing HIV transmission. And it can be dangerous to an agency's health to fight city hall. Few agencies can afford to ignore the fact that the defendant—the government—is a substantial, if not the chief, source of their funding, so that the official their lawyers depose today may be ruling on their latest grant proposal tomorrow. Under these circumstances, many educators will consciously or unconsciously censor themselves, adapting their messages to do the best they can within the rules. People at risk of HIV pay the price of silence.

The opportunity costs, too, are incalculable, precisely because HIV education is still largely in an experimental stage. We do not know exactly what will work, and the only way to learn is through rigorous trial and error. Instead of channeling energy into program innovations and evaluation, instead of encouraging a diversity of approaches, the government has built barriers and fostered homogeneity.

Finally, the Constitution, as interpreted by our Supreme Court, also does little or nothing to alleviate the effects of money and power (or the lack of them) on free speech. As Professor David Kairys has trenchantly observed, "We . . . are allowed to demonstrate, picket, hand out literature, gather in the streets, sing, chant, yell, and scream—all of which effectively amounts to a *display of displeasure or discontent*, without the means to explain why we are displeased, much less to actually participate in any social dialogue.''[72] The ideas of those who do not own, or cannot purchase, access to the mass media, are filtered, if not entirely ignored, by those who do, as the career of ACT-UP vividly illustrates.

CONDOMS AND NEEDLES

Condoms and needles are basic tools of HIV prevention, but their distribution has proven to be enormously controversial. The battles over condoms have been primarily political—most notably in the several cities that have introduced condoms into the schools. In one instance, however, a group of Philadelphia parents went to court to stop their school board from giving condoms to high school students on request, arguing among other things that condom distribution was an incitement to sodomy and that the "opt-out" provision—under which parents could contact the school and exclude their children from the program—was a burden on parental rights. Given the authority of school boards to make policy decisions, the suit has little chance of success.[73] (In one even more bizarre episode of legal misjudgment, the freeholders of Burlington County, New Jersey, voted to *stop* city health workers from providing free condoms along with HIV educational material, based on the exceedingly remote possibility of a products liability lawsuit by a person infected because of a defective condom.[74]) Distributing needles, however, has put educators face-to-face with a web of criminal drug laws.

The nation's first needle-exchange programs began in Tacoma, Washington, and New York City in 1988. (The New York program's low enrollment ceiling—only 300 participants—and inconvenient downtown location doomed it to irrelevancy as both scientific experiment and public health measure; it was shut down by David Dinkins when he succeeded Ed Koch as mayor.[75]) Subsequently, significant programs have been initiated by health agencies or private activists in a small number of cities including Seattle, Spokane, Portland, New York City, Boulder, New Haven, San Francisco, Philadelphia, Boston, and Honolulu.[76]

Standing in the way of needle exchange are state laws that strictly control the possession, distribution and sale of hypodermic needles and syringes. Most of the high prevalence states, including New York, New Jersey, Connecticut, Pennsylvania, Massachusetts, Illinois, and California, specifically outlaw the sale or possession of needles without a prescription.[77] Forty-five states and the District of Columbia have enacted drug paraphernalia laws, which make it a crime to deliver, or possess with intent to deliver, virtually any item that could be used in connection with illegal drug use, with the knowledge that it will be so used. These laws would seem to apply squarely to clean needle workers, who pass out injection equipment knowing, indeed hoping, that it will be used by the recipients for their drug injection. Moreover, the definition of "drug paraphernalia" in these laws is so broad that it could conceivably be read to include bleach distributed with the intent that it be used to clean drug needles, although no one to date has invoked that argument against a bleach program. (For more on drug paraphernalia and prescription laws, see chapter 8.)

In some places, needle exchangers sought changes in drug paraphernalia laws to make clear that what they were doing was legal. The programs in New Haven and Hawaii went forward under special legislation authorizing distribution on an experimental basis. New York City's experimental program was initiated under the state health commissioner's authority to waive the drug laws when necessary to preserve public health.[78]

Health officials in Tacoma and Spokane, faced with a state attorney general's opinion that needle-exchange programs violated Washington's drug paraphernalia law, went to court for a judicial declaration that their broad discretion under state health law to fight disease included the power to pass out needles. The trial courts sided with the public health officials. Describing needle exchange as another useful tool in the war on drugs, the judge in Spokane read the paraphernalia law to exempt from liability "any authorized state, county, or municipal officer who is engaged in the lawful performance of his or her duties."[79]

In other places, needle exchangers have simply taken the position that what they are doing is not against the law. The drug paraphernalia laws were passed before anyone had ever heard of HIV. The intention of their drafters was to discourage the drug trade by preventing the commercial sale of injection equipment. Needle exchange is intended to prevent HIV transmission, not increase drug use. Indeed, effective needle exchange discourages the sale of needles from less reliable sources.

This interpretation of the drug paraphernalia laws, although contrary to the plain statutory language, is winning acceptance in current practice and case decisions. Needle exchange still takes place in New York, where members of ACT-UP distribute 120,000 needles annually at five sites in Brooklyn, Manhattan, and the Bronx.[80] In San Francisco, the largest needle program in the nation persists despite the apparent prohibition under California law. The National AIDS Brigade, based in Boston, has a bicoastal network actively engaged in needle exchange in major cities. Portland's program has gone on for years without the interference of police and prosecutors.

In all these places, law enforcement officials are exercising their discretion not to treat needle exchange as a crime.[81]

Even when health workers have been arrested and brought to trial, judges and juries have so far been unwilling to convict them. Jury members who sympathize with a needle exchanger have the power to simply vote not guilty, however clearly the law may call for conviction. This is referred to as "jury nullification." In a number of cases, defendants have successfully used the "necessity defense," under which they admit to breaking the law but plead that their crime was necessary to avert an even greater evil. In New York, a judge accepted the defense and acquitted eight people arrested at a needle-exchange site in lower Manhattan. The factors she considered are representative of the necessity defense nationwide: the defendants reasonably believed that their actions were necessary to prevent an imminent harm to others; the defendants themselves did not create the emergency they were trying to alleviate; breaking the needle possession law did less harm than would an addict's using a dirty needle instead; there were no better options open to the exchangers for reducing transmission through drug use; and the legislature had not contemplated a situation like this when it passed the possession law, long before the epidemic began.[82] The necessity defense has also prevented convictions in cases in Boston and New Jersey, as well as a case in California in which the jury foreman not only voted to acquit but went out and joined the program.[83]

Although there are few signs that needle exchange will receive enthusiastic government support as part of the national public health policy against AIDS, government officials are generally not eager to continue treating as criminals private citizens who distribute needles on their own. Commentators, including the National Commission on AIDS, have advocated repealing prescription and possession bans, narrowing paraphernalia laws to allow possession of needles, and removing any threat of criminal penalties against appropriate sellers of needles such as pharmacists.[84]

CONCLUSION

Political leaders—the people who vote the funds and set the terms for HIV education—have so far failed to rise above ambivalence about HIV, sex, and death, leaving us with a socially marginalized HIV education program encumbered with counterproductive restrictions. As recently as December 1991, President Bush, still silent about most HIV issues, went out of his way to condemn the distribution of condoms to children in the Philadelphia schools. After announcing that passing out condoms would not affect behavior, the president told a local television audience that "just passing out condoms, giving up on lifestyle and giving up on family and fundamental values is [not] correct." He also came out against needle exchange because it "would encourage drug use."[85]

Neither can we expect courts to order us back onto a more productive and effective course. Cases like *Doe v. Borough of Barrington,* where a judge imposed upon a town a duty to educate its police, are exceptional. Although HIV advocates may see education policy as a matter of life and death, the dominant view from the bench is that it presents disputes about money, policy and values that courts ought not to resolve. Indeed, judges often recast plaintiffs' complaints about the merits of a government action into questions about the judiciary's own authority to act.

The role of the legal system *in* HIV education, however, goes beyond disputes *about* HIV education. Whenever a court resolves a case of discrimination or invasion of privacy or negligent transmission of the virus, it is educating the public as well as deciding a substantive legal issue. When a legislature passes a law protecting, for example, the confidentiality of HIV-related information, it is putting its support behind the view that identification of the infected is not medically necessary.[86] Inaction, too, sends a message.

The legal system's potential to educate or confuse the public about HIV is clearly seen in a comparison of two major social disputes about HIV: the schooling of infected children, and the practice of medicine by infected health care workers. In the mid 1980s, a number of children with HIV, the most famous of whom was Ryan White, were prevented from attending school. Frightened parents demonstrated, threatening a boycott if any HIV-infected children were ever admitted. The emotionally charged stories naturally generated substantial media attention, much of it focusing more on the dramatic anxieties than on the medical facts.

In the face of this, health authorities firmly recommended no substantial restrictions on child attendance, and across the country courts backed them up. In so doing, the courts performed a ritual as well as a legal function: the evidence was presented by both sides to an apparently neutral decisionmaker whose only interest was in finding the truth. While the decisions might not always inspire confidence in the critical reader (one decision, for example, relied for basic medical facts on an article in *Reader's Digest*), by matching the behavioral norm (don't discriminate) with the official risk assessment (there's no need to discriminate), courts reassured the public that health officials were truthful and reasonable in their recommendations.

Where courts ordered HIV-infected children admitted to school, community opposition tended to recede, and by the end of the 1980s the education of children with
HIV had ceased to be a major source of controversy.[87]

Events have moved very differently with respect to infected health care
workers. For many years, health officials accurately, if imprudently, treated transmission of HIV from health care worker to patient as the vanishingly small risk
it is. When the story broke that some very appealing, White, middle-class people
in Florida had apparently been infected during visits to their dentist, the CDC was
unprepared. As the story grew, the CDC waffled on its assessment of the risk,
and the public perception grew that being infected by a doctor was a serious
possibility worth worrying about.

This misperception of risk has so far been strongly validated by courts and
legislators. In closely watched decisions, several courts have ordered that past and
prospective patients be notified of a doctor's HIV infection, and have allowed mandatory testing of health care workers suspected of having HIV. The judges' opinions
essentially conceded that the risk of actual transmission was exceedingly low, basing
their decisions instead on the patient's "right to know."[88] Ironically, the effect of
the decisions has been to validate the perception that a patient *needs* to know—that
is, that the risk is significant. This perception has only been bolstered by legislative
efforts to punish infected health care workers who practice without informing their
patients.[89]

Questions of what kind of education policy we are going to pursue remain
squarely in the political realm. Were we serious as a nation about changing dangerous
behavior, our president would be supporting, rather than questioning, condom distribution in schools. Content restrictions on educational materials would be lifted.
Studies of American sexual behavior would be allowed to go forward. In all fifty
states, laws inhibiting needle distribution would be amended. In the private sector,
the mass media would accept ads for condoms, and federally funded public service
announcements would be more explicit and frequent. And that would simply be
removing the obstacles. Ten years into the epidemic, our acts still betray an ambivalence to HIV education and an indifference to our failure to pursue it. HIV
education is a form of social change, which makes it worth a fight—and which
means that it will not happen without one.

NOTES

1 For excellent discussions of education, upon which I have generally based my account, see National Commission on Acquired Immune Deficiency Syndrome, *America Living With AIDS: Transforming Anger, Fear, and Indifference into Action* 18–44 (1991); Francis & Chin, *The Prevention of Acquired Immunodeficiency Syndrome in the United States: An Objective Strategy for Medicine, Public Health, Business, and the Community,* 257 J.A.M.A. 1357 (1987); Freudenberg, *AIDS Prevention in the United States: Lessons from the First Decade,* 20 Int'l Health Services 590, 597–98 (1990); E. Chelimsky, *Educating People at Risk for AIDS,* 27 (General Accounting Office testimony to Senate Committee on Governmental Affairs, June 8, 1988); *see also* Amsel, *Introducing the Concept "Community Prevention,"* in AIDS and Intravenous Drug Use: Future Directions for Community-Based Prevention Research vii (C. Leukefeld, R. Battjes & Z. Amsel eds. 1990) [hereinafter AIDS and Intravenous Drug Use]; Citizens Commission on AIDS for New York City and Northern New Jersey, AIDS Prevention and Education: Reframing the Message (1989). The best review of federal efforts to date is H. Schietinger, Good Intentions: A Report on Federal HIV Prevention Programs (1991) (available from AIDS Action Council, 2033 M. Street N.W., Suite 802, Washington, D.C. 20036).

2 *See, e.g.,* Bell, *et al., Evaluating the Outcomes of AIDS Education,* 2 AIDS Educ. & Prevention 82 (1990); Fullilove, *et al., Black Women and AIDS Prevention: A View Towards Understanding the Gender Rules,* 27 J. Sex Res. 47, 57 (1990); Friedman, *et al., Health Education for IV Drug Users,* in AIDS and IV Drug Abusers 199, 211–13 (R. Galea, B. Lewis & L. Baker eds. 1988); *see also* Neaigus, *et al., Effects of Outreach Intervention on Risk Reduction Among Intrave-*

nous Drug Users, 2 AIDS Educ. & Prevention 255 (1990) (describing intravenous drug users' receptivity to educational efforts facilitated by ex-users).

3 *See* R. Bayer, Private Acts, Social Consequences: AIDS and the Politics of Public Health 101–136 (1989); Ginzburg, *et al., Health Education and Knowledge Assessment of HIV Diseases among Intravenous Drug Users,* in AIDS and IV Drug Abusers, note 2 above, at 185, 193; Jackson, *et al., The Role of Drug Abuse Treatment Programs in AIDS Prevention and Education Programs for Intravenous Drug Users: The New Jersey Experience,* in AIDS and Intravenous Drug Use, note 1 above, at 167, 178–80; *This Court Offers Condoms with Prostitutes' Sentences,* N.Y. Times, Mar. 20, 1991, at B1; *see also* Pyle, *Counselors Take AIDS Battle to the Streets,* L.A. Times, Apr. 9, 1991, at B1 (" 'You've got to do essentially a marketing campaign. . . . Instead of marketing Reeboks or Coca-Cola, you're marketing risk reduction and to market anything you've got to hand out free samples.' ").

4 For his many insights into the social control of sexuality, I rely on M. Foucault, The History of Sexuality (R. Hurley trans. 1978).

5 *See, e.g.,* National Commission on Acquired Immune Deficiency Syndrome, note 1 above, at 24–25; Friedman, note 2 above, at 199, 208–09, 211; Maccoby, *Communication and Health Education Research: Potential Sources for Education for Prevention of Drug Use,* in AIDS and Intravenous Drug Use, note 1 above, at 1.

6 *See* Schinke, *et al., African-American and Hispanic-American Adolescents, HIV Infection, and Preventive Education,* 2 AIDS Educ. & Prevention 305 (1990); Franzini, *et al., Promoting AIDS Risk Reduction Via Behavioral Training,* in 2 AIDS Educ. & Prevention 313 (1990); Fullilove, *et al.,* note 2 above, at 60–61.

7 *See, e.g.,* Gostin, *The Interconnected Epidemics of Drug Dependency and AIDS,* 26 Harv. C.R.-C.L. L. Rev. 113, 162–81 (1991); Selwyn, *et al., Knowledge About AIDS and High Risk Behavior Among Intravenous Drug Users in New York City,* in AIDS and IV Drug Abusers, note 2 above, at 215, 224–26.

8 *See* Serrano, *The Puerto Rican Intravenous Drug User,* in AIDS and Intravenous Drug Use, note 1 above, at 24, 29.

9 *See, e.g.,* Fox, *Chronic Disease and Disadvantage: The New Politics of HIV Infection,* 15 J. Health Pol'y, Pol. & Law 341, 345 (1990); *The Health Status of the United States,* Federal News Service, Apr. 8, 1991 [hereinafter *Health, United States*]; Chu, *et al., Impact of the Human Immunodeficiency Virus Epidemic on Mortality in Women of Reproductive Age, United States,* 264 J.A.M.A. 225 (1990).

10 *Health, United States,* note 9 above; Aral & Holmes, *Sexually Transmitted Diseases in the AIDS Era,* Sci. Am., Feb. 1991, at 62; *see also* Sullivan, *Effects of Discrimination and Racism on Access to Health Care,* 266 J.A.M.A. 2674 (1991) (Secretary of Health and Human Services notes "clear, demonstrable, undeniable evidence of discrimination and racism in our health care system").

11 For an eloquent account of the issue, see Dalton, *AIDS in Blackface,* 118 Daedalus 3219 (1989).

12 Freudenberg, note 1 above, at 597–98.

13 Surgeon General's Report on Acquired Immune Deficiency Syndrome 14, 28 (1986); *see, e.g.,* Institute of Medicine, National Academy of Sciences, Confronting AIDS: Directions for Public Health, Health Care and Research 96–112 (1986) [hereinafter Confronting AIDS]; Roper, *Current Approaches to Prevention of HIV Infections,* 106 Pub. Health Reports 111 (1991). *But see* Dannemeyer & Franc, *AIDS-Policies and Prospects: The Failure of AIDS-Prevention Education,* Pub. Interest, Summer 1989, at 47.

14 *See* Winkenwerder, *et al., Federal Spending for Illness Caused by the Human Immunodeficiency Virus,* 320 New Eng. J. Med. 1598, 1600 table 2 (1989); H. Schietinger, note 1 above, pt. 2 at 3 fig. 1.

15 *See* Evaluating AIDS Prevention Programs 51–52, 83–86, 102–03 (S. Coyle, R. Boruch & C. Turner expanded ed. 1991); Roper, note 13 above, at 113–15; H. Schietinger, note 1 above, pt. 2 at 21 & 10–14 figs. 8–9, 3 fig. 1, pt. 5 at 5; *see also Publicly Funded HIV Counseling and Testing—United States, 1985–1989,* 39 MMWR 137, 140 (1990)("Of all HIV prevention efforts, counseling and testing activities receive the highest level of resource support from the CDC.").

16 *See Publicly Funded HIV Counseling and Testing—United States, 1985–1989,* note 15 above; Higgins, *et al., Evidence for the Effects of HIV Antibody Counseling and Testing on Risk Behaviors,* 266 J.A.M.A. 2419 (1991); H. Schietinger, note 1 above, pt. 2 at 25.

17 *See* H. Schietinger, note 1 above, at 21–24; Higgins, *et al.,* note 16 above; Roper, note 13 above; Zenilman, *et al., Effect of Posttest Counseling on STD Incidence,* 267 J.A.M.A. 843 (1992).

18 On the controversy over testing, see generally R. Bayer, note 3 above, at 101–36.

19 Evaluating AIDS Prevention Programs, note 15 above, at 51–52, 83–86, 102–03; Roper, note 13 above, at 114; *see* Bailey, *AIDS Prevention: A Sad State of Affairs,* Psychology & AIDS Exchange, Apr. 1991, at 2.

20 Roper, note 13 above, at 112–13; H. Schietinger, note 1 above, pt. 2 at 19–20.

21 Roper, note 13 above, at 112; *see* H. Schietinger, note 1 above, pt. 2 at 16–19; *see also HIV-Infection Prevention Messages for Injecting Drug Users: Sources of Information and Use of Mass Media—Baltimore, 1989,* 40 MMWR 465, 466 (1991) (television was primary source of information about HIV for almost half of surveyed drug users).

22 *Social Barriers to AIDS Prevention,* in Committee on AIDS Research and the Behavioral, Social and Statistical Sciences, National Academy of Science, AIDS: Sexual Behavior and Intravenous Drug Use 372, 376–78 (Turner, Miller & Moses eds. 1989); Bernstein, *Condoms: TV's Dirty Little Secret,* L.A. Times, Oct. 19, 1990, at F1; Hastings, *Fox OKs Condom Ads for Broadcast,* Phila. Gay News, Nov. 22–23, 1991, at 12; Blendon, Donelan & Knox, *Public Opinion and AIDS: Lessons for the Second Decade,* 267 J.A.M.A. 981 (1992).

23 *See HIV-Infection Prevention Messages for Injecting Drug Users: Sources of Information and Use of Mass Media—Baltimore, 1989,* note 21 above, at 467; H. Schietinger, note 1 above, pt. 2 at 18.

24 *See* National Commission on Acquired Immune Deficiency Syndrome, note 1 above, at 34–6; H. Schietinger, note 1 above; Evaluating AIDS Prevention Programs, note 15 above.*But see, e.g.,* Siegel, *et al., Bleach Programs for Preventing AIDS among IV Drug Users: Modeling the Impact of HIV Prevalence,* 81 Am. J. Pub. Health 1273 (1991).

25 *See generally* Freudenberg, note 1 above; Blendon, Donelan & Knox, note 22 above; Kagay, *Poll Finds AIDS Causes Single People to Alter Behavior,* N.Y. Times, June 18, 1991, at C3.

26 *See, e.g.,* Centers for Disease Control, *HIV/AIDS Knowledge and Awareness of Testing and Treatment—Behavioral Risk Factor Surveillance,* 267 J.A.M.A. 27 (1992); C. McKenna & M. Young, Knowledge, Attitude and Behavior Concerning AIDS 2–3 (1990) (available from Pennsylvania State Data Center, Institute of State and Regional Affairs, Penn State Harrisburg, Middletown, PA 17057); McNally, *et al.,* AIDS Related Knowledge and Behavior Among Women 15–44 Years of Age: United States, 1988 (1991) (available from National Center for Health Statistics, Hyattsville, Md.); Selwyn, *et al.,* note 7 above, at 215, 219–20.

27 *See, e.g.,* Freudenberg, note 1 above, at 590–91; McNally, *et al.,* note 26 above.

28 Kolata, *Drop in Casual Sex Tied to AIDS Peril,* N.Y. Times, May 15, 1991, at A22; *see* Kagay, note 25 above; McNally, *et al.,* note 27 above.

29 Fisher & Misovich, *Evolution of College Students' AIDS-Related Behavioral Responses, Attitudes, Knowledge, and Fear,* 2 AIDS Educ. & Prevention 322 (1990). *See generally* Blendon, Donelan & Knox, note 22 above.

30 Sonenstein, *et al., Sexual Activity, Condom Use and AIDS Awareness Among Adolescent Males,* 21 Fam. Plan. Persp. 152 (1989); *see also* Moran, *et al., Increase in Condom Sales following AIDS Education and Publicity, United States,* 80 Am. J. Pub. Health 607 (1990).

31 Becker & Joseph, *AIDS and Behavioral Change to Reduce Risk: A Review,* 78 Am. J. Pub. Health 395, 407 (1988).

32 San Francisco Department of Health, The Young Men's Survey, June 4, 1991 (documenting results of survey of gay men aged seventeen to twenty-five); *see* Lambert, *Relapses Into Risky Sex Found in AIDS Studies,* N.Y. Times, June 22, 1990, at A18. *See generally* National Commission on Acquired Immune Deficiency Syndrome, note 1 above.

33 *See* chapter 8 in this volume; *see also* Byrd, *Low Rate of Condom Use Found,* Philadelphia Inquirer, Dec. 13, 1991, at 10A (survey of 6,104 sex partners of IV drug users found that 58 percent of men and 63 percent of women had not used condoms in previous six months).

34 Des Jarlais, *et al., Risk Reduction of AIDS Among IV Drug Users,* in AIDS and IV Drug Abusers, note 2 above, at 75, 105; Ginzburg, *et al.,* note 3 above, at 185, 193–94; Gostin, note 7 above, at 124–25, 138–62; Navarro, *Yale Study Reports Clean Needle Project Reduces AIDS Cases,* N.Y. Times, Aug. 1, 1991, at A1; Neaigus, note 2 above, at 258–259, 268–69; Pyle, note 3 above; Sel-Aug. 1, 1991, at A1; Neaigus, note 2 above,

at 258–259, 268–69; Pyle, note 3 above; Selwyn, *et al.*, note 7 above, at 220; *Clean Needles and AIDS,* N.Y. Times, July 10, 1991, at C11; Personal Communication, Kevin McKinney, AIDS Surveillance Field Coordinator, San Francisco Department of Public Health (July 9, 1991). Experience overseas suggests that needle-exchange programs do not seem to encourage drug use or deter people from getting treatment. Rather, exchange is associated with decreases in needle sharing and venereal disease and helps to direct people into treatment. Stryker, *IV Drug Use and AIDS: Public Policy and Dirty Needles,* 14 J. Health Pol'y, Pol. & L. 719, 725–26 (1989).

35 McNally, *et al.*, note 26 above.

36 Aral & King, note 10 above, at 62.

37 National Commission on Acquired Immune Deficiency Syndrome, note 1 above, at 38–9; H. Schietinger, note 1 above, pt. 5 at 1–5.

38 *See, e.g.,* California v. Three 3 MCS, Inc., No. C685816 (Cal. Super. Aug. 30, 1988).

39 *See* Bean v. Board of Supervisors, No. 0640618 (Cal. Super. filed Mar. 18, 1987) (citing Cal. Health & Safety Code § 3110).

40 42 U.S.C. § 1983 (1988).

41 *See generally* City of Canton v. Harris, 489 U.S. 378 (1989); Monnell v. Department of Social Servs., 436 U.S. 658 (1978).

42 Doe v. Borough of Barrington, 729 F. Supp. 376, 390 (D.N.J. 1990).

43 *See, e.g.,* Fla. Stat. Ann. § 233.0672 (West Supp. 1991); Ill. Ann. Stat. ch 22, para. 27–9.1 (Smith-Hurd 1992); Ind. Code Ann. § 20–8.1–11–2 (Supp. 1991); La. Rev. Stat. Ann. § 17:281(3) (West Supp. 1992); Okla. Sta. Ann. tit. 70 § 11–103.3 (West 1989); Utah Code Ann. § 53A–13–101 (1989); *see also* Nev. Rev. Stat. Ann. § 389.065 (Michie 1991) (requiring written consent of parent or guardian as condition of

child's participation); Wash. Rev. Code Ann. § 28A.230.070 (West Supp. 1991) (parents and guardians must be notified, provided with opportunity to review materials). *See generally Guidelines for Effective School Health Education to Prevent the Spread of AIDS,* 37 MMWR S–2 (1988); Gostin, *Public Health Strategies for Confronting AIDS,* 261 J.A.M.A. 1621 (1989).

44 Cal. Civ. Code §§ 4201.5, 4300(c) (Deering 1991); Ga. Code Ann. § 19–3–35.1(c) (Michie 1990); Haw. Rev. Stat. § 572–5(d) (1990); Ind. Code Ann. §§ 31–7–3–3, 31–7–3–3.5 (Burns 1990); Mich. Comp. Laws Ann. §§ 333.5119-.5121 (West 1991); R.I. Gen. Laws § 15–2–3 (1990); Va. Code Ann. § 20–14.2 (Michie 1990); W. Va. Code § 16–3C–2(h) (1991); *see also* Tex. Fam. Code Ann. § 1.07(e) (West 1991); Tex. Health & Safety Code Ann. § 81.102 (West 1991) (Board of Health may mandate pre-marital HIV testing if HIV seropositivity rate goes up to 0.83 percent or above); Utah Code Ann. § 30–1–2(1) (1990) (marriage involving person with AIDS void). *See generally* Gostin, note 43 above.

45 *See, e.g.,* People v. Patillo, 4 Cal. App. 1576 (1992); Md. Health-Gen Code Ann. § 18–401 (1991); W. Va. Code § 16–3C–2(f)(2) (1990) (mandating HIV testing of people convicted of sex crimes); Cal. Penal Code § 1202.6 (Deering 1991) (same); Mich. Comp. Laws Ann. § 333.5129 (West Supp. 1991) (mandating distribution of HIV transmission information for people arrested and charged with sex crimes).

46 Philadelphia, Pa., Code app. § 9–1700 (1991).

47 *N.Y.C. Transit Auth. Agrees to Strengthen Employee HIV Protection,* AIDS Litig. Rep. (Andrews) at 4945 (1990) (settlement of New York v. New York City Transit Auth., No. 41627/90) (N.Y. Supreme Ct. July 19, 1990)) (applying N.Y. Labor Law §§ 875 *et. seq.*). *See generally* M. Rothstein, Occupational Safety and Health Law 225–30 (3d ed. 1990).

48 *Occupational Exposure to Bloodborne*

Pathogens, 29 C.F.R. § 1910.1030 (1991). *See generally* M. Rothstein, note 47 above.

49 *See* Ware v. Valley Stream High School Dist., 75 N.Y.2d 114, 551 N.Y.S.2d 167 (1989).

50 *Compare* Wisconsin v. Yoder, 406 U.S. 205 (1972) *with* Employment Div. v. Smith, 110 S. Ct. 1595, 1598–1601 & n.1 (1990). On the authority of school boards to prescribe the curriculum, see generally Board of Educ. v. Pico, 457 U.S. 853 (1982); Annotation, *Validity of Sex Education Programs in Public Schools,* 82 A.L.R.3d 579 (1978 & Supp. 1990); Annotation, *Validity of State Regulation of Curriculum and Instruction in Private and Parochial Schools,* 18 A.L.R.4th 649 (1982 & Supp. 1990).

51 *Ware,* 551 N.Y.S.2d at 172–77. *See generally Developments in the Law—Religion and the State,* 100 Harv. L. Rev. 1606, 1703–15 (1987). On the need for and effectiveness of HIV education for school children, see Gilchrist, *The Role of Schools in Community-Based Approaches to Prevention of AIDS and Intravenous Drug Use,* in AIDS and Intravenous Drug Use, note 1 above, at 150.

52 *Revision of Requirements for Content of AIDS-Related Written Materials, Pictorials, Audiovisuals, Questionnaires, Survey Instruments, and Educational Sessions in Centers for Disease Control Assistance Programs: Notice,* 57 Fed. Reg. 10793 (March 30, 1992); *Revision of Requirements for Content of HIV/AIDS Related Written Materials, Pictorials, Audiovisuals, Questionnaires, Survey Instruments, and Educational Sessions, in Centers for Disease Control Assistance Programs,* 55 Fed. Reg. 23414 (June 7, 1990); *Cooperative Agreements for Minority and Other Community-Based Human Immunodeficiency Virus (HIV) Prevention Projects Program Announcement and Availability of Funds for Fiscal Year 1989,* 54 Fed. Reg. 663 (Jan. 9, 1989); *Cooperative Agreements for Acquired Immunodeficiency Syndrome (AIDS) Prevention & Surveillance Projects Program Announcement and Notice of Avail-*

ability of Funds for Fiscal Year 1988; Amendment, 53 Fed. Reg. 3554, 6034–35 (February 29, 1988); *Program Announcement and Notice of Availability of Funds for Fiscal Year 1986; Cooperative Agreements for Acquired Immunodeficiency Syndrome (AIDS): Health, Education and Risk Reduction Programs,* 51 Fed. Reg. 3427, 3431 (January 27, 1986) [emphasis added] [hereinafter 1986 Guidelines]; *see* Gay Men's Health Crisis v. Sullivan, 733 F.Supp. 619, 624 (S.D.N.Y. 1989) [hereinafter GMHC I]; Gay Men's Health Crisis v. Sullivan, No. 88 Civ. 7482 (SWK) (May 11, 1992) [hereinafter GMHC II].

53 Pub. L. No. 100–202, 101 Stat. 1329 (1987).

54 Pub. L. No. 100–436, 102 Stat. 1680 (1988) (emphasis added); *see* Institute of Medicine, National Academy of Sciences, Confronting AIDS: Update 1988, at 7 ("Explicit information on the risks associated with gay sex and the way those risks can be minimized does not 'promote or encourage' homosexual activities. Its sole function is to help homosexuals avoid an illness that endangers their lives and those of their sexual partners and costs the nation billions of dollars.").

55 986 Guidelines, note 52 above, *see* GMHC I, 733 F.Supp. at 624.

56 GMHC II, slip op. at 44 n. 39, 56–57, 59–62.

57 GMHC I, 733 F.Supp. at 627.

58 Chevron USA Inc. v. National Resources Defense Council, 467 U.S. 837, 843–44, 865 (1984).

59 42 U.S.C. §§300ee–16(a)(6)(A), (d) (1988).

60 GMHC II, slip op. at 32; *see* Miller v. California, 415 U.S. 15, 24–25 (1973).

61 *See, e.g.,* Grayned v. City of Rockford, 408 U.S. 104, 108–09 (1972). *See generally* Amsterdam, *The Void-for-Vagueness Doctrine in the Supreme Court,* 109 U. Pa. L. Rev. 67 (1960).

62 GMHC II, slip op. at 37–38.

63 GMHC I, 733 F.Supp. at 638–39; GMHC II, slip op. at 33, 40.

64 Perry v. Sindermann, 408 U.S. 593 (1972); Sherbert v. Verner, 374 U.S. 398 (1963); Speiser v. Randall, 357 U.S. 513 (1958); Bella Lewitzky Dance Co. v. Frohnmayer, 754 F.Supp. 774, 785 (C.D. Cal. 1991) (government may not attach unconstitutional conditions to funding). *But see* Regan v. Taxation With Representation, 461 U.S. 540 (1983); Harris v. McRae, 448 U.S. 297 (1980); Maher v. Roe, 432 U.S. 464 (1977) (limits on use of subsidy do not infringe rights). *See generally* L. Tribe, American Constitutional Law §11–5, at 781–84 (2d ed. 1988); Epstein, *Unconstitutional Conditions, State Power and the Limits of Consent,* 102 Harv. L. Rev. 4 (1988); Fiss, *State Activism and State Censorship,* 100 Yale L.J. 2087 (1991); Sullivan, *Unconstitutional Conditions,* 102 Harv. L. Rev. 1413 (1989).

65 Rust v. Sullivan, 111 S. Ct. 1759, 1778 (1991) (Blackmun, J., dissenting).

66 *See* Miami Herald v. Tornillo, 418 U.S. 241 (1974) (striking down a Florida statute compelling newspapers to grant a "right of reply" to political candidates); Red Lion Broadcasting Co. v. FCC, 395 U.S. 367 (1969) (upholding fairness doctrine).

67 Kupona Network v. Chicago Transit Auth., No. 89C 6908, AIDS Litig. Rep. (Andrews) at 3402 (N.D. Ill. filed Sept. 13, 1989); *see* Simmons, *CTA Rejects AIDS Prevention Ad,* Windy City Times, Dec. 1, 1988, at 1.

68 Perry Educ. Ass'n v. Perry Local Educ. Ass'n, 460 U.S. 37 (1983); U.S. v. Kokinda, 110 S. Ct. 3115, 3133 (1990) (Brennan, J., dissenting); Greer v. Spock, 424 U.S. 828 (1976). *See generally* L. Tribe, note 64 above, § 12–24, at 993; Post, *Between Governance and Management: The History and Theory of the Public Forum,* 34 U.C.L.A. L. Rev. 1713 (1987).

69 Lehman v. Shaker Heights, 418 U.S. 298, 303 (1974).

70 Planned Parenthood Ass'n v. Chicago Transit Auth., 767 F.2d 1225 (7th Cir. 1985).

71 Washburn, *Anti-AIDS Poster Gets CTA's OK,* Chicago Tribune, June 5, 1990, at Chicagoland 1; Pearson & Wagner, *Senate Votes to Ban AIDS Posters from CTA,* Chicago Tribune, June 23, 1990, at News 1.

72 Kairys, *Freedom of Speech,* in The Politics of Law: A Progressive Critique 237, 261 (D. Kairys rev. ed. 1990).

73 *See* Parents United for Better Schools v. School Dist. of Phila., Jan. Term 1992, No. 1389 (Common Pleas Phila. County filed Jan. 13, 1992). Major cities with full-scale or pilot condom programs in the schools include New York, Philadelphia, Los Angeles, San Francisco, Chicago, Baltimore and Seattle. *Los Angeles to Distribute Condoms in High Schools,* N.Y. Times, Jan. 23, 1992, at A17.

74 Campbell, *Condom Giveaway Halted,* Philadelphia Inquirer, Apr. 11, 1991, at 4B.

75 Stryker, note 34 above, at 726–27; Jackson, *Clean Needles or Dirty Reality,* Boston Globe, July 27, 1990, at 13.

76 Goldstein, *Clean Needle Programs for Addicts Proliferate; Some Are Legal, Others Depend on Uneasy Truce With Officials,* Washington Post, April 23, 1991, at Z6; Lambert, *Protesters Test State Needle Laws,* N.Y. Times, April 14, 1991, sec. 4, at 6.

77 The other states are Delaware, Rhode Island, New Hampshire, and Maine, as well as the District of Columbia. For an authoritative discussion of the law and policy of AIDS and IV drug use, see Gostin, note 7 above, at 139–43.

78 *See* Gostin, note 7 above, at 150 n.141; Williams, *"We'd All Be Dead Without You"—Needle Swap Challenged,* Seattle Times, May 6, 1991, at B3; Conn. Gen. Stat. § 19a–124 (1990); 1990 Hi. Act 280 § 2(b). Provisions allowing state health authorities to exempt certain items from drug paraphernalia laws are not unusual, and may be the most expeditious vehicle for clarifying the legal status of needle-exchange programs. *See,* *e.g.,* 35 Pa. Stat. Ann. § 780–105 (Purdon 1977).

79 *See, e.g.,* Spokane County Health Dist. v. Brockett, No. 90–2–03535–7 (Super. Ct. Wash. May 7, 1991).

80 Sachar, *Activists on Trial for Providing Needles,* N.Y. Newsday, Apr. 9, 1991, at 23.

81 Longcope, *AIDS Activists Have Hopes for Bill to Legalize Needles,* Boston Globe, May 4, 1991, at Metro 28 (citing Assistant District Attorney Kennedy of Palo Alto regarding charges pressed against Jon Parker for needle distribution: "I am dropping the charges and recalling the warrant for him. I have better things to do."); *see also* 1989 Washington Attorney General's Opinion No. 13, 1989 Wash. AG LEXIS 14, *17–18 (prosecutors would weigh all factors, not necessarily charge health worker with violation of needle law).

82 People v. Bordowitz, No. 90N028423, AIDS Litig. Rep. (Andrews) 6,564 (June 25, 1991); *see also* People v. Cezar, 149 Misc. 2d 620, 573 N.Y.S.2d 352 (N.Y. Crim. Ct. 1991) (overturning conviction of activist arrested for possessing used syringes). *See generally* Arnolds & Garland, *The Defense of Necessity in Criminal Law: The Right to Choose the Lesser Evil,* 65 J. Crim. L. & Criminology 289, 298 (1974).

83 *See* Gross, *In Fulfilling Civic Duty, Juror Finds New Cause,* N.Y. Times, May 6, 1991, at A10.

84 National Commission on Acquired Immune Deficiency Syndrome, Report: The Twin Epidemics of Substance Use and HIV (1991); *see* Grahm, *Activists Divided on Effi-*

cacy of Needle Exchange Program, Boston Globe, Jan. 29, 1991, at 1p.

85 *Bush Faults Some AIDS Programs,* Philadelphia Inquirer, Dec. 18, 1991, at 8A.

86 For a concise review of the legal and sociological research on the educative function of law and its role in the HIV epidemic, see Roden, *Educating Through the Law: The Los Angeles AIDS Discrimination Ordinance,* 33 U.C.L.A. L. Rev. 1410 (1986); *see also* Weinstein, *Employment Discrimination: AIDS Education and Compliance with the Law,* 1 Temple Pol. & Civ. Rts. L. Rev. 85 (1992) (discussing educative potential of Americans With Disabilities Act).

87 *See, e.g.,* Martinez v. School Bd., 861 F.2d 1502 (11th Cir. 1988); Doe v. Belleville Pub. School Dist., 672 F. Supp. 342 (S.D. Ill. 1987); Ray v. School Dist., 666 F. Supp. 1524 (M.D. Fla. 1987). *See generally* Cooper, *AIDS Law: The Impact of AIDS On American Schools and Prisons,* 1987 Ann. Surv. Am. L. 117; Kass, *School Children with AIDS,* in AIDS and the Law: A Guide for the Public 66 (H. Dalton, S. Burris & the Yale AIDS Law Project eds. 1987).

88 *In re* Application of Milton S. Hershey Med. Ctr., 595 A.2d 1290 (Pa. Super 1991); Estate of Behringer v. The Med. Ctr. at Princeton, 592 A.2d 1251 (N.J. Super 1991); Leckelt v. Hospital Dist., 909 F.2d 820 (5th Cir. 1990).

89 *See* Pub. L. No. 102–141, 105 Stat. 834 (1992). *See generally* Marshall, *et al., Patients' Fear of Contracting the Acquired Immunodeficiency Syndrome from Physicians,* 150 Archives Internal Med. 1501 (1990).

7 Testing, Disclosure, and the Right to Privacy

Scott Burris

Our society has the technological capacity to accurately identify people with HIV and to gather, store, and selectively disseminate medical information about them. We lack a broad social consensus about how to use that capacity. Public health authorities and expert advisory panels have generally supported voluntary testing and the strict protection of medical confidentiality. A few on the lunatic fringe have sought widespread use of involuntary testing and dissemination of HIV information. More recently, some leaders in mainstream medical circles have complained that HIV has been treated "exceptionally" and that testing and disclosure should henceforth be governed by the same rules that supposedly apply to other diseases. The public, at least as portrayed in the media, oscillates among indifference, sympathy, and fear. More and more, disputes about privacy and HIV are being settled by legislators and judges. How well lawmakers are doing is my subject in this chapter.

In our legal tradition, issues of HIV testing and the dissemination of medical information fit into the portmanteau category of "privacy." Reflecting the diversity of its many roots and meanings, privacy is protected—and privacy issues are analyzed—under many different legal doctrines. Under the federal Constitution, there is a developing right to keep personal information private (called "informational privacy") and to be free to make certain important decisions about what happens to one's own body (referred to as "autonomy"). The Constitution also protects a more specific right to be free of unreasonable searches and seizures, including unreasonable searches of the human body and "seizures" of blood. States also protect privacy through their own constitutions; through tort rules governing defamation, invasion of privacy, and the doctor-patient relationship; and, increasingly, through laws passed specifically to govern HIV testing and medical record-keeping. Many states have also enacted laws mandating testing or the release of information in specific situations, such as after a conviction for rape.

115

Despite its many legal forms, the law of privacy is becoming increasingly homogenized. Legal analysis is dominated by the metaphor of "balancing," a shorthand for the idea that privacy will be protected only if the court believes that the costs and benefits of protecting it "outweigh" those that would flow from not doing so. This analysis, despite if not because of its simplicity, obscures the very issues that are most important to recognize and imperative to resolve: What interests should be considered? What *is* reasonable? Who should decide? What criteria should apply? Indeed, the technique of balancing invites lawmakers to think about HIV privacy issues as if they necessarily depended on a choice between competing rights—of patients, of crime victims, of the infected, of society. Few cases are really that simple. A rational decisionmaker would want to know what social or personal problem a breach of privacy purports to solve, what alternative measures are available, and how breaching privacy here will affect other people and their behavior. Speaking the often imprecise language of "rights," in pursuit of the elusive "reasonable" balance, judges and legislators in HIV matters are developing privacy policies that often have less to do with public health than with the mass psychology of epidemic disease.

I begin this survey of privacy law by describing the technology of HIV testing and the development of a consensus among health authorities in favor of privacy. Thereafter I will discuss state testing and confidentiality laws written specifically to cover HIV, other state laws affecting medical privacy, the privacy protections offered by the federal Constitution, and the ways in which judicial analysis can go astray under all these doctrines. I conclude with a brief consideration of state tort law doctrines, such as defamation, that can be used to address publication of HIV-related information. To keep the law in context, I will focus on the story of one young doctor who tested positive for HIV, a story that captures all the essential medical, moral, and legal ambiguities that constitute our patchwork national policy on HIV testing and confidentiality.

MEET JOHN DOE

On May 19, 1991, Dr. John Doe, an obstetrical resident rotating between Harrisburg Hospital and Milton S. Hershey Medical Center in central Pennsylvania, was assisting in an operation at Harrisburg. The lead surgeon inadvertently cut Dr. Doe with a scalpel that had the patient's blood on it. Dr. Doe regloved and continued with the procedure. This was, as far as Dr. Doe could recall, the first time he had suffered a serious cut in surgery. Following guidelines promulgated by the Centers for Disease Control (CDC), he underwent testing for HIV and hepatitis B the next day.[1] (The issue of HIV-infected health care workers is discussed in detail in chapter 17.)

THE HIV TESTS

There is no test for AIDS, nor a readily available test for the virus associated with the disease. The two most commonly used "AIDS tests," the enzyme-linked immunosorbent assay (ELISA) and the Western Blot, actually detect antibodies created by the immune system in response to HIV infection. In 1992, the government approved a ten-minute antibody test, which may replace the ELISA in regular use. Tests have also been developed that detect the virus itself, but these "antigen" tests are still too complicated and expensive to compete with the antibody tests for most uses.

As is standard practice, Dr. Doe's blood was initially subjected to an ELISA test. The ELISA is inexpensive and easy to administer; a test kit costs under five dollars, and the results can be read by a machine. (None of the prices in this discussion include the costs of drawing blood and providing counseling, which can easily add twenty to thirty dollars to the total.) It is, therefore, the primary HIV test. Because it was designed for use in screening the nation's blood supply, it errs on the side of showing a positive result. False-negative results are rare. This makes it highly reliable for detecting people who are infected but also means that many if not most of its positive results are false. Depending on the brand of the test kit and the prevalence of HIV in the population, up to 70 percent of positive ELISA tests cannot be confirmed by further testing.[2] Dr. Doe's first ELISA came back positive on May 21.

Because so many of those who test positive on a first ELISA will actually be uninfected, it is common medical practice to confirm a positive ELISA by performing a second ELISA and, if the result remains positive, by conducting a Western Blot. The Western Blot is much more expensive, running between fifty and sixty dollars, and must be interpreted by a technician. It is a "complex and very labor intensive" test, the interpretation of whose results can vary according to the lab and even the technician doing the interpreting. Depending upon the prevalence of the virus in the population being tested, 30 to 80 percent of repeatedly positive ELISA results are determined to have been false by Western Blot. The Western Blot, too, can produce false positives, although new antigen tests can be highly effective in identifying false-positive Western Blots.[3] Dr. Doe's positive Western Blot confirmed the diagnosis of HIV infection on May 28.

The antibody tests do produce some false negatives, almost all of which are the result of the latency period between infection with HIV and the development of antibodies. This so-called window period is normally about six weeks, although a few studies, now doubted by most scientists, have found that some infected people might remain antibody negative for as long as two years. (Dr. Doe's positive test result, obtained so soon after his exposure, showed that he had *not* gotten his HIV from the scalpel cut.) It is also possible for people who do develop antibodies to lose them as their symptoms progress. Finally, a substantial source of false test results, both positive and negative, is human error: if the test is badly performed, or the proper confirmatory tests are not run, the reliability of the testing process plummets.

Dr. Doe's confirmed positive result was certainly correct. The overall accuracy of a series of ELISAs and Western Blots is as good as or better than that of most other common diagnostic tests, and Doe's tests were performed by a competent lab.[4] This does not imply, however, that the same tests could reliably be used for mass population screening. Because of the window period alone, no testing program can guarantee that all infected people will be identified. Considering, as well, the errors associated with sloppy techniques, and the costs of the frequent retesting that would be needed to weed out false negatives, the use of screening as a primary means of addressing HIV would be a misuse of a good medical tool. (For more on the tests, see chapter 2.)

THE HOSPITALS' RESPONSE TO THE INFECTED PHYSICIAN

Dr. Doe learned of his initial positive ELISA test on May 21—and so, apparently, did several other people at the Harrisburg Hospital. To begin with, his test result was placed into the computerized medical record system, to which more than a hundred hospital staffers had access.[5] Dr. Doe told a few of his supervisors, and those who knew apparently made their own decisions about who else needed to be told. Very quickly his case was a major topic of discussion among the top staff at both hospitals.

The CDC guidelines then in effect took the position that the chances of transmission from an infected health care worker to a patient were extremely low and could be even further reduced by strict adherence to "universal precautions." The guidelines did not suggest that infected health care workers be prevented from practicing surgery or any other specialty, or that past patients be informed or tested unless there was a known exposure to the provider's blood.[6] These 1987 guidelines were, however, politically if not medically out of date, and the hospitals ignored them. Dr. Doe's diagnosis was delivered at a time of peak interest in the issue of HIV transmission by health care workers. The story of five people in Florida, infected through some sort of contact with dentist David Acer, had become, through repetition in the media, a nationwide epidemic, and the subject of heated deliberations in Congress, professional organizations, and public health agencies. It was widely known that the CDC was preparing a revised set of guidelines and was under considerable pressure to recommend at least some restrictions on the practice of surgical procedures by infected health care workers.

Although the hospitals' decisionmakers, like most medical and public health authorities, believed that Dr. Doe posed little if any risk to his patients, this was not necessarily their main concern. The American Medical Association had decided that HIV-infected physicians "have an ethical obligation not to engage in any professional practice which has an identifiable risk of transmission," no matter how low, without securing in advance the patient's informed consent to run the risk.[7] One widely reported court decision had suggested that a patient had a right under the tort law of informed consent to be told when a provider was infected, despite the low risk of transmission.[8] Tort defense lawyers were advising their hospital clients that hospitals might be found to have a legal duty to restrict the practice of HIV-infected physicians on staff, and to notify past patients. "One of the great problems here is not just the possibility of infection," one Harrisburg Hospital official later testified,

> but is anxiety on the part of the public and our patients. It is my understanding that there are many more suits in regard to that in some of the other institutions that involve this sort of situation than people who sue because they think they have gotten the infection. They sue because of the anxiety and upset that they have suffered and so as an institution we wish to do as much as possible to allay that and that is the course we have set on and this is the reason why we think we need to not behave in a way that makes anyone doubt our credibility.[9]

In other words, even if the risk of HIV transmission was low, the risk of litigation was significant.

By June 3, the hospitals had decided not only that Dr. Doe was finished as a surgeon, but also that many of his past patients would have to be informed of his infection and that the whole thing needed to be resolved on an emergency basis. At this point, they faced the question of whether telling these patients would be legal.

HIV-SPECIFIC STATE TESTING AND CONFIDENTIALITY LAWS

The Voluntarist Consensus

Just six months earlier, the Pennsylvania General Assembly had enacted a comprehensive law governing HIV testing and informational privacy. The law, which would be tested for the first time in the matter of Dr. Doe, was the product of a nationwide movement to encourage voluntary testing and improved medical care for people with and at risk of HIV.

By the time the human immunodeficiency virus was discovered, and a test was developed to identify those who carried it, no one with any serious understanding of public health was proposing large-scale use of voluntary screening, disclosure, and isolation as means of controlling the epidemic. There were already so many people infected that such a course would have been logistically impossible and economically prohibitive. It would also have engendered tremendous opposition, which, regardless of the merits of the dispute, made it even more unlikely to succeed. The chilling example of the mass imprisonment of Japanese Americans during World War II only underlined the incompatibility of a status-based quarantine with the better angels of our national nature. Nevertheless, arguments about drastic measures like quarantine grabbed the headlines and helped perpetuate the faulty metaphor of the epidemic as a war between the sick and the well.

There is a popular misperception that voluntarist policies represent a departure from a tradition of coercive measures, a departure attributable to the self-interested efforts of a powerful gay, civil liberties lobby. In fact, systematic coercion to promote public health has a dubious history. The harsh forms of quarantine and ostracism in pre-modern times had as little impact on disease as prayer and alchemy. Modern medical knowledge has reduced, rather than increased, the need for quarantine and isolation, and has, with most diseases, succeeded in offering the best possible inducement to voluntary treatment, a cure. In the United States, public health efforts to force large numbers of people into treatment—notably the World War I–era campaign against venereal disease—failed to reduce prevalence, even as public education and voluntary testing were working well. Programs to induce *voluntary* behavior change—in smoking, eating, drinking—have moved to the forefront of public health work, with important success, while the nation's experiment with Prohibition to prevent alcohol abuse was a total failure, and the war on drugs repeats the mistake.[10] (For more on the history of public health and communicable disease, see chapter 3.)

Believers in a supposed tradition of coercive measures often point to school vaccination requirements, premarital disease screening, or disease reporting. For the most part, these "mandatory" programs have run smoothly not because of coercion, but because of broad public acceptance of their goals and methods. When motives are disputed, or harm to the subjects is potentially great, the levels of compliance are very different. Illinois' unhappy experience with premarital HIV screening indicates what happens when the social consensus breaks down: during the first six months of the program, marriage license applications dropped by nearly one-fourth as people married out of state or not at all. When the program was abandoned, one year after its inception, the state had located 8 HIV-positive people, from a pool of 70,846 applicants, at a cost of $312,000 each. The episode also demonstrates that compulsion in the world of public health is largely an illusion. Outside the criminal justice system, what we really mean by terms like *mandatory testing* is that some benefit, like medical care or a marriage license, is made contingent upon being tested. Those unwilling to be tested simply forego the benefit.[11]

It is certainly true that concern for the sensibilities of the infected, if not for their civil rights, has strongly influenced the shape of the public health response to HIV. In large part, however, public health policymakers have tried to avoid alienating people at risk because policies of consensus and cooperation are likely to prevent more HIV transmission than policies of confrontation, and because ineffective coercive policies are useless if not harmful. The social status, values, and political attitudes of those at risk of acquiring HIV are part of the social context in which the disease operates, and must be addressed in health policy. Measures that focus on the virus and ignore the characteristics of the people it infects will fail.[12]

People who think that the politicization of HIV policy makes this disease different from health threats of the past have forgotten their history. Political fights have shaped public health measures from tuberculosis reporting, to venereal disease control, to water fluoridation, to no-smoking campaigns, all of which have been implemented through a process of social negotiation in agencies, legislative lobbies, and the courts of law and public opinion. Indeed, the only health measures that have not been forged in political controversy have been the ones that nobody cared much about.[13]

The General Rule of Confidentiality and Informed Consent

The public health consensus in support of privacy protections and against coercion led a majority of states to adopt measures in the late 1980s governing HIV testing and confidentiality. By the end of 1991, thirty-six states had enacted legislation requiring informed consent for HIV testing, and virtually every state provided some degree of protection for the confidentiality of HIV information.[14] The earliest statutes, passed in 1985 and 1986, generally focused on the HIV test itself. California's 1985 statute, for example, required informed consent for all testing, forbade any person from identifying anyone who had taken an HIV test, and set out criminal and civil penalties for violators. (In later years, various exceptions were added, notably authorizing disclosure to spouses, needle and sex partners, and various health care providers.[15])

A second wave of statutes began emerging in 1988. These tended to expand the range of counseling required and information protected, but also to set forth more and more detailed exceptions. Pennsylvania's law, based on similar "second-generation" statutes in Washington, Florida, New York, and Connecticut, is typical.[16]

Confidentiality. The Pennsylvania law created a categorical rule against disclosure not just of test results, but of any "confidential HIV-related information" obtained "in the course of providing any health or social service or pursuant to a release." "Confidential HIV-related information" was broadly defined as information that a person "has been the subject of an HIV-related test, or has HIV, HIV-related illness or AIDS, or any information which identifies or reasonably could identify an individual as having one or more of these conditions, including information pertaining to the individual's contacts." Thus the law could be violated not only by actually releasing an infected person's name itself, but also by conduct, like putting a distinctive mark on an infected person's medical file, that could be expected to tip off third parties about the person's diagnosis.[17]

The Pennsylvania lawmakers deliberately did not create a general right of privacy, applicable to anyone in possession of HIV-related information. The rule of confidentiality applies chiefly to those who acquire the information in the course of providing a health or social service. Within those fields, however, the duty to protect privacy applies at every level, from billing clerks to chiefs of surgery. The law's protection also extends to perhaps unexpected agencies: courts will probably not include prisons in the definition of social service providers, but any prison employees providing medical care or social services are fully bound by the law.[18]

Confidentiality laws like Pennsylvania's generally require a patient's written authorization before information can be released. A general consent form is not sufficient; it must specifically state who is to get the information, for what purpose, and for what period of time the consent remains valid.[19] The written release is also a mechanism for extending the law's privacy obligation beyond the realm of health and social services, because *anyone* who obtains information pursuant to a written release is fully bound by the law. Thus, a construction worker who tells her boss that she is infected has no privacy protection under the law but is fully covered if her boss learns of her condition through a written release of information from her doctor.[20]

Without a patient's written release, disclosure is allowed only if it falls within one of twelve other specific exceptions provided in the statute. As under most other confidentiality laws, information can be disclosed without a release to health departments and hospital oversight agencies and, naturally, to the subject of the test and the physician who ordered the test.[21] Other exceptions, more problematic, will be discussed below.

Informed Consent for Testing. The testing provisions of HIV privacy laws were intended to promote both voluntary testing and risk-reduction counseling. The Pennsylvania law not only prohibits virtually all HIV testing without the patient's informed consent, but also requires that anyone considering a test be given pre-test counseling including "an explanation of the test, . . . its purpose, potential uses, limitations and the meaning of its results," as well as "information regarding measures for the prevention of, exposure to and transmission of HIV." Those who choose to be tested must be offered, along with the test results, "the immediate opportunity for individual, face-to-face counseling" about the meaning of the results, how to avoid transmission of HIV, and the benefits and availability of partner notification services. If the result is positive, the law also requires counseling about available medical and mental health services.[22] Dr. Doe, by the way, did sign a written consent form but received no counseling before or after the test, either because of ignorance of the law or the questionable belief that, as a doctor, he already had all the information he needed. (For more on HIV testing and counseling as a prevention strategy, see chapter 6.)

Laws governing testing and counseling, unlike confidentiality provisions, tend to have very few exceptions. In most states, informed consent and counseling are not required in connection with "blinded" medical research, where the researcher has no way of identifying the research subject. Counseling and consent are also generally not required for screening donations of blood or other tissues, although post-test counseling must normally be offered if the donor is informed of the result. Like a number of other states, Pennsylvania also creates an exception to counseling and informed consent when the test is necessary to help a patient in a medical emergency, although it is not clear what sort of emergency would entail the need for immediate HIV testing.[23]

The legal recognition of patients' right to decide whether or not to take an HIV test has been widespread, but not universal. Illinois allows a physician to test without counseling or consent if he or she believes it to be medically indicated for diagnosis and treatment and has obtained general consent to provide treatment. Fourteen states have no statutory informed consent rule for HIV testing at all.[24] Every state's law protects the privacy right of patients to make informed decisions about whether or not to accept medical care, including testing, but the general law of informed consent has not yet been interpreted to require the sort of specific, written informed consent for HIV testing required by HIV privacy laws. Studies indicate that involuntary HIV testing under cover of a general consent to treatment is common.[25] (For more on testing patients and their rights of informed consent, see chapter 17.)

The Pennsylvania law, like many others, has a provision designed to minimize the damage of incorrect test results. The statute specifically prohibits notifying a patient of a positive test result until standard confirmatory testing has been performed.[26] In Dr. Doe's case, this rule was violated. A week before his diagnosis was confirmed by a Western Blot, he was listed as HIV-positive on the hospital computer, and significant decisions about his future were being made. It is indicative of the hysteria with which his case was treated that so many important decisions were made on the basis of results that stood a good chance of being incorrect.

Major Exceptions to the Privacy Rules

Most HIV privacy laws contain exceptions responsive to genuine, and not-so-genuine, "needs to know." In addition, many states have passed mandatory testing and disclosure provisions that override the general policy of voluntariness and nondisclosure. Some of these exceptions respond to the demands of well-organized interest groups. Funeral directors, for example, have been successful in many states in securing notification whenever the deceased had HIV, despite the fact that they ought to be using the same universal precautions as health care workers, and despite strong anecdotal evidence of HIV discrimination in the industry.[27] Insurers, too, have often won special testing privileges and relaxed confidentiality rules.[28]

Testing Patients and Releasing HIV-Related Information to Their Health Care Providers. In setting out to regulate medical privacy, state legislatures inserted themselves into the physician-patient relationship in a significant, and potentially disruptive, way. The drafters of HIV privacy laws have had to figure out how to protect privacy without interfering with the free flow of information needed for good medical care. Increasingly, they have also had to deal with the demands of some health care workers who say they need to know their patients' HIV status, under at least some circumstances, to deal appropriately with their own risk of infection.

When Dr. Doe was tested for HIV, he became a patient as well as a doctor. The Pennsylvania law allows disclosure of a patient's HIV information without a release within a health care institution to any staff member "involved in the medical care or treatment of the subject." Outside the hospital setting, health care providers' access to information without the patient's release is more limited. Even if physicians (or dentists or chiropractors) in private practice are providing care to a person with HIV, they may not be told of the patient's HIV status unless they need to know in order to provide care in an emergency, or unless their advice on diagnosis or treatment of the patient has specifically been sought.[29]

Pennsylvania's law on routine testing and disclosure reflects the customary ethical view that a physician acts for the patient's benefit, not his or her own, and therefore that any medical test or disclosure of information should be only for the good of the patient. Other states, like New York and Washington, also give legal force to this ethical approach by tying disclosure to the needs of the patient or the usual custom of the profession.[30]

At the same time, many states, including Pennsylvania, have responded to health care workers' fear of HIV by hinging at least some patient testing and disclosure of information on the supposed need of the health care provider (and others who may have some custodial responsibilities for the patient, such as prison guards) to be notified on occasion of a patient's status for their own protection. The loosest of these laws apparently assume that people with HIV are intrinsically dangerous and do not require any evidence that the health care provider obtaining the test or disclosure actually faces exposure to HIV in a manner capable of transmitting it.[31] A few states authorize disclosure of HIV status to first responders, police, and firefighters who have had contact with someone who is subsequently diagnosed as HIV-infected.[32]

Pennsylvania is one of about a dozen states that have tried to set a slightly higher standard, limiting patient testing and disclosure for the benefit of a health care provider or other person to cases in which there has been a demonstrably "significant exposure," usually defined as contact with blood or body fluids in a manner that could transmit HIV. These laws most frequently "protect" health care workers but sometimes also cover first responders and police and firefighters. The rationale for these provisions is not that testing the source of the exposure will determine whether the exposed person was infected—obviously it will not—but that the patient's result can assist the exposed person to evaluate the overall likelihood of infection, and provide some level of psychological comfort.

The various "significant exposure" laws differ primarily in the formal procedures they require to establish that an exposure has occurred, that it is "significant," and that the patient will not consent to testing.[33] In practice, however, the requirement that an exposure be certified by a neutral physician as significant is probably little protection against unnecessary testing: as the term is typically defined, almost any contact with patients' blood or body fluid could qualify. But elaborate procedures may accomplish a reduction in panic: exposed health care providers who are required to consult with a physician will, one hopes, learn enough to put the risk into context and reduce their anxiety level. In any event, most patients readily agree to testing for the benefit of a health care worker after an exposure, even without the threat of compulsion.[34]

In Dr. Doe's case, there was no question of disclosing his HIV status to the doctors caring for him as a patient. They all knew. The issue the hospitals had decided to bring to a court was whether to disclose information about him as a doctor to his former patients. On this the Pennsylvania law was silent. Indeed, as of April 1992, only two states had laws clearly authorizing the involuntary testing of health care providers or disclosure of information about them to patients, although the issue was on many legislative agendas.[35] (For more on the controversy, see chapter 17.)

Physician Warnings to Third Parties. One of the most confused debates in health policy has concerned the proper role of physicians in warning third parties of a risk of exposure to HIV created by one of their patients. Both medical ethics and the common law leave health care providers in considerable doubt about whether their duty to protect a patient's privacy or a third party's safety should prevail in any particular situation.

Almost half the states have dealt with this dilemma in their HIV privacy or general public health laws, almost all by giving the physician the freedom to disclose or not without fear of legal penalty either way. The laws vary in their specificity in defining who can be warned and under what circumstances. The most narrowly tailored of these provisions allow notification only of people with whom the patient is likely to have sex or share needles in the future, and then only after the physician has offered counseling to the patient and warned the patient that notification is going to take place. Normally, these laws require that the patient's identity not be revealed. (Maryland's is exceptional in *requiring* that the identity be revealed.)[36]

Other states have been less exacting, allowing disclosure to contacts or family members without specifying intermediate steps and even, in a few places, without reason to believe that the people notified are at risk. These laws are unnecessarily broad. Evidence that such loose notification laws are based less on public health imperatives than on the desire to mark the infected can be found in Georgia's statute, which allows disclosure not just to a spouse or sexual partner but to a patient's child if the physician "reasonably believes" that the child is at risk of being infected. It is, unfortunately, not out of the question that a child could also be a patient's "sexual partner," but there are certainly few situations in which a physician's belief that a patient's child is otherwise at risk could ever be reasonable.[37] The Pennsylvania confidentiality law limits such warnings to sexual or needle-sharing partners of the infected patient, so it could not be read to authorize disclosure to Dr. Doe's patients as "third parties at risk."

These notification rules almost universally apply to physicians only, despite concerns by other health care and mental health professionals about their own legal duties. A general confidentiality rule, however, actually clarifies their obligations as well. The duty to warn third parties is a product of judge-made common law. A legislative enactment requiring nondisclosure of HIV-related information supersedes the judicial rule, and therefore should protect social workers, nurses, psychologists, and others from being successfully sued for failure to warn. (For more on the common law governing physician warnings, see chapter 17.)

No matter what the law says, health professionals have difficult choices to make when faced with a patient in denial. Should they work with the patient to overcome the barriers to notification or abstinence from unsafe behavior? Search out and notify the person at risk? Hand the problem off to health authorities? The answers have much more to do with professional judgment than with the law, and, in fact, the role of the law may loom larger in theory than in practice: no court in an HIV case has found a professional liable for warning or for failing to warn, nor has any patient challenged the constitutionality of a warning law. A person with HIV, engaging in behavior he or she knows is dangerous, is not a likely plaintiff in a lawsuit against a doctor who intervened to protect a third party, particularly if the warning was done sensitively and as a last resort.

Mandatory Testing and Disclosure in Institutions. Some states authorize involuntary testing of, and disclosure of information about, people in prisons, mental hospitals, juvenile facilities, and residential centers for the developmentally disabled. Sometimes this is limited to situations where testing is for the medical benefit of the subject, but more often it is justified by administrative convenience or by a supposed need to inform various personnel for their safety.[38] A few states have enacted laws permitting or requiring the notification of school officials when a health care provider has identified a school-age child as HIV-positive.[39] Disclosure and testing in the course of foster care and adoption placements are common.[40]

The law on such testing remains unclear. Testing of prison inmates has been upheld on many occasions, but testing of other institutionalized people has not even been challenged. A Nebraska state agency's effort to test employees of institutions for the developmentally disabled was firmly rejected as a violation of the Fourth Amendment.[41] Testing that is supposedly justified by a need to protect staff or other residents is most suspect on the medical facts and the best candidate for judicial invalidation. Testing that is justified by an institution's duty to meet the medical needs of its charges would present a more complicated set of issues to a court: forcing someone to be tested for his or her own good is paternalistic and subject to abuse, but early identification is now certainly beneficial for the patient. The outcome of any legal challenge could well depend upon how truly administrators have pursued patient welfare over other, less altruistic ends. Dr. Doe's case is exemplary: he was tested, for his medical benefit, after exposure to a patient's blood, but the results were used by his employers to cut off his surgical career.

Mandatory Testing and Disclosure in the Criminal Justice System. Mandatory testing and disclosure of information is steadily becoming more common in the criminal justice system. Legislatures, or judges acting on their own, have authorized the testing of people convicted of (or in some instances merely charged with) prostitution,[42] sex crimes,[43] drug offenses,[44] and assaulting a public safety officer.[45] In some states, the results are filed with the local district attorney; if the subject is arrested again for a crime involving a risk of HIV transmission, the earlier results can be used as the basis for a more serious charge or a longer sentence.[46]

Invasions of the privacy of people charged with or convicted of crimes, especially if sanctioned by the legislature, are unlikely to be overturned by courts, even if the measures serve no real public health purpose. The people being tested are widely despised, while the people for whose supposed benefit the testing is being done—like rape survivors or police officers—excite compassion. Moreover, sexually transmitted disease testing of people held on "morals charges" has been allowed for decades. Unfortunately, legislators are much quicker to impose mandatory testing and disclosure than to appropriate funds for HIV counseling for people who have been assaulted or for intensive educational interventions among prostitutes and their customers.[47] (For more on HIV as a criminal matter, see chapter 11.)

Testing and Disclosure by Court Order. Pennsylvania's law, like most of the newer, more comprehensive confidentiality laws, has a mechanism allowing people who wish to conduct an HIV test or to release or receive HIV-related information, but who are prevented from doing so by the law, to apply to a court for special permission. Such laws commonly provide for expedited proceedings, as well as the use of pseudonyms and sealed records to prevent the proceeding itself from disclosing the subject's identity.[48] This was the provision under which Dr. Doe's employers sought court permission to notify his patients of his infection.

Permission can be granted only if the applicant demonstrates a "compelling need" for the test or disclosure that cannot be met in any other way. This on its face sets a high standard. Moreover, like any state law, the provision for court-ordered testing or disclosure could not be interpreted to authorize a breach of privacy the U.S. Constitution would forbid. As did other states, Pennsylvania's legislature explicitly invited a balancing analysis by instructing the courts to weigh the interest in testing or disclosure against not only the subject's privacy interest, but the public health interest in HIV confidentiality.[49] In Dr. Doe's case, the hospitals evidently saw this provision as a way to minimize their chances of being sued: if a court approved the release, they could not be sued for a breach of confidentiality by Dr. Doe; if the court withheld permission, the hospitals would, presumably, be insulated from later suits by patients claiming they should have been told.

Enforcing State Confidentiality Laws

State HIV confidentiality and testing laws make a strong statement in favor of privacy, but they vary considerably in their bite. With some exceptions, they depend upon the injured individual to take up the legal cudgel against the violator. Unfortunately, loss of one's privacy is often more painful emotionally than economically. Without the lure of high dollar damages, few attorneys will prosecute "breach of privacy" cases except at their high hourly rates, and people without lawyers rarely win cases.

Some states, but not Pennsylvania, have dealt with this by setting specified minimum damages for each violation. In New York, for example, a wrongdoer is subject to a civil penalty of up to $5,000 for each violation, which can add up quickly if the violator has disclosed the information to many people. Moreover, willful violation of the confidentiality law is also a misdemeanor crime, prosecuted by the state at its expense. In some states, the losing defendant in a civil suit can be made to pay the plaintiff's attorneys fees, a provision that encourages attorneys to accept cases without charging fees up front. Some states specifically allow suits for injunctions to prevent a threatened release of information; in most others, courts would have the authority to issue such injunctions even without specific statutory authorization.[50]

OTHER STATE LAW PROTECTING MEDICAL PRIVACY

The two hospitals that employed Dr. Doe went to court under the confidentiality law for permission to notify his patients that he had HIV. Privacy interests, however, tend to overlap. In considering whether the hospitals had a compelling need to release information about Dr. Doe, both sides and the court were well aware of the long-standing regard of the legal system for the privacy of the medical relationship.

Doctors have an ethical duty not to reveal information given to them in confidence by their patients. In a number of cases, courts have used this ethical duty to protect patient privacy as the basis for a legal duty to do so. Of most importance for Dr. Doe was the case of *Estate of Behringer v. The Medical Center at Princeton*. There, too, a hospital physician was tested for HIV at his own institution. Within hours of receiving his test result, he was getting phone calls from colleagues who had learned of his infection through the staff grapevine. A New Jersey court found that the hospital's release of information to colleagues breached a duty to keep a patient's sensitive medical information confidential. While this part of the decision supported Dr. Doe's position against release, The *Behringer* judge also accepted the hospital's position that a doctor's HIV infection posed enough of a risk to patients to justify Behringer's doctors in informing hospital management of his infection.[51]

Doctor Doe's HIV-related medical records enjoyed no significant protection under general state law governing medical records. Indeed, a patient's medical records are not, legally speaking, the patient's records at all: they are the property of the medical provider who has compiled them. Many states, including Pennsylvania, have found it necessary to enact laws that guarantee patients' right to examine and copy their own records. Thus, although there are many laws across the country that regulate how records are kept, very few of them directly protect patient privacy. This was highlighted, in an extreme case, when a South Carolina entrepreneur bought the patient files of a retiring doctor at an auction, planning to resell the practice to another doctor. Though it was shocking to patients, and struck some medical ethicists as improper, in the eyes of the law it was a perfectly legal sale of goods.[52] (Privacy in the medical relationship is discussed in more detail in chapter 17.)

CONSTITUTIONAL PRIVACY RIGHTS

The question formally presented in the hospital's petition to notify Dr. Doe's patients of his infection was one of state law: did the facts indicate a "compelling need" for release of information? The Constitutional law of privacy was, nevertheless, an integral part of the legal argument. In the same way that the Supreme Court's decision that communicable diseases could be "handicaps" defined the legal debate on HIV discrimination, the Court's recognition that medical decision-making and informational privacy had constitutional protection made any HIV testing or disclosure a matter of privacy as well as public health.

The Right of Privacy

The federal Constitution and many state constitutions protect the privacy of medical information against government intrusion, although in all but a few state constitutions the right of privacy is not explicitly stated. Instead, it has been derived by judges from the general tenor and purposes of these fundamental charters.[53] Privacy protection has been found by courts to be particularly necessary for HIV-related information:

> Society's moral judgments about the high-risk activities associated with the disease, including sexual relations and drug use, make the information of the most personal kind. Also, the privacy interest in one's exposure to the AIDS virus is even greater than one's privacy interest in ordinary medical records because of the stigma that attaches with the disease. The potential for harm in the event of a nonconsensual disclosure is substantial . . . [including] the stigma and harassment that comes with public knowledge of one's affliction with AIDS. The hysteria surrounding AIDS extends beyond those who have the disease. The stigma attaches not only to the AIDS victim, but to those in contact with the AIDS patient and to those in high risk groups who do not have the disease.[54]

Even in instances where courts have found release of information to be justified, they have usually been careful to make the disclosure as narrow as possible.

The right of privacy also encompasses the freedom autonomously to choose or refuse medical care and to decide for oneself when to release sensitive information to others. As one court explained, "there are few decisions over which a person could have a greater desire to exercise control than the manner in which he reveals [an HIV] diagnosis to others."[55] The analysis of privacy as a right to make important decisions about one's own body and health has been developed in cases involving sexual issues, including contraception, abortion, and homosexual intercourse. In the early cases, "privacy as autonomy" was treated by the Supreme Court as an essential attribute of personhood, a fundamental right subject to the most stringent constitutional protection. In the social battle about abortion over the last twenty years, the right to make basic decisions free of government interference has been repeatedly cut back, and its future is far from clear. The refusal of the Supreme Court to even recognize a privacy interest in consensual homosexual intercourse was another ominous sign of retrenchment.[56]

The practical strength of any constitutional right is reflected by the test the courts use to enforce it. When judges strongly back a right, they allow government infringement only when it serves a compelling state interest. When judges believe the right to enjoy minimal protection, they require from the state only that its interference be rationally related to a legitimate interest. Between these poles of scrutiny are the various balancing and multifactor checklist sorts of tests, which purport to identify key interests or issues that will help a court decide how strongly to enforce a right in a particular case. Privacy's relative youth as an independent constitutional right, and the several different sorts of interests that the right protects, have left courts in some confusion about which test or tests to use. Indeed, just about every available test has been used in one HIV-related case or another.[57] (For more on the traditional forms of analysis in constitutional law, see chapter 14.)

The results in HIV-related cases have been as varied as the forms of analysis. While there is widespread agreement that the right of privacy protects people with HIV, and even that testing or disclosure without a good reason should be discouraged, there is little consistency on the question of what constitutes a good reason. Courts have found it to be a violation of privacy for a police officer to tell a person's neighbors that he has HIV, for a prison to involuntarily transfer infected inmates to a known "AIDS-only" dormitory, for prison medical staff to discuss an inmate's infection with nonmedical personnel, and for blood donors' identities to be revealed to private parties suing blood banks for providing HIV-infected blood. Other courts, however, have found that privacy is not violated when a military officer reveals a civilian employee's infection to other officers, when a prison segregates its infected inmates, and when blood donor names are released to private litigants.[58]

The HIV epidemic has brought more claims of privacy and thus has placed greater pressure on courts to clarify the rules. Courts in AIDS cases are generally recognizing that both autonomy and informational privacy are worthy of real protection under the Constitution. What may be decisive in the future of privacy law is the degree to which courts are willing to accommodate government desires to test or disclose. While no certain trend has developed in the formal doctrine, in practice the balancing approach seems to be carrying the day. This guarantees that comparable cases will continue to be decided in opposite ways for some time to come.

The Fourth Amendment

Individual privacy is also protected by the Fourth Amendment, which establishes "the right of the people to be secure in their persons, houses, papers, and effects, against unreasonable searches and seizures by government or its agents." Like a seizure of medical records, a blood test is a search that can reveal intimate personal information. A person has a reasonable expectation that bodily autonomy and the privacy of medical information will be respected. All of this places HIV testing by the government or its agents squarely within the ambit of Fourth Amendment protection.[59] As with the right to privacy, the analysis only begins with a finding that medical information is generally protected by the Fourth Amendment. The actual degree of privacy protection under the Fourth Amendment depends on the case-by-case application of the legal rules.

Much of the modern development of the Fourth Amendment came in the criminal context, where the determinant of reasonableness was whether a magistrate had issued a search warrant based on "probable cause" to believe that a search would produce evidence of a crime.[60] Although the Supreme Court recognized that government searches outside the criminal law area—for example, to enforce workplace safety laws—were different, it nevertheless usually required a warrant (or at least a clear set of regulatory standards dictating when a search would occur), and some level of individualized suspicion, before accepting a search as "reasonable."[61] These requirements made mass government screening difficult, and, indeed, put a substantial burden on the government to show why even an individual test ought to be coerced. In the 1980s, however, the Supreme Court developed a broad exception to the usual Fourth Amendment rules for cases "when 'special needs, beyond the normal need for law enforcement, make the warrant and probable-cause requirement impractical.' "[62]

The "special needs" exception is framed in narrow terms, applying, according to the Court, only "in limited circumstances, where the privacy interests implicated by the search are minimal, and where an important governmental interest furthered by the intrusion would be placed in jeopardy by a requirement of individualized suspicion."[63] In most cases, Justice Scalia explained, "the question comes down to whether a particular search has been 'reasonable,' [and] the answer depends largely upon the social necessity that prompts the search."[64] Perhaps more important than the narrow language of the special-needs decisions, however, is their tenor, which reflects the ascendancy on the high court of jurists who are more likely to resolve conflicts between government power and individual rights in favor of the government.

As with privacy, judges assessing the reasonableness of HIV testing under the Fourth Amendment have reached varying and even contradictory decisions, and will continue to do so for some time. Courts have both upheld and overturned laws allowing the testing of prostitutes.[65] One decision refused to allow testing of care providers in a facility for the developmentally disabled because "the risk of transmission of the disease from the staff to the clients . . . is minuscule, trivial, extremely low, extraordinarily low, theoretical, and approaches zero." Another court, although accepting that "the probability that a health care worker will transmit HIV to a patient may be extremely low," upheld testing of a licensed practical nurse because "the potential harm of HIV infection is extremely high."[66] In line with the statist orientation of the Rehnquist Supreme Court, judges have tended to side with legislatures in challenges to HIV testing and disclosure laws, however ill-conceived. In particular, the special needs approach has been used by lower court judges to uphold mandatory testing schemes that were defended as serving public health, rather than criminal justice, goals.[67] Courts have been somewhat stricter in analyzing ad hoc testing conducted by lesser government agencies or individual officials.[68]

THE HOSPITALS' "COMPELLING NEED"

The two hospitals asked the Pennsylvania courts to allow them to notify more than 350 patients who had undergone an operation by, or in the presence of, Dr. Doe. Dr. Doe's recollection was that he had never exposed a patient to his blood. The surgical records, which were supposed to note cuts, did not reveal any. Neither did they always indicate, as one might have expected them to, "whether Dr. Doe simply observed; had contact with the patient other than in an invasive procedure; or was significantly involved in an invasive procedure in which he employed a blade or needle."[69] Yet despite the fact that there was an extremely low risk that anyone would have been infected through an exposure, further discounted by the low probability that anyone had been exposed at all, the hospitals quickly got their court order for release to the full list of patients, and the order was shortly upheld on appeal. How did the hospitals, and the courts, justify the conclusion that there was a compelling need for release? Essentially, they succeeded by making a virtue of the very absence of necessity, turning the lack of evidence of risk into a compelling medical mystery.

THE THUMBS ON THE JUDICIAL SCALES

Privacy enjoys extraordinarily strong protection in theory. Once privacy is placed in the scales of justice, however, all bets are off. Asking whether one party's rights are more important than another's is often the wrong question to start with, and deciding how much particular interests "weigh" is a precarious business indeed. For some judges, the various balancing tests developed in the privacy precedents are just confusing—poor analytic tools that do not help the decisionmaker understand the case. For other judges, the language of balancing is a convenient way of rationalizing a decision made in the gut or wherever else the political instinct resides. HIV cases like Dr. Doe's are a catalogue of the ways balancing can go wrong.[70]

A crisis and a "reasonable" balance rarely coexist. By treating Dr. Doe's infection as an emergency, the hospitals deftly assumed that which was to be proven: that human life was at stake and every minute counted.[71] Ironically, the confidentiality law helped them do this. The court-ordered release provision, with its expedited procedures, was designed with emergencies in mind. The petition for release was filed on June 10; the first hearing took place that day and the next. The court allowed Doe's attorney another day and a half to file a brief and issued its decision to allow the full release sought by the hospitals on June 14. The appeals court refused to delay the release, which took place on June 19, but ordered the case briefed and argued on an emergency schedule. The appeal was heard July 10, and the opinion allowing the release that had already occurred was issued on July 30. The entire question of what to do about HIV-infected health care workers in Pennsylvania was effectively settled in less than two months, long before any public health consensus had been achieved.

To cast any HIV issue as a conflict between the intangible privacy rights (or even the palpable economic interests) of a person with HIV and the welfare of someone who may have been infected with HIV is to fiddle the scales at the outset. One hardly needs to be a Las Vegas oddsmaker to predict on which side the smart money will land. Given that it would never be reasonable to place one person's reputation or pocketbook above another's life, the only important question is whether someone's life is, in fact, at significant risk. Too often, however, courts in HIV cases find ways to dodge this question.

Any risk assessment has at least two components: the chances of a bad thing happening, and the gravity of the harm that will be caused if it does.[72] As the chances of anything happening decline, the consequences must get worse to make the overall risk significant. Few people avoid eating fish because of the low chance of choking to death on a bone. On the other hand, a very low risk of a nuclear reactor accident is significant because of the potential for catastrophic damage. While the numbers are important, any risk assessment is ultimately a value choice, not a scientific conclusion. Indeed, people's fear often has much less to do with the actual chances of something happening than with factors like how outrageous the harm seems and how heavily it is reported in the media. Statistically, Dr. Doe presented less of a risk to his patients than a salmon on a dinner plate. As can happen in HIV cases, however, he was treated like a Chernobyl.

In some early HIV cases, it appeared that courts would not consider the consequences of transmission at all if the chances of harm actually occurring were very low. Judges rejected the proposition that uncertainty as to the precise level of risk justified treating the risk as significant. "Little in science can be proved with complete certainty," one court noted, and to require it would place "an impossible burden of proof" on people like Dr. Doe.[73] Another wrote:

> There was testimony in this case that there can be no guarantee that the [agency's] clients could not possibly contract the AIDS virus, and thus the policy is necessary because of the devastating consequences of the disease. . . .
> . . . This policy ignores the current state of medical knowledge which establishes that the AIDS virus is not contracted by casual contact. The defendants are simply asking that this Court approve their policy because it is better to be safe than sorry.[74]

In recent years, this approach has been challenged, particularly in cases involving health care workers. A common judicial move is to replace probability of harm with possibility of harm as the threshold question.[75]

The chance of Dr. Doe infecting a patient was a compound of two risks: the chances that an exposure to his blood could infect a patient and the chances that any patient had actually been exposed to his blood. Both chances were extremely low, and, in conventional probability analysis, should have been multiplied to produce an even lower figure. Although the precise value of the final figure was unknown and unknowable, it approached zero. The *Doe* court itself noted that the "chances of transmitting the HIV virus via surgical procedures is very slim—one commentator has estimated the chances to be 1/48,000," but the court focused on the fact that, no matter how low the chances of transmission, "the *potential* is nevertheless there."[76]

Asking whether transmission can possibly happen or not, rather than how likely it is to happen, works a powerful change in the outcome: if we cannot tell whether the risk is one in five thousand or one in forty-eight thousand, then some courts behave as if we are entitled to treat it as one in one hundred. The "potential" can be magnified by loose mathematics and irrelevant statistics. The risk that Dr. Doe himself posed was multiplied by the risk posed by all infected health care workers: "When one begins to calculate how many individuals may be subject to the same risk by the same medical worker, multiplied by the aggregate of infected health care workers, the numbers become staggering." His personal record of not being cut and complying with barrier precautions was washed out by reference to studies that purported to show that "a surgeon will cut a glove in approximately one out for four cases, and probably sustain a significant cut in one out of every forty cases."[77]

By the time it has gone this far, a court is well placed in its argument to throw aside the notion that the chances of harm matter at all in a risk assessment. In a phrase which has turned up in various guises in too many HIV cases, the Superior Court opined: "Surely it is no consolation to the one or two individuals who become infected after innocently consenting to medical care by an unhealthy doctor that they were part of a rare statistic."[78] This is as true as it is simpleminded: it is just as true that no one, if she thought it possible, would want to be a person with HIV exposed to professional ruin or worse, simply to salve irrational fears of a vanishingly tiny risk of transmission.

Freed of the need to consider probability, it is disturbingly easy for a judge to paint a person with HIV as the embodiment of disaster. If Doe exposed someone, and that person was infected, that person would surely die. And why stop there? The hospitals raised the possibility of further infection of spouses, breast-feeding infants, even recipients of the infected patients' blood. It takes little more than logic and imagination to place any person with HIV at the center of a mini-epidemic. If the possibility of death, however unlikely, is enough to create a compelling reason to test or disclose, people with HIV will always lose.[79]

The balancing analysis creates problems beyond the realm of risk assessment. Most significantly, its bilateral comparison of one party's rights against another's often orphans the public interest. Questions of confidentiality and informed consent for testing are important to society, not just to individuals. While claims that *any* breach of privacy will "drive the infected underground" are hard to substantiate, it is reasonable to believe that pointless invasions of privacy do not need to be too harmful to do more harm than good.[80] More concretely, most schemes for involuntarily identifying people with HIV are expensive, using resources that could be better deployed in more effective programs. The rule that many lawyers will generalize from Dr. Doe's case—that all infected practitioners must inform their patients—presupposes a requirement that health care workers know their HIV status. This, in turn, means that health care workers must be tested. The Pennsylvania

Health Department estimated that it would cost $13.8 million to test and counsel each of the state's health care workers for HIV one time—just about what the state and federal governments annually spend on all Pennsylvania AIDS prevention programs combined. And an effective screening program would require two to four tests per year.[81] Yet none of this was seriously addressed in the *Doe* case.

Moreover, the price of testing is not the only cost. There is also the loss of the social investment in the infected workers who can no longer practice in their field of specialization, or at all. This loss is difficult to quantify, but it clearly is far more than zero. Over time, as screening prevents the infected from entering training, this may diminish somewhat, but through professional and lifestyle exposures, health care workers will continue to be infected at a rate comparable to that of others in the same demographic groups, so this cost will never disappear. Another, more intangible cost is the disincentive this policy, and this manner of making policy, creates for health care workers to provide care to the known infected.[82] The court in the *Doe* case simply did not examine these issues, because it saw itself confined to deciding whether a patient's "right to know" outweighed Dr. Doe's right to privacy. This sort of faulty analysis is all too common in HIV privacy cases, and will continue to stand in the way of a rational, effective response to the epidemic.

DR. DOE AND THE PRESS

Reporters had no trouble figuring out who Dr. Doe was. Even though the case was filed under a pseudonym and the record was closed, the public docket in the court clerk's office showed that the two hospitals had filed an application with respect to an anonymous doctor. The grapevine readily revealed that the case had to do with HIV, which brought the local newspaper into court claiming a First Amendment right to see the record and have access to any further proceedings. Once the hospitals sent letters to Doe's patients and held a news conference, reporters knew that Doe was an obstetrics resident on leave, a description which, they quickly learned, applied to only one person.

Dr. Doe's attorney did not oppose unsealing the record, because Doe's name had never been uttered in court or included in any filing. The attorney did, however, convince the local newspaper that it would run afoul of the Pennsylvania confidentiality law if it published the doctor's name. Unfortunately, this says more about the persuasiveness of a good lawyer than the strength of the law. The newspaper did not learn Doe's name through a written release, or in the course of providing a health or social service, and so was not covered by the law at all.[83] Nor would Dr. Doe have had much of a case under the general tort law of privacy.

Invasion of Privacy, Defamation, and Libel

Defamation is a false statement that injures a person's reputation: if the statement is made orally, it is called slander; if made in writing, it is libel. The essence of the tort is not damage to self—such as emotional pain and suffering—but injury to reputation. Accusing someone of being infected with an incurable, stigmatizing disease certainly qualifies as defamation, and in most states would justify a suit even without proof of actual monetary damages.[84]

Defamation would be of limited value in protecting the privacy of Dr. Doe, or anyone else with HIV, because, by definition, the plaintiff can win the case only if the defendant's statement is false. On the other hand, defamation is a useful cause of action for people merely perceived to be infected. In one case, a jury awarded $100,000 in damages to an uninfected Georgia school teacher whose ex-boyfriend posted signs stating that she had AIDS. In another, a small-town man was awarded $25,000 in a suit against an acquaintance who spread a rumor that he had AIDS.[85]

Invasion of privacy, in contrast to defamation, does not focus on injury to one's reputation; rather, the underlying principle is that an individual simply has the right to be left alone. There are several different types of invasion of privacy claim, two of which may be implicated by the release of HIV information: public disclosure of embarrassing private facts and placing an individual in a false light in the eyes of the public.

The tort of publishing private facts is the other side of the coin of defamation, protecting correct information whose release to the public would strike a reasonable person as highly offensive and objectionable. Publicly identifying a person as having HIV, with or without information about the behavior that led to it, would probably satisfy that requirement. Claims of "false light" invasion of privacy are usually brought by people who have been made the object of pity or ridicule by being linked with some sensational or newsworthy event in a way that misstates their actual involvement. To be actionable, the false publicity must be of the sort that would be highly objectionable to a reasonable person. In an HIV-related case that exemplifies the false light situation, a woman sued a newspaper for showing a picture of her and her child in connection with an article that talked about children with AIDS.[86]

The defamation and invasion of privacy torts are significantly limited by constitutional protections afforded to the free exchange of information and ideas. If the information is about a matter of public interest, or the subject of the information is a public figure—and both these terms tend to be broadly defined—then publication will be protected by the First Amendment unless the plaintiff can show that the information not only was untrue, but was published with malicious disregard of its falsity. In the case of true information lawfully obtained about a matter of public significance, liability for breach of privacy will be imposed only if it would serve "a state interest of the highest order."[87] This is why Arthur Ashe, the famous tennis player, could not use the law to prevent the media from revealing his HIV disease. Dr. Doe, who might have been able to satisfy the threshold requirements of the invasion of privacy tort, would still probably have failed in a claim against the local press because of the high news value of his condition.[88] By trying so hard to remain private, he had become a public figure.

Ironically, recovering under any of these tort theories requires the plaintiff to invoke the stigma of HIV even as she may be trying to fight it. A person with HIV is put in the unpleasant situation of arguing that it is shameful to be identified as having HIV in order to win, and a court decision that ultimately protects the privacy of people with HIV may do so by, in essence, perpetuating negative attitudes. It is apparently realistic, but nevertheless troubling, that courts can find that a "reasonable" person regards as repulsive and shameful the condition of being HIV-infected.

EPILOGUE

Dr. Doe has, hopefully, retreated into obscurity in a nonsurgical field. In due course, the hospitals were sued by some of the people they had notified. Not one was infected but all claimed emotional and physical harm from their fear. Ironically, the same hospital lawyers who had argued that the institutions had a compelling need to notify because of the risk, now argued that the hospitals had no duty to detect, or warn patients in advance about, HIV-infected staff members because the risks were so low. Indeed, they heatedly asserted that tort law could not require such measures, because the patients' interest in knowing was outweighed by Doe's and the public's interest in privacy.[89]

The protection of privacy is important for an effective public health response to HIV in a just society. Testing and disclosure programs too often reflect a preoccupation with low but frightening risks and a preference for identifying people whose exposure is unusual over providing services to the easy-to-identify. The claim that privacy is in conflict with public health too often reflects underlying disdain for those with, or at risk of, HIV. It looks as if we will continue to praise privacy, and often even protect it, while allowing it to be needlessly compromised on too many occasions. This is unsurprising, if not inevitable. HIV is frightening, and there is much we do not know. Privacy itself is an elusive good. We are a society that values the free, convenient flow of information. We are often impatient with rules and forms. Broad rules of privacy can interfere with appropriate, beneficial transfer of information and with the exercise of professional judgment just where an educated discretion is the best guide to conduct. While strong privacy laws are important, a privacy policy will succeed in the long run only if it becomes a widely accepted privacy ethic. Everyone who comes into possession of HIV information, or who is in a position to do HIV testing, must understand the importance of privacy to both the individual and the society, and act, whatever the legal rules, in a manner that reflects that importance.

NOTES

1 This account is drawn from the transcripts of the trial-level hearing, two lower court decisions in the case, and Dr. Doe's petition for allocatur (review) by the Pennsylvania Supreme Court. I represented the American Civil Liberties Union of Pennsylvania as a friend of the court. See *In re* Application of Milton S. Hershey Med. Ctr., 595 A.2d 1290 (Pa. Super. Ct. 1991).

2 This discussion of the test is drawn generally from Sloand, *et al.*, *HIV Testing: State of the Art*, 266 J.A.M.A. 2861 (1991); Bloom & Glied, *Benefits and Costs of HIV Testing*, 252 Science 1791 (1991); Field, *Testing for AIDS: Uses and Abuses*, 16 Am. J. L. & Med. 33 (1990); Pauker, *HIV Screening: Nosocomial Epidemiologic Risks and Decision Analysis*, 18 L. Med. & Health Care 33 (1990); Rhame & Maki, *The Case for Wider Use of Testing for HIV Infection*, 320 New Eng. J. Med. 1248 (1989); Rothstein, *Screening Workers for AIDS*, in AIDS and the Law: A Guide for the Public 126 (H. Dalton, S. Burris and the Yale AIDS Law Project eds. 1987); Wiess & Thierr, *HIV Testing is the*

Answer—What's the Question? 319 New Eng. J. Med. 1010 (1988).

3 Sloand, *et al.*, note 2 above; Busch, *et al.*, *Reliable Confirmation and Quantitation of Human Immunodeficiency Virus Type 1 Antibody Using a Recombinant-antigen Immunoblot Assay*, 31 Transfusion 129 (1991); Read, *et al.*, *Comparison of Three HIV Antigen Detection Kits in Sequential Sera from a Cohort of Homosexual Men*, 4 J. AIDS 717 (1991).

4 Gross, *HIV Antibody Testing: Performance and Counseling Issues*, New Eng. J. Pub. Pol'y, Winter/Spring 1988, at 189, 191–93; Meyer & Pauker, *Screening for HIV: Can We Afford the False Positive Rate?* 317 New Eng. J. Med. 238 (1987). *But see* Burke *et al.*, *Measurement of the False Positive Rate in a Screening Program for Human Immunodeficiency Virus Infections*, 319 New Eng. J. Med. 961 (1988). *See generally* Cates & Handsfield, *HIV Counseling and Testing: Does It Work?* 78 Am. J. Pub. Health 1533 (1988).

5 *See* Cohen, *HIV/AIDS Confidentiality: Are Computerized Medical Records Making Confidentiality Impossible?* 4 Software L.J. 93 (1990).

6 *Recommendations for Prevention of HIV Transmission in Health Care Settings,* 36 MMWR 3S (Supp. 2 1987).

7 American Medical Association, Statement on HIV Infected Physicians (Jan. 17, 1991).

8 Behringer v. The Med. Ctr. at Princeton, 592 A.2d 1251 (N.J. Super. Ct. 1991).

9 Transcript of Proceedings, June 10, 1991, at 51–52 (Dr. George Rohrer), Doe v. Hershey Medical Center, No. 91–2531 (Pa. C.P. filed June 10, 1991) [hereinafter Doe Transcript].

10 *See* A. Brandt, No Magic Bullet: A Social History of Venereal Disease in the United States Since 1880 (expanded ed. 1987); J. Duffy, The New Sanitarians 205–19 (1990); Musto, *Quarantine and the Problem of AIDS,* in AIDS: The Burdens of History 67 (D. Fox & E. Fee eds. 1988). The main proponents of the current attack on "AIDS exceptionalism" are Ronald Bayer, *Public Health Policy and the AIDS Epidemic, An End to HIV Exceptionalism?* 324 New Eng. J. Med. 1500 (1991), and Marcia Angell, *A Dual Approach to the AIDS Epidemic,* 324 New Eng. J. Med. 1498 (1991).

11 *See* Turnock, *et al.*, *Mandatory Premarital Testing for Human Immunodeficiency Virus: The Illinois Experience,* 261 J.A.M.A. 3415 (1989); Bayer, Levine & Wolf, *HIV Antibody Screening: An Ethical Framework for Evaluating Proposed Programs,* 256 J.A.M.A. 1768 (1986); *see also* Cates & Handsfield, note 4 above.

12 *See* A. Brandt, note 10 above; R. Bayer, Private Acts, Social Consequences: AIDS and the Politics of Public Health 232–34 (1989); *see also* New York State Sch. Bds. Ass'n v. Sobol, 168 App. Div. 2d 188 (N.Y. App. Div. 1991) (upholding requirement of religious representation on school AIDS panels

against Establishment Clause challenge), *aff'd,* 591 N.E.2d 1146 (N.Y. 1992).

13 *See, e.g.,* Brandt, note 10 above; Fox, *Social Policy and City Politics: Tuberculosis Reporting in New York, 1889–1900,* 49 Bull. Hist. Med. 169 (1975); Musto, note 10 above; Porter & Porter, *The Enforcement of Health: The British Debate,* in AIDS: The Burdens of History, note 10 above, at 97; C. Rosenberg, The Cholera Years: The United States in 1832, 1844 and 1866 (rev. ed. 1987); *see also* Wachter, *AIDS, Activism and the Politics of Health,* 326 New Eng. J. Med. 128 (1992) (describing success of AIDS advocates in political action).

14 Albert, *et al.*, AIDS Practice Manual app. A (3d ed. 1991); Gostin, *Public Health Strategies for Confronting AIDS: Legislative and Regulatory Policy in the United States,* 261 J.A.M.A. 1621 (1989).

15 1985 Cal. Stat. ch. 22, § 1 (codified as amended at Cal. Health & Safety Code §§ 199.20-.27 (West 1990)); 1986 Me. Laws 711 (codified as amended at Me. Rev. Stat. Ann. tit. 5, § 19203 (West 1989 & Supp. 1990)); 1986 Mass. Acts 241 (codified as amended at Mass. Gen. Laws. Ann. ch. 111, § 70F (West Supp. 1991)); 1985 Wis. Laws 29, § 1962gm (codified as amended at Wis. Stat. Ann. §§ 146.025 -.0255 (West 1989 & Supp. 1990)). Hawaii's 1986 statute was an exception, in that it applied to sexually transmitted diseases generally, covering "all information and records containing any information which identifies any person who has or may have any condition related to a sexually transmitted disease." It was later amended to apply only to HIV. 1986 Haw. Sess. Laws 161 (codified as amended at Haw. Rev. Stat. Ann. § 325–101 (Michie 1988)). *See generally* Dunne & Serio, *Confidentiality: An Integral Component of AIDS Public Policy,* 7 St. Louis U. Pub. L. Rev. 25, 31–32 (1988).

16 Pa. Stat. Ann. tit. 35, §§ 7601 *et seq.* (Supp. 1991); *see, e.g.,* Conn. Gen. Stat. §§

19a–581 to –590 (1991); Fla. Stat. Ann. §
381.004 (West Supp. 1992); N.Y. Pub.
Health Law §§ 2780 *et seq.* (McKinney
Supp. 1991); Wash. Rev. Code. Ann. §
70.24.105 (West Supp. 1991); *see also* Ariz.
Rev. Stat. Ann. § 36–664 (West Supp. 1990);
N.C. Gen. Stat. §§ 130A–143 (Michie 1990);
N.J. Stat. Ann. §§ 26:5C–5 to –14 (West
Supp. 1991). *But see* Ill. Ann. Stat. ch. 111
1/2, para. 7309 (Smith-Hurd 1988 & Supp.
1991) (test result only); Iowa Code Ann. §§
141.22, 141.23 (1989) (same); Tex. Health &
Safety Code Ann. § 81.103 (West Supp.
1991) (same). Florida's statute has been nar-
rowed by a number of amendments since its
passage in 1988. For a cogent account of how
a narrow and protective privacy law was undermined by political pressure for mandatory
testing, see Waters, *Florida's Involuntary
AIDS Testing Statutes,* 19 Fla. State U. L.
Rev. 369 (1991).

17 Pa. Stat. Ann. tit. 35, § 7607(a); *accord*
N.Y. Pub. Health Law § 2782; *see* Nolley v.
Erie County, 776 F. Supp. 715 (W.D.N.Y
1991) (jail's policy of placing red sticker on
files of HIV-infected prisoners ''reasonably
could identify'' such prisoners as infected).

18 Pa. Stat. Ann. tit. 35, § 7603 (1991); *accord, e.g.,* N.Y. Public Health Law § 2780;
see, e.g., Inmates of New York State with
Human Immune Deficiency Virus v. Cuomo,
No. 90-CV–252, 1991 WL 16032 (N.D.N.Y
Feb 7, 1991) (applying New York law in
prison litigation); Attorney General v. Biome-
tric Profiles, 533 N.E.2d 1364 (Mass. 1989)
(state confidentiality law does not protect
commercial testing company from state investigation of its activities); Urbaniak v. Newton,
226 Cal. App. 3d 1128 (1991) (law prohibiting release of test results did not cover disclosure of HIV information obtained by voluntary
oral statement by subject); Van Straten v.
Milwaukee Journal Newspaper-Publisher, 447
N.W.2d 105 (Wis. Ct. App. 1989), *cert. denied,* 110 S. Ct. 2626 (1990) (state confidentiality law did not apply to information

obtained from sources other than health care
providers and blood banks).

19 Pa. Stat. Ann. tit. 35, § 7607; *accord,
e.g.,* Ariz. Rev. Stat. Ann. § 36–664E; N.Y.
Pub. Health Law § 2780(9).

20 Pa. Stat. Ann. tit. 35, § 7607 (b); *accord,
e.g.,* N.Y. Public Health Law § 2782 (3); *see*
Conn. Gen. Stat. §§ 19a–583
to –585.

21 Pa. Stat. Ann. tit. 35, § 7607(a); *see,
e.g.,* Conn. Gen. Stat. § 19a–583(a); Fla.
Stat. Ann. § 381.609(3)(f); Haw. Rev. Stat. §
101; N.Y. Pub. Health Law § 2782(1); *cf.*
Wash. Rev. Code. Ann. § 70.24.105; *see
also* McBarnette v. Feldman, No. 15978/91,
1992 WL 67233 (N.Y. Sup. Ct. Jan. 30,
1992) (HIV confidentiality law no bar to
health department access to patient medical
records in public health investigation).

22 Pa. Stat. Ann. tit. 35, § 7604; *see CA
Couple Awarded $443,000 in Suit over HIV
Result Notification,* AIDS Litig. Rep. (Andrews) 8385 (July 14, 1992) (suit claiming violations of 1989 state law requiring
counseling services be provided to insurance
applicants who test HIV-positive).

23 Pa. Stat. Ann. tit. 35, § 7605(g); *accord,
e.g.,* Cal. Health & Safety Code § 199.22;
Fla. Stat. Ann. §§ 381.609(3)(f); Haw. Rev.
Stat. § 325–16(b)(1); N.Y. Pub. Health Law
§ 2781(6); Wash. Rev. Code. Ann. §
70.24.105(2)(d); *see also* Conn. Gen. Stat. §
19a–583(a)(5) (allowing testing by medical
examiner called in to determine cause of
death).

24 Ill. Ann. Stat. ch. 111 1/2, para. 7309
(Smith-Hurd 1988 & Supp. 1991); *see* Albert,
et al., note 14 above, app. A.

25 *See, e.g.,* Cruzan v. Director, Missouri
Dep't of Health, 110 S. Ct. 2841 (1990);
Lewis & Montgomery, *The HIV-Testing Policies of U.S. Hospitals,* 264 J.A.M.A. 2764
(1990). *See generally* A. Rosoff, Informed
Consent: A Guide for Health Care Providers
3–8 (1981); 2 Louisell & Williams, Medical

Malpractice § 22.04 (1990). For a state-by-state summary of statutes and decisions governing informed consent, see *id.* § 22.19.

26 Pa. Stat. Ann. tit. 35, § 7605(c); *accord, e.g.,* Fla. Stat. Ann. § 381.004(3)(d). For a strong critique of laws requiring disclosure of results to the subject, see Closen, *Mandatory Disclosure of HIV Blood Test Results to the Individuals Tested: A Matter of Personal Choice Neglected,* 22 Loy. U. Chi. L.J. 445 (1991).

27 *See, e.g.,* Pa. Stat. Ann. tit. 35, § 7607(a)(11); Iowa Code Ann. § 141.25 (West 1989); Kan. Stat. Ann. § 65–2438 (1989).

28 *See, e.g.,* Pa. Stat. Ann. tit. 35, § 7605(h); Conn. Gen. Stat. §§ 19a–582(e)(9), 19a–586; Fla. Stat. Ann. § 381.609; N.Y. Pub. Health Law §§ 2782(1)(i),(j).

29 Pa. Stat. Ann. tit. 35, §§ 7607(a)(4), (6).

30 N.Y. Pub. Health Law § 2782(1)(d); Wash. Rev. Code. Ann. § 70.24.105(6); *see also* Fla. Stat. Ann. § 381.004(3)(f)(2) ("need to know"); *cf.* N.J. Stat. Ann. § 26:5C–8 (medical personnel "directly involved" in treatment or diagnosis); N.C. Gen. Stat. §§ 130A–143, 130A–148 (Michie 1990) (release to "health care professional providing medical care to the patient").

31 *See* Tex. Health & Safety Ann. § 81.103; Md. Health-Gen. Code Ann. § 18–213 (1990); Wyo. Stat. Ann. § 35–4–132(c) (Michie Supp. 1991); *see also* Ga. Code Ann. § 24–9–47(i)(1) (Harrison 1990) (allows disclosure from one health care provider to another providing care if disclosure is "reasonably necessary" to protect against risk of infection); Tex. Health & Safety Ann. § 81.102 (allows testing "on the person that could expose health care personnel to AIDS or HIV infection" in an operation); *cf.* Haw. Rev. Stat. § 325–16(b)(6) (authorizing a treating doctor to test if patient is "incapable" of consenting and doctor has "reason to believe that the safety of health care providers may be affected due to exposure to the blood or body

fluids of a patient suspected of possible HIV infection").

32 *See, e.g.,* R.I. Gen. Laws § 23–28.36–3; Ala. Code § 22–11A–39 (1990).

33 *Compare* Wis. Stat. Ann. § 146.025(4) *and* Conn. Gen. Stat. §§ 19a–582(e)(5), 19A–583(a)(7) *and* Fla. Stat. Ann. § 381.004(3)(i)(10) *and* Pa. Stat. Ann. tit. 35, § 7606 (relatively strict formal requirements) *with* Ill. Stat. Ann. ch. 111 1/2, paras. 7307, 7309 (no effort to secure informed consent required; testing based on one physician's judgment that exposure could result in transmission) *and* Tex. Health & Safety Ann. § 81.102(a)(4)(D) (allowing post-exposure testing under any circumstances set forth in a health care provider's infectious disease protocols) *and* Va. Code § 32.1–45.1 (Michie Supp. 1991) (consent deemed granted when patient accepts care).

34 *See generally* Furrow, *AIDS and the Health Care Provider: The Argument for Voluntary HIV Testing,* 35 Vill. L. Rev. 823 (1989); Turkington, *Confidentiality Policy for HIV-Related Information: An Analytic Framework for Sorting Out Hard and Easy Cases,* 34 Vill. L. Rev. 871 (1989).

35 Va. Code § 32.1–45.1(B) (participation in health care provision deemed consent to testing and release of information to person exposed); Ill. Stat. Ann. ch. 111 1/2, para. 7405.5 (requiring state health department to notify present and former patients, regardless of possible exposure, when it learns a physician is infected); *see also* Treasury, Postal Service and General Government Appropriations Act of 1992, Pub. L. No. 102–141, § 633, 105 Stat. 834, 876–77 (requiring states, within one year, to implement CDC guidelines, or equivalent measures, to protect patients from HIV during surgery); McBarnette v. Feldman, No. 15978/91, 1992 WL 67233 (N.Y. Sup. Ct. Jan. 30, 1992) (authorizing health department to obtain list of patients of HIV-infected dentist under department's general authority to protect public health).

36 *See, e.g.*, Cal. Health & Safety Code §
199.25; Conn. Gen. Stat. § 19a–584; Ind.
Code Ann. § 16–1–10.5–11.5 (West 1992);
Md. Health-General Code Ann. § 18–337;
N.Y. Public Health Law § 2782(4); *see also*
Ariz. Rev. Stat. Ann. § 36–664(K) (West
Supp. 1991) (authorizing people who know of
third party at risk to submit the names of both
people to health department, which will then
send a trained counselor to contact person at
risk).

37 Ga. Code Ann. § 24–9–47 (Harrison
1990); *see* Tex. Health & Safety Ann.
§81.103 (to spouse by physician ordering
test).

38 *See, e.g.*, Cal. Health & Safety Code §
199.222 (involuntary prisoner testing/disclo-
sure); Wash. Rev. Code Ann. § 70.24.105(4)
(disclosure of sexually transmitted disease or
HIV infection "for disease prevention or control and for protection of the safety and security of staff, offenders and the public"); Pa.
Stat. Ann. tit. 35, § 7607 (a)(12) (disclosure
of HIV information to employees of juvenile,
mental health, and mental retardation facilities
who have general authorization to receive
medical information and are responsible for
medical care of subject); R.I. Gen. Laws §
23–6–22 (permitting disclosure to state
agency responsible for minors under care of
state); Wis. Stat. Ann. § 146.025(2)(a)(3) (involuntary testing of mental health/mental retardation center residents if medical director
determines patient conduct poses significant
risk of transmission to other patient).

39 *See, e.g.*, Fla. Stat. Ann. § 384.25(5); Ill.
Ann. Stat. ch. 111 1/2, para. 22.12(a): R.I.
Gen. Laws § 5–37.3–4(b)(13).

40 *See, e.g.*, N.Y. Pub. Health Law § 2782
(h); Wash. Rev. Code. Ann. § 70.24.105(2)(j);
cf. N.C. Gen. Stat. § 130A–148(h)(Michie
1990) (testing of minors without consent of parent or guardian in cases of suspected abuse).

41 *See* chapter 12; Glover v. Eastern Neb.
Community Office of Retardation, 686 F.

Supp. 243 (D. Neb. 1988), *aff'd*, 867 F.2d
461 (8th Cir.), *cert. denied*, 493 U.S. 932
(1989).

42 *See, e.g.*, Ark. Stat. Ann. § 16–82–101
(Michie Supp. 1989); Fla. Stat. Ann. §
381.004 (3)(i)(1)(a); Idaho Code § 39–604(3)
(Supp. 1991); Wash. Rev. Code. Ann. §
70.24.340(1)(b); *see also* Love v. Superior
Court, 276 Cal. Rptr. 660 (Ct. App. 1990)
(upholding California testing law). *But see* Illinois v. Madison, No. 88–123673 (Ill. Cir.
Ct. Aug. 3, 1989) (Illinois prostitute-testing
statute unconstitutional), *rev'd sub nom.* Illinois v. Adams, 1992 Ill. LEXIS 107 (July
30, 1992).

43 *See, e.g.*, Ga. Code Ann. § 27–2540;
Idaho Code § 39–604(3); Wash. Rev. Code.
Ann. § 70.24.340(1)(a); Virgin Islands v.
Roberts, 756 F. Supp. 898 (D.V.I. 1991).

44 *See, e.g.*, Idaho Code § 39–604(3); Wash.
Rev. Code. Ann. § 70.24.340(1)(c); *see also*
People v. C. S., 583 N.E.2d 726 (Ill. App.
Ct. 1991) (upholding Illinois testing law); *cf.*
W. Va. Code § 16–3C–2(f)(4) (health depart-
ment may order testing of IV drug users who
endanger public health).

45 *See, e.g.*, Cal. Health & Safety Code §
199.97; Fla. Stat. Ann. § 796.08(7)(a); Johnetta J. v. Municipal Court, 267 Cal. Rptr.
666 (Ct. App. 1990) (upholding California
testing law).

46 *See, e.g.*, Nev. Rev. Stat. Ann. §§
201.356, 201.358 (Michie 1991); *Love*, 276
Cal. Rptr. at 663 & n.4; *C. S.*, 583 N.E.2d
at 730–31.

47 *See* Reynolds v. McNichols, 488 F.2d
1378 (10th Cir. 1973) (upholding VD testing
of prostitutes). For a thorough, readable and
incisive policy analysis of HIV testing, see
Field, note 2 above.

48 Pa. Stat. Ann. tit. 35, § 7608; *accord*
N.Y. Pub. Health Law § 2785 (disclosure
only); Iowa Code § 141.23 (1991). Courts
have the authority to allow litigants with HIV
to proceed under pseudonyms, and to seal

records, even in the absence of HIV confidentiality laws. *See, e.g.,* Doe v. Shady Grove
Adventist Hosp., 598 A.2d 507 (Md. Ct.
Spec. App. 1991).

49 Pa. Stat. Ann. tit. 35, § 7605(g)(2); *accord, e.g.,* Fla. Stat. Ann. § 381.609(3)(f)(9);
Iowa Code § 141.23(1)(g); Wash. Rev. Code
Ann. § 70.24.105(2)(f); *cf.* People v. Anonymous, 582 N.Y.S.2d 350 (Sup. Ct. 1992)
(prostitute "waived" confidentiality protection against testing by stating she was
infected).

50 *See, e.g.,* N.Y. Public Health Law §
2783(1); Fla. Stat. Ann. § 381.609(6)(b) (intentional violation a misdemeanor crime); N.C.
Gen. Stat, § 130A-148(i) (civil action limited
to injunctive or declaratory relief for testing or
confidentiality violations outside employment
sphere, attorney fees); Pa. Stat. Ann. tit. 35, §
7610 (civil action); Wash. Rev. Code. Ann. §§
70.24.080, 70.24.084 (civil action, attorney
fees, $1,000 minimum damages for negligent
violation, $2,000 for willful violation; violation
a misdemeanor crime); *see also* V. v. State, 566
N.Y.S.2d 987 (Ct. Cl. 1991) (New York confidentiality law read to authorize private lawsuit
by injured individual); Urbaniak v. Newton,
No. 870 679, AIDS Litig. Rep. (Andrews)
7006 (Cal. Super. Ct. Sept. 13, 1991) (awarding $79,000 attorney fee in HIV confidentiality
case).

51 Estate of Behringer v. The Med. Ctr. at
Princeton, 592 A.2d 1251 (N.J. Super 1991);
see Anderson v. Strong Memorial Hosp., 531
N.Y.S.2d 735 (Sup. Ct. 1988)(breach of confidentiality claim stated when a patient allowed himself to be photographed based on
his doctor's and a nurse's assurance he would
not be recognizable, and recognizable picture
was published in newspaper); 2 G. Trubow,
Privacy Law and Practice § 7.02[1] (1989);
W. Roach, Jr., S. Chernoff & C. Esley,
Medical Records and the Law 153–57
(1985)[hereinafter Medical Records and the
Law]; Note, *Breach of Confidence: An
Emerging Tort,* 82 Colum. L. Rev. 1426
(1982). *But see* Dotson v. St. Mary's Hosp.,

No. 090017, 1990 WL 284370 (Conn. Super.
Ct. May 2, 1990).

52 *See* 2 G. Trubow, note 51 above, §
7.02[3]; Uniform Health Care Information
Act, 9 U.L.A. 478 (1988); Medical Records
and the Law, note 51 above, at 62–66;
Smothers, *Side Effects of a Bid on Medical
Files,* N.Y. Times, Aug. 14, 1991, at A10;
Baxley, *On the Auction Block: Your Personal
Medical Records,* Philadelphia Inquirer, Sept.
1, 1991, at 14A. In a few states, however,
improper disclosure may be punishable as a
crime. Medical Records and the Law at 141–
42; *see also* R.I. Gen. Laws § 5–37.3–4
(Supp. 1991).

53 *See, e.g.,* Whalen v. Roe, 429 U.S. 589,
599–600 (1977); Fraternal Order of Police v.
City of Philadelphia, 812 F.2d 105 (3d Cir.
1987); United States v. Westinghouse Elec.
Corp., 638 F.2d 570, 577 (3d Cir. 1980);
Stenger v. Valley Hospital Center, 563 A.20
531, *aff'd,* 1992 Pa. LEXIS 344 (1992). *See
generally* Chlapowski, *The Constitutional
Protection of Informational Privacy,* 71 B. U.
L. Rev. 133 (1991); Kreimer, *Sunlight, Secrets and Scarlet Letters: The Tension Between Privacy and Disclosure in
Constitutional Law,* 140 U. Pa. L. Rev. 1
(1991); Rubenfeld, *The Right of Privacy,* 102
Harv. L. Rev. 737 (1989); Turkington, *Legacy of the Warren and Brandeis Article: The
Emerging Unencumbered Constitutional Right
to Informational Privacy,* 10 N. Ill. U. L.
Rev. 479 (1990). On state constitutional protections, see *e.g.,* State v. Farmer, 805 P.2d
200, 208 (Wash. 1991); *In re* June 1979 Allegheny County Investigating Grand Jury, 425
A.2d 73 (Pa. 1980). *See generally* Silverstein, *Privacy Rights in State Constitutions:
Models for Illinois?* 1989 U. Ill. L. Rev. 215.

54 Doe v. Barrington, 729 F. Supp. 376, 384
(D.N.J. 1990) (citations omitted); *accord,
e.g.,* Doe v. City of Cleveland, 788 F.Supp.
979 (N.D. Ohio 1991); Inmates of New York
State with Human Immune Deficiency Virus
v. Cuomo, No. 90-CV-252, 1991 WL 16032
(N.D.N.Y. Feb. 7, 1991); Woods v. White,

689 F. Supp. 874 (W.D. Wis. 1988), *aff'd,*
899 F.2d 17 (7th Cir. 1990). *But see* Harris
v. Thigpen, 727 F. Supp. 1564 (M.D. Ala.
1990), *aff'd in part, vacated in part,* 941
F.2d 1495 (11th Cir. 1991); Plowman v.
United States Dep't of Army, 698 F. Supp.
627 (E.D. Va. 1988).

55 Doe v. Coughlin, 697 F. Supp. 1234,
1237 (N.D.N.Y. 1988); *see* Hawaii Psychiatric Soc'y v. Ariyoshi, 481 F. Supp. 1028,
1038 (D. Haw. 1979) (privacy protects freedom to choose when to reveal thoughts and
feelings). *But cf.* Local 1812, Am. Fed. Gov.
Emp. v. Department of State, 662 F. Supp.
50, 53 (D.D.C. 1987) (psychological consequences of learning one's HIV status do not
raise privacy issue).

56 *See* Bowers v. Hardwick, 478 U.S. 186
(1986); Webster v. Reproductive Health
Servs., 492 U.S. 490 (1989); Roe v. Wade,
410 U.S. 113 (1973); Griswold v. Connecticut, 381 U.S. 479 (1965). *See generally* Kreimer, note 53 above.

57 *See* Plowman, 698 F. Supp. 627 (E.D.
Va. 1988) (applying rational basis test to informational privacy issue); Johnetta J., 267
Cal. Rptr. 666, 683 (Ct. App. 1990) (applying compelling state interest test to California
constitutional privacy claim against mandatory
testing and disclosure of HIV information);
Doe v. Borough of Barrington, 729 F. Supp.
376, 385 (D.N.J. 1990) (citing McKenna v.
Fargo, 451 F. Supp. 1355 (D.N.J. 1978) (applying compelling state interest test to informational privacy claim), *aff'd,* 601 F.2d 575
(3d Cir. 1979). *See generally* Snyder v. Mekhjian, 593 A.2d 318, 319 (N.J. 1991) (Pollock, J., concurring); Chlapowski, note 53
above, at 146.

58 *Compare Borough of Barrington,* 729 F.
Supp. 376 *and* Woods v. White, 689 F.
Supp. 874 (W.D. Wis. 1988) (revelation violates privacy) *with* Plowman, 698 F. Supp.
627 (E.D. Va. 1988) (officer's revelation did
not violate employee's privacy). *Compare*
Doe v. Coughlin, 697 F. Supp. 1234
(N.D.N.Y. 1988) (transfer to HIV-only dorm

violates privacy) *with* Harris v. Thigpen, 727
F. Supp. 1564 (M.D. Ala. 1990) (segregation
does not violate privacy), *aff'd in part, vacated in part,* 941 F.2d 1495 (11th Cir.
1991). *Compare* Bradway v. American Nat'l
Red Cross, 132 F.R.D. 78 (N.D. Ha. 1990)
and Rasmussen v. South Florida Blood Bank
Inc., 500 So. 2d 533 (Fla. 1987) (release of
donor names violates privacy) *with Snyder,*
593 A.2d at 319 (release does not violate
privacy).

59 *See, e.g.,* Glover v. Eastern Neb. Community Office of Retardation, 686 F. Supp.
243 (D. Neb. 1988), *aff'd,* 867 F.2d 461 (8th
Cir.), *cert. denied,* 493 U.S. 932 (1989); Virgin Islands v. Roberts, 756 F. Supp. 898,
901–04 (D.V.I. 1991). *See generally* Skinner
v. Railway Labor Executives Ass'n, 489 U.S.
602, 617 (1989); Schmerber v. California,
384 U.S. 757 (1966).

60 *See, e.g.,* Terry v. Ohio, 392 U.S. 33
(1968); Winston v. Lee, 470 U.S. 753 (1985).

61 *Skinner,* 489 U.S. at 637–39 (Marshall,
J., dissenting); *see, e.g.,* Donovan v. Dewey,
452 U.S. 594 (1981); Marshall v. Barlow's,
Inc., 436 U.S. 307 (1978); Camara v. Municipal Court, 387 U.S. 523 (1966). *See generally* Note, *AIDS and Rape: The Constitutional
Dimensions of Mandatory Testing of Sex Offenders,* 76 Cornell L. Rev. 238, 246–49
(1990).

62 *Skinner,* 489 U.S. at 619–20 (quoting
Griffin v. Wisconsin, 483 U.S. 868 (1987));
National Treasury Employees Union v. Von
Raab, 489 U.S. 656 (1989); New Jersey v. T.
L. O., 469 U.S. 325 (1985).

63 *Skinner,* 489 U.S. at 624.

64 *Von Raab,* 489 U.S. at 680 (Scalia, J.,
dissenting).

65 *Compare Love,* 276 Cal. Rptr. at 660 *with*
People v. Madison, No. 88–123673 (Ill. Cir.
Ct. Aug. 3, 1989) *rev'd sub nom* Illinois v.
Adams, 1992 Ill. LEXIS 107 (July 30, 1992).

66 *Compare Glover,* 686 F. Supp. at 250–51
with Leckelt v. Board of Comm'rs, 909 F.2d
820, 829 (5th Cir. 1990).

67 See, e.g., Love, 276 Cal. Rptr. 660 (Ct. App. 1990); Johnetta J., 267 Cal. Rptr. 666 (Ct. App. 1990); Anonymous Fireman v. City of Willoughby, 779 F. Supp. 402 (N.D. Ohio 1991).

68 Compare Dunn v. White, 880 F.2d 1188 (10th Cir. 1989)(upholding prison's mandatory testing program) with Walker v. Sumner, 917 F.2d 382 (9th Cir. 1990)(individual officer's use of stun gun to force prisoner to take HIV test violated Fourth Amendment) and Barlow v. Ground, 943 F.2d 1132 (9th Cir. 1991) (warrant required to test arrestee for HIV).

69 In re Application of the Milton S. Hershey Medical Ctr., No. 2541 S 1991, slip op. at 5 (C.P. Pa. June 14, 1991).

70 For a critique of balancing, see Aleinikoff, Constitutional Law in the Age of Balancing, 96 Yale L.J. 943 (1987).

71 Doe Transcript, note 9 above, at 16.

72 See Burris, Rationality Review and the Politics of Public Health, 34 Vill. L. Rev. 933 (1989).

73 Chalk v. United States District Court, 840 F.2d 701, 707 (9th Cir. 1988).

74 Glover, 686 F. Supp. at 250–51.

75 See, e.g., Leckelt, 909 F.2d at 829.

76 In re Application of Milton S. Hershey Med. Ctr., 595 A.2d 1290, 1296 (Pa. Super. Ct. 1991).

77 Id. at 1292 n.3, 1296 (quoting Gostin, HIV Infected Physicians and the Practice of Seriously Invasive Procedures, 19 Hastings Center Rep. 32, 33 (1989)).

78 Id. at 1296.

79 Doe Transcript, note 9 above, at 15; see, e.g., Doe v. Coughlin, 518 N.E.2d 536, 542 & n.3 (N.Y. 1987), cert. denied, 488 U.S. 879 (1988).

80 See Doe v. Puget Sound Blood Ctr., 819 P.2d 370 (Wash. 1991).

81 Pa. Dep't of Health, Testing Health Care Workers for HIV—Costs, Benefits, and

Options, HIV/AIDS Update, July 1991, at 2–3. See generally Bloom & Glied, note 2 above.

82 Gostin, The HIV-Infected Health Care Professional: Public Policy, Discrimination, and Patient Safety, 18 L. Med. & Health Care 303 (1990); Barnes, et al., The HIV-Infected Health Care Professional: Employment Policies and Public Health, 18 L. Med. & Health Care 311 (1990).

83 Cf. In re Application of Multimedia KSDK, Inc., 581 N.E.2d 911 (Ill. Ct. App. 1991) (Illinois confidentiality law did not prohibit press from publishing HIV-related information disclosed in open court proceedings).

84 This discussion relies generally on Prosser & Keeton on the Law of Torts §§ 111–117 (W. Keeton 5th ed. 1984); see also Medical Records and the Law, note 51 above, at 146–53; 2 G. Trubow, note 51 above, § 7.06[3].

85 Snipes v. Mack, 381 S.E.2d 318 (Ga. Ct. App. 1989); McCune v. Neitzel, 457 N.W.2d 803 (Neb. 1990); see also Tulsa TV Station, Snack Pie Maker Denies AIDS Defamation Charges, AIDS Litig. Rep. (Andrews) 4830 (1990) (worker who claimed he had been fired because his brother had AIDS brought suit for, inter alia, defamation and libel, after local television broadcast a story saying that he had AIDS); Lee v. Calhoun, 948 F.2d 1162 (10th Cir. 1991) (upholding dismissal of HIV-infected plaintiff's defamation claim based on truth of the statement).

86 Hillman v. Columbia County, 474 N.W.2d 913 (Wis. Ct. App. 1991); Hammonds v. Cox Enters. Inc., No. D80918, AIDS Litig. Rep. (Andrews) 5084 (Super. Ct. Ga. filed July 24, 1990); Atlanta Woman Settles Suit Over Allegedly Libelous Photograph, AIDS Litig. Rep. (Andrews) 6005 (1991)(settlement of Hammonds). But see Anderson v. Strong Memorial Hosp., 531 N.Y.S.2d 735 (Sup. Ct. 1988) (New York recognizes no privacy action for publication of photo).

In a 1991 decision, the Supreme Court

held that the First Amendment did not protect a newspaper from liability for failure to honor a promise to keep a news source confidential. Cohen v. Cowles Media Co., 111 S. Ct. 2513 (1991). By analogy, a photographer's promise that a picture would not be used in a damaging way or a reporter's promise not to reveal the name of a person with HIV would also be enforceable. *See* Anderson v. Strong Memorial Hosp., 573 N.Y.S. 2d 828 (Sup. Ct. 1991).

87 *See, e.g.,* Smith v. Daily Mail Pub. Co., 443 U.S. 97, 103 (1979).

88 *See, e.g.,* Dorsey v. National Enquirer, Inc., 952 F.2d 250 (9th Cir. 1991) (upholding dismissal of Englebert Humperdinck's claim of defamation because newspaper had accurately reported statements made in court papers in the public record); Van Stratten v. Milwaukee Journal, 447 N.W.2d 105 (Wis. App. 1989) (inmate with HIV made himself a public figure by attempting suicide).

89 Wohlgemuth v. Milton S. Hershey Medical Ctr., No. 2694-S-1991 (C.P. Pa. Jan. 30, 1992)(order denying defendant's motion to dismiss HIV-exposure claims).

8

Drug Dependency and HIV

Larry Gostin

Needle sharing among drug-dependent people is fueling the modern human immunodeficiency virus (HIV) epidemic. The transmission of HIV occurs when infected drug users self-administer heroin, cocaine, amphetamines, or other drugs through an injection into a vein, under the skin or into a muscle ("skin popping"). The needle, syringe, and possibly the "cooker" (a spoon or bottle cap used to dissolve the drug in water prior to injection) may contain small amounts of HIV-infected blood. To ensure that no trace of the drug remains in the syringe, the user often draws his or her blood into the syringe and reinjects it into the vein, a practice known as "booting." The "works" (injection equipment) are then shared with another drug-dependent person who draws his or her own blood into the syringe, mixing it with the blood from the partner. Thus, syringe and needle sharing is a highly efficient method of transmitting an infection.[1]

Cocaine also affects the HIV epidemic in two significant ways. First, cocaine can be injected. Indeed, intravenous (IV) cocaine users have to inject more frequently than heroin users to achieve the same high, thus posing a greater risk of transmission of HIV. Currently, there is no chemical treatment for cocaine use comparable to methadone for heroin use.[2] Second, the exchange of sex for cocaine, particularly in crack houses, is fanning the HIV epidemic.[3]

The needle-borne HIV epidemic is a public health problem of broad dimensions. Intravenous drug users are the second-largest risk group for HIV infection in the American population. Twenty-nine percent of all cases of AIDS reported to the U.S. Centers for Disease Control (CDC) involve IV drug users.[4] The serological prevalence of HIV in the IV drug use community is higher still. Epidemiological studies in major urban areas, particularly New York, Northern New Jersey, and Connecticut, demonstrate HIV seroprevalence rates of 50 percent or more.[5] Moreover, HIV disease in drug-dependent populations is an epidemic that strikes disproportionately the urban poor, African Americans, and Hispanics.[6] The risk factors are related to behavior,

not race. Dawson explains that "to label a pigment as a risk factor is to promote
... racist notions that have hampered HIV research, thwarted access to care, and
tainted educational efforts about HIV."[7] Ethnographic studies of this population
describe it as "street drug abusers," of which the vast majority is homeless, unemployed, or underemployed. Many also suffer from multiple physical dependencies
on drugs and alcohol.[8] These studies point to the vulnerability of the drug-dependent
population and its frequent inability to meet its own health care needs.

HIV among IV drug users is also the single most important source for the spread
of the infection to nonrisk groups. It is likely that if heterosexual transmission of
HIV becomes self-sustaining, IV drug users will be the source of infection.[9] Nearly
72 percent of all heterosexual cases of AIDS reported in the United States involve
persons who have had sexual contact with an IV drug user.[10] The connection between
pediatric AIDS and IV drug use is even more striking. Seventy-nine percent of all
children born infected with HIV have a mother who either was an IV drug user or
had sexual relations with an IV drug user.[11]

Drug dependence and HIV are America's two most pressing epidemics, interconnected by a cycle of urban poverty, physical dependence, and a culture of sharing
needles and syringes. Extant political strategies to curb these interconnected epidemics involve two traditional approaches. The first—law enforcement and interdiction—is designed to limit the supply of illicit drugs to the marketplace. The second
strategy to combat the drug and HIV epidemics involves reducing the demand for
illicit drugs. Education, counseling, and treatment (detoxification, maintenance, and
rehabilitation) are all designed to reduce dependence on drugs, and are called demand-side policies. For those who cannot stop drug use, public health strategies
seek to alter dangerous sharing behavior or to encourage the sterilization of works.

Supply-side and demand-side policies are often in conflict, and this conflict
reduces the efficiency of the programs and thwarts the public health goals that
underlie both types of policies. For example, counseling, education, and outreach
programs designed to teach drug-dependent people safer ways to engage in unlawful
behaviors appear to condone or even foster drug use. The conflict between supply-
side and demand-side policies is also reflected in the relative funding that the federal
government commits to law enforcement and public health. Less than two decades
ago only 44.1 percent of the federal drug-abuse budget went to activities related to
interdiction, eradication, and other law enforcement measures, with the remaining
funds going to drug treatment, prevention, and education. In the last decade, however, expenditures for law enforcement rose substantially to between 73 percent and
82 percent of the drug-abuse budget.[12] The increase in the enforcement budget reflects
the current government philosophy that strong supply-side efforts that emphasize

the criminal and immoral aspects of drug use will yield health benefits for the public. My theme is that government should pursue a consistent policy on drug use that explicitly prefers therapeutic and public health goals to law enforcement goals when these two are in conflict. Such a preference for therapeutic goals is needed because of the seriousness of the HIV epidemic and because the sweep of criminal prohibitions and government regulation often renders public health measures ineffective. The human tragedy of the drug and HIV epidemics is not simply that people are acting unlawfully or immorally, but that drug dependency is destructive to a person's health and to the health of the community. The goal of supply-side policies should be to protect the health and safety of the individual and the community, not simply to punish "immoral, self-gratifying" behavior. Thus, the measure of effectiveness of those policies should be whether they succeed in lowering rates of drug dependency and needle-borne transmission of infection. If supply-side policies fail this test, they defeat the very objective for which they were formulated and lose their validity.

The nation's law enforcement strategy to curb the drug dependency and HIV epidemics has not been successful. The rate of serious drug use and the needle-borne spread of HIV are both growing in ways that are profoundly detrimental to the health of the public. The decline in casual drug use is a notable achievement of efforts to reduce illicit drug use.[13] However, this reduction in casual drug use may reflect prevention and education efforts in schools and significant cultural changes rather than the effectiveness of current law enforcement techniques. Moreover, the decline in casual use is more than offset by a marked increase in drug dependency and regular use of highly addictive drugs such as cocaine.[14] The United States has not attempted a comprehensive public health approach to confront the dual epidemics of drugs and HIV. Yet scientific studies show that public health policies will be effective in reducing the demand for drugs, the sharing of drug-injection equipment, and the overall risk of HIV infection. Consistent with these studies and with a focus on demand-side policies, I present three strategies for controlling the spread of HIV in the drug-dependent population: prevent the sharing of drug-injection equipment; ensure that drug-dependent people use sterile injection equipment; and provide medical treatment and rehabilitation so that drug users are no longer dependent on drugs or can satisfy the craving through lawful use of a prescribed drug such as methadone.

None of these strategies, standing alone, will significantly impede the spread of HIV in the drug-dependent population. But the cumulative effect of education, counseling, and outreach to reduce the sharing of works; of clean-needle programs to increase the use of sterile injection equipment; and of comprehensive medical treatment in specialized and mainstream health facilities to reduce dependence on drugs provides the best opportunity to impede the needle-borne HIV epidemic.

EDUCATION ABOUT RISK AVOIDANCE PRACTICES:
PUBLIC POLICIES DESIGNED TO REDUCE SHARING OF
DRUG PARAPHERNALIA

The sharing of works is the most critical factor in the transmission of HIV in the IV drug use population.[15] Works are usually shared out of practical necessity, but sometimes the sharing occurs as part of the drug subculture, as a form of social bonding or camaraderie within the group.[16] Drug-dependent people share works with sexual partners, members of a friendship group or other users in a "shooting gallery."[17] A shooting gallery is a place where a person can inject illicit drugs. Most galleries are located near a "copping" place where drugs can be purchased. Needles are sometimes obtained "free" with the drug purchase; others, kept by dealers for renting or lending to customers, are called "house works." After the house works are used, they are returned and used again by another customer. Needles and syringes may be used repeatedly in this way until they become clogged with blood, too dull to use, or broken.[18] Most users in research studies report that they obtain their needles from street sellers and shooting galleries.[19] Injection equipment is also obtained from doctors, pharmacies, or diabetics. Some sellers steal needles from hospital garbage bins or forge prescriptions. Shooting galleries and house works are particularly detrimental to the public health because they involve sharing needles beyond a small group of friends or sexual partners. Safety-conscious users, however, cannot rely on dealers and shooting gallery proprietors as a safe source of sterile equipment, since these dealers and proprietors sometimes repackage contaminated needles and syringes and sell them as new.[20] Since sterile injection equipment is not readily available, education programs must teach drug users how to sterilize the needles and syringes by themselves.

Current education programs have successfully disseminated basic information about how AIDS is transmitted.[21] However, a striking dissonance still exists between what IV drug users know and how they behave. Even though many addicts know that sharing is a high-risk behavior, they continue to share works because drug-dependent people going through withdrawal are concerned primarily with a rapid injection of heroin or cocaine.[22] Several studies also suggest that the sexual behavior of drug users is highly resistant to change.[23] Risk-reduction education must also be designed to overcome the ingrained behavior of needle sharing and to help form new patterns of behavior in the drug-dependent population. Although complete abstention from drug use is an admirable goal, for many it will never be achieved. If society truly desires to promote health and save lives among persons who continue to inject drugs, risk-reduction education is critically important.

Can Education Work?

Public and political opposition to risk-education programs is evident across the nation. Opponents often argue that these programs are unlikely to be effective because of the inherent characteristics of the IV drug-using population: physiological dependence, illiteracy, and lack of formal education. Opponents of risk reduction also argue that drug users have a fundamental lack of concern about their health. Finally, opponents point to the difficulty of reaching a group engaged in a criminal enterprise that the dominant population regards with hostility.

Arguments that risk-reduction programs cannot be effective ignore relevant data. Studies show that an overwhelming majority of users know and understand the behavior that puts them at risk for HIV infection. More significantly, drug-dependent people have shown a willingness to change socially ingrained activities—evidenced by greater use of sterile injection equipment, fewer needle-sharing partners, and less IV drug use—when provided with education and counseling and given the means to change their behavior. As a result of risk-reduction programs, drug users are demanding that dealers and proprietors of shooting galleries provide sterile injection equipment. They have also sought out public health department programs, such as bleach and sterile needle distribution, and drug treatment.[24]

Unfortunately, current education policies make it difficult to provide effective messages to users. Federal and many state laws require a focus on abstinence in HIV education, on moral rather than public health or legal grounds. (See chapter 6.) Legislatures must understand that behaviors of a physically addicting or socially habitual nature are difficult to alter. Drug users require focused, graphic information about the safer use of drug paraphernalia, where it can be obtained, and the most effective methods for needle sterilization. Thus, the information must be explicit, understandable, and directly relevant to the target audience.

Proposals for an Effective Education Program

Risk-reduction theory and research provide useful leads for developing effective education programs and policies. Two components of efficacious educational programs are promoting knowledge about how to behave more safely to avoid contracting HIV and altering social organizations and cultural rituals surrounding the sharing of drug-injection equipment. The critical variables are the process of dissemination and the content of the educational messages.

Existing public health education programs have broadly accomplished the goal of providing basic information to drug users about HIV transmission. Drug users demonstrate high knowledge of the fact that sharing equipment can transmit HIV. Educational programs should move beyond providing basic information about how HIV is transmitted and start including practical and simple instruction on the safest and most convenient methods for sterilizing injection equipment. Of the various methods of effective sterilization, most public health officials advocate the use of household bleach because it is both readily available and highly effective in decontaminating the equipment. Immersion of a hypodermic needle and syringe in a diluted bleach solution (10:1) will effectively decontaminate the works. Other methods are less convenient or effective. Boiling the works can kill the virus, but the fifteen minutes needed for this to be effective is too long for a drug user to wait when in withdrawal. A 70-percent solution of isopropyl alcohol can also kill the virus, but this is a substance that drug users might be tempted to ingest, causing health risks of its own. Moreover, IV drug users may employ the lesser strengths of alcohol found in wine, beer, or gin, in the mistaken belief that they are effective disinfectants.

Some drug users report that even if they did have access to sterile equipment, they would still share works because others in their social group continue to do so. Sharing is associated with initiation into IV drug use and, thereafter, serves as a social bonding mechanism. In order to change an individual's sharing behavior, education, counseling, and outreach must seek to change practices in the social organizations to which users belong.

Penetrating the insular culture of IV drug users to alter the social fabric of the group is particularly daunting. The most effective ways of altering the social organizations and cultural rituals of drug users involve understanding their language, culture, and thinking; gaining their trust by providing services rather than punishment; and using the communication networks in their communities. Innovative programs use current and former addicts to provide HIV education, bleach or alcohol for sterilization, and access to services and welfare benefits.

Visible signs that public programs are motivated by a desire to protect the health and lives of drug-dependent people, rather than to stigmatize and punish them, may make it easier for an addict to look beyond his immediate social circle for support. Present policies that hold drug users criminally and morally accountable for their behavior drive them underground and reduce their exposure to alternate forms of behavior. Clear policies and practices unequivocally directed toward the health of the drug-dependent population are more likely to aid in reducing the subculture's influence on users' behavior.

Reaching Out to the Drug-Dependent Population:
Increasing Access Points for Education and Counseling

Drug users are generally criminalized, marginalized, and unorganized, making them hard to reach with a public health message. The problem of reaching drug subcultures can be approached in three ways. First, support, self-help, and advocacy groups for drug-dependent people might be formed, analogous to the groups that have been so successful in the gay community. Second, addicts can be reached through the use of former addicts who volunteer or who are paid by public health departments to interact with drug users in shooting galleries, hotels, and "copping places."

Third, educational programs must be located in places where users are likely to go. The two systems that have the most contact with the drug-use community are the health care and criminal justice systems. A comprehensive health care structure that could be used to provide detailed education about practice methods for safer drug injection already exists. Educational programs could operate from numerous health care outlets around the country: physicians' offices, emergency rooms, group health clinics, health maintenance organizations, community hospitals, and clinics for the treatment of substance abuse and sexually transmitted diseases. Use of existing health care outlets for new educational initiatives would be inexpensive. Furthermore, integrating education into the health care system would ensure frequent exposure to education since drug users often have multiple medical needs that require interaction with the health care system.

Drug users also have frequent contact with the criminal justice system. Key points of contact are arrest, trial, and post-sentencing procedures. Wide-ranging powers already exist to require testing, education, and treatment of criminal defendants. These powers could be exercised as a condition of bail, probation, or other disposition. Requiring a drug user to attend testing, education, and treatment programs as an alternative to incarceration would be more protective of the public health and safety than current nonmandatory measures. Without systematic attempts to alter their dependent behaviors, drug users are likely to continue their habits both in prison and after they leave.

STRATEGIES FOR INCREASING THE SUPPLY OF STERILE INJECTION EQUIPMENT

Sharing drug-injection equipment is not merely a learned response or a function of the unfathomable culture and routines of the drug world. Sharing is also the direct result of a conscious policy choice to maintain a limited supply of needles and syringes, denying drug users any realistic opportunity to engage in safer behavior. Policy choices to make sterile injection equipment more available to IV drug users are fraught with political, legal, and moral conflicts. The dominant society has an ideological objection to making injection equipment available to IV drug users. The majority argues that such policies detract from educational messages directed to the general public, to school children, and to residents of urban areas to "just say no" to drugs. They argue that legalizing possession of clean needles, and, particularly, distributing them, appears to condone and encourage drug use because it provides the means for injecting illicit and dangerous substances into the body.

Minority communities and church groups in poor inner-city areas are particularly vehement in their opposition to clean-needle programs. Understanding the depth of feeling and the reasoning behind such opposition is critical to future policy development in this area. The intensity of feeling is manifested in characterizations of the drug epidemic and of the distribution of needles or even bleach as genocidal campaigns. One prominent voice in the African American community describes the cocaine epidemic as "Genocide, 1990s style": "when the spirit of a people is destroyed, when the culture of a people is eradicated, when basic human relationships are ripped apart, when large numbers of people are killed because of drug-related crimes and overdoses, I am talking about the spiritual and physical death of a race." The social disintegration, economic drain, morbidity, and mortality associated with the drug epidemic in poor African American and Hispanic communities should not be underestimated. Community leaders argue that clean-needle programs may increase the number of injections by current users and entice new recruits into IV drug use while having only a negligible effect on the spread of HIV infection. Even if there are no data demonstrating these harmful effects of clean-needle programs, there is revulsion at the thought that poor, minority communities will bear the risk of experimentation.[25]

A clean-needle program forced upon an untrusting community will almost certainly fail. My purpose is not to force clean-needle programs upon minority communities, but to present data showing that clean-needle programs, in combination with an array of health care, prevention, and educational services, would stem the epidemics of drug use and HIV infection that have overwhelmed minority communities. The policy analysis may be framed in this question: if we were to start with no prohibitions on the sale and distribution of drug paraphernalia—and with no political symbolism attached to such distribution—would we adopt policies strictly limiting the supply of sterile injection equipment?

Present Statutory Limitations on the Sale, Distribution, or Possession of Syringes and Needles

Broadly speaking, there are two categories of legislation that directly affect the supply of sterile drug-injection equipment: drug-paraphernalia laws and needle-prescription laws.

Drug-Paraphernalia Laws. Drug-paraphernalia laws are in effect in virtually every state in the nation. These statutes ban the manufacture, sale, distribution, or possession of a wide range of devices if it is known that they may be used to introduce illicit substances into the body. Drug-paraphernalia laws, therefore, require criminal intent to supply or use the equipment for an unlawful purpose.[26] Selling or distributing hypodermic needles and syringes where there is no knowledge that they will be used to inject illicit drugs are not offenses under these statutes. Thus, a pharmacist who sells hypodermic syringes and needles over the counter, believing they will be used by a diabetic to inject insulin, commits no offense under drug-paraphernalia laws.

The modern trend toward comprehensive drug-paraphernalia laws began with the formulation of a model act by the Drug Enforcement Administration of the Department of Justice in 1979.[27] At least forty-seven states and the District of Columbia have enacted the model act or similar legislation. In 1986, the federal government expanded paraphernalia prohibitions by enacting an umbrella statute designed to reach any activity involving paraphernalia crossing interstate lines. Although the Mail Order Drug Paraphernalia Control Act was originally designed to prohibit use of the postal service to send drug-injection equipment, the plain language of the statute extends to "any offer for sale and transportation in interstate or foreign commerce" of drug paraphernalia. The Act also contains a broad definition of drug paraphernalia, and it has survived constitutional scrutiny.[28]

Drug-paraphernalia laws erect formidable obstacles for IV drug users attempting to comply with public health advice to use sterile injection equipment. Even if the user can buy a sterile hypodermic syringe over the counter, he still can be prosecuted under these statutes if the syringe is found in his possession. In order to escape prosecution the user must demonstrate that she has a valid medical purpose for possessing the equipment. Drug-paraphernalia laws, therefore, not only significantly limit the supply of sterile equipment on the street, but also provide a marked disincentive for users to have sterile equipment in their possession when they frequent a copping place. Since this is precisely the time users most need to have a sterile hypodermic in their possession, drug-paraphernalia laws constitute a significant barrier to effective public health practices.

Needle-Prescription Laws. Drug-paraphernalia laws do not prohibit or regulate the sale of hypodermics if the seller has no reason to believe that the equipment will be used for injection of illicit drugs. Accordingly, over-the-counter sales of hypodermic syringes and needles are permitted in most states. Pharmacists are not obliged to question the buyer's intention in purchasing the equipment, and wide variations in sales practices exist. Some pharmacists will sell to any buyer, while others will not sell to a buyer who shows visible signs of IV drug use or who is unable to present a plausible medical justification for his request to purchase the equipment.[29]

Eleven states and the District of Columbia significantly restrict over-the-counter sales of hypodermic needles and syringes. These jurisdictions' "needle-prescription" laws, dating back to the New York Boylan-Town Act of 1914, prohibit the sale, distribution, or possession of hypodermic syringes or needles without a valid medical prescription.[30] Needle-prescription laws are more onerous than drug-paraphernalia laws because they do not require criminal intent.[31] Under needle-prescription laws, physicians may write prescriptions for hypodermic syringes and needles for patients under their care only if there is a legitimate medical purpose for them to do so. A wholesale druggist or surgical supplier must keep careful records of the sale of syringes and needles. People charged with illegal possession of a hypodermic syringe or needle have the burden of proving that they have sufficient authority or license to possess them.[32]

The Public Health Impact of Limiting the Supply of Sterile Injection Equipment

The demand for sterile injection equipment vastly outstrips its supply. Of people selling injection equipment, the great majority reports that the illicit market is thriving. The over-the-counter cost of a hypodermic syringe and needle can be as low as twenty-five to fifty cents. Yet the cost on the black market is about three dollars and sometimes as high as ten dollars.[33] Although this price appears to be low relative to the cost of drugs, the extremely high number of injections, particularly among cocaine users, means that numerous hypodermics are required over time. Some users will pay the additional cost of new injection equipment, but they still must rely on the integrity of dealers. And some users will save the cost of new equipment by borrowing house works or sharing with friends. Restricting the supply of sterile injection equipment thus increases the incidence of unsafe sharing practices and unnecessarily aggravates the HIV epidemic.

Proposals for Statutory Reform Consistent with Public Health Objectives

Drug-paraphernalia laws have two ostensible objectives, neither of which they achieve. The first is to discourage illicit drug use. However, no data support the proposition that access to sterile injection equipment causes people to begin, continue, or increase iv drug use. The percentage of iv drug users in the United States has been relatively stable for many years, both before and after the introduction of drug-paraphernalia statutes.

The second objective of drug-paraphernalia laws is to give law enforcement officers an additional ground upon which to arrest drug users. If the police cannot charge a person for possession of illicit drugs, they can still sustain a charge of possession of drug paraphernalia. However, this is probably the most pernicious aspect of paraphernalia laws. To avoid potential prosecution, iv drug users have learned not to carry with them any of their equipment.[34] Therefore, they are forced to use the often-contaminated equipment that they can rent or share at a shooting gallery or hotel. Drug users have even been arrested for carrying vials of bleach, based upon the questionable legal theory that household bleach used to sterilize injection equipment can be classified as drug paraphernalia.[35] Ironically, under this theory, drug users attempting to engage in safer behavior would be the ones most likely to be punished.

Narrow the Focus of Drug-Paraphernalia Laws. Drug-paraphernalia laws, if they are to be consistent with public health objectives, should focus their prohibitions on only the sale, rental, or distribution of drug-injection equipment by unauthorized people, not on possession. These prohibitions would apply to a drug dealer or proprietor of a shooting gallery, but not to a health care professional, pharmacist, or druggist. The law would regulate the sale of hypodermic syringes and needles in much the same way as existing law—ensuring that they are sold only in appropriate places (for example, pharmacies and not candy stores) by trained and experienced professionals, and in a safe, sterile condition. However, there would be no pretense that the authorized seller did not know what the equipment was going to be used for. More important, the drug-dependent person would not be chilled from buying, possessing, or using the sterile injection equipment by the threat of criminal sanctions. Any sale or distribution of equipment by an unauthorized person, however, would continue to be subject to criminal penalties.

A new law that focuses on illicit sale of hypodermics, but not on authorized sale and purchase, would have the benefit of allowing drug users to possess sterile equipment, thus encouraging safer injection practices. It would also quickly end the thriving black market for the sale of hypodermic syringes and needles, which poses a significant danger to the health of the public, because sterile injection equipment would be readily available to the drug-dependent person at an inexpensive price.

Repeal Needle-Prescription Laws. Along with modification of drug-paraphernalia laws, some states would also need to repeal needle-prescription laws to allow pharmacists and other authorized retailers to sell hypodermics over the counter, without a medical prescription. This repeal would be less controversial than needle-distribution programs because the state would not be directly involved in the distribution of drug-injection equipment. Moreover, repeal of these laws would have no revenue impact for state legislatures. It would simply remove the state as an affirmative obstacle to providing IV drug users with the sterile equipment necessary to protect their health.

Repeal of needle-prescription legislation is already supported by respected public health and bar associations, including the National Commission on AIDS.[36] More important, thirty-nine states and several European nations already permit over-the-counter sales of hypodermic syringes and needles. Experience in these jurisdictions shows that they are better able to control the needle-borne spread of HIV, and that allowing over-the-counter sales does not result in greater drug use.

Repeal of needle-prescription statutes need not mean that the state must abandon any attempt to regulate the sale of hypodermic needles and syringes. State legislators concerned with the sensitivity of local communities can require that sales take place only in certain locations, such as pharmacies, and that the equipment not be placed on display in view of customers. At the least, policymakers owe drug-dependent people the opportunity and means for protecting themselves and others from the needle-borne spread of HIV.

Another alternative would be to loosen the legal regulations on prescriptions for sterile needles. Physicians could prescribe a sterile needle expressly for the purpose of preventing transmission of disease through dirty equipment. Such prescriptions could be filled at specially licensed pharmacies or distribution centers, where HIV education programs could occur. Clearly, there are practical problems with this approach. Physicians who generally do not practice in the drug-dependency area would be faced with hard choices, and physicians and pharmacists might feel uncomfortable with such a legal responsibility. Such discomfiture, however, could be addressed through separately licensing these practitioners or pharmacies. Additionally, state licensure boards could mandate continuing education programs that would address the scope of the practitioners' duties and constraints in this area.

Affirmative Measures: State-Sponsored Efforts to Increase the Supply of Sterile Injection Equipment

The most frequently mentioned advantage of repealing needle-prescription statutes is also the proposal's most notable deficiency. Relying on private sales, as opposed to public distribution, is politically easy because the state can claim that it plays no direct role in supplying a disfavored population with the tools to abuse drugs. However, if the state is not a player in needle distribution, it loses a valuable opportunity to provide services to a hard-to-reach population.

The best way to reach underserved populations is to offer them benefits and services. Offering sterile syringes and needles breaks down barriers of distrust by demonstrating the state's humane commitment to the health and well-being of drug-dependent people. Needle-distribution programs can also provide critically important points of access for education, HIV testing and counseling, distribution of bleach and condoms, and medical services including primary care and treatment for drug dependency or sexually transmitted diseases. Needle-distribution programs can take many forms, ranging from established government distribution centers to on-the-street distribution by ex-addicts or even vending machines. Most versions of needle distribution are called "needle exchange" because drug-dependent people can exchange used needles for sterile ones. In this way the state keeps control over the number of needles in circulation.

Experience with Needle Exchange and Bleach Distribution in the United States. Needle-exchange programs in the United States are politically charged, and their establishment, even on an experimental basis, has been seriously delayed. The overarching message of law enforcement and community leaders is that drug use is profoundly detrimental to a person's health and to the social fabric of local neighborhoods. Most drug opponents actively denounce clean-needle programs, fearing that such programs will lead to an increase in drug use because of the mixed message needle exchange seems to send. While Boston leaders debated whether to adopt a needle-exchange program, Cardinal Bernard F. Law, Catholic archbishop of Boston, said, "The answer to drugs must be an unequivocal no. It is difficult to say that convincingly while passing out clean needles." Law enforcement and community leaders recognize the conflict between legal and moral dictates and public health objectives, but consistently press for punitive measures to deal with the drug problem.[37]

Needle-exchange programs cannot proceed without the cooperation of the very groups that traditionally oppose them—law enforcers and community leaders. The conflict between public health and criminal justice is well illustrated by the dilemmas inherent in needle exchange: public health officials in some of the highest sero-prevalence cities cannot establish exchange programs without first obtaining authorization from the state under needle-prescription laws; the police must agree not to arrest and the district attorney not to prosecute people using drug paraphernalia distributed under the needle-exchange program; and community leaders must agree to the location of needle distribution centers, which, if they are to be effective, need to be situated in poor urban areas.

Needle-exchange programs were proposed as early as 1986, when the Institute of Medicine stated that "it is time to begin experimenting with public policies to encourage the use of sterile needles and syringes by removing legal and administrative barriers to their possession and use."[38] Needle-exchange programs that were strongly supported by city public health departments were successfully blocked in Boston, San Francisco, Los Angeles and Chicago.[39] The nation's first needle-exchange program, in New York City, experienced significant problems in formation and operation. The Portland, Oregon needle-exchange program also initially experienced problems. The program was less controversial than others because it was run by a nonprofit social services agency administering a grant from the American Foundation for AIDS Research. In addition, the state already allowed over-the-counter sales of hypodermic syringes and needles. Nonetheless, implementation of the program was delayed because of the difficulty in obtaining insurance and because of legal challenges to the program. In responding to political pressures, Portland's mayor stressed that the program did not actually involve the city itself in the distribution of injection equipment. Needle-exchange programs have also been established in Tacoma, Washington; Boulder, Colorado; New Haven, Connecticut; Philadelphia, Pennsylvania; and Hawaii. Their apparent success in reducing HIV transmission without increasing drug use has helped win credibility for needle exchange in major cities. (For more on needle-exchange programs and the law, see chapter 6.)

Another way for the state to increase the supply of sterile injection equipment is to distribute disinfectants to the drug-dependent population. Innovative programs that distribute vials of bleach to encourage sterilization of works are already under way in New York, New Jersey, and San Francisco. IV drug users are instructed to rinse their works with household bleach and then twice with water so that traces of the bleach are not injected.[40]

The importance of actually distributing vials of bleach is illustrated by experiences with bleach programs in Baltimore. The public health departments there distributed detailed information about AIDS, including directions on how to sterilize needles and syringes through boiling or the use of alcohol and bleach. Residents of neighborhoods that participated in these outreach programs had significantly greater knowledge of what constitutes dangerous behavior than those in neighborhoods that did not participate. Yet no significant differences were measured in the number of injections, sterilizations, or sharing practices in the "knowledgeable" neighborhoods.[41]

The importance of providing an array of means to comply with public health advice is reinforced by ethnographic studies of behavior while in withdrawal. Withdrawal has been shown to be a critical factor retarding safer injection practices. The severe physical discomfort and the craving for relief drives users to resort to any readily available needle and syringe for injecting the drug. Asking a drug-dependent person to prolong withdrawal in order to obtain uncontaminated injection equipment virtually guarantees failure in risk-reduction efforts. The design of public health programs must ensure that IV drug users have immediate, unimpeded access to sterile equipment prior to the time of injection. Distributing vials of bleach, coupled with education about their proper use, will achieve just that goal.

The Experience with Needle Exchange Abroad. Needle-exchange programs in other parts of the world have not usually encountered the same political and public obstacles they face in the United States. Many countries have been able to harmonize effectively the objectives of law enforcement and public health and have gained broad consensus for needle-exchange programs. Outlets for sterile injection equipment have been established in a number of countries in Western Europe, as well as in Canada and Australia.[42] Government-sponsored research in Australia, Great Britain, and the Netherlands concluded that the distribution projects were successful and made recommendations for their continuation.[43] Preliminary results indicate that the availability of sterile injection equipment has not increased drug use. More significantly, these results also show some decline in HIV seroprevalence rates.[44] The programs also tend to attract people with no prior contact with drug treatment programs.

Evaluation of Needle-Exchange Programs: Meeting Valid Public Health Objectives. Preliminary data show that needle exchange, in conjunction with other strategies, could be an effective public health policy to slow the drug and HIV epidemics. Admittedly, the data collected from needle-exchange programs in the United States and abroad are decidedly insufficient because of small sample size and methodological concerns. Comparative research is also difficult to evaluate, since data from one country are not necessarily transferable to another culture. Still, the urgency associated with drug use and the needle-borne transmission of infectious disease suggests that programs that show some promise of being effective ought to be more carefully evaluated.[45]

Perhaps the most promising aspect of the various studies is the indication of the potential value of needle exchange as a bridge to drug treatment and to a wide array of other health and social services. Although drug users often have pressing health and welfare needs, they are exceedingly difficult to reach. Offering a benefit to drug users facilitates positive contact with them. Using needle exchange as a way to offer drug users HIV testing, counseling, sex education, treatment referrals, housing, and social support is well worth the moderate cost of exchange programs.

However, exchange programs that thrust services on clients have difficulty attracting and keeping clients. Programs that "don't preach" and only distribute needles have lower client attrition. To be sure, it is difficult to attract and keep illicit drug users within any traditional public health program. Nonetheless, it makes little sense to give up a major benefit of the program in order to attract clients. Instead, exchange programs should be designed and advertised with the user in mind: they should operate out of convenient and nonthreatening locations; the staff should be attuned to the drug culture; the services should be offered in a noncoercive manner; the programs should be confidential; and nondiscrimination on the basis of HIV infection should be the norm.

An explicit goal of exchange programs is reducing the incidence of needle sharing. Data show that the longer users attend exchange programs, the more likely they are to report significant reductions in sharing behavior. Moreover, the longer they attend, the more likely it is that the exchange program will be their exclusive source of injection equipment. The incidence of needle-borne transmission will be reduced if users alter their usual sharing behavior and rely upon public health programs instead of dealers and shooting gallery proprietors for their works. Evidence of reduced sharing suggests that drug users are aware of AIDS risks, concerned about their health, and willing to alter their behavior to avoid needle-borne infections.

It is extraordinarily difficult to demonstrate that reduced HIV seroprevalence rates are due to the establishment of needle-exchange programs. So many factors affect the rate of HIV transmission that the effect of one cannot be scientifically measured. Nevertheless, widespread sharing in cities with tight restrictions on needle supply has been linked to the disproportionately high prevalence of HIV in those cities. For example, New York has both needle-prescription and drug-paraphernalia laws and a seroprevalence rate among IV drug users of from 50 to 60 percent.[46] HIV seroprevalence rates are lower in cities that make sterile injection equipment more readily available, such as Amsterdam. While these figures establish no definite causal link between limits on sterile injection equipment and the HIV seroprevalence rate, they do indicate that supply limitations are not decreasing seroprevalence rates and that readily accessible supplies are not resulting in a feared increase in HIV infection.[47] An important advantage exchange programs have over programs that simply distribute injection equipment is that they reduce the supply of contaminated needles in circulation. More established programs such as the one in Amsterdam have experienced excellent rates of one-for-one exchanges.

Needle-exchange programs do not cause the various harms feared by their opponents.[48] Government-sponsored researchers in the United States and abroad have concluded that there is no measurable increase in drug use associated with needle exchange. Drug users who participate in exchange programs have demonstrated either the same or lower rates of drug injection as other drug users over the same time periods.[49] Longitudinal studies of programs such as the Amsterdam exchange could detect no increase in drug injection over time. Indeed, one study showed no increase in the rate of drug injection in clients at a methadone clinic that operated adjacent to the needle-exchange program.[50]

The concern that needle-exchange programs appear to sanction an unlawful and unhealthy activity, particularly in vulnerable minority areas already ravaged by the drug epidemic, could be addressed through the dissemination of culturally appropriate anti-drug messages at exchange centers. These messages should stress that exchange programs are designed to help drug users reduce their dependence through counseling and treatment. A more difficult problem with needle-exchange programs is that they may be thrust on local communities without consultation and without a comprehensive strategy for combating drug abuse. Needle-exchange programs would be more palatable to those communities as part of a comprehensive and well-funded package of services—education, drug treatment, and health care—designed to interrupt the cycle of poverty, drug use, and AIDS.

PROVIDING TREATMENT TO CONFRONT THE DUAL EPIDEMICS OF DRUG DEPENDENCY AND HIV

A thirty-four-year-old crack addict from the South Bronx decided he wanted to get well. After being turned away from numerous treatment clinics and hospitals, he gave up on the health care and drug treatment systems and sought treatment through the criminal justice system. He smashed windows in two police stations and displayed a hypodermic syringe and a crack vial through a third window, but his efforts to be arrested were unavailing.[51] This user's experience in New York City reflects conditions in most of America's large urban areas, where there are waiting lists of up to six months or more for drug treatment programs.[52]

The lifestyles of drug-dependent people often drive them to seek immediate relief from the physical and psychological effects of drugs. A user cannot be relied upon to reappear for a treatment slot that becomes available at some future time. For this reason, the goal of public health must be treatment on demand.[53] Delays in providing treatment for IV drug users cost human lives and scarce health care dollars. Drug dependency contributes substantially to the spread of HIV. A drug user who is turned away from treatment will in all probability continue the dangerous cycle of drug dependency, needle sharing, crime, and prison. Imprisonment does not address the problem: when the user is released from prison, the cycle will probably repeat itself.[54] The result is a spiral of drug use, violence, and HIV infection.

Provision of treatment services does not generate the same political conflicts as other strategies for confronting drug dependency and AIDS because the public health goal of treatment is consistent with prevailing moral values and criminal proscriptions. Nevertheless, existing treatment services are inadequate. The government and the public apparently undervalue rehabilitation as a policy option because of the belief that "treatment does not work."[55] This insupportable perception is based upon outdated and inaccurate scientific studies, the poor performance of treatment programs that lacked an adequate number of experienced personnel, and the absence of sufficient funding and commitment to make the programs work. Moreover, asking the question "Does treatment work?" is an overly simplistic approach to analyzing the benefits of treatment, because many variables affect the process and ultimate outcomes of treatment. A more appropriate question is whether treatment can work, if properly conceived, funded, and administered.

Can Treatment Work?

Treatment Evaluation Studies: Achieving Enduring Reductions in Drug Use and Criminality. Two major evaluative research projects have led social scientists to the nearly unanimous conclusion that treatment works: the Treatment Outcome Prospective Study (TOPS) and the National Treatment System Based on the Drug Abuse Reporting Program (DARP).[56] The TOPS project was a longitudinal study of 11,750 people admitted to thirty-seven treatment programs in ten cities from 1979 to 1981. The treatments studied were methadone maintenance, residential therapeutic treatment (therapeutic community treatment), and out-patient detoxification treatment. The participants were tracked for five years.

The TOPS study showed that each of the treatments was effective in causing significant and enduring declines in drug use. Overall, fewer than 20 percent of the participants in any of the treatments were regular users of the drugs studied three to five years after entering the program. These effects were evident for non-opioid as well as opioid drugs. Even under the most rigorous outcome standard, abstinence from cocaine, the treatment was successful. Abstinence rates in the year after treatment ranged from between 40 to 47 percent among the three treatments.[57] The DARP study, conducted before TOPS, involved almost forty-four thousand admissions to treatment, and showed similar abstinence and improvement rates.[58]

Numerous smaller studies have repeatedly reaffirmed the findings of TOPS and DARP: treatment is effective in reducing drug use; treatment's effectiveness increases with duration; and treatment achieves results that endure over time. The research literature focused upon treatment for opioid use because opioid drugs had been the drugs of choice.[59] However, non-opioid drugs, particularly injectable and crack cocaine, have emerged as the most frequently used drugs in the late 1980s and the early part of this decade. Treatment and program evaluation for cocaine use has been less rigorous than that for opioid drugs. Nevertheless, some studies have reported similar levels of treatment efficacy for cocaine abuse.[60]

In addition to reducing drug use, treatment reduces crime. The association between drug use and crime is inescapable. Many drug-dependent people commit their crimes as a means of obtaining money to purchase their drugs. Jails, courts, and prosecutors in major urban areas are overloaded with drug-dependent offenders. However, because of case overload, most offenders receive little or no prison time and no treatment.[61] Social scientists almost universally report that reducing demand for drugs through prevention and treatment reduces the level of drug-related criminal activity. Both the TOPS and DARP studies concluded that treatment produces a dramatic decrease in criminal behavior.[62]

TOPS, DARP, and the host of smaller studies point to the conclusion that treatment can work. Convincing policymakers and the general public of this fact is the next important step toward ensuring that treatment programs receive the attention and funding they deserve.

Methadone Maintenance Programs. Methadone hydrochloride maintenance is a mainstay of the drug treatment system. Methadone, given to heroin addicts at clinically appropriate daily doses, mimics the effects of the drug so that withdrawal cravings are reduced or eliminated.[63] Methadone maintenance has been exhaustively studied and has been demonstrated to be safe and effective.[64] Intravenous drug abusers achieve immediate and substantial reductions in heroin use while on methadone maintenance. Studies have shown that a significant percentage of drug users abstain from illicit opiate use while in treatment.[65] Positive effects are strengthened the longer they remain in the maintenance program.[66]

Methadone treatment has features that make it particularly effective in impeding the needle-borne spread of HIV. It has the highest client retention rate of all of the treatment modalities.[67] Client retention is important because length of treatment is one of the best predictors of successful outcome.[68] Methadone treatment also lowers risk behavior for HIV transmission by significantly reducing the number of injections and the sharing of injection equipment. Although reductions in injections and sharing are evident across the range of treatments, methadone maintenance has the most pronounced effect.[69] HIV seropositivity of addicts enrolled in methadone maintenance is also consistently lower than that of addicts not in treatment.[70]

Despite the overwhelming evidence of methadone's ability to combat the dual epidemics of HIV and drugs, such programs remain highly controversial. The concerns of opponents of methadone expansion are not well articulated, but can be grouped into three categories: methadone merely substitutes one long-term addiction for another;[71] methadone clients suffer from prejudice and are viewed as dangerous and antisocial;[72] and methadone treatment is itself immoral because of society's expressed preference for a drug-free lifestyle.[73]

These essentially ideological objections to methadone maintenance are hardly powerful given the practical effectiveness of the drug. We may be bewildered by the chemical reasons why the body seems to adapt so well to the long-term narcotic effects of methadone, and we may prefer, both morally and socially, a person who is drug-free. Yet, few public health interventions have been demonstrated to be as effective and safe as methadone. Substantial expansion of methadone maintenance would be a potent tool for reducing drug abuse, crime and HIV transmission.

Compulsory versus Voluntary Treatment. Drug treatment professionals understandably have been reluctant to recommend compulsory interventions when there are long waiting lists for people actively seeking treatment. Compulsory intervention also contravenes the intuition that drug-dependent people must be self-motivated in order to benefit from treatment. This intuition, however, is simply not borne out by the relevant data. In fact, there appears to be little difference in the efficacy of treatment between those who volunteer for it and those who are coerced into it.[74]

Compulsory treatment for drug abuse can be accomplished through civil commitment or through the criminal justice system. Twenty-five states have civil commitment statutes in effect. The Federal Narcotic Addict Rehabilitation Act (NARA) also authorizes compulsory admission for drug treatment. Studies of the effectiveness of civil commitment in the decade from 1965 to 1975, when it was actively used, demonstrate that it was at least as effective as voluntary treatment. Despite the continuing statutory authority for civil commitment, however, relatively few drug-dependent people have been civilly detained and treated since the mid–1970s.[75]

Mandatory treatment through the criminal justice system is also authorized under numerous statutes that provide for treatment as a condition of release on bail, probation, and parole.[76] While treatment under many of these schemes is technically voluntary, failure to agree to and carry out the treatment program can result in incarceration. Under this scheme the drug-dependent person clearly has a vested interest in opting for treatment.

Extensive research has been undertaken concerning the success of mandatory treatment in the criminal justice system. The criminal justice system is nearly twice as likely as any other source to refer young users into treatment.[77] Both the TOPS and DARP studies show benefits to people under mandatory treatment equal to, or greater than, the benefits of voluntary treatment. The major model for treatment in the criminal justice system is the Treatment Alternatives to Street Crime (TASC) program. The goals of TASC are to identify drug users who come into contact with the criminal justice system, to refer them to clinically appropriate treatment, to monitor their progress, and to return violators to the criminal justice system. The TASC program employs creative strategies including deferred prosecution, community sentencing, diversion to the civil treatment system, and pre-trial intervention to help funnel drug users into treatment. The program also utilizes traditional strategies such as probation and parole supervision.[78]

More than forty evaluations of TASC have concluded that it has intervened effectively to reduce drug abuse and criminal activity and that it has identified previously unrecognized drug-dependent people. Indeed, researchers have concluded that criminal justice treatment clients do as well as or better than clients in other drug abuse treatment programs. Successes of compulsory treatment include significantly reduced drug use and criminal activity and increased employment and social coping skills. Similarly successful outcomes are evident for prison-based treatment and aftercare for probationers and parolees.[79]

Compulsory treatment's proven effectiveness may persuade even groups that are morally opposed to drug use to choose treatment over punitive measures. A mandatory treatment program could make a user's otherwise useless time in the criminal justice system highly productive. Since a clear nexus exists between treatment duration and treatment success, extended treatment in the criminal justice system would significantly increase the probability of a positive outcome. Despite the limits it places on personal autonomy, compulsory treatment promises a brighter future for drug-dependent persons than currently practiced punitive measures.

**Present Treatment Programs: The Gulf between Treatment Needs
and Service Availability**

Politicians and public opinion polls alike place drug abuse and the needle-borne spread of HIV infection among the country's most pressing social problems. Total federal funds budgeted for drug programs increased from $1.5 billion in Fiscal Year 1980 to $5.669 billion in Fiscal Year 1989. For Fiscal Year 1991, the administration proposed a total of just over $10.6 billion.[80] The rise in funding, the National Drug Control Strategy, and the tough public talk about a "drug war" reflect the federal government's social priorities.[81] But noticeably absent from the spending, planning, and rhetoric is a comprehensive strategy for treatment and prevention. Surprisingly, no exact government figures are kept on the percentage of federal funds that go to treatment and prevention as opposed to law enforcement, eradication, and interdiction. But by any account, the percentage is low. Two decades ago more than 50 percent of the total drug-abuse budget went to treatment and prevention; it was reduced to between 18 and 27 percent during the Reagan years and was approximately 29 percent for Fiscal Year 1991.[82]

Expert commission and press reports have repeatedly drawn attention to the inability to meet treatment needs across the nation. States estimate that less than 12 percent of the more than twelve million drug-dependent people needing treatment are actually receiving treatment services. As of September 25, 1989, 66,766 people in forty-four states responding to a national survey were on treatment waiting lists; half of these people had been waiting for at least thirty days, and in many major urban states and the District of Columbia, between 90 and 100 percent of the people on the lists had waited at least thirty days. In some areas, addicts can wait for six months to a year for treatment. Waiting lists, moreover, may be grossly understated because many programs are so full that they do not add people to their lists. Addicts on waiting lists exhibit increased involvement in crime and less interest in entering treatment. The absence of adequate treatment services is also evident in correctional facilities. Studies indicate that the vast majority of inmates who are seriously drug dependent are not in treatment.[83]

The relatively low percentage of expenditure on demand reduction and the long waiting lists for treatment are symbolic of society's perception of drug-dependent people as morally blameworthy rather than ill, and of the low value given to treatment relative to punishment. Expenditures on demand reduction to bridge the gulf between services and current needs would not only be a symbol of humanity toward a historically reviled and vulnerable population, but would also be a cost-effective way to reduce drug abuse and crime.

The Cost-Effectiveness of Drug Treatment

The Presidential Commission on the HIV Epidemic observed that treatment on demand can save money as well as lives. At a purely economic level, the Commission reported, the annual cost of keeping a person in prison is $14,500, but as little as $3,000 is needed for drug treatment. More recently, the National Commission on AIDS starkly compared the cost of a new treatment slot ($11,000) with the cost of a new prison bed ($92,000).[84] The cost of treatment compares favorably with the $50,000 or more lifetime cost of treating a person with AIDS.[85] Comprehensive cost-benefit studies conclude that state-level funding of drug-abuse programs is economically justified. The studies focused on reduced arrest, prosecution, and incarceration costs; reduced loss resulting from property theft; reduced social costs due to an improved labor market; and reduced medical treatment costs. The TOPS study concluded that there was an 11 to 30 percent decline in these indirect costs as a consequence of drug-abuse treatment. Another study found a cost-benefit ratio of 1:11.54—for every dollar spent for effective drug treatment, $11.54 of social costs is saved.[86]

Expanding Access to Demand Reduction Services

If policymakers concur that prevention and treatment—properly designed, funded, and executed—is beneficial to the individual and is cost effective, the remaining question is how best to reach the drug user to reduce demand. Virtually all treatment services are delivered through traditional drug treatment facilities that are separated from the mainstream health care system. Drug treatment occurs, if at all, when a drug user himself seeks out services, has the persistence to wait his turn on the list, and voluntarily remains in treatment for the duration necessary to obtain results. This system is, at best, haphazard and idiosyncratic and, at worst, designed to perpetuate the revolving door between drug use, needle sharing, and brief stays in detoxification or in prison. This pattern suggests that the current segregated treatment system is capable neither of recruiting large numbers of drug users nor of keeping them in treatment.

Two distinct foci for enhancing the capacity to identify and treat drug-dependent persons are the health care and criminal justice systems. Large numbers of otherwise unrecognized and untreated drug users come into contact with both systems. It simply makes no sense to have a seriously dependent person pass through an emergency room, hospital, courtroom, or prison and fail to identify him or her as a person who needs treatment. Even if the person is properly identified, these settings presently have insufficient capacity to provide treatment or even to make a referral. The settings are not designed or funded to provide treatment, and staff members are inadequately trained and experienced to provide expert care for seriously drug-dependent people. Both the health care and criminal justice systems could remedy these problems.

The Health Care System. Seriously drug-dependent people are likely to have multiple health problems, not only because of the physical and psychological effects of their dependency, but also because they are likely to be poor, malnourished, even homeless. As a result of their multiple health problems, drug-dependent people are likely to come into contact with the health care system in traditional venues such as hospitals, emergency rooms, community health and mental health centers, family physician offices, health maintenance organizations, and the like.

The number of drug-related hospital admissions increased by 121 percent between 1985 and 1988. Included in this figure is a twenty-eight-fold increase in hospital admissions involving smoked cocaine (crack).[87] Unidentified drug users, many already HIV-positive, pass through the health care system. Blinded studies of sentinel hospitals throughout the United States suggest that as many as eighty thousand cases of HIV infection pass undetected through American hospitals each year. In large urban areas up to 50 percent or more of these cases of HIV infection are likely to be among unrecognized and untreated IV drug users. Studies of medical centers and emergency rooms indicate that a substantial number of patients have recently used an illicit drug, and many may be seriously dependent.[88]

Even if seriously drug-dependent people were identified in traditional health care settings, they would be unlikely to receive the expert care needed to ameliorate their long-term dependencies. Traditional medicine is ill prepared, at the most fundamental levels, to provide effective drug-abuse treatment. Medical training in the area of drug abuse is quite poor. Even primary care physicians themselves feel incompetent to treat substance abuse. The beliefs of physicians are confirmed by studies showing pitifully low levels of accuracy in identifying and diagnosing substance abuse. Physicians have had little reason to study substance abuse, because addicts are either shipped off to prison or never identified. It is likely that if public health objectives prevailed, medicine would quickly respond with better education and more active practice.[89]

Physicians cannot legally prescribe methadone—the government-sanctioned chemical treatment for opiate abuse—unless they are specifically approved for the purpose, and approval is not granted unless they comply with detailed regulations concerning staff-patient ratios, counseling, and paperwork.[90] The objectives of the regulations are to ensure in-depth psychological and medical care and counseling, and to prevent methadone maintenance centers from becoming mere "watering holes" to continue addiction. However, the regulations have had the effects of stifling the growth of methadone maintenance programs and discouraging ordinary health care providers from offering drug-abuse treatment at all. Consider the typical case where a seriously dependent person is in an emergency room or is an in-patient in a city hospital. The provider can treat all of the physical conditions associated with drug use, but is unable to prescribe anything related to the primary diagnosis of drug dependency. The provider's only realistic option is to place the patient on a waiting list for a separate drug treatment slot.

The Department of Health and Human Services has already issued proposed rules, in response to the HIV epidemic, to ease the regulatory burden on methadone maintenance programs. The proposed rules authorize minimum-service therapy to patients awaiting comprehensive maintenance treatment, and require counseling on the avoidance of HIV transmission. Professionals providing minimum-service maintenance are required to provide a medical examination and services, but not rehabilitative services and routine urine screening. These are regarded as interim measures until the client can be transferred to a comprehensive program.[91]

Although both drug-dependent people and physicians believe that drug treatment services should be more fully integrated into the health care system, and although the health care system has the unique capacity to identify and care for patients, there remain systematic problems in utilizing the mainstream health care system for these purposes. Integrating drug treatment into primary care, hospitals, community health and mental health centers, health maintenance organizations and other provider settings will require a sizable influx of resources for training, facilities, and staff. It will also require fundamental reform of federal regulations to allow physicians to prescribe methadone and future chemical treatments in the same way that they can currently prescribe in other areas of medicine.

The Criminal Justice System. Drug abuse is placing an extraordinary strain on law enforcement, courts, and prisons. Considerable evidence exists showing the close relationship between drug use and crime. The Drug Use Forecasting (DUF) program of the National Institute of Justice monitors drug use among recently arrested people in selected cities. Members of the DUF staff obtain voluntary, anonymous urine specimens from a sample of male arrestees from twenty-two cities. The prevalence of recent cocaine use among arrestees is striking (at least 50 percent). This figure is, moreover, an underestimate since DUF significantly limits the participation in its studies of people who are arrested on charges of possession or sale of drugs. The finding that at least 20 percent of drug injectors in this study reported sharing needles indicates that there is a continuing risk for the spread of HIV and other blood-borne infections.[92] Between 75 and 83 percent of people incarcerated reported they had used drugs in the past, and between one-third and two-fifths reported they were under the influence of an illegal drug at the time of the offense.[93]

Many prisoners take drugs even after they are incarcerated and often share injection equipment with other prisoners. One rural prison system reported that 26.9 percent of the inmate samples tested positive for illicit drugs. Although the prison system was able to lower this rate to 9.2 percent with routine drug screening and punishments, it indicates that drug use among inmates can be substantial.[94]

Despite the large number of drug-dependent people coming into contact with the criminal justice system, there are few comprehensive treatment programs. One national survey found that only 4 percent of state prison inmates received any treatment, and almost half the nation's prison inmates were not served by any identifiable drug-abuse treatment program.[95] For many in the criminal justice system, routine urine testing is the only "treatment" provided. The criminal justice system, particularly in corrections, often presents ideological, economic, and practical reasons for not providing treatment for more people. This resistance to establishing effective drug treatment programs reflects once again the tension between the preventive and punitive goals of criminal justice and rehabilitation. Even if this conflict could be resolved, severe prison overcrowding and the strain on resources make the provision of effective treatment very difficult.

The TASC program has already shown that a demand reduction model works better, is more humane, and costs less than the model of punishment and retribution that has dominated government thinking for the last decade and more. Furthermore, making a real commitment to treatment might help ease present constitutional and civil rights concerns that limit the justice system's attempts to identify drug users. Planners should carefully consider the future savings associated with effective treatment when attempting to work within present budgetary constraints.

CONCLUSION

Drug use and the needle-borne spread of infection are primarily public health problems. Seriously drug-dependent people are neither uncaring about the effects of drug use and HIV on themselves or their partners, nor unable to change their behaviors if given the education, means, and services to do so. As human beings they are more ill than bad, and they are unable to escape from their physical dependencies by admonitions to "just say no" or the imposition of draconian criminal penalties. Social science research has provided a clear agenda for confronting the dual epidemics of drug dependency and HIV, if the national will and resources are devoted to achieving this end.

NOTES

1 See Des Jarlais, Friedman & Strug, *AIDS and Needle Sharing Within the IV Drug Use Subculture*, in The Social Dimensions of AIDS: Methods and Theory 111 (D. Feldman & T. Johnson eds. 1986); Ginzburg, *Intravenous Drug Abusers and HIV Infection: A Consequence of Their Actions*, 14 L., Med. & Health Care 268 (1986); Stryker, *IV Drug Use and AIDS: Public Policy and Dirty Needles*, 14 J. Health Pol'y, Pol. & L. 719 (1989).

2 National Institute on Drug Abuse, U.S. Dep't of Health and Human Services, NIDA Monograph No. 88, Mechanisms of Cocaine Abuse and Toxicity (1988) [hereinafter NIDA Monograph No. 88].

3 Fullilove, *et al.*, *Risk of Sexually Transmitted Disease among Black Adolescent Crack Users in Oakland and San Francisco*, 263 J.A.M.A. 851 (1990).

4 Centers for Disease Control, HIV/AIDS Surveillance: U.S. Cases Reported Through September 1990, at 8 (1990) [hereinafter Centers for Disease Control, Sept. 1990]; Stoneburner, *et al.*, *A Larger Spectrum of Severe HIV–1-Related Disease in Intravenous Drug Users in New York City*, 242 Science 916 (1988).

5 See Des Jarlais, *et al.*, *Intravenous Drug Use and the Heterosexual Transmission of the Human Immunodeficiency Virus: Current Trends in New York City*, 87 N.Y. St. J. Med. 283 (1987); Des Jarlais, Friedman & Stoneburner, *HIV Infection and Intravenous*

Drug Use: Critical Issues in Transmission Dynamics, Infection Outcomes, and Prevention, 10 Rev. Infectious Diseases 151 (1988); Robertson, *et al.*, *Epidemic of AIDS Related Virus HTLV-III/LAV Infection among Intravenous Drug Users*, 292 Brit. Med. J. 527, 529 (1986).

6 Centers for Disease Control, Sept. 1990, note 4 above, at 12; *see also* Des Jarlais & Friedman, *HIV Infection among Persons who Inject Illicit Drugs: Problems and Prospects*, 1 J. AIDS 267, 269 (1988).

7 Dawson, *HIV in Intravenous Drug Users*, 322 New Eng. J. Med. 632 (1990).

8 Feldman & Biernacki, *The Ethnography of Needle Sharing among Intravenous Drug Users and Implications for Public Policies and Intervention Strategies*, in National Institute on Drug Abuse, U.S. Dep't of Health and Human Services, NIDA Monograph No. 80, Needle Sharing among Intravenous Drug Abusers: National and International Perspectives 28 (1988) [hereinafter NIDA Monograph No. 80].

9 National Research Council, AIDS: Sexual Behavior and Intravenous Drug Use 2186 (C. Turner, H. Miller & L. Moses eds. 1989) [hereinafter National Research Council Report].

10 Centers for Disease Control, Sept. 1990, note 4 above, at 9; Des Jarlais & Friedman, *The Psychology of Preventing AIDS among Intravenous Drug Users*, 43 Am. Psychologist 865 (1988).

11 Centers for Disease Control, Sept. 1990, note 4 above, at 9.

12 Brecher, *Needles and the Conscience of a Nation,* 1 Drug Pol'y Letter 5–6 (1989).

13 National Institute on Drug Abuse, U.S. Dep't of Health and Human Services, National Household Survey on Drug Abuse: Population Estimates 1988 (1989).

14 The White House, National Drug Control Strategy 1 (1989).

15 *See, e.g.*, Becker & Joseph, *AIDS and Behavioral Change to Reduce Risk: A Review,* 78 Am. J. Pub. Health 403 (1988); Schoenbaum, *et al., Risk Factors for Human Immunodeficiency Virus Infection in Intravenous Drug Users,* 321 New Eng. J. Med. 874 (1989).

16 *See* Conviser & Rutledge, *The Need for Innovation to Halt AIDS among Intravenous Drug Users and Their Sexual Partners,* 3 AIDS & Pub. Pol'y J. 43 (1988); Des Jarlais, *et al., Heterosexual Partners: A Large Risk Group for AIDS,* 2 Lancet 1346 (1984); Des Jarlais, *et al., The Sharing of Drug Injection Equipment and the AIDS Epidemic in New York City: The First Decade,* in NIDA Monograph No. 80, note 8 above, at 160, 163–64 [hereinafter Des Jarlais, *et al., Sharing Drug Injection Equipment*]; Des Jarlais & Friedman, note 10 above, at 869; Dolan, *et al., Characteristics of Drug Abusers that Discriminate Needle-Sharers,* 102 Pub. Health Rep. 395 (1987); Friedman, Des Jarlais & Sotheran, *AIDS Health Education for Intravenous Drug Users,* 13 Health Educ. Q. 383, 385 (1986); Feldman & Biernacki, note 8 above, at 32–34.

17 Des Jarlais & Friedman, *Transmission of HIV among Intravenous Drug Users,* in AIDS: Etiology, Diagnosis, Treatment and Prevention 385 (V. DeVita, S. Hellman & S. Rosenberg eds. 1988).

18 Des Jarlais, *et al., Sharing Drug Injection Equipment,* note 16 above, at 164; *see also* Hopkins, *Needle Sharing and Street Behavior in Response to AIDS in New York City,* in

NIDA Monograph No. 80, note 8 above, at 18, 24 (in one study, users said they used the same needle to inject drugs 1 (19 percent), 2–5 (36 percent), 6–21 (31 percent), more than 21 (11 percent) times).

19 D'Aquila & Williams, *Epidemic Human Immunodeficiency Virus (HIV) Infection among Intravenous Drug Users,* 60 Yale J. Bio. Med. 545, 553 (1987); Hopkins, note 18 above, at 25.

20 Des Jarlais & Hopkins, *Free Needles for Intravenous Drug Users at Risk for AIDS: Current Developments in New York City,* 313 New Eng. J. Med. 23 (1985).

21 *E.g.*, Des Jarlais & Friedman, *HIV Infection among Intravenous Drug Users: Epidemiology and Risk Reduction,* 1 AIDS 67, 70 (1987); Feldman & Biernacki, note 8 above, at 14; Friedman, Des Jarlais & Sotheran, note 16 above, at 386; Selwyn, *et al., Knowledge About AIDS and High Risk Behavior among Intravenous Drug Abusers in New York City,* 1 AIDS 247 (1987).

22 Becker & Joseph, note 15 above; D'Aquila & Williams, note 19 above, at 553; Des Jarlais, Friedman & Hopkins, *Risk Reduction for the Acquired Immunodeficiency Syndrome among Intravenous Drug Users,* 103 Annals Internal Med. 755 (1985); Stimson, *et al., HIV Transmission Risk Behavior of Clients Attending Syringe-Exchange Schemes in England and Scotland,* 83 Brit. J. Addiction 1449 (1988) (drug users in the sample reported that they shared injection equipment because of the scarcity of equipment (51 percent), need for a fix (50 percent) and/or peer influence (35 percent)).

23 Des Jarlais & Friedman, note 6 above, at 270; Des Jarlais & Friedman, *The Psychology of Preventing AIDS among Intravenous Drug Users,* 43 Am. Psychologist 865, 866–67 (1988).

24 Becker & Joseph, note 15 above, at 403; Des Jarlais & Friedman, *HIV and Intravenous Drug Use,* 2 AIDS S65, S65–66, S70–71 (Supp. 1, 1988); Des Jarlais & Friedman, note 21 above, at 73; Des Jarlais, Friedman & Hopkins, note 22 above, at 758; Des Jarlais, Friedman & Stoneburner, note 5 above, at 156; Friedman, *et al.*, *AIDS and Self Organization among Intravenous Drug Users,* 22 Int'l J. Addiction 201 (1987); Friedman, Des Jarlais & Sotheran, note 16 above; Guydish, *et al.*, *Changes in Needle Sharing Behavior among Intravenous Drug Users: San Francisco, 1986–1988,* 80 Am. J. Pub. Health 995 (1990); Robertson, Skidmore & Roberts, *Infection in Intravenous Drug Users: A Follow-Up Study Indicating Changes in Risk-Taking Behaviour,* 83 Brit. J. Addiction 387 (1988); Selwyn, *et al.*, note 21 above; *Risk Behavior for HIV Transmission among Intravenous Drug Users Not in Treatment,* 39 MMWR 273 (1990). Similar reductions in needle sharing are reported in Europe, including parts of Italy, France, and the United Kingdom. Olievenstein, *Drug Addiction and AIDS in France in 1987,* in NIDA Monograph No. 80, note 8 above, at 114; Stimson, *Injecting Equipment Exchange Schemes in England and Scotland,* in NIDA Monograph No. 80, note 8 above, at 89; Tempesta & Di Giannantonio, *Sharing Needles and the Spread of HIV in Italy's Addict Population,* in NIDA Monograph No. 80, note 8 above, at 100.

25 Williams, *Crack is Genocide, 1990s Style,* N.Y. Times, Feb. 15, 1990, at 31; *see* Kolata, *Black Group Assails Giving Bleach to Addicts,* N.Y. Times, June 17, 1990, at 20; Marriott, *Needle Exchange Angers Many Minorities,* N.Y. Times, Nov. 7, 1988, at 1. *See generally* Dalton, *AIDS in Blackface,* 118 Daedalus 205 (1989).

26 *See, e.g.,* Village of Hoffman Estates v. The Flipside, Hoffman Estates, Inc., 455 U.S. 489, *reh'g denied,* 456 U.S. 950 (1982). For a state-by-state breakdown of these laws, see Gostin, *The Interconnected Epidemics of Drug Dependency and AIDS,* 26 Harv. C.R.-C.L. L. Rev. 114 (1991).

27 Model Drug Paraphernalia Act (Drug Enforcement Administration 1979), *reprinted in*

Note, *The Model Drug Paraphernalia Act: Can We Outlaw Headshops—and Should We?* 16 Ga. L. Rev. 137 (1981).

28 21 U.S.C. § 857 (1988); *see* 132 Cong. Rec. H6655–56 (daily ed. Sept. 11, 1986) (statement of Rep. Levine); United States v. Main Street Distributing, Inc., 700 F. Supp. 655 (E.D.N.Y. 1988).

29 The scant literature on this issue suggests that there is wide variability in the practices and attitudes of pharmacists in relation to AIDS and drug abuse. Glanz, Byrne & Jackson, *Role of Community Pharmacies in Prevention of AIDS among Injecting Drug Misusers: Findings of a Survey in England and Wales,* 299 Brit. Med. J. 1076 (1989); Goldberg, *AIDS and Intravenous Drug Use,* 294 Brit. Med. J. 906 (1987).

30 National Association of Boards of Pharmacy, 1988–1989 Survey of Pharmacy Law Including All 50 States, D.C. and Puerto Rico 42 (1989) (significant restrictions on over-the-counter sales in California, Connecticut, Delaware, Illinois, Maine, Massachusetts, New Hampshire, New Jersey, New York, Pennsylvania and Rhode Island); *see, e.g.,* La. Rev. Stat. Ann. § 40 (West 1977); Mass. Gen. Laws Ann. ch. 94C, § 27 (West 1990); N.Y. Penal Law § 220.45 (Consol. 1989). *See generally* Committee on Medicine & Law, Ass'n of the Bar of the City of New York, *Legalization of Non-Prescription Sale of Hypodermic Needles: A Response to the AIDS Crisis,* 41 Rec. A. B. City N.Y. 809, 811 (1986) [hereinafter N.Y.C. B. A., *Legalization*].

31 *See* People v. Bellfield, 230 N.Y.S.2d 79 (Sup. Ct. N.Y. 1961), *aff'd,* 183 N.E.2d 230 (N.Y. 1962). *But see* State v. Birdsell, 104 So. 2d 148 (La. 1958).

32 *See, e.g.,* Commonwealth v. Jefferson, 387 N.E.2d 579 (Mass. 1979); Mass. Gen. Laws Ann. ch. 94C, § 27 (West 1990).

33 Des Jarlais, Friedman & Hopkins, note 22 above, at 758; Morgan, *Inside a Shooting Gallery: New Front in the AIDS War,* N.Y.

Times, Feb. 6, 1988, at B1; *see also* Des Jarlais & Friedman, note 23 above, at 866; Hopkins, note 18 above, at 26.

34 American Medical Association, *Reducing Transmission of Human Immunodeficiency Virus (HIV) among and through Intravenous Drug Abusers,* 4 AIDS & Pub. Pol'y J. 3, 143 (1987); Connors & Galea, Anthropological Investigations of the Meaning and Practices of Needle Use and Sharing among Intravenous Drug Users (IVDU), presented at the Fourth Int'l Conf. on AIDS, Stockholm (June 1988).

35 *See* Stryker, note 1 above, at 729.

36 *See* National Commission on Acquired Immunodeficiency Syndrome, Report: The Twin Epidemics of Substance Use and HIV (1991); N.Y.C. B. A., *Legalization,* note 30 above, at 809; American Bar Association, AIDS: The Legal Issues: Discussion Draft of the ABA AIDS Coordinating Committee 233 (1988); Committee on Law and Reform of the New York County Lawyers Association, Report on Drug Related AIDS and the Legal Ban on Over-the-Counter Hypodermic Needle Sales 1 (Jan. 12, 1988) (unpublished manuscript on file with the American Society of Law and Medicine, Boston, Mass.) [hereinafter Committee on Law and Reform Report].

37 *Bostonians Split on Mayor's Idea of Needle Swap,* N.Y. Times, Mar. 24, 1988, at A16; *see also* Primm, *Needle Exchange Programs Do Not Solve the Problem of HIV Transmission,* AIDS Patient Care, Aug. 1989, at 18, 20.

38 Institute of Medicine, National Academy of Sciences, Confronting AIDS: Directions for Public Health, Health Care, and Research 110 (1986).

39 Gostin, note 20 above, at 150.

40 Chaisson, *et al., HIV, Bleach, and Needle Sharing,* 20 Lancet 5 (1987); Des Jarlais & Friedman, note 23 above, at 865–70; Jackson, *et al., A Coupon Program—Drug Treatment and AIDS Education,* 24 Int'l J. Addiction 1035, 1035–51 (1990).

41 McAuliffe, Breer & Doering, *An Evaluation of Using Ex-Addict Outreach Workers to Educate Intravenous Drug Users About AIDS,* 4 AIDS & Pub. Pol'y J. 218 (1989).

42 *See* Bardsley, Turvey & Blatherwick, *Vancouver's Needle Exchange Program,* 81 Can. J. Pub. Health 39 (1990); Blatherwick, *How to "Sell" a Needle Exchange Program,* 80 Can. J. Pub. Health 26 (1989); Fox, Day & Klein, *The Power of Professionalism: Policies for AIDS in Britain, Sweden, and the United States,* 118 Daedalus 93 (1989); *see also* Karpen, *A Comprehensive World Overview of Needle Exchange Programs,* AIDS Patient Care, Aug. 1990, at 26; Wodak, *Needle Exchange Succeeding in Australia,* N.Y. Times, Mar. 26, 1990, at A16.

43 Wolk, Wodak & Guinan, HIV Seroprevalence in Syringes of Intravenous Drug Users Using Syringe Exchanges in Sydney, Australia, presented at the Fourth Int'l Conf. on AIDS, Stockholm (June 1988) (reported in Des Jarlais, *AIDS Prevention Programs for Intravenous Drug Users: Diversity and Evolution,* 1 Int'l Rev. Psychiatry 101, 102 n.19 (1989); *see also* Buning, van Brussel & van Santen, *Amsterdam's Drug Policy and Its Implications for Controlling Needle Sharing,* in NIDA Monograph No. 80, note 8 above, at 59 (1988); Hart, *et al., Evaluation of Needle Exchange in Central London: Behaviour Change and Anti-HIV Status Over One Year,* 3 AIDS 261 (1989); Morrison & Plant, *Drug Problems and Patterns of Service Use amongst Illicit Drug Users in Edinburgh,* 85 Brit. J. Addiction 547 (1990); Stimson, *AIDS and HIV: The Challenge for British Drug Services,* 85 Brit. J. Addiction 329 (1990); Wolk, *et al., HIV-Related Risk Taking Behavior, Knowledge and Serostatus of Intravenous Drug Users in Sydney,* 152 Med. J. Austl. 453 (1990).

44 *See* Joseph & Des Jarlais, *Needle and Syringe Exchange as a Method of AIDS Epidemic Control,* AIDS Update, Sept.-Oct. 1989, at 3–4; Raymond, *U.S. Cities Struggle to Implement Needle Exchange Despite Ap-*

parent Success in European Cities, 260
J.A.M.A. 2620, 2621 (1988); Robert, *et al.,*
Behavioral Changes in Intravenous Drug
Users in Geneva: Rise and Fall of HIV Infec-
tion, 1980–1989, 4 AIDS 657 (1990).

45 *See generally* Wood, *Needle Exchange*
Programs Stop AIDS!, 4 AIDS Patient Care
14 (1990).

46 Institute of Medicine, National Academy
of Sciences, Confronting AIDS: Update 1988,
at 84; New York City Dep't of Health, the
Pilot Needle Exchange Study in New York
City: A Bridge to Treatment 4 (1989).

47 *See generally* Des Jarlais, *AIDS Preven-*
tion Programs for Intravenous Drug Users:
Diversity and Evolution, 1 Int'l Rev. Psychiatry 101, 102 (1989).

48 *See* O'Brian, *Needle Exchange Programs:*
Ethical and Policy Issues, 4 AIDS & Pub.
Pol'y J. 75, 79 (1989).

49 *See* Joseph & Des Jarlais, note 44 above.

50 *See* Wodak, *Needle Exchange Succeeding*
in Australia, note 42 above.

51 Lambert, *Fight in War of Drugs and*
AIDS, N.Y. Times, Dec. 23, 1988, at B1.

52 Institute of Medicine, National Academy
of Sciences, note 38 above, at 108–09; *see*
Institute of Medicine, National Academy of
Sciences, note 46 above, at 84–85; Presidential Commission on the Human Immunodeficiency Virus Epidemic, Report 94–104
(1988).

53 *See, e.g.,* Presidential Commission on the
Human Immunodeficiency Virus Epidemic,
note 52 above, at 94–104; National Commission on Acquired Immunodeficiency Syndrome, note 36 above, at 6–10.

54 *See generally* Majority Staffs of the Sen-
ate Judiciary Committee and the International
Narcotics Control Caucus, Fighting Drug
Abuse: A National Strategy 66–71 (1990).

55 Martinson, *What Works?—Questions and*
Answers About Prison Reform, 35 Pub. Inter-
est 48 (1974); *see* National Criminal Justice
Ass'n, U.S. Dep't of Justice, Treatment Op-

tions for Drug-Dependent Offenders: A Re-
view of the Literature for State and Local
Decisionmakers 9–10 (1990) [hereinafter
Treatment Options].

56 R. Hubbard, *et al.,* Drug Abuse Treatment: A National Study of Effectiveness
(1989) [hereinafter The TOPS Study]. The
primary source for the DARP study is found in
The Effectiveness of Drug Abuse Treatment:
Evaluation of Treatment Outcomes for 1971–
1972 DARP Admission Cohort (S. Sells & D.
Simpson eds. 1976) [hereinafter DARP]. One
important caveat, however, is that neither
TOPS nor DARP were controlled trials. Controlled trials to evaluate drug treatment outcomes are badly needed.

57 The TOPS Study, note 56 above, at 102–
21.

58 *See generally* Simpson, *National Treat-*
ment System Evaluation Based on the Drug
Abuse Reporting Program (DARP) Followup
Research, in National Institute on Drug
Abuse, U.S. Dep't of Health and Human
Services, NIDA Monograph No. 51, Drug
Abuse Treatment Evaluation: Strategies,
Progress and Prospects 29 (1984 & reprint
1986, 1988) [hereinafter NIDA Monograph
No. 51].

59 *See, e.g.,* National Institute on Drug
Abuse, U.S. Dep't of Health and Human Ser-
vices, NIDA Monograph No. ADM 83–1281,
Research on the Treatment of Narcotic Addic-
tion: State of the Art (1983) [hereinafter
NIDA Monograph No. ADM 83–1281];
Simpson & Savage, *Drug Abuse Treatment*
Readmissions and Outcomes, 37 Archives
Gen. Psychiatry 896 (1980).

60 *See, e.g.,* National Institute on Drug
Abuse, note 13 above, at 29–39; Simpson, *et*
al., Addiction Careers: Etiology, Treatment,
and 12-year Follow-up Outcomes, 16 J. Drug
Issues 107 (1986).

61 Greenberg & Adler, *Crime and Addiction:*
An Empirical Analysis of the Literature,
1920–1973, 3 Contemp. Drug Probs. 221
(1974); Treatment Options, note 55 above, at

1–2; The TOPS Study, note 56 above, at 1, 152, and ch. 6; U.S. General Accounting Office, Controlling Drug Abuse: A Status Report 19 (1988).

62 The TOPS Study, note 56 above, at 128; Simpson, note 58 above, at 31–33.

63 *See* Dole, *Implications of Methadone Maintenance for Theories of Narcotic Addiction*, 26 J.A.M.A. 3025 (1988).

64 *See* Cooper, *Methadone Treatment and Acquired Immunodeficiency Syndrome*, 262 J.A.M.A. 1664 (1989); Kreek, *Health Consequences Associated with the Use of Methadone*, in NIDA Monograph No. ADM 83–1281, note 59 above, at 456; The TOPS Study, note 56 above, at 5.

65 *See* McLellan, *et al.*, *Is Treatment for Substance Abuse Effective?* 247 J.A.M.A. 1423 (1982).

66 *See* Simpson, note 58 above, at 33.

67 *See* Cooper, note 64 above, at 1664; Dole, *Methadone Treatment and the Acquired Immunodeficiency Syndrome Epidemic*, 262 J.A.M.A. 1681 (1989).

68 Within the first three months of treatment, only 14 percent of new methadone patients drop out, while 40–50 percent drop out in other modalities. *Id.*

69 *See* Ball, *et al.*, *Reducing the Risk of AIDS Through Methadone Maintenance Treatment*, 29 J. Health & Soc. Behav. 214 (1988).

70 *See* Cooper, note 64 above, at 1665.

71 D'Amico, *Methadone Treatment and Acquired Immunodeficiency Syndrome*, 263 J.A.M.A. 658 (1990); *see* Kirn, *Methadone Maintenance Treatment Remains Controversial Even After 23 Years of Experience*, 260 J.A.M.A. 2970 (1988).

72 *See* Senay, *Methadone Maintenance Treatment*, 20 Int'l J. Addiction 803 (1985).

73 Rosenthal, *Methadone Clone: A Bad Quick Fix*, N.Y. Times, July 1, 1989, at 23; *see* Cooper, note 64 above, at 1665.

74 *See* Anglin, Brecht & Maddahian, *Pretreatment Characteristics and Treatment Performance of Legally Coerced versus Voluntary Methadone Maintenance Admissions*, 27 Criminology 537 (1989); Leukefeld & Tims, *Compulsory Treatment: A Review of Findings*, in National Instute on Drug Abuse, U.S. Dep't of Health and Human Services, NIDA Monograph No. 86, Compulsory Treatment: Research and Clinical Practice 236 (1988) [hereinafter NIDA Monograph No. 86]; *see also* Anglin, *The Efficacy of Civil Commitment in Treating Narcotic Addiction*, in NIDA Monograph No. 86, above, at 31–32; Maddux, *Clinical Experience with Civil Commitment*, in NIDA Monograph No. 86, above, at 35.

75 Anglin, *The Efficacy of Civil Commitment in Treating Narcotics Addiction*, 18 J. Drug Issues 527 (1988); Anglin & McGlothlin, *Outcome of Narcotic Addict Treatment in California*, in NIDA Monograph No. 51, note 58 above, at 109; Bursten, *Post-Hospital Mandatory Outpatient Treatment*, 143 Am. J. Psychiatry 1255 (1988); Herrington, *Outpatient Commitment: A Care Option Offering Structured Therapy with Less Restriction*, Psychiatric News, Feb. 7, 1986, at 7; Inciardi, *Compulsory Treatment in New York: A Brief Narrative History of Misjudgment, Mismanagement, and Misrepresentation*, 18 J. Drug Issues 547 (1988); Lindblad, *Civil Commitment Under the Federal Narcotic Addict Rehabilitation Act*, 18 J. Drug Issues 595 (1988); NIDA Monograph No. 86, note 74 above; Rosenthal, *The Constitutionality of Involuntary Civil Commitment of Opiate Addicts*, 18 J. Drug Issues 641 (1988); Winick, *Some Policy Implications of the New York State Civil Commitment Program*, 18 J. Drug Issues 561 (1988). *See generally* W. McGlothlin & M. Anglin, Compulsory Treatment of Opiate Dependence (1988).

76 *See, e.g.*, Ala. Code § 12–23–7 (Supp. 1991); Neb. Rev. Stat. § 29–2262(4) (Supp. 1991).

77 Leukefeld & Tims, note 74 above, at 239–40. *See generally* E. Wish, M. Toborg & J. Ballassai, Identifying Drug Users and Monitoring Them During Conditional Release: Issues and Practices (1988); M. Stitzer & M. McCaul, Criminal Justice Interventions with Drug and Alcohol Abusers: The Role of Compulsory Treatment (1987); NIDA Monograph No. 86, note 74 above.

78 *See* Cook & Weinman, *Treatment Alternatives to Street Crime,* in NIDA Monograph No. 86, note 74 above, at 99; Hubbard, *et al., The Criminal Justice Client in Drug Abuse Treatment,* in NIDA Monograph No. 86, note 74 above, at 57.

79 J. Baglin, The Impact of the Federal Drug Aftercare Program 5–6 (Federal Judicial Center 1986); H. Wexler, A Model Prison Rehabilitation Program: An Evaluation of the "Stay'n Out" Therapeutic Community (1988); Anglin, Brecht & Maddahian, note 74 above, at 553–54; Hubbard, *et al., The Criminal Justice Client in Drug Abuse Treatment,* in NIDA Monograph No. 86, note 74 above, at 76; Platt, Perry & Metzger, *The Evaluation of a Heroin Addiction Treatment Program within a Correctional Program,* in Effective Correctional Treatment (R. Ross & P. Gendreau eds. 1980); *see also* Leukefeld & Tims, note 74 above, at 238. *See generally* Treatment Options, note 55 above, at 9.

80 National Association of State Alcohol and Drug Abuse Directors, Treatment Works: A Review of 15 Years of Research Findings on Alcohol and Other Drug Abuse Treatment Options 3 (1990) [hereinafter Treatment Works].

81 *See* The White House, National Drug Control Strategy: Budget Summary (1990) [hereinafter Budget Summary]; The White House, note 14 above.

82 *See* Brecher, *Needles and the Conscience of a Nation,* note 12 above, at 5–6; Budget Summary, note 81 above.

83 Brown, *et al., The Functioning of Individuals on a Drug Abuse Treatment Waiting List,* 15 Am. J. Drug & Alcohol Abuse 261 (1989); National Commission on Acquired Immunodeficiency Syndrome, note 36 above, at 7–10; Treatment Works, note 108 above, at app. I.; U.S. Conference of Mayors, The Anti-Drug Abuse Act of 1986: Its Impact in Cities One Year After Enactment—A 42-City Survey 1 (1987); *see* J. Petersilia, Which Inmates Participate in Prison Treatment Programs? 7 (1978); J. Petersilia & P. Honig, The Prison Experience of Career Criminals 32 (1980); *see also* Kerr, *U.S. Drug "Crusade" is Seen as Undermining Itself,* N.Y. Times, Oct. 26, 1987, at A1; Malcolm, *In Making Drug Strategy No Accord on Treatment,* N.Y. Times, Nov. 19, 1989, at A1.

84 Treatment Works, note 80 above, at 25; National Commission on Acquired Immunodeficiency Syndrome, note 36 above, at app. A.

85 *See* Fox, *The Cost of AIDS: Exaggeration, Entitlement, and Economics,* in AIDS and the Health Care System 197 (L. Gostin ed. 1990).

86 V. Tabbush, The Effectiveness and Efficiency of Publicly Funded Drug Abuse Treatment and Prevention Programs in California: A Benefit Cost Analysis 94 (1986); The TOPS Study, note 56 above.

87 The White House, note 14 above, at 3.

88 *See* Bailey, *Cocaine Detection During Toxicology Screening of a University Medical Center Patient Population,* 25 J. Clinical Toxicology 71 (1987); Gordin, *et al., Prevalence of the Human Immunodeficiency Virus and Hepatitis B Virus in Unselected Hospital Admissions: Implications for Mandatory Testing and Universal Precautions,* 161 J. Infectious Diseases 14 (1990); Kelen, DiGiovanna & Bisson, *Human Immunodeficiency Virus Infections in Emergency Department Patients,* 262 J.A.M.A. 518 (1989); Lindenbaum, *et al., Patterns of Alcohol and Drug Abuse in an Urban Trauma Center: The Increasing Role of Cocaine Abuse,* 29 J. Trauma 1654 (1989); Marzuk, *et al., Prevalence of Recent Cocaine Use among Motor Vehicle Fatalities* *in New York City,* 263 J.A.M.A. 250 (1990); St. Louis, *et al., Seroprevalence Rates of Human Immunodeficiency Virus Infection at Sentinel Hospitals in the United States,* 323 New Eng. J. Med. 213 (1990); Soderstrom, *et al., HIV Infection Rates in a Trauma Center Treating Predominantly Rural Blunt Trauma Victims,* 29 J. Trauma 1526 (1989).

89 *See, e.g.,* Bigby, *Substance Abuse Education During Internal Medicine Training,* 74 J. Gen. Internal Med. 74 (1989); Fassler, *Views of Medical Students and Residents on Education in Alcohol and Drug Abuse,* 60 J. Med. Educ. 562 (1985); Helwick, *Substance Abuse Education in Medical School: Past, Present, and Future,* 60 J. Med. Educ. 707 (1985); Kennedy, *Chemical Dependency: A Treatable Disease,* 81 Ohio St. Med. J. 77 (1985); Lewis & Gordon, *Alcoholism and the General Hospital: The Roger Williams Intervention Program,* 59 Bull. N.Y. Acad. Med. 181 (1983). *See generally* Gottlieb, Mullen & McAlister, *Patients' Substance Abuse and the Primary Care Physician: Patterns of Practice,* 12 Addictive Behav. 23 (1987).

90 21 C.F.R. § 291 (1990) (the Methadone Regulation).

91 U.S. Dep't of Health & Human Services, FDA & NIDA, *Methadone in Maintenance and Detoxification: Joint Revision of Conditions for Use,* 54 Fed. Reg. 8954, 8973–74 (1989) (to be codified at 21 C.F.R. § 291).

92 *Urine Testing for Drug Use among Male Arrestees—United States 1989,* 38 MMWR 780 (1989); *see also* National Institute of Justice, *DUF: Drug Use Forecasting* (1989) (the incidence of cocaine use tripled in two years).

93 Bureau of Justice Statistics, U.S. Dep't of Justice, Drugs and Crime Facts 1989, at 5.

94 Vidgal & Stadler, *Controlling Inmate Drug Use Cut Consumption by Reducing Demand,* Corrections Today, June 1990, at 96; *see also* Carvell & Hart, *Risk Behaviours for HIV Infection among Drug Users in Prison,* 300 Brit. Med. J. 1383 (1989).

95 F. Tims, Drug Abuse Treatment in Prisons 13 (National Institute on Drug Abuse, Research Report No. ADM 86–1149, 1981, reprinted 1986).

III HIV in the Public Sector

9 HIV Screening & Discrimination: The Federal Example

Donna I. Dennis

In four settings over which it exercises complete control—the military, the Foreign Service, the Job Corps, and immigration policy—the United States government has required HIV testing and has excluded, restricted, or expelled people who test positive for HIV antibodies. This chapter will describe in detail each of the government's HIV screening programs and the legal challenges to them.

A theme pervading the federal government's response to HIV is the contrast between what it advises for and requires of others and what it does itself as employer and program administrator. The most striking manifestation of this theme is the government's rejection of the advice of its own public health officials, including the surgeon general, the Centers for Disease Control (CDC), and the secretary of health and human services. Although those experts have argued that mandatory testing, nonconsensual disclosure of personal medical information, and categorical exclusion or restriction of HIV-infected men and women are not only unnecessary but in fact create the wrong incentives for safeguarding both individual and public health, these are the HIV measures that federal agencies have embraced.[1]

Similarly, the government's policies conflict with its professed support of antidiscrimination laws for people with disabilities. Announcing his approval of the expansive protections afforded people with AIDS and HIV by the Americans with Disabilities Act (ADA), President Bush declared: "We're in a fight against a disease—not a fight against people. And we will not and must not in America tolerate discrimination."[2] Yet the government's treatment of people with HIV within its ranks does not mesh with the ADA, a sweeping law that, beginning in July 1992, will prohibit discrimination on the basis of disability by any employer with more than twenty-five employees.

The government's HIV policies do not even implement the current federal law that prohibits federal agencies and recipients of federal funding from dis-

187

criminating against people with disabilities, or those perceived to be disabled, and that calls on the federal government to undertake affirmative action on their behalf.[3] As interpreted by the United States Supreme Court and lower federal courts, the Rehabilitation Act (1) bars discrimination against people who are disabled, or are regarded as disabled, who can perform the essential elements of a job or program; (2) requires an individualized, case-by-case assessment of whether people with disabilities are otherwise qualified; (3) prohibits the disqualification of disabled people on alleged grounds of safety unless their employment or program participation poses a significant risk to the safety of others or a probability of substantial, imminent harm to themselves; and (4) in the event that some disabled people cannot perform the essential functions of a job or program, requires reasonable accommodations, including modification of equipment and work schedules, that would enable them to do so. Most important, the Supreme Court has admonished that courts (and therefore, by implication, employers and program administrators covered by the Act) "should defer to the medical judgments of public health officials."[4] As I will show, the federal government has violated each of those strictures with alarming frequency.

The government's pattern of non-acquiescence to its own public health experts and to basic principles of nondiscrimination has been viewed sympathetically by the federal judiciary. Some courts have struck down state and local efforts to screen employees for HIV or to restrict HIV-infected people within the workplace because the measures were contrary to public health wisdom and were discriminatory.[5] But courts have been reluctant to apply the same level of scrutiny to federal HIV policies. Instead, judges have left a record of complicity with the government's strong-arm tactics. Indeed, the cases contesting federal HIV screening procedures, procedures which to date have withstood every legal challenge, provide a clear and disturbing picture of a statist orientation within the judiciary. This orientation must change if future attacks on the government's HIV policies are to succeed.

I conclude with a brief exploration of the intersections between the HIV screening programs discussed here and historical patterns of official discrimination, particularly against gay people. Just as one cannot understand the federal government's continued ability to weed out HIV-positive people without noting exceptional judicial deference, one cannot fully comprehend its desire to do so without considering its longstanding resistance to allowing anyone to represent the United States who does not conform to a narrow and exclusive definition of what it means to be an American.

THE MILITARY

Mandatory Testing, Exclusion, and Reassignment

The armed forces' HIV program began innocuously enough on March 13, 1985, when the director of the Military Blood Program ordered his personnel to test all donated blood for HIV. The director's order, however, went on to require civilian blood agencies to report to military authorities the names of servicemembers who tested positive. On August 30, 1985, the Department of Defense (DOD) ordered testing of all applicants for the armed services, including the National Guard, the reserves, advanced ROTC programs, and military academies. At that time, the DOD did not disclose what would happen to recruits who tested positive.[6]

Shortly thereafter, on October 24, 1985, Defense Secretary Casper Weinberger issued a memorandum expanding the military's screening program to include all 2.1 million active duty personnel. He also provided the first detailed description of the military's HIV policy. Under Secretary Weinberger's orders, recruits who tested positive were to be denied entry to the armed forces. This exclusion was justified on the grounds that (1) HIV infection existed prior to service; (2) the DOD would avoid potential medical costs and the possibility that infected recruits would not complete their service commitments; (3) HIV-infected recruits might be harmed by immunizations administered in basic training; (4) HIV-infected people would be unable to participate in battlefield blood transfusions or other blood donation programs; and (5) it was impossible to distinguish between HIV-positive people who would develop AIDS and those who would remain healthy.[7] According to the same orders, enlisted personnel who tested positive were to be referred for medical evaluations. Those who manifested no signs of clinical illness or immunological deficiency would be retained, but their assignments could be limited in order to protect the health and safety of themselves as well as of others. Personnel with clinical symptoms of AIDS would be medically retired.

On August 25, 1986, the DOD expanded its policy by beginning to expel seropositive students already enrolled in officer candidate programs, ROTC programs, and service academies. Recoupment of scholarships and the like was prohibited only if HIV was the *sole* reason for expulsion. (The narrowness of this prohibition reflects the DOD's recent practice of requiring gay students forced to leave ROTC programs to return scholarship money.[8])

On April 20, 1987, Secretary Weinberger issued a revised memorandum on HIV policy, which expanded the restrictions on HIV-infected servicemembers to prohibit them from being stationed overseas. In addition, it barred members of the reserves who tested positive from extended active duty (duty for more than thirty days), except in time of mobilization and on the decision of the secretary of the military department concerned. Reservists not on active duty who could not be used by the Selected Reserves were to be involuntarily transferred to the Standby Reserves, with concomitant loss of certain benefits. The memorandum also instituted contact tracing. Medical personnel were encouraged to ask servicemembers to identify any people they might have exposed to HIV. The secretary required that the names of civilian contacts be released to civilian health authorities unless local law prohibited release. Military contacts were to be traced by the military, counseled about the possibility of HIV infection, and tested without any requirement of consent.[9]

On August 4, 1988, the deputy secretary of defense renewed the HIV policies set forth in the 1987 Weinberger memorandum. The 1988 memorandum also enacted a contact-tracing procedure for the reserves, which allowed military doctors to contact the spouses of reservists who tested positive. On December 29, 1988, the DOD issued final rules extending the compulsory testing program to civilian DOD employees who were assigned or being moved to countries that required HIV testing. People who tested positive would be either barred from the country or reported to local health authorities, as specified by the host nation.[10]

On April 16, 1991, the DOD published its complete policy on AIDS and HIV in the form of rules in the Federal Register.[11] The rules continue the HIV screening programs set forth in prior administrative memoranda. However, they offer no rationale for the policies, including the categorical exclusion of HIV-positive recruits, nor for the stark contrast between those policies and the views of government public health officials who oppose the blanket exclusion or restriction of HIV-infected people in other settings. Presumably, the military intends to rely on the justifications offered when it first formulated its screening programs. Yet those justifications, superficially plausible in 1985, do not withstand any level of scrutiny now.

The military's first rationale—that HIV infection existed prior to service—only begs the question of whether the infection by itself impairs performance in a way that warrants categorical exclusion. The second argument—that HIV-infected people must be rejected to avoid potential medical costs and the possibility that they would not complete their service commitments—is weightier. That claim, however, is seriously undercut by recent medical data. Because of HIV's prolonged latency period (a time continually extended by the development of drugs to prevent the occurrence of disease), most recruits who test positive and are asymptomatic will be able to fulfill their service commitments in good health and without incurring abnormally high medical costs. (See chapter 2.) Denying employment to an entire category of military personnel because a few among them might not complete their tours of duty is an overzealous and unduly restrictive response.

The military's concern that HIV-positive recruits might be harmed by vaccines given at basic training could certainly be addressed in a less drastic manner. Nor can the military justify its blanket exclusion of otherwise healthy HIV-positive recruits on the ground that they will contaminate the military blood supply. The armed forces have screened all blood for HIV since 1985. During the Persian Gulf war, the Army used civilian blood agencies to procure the blood necessary for casualties so that it would not need emergency blood donations from active servicemembers.[12]

Finally, the military's inability to determine which people will eventually develop AIDS—essentially a restatement of its second argument—is not a rational justification for excluding HIV-positive recruits. After all, it is impossible to determine whether any particular recruit will remain free of serious illness during military service. The fact that some people with HIV may develop AIDS during their tours of duty does not warrant an irrebuttable presumption that every HIV-infected applicant is unfit.

Similarly, the military's broadly articulated interests in evaluating the condition of servicemembers and preserving force readiness cannot justify the blanket ban on overseas service for currently enlisted servicemembers who are infected. The military already monitors the medical condition and HIV status of service personnel while they are stationed abroad, just as it must be concerned with the medical condition of personnel stationed at home. Although medical evidence does not support the military's view that asymptomatic people are so impaired as to impede the readiness of their units, HIV infection may in some cases progress to clinical illness and limit a servicemember's capacities. Those circumstances, however, can be dealt with as they arise and do not require a blanket limitation.

Thus, none of the military's justifications warrant its all-encompassing policy of exclusion and reassignment. Its policies not only contradict the advice of public health experts by presumptively restricting the activities of HIV-positive men and women, but they also undermine a principle that the government otherwise professes to support: that people with disabilities should have the opportunity to work so long as they are able, with reasonable accommodation, to perform the essential functions of the job.

Lack of Confidentiality

The military's policies also conflict with the views of public health officials by failing to protect the confidentiality of personal HIV information. The DOD's contact-tracing program provides an obvious route for the disclosure of seropositivity. Furthermore, the memoranda instituting HIV testing nowhere require or even encourage medical authorities to keep their patients' HIV status confidential. In fact, servicemembers' medical files, which include HIV test results, are routinely sent without their permission to the office of their commanders, where anyone with access to files can readily learn who is HIV positive. To make matters worse, some commanding officers apparently have exposed the status of servicemembers by conspicuously reassigning them to menial tasks, housing them in special HIV-only barracks, and tolerating public harassment.[13]

An even more serious problem for HIV-infected servicemembers is the lack of protection provided for their disclosures to doctors of drug use or homosexual activity. Under military law, both homosexuality and drug use are grounds for dishonorable discharge and even court-martial. A discharge that is less than honorable may result not only in life-long stigma, but also in loss of veterans' benefits, including care in a Veterans Administration hospital.[14]

When faced with discharge or court-martial, servicemembers who have tested positive have understandably been reluctant to tell their doctors how they acquired HIV infection. To encourage disclosure, the 1985 Weinberger memorandum ordered that the results of HIV tests, and admissions of drug use or sexual activity made in post-test interviews, could not be used to procure a dishonorable discharge or to punish a servicemember in a court-martial under the Uniform Code of Military Justice. Yet information about homosexuality or drug use gained in epidemiological interviews could still trigger an honorable discharge, either on grounds of medical disability or under a catchall clause permitting discharge "for the convenience of the Government." As a result, it became quite common for patients to confess homosexuality to doctors who promised them confidentiality, only to find themselves administratively discharged "for the convenience of the Government" as soon as the information was passed along to their commanders.[15]

In the fall of 1986, widespread reports that many servicemembers were not being candid about the sources of their HIV infection prompted Congress to intervene. As part of the Defense Authorization Act, Congress prohibited any "adverse personnel action" based on information disclosed by HIV-positive servicemembers during HIV-related medical evaluations. Adverse action was defined as a court-martial, nonjudicial punishment, involuntary separation for other than medical reasons, administrative or punitive reduction in grade, denial of promotion, unfavorable entry in a personnel record, bar to reenlistment, and any other action considered by the secretary to be adverse.[16]

Following the law's passage, Secretary Weinberger revised his HIV policy to incorporate the additional limits on the use of information elicited during epidemiological interviews. Not surprisingly, the provisions of the resulting 1987 Weinberger memorandum, which remain in effect today, largely circumvent the Congressional ban by creating a new category of purportedly "non-adverse" personnel actions. Those non-adverse actions include reassignment, denial or revocation of a security clearance, suspension or termination of access to classified information, and removal from flight status or "other duties requiring a high degree of stability or alertness such as explosive ordnance disposal or deep-sea diving." In addition, the military continues to permit military commanders to receive the medical files of their subordinates and to instigate "independent" investigations into the sexual practices or drug use of anyone who tests positive for HIV. The investigations can lead to the full array of available penalties, including dishonorable discharge or court-martial. In the Navy, for example, the commander of any seropositive person who is retained receives a letter containing instructions on how to handle the individual. It reads: "Ensure the member is aware he is being retained on active duty despite statistics which indicate that 90 percent of all individuals having the HIV antibody are homosexual or drug abusers. He is not being labeled as such unless his actions reflect otherwise. If his actions reflect such behavior, he will be subject to disciplinary action and/or administrative separation."[17]

Segregation

One of the most egregious manifestations of the military's quest to cleanse itself of HIV came to light in 1989, with reports of a segregated barracks for HIV-infected soldiers at Fort Hood, Texas. The commanding officer at Fort Hood ordered approximately fifty of the seventy soldiers who tested positive after a periodic screening to be moved from their units to the third floor of one of the barracks. Soldiers at Fort Hood said that the building was commonly referred to as "HIV hotel" and "the leper colony." The HIV-infected soldiers also charged that the military police scrutinized their behavior with extra vigor and searched their property for evidence of homosexuality. A report by the Office of the Inspector General confirmed that the base commander at Fort Hood removed HIV-infected soldiers from their duties and reassigned them to sweeping floors and mopping latrines. The report also found that commanding officers allowed the infected soldiers to be publicly harassed, a situation that drove one of them to attempt suicide. The negative publicity appears, for now at least, to have halted the segregation of HIV-infected soldiers at Fort Hood.[18]

Court-Martial

The 1987 Weinberger memorandum introduced a provision permitting the dishonorable discharge or court-martial of servicemembers for noncompliance with "lawfully ordered preventive medicine procedures." Although the military instructs medical personnel to counsel servicemembers on how to avoid HIV transmission, the "cornerstone of the military's AIDS policy" has become the issuance of safe-sex orders to infected personnel by their commanding officers.[19]

The standard order, individually given to seropositive servicemembers, requires them to inform all prospective sexual partners, medical personnel, and dental care providers of their HIV status. It also commands them to avoid any exchange of blood or bodily fluids, including saliva (which is not thought to be an effective vehicle for transmission), during sex. Those who have violated the orders have been vigorously prosecuted and severely punished, not only for disobeying an order but for reckless endangerment and aggravated assault by means likely to produce death or grievous bodily harm. Convictions have resulted in sentences of up to six years in military prison.[20]

Although the military's emphasis on punishment is not unusual or surprising, the vindictiveness animating some of its prosecutions in the context of HIV clearly falls beyond the pale. A memorandum addressed to military prosecutors from the Trial Counsel Assistance Program posed this question: "Anxious to take on an AIDS case? . . . Your smorgasbord of possible charges includes sodomy, of course, but the more adventurous of you will want to see if an assault or order-violation (failure to follow 'safe-sex' procedures) specification fits your facts." The instruction concludes: "Consider scoring early points with members or judge by having surgical gloves and masks ready for their use in the courtroom. Good hunting, and remember, even if the accused is acquitted, you'll still get the death penalty."[21]

Marine Sergeant John Roantes is one of those who has been hunted. He was charged with reckless endangerment, willful disobedience of an order, and making a false official statement. These charges carried a sentence of more than twelve years in military prison, forfeiture of pay, and dishonorable discharge. His alleged crime: failing to disclose to a dental hygienist, who wore gloves and a mask while cleaning his teeth, that he had tested positive for HIV. Although Sergeant Roantes eventually was permitted to plead guilty to the charge of disobeying an order, his original indictment illustrates the often irrational and draconian nature of the military's response to HIV.[22]

The Military's Policies in the Courts

Legal challenges to the military's HIV policies face substantial obstacles, which derive largely from the courts' habit of reflexively acceding to the federal government within the broadly defined arena of military policy. The federal judiciary views the armed forces as a "specialized society separate from civilian society," which relies "of necessity on a hierarchical structure of discipline and obedience to command."[23] According to this view, the separateness of military society and its need for discipline justify intense regulation of the individual, which the military carries out through a separate system of military justice and a separate criminal code, the Uniform Code of Military Justice. The solicitude shown by the federal courts has allowed the armed forces to devise personnel policies unfettered by constitutional or statutory concerns for individual rights.

To avoid interfering with military policies, courts often resort to the device of jurisdiction. Federal judges scrupulously require servicemembers to exhaust internal military remedies before they will hear servicemembers' claims.[24] Even then, the courts often refuse to entertain constitutional arguments or statutory claims of discrimination out of deference to the military's alleged need to manage its own affairs.[25] If and when servicemembers do get their day in federal court, judges usually defer without much analysis to the military's routine assertion of its need to intrude on individual rights in order to preserve discipline or combat readiness. The courts have upheld the armed forces' right to discipline or remove servicemembers for wearing yarmulkes,[26] for circulating petitions without permission of a base commander,[27] or for homosexuality,[28] all in honor of the military's special status and its need to "foster instinctive obedience, unity, commitment and esprit de corps."[29]

The military's HIV employment policies have been reviewed in only three cases. The first of these involved Robert Plowman, a civilian who worked as a music specialist for the Army Moral Support Fund in South Korea. In April 1986, he was admitted to the Army infirmary for treatment of an injury, and his blood was tested for HIV without his knowledge. An Army doctor reported Plowman's positive test result to Plowman's commander, and he in turn discussed Plowman's HIV status with four other Army officials. The commander then convened a meeting with Plowman and those four officials. Allegedly he forced Plowman to resign by threatening to notify South Korean civilian authorities of his condition. In *Plowman v. Department of the Army*, Plowman raised two important issues: (1) does nonconsensual testing of civilians violate their Fourth Amendment right to be free of unreasonable searches? and (2) does the constitutional right of privacy require the

Army to keep the personal medical information of civilian employees confidential?[30] (For more on these rights, see chapter 7.)

The court disposed of Plowman's claims without truly addressing either one. Under the doctrine of "qualified immunity," a government official cannot be liable for violating someone's constitutional rights unless it was "clearly established" in earlier court decisions that the sort of thing the official did was illegal. If the official could reasonably believe what he or she was doing was legal, the official cannot be sued even if the belief was incorrect. By resorting to qualified immunity as a basis for its decision, a court can focus on what a defendant thought rather than on what the law requires. In Plowman's case, the court granted the defendant qualified immunity because, even though other courts had found constitutional violations under similar circumstances, the rights to be free of involuntary HIV testing and disclosure in the military context were not so clearly established that the defendant should have respected them. Indeed, the court, on the basis of scant evidence and the Army's declarations, opined that patient screening to protect health care workers was a "medical necessity," and that the disclosure was "no broader than reasonably necessary to determine how to proceed in a sensitive situation."[31]

In accepting the government's superficial and unsupported rationalizations for the testing and disclosure, the court did not require the military to explain why it was departing from the position of leading public health authorities that testing patients is a poor way to protect health care workers.[32] Nor did the court require the government to explain exactly what was "sensitive" about a civilian employee in a music and theater morale program having HIV, why any action on the part of the commander was called for, and therefore why it was necessary for the commander to tell anyone else at all.

The military's policy of excluding HIV-infected people from service came under attack (but again, not much scrutiny) in Doe v. Garrett.[33] Doe was a Navy recruiter whom the Navy refused to reenlist for active duty after he had tested positive for HIV. At the time, Doe was healthy, had no symptoms of AIDS, and possessed a superior record of service as a recruiter. He challenged the Navy's decision primarily as a violation of the Rehabilitation Act, which prohibits discrimination on the basis of HIV "in any program or activity conducted by any Executive agency" of the federal government.[34] (For more on the Rehabilitation Act, see chapter 13.)

A threshold question of tremendous importance to Doe, and to other HIV-infected servicemembers, was whether members of the armed forces could avail themselves of the protections of the Rehabilitation Act. Even though the clear language of the Act itself makes no exception for uniformed military personnel, both the trial and appellate courts chose to follow court decisions under Title VII (the separate federal statute banning employment discrimination on the basis of race, religion, sex, or national origin) that have excluded servicemembers from coverage.[35] In addition, the appeals court declared itself bound by an earlier case which had held that the military's statutory authority to prescribe qualifications for service overrides servicemembers' rights to nondiscrimination under the Act.[36]

As a second line of attack, Doe argued that the Navy's refusal to reenlist him violated his right to procedural due process under the United States Constitution. The district court refused to exercise jurisdiction over Doe's constitutional claim, holding that a review of the Navy's HIV policy "would constitute a significant and ill-advised intrusion into the sensitive realm of the military personnel decision-making process."[37] In the court's view, the military should have exclusive power to determine physical requirements for service, including the power to conclude that HIV-infected people are not qualified for active duty, no matter how little that conclusion comports with medical fact. By reading servicepeople out of the Rehabilitation Act and declining jurisdiction over Doe's constitutional claims, *Doe v. Garrett* made the military's policy of weeding out HIV-positive personnel virtually immune from constitutional or statutory review.

Doe v. Marsh upheld restrictions on the training and assignments of HIV-positive men and women. Doe, an HIV-positive soldier, was stripped of the opportunity to change his military specialty from ammunitions to construction, solely because of his HIV test results. As in *Doe v. Garrett,* the court refused to consider Doe's Rehabilitation Act claim on the ground that the Act did not give uniformed military personnel a right to sue.[38]

Although the court did hear Doe's constitutional claim, it subjected the Army policy to the most deferential standard of review, accepting on its face the Army's assertion that the limitation on schooling was "designed to ensure a systematic evaluation and study of the natural progression of the disease." The court did not require the Army to produce any evidence that its policy was in fact a rational means of advancing its stated scientific goals, but simply accepted the Army's discrimination as "rational and, indeed, salutary." Once again, a court validated governmental HIV restrictions in the absence of a demonstrated medical basis for the policy.[39]

THE FOREIGN SERVICE

On November 22, 1986, the Department of State became the second government agency to commence forced HIV testing. Its policy requires HIV screening for all applicants, as well as all Foreign Service employees who seek to qualify or who have qualified for worldwide service. Family members of those who have qualified to go overseas are also tested. Any applicant who tests positive is rejected for employment. Current members of the Foreign Service who test positive and are asymptomatic, or who have spouses or dependent children who test positive, are barred from most posts outside the United States. Employees with signs of clinical illness or immune suppression, or with family members having those characteristics, are barred altogether from service abroad. The State Department also rejects applicants for the Peace Corps who test positive.[40]

The Foreign Service was the target of the first legal challenge to a federal screening policy. In *Local 1812, American Federation of Government Employees v. Department of State*, the Foreign Service officers' union sought a preliminary injunction against the State Department, contending that mandatory testing violated its members' constitutional rights to privacy and freedom from unreasonable searches. Local 1812 further argued that the restrictions on assignments of HIV-positive members contravened the Rehabilitation Act. Judge Gesell of the United States District Court for the District of Columbia denied Local 1812's request to stop the testing.[41]

The court evaluated the union's constitutional objections in light of the competing interests of the employees and the government. As a threshold matter, the court viewed as minimal the intrusion created by adding an HIV test to the extensive battery of medical tests already required for officers and their families. According to the government, its interest lay in protecting the health of employees and their "fitness for duty in a specialized government agency." Because the State Department's asserted interests did not relate to the prevention of HIV transmission, Local 1812's medical evidence that mandatory testing did not promote public health was deemed irrelevant. The court went on to rule that the government's interest in imposing HIV testing outweighed the already limited privacy interests of its employees.[42]

The court gave short shrift to the union's Rehabilitation Act claim. Under the Act, federal agencies may not limit the employment of people with disabilities who are otherwise qualified; to be "otherwise qualified" is to be able to perform the essential functions of the job. The Act also requires federal employers to make reasonable accommodations, such as restructuring jobs or providing additional equipment, to enable disabled people to perform these essential functions. Local 1812 argued that because asymptomatic HIV-positive people were currently able to perform their assignments and could remain healthy for years, they were "otherwise qualified" for their two- or three-year tours of duty overseas. The State Department, however, did not contend that seropositivity had an adverse effect on the current work performance of infected employees, but that service in areas where poor medical conditions prevailed would endanger the HIV-infected workers themselves. The court agreed. It held that the additional risk of harm that HIV-infected people would face as a result of overseas service, through the possibility of contracting exotic diseases at foreign posts or receiving inadequate medical treatment at remote stations, was sufficiently great to render them unqualified for worldwide duty. The court therefore found the government's concern for employee safety sufficient to justify excluding HIV-positive applicants altogether and barring current HIV-positive members from most overseas posts. The court further ruled that the accommodation necessary to render HIV-infected employees qualified for overseas duty, such as upgrading medical care at foreign posts, was more than the Rehabilitation Act required.[43]

Local 1812 provides another illustration of the state-centered orientation of the judiciary in federal HIV cases. The court uncritically accepted the State Department's medical evidence that foreign employment could be dangerous to HIV-infected officers, even though medical experts produced by Local 1812 sharply contested that conclusion. In particular, the court relied heavily on evidence of the harmful misdiagnosis of two cases of AIDS in foreign posts. Yet the court failed to consider evidence offered by Local 1812 that misdiagnoses of AIDS were highly unlikely after the first few years of the epidemic, when even U.S. doctors had misdiagnosed symptoms. While focusing on the State Department's worst-case scenarios, the court took little notice of the wide-ranging medical evidence adduced by Local 1812 showing that most HIV-infected people, whether at home or abroad, remain asymptomatic and fully capable of fulfilling their employment obligations for many years after infection.[44]

In authorizing the government's HIV screening procedures, the court also ignored settled rules of law. First, the court's validation of the government's categorical exclusion of infected applicants and limitation of assignments for infected servicemembers flies in the face of the well-established rule that employers should undertake *individualized* assessments of whether disabled people are "otherwise qualified" to perform particular jobs. Indeed, Congress's recognition that adverse employment decisions should not be based on generalized assumptions lies at the heart of the Rehabilitation Act.[45] Local 1812's lapse in applying the correct legal standard is particularly striking in view of the fact that the government did not demonstrate that most of the HIV-positive individuals denied jobs or overseas posts would suffer a significantly greater risk of serious harm than other employees as a result of health conditions in foreign posts.

Since the Foreign Service always requires a comprehensive physical examination prior to overseas assignment, the government's purported concern for employee safety could easily be addressed on a case-by-case basis at minimal extra cost. If an examination revealed that a particular diplomat was extremely vulnerable to opportunistic infections found abroad, that person could then be barred from overseas service or, if already stationed overseas, returned to the United States. Any inconvenience caused by transferring employees to posts with sophisticated medical care in the event they become ill should fall within the general duty to make reasonable accommodations imposed by the Rehabilitation Act, and especially within a federal employer's special duty to take affirmative steps to accommodate disabled workers.[46]

The court's analysis in *Local 1812* is flawed in another respect. Permitting an employer to deny employment based on the mere possibility of future illness undermines the Rehabilitation Act's premise that qualified disabled people should be permitted to work. Other courts have carefully scrutinized employer claims of this sort in order to avoid "allowing remote concerns to legitimize discrimination . . . [and to] vitiate the effectiveness of section 504 of the Act."[47] Specifically, employers seeking to deny or restrict employment on safety grounds have been required to make a case-by-case evaluation of the work and medical history of each disabled applicant or employee, along with an individual finding that no reasonable accommodation would allow the person to perform the essential functions of the job without a "reasonable probability of substantial, imminent harm."[48] Abstract generalizations about the possibility of future injury, such as those adduced in *Local 1812*, fall far short of the accepted standard.

Finally, one should consider whether courts should ever permit an employer to limit the opportunities of people with disabilities out of concern for their safety.[49] The danger of such a course is that employers will discriminate against workers with disabilities while professing to protect them. In *United Auto Workers v. Johnson Controls, Inc.*, a recent sex discrimination case under Title VII, the Supreme Court made clear that employment discrimination in the name of paternalism is illegal. The Court declared that employer appeals to employee safety do not justify denial of employment unless the allegedly dangerous characteristic "actually interferes with the employee's ability to perform the job."[50] In *Local 1812*, the Foreign Service failed to show that HIV infection interfered with the servicemembers' ability to perform their jobs, and the court refused to confront or even to acknowledge the grave threat that employer paternalism poses for the employment rights of people with disabilities.

THE JOB CORPS

The Job Corps is a federal program designed to provide vocational training and education to disadvantaged, inner-city teenagers so that they may become "more responsible, employable, and productive citizens."[51] On December 19, 1986, the Department of Labor joined the ranks of federal agencies conducting HIV screening by ordering the testing of all students entering residential Job Corps programs. Under the Department's initial policy, members of the Job Corps who tested positive were automatically terminated from the program. The Job Corps defended its insistence on an HIV-free environment by asserting that people from socioeconomically disadvantaged backgrounds often had a "significant history of drug use and/or sexual experimentation," and therefore were likely to transmit the virus.[52]

In response to two lawsuits filed against the program, the Department of Labor modified its policy on July 24, 1989.[53] The new policy continues to require HIV testing for Job Corps students entering residential programs and termination of those who refuse to take the test. Instead of automatically expelling corpsmembers who test positive, the Job Corps now subjects them to a battery of psychological tests, which include intensive questioning about their sexual desires and practices, in an effort to determine whether they will transmit HIV to others. Only students who pass those tests can remain in the program. Entering students who test positive, but not those who test negative, must repeat the HIV tests and psychological assessments on a quarterly basis.

In July 1988, James Dorsey sued the Department of Labor over the Job Corps' mandatory testing policy and his termination from the residential program after he tested positive.[54] After he filed his suit, the Job Corps revised its policy and readmitted him. Dorsey then amended his complaint to challenge the revised policy. He now alleges that forced HIV testing is an unreasonable search that violates the Fourth Amendment, and an invasion of his Fifth Amendment right to privacy. He also maintains that the Job Corps' HIV policy discriminates against infected corpsmembers by repeatedly subjecting them to intrusive tests and demeaning psychological evaluations, in effect placing on them the burden of disproving any theoretical possibility of harm.

Arguments in *Dorsey v. Department of Labor,* now pending in the United States District Court for the District of Columbia, have focused on whether the program is reasonable from a medical point of view. The Department of Labor cites three reasons for testing Job Corps participants: to determine whether the Job Corps can provide adequate health care; to determine whether individual HIV-positive students present a risk of transmitting the virus; and to provide psychological and medical care for HIV-infected students. Weighed against those interests, the government argues, the personal intrusion caused by the testing is minimal. (Like the Foreign Service, the Job Corps already requires blood samples from entering corpsmembers.)

The government's arguments, however, are not persuasive, particularly in an educational setting like the Job Corps. First, because HIV testing does not indicate whether students are currently suffering from any of the infections that characterize AIDS, or whether they will develop any such infections during the two-year Job Corps program, testing does not well serve the government's alleged need to determine whether its health care facilities are adequate to care for the medical conditions of students. Those who do become too ill for the Job Corps can be dismissed under generally applicable guidelines already in force.

Second, as Dorsey has asserted, medical authorities agree that coercive approaches to HIV, and mandatory testing in particular, are ineffective and, indeed, counterproductive. Furthermore, the Job Corps' resort to coerced testing would appear to conflict with its stated goal of assisting disadvantaged teenagers in becoming responsible, self-reliant adults.[55]

Third, the Job Corps has not demonstrated that it actually provides health care benefits to HIV-positive applicants that justify the intrusion caused by HIV testing. It apparently offers little in the way of constructive counseling or medication to prevent the development of clinical symptoms. In fact, according to Dorsey, psychological monitoring and repeated testing inflict harm on HIV-positive students by subjecting them to harassment and stress.[56]

The periodic testing and psychological evaluation of students who test positive, but not those who initially test negative, would also appear to run afoul of the Rehabilitation Act's prohibition of discrimination in federal programs. The Job Corps contends that the tests are necessary to ensure that HIV-positive students do not transmit the virus to others. Yet courts in other contexts have not required HIV-positive people to undergo psychological tests or to disprove every theoretical risk of transmission. Instead, they have focused on whether public health experts find a "significant risk" of harm to others.[57] The fact that the HIV-infected people in the Job Corps are from disadvantaged backgrounds should not alter the burdens imposed on them. Without evidence that a particular student has engaged in conduct that places other students at significant risk, repeated testing and surveillance of his behavior unfairly stigmatize and discriminate against him on the ground of his HIV infection. Moreover, the psychological "assessments" that the Job Corps undertakes lack the kind of predictive precision that might conceivably justify their intrusive and discriminatory impact.

In short, the Department of Labor's alleged aims do not justify, nor are they served by, the coercive and discriminatory measures it has chosen. On the contrary, data from the Job Corps testing program demonstrate that underprivileged adolescents are at increasing risk of infection, which the Corps is doing nothing to reduce.[58] The Job Corps' justification for HIV testing is even weaker than that of the Foreign Service, which at least could argue that it is a specialized agency with singular fitness requirements. The Job Corps, on the other hand, is an educational program designed to assist underprivileged teenagers. Weeding out or penalizing HIV-positive participants sends a message to disadvantaged teenagers with HIV infection that they have no chance to escape from the cycle of poverty and joblessness that programs like the Job Corps were designed to break.

THE IMMIGRATION AND NATURALIZATION SERVICE

A blatant illustration of the way in which the government has flouted the findings of its own public health experts has been the continuing controversy over whether HIV infection should be a ground for excluding aliens from this country. The issue was first joined in 1987, when Congress enacted a law, commonly known after its Senate sponsor as the Helms Amendment, requiring the exclusion of HIV-infected aliens as carriers of a "dangerous contagious disease."[59]

As a result of this classification, all immigrants were tested for HIV and those who tested positive were excluded, including applicants seeking adjustment of status to permanent residence, applicants for amnesty, and refugees.[60] Although the United States has not routinely tested non-immigrants such as tourists, students, and other travellers to the United States, those whom immigration officials learned were HIV-positive were subject to exclusion as well.

The Helms Amendment provoked a torrent of criticism from scientific and human rights authorities. The restrictions placed on international travel and temporary residency sparked particularly vehement opposition. Critics were quick to point out that the United States was much more an exporter than an importer of HIV and that casual, everyday contact with HIV-positive travellers posed no public health threat to U.S. residents.[61]

A pivotal incident in the struggle to reverse the restrictions was the exclusion in 1989 of a Dutch health educator, Hans Paul Verhoef, who was travelling to a lesbian-gay health conference. Customs officials in Minneapolis, Minnesota, discovered AZT in Verhoef's luggage and gave him the choice of leaving the country or being held in a state prison pending an exclusion hearing. Mr. Verhoef chose to resist the pressure from the Immigration and Naturalization Service (INS) to depart and instead applied for a waiver. Although the Minneapolis office initially granted Verhoef a waiver, INS headquarters overruled the local office, concluding that the public health benefits conferred by his attendance at the conference did not offset the risk he posed to public health by entering the country. The evidence inspiring that decision was apparently Mr. Verhoef's possession of sexual paraphernalia in his luggage.

Although the INS's decision was eventually reversed by an immigration judge, who approved a waiver of the HIV exclusion and ordered Verhoef admitted for three weeks upon the posting of a $10,000 bond, the spectacle of the United States preventing a person with AIDS from attending an AIDS health conference provided a powerful weapon for opponents of the U.S. policy. Widespread criticism of the INS' handling of the affair led many members of Congress to question the wisdom of excluding HIV-infected travellers, and forced the Bush administration to make waivers available to temporary visitors who sought to attend conferences, obtain medical treatment, conduct business, or visit relatives in the United States.[62] HIV-infected tourists, however, continued to be subject to exclusion.

The virtually unanimous outcry by public health and human rights authorities against the HIV exclusion led Congress to repeal the Helms Amendment in 1990. As part of the Immigration Act of 1990, Congress directed the secretary of health and human services to draw up a new list of diseases that would be grounds for excluding aliens. Seeking to remove politics and prejudice from the selection process, Congress specifically admonished Health and Human Services (HHS) that the list should contain only "communicable disease[s] of public health significance."[63]

In response to Congress, HHS Secretary Louis Sullivan proposed that only infectious tuberculosis be categorized as a "communicable disease of public health significance." Based on the advice of the nation's leading scientific experts—the CDC, the Public Health Service, the American Medical Association, and the American Public Health Association—Secretary Sullivan concluded that the entry of HIV-positive aliens would not pose a public health threat to the country. In his proposed rules, Secretary Sullivan reiterated the consensus of the public health community that casual contact does not transmit HIV and that universal education, not exclusion of HIV-infected people, is the "best defense" against AIDS.[64] In a remarkable act of defiance of both public health wisdom and the will of Congress, the Justice Department directed HHS to repeal the proposed rules and to restore HIV to the list of excludable diseases.[65] Interim regulations issued on May 31, 1991, continued testing of immigrants and exclusion of those who tested positive, pending further review of the policy.

The Bush administration initially defended the HIV exclusion on two grounds: HIV-infected aliens would spread the virus to U.S. citizens, and HIV-infected immigrants would burden the health care system.[66] Faced with the opposition of public health authorities, the Bush administration quickly abandoned any public health justification for the HIV exclusion. Instead, on August 1, 1991, government officials declared that admitting HIV-infected immigrants would be too costly for the United States, and that the INS would continue the ban on that basis alone.[67] As a practical matter, the effect of the new policy is to maintain the testing and exclusion requirements for would-be immigrants but to drop them for people seeking to enter the country temporarily.

The government's economic justification for immigrant screening has little persuasive power. The known costs of HIV testing are likely to be much greater than any potential costs imposed on the health care system by HIV-infected immigrants. The government itself estimates that only 600 out of the 600,000 or more applicants for permanent residence status each year would test positive. In 1989, only 420 would-be immigrants were barred from the United States on the grounds of HIV infection. By contrast, over a million U.S. residents are already thought to be infected.[68]

Additional evidence suggests that the cost-saving argument is a pretext for discrimination rather than a legitimate concern. Immigrants have always been required to demonstrate their ability to support themselves and to be sponsored by their families or employers. In fact, there has long been a "public charge" provision that excludes from entry individual immigrants and non-immigrants who are likely to need government assistance.[69] But the United States has never before excluded as public charges an entire class of people on the basis of the potential long-term costs of their illness. Case-by-case evaluation has always been the standard. The special treatment accorded HIV has led some members of the public health community to question whether the government is using HIV as a proxy for "a lifestyle some despise."[70]

Putting aside the wisdom of screening immigrants for HIV, the INS's administration of the program also presents cause for concern. Advocates for immigrant communities have reported that the doctors designated by the INS to give HIV tests in the United States do not provide pre- or post-test counseling, as required by law in some states, do not obtain prior, written informed consent, also required by law in some states, and do not conduct confirmatory tests of initial positive results.[71] In addition, those advocates have charged that the doctors fail to inform immigrant applicants personally of test results, disclose applicants' HIV status to third parties without their consent, and neglect to inform aliens seeking amnesty of their legal right to obtain a waiver of the HIV exclusion. These conditions are aggravated for the majority of immigrants, who are tested outside the United States and often in countries where reliable testing facilities and confidentiality protections do not exist.[72]

Immigration Cases

Whatever course immigration policy eventually takes, it is virtually certain that the judiciary will have little role in its formulation or review. As it has with the military, the judiciary has deferred reflexively to federal action in the area of immigration. The government possesses virtually unbounded power to exclude aliens from the United States, largely because the Supreme Court has not regarded aliens seeking admission as possessing any constitutional rights that could constrain government action.[73] Consequently, courts have not hesitated to uphold governmental authority to exclude aliens on health-related grounds,[74] or on the basis of any other quality deemed undesirable. Congress's authority to exclude gay aliens, for example, was long upheld by the Supreme Court,[75] although Congress itself finally repealed the exclusion as part of the Immigration Act of 1990.

Considering the absence of meaningful judicial review of government policies in the area of immigration, it is hardly surprising that no case has been brought challenging the exclusion of HIV-infected aliens from the United States. The policy's seeming immunity from legal challenge has, however, strengthened other forms of resistance, particularly boycotts and lobbying. Coordinated methods of protest and political pressure—rather than litigation—offer the best hope for lifting the HIV ban on immigration, as well as for reforming the military and other federal operations that the courts have been unwilling to touch.

CONCLUSION

The federal government has aggressively implemented a series of measures designed to purify its ranks by identifying, rooting out, or containing people with HIV. Furthermore, the federal judiciary has displayed a complete lack of commitment to restraining the government's coercive and exclusionary impulses, even allowing for its traditional deference to the executive branch.

The government's response to HIV should not be viewed in isolation, however.

It is part of a larger problem: the profound uneasiness of this nation's leaders with any deviation from what they perceive to be the normal and, indeed, the ideal American, a model that historically has been able-bodied, heterosexual, and White.[76] The government's uneasiness with any form of difference appears particularly clearly when it is in the position of choosing who may belong to groups that represent the United States in some way, such as the military, the Foreign Service, the Job Corps, and the body politic itself.

Most obviously and directly, the government's HIV policies have thwarted the struggle of people with disabilities or perceived disabilities for full integration into the social and economic life of this country. Yet the federal response to HIV is also a forceful reminder that this nation's ideal of the citizen continues to exclude one of the communities that has been closely associated with AIDS: gay people. It cannot be overlooked that the United States has instituted the most stringent HIV screening in three areas where it historically has practiced extreme anti-gay discrimination: in the military, in the Foreign Service, and in immigration.

In the military, for example, unrepentant discrimination against gay people has been official policy since 1943. Between 1975 and 1985, the military discharged 15,000 servicemembers because of allegations of homosexuality.[77] This policy intensified during the Reagan administration with the issuance, in 1982, of a DOD directive designed to make it even easier for the government to screen out gay people seeking to enter or remain in the armed forces. The directive, which is still in effect, states that "homosexuality is incompatible with military service" and broadens the definition of homosexual to include anyone who "engages in, desires to engage in, or intends to engage in homosexual acts."[78] The effect of the regulation is to sanction the discharge not only of servicemembers who engage in homosexual conduct, but also of those who have a homosexual or bisexual orientation.[79]

The release of studies commissioned by the DOD, documenting the laudable contributions of gay servicemembers, has not abated military discrimination against gay people.[80] A July 1990 Navy bulletin that urged commanders to root out lesbians typifies the military's current policy in its animosity toward gay servicemembers and its irrational, self-defeating logic. The bulletin condemns lesbian sailors as "predator[s]" who are bad for morale at the same time that it praises them as "hardworking, career-oriented, willing to put in long hours on the job and among the command's top professionals."[81] Even in times of military crisis, the government perceives purging gay people from its midst as more important than promoting professional competence and commitment. Thus far, federal courts have upheld the military's homophobic policies.[82]

Although the Foreign Service does not publish an explicit policy banning gay people, it, too, discriminates against them. Members of the Foreign Service must receive security clearances. This requirement has typically been used by the federal government to deny positions to gay men and lesbians on the alleged ground that they are security risks.[83]

Immigration policy has also been a vehicle for homophobic bias in American history. In 1952, Congress passed the McCarran-Walter Act, which barred those "afflicted with psychopathic personality" from the United States.[84] In 1965, the Act was amended to add an exclusion for aliens "afflicted with . . . sexual deviation."[85] In 1967, the Supreme Court ruled that it was "beyond a shadow of a doubt" that Congress, in enacting the McCarran-Walter Act, had intended the phrase "psychopathic personality" as a term of art to mean people "afflicted with homosexuality."[86] Consequently, the Court sanctioned the exclusion of aliens solely on the ground that they were gay. The provision banning gay people from the United States as "psychopath[s]" remained in effect until October 1990.[87] Just as Congressional homophobia played a role in the 1987 bill banning entry of HIV-infected aliens, so the repeal of the homosexual exclusion was linked in the Immigration Act of 1990 with repeal of the HIV ban.

It should be noted that United States policies in these areas have historically been marked by blatant racism as well as homophobia. In the military, for example, African Americans were officially excluded from service until the late 1940s by caps on their enlistment. Those who could enlist were assigned to segregated units and limited to particular job categories, usually kitchen and custodial work. Although some Black men were allowed to fight in segregated units, often they were excluded from combat duty and overseas service.[88] The military's current HIV policy—excluding infected recruits, prohibiting overseas duties for HIV-positive servicemembers, and apparently reassigning infected personnel to menial jobs and separate living quarters—eerily echoes the experience of African Americans in the armed forces.

Throughout the first half of this century, the United States also pursued an expressly racist immigration policy. It designed quotas to exclude or limit the entry of people from non-White races or ethnic groups perceived to be undesirable or inferior.[89] The desire to keep the country untainted by immigrants with HIV is reminiscent of past government efforts to restrict the immigration of members of stigmatized racial and ethnic groups.

Although the United States no longer bars people of color from entering the country or serving in the armed forces, racist attitudes persist in the government's present HIV programs. In the Job Corps, for example, the government has imposed mandatory testing on all applicants—a large percentage of whom are people of color—and has sought either to exclude HIV-positive applicants or to require them to prove that they do not pose a risk to others as a condition of remaining in the Corps. At the same time, it has rejected effective strategies for teaching adolescents who are at high risk for HIV infection about measures to prevent transmission.[90] The government's repressive response to HIV among applicants for the Job Corps is certainly odd in view of the program's stated educational purpose. Yet the response is consistent with the government's historical treatment of people of color as less than full-fledged citizens. In particular, the adoption of HIV screening devices in the Job Corps appears to stem from the disturbing assumption that coercive and punitive measures are most appropriate for controlling the behavior of people of color, and poor people of color in particular.[91]

The parallels between HIV screening programs and historical patterns of discrimination should make courts skeptical of governmental claims that those programs are necessary and narrowly tailored. The lack of medical purpose behind the policies should make the resort to coercion and discrimination even more suspect. Indeed, the federal government's own laws relating to disability and perceived disability require accommodation of those with a difference—not a blanket exclusion.

The collective teachings of history, science, and antidiscrimination law demand that the courts subject the government's screening programs to more than the cursory, deferential standard of review that they have so far embraced. Until that happens, other means of change must be pursued aggressively in order to correct the pernicious notion that HIV-infected people are not fit to serve, or even gain admission to, the United States.

NOTES

1 *See, e.g.,* U.S. Department of Health and Human Services, *Proposed Rulemaking on Medical Examination of Aliens,* 56 Fed. Reg. 2484 (1991) (to be codified at 42 C.F.R. pt. 34); Report of the Surgeon General on Acquired Immune Deficiency Syndrome (1987); *Recommendations for Preventing Transmission of Infection with Human T-Lymphotropic Virus Type III, Lymphadenopathy-Associated Virus in the Workplace,* 34 MMWR 681, 691 (1985); Presidential Commission on the Human Immunodeficiency Virus Epidemic, Report: June 1988 at 113; Institute of Medicine, National Academy of Sciences, Confronting AIDS: Update 1988, at 62–64, 69–76; *Prevention and Control of Acquired Immune Deficiency Syndrome: An Interim Report,* 258 J.A.M.A. 2097, 2100 (1987).

2 President Bush made this statement in an address to the National Leadership Coalition on AIDS on March 29, 1990. 5 AIDS Pol'y & L., Apr. 4, 1990, at 1; *see* Johnson, *Reagan, Spurning Tougher Move, Orders Anti-Bias Rules on AIDS,* N.Y. Times, Aug. 3, 1988, at A1.

3 29 U.S.C.A. § 791 *et seq.* (West Supp. 1991); *see also* 29 C.F.R. § 1613.703 (1990)

(EEOC guidelines) ("Federal Government shall become a model employer of handicapped individuals").

4 School Board of Nassau County v. Arline, 480 U.S. 273, 287 & nn.16–17, 288 (1987); Chalk v. United States District Court, 840 F.2d 701, 705, 707–08 (9th Cir. 1988); Bentivegna v. United States Department of Labor, 694 F.2d 619, 623 (9th Cir. 1982); see also 29 C.F.R. § 1613.704(b) (1990).

5 See, e.g., Glover v. Eastern Nebraska Community Office of Retardation, 867 F.2d 461 (8th Cir.) (mandatory HIV testing of employees in facilities for care of mentally retarded people struck down as violation of Fourth Amendment rights of employees), cert. denied, 493 U.S. 932 (1989); Chalk, 840 F.2d 701 (removal of teacher with AIDS from classroom violates Rehabilitation Act).

6 A. Polk (director, Department of Defense Military Blood Program Office), Memorandum: Military Implementation of Public Health Service Provisional Recommendations Concerning Testing Blood and Plasma for Antibodies to HTLV-III (Mar. 13, 1985); W. Taft (deputy secretary of defense), Memorandum: HTLV-III Testing (Aug. 30, 1985); see also Boffey, Military Services Will Be Screened for AIDS Evidence, N.Y. Times, Oct. 19, 1985, § 1, at 1.

7 C. Weinberger, Memorandum: Policy on Identification, Surveillance, and Disposition of Military Personnel Infected with Human T-Lymphotropic Virus Type III (HTLV-III) (Oct. 24, 1985); see also Top Pentagon Health Official Recommends Keeping Policy on AIDS, N.Y. Times, Dec. 18, 1986, at B31; Keller, Military Says It Will Use AIDS Replies in Ousters, N.Y. Times, Oct. 29, 1985, at A1.

8 Pentagon Extending its AIDS Curb Issued to R.O.T.C.'s, N.Y. Times, Sept. 14, 1986, § 1, at 34; see Lewin, Gay Cadet Is Asked to Repay R.O.T.C. Scholarship, N.Y. Times, Mar. 2, 1990, at A10.

9 C. Weinberger, Memorandum: Policy on Identification, Surveillance, and Administration of Personnel Infected with Human Immunodeficiency Virus (HIV) (Apr. 20, 1987) ; see Military To Help Civilians on AIDS Warnings, N.Y. Times, Apr. 23, 1987, at A20.

10 W. Taft, Memorandum: Policy on Identification, Surveillance, and Administration of Personnel Infected with Human Immunodeficiency Virus (Aug. 4, 1988); Compliance with Host Nation HIV Screening Requirement for DOD Civilian Employees, 53 Fed. Reg. 52, 693 (1988) (codified at 32 C.F.R. § 58); Military AIDS Testing Plan Is Extended by the Pentagon, N.Y. Times, Aug. 14, 1988, § 1, at 12.

11 Human Immunodeficiency Virus (HIV-1), 56 Fed. Reg. 15,281–01 (1991) (to be codified at 32 C.F.R. pt. 58).

12 Kolata, Civilian Agencies Sending Blood to Augment Military's Gulf Supply, N.Y. Times, Jan. 17, 1991, at A19.

13 See Garrett, The Army's War against AIDS, N.Y. Newsday, Feb. 27, 1989, at 6.

14 C. Williams & M. Weinberg, Homosexuals and the Military 34–35 (1971); Keller, note 7 above, at A1.

15 Keller, note 7 above, at A13; see also Boffey, Of AIDS and the Lack of Confidentiality, N.Y. Times, Aug. 10, 1985, § 1, at 7.

16 Pub. L. 99–661, Div. A, Title VII, § 705 cc, 100 Stat. 3904 (1986); see Budahn, Hill Bars 'Adverse Action' against AIDS Carriers, Air Force Times, Nov. 3, 1986.

17 COMNAVMILPERSCOM LETTER, From: Commander, Navy Military Personnel Command, 1300 Ser. N453/(2)(d); see also Rivera, The Military, in AIDS and The Law: A Guide for the Public 221, 230–32 (H. Dalton, S. Burris & Yale AIDS Law Project eds. 1987).

18 Garrett, note 13 above; Army Faulted For AIDS Actions, Columbus Dispatch, July 2, 1989, at 2A.

19 Milhizer, *Endangering Others, The Military's Approach for Controlling HIV Transmission*, Judges' J., Summer 1990, at 34.

20 *Id.; see, e.g.,* United States v. Johnson, 30 M.J. 53 (C.M.A.), *cert. denied,* 111 S. Ct. 294 (1990); United States v. Stewart, 29 M.J. 92 (C.M.A. 1989) ; United States v. Womack, 29 M.J. 88 (C.M.A. 1989); United States v. Woods, 28 M.J. 318 (C.M.A. 1989). *See generally* Anderson *et al., AIDS Issues in the Military,* 32 A.F. L. Rev. 353, 363–66 (1990).

21 This memorandum, signed by Major Cal Scovel, was obtained by Captain William R. Fisher during discovery in the Roantes case. Personal communication, Capt. William R. Fisher, Esq. (Nov. 2, 1990).

22 Personal communication, Capt. William R. Fisher, Esq. (Nov. 2, 1990); *Marine Faces Court-Martial for Not Disclosing HIV to Hygienist,* AIDS Litig. Rep. (Andrews) 2505 (Apr. 14, 1989).

23 Parker v. Levy, 417 U.S. 733, 743–44 (1974).

24 *See, e.g.,* Mindes v. Seamen, 453 F.2d 197 (5th Cir. 1971).

25 *See, e.g.,* Chappell v. Wallace, 462 U.S. 296 (1983). *See generally Mindes,* 453 F.2d 197; Gorenstein, *Judicial Review of Constitutional Claims against the Military,* 84 Colum. L. Rev. 387 (1984).

26 Goldman v. Weinberger, 475 U.S. 503 (1986).

27 Brown v. Glines, 444 U.S. 348 (1980).

28 Ben-Shalom v. Marsh, 881 F.2d 454 (7th Cir. 1989), *cert. denied,* 494 U.S. 1004 (1990); Woodward v. United States, 871 F.2d 1068 (Fed. Cir. 1989), *cert. denied,* 494 U.S. 1003 (1990); Dronenberg v. Zech, 741 F.2d 1388 (D.C. Cir. 1984); Beller v. Middendorf, 632 F.2d 788, 812 (9th Cir. 1980), *cert. denied,* 452 U.S. 905 (1981).

29 *Goldman,* 475 U.S. at 507.

30 Plowman v. Department of the Army, 698 F. Supp. 627 (E.D. Va. 1988).

31 *Id.* at 631–37. For more on qualified immunity, see Anderson v. Creighton, 483 U.S. 635 (1987); Harlow v. Fitzgerald, 457 U.S. 800 (1982).

32 CDC, *Recommendations for Prevention of HIV Transmission in Health-Care Settings,* 258 J.A.M.A. 1441, 1449 (1987); *see also* Altman, *Mandatory Tests for AIDS Opposed at Health Parley,* N.Y. Times, Feb. 25, 1987, at A1.

33 903 F.2d 1455 (11th Cir. 1990), *cert. denied,* 111 S. Ct. 1102 (1991).

34 29 U.S.C. § 794 (1988).

35 *Garrett,* 903 F.2d at 1458–61; *see, e.g.,* Roper v. Department of the Army, 832 F.2d 247 (2d Cir. 1987); Gonzalez v. Department of the Army, 718 F.2d 926 (9th Cir. 1983).

36 *Garrett,* 903 F.2d at 1461–62 (citing Smith v. Christian, 763 F.2d 1322 (11th Cir. 1985)). *But see, e.g.,* Doe v. Attorney General, 941 F.2d 780 (9th Cir. 1991) (physician with AIDS had private right of action under § 504 of Rehabilitation Act against Federal Bureau of Investigation for refusing to send agents to physician for physical examinations despite contract).

37 Doe v. Ball, 725 F. Supp. 1210, 1216 (M.D. Fla. 1989), *aff'd sub nom.* Doe v. Garrett, 903 F.2d 1455 (11th Cir. 1990), *cert. den.,* 111 S. Ct. 1102 (1991).

38 Doe v. Marsh, No. 89–1383–0G, AIDS Litig. Rep. (Andrews) 4117 (D.D.C. Feb. 8, 1990).

39 *Id.* at 4123.

40 U.S. Department of State, Department Notice: AIDS Testing (Nov. 22, 1986); U.S. Peace Corps, Medical Information For Applicants (Nov. 1, 1990); *see also State Department to Require Testing for Foreign Service,* 1 AIDS Pol'y & L., Dec. 3, 1986, at 1.

41 Local 1812, Am. Fed'n of Gov't Emp. v. Department of State, 662 F. Supp. 50 (D.D.C. 1987).

42 *Id.* at 53.

43 *Id.* at 54 n.7.

44 *See* Plaintiff's Reply Memorandum In Support of Motion for Preliminary Injunction at 11–12, *Local 1812*, 662 F. Supp. 50 (D.D.C. 1987) (No. 87–0121); *see also* 662 F. Supp. at 54 (conceding that "persons may under normal circumstances in the United States carry HIV for years, be completely well, and perform efficiently").

45 *See* School Bd. of Nassau County v. Arline, 480 U.S. 273, 287 (1987).

46 *See* 29 U.S.C.A. § 791 (West Supp. 1991). Reasonable accommodations are those that do not place "undue hardships" on the operations of the agency or other employer. 29 C.F.R. § 1613.704 (1990). In one recent case, a U.S. district court required the U.S. Postal Service to accommodate an employee with HIV disease by transferring him to a post with adequate medical facilities even when seniority requirements had to be waived to accomplish the transfer. Buckingham v. Postal Service, 55 Empl. Prac. Dec. (CCH) ¶ 40,594 (C.D. Cal. Feb. 15, 1991).

47 Bentivegna v. Department of Labor, 694 F.2d 619, 623 (9th Cir. 1982).

48 Mantolete v. Bolger, 767 F.2d 1416, 1422–23 (9th Cir. 1985) (mere showing of "elevated risk" of injury not sufficient); *see also* Ackerman v. Western Electric Co., Inc., 643 F. Supp. 836, 851 (N.D. Cal. 1986) (applying probability of substantial and imminent harm standard to state law analogous to Rehabilitation Act), *aff'd*, 860 F.2d 1514 (9th Cir. 1988).

49 *See* Curran, *Mandatory Testing of Public Employees For The Human Immunodeficiency Virus: The Fourth Amendment and Medical Reasonableness*, 90 Colum. L. Rev. 720, 748–49 (1990).

50 United Auto Workers v. Johnson Controls, Inc., 111 S. Ct. 1196, 1198 (1991); *see also* Dothard v. Rawlinson, 433 U.S. 321, 335 (1977) (risk to Title VII plaintiff posed by particular job is not sufficient to establish either a bona fide occupational qualification defense or a business necessity defense).

51 29 U.S.C.A. § 1691 (1985).

52 Job Corps Bulletin No. 86–58 (Dec. 19, 1986).

53 Job Corps Bulletin No. 89–03 (July 24, 1989).

54 Dorsey v. Department of Labor, No. 88–1898 (D.D.C. filed July 12, 1988).

55 *See* Hein, *Mandatory HIV Testing of Youth: A Lose-Lose Proposition*, 266 J.A.M.A. 2430 (1991) (editorial); Institute of Medicine, Nat'l Acad. of Sciences, *HIV Infection and AIDS* 5 (1988); *see also* Medical Examination of Aliens, 56 Fed. Reg. 2484 (1991) (to be codified at 42 C.F.R. pt. 34) (proposed Jan. 23, 1991).

56 *See* Plaintiff's Memorandum in Support of His Renewed Motion for Partial Summary Judgment on His Administrative Procedure Claim and in Opposition to Defendants' Summary Judgment Motion at 8–9, 25, *Dorsey* (No. 88–1898).

57 *See, e.g.*, Chalk v. United States District Court, 840 F.2d 701, 707–08 (9th Cir. 1988).

58 St. Louis, *et al.*, *Human Immunodeficiency Virus Infection in Disadvantaged Adolescents: Findings from the U.S. Job Corps*, 266 J.A.M.A. 2387 (1991).

59 Pub. L. No. 100–71, § 518, 101 Stat. 475 (1987). Accordingly, HHS issued rules, effective December 1, 1987, placing HIV infection on the list of dangerous contagious diseases. 42 C.F.R. §§ 34.2(b), 34.4(a) (1987). For an account of the bureaucratic response to the Helms Amendment, see Lynch, *Medical Exclusion and Admissions Policy: Statutes and Strictures*, 23 N.Y.U. J. Int'l L. & Pol. 1001 (1991). *See generally* Chang-Muy, *HIV/AIDS and International Travel: International Organizations, Regional Governments, and the United States Respond*, 23 N.Y.U. J. Int'l L. & Pol. 1047 (1991).

60 The Immigration Reform And Control Act of 1986 and the Refugee Act of 1980 provide for waivers of the HIV exclusion at the discretion of the Attorney General if applicants can show compelling family unity, humanitarian, or public interest grounds. 8 U.S.C.A. §§ 1255a (d)(2)(B), 1160 (c)(2)(B) (West Supp. 1991). The INS, however, has required HIV-infected aliens to make an additional showing that: (1) the danger to the public health of the United States created by their admission to the country would be minimal; (2) the possibility of spread of the disease created by their admission would be minimal; and (3) there would be no cost incurred by any U.S. government agency without prior consent of that agency. J. Puleo (INS Assistant Commissioner for Examinations), Cable to INS Regional Offices (March 2, 1988), *reprinted in* 65 Interpreter Releases 239 (Mar. 14, 1988). The strenuous requirements of the INS have made waivers virtually impossible to obtain without legal representation, a luxury that many applicants for legalization have not had.

61 *See* United Nations High Commission for Refugees, Inter-Office Memorandum No. 70/88: UNHCR Policy and Guidelines Regarding Refugee Protection and Assistance and Acquired Immune Deficiency Syndrome (AIDS) (May 6, 1988); T. Stoltenberg (United Nations High Commissioner for Refugees) Letter to INS Commissioner G. McNary (Aug. 24, 1990); *Global Offensive against AIDS,* 258 J.A.M.A. 11 (1987) (comments of World Health Organization); *see also* National Commission On AIDS, Annual Report to the President and the Congress 50–54 (1990); Hilts, *Disease Control Center Says AIDS Shouldn't Bar U.S. Entry,* N.Y. Times, Feb. 28, 1990, at A24; Okie, *Public Health Experts Raise Doubts on Plan to Test Immigrants for AIDS,* Wash. Post, July 15, 1987, at A14.

62 *See* Boodman, *U.S. Ban on Tourists with HIV Surprises Some Lawmakers,* Wash. Post, Apr. 19, 1989, at A2; Johnston, *U.S. Will Ease Visa Restrictions for Some Who Suffer from AIDS,* N.Y. Times, May 19, 1989, at D16; Letter of Gene McNary (INS Commissioner) to Maureen Byrnes (National Commission on AIDS), June 19, 1990 (outlining U.S.

policy on admitting non-immigrants with HIV to the U.S.).

63 Immigration Act of 1990, P.L. 101–649, 104 Stat. 4978; 136 Cong. Rec. H13229 (daily ed. Oct. 26, 1990). The Conference Report states that the change was intended "to insure that this exclusion will apply only to those diseases for which admission of aliens with such disease would pose a public health risk to the United States." *Id.* at H13238. The Conference Report also provides that the determination of what diseases constitute a public health threat "shall be based on current epidemiological principles and medical standards."

64 *Medical Examination of Aliens,* note 55 above, at 2484–85.

65 Pear, *Ban on Aliens with AIDS to Continue for Now,* N.Y. Times, May 30, 1991, at A23.

66 *Medical Examination of Aliens,* 56 Fed. Reg. 25,000 (1991) (to be codified at 42 C.F.R. pt. 34) (proposed May 31, 1991).

67 *See* Gladwell, *U.S. Won't Lift HIV Immigration Ban,* Wash. Post, Aug. 2, 1991, at A1; Hilts, *U.S. Planning to Allow Visits by People with AIDS,* N.Y. Times, Aug. 2, 1991, at B2.

68 Pear, note 65 above, at A23; U.S. Department of Health and Human Services, *HIV Prevalence Estimates and AIDS Case Projections for the United States: Report Based upon a Workshop,* 39 MMWR 1 (1990).

69 8 U.S.C.A. § 1182(a)(4) (West Supp. 1991).

70 Fineberg (dean of Harvard School of Public Health), *False Aim against AIDS,* N.Y. Times, July 31, 1991, at A19.

71 *See, e.g.,* M. Barnes, Director of Policy, New York State AIDS Institute, Letter to S. Blackman, acting district director, INS (Dec. 15, 1989) (informing INS that administration of HIV tests by INS-designated civil surgeons in New York does not comply with Article 27-F of New York State Public Health Law).

72 Current regulations require immigrant applicants to undergo HIV testing abroad rather than at their point of entry into the United States. *Medical Examination of Aliens*, note 66 above, at 25002–03 (to be codified at 42 C.F.R. § 34.3(b)(4)). For a summary of abuses of mandatory testing, see AIDS Legal Council, *et al* ., Policy Paper: Immigration and Naturalization Service HIV Antibody Testing: No Justification for Exclusion of Immigrants and Refugees (April 1990) (available from Coalition for Immigrant and Refugee Rights and Services, 2111 Mission Street, Room 401, San Francisco, CA 94111); *see also* 68 Interpreter Releases 55 (Jan. 14, 1991) (complaint by Hawaii Governor's Committee on AIDS that INS civil surgeons not following state testing guidelines).

73 *See, e.g.,* Kleindienst v. Mandel, 408 U.S. 753, 766 (1972) ; Knauff v. Shaughnessy, 338 U.S. 537, 544 (1950); Fiallo v. Bell, 430 U.S. 787 (1977). *See generally* Developments in the Law, *Immigration Policy and the Rights of Aliens*, 96 Harv. L. Rev. 1286 (1983); Hahn, *Constitutional Limits on the Power to Exclude Aliens*, 82 Colum. L. Rev. 957 (1982).

74 *See, e.g.,* Zartarian v. Billings, 204 U.S. 170 (1907).

75 Boutilier v. INS, 387 U.S. 118 (1967).

76 For an excellent discussion of the historical intolerance of state authorities and others for the "humanity of difference," see Wolfson, *Civil Rights, Human Rights, Gay Rights: Minorities and the Humanity of the Different,* 14 Harv. J.L. & Pub. Pol'y 21 (1991).

77 Developments in the Law, *Sexual Orientation and the Law,* 102 Harv. L. Rev. 1508, 1554 (1989) [hereinafter *Sexual Orientation and the Law*]. cb. *See generally* Rivera, *Queer Law: Sexual Orientation in the Mid-Eighties—Part II,* 11 U. Dayton L. Rev. 275, 287 (1986).

78 Department of Defense, Directive No. 1332.14, encl. 3, § H.1.b.1. (1982) (Enlisted Administrative Separations); *see also* Rivera, note 77 above, at 297.

79 *See* Watkins v. United States Army, 875 F.2d 699, 714 (9th Cir. 1989) (Norris, J., dissenting) ("under the Army's regulations 'homosexuality,' not sexual conduct, is clearly the operative trait for disqualification"), *cert. denied,* 111 S. Ct. 384 (1990).

80 *See* Department of Defense Personnel Security Research and Education Center, Nonconforming Sexual Orientations and Military Suitability (Dec. 1988) (PERS-TR–89–002).

81 J. Donnell (Vice Admiral, Commander of Navy's Surface Atlantic Fleet), Administrative Message (July 24, 1990); *see* Gross, *Admiral Praises Lesbians but Urges Their Dismissal,* N.Y. Times, Sept. 2, 1990, § 1, at 70.

82 *See* Ben-Shalom v. Marsh, 881 F.2d 454 (7th Cir. 1989), *cert. denied,* 110 S.Ct. 1296 (1990); Woodward v. United States, 871 F.2d 1068 (Fed. Cir. 1989), *cert. denied,* 110 S. Ct. 1295 (1990); Dronenberg v. Zech, 741 F.2d 1388 (D.C. Cir. 1984); Beller v. Middendorf, 632 F.2d 788, 812 (9th Cir. 1980), *cert. denied,* 452 U.S. 905.

83 *Sexual Orientation and the Law,* note 77 above, at 1556.

84 Ch. 477, tit. II, ch. 2, § 212, 66 Stat. 182 (1952) (codified as amended at 8 U.S.C. § 1182(a)(4) (1988)).

85 Pub. L. No. 89–236, § 15 (b), 79 Stat. 919 (1965) (codified as amended at 8 U.S.C. § 1182 (a)(4) (1988)).

86 Boutilier v. Immigration Service, 387 U.S. 118, 120, 123 (1967).

87 In 1979, however, the Public Health Service ceased the practice of certifying aliens as psychopaths simply because they were gay, a change that has made it more difficult for the INS to exclude gay aliens. *Sexual Orientation and the Law*, note 77 above, at 1661.

88 Dudziak, *Desegregation as a Cold War Imperative*, 41 Stan. L. Rev. 61, 72 (1988).

89 *See generally* 1 C. Gordon & S. Mailman, Immigration Law & Procedure § 2.02 (1991).

90 *See* Hein, note 55 above; St. Louis, *et al.*, note 58 above.

91 Indeed, all of the groups singled out for mandatory testing, except the Foreign Service, consist disproportionately of people of color. For example, the top ten countries of birth of immigrants in 1989, accounting

for two-thirds of the immigrants admitted, were: Mexico, El Salvador, the Philippines, Vietnam, Korea, China, India, the Dominican Republic, Jamaica, and Iran. U.S. Immigration and Naturalization Service, Statistical Yearbook of the Immigration and Naturalization Service xviii (1989). In 1989, 75 percent of amnesty applicants, who must submit to HIV tests to legalize their status in the United States, were Latino. *Id* . at xiii. The U.S. military also consists disproportionately of members of racial minorities, African Americans in particular. *See* Wilkerson, *Blacks Wary of Their Big Role as Troops*, N.Y. Times, Jan. 25, 1991, at A1.

10 Reproduction and Parenting

Taunya Lovell Banks

Although adult males continue to constitute the majority of people living with HIV disease in the United States, HIV infection among women and children is on the rise. Nationally, women make up 11.5 percent of AIDS cases, and in some areas of the Northeast the figure is closer to 25 percent and growing.[1] Because most women with HIV disease are of childbearing age, as their numbers have grown so has the number of pediatric AIDS cases. Already, HIV infection is among the ten leading causes of death for children between one and four years of age.[2] Given our relative success in stemming transfusion-related and blood products–related transmission of HIV, the vast majority of pediatric cases, and virtually all new ones, involve transmission from mother to child before or during birth (perinatal transmission).[3]

As the number of pediatric AIDS cases continues its steep rise (in 1991, an estimated 2,200 HIV-infected babies were born, as compared with 1,500 in 1990),[4] government officials at all levels have pressed for more effective measures to stem vertical transmission. Often, these measures bear heavily upon the reproductive freedom of HIV-positive women. Although many such women will voluntarily choose to forego pregnancy when fully and sensitively informed about the risks of perinatal transmission, others will not, preferring to take the two-in-three chance that their babies will be born uninfected.[5] Public health measures designed to dissuade women from freely exercising this option raise serious constitutional issues. Similarly, measures that pressure HIV-positive women to terminate existing pregnancies are constitutionally suspect.

When women with HIV elect to bring pregnancies to term, a host of parenting, child care, and custody issues arise. Who will serve as the child's primary caretaker? If the child is also infected, who will assure that its special needs are met? If the mother is the primary caretaker and questions are raised regarding her capacity to parent, how should they be resolved? If she becomes too disabled to continue functioning as a parent, who will take over? Who will take over if she dies?

Perinatal HIV transmission highlights the inadequacies of existing mechanisms for assisting families in crisis. Our social service systems have failed to plan for the problems that predictably arise when HIV-positive adults seek to care for small children, much less those that arise when both parents and children are infected. When the primary caregiver is female, poor, and/or non-White, it is almost impossible for the family to remain intact without help. Yet social support services for families are given low priority by government, and agency policies are often hostile to the families that need help the most—single-parent families headed by poor women and women of color. Existing programs provide inadequate options for temporary child care and family support when parents become ill or incapacitated. The emphasis in most cases is on foster care, which disrupts families by removing children from their homes rather than providing in-home support services for sick parents and children.

Many of the reproduction and parenting issues affecting HIV-positive women in America reflect continuing race, sex, and class bias in the delivery and quality of health care and related social services.[6] For example, the absence of women's unique concerns in scientific and clinical discussions about HIV, until relatively recently, reflects the continuing institutional sexism in medical research. But even when interest is expressed in HIV-positive women, the focus is on their role as transmitters of the disease rather than on the women themselves.[7] Women have little input into HIV policies, reflecting the tendency of health care providers to adopt paternalistic attitudes toward female patients, discounting their complaints and concerns in the belief that women have no role in determining their own medical treatment. In addition, treatment protocols are geared to the ways in which the disease is manifested in men, and women may therefore be misdiagnosed and may receive inadequate treatment once the disease is diagnosed.[8]

Health policies designed to minimize vertical transmission must take into account the fact that an overwhelmingly disproportionate number of HIV-positive women are Black and Latina and are in their childbearing years,[9] and that a disproportionate number of them are poor[10] and are drug users or the sexual partners of drug users.[11] This is significant, because in this country poor women and women of color have traditionally been discouraged and even coerced by health care and social service agencies to forego pregnancy.[12] Thus, care must be taken lest race, sex, class, and lifestyle biases bear heavily on the reproductive and parenting rights of women with HIV.

REPRODUCTION ISSUES

HIV Testing of Fertile Women

Currently, the Centers for Disease Control (CDC) recommends that all fertile women at risk for HIV infection be routinely tested.[13] Given the sharp increase in HIV infection among women and the risk of perinatal transmission, it seems likely that future recommendations will advise that all women of childbearing age be tested. Further, there is reason to believe that much of this testing will take place without the women's consent. A survey of 560 randomly selected nongovernment hospitals has shown that many hospitals do not obtain patient consent to HIV antibody tests.[14] In addition, 3 to 4 percent of the hospitals surveyed never or only sometimes informed patients of positive test results.[15]

Undoubtedly, voluntary testing of fertile women should be encouraged to minimize the risk of perinatal transmission, and testing is most valuable if it occurs before pregnancy. At that point, an HIV-positive woman can make an informed choice about whether to become pregnant. Such testing, however, raises a troubling issue: what information should be provided to women who test positive? Under the circumstances, counselors should take a "nondirective" approach, providing the client with relevant information in a nonjudgmental manner and taking no position on the issue of childbearing, leaving that decision to the woman.

The push for routine testing of fertile women raises the very real concern that states will use test results to identify women with HIV so they can be counseled not to reproduce. Such "directive counseling" denies women the opportunity to receive an unbiased assessment of their medical situation and make an informed personal decision free of coercive influences. Currently, HIV counseling is not regulated, and many health care professionals quietly advocate that HIV-positive fertile women be counseled to forego pregnancy and, in some cases, to be sterilized.[16]

Even when coercion is not intended, directive counseling presents substantial risks. For one thing, such counseling undercuts individual patient autonomy. Health care workers who provide counseling may not know what is best and may sometimes assume, based on sex, race, class, and substance-use history, that the patient is irresponsible. Directive HIV prenatal counseling may be insensitive to the different cultural values about reproduction and group identity held by many of the women counseled. These programs often fail "to be sensitive to the special value of children for Black and Latina women. . . . [Planners must realize that culturally] the ability to reproduce was seen as a powerful tool in the fight for liberation."[17] Much of the sterilization abuse directed at poor women and women of color during this century was based on similar assumptions.

Directive counseling also raises the possibility that women with HIV may wrongfully believe that compliance with the counselor's recommendation is a necessary condition of continued medical treatment. Since directive counseling in this context may substantially interfere with the reproductive choices of these women, especially where they have limited access to health care, it raises serious right-to-privacy concerns when supported or carried out by government.[18]

HIV Testing of Pregnant Women

There are calls for routine HIV testing of pregnant women.[19] But routine testing during pregnancy is even more problematic than screening all fertile women. The goals of prenatal HIV testing are muddy at best. It is said that testing facilitates the counseling of infected women regarding the impact of HIV on pregnancy and the effect of pregnancy on the progression of the disease; the risk of transmission to the fetus; and the risk of transmission to sexual partners and possible infection in older children.[20] Another unstated goal of prenatal testing may be preventing HIV-positive mothers from giving birth to healthy children who may soon become wards of the state when their mothers die.

Putting aside the question of whether it is in the interest of an HIV-negative fetus to be born to an HIV-positive mother, the *articulated* benefits of prenatal HIV testing are questionable at best. We simply do not know enough about the impact of HIV on pregnancy, nor about the effect of pregnancy on the progression of the disease, to counsel women on these issues. Although early reports expressed concern that pregnancy accelerated the disease process, there is little evidence to support this theory. In fact, a recent review of the scientific literature on HIV in women suggests that pregnant women who are infected should be treated no differently than their nonpregnant counterparts, "unless there are documented and compelling fetal concerns that would justify a modification of those standards."[21] Further, since the effect of abortion on pregnant HIV-positive women is likewise unknown, counseling pregnant women to abort could put them at greater risk than counseling them to continue the pregnancy.

On the other hand, prenatal HIV testing may have some health benefits for women, since prenatal care may be more readily available for women with limited access to care and prenatal clinics are often where women first learn of their infection. Both the length and quality of life for all HIV-infected women can be improved by early diagnosis and treatment. However, pregnant women with HIV must be treated as individuals, independent of the fetus they carry. This means that they should be fully informed of the risks and benefits of HIV therapies.[22] Yet women are being targeted for routine HIV testing because they are pregnant and can transmit the virus perinatally. To date, the primary articulated concern is not with women themselves, but with women as vectors of HIV transmission.

Justifications for testing that center on the putative benefits to the fetus are also questionable. We do not know precisely when perinatal transmission occurs, nor by what mechanism. Studies indicate that the rate of maternal-to-fetal transmission in some women may be as high as 45 percent and in others as low as 12.9 percent.[23] Thus, the risk of transmission in any particular case cannot accurately be predicted. In addition, there is at present no approved treatment for fetuses of HIV-positive women.[24] Therefore, setting aside the idea of terminating the fetus for its own sake, there is nothing to be gained by prenatal (as against neonatal) testing.

Even if effective treatments were available for the fetus, prenatal HIV testing raises a potential conflict of interest between the pregnant woman and her fetus. In some experiments, still in the early stages, pregnant women are being given AZT in hopes of benefitting the fetus. Initially, at least one of these studies called for the mother's AZT to be discontinued once the child was born, since only the fetus, and not the woman, was the subject under study.[25]

This study is particularly worrisome. It is a fetus-centered study that treats women as vectors and raises potential conflicts of interest between mother and fetus because AZT may benefit the fetus while harming the mother. In addition, pregnant women may be coerced into continuing their pregnancies because participation in experimental protocols is the only way they can get medical treatment. Whereas pregnant women with HIV should have access to treatment protocols, fetus-centered protocols that treat pregnant women as vectors may not serve their best interests. These protocols should be closely scrutinized before approval to insure that both mother and fetus derive comparable benefits. We need to make sure that women with limited access to health care are not exploited by treatment protocols that seem to offer an opportunity for enhanced care.

Given the current demographics of HIV disease in women, pregnant women may be compelled to be treated once treatment becomes available for fetuses. There are already a few cases, although not involving women with HIV in which courts have ordered forced prenatal invasions. Many of these cases involve poor women of color. A recent study of physician and hospital court-ordered obstetrical intervention found that 81 percent of the women involved were Black, Asian, or Latina. All of them were treated in teaching hospital clinics or were receiving public assistance.[26] Forced prenatal invasion of an otherwise legally competent pregnant woman is always inappropriate, because too often it subordinates the woman's bodily autonomy to the fetus. In addition, judges may not trouble themselves to balance the competing maternal-fetal interests when the women in question are Black or Latina.

These competing maternal-fetal interests are also present when pregnant HIV-infected women are counseled. People who counsel these women may find it difficult to decide whether their primary duty is to the prospective parent, the fetus, or society. This conflict is also reflected in the current scholarly dialogue over fetal rights and the rights of pregnant women to refuse treatment intended to benefit the fetus, or to engage in conduct that may harm the fetus.[27] Even when the counselor is clear on where her or his obligation lies, it is not easy for the prospective parent to decide whether to risk her health for that of the fetus, or vice versa. Her choice should be informed and uncoerced, based on all of the available information.

Health care providers who use prenatal HIV testing primarily to identify infected pregnant women so that they can be counseled to abort may well violate federal and (to a lesser extent) state law by interfering with the reproductive choices of women with a protected disability.[28] (For more on antidiscrimination law, see chapter 13.) When the health care provider is a government entity, directive counseling to abort may also violate women's constitutional right to privacy.[29] It would be truly odd if the Constitution were held, in some circumstances, to protect a woman's right to abort a fetus over the state's objection but not to protect her right to bring it to term. Even if *Roe v. Wade* is overturned, the constitutional argument against coercing HIV-positive pregnant women to abort would be strengthened to the extent that the reversal would be premised on rights inhering in the fetus, or on the protectability of fetal life.

There is no compelling rationale for directive counseling of pregnant women with HIV. Purely financial arguments, such as limiting the cost to society of caring for seriously ill newborns and orphans, cannot be allowed to override the fundamental right to procreate.[30] Even if the state asserts an interest in protecting potential life, forced or coerced abortion terminates, rather than protects, that life. In addition, if the state argues that protecting societal health is a compelling governmental interest, there is little evidence that routine or compulsory HIV prenatal testing coupled with directive counseling is sufficiently narrowly tailored to achieve that goal.

Constitutional concerns aside, directive counseling that pressures women to terminate their pregnancies is foolish and cruel in a society that does not make abortions readily available to poor women of color.[31] Not only are Medicaid funds unavailable in most states for even therapeutic abortions,[32] but many clinics refuse to perform abortions on HIV-positive women.[33] Nor is prenatal HIV testing a sensible means of protecting health care workers from on-the-job exposure. Often there is no time to test for HIV, and even when there is, some infected patients may not have developed detectable antibodies. Thus, the only reliable way for health care workers to avoid infection is to follow the universal precautions recommended by the CDC.

To the extent that support for directive counseling reflects the perception of some health care providers that women generally—and especially poor women, women of color, and drug users—are irresponsible, such counseling is incompatible with the ideal of patient autonomy that is at the heart of the doctrine of informed consent. Directive counseling not only impermissibly interferes with women's procreational choices, but it also denies women the right to participate in treatment decisions affecting their bodies. Any counseling of HIV-positive women that directs them to be sterilized or to seek an abortion if they are pregnant fails to treat them as important participants in health care decisions affecting them.

Finally, prenatal HIV testing is analogous to prenatal testing for genetic diseases. Like HIV, genetic disorders can be transmitted vertically from mother to child, and many genetic disorders are not treatable before birth. Directive counseling is considered inappropriate in these circumstances, and it should be considered similarly inappropriate in prenatal HIV counseling.[34]

This is not to say that routine HIV prenatal testing, preceded by informed consent and accompanied by *nondirective* counseling, could never be appropriate. Testing would be most useful to women if (1) it provided information that could be used to improve the treatment outcome of women with HIV, and (2) women identified as infected had meaningful access to medical care. Since we do not know enough about the impact of pregnancy on HIV-positive women, the first condition cannot be satisfied. In addition, we have no mechanism for guaranteeing that these women will have access to medical care. In fact, recent studies suggest that many already have less access to medical care than most Americans. For example, in one study only 61 percent of Black women, compared to 79 percent of White women, received prenatal care during the first three months of pregnancy.[35] Thus, the practical value of prenatal HIV testing is questionable. We must therefore find other, more appropriate ways of preventing perinatal transmission that do not interfere with women's reproductive freedom.[36]

HIV Testing of Newborns

From the perspective of newborn children, neonatal testing may well be justified because early detection of possible HIV exposure will determine whether prophylactic treatment is indicated. It is far from clear whether knowledge of a newborn's HIV status will significantly reduce or delay illness or death.[37] Neonatal HIV testing is distinguishable from other neonatal testing in that, even if antibodies are found, there is no truly accurate way of telling whether they are the mother's or the newborn's.[38] However, there are relatively benign prophylactic measures for infants who carry their mother's antibodies, and the strong possibility (one in three) of actual infection also has a bearing on medical treatment for other conditions. Recent studies suggest that methods may be available in the near future to detect perinatally acquired HIV infection in infants as young as six months.[39] These are very preliminary findings, however, and have yet to be tested on large numbers of infants and in clinical settings.

Even if early detection of HIV becomes possible, neonatal testing raises potential conflicts between mother and infant. The newborn's test results reflect the mother's HIV status. This information will likely be placed in her medical records and will become broadly available to a wide range of health care and social service staff members. Confidentiality within hospitals is notoriously difficult to maintain, and inappropriate disclosure of the mother's infection could subject her to discrimination and render her uninsurable.

Since neonatal HIV testing thus poses real risks for mothers, it should not be performed without their informed consent unless there is a high degree of probability that knowledge of the newborn's status will significantly reduce or delay illness or death. Given the present uncertainty, even though neonatal HIV testing may be appropriate in many circumstances, routine testing without the express consent of the newborns' parents or guardians is not justified.

Finally, an infected woman whose status is disclosed through neonatal testing might be criminally prosecuted if she knew she was HIV-positive before becoming pregnant. Although no such prosecutions have been sought as of this writing, there have been attempts to prosecute pregnant drug users for knowingly transmitting drugs to their children perinatally.[40] Further, a woman who decides to become pregnant after learning of her HIV status may be characterized as a neglectful or abusive parent because she gives birth to a child who may be HIV-positive.[41] This determination could result in loss of custody. Although it is unlikely that these actions would be successful, the possibility that they might be initiated against women with HIV should not be discounted. Therefore, the privacy interest of the mother should always be considered before unconsented neonatal HIV testing is authorized. (For more on the law of medical confidentiality and informed consent for testing, see chapter 7.)

FAMILY ISSUES

Impact of the Changing Demographics of HIV

Most early HIV-related family law cases involved disputes between parents over child custody or visitation rights when the father was gay.[42] Much more common these days, however, are disputes between parents and the state. Problems typically arise when the custodial parent—usually a woman—is HIV-positive, and the state questions and impedes her attempt to make temporary or permanent custody arrangements for her children or questions her ability to care for her child, who may also be infected. (Although some HIV-positive fathers are custodial parents, and many of the problems described would apply to them, this section focuses on mothers with HIV who are single parents.)

Much of family law relating to child care operates on the assumption that most children live in two-parent homes. Thus, when one parent is sick or dies, the remaining parent continues to care for and have custody of the children. As a result, both the legal and social systems governing child custody are geared to the problems most commonly faced by financially stable, middle-income, two-parent families. Unfortunately, this is not the environment in which most HIV-positive parents live, and their parenting needs are often not adequately addressed.

The Typical HIV-Positive Parent

According to the statistics, many custodial parents with HIV are women with young dependent children. A New York study of HIV-positive mothers found that they were more likely than HIV-positive fathers to be the custodial parent of children under ten years of age.[43] When these women are involved in a steady relationship, their partners are usually also infected and may be dying as well. So some women with HIV are the primary caretakers for adult partners as well as for dependent children.

Unfortunately, most social policies aimed at seropositive women fail to consider the special needs of these caretakers: the policies focus narrowly on preventing pregnancy and fail to provide adequate health care and social services to keep families healthy and together. For example, Medicaid and private insurance reimbursement schemes either do not cover or do not adequately reimburse for home care for HIV-positive mothers or their children. These gaps in critical services undermine the capacity of women with HIV to seek care for themselves, and thus impair their ability to care for their children and adult partners.

Even when infected women have access to health care, their children may still suffer because existing support services suppose that there are two potential caregivers in the home. For example, a mother with HIV may not be sick enough to require a visiting home health-care attendant for herself but may be too sick to care adequately for a child who also has HIV. No support is provided because of the underlying assumption that a second parent is available to care for the children. When a home health-care attendant is provided, the attendant's job does not include child care, again on the assumption that someone else is available. Thus children of dying mothers may be neglected in the process.

Poor single-parent mothers with HIV face other problems more directly related to their gender and income. For example, health care providers have a tendency to override the traditional right of parents to make decisions regarding their children's care when the parent is poor, female, and HIV-positive. In one Maryland case a mother was reported for medical neglect when she threatened to remove her HIV-infected child from the hospital after a disagreement with the attending physician over treatment. The mother felt that treatment should not proceed because the hospital had not instituted adequate measures to insure that the child's medical records would remain confidential.[44] Similarly, a mother's refusal to let her child take AZT because of concerns about its toxicity might also be construed as medical neglect. In such circumstances, the health care provider's reluctance to defer to parental authority and readiness to report the mother to a child protection agency might well reflect the fact that the patient is a woman, is poor, is probably Black or Latina, and is most likely a drug user or the sexual partner of one. Given those attributes, the provider might unconsciously assume that the mother is not competent to make health care decisions for her child and might be outraged that she has had the temerity to challenge the provider.

Similarly, medical authorities are often blind to the fact that failure to keep a doctor's appointment may say more about a city's public transportation system than it does about a parent's commitment to her children. Thus, a mother who fails to bring her fifteen-month-old HIV-negative child into the hospital for follow-up testing might be unfairly charged with medical neglect. This overeagerness to seek state intervention when parenting falls below some ideal level that bears little relationship to reality, especially for poor parents, must be reassessed. Too often intervention by the state means removing children from their homes.

Temporary Disability or Death

Ultimately, every custodial mother with HIV will have recurrent instances of hospitalization. In these circumstances she may have to relinquish custody either temporarily or permanently. However, family members who volunteer to care for her dependent children receive little or no financial support for temporary care. If the cooperating family member is on public assistance, extensive documentation is required before Aid to Families with Dependent Children (AFDC) funds can be obtained and the children put on the family member's budget.[45] In addition, foster care funds usually are not available where the family member is employed, and informal child care arrangements are not effective when the mother is so disabled that she will never be able to care for her dependent children.

Most important, it is often difficult for a seriously ill mother to retain custodial rights when her dependent children must be cared for outside of the home. To avoid loss of custody, some lawyers recommend that HIV-positive mothers use a letter or other written notarized document to grant a power of attorney to a family member, giving that person some authority to care for the children and make necessary decisions for their well-being. In this instance, the power of attorney operates as an informal temporary guardianship. This mechanism is favored by poor single parents because it is much faster than formal guardianship and does not involve going to court. In some states a power of attorney can be used to grant another unrelated person temporary custody.[46] This device may be useful when the mother is estranged from her family but has family-like contacts with unrelated people.

However, a power of attorney is sometimes not recognized as legally valid by schools, health care providers, or courts, and is thus not fully effective in fulfilling the mother's intentions. Even when legally recognized, a power of attorney will not be effective in permanent or long-term custody situations or in situations where the parent is mentally incapacitated.[47] A power of attorney is good only for a limited period of time and requires periodic renewal. It is thus inappropriate for an HIV-infected parent who has periodic physical or mental lapses, because it cannot spring into action when the parent is incapacitated and then lapse when the parent is well enough to continue her parenting duties.

To avoid the legal uncertainties of a power of attorney, a mother with HIV might want a temporary or permanent guardian appointed for her children. A guardian stands in the shoes of the parent, is legally responsible for the children's well-being, can receive benefits for the children, and can make medical and other decisions for their benefit. There are, however, some disadvantages to guardianship. For example, in some states the appointment of a guardian means that the parent permanently relinquishes all parental rights and loses all control over fundamental decisions affecting her children. In other states the parent retains some, but not all, parental rights and can make decisions about the children's care with the consent of the guardian. In these states, when the parent and the guardian disagree over fundamental decisions, there is an element of uncertainty about the extent of the parent's rights.

Even when the parent is willing to relinquish custody temporarily or permanently, the guardianship option may be particularly difficult for a poor HIV-positive mother because she will usually need legal assistance in petitioning the court to appoint a guardian, and the process can take several months. In the meantime, she may be too sick to care for her children and may be forced to make informal, legally ineffective child care arrangements or place her children in foster care.

In situations where family members are willing to care for the children but need financial assistance, some lawyers suggest that the mother voluntarily surrender her children to foster care on a temporary basis and request that they be placed with relatives, in what is commonly called "kinship foster care." This arrangement has certain advantages. Relatives, who otherwise may be financially unable to provide for the children, are given the same monthly allowances as nonrelated foster parents, and the children, emotionally upset about the illness of their custodial parent, remain with family members. However, all foster care homes must be reviewed and approved by the appropriate agency. This process takes time, and in the interim the children, now wards of the state, may remain in state custody or be placed with strangers. Further, while the relatives may want to care for the children, they may be unwilling to undergo the government scrutiny and monitoring of their lives required by the foster care system, and the children may remain with strangers. Perhaps even more important to the mother, surrendering her children to foster care means relinquishing custody.

There are other disadvantages to foster care. The state controls the parent-child relationship and can dictate many things, including the time and frequency of parental visits. As a result, it may be difficult for the HIV-positive parent to regain custody of her children, or even to visit them regularly, once her circumstances have improved. This is especially true when the children are receiving certain benefits such as AFDC, Medicaid, and Social Security Disability.

Once the parent surrenders control of her children, either to the foster care system or to a legal guardian, any benefits the children receive are transferred to the foster parents or guardian, thus reducing the parent's income, often substantially. The parent may not be able to maintain the current home and may lose some of her health care benefits as well. Only through more informal, but less legally effective, child care arrangements can she both retain legal custody and avoid losing public benefits provided for the children. Thus, the legal and social structures often work against the HIV-infected mother who is eager to play a major role in raising her children although she is ill.

There are even more problems when the custodial parent dies. When no guardian has been appointed, the children may be placed with strangers in foster care until they can be adopted. When guardianship proceedings have been initiated before the parent's death, the court may appoint a temporary unrelated guardian to make necessary decisions for the children pending final resolution of the guardianship petition. This shifting of environments can be particularly upsetting for young children who have just lost their mother.

By law, in most states, the surviving noncustodial parent has the right to custody of any children. This parent is preferred over other family members, even when the parent had little or no prior involvement with the children. However, some custodial parents may object to the surviving parent's obtaining custody. In this instance, a terminally ill HIV-positive custodial parent needs to resolve the care issue before she dies, since she may have evidence of the surviving parent's unfitness that might help other family members obtain custody. To do this, the custodial parent must not only arrange for the appointment of a guardian for her children, but must also be prepared, in some states, to initiate action to terminate the soon-to-be surviving parent's rights. The process may take many months, draining the limited energies of the terminally ill parent.

Some of the child care problems created when the parent is temporarily ill could be alleviated if there were sufficient in-home support services so that the child could remain at home and the parent and child could be cared for together. Studies of the cost of in-home (as opposed to hospital) care for HIV-positive people indicate that home care is much cheaper and seems to have a more positive psychological effect on the patients. In addition, both mothers and children benefit when they are kept together.[48] Considering the most likely alternative—long-term foster care in numerous foster homes—and the likely consequence of such arrangements—severe emotional disturbance—it may be far preferable for dependent children to remain with a sick parent as long as possible.[49] It may also benefit the mother's health if her children are present and her family is intact. There is anecdotal evidence that maintenance of family structure and continued interaction with family members can prolong the life of terminally ill people.

Some of these concerns led in 1980 to the enactment of the federal Adoption Assistance and Child Welfare Act. Congress wanted to encourage states to adopt reforms that would protect children at home, thus reducing the number of children in foster care, and provide family-focused rehabilitative services in situations where children had been removed from their homes.[50] Under the Act, state foster care systems that receive federal funds must make "reasonable efforts" to prevent removing children from their homes.[51] Reasonable efforts could include family advocacy measures such as homemaking services, transportation to and from health care providers, crisis counseling, drug and alcohol abuse counseling where necessary, and provision of temporary child care.

The extent of a state's obligation to affirmatively take preventive steps to avoid removing children from their homes is unclear.[52] Although the secretary of the Department of Health and Human Sevices can hold states accountable for failing to take appropriate steps to keep families intact, the rights created by the Act are not enforceable in lawsuits brought by private citizens under federal civil rights law.[53] In addition, social workers who wrongfully remove children from their homes are immune from suit.[54]

When Parenting Abilities Are Questioned

Our legal system usually assumes that parents, especially mothers of young children, are the most caring and knowledgeable custodians of their children. In fact, most HIV-positive mothers are not only ready and able to take care of their children, but also go to extraordinary lengths to do so, often neglecting their own health in the process. By contrast, there are some mothers with HIV whose lives are so disorganized—due to illness, drug use, financial problems, and so forth—that they have little interest in caring for their children. Then too, there are women whose lives are in a shambles at the time of their children's birth, leading them to give up custody, who later regain some control and want their children back.

Unfortunately, government agencies seldom draw distinctions between HIV-positive mothers when making child custody decisions. Instead, state-initiated custody disputes often reflect the perception of many decisionmakers that HIV-infected mothers are bad and that their infected children are "innocent victims."[55] The "bad mother" label attaches in part because the mother's biological responsibility for the child's status is converted into a kind of moral responsibility. (Tellingly, this type of conversion does not usually occur with mothers of infants who have serious genetic defects.)

Black women are especially stigmatized, because the inseparable combination of their race and gender results in their devaluation as mothers.[56] Economically needy parents are also perceived this way. Thus, when a mother is HIV-positive, Black, and poor, the cumulative biases cannot help but influence how health care and social service workers judge her conduct as a parent. True, when the mother is also a drug user, the "bad mother" label may have more validity, although not invariably. Yet this labeling, whether accurate or not, influences attitudes about the mother and her parenting skills that can result in the wrongful removal of children from her home.

Similarly, mothers with HIV may be more likely to be accused of neglect by social service agencies and to have their children removed by the state. This is especially true for the large number of HIV-infected women identified as drug users. Drug-using mothers may lose custody because their drug status alone is seen as evidence of child neglect. Further, child neglect proceedings are often instituted when neonatal testing discloses illicit drug use by the mother.[57] The child-neglect label attaches even though the mother may have tried unsuccessfully to enter a drug treatment facility. Yet health and social services workers, when assessing the existence of neglect, may act to punish the mother because she has not obtained treatment for her drug problem.

The absence of drug treatment facilities for female drug users, especially pregnant women, makes rehabilitation exceedingly difficult to pursue. Even when a drug-using woman is not pregnant, few of the treatment programs that admit women allow mothers to reside on the premises with their children.[58] Thus drug-using mothers who are also HIV-positive have few support mechanisms to help them handle their addiction while keeping their families together; yet government agencies may be quick to sever family bonds and take children from loving parents because of their drug status.

Drug users die faster after HIV diagnosis than non-users, yet it has not been determined whether drug users' infection advances more rapidly to AIDS and death. One possible explanation may be that drug users generally are in poorer health because they do not take good care of themselves and get inadequate nutrition.[59] Consequently, they may be less able to attend to the basic needs of their children. Unless local social service agencies are pressured to provide support services to keep their families intact, active drug users may be even more likely than other HIV-positive parents to lose custody of their children because of poor health. Social support services, as well as medical care, are necessary components of adequate care for HIV-infected parents.

Whether or not the mother's own poor health justifies removal of her children, physically abusing them and neglecting their medical needs are certainly appropriate grounds for state intervention. However, charges of medical neglect should be viewed with caution since they often reflect the racial, class, and lifestyle assumptions of the person who lodged them. Thus, Black children tend to be significantly overrepresented in child abuse and neglect reportings. Further, the parents most often reported for child neglect are young single women who are on public assistance.[60] Many of the parents and children whose lives are affected by HIV fit these profiles.

Since abuse and neglect charges often stem from the perception that poor and non-White mothers are incapable of being good parents, we should look closely at what agencies characterize as medical neglect. All too often the neglect charged is simply the parent's inability to provide adequate health care due to lack of transportation, failure to maintain Medicaid benefits or provide proof of eligibility, or the existence of more pressing family problems that need to be addressed. Home-based support services could substantially reduce this alleged neglect. Here again, social service policies are not designed to assist poor HIV-positive mothers in handling their family-related problems and keeping their families intact.

An HIV-infected parent also may be reported for medical neglect for reasons related to, but distinct from, her HIV status. For example, several mothers who gave birth to babies with narcotic toxicity have lost custody of their children on grounds of neglect.[61] Most of these mothers were Black, and many were also HIV-positive. Although one court has concluded that removing newborns with narcotic toxicity from their mothers is an unconstitutional restriction on the integrity of the pregnant woman, most states continue this practice.[62]

Many child advocates oppose removing children from their homes solely on account of medical neglect, in light of the myriad inadequacies of foster care.[63] Whether or not one adopts that position, efforts to remove children based only on allegations of child neglect should be closely scrutinized, especially in light of the state's obligations under the Adoption Assistance and Child Welfare Act. Unfortunately, Black and Latino parents are less likely to receive the support services encouraged by the Act, and their children are therefore overrepresented in foster care.[64]

The State as Substitute Parent

There is a growing number of HIV-positive children whose care has been entrusted to state social services agencies.[65] It is estimated that in New York City alone, 50,000 to 100,000 children will lose at least one parent to AIDS in this generation, and of this number 20,000 will lose one parent by 1995. Many of these children will become wards of the state. As noted previously, many "chemically dependent HIV-positive women may be unable or unwilling to care for their children" and may make no arrangements for transferring custody.[66] Since appropriate care settings within the children's extended family may be impossible, the next-best placement is often in foster or small group homes. According to one study, approximately 26 percent of all HIV-infected children who do not live with their parents live in foster care.[67]

HIV Testing and Confidentiality. State social service agencies often face difficult problems when acting as substitute parents. One problem concerns the right of infected children to confidentiality regarding their HIV status when they are placed in foster care. Two questions often arise in this situation: whether the state agency may test children in foster care for HIV antibodies and whether it may include information about their HIV status in their files.

Some states may attempt testing without parental consent when placing children in foster care. The CDC recommends that agencies routinely screen children thought to be at risk before placing them in foster or adoptive homes.[68] However, federal regulations suggest that, in the absence of parental consent, a child advocate be appointed before testing occurs.[69] The argument in favor of testing is that infected children should be identified so that they can receive appropriate medical care, including access to AZT and experimental treatment protocols. This argument is stronger today, since HIV-positive children are no longer denied access to experimental drugs. However, "the treatment arsenal is meager."[70] At least one commentator appropriately suggests that testing should occur only if "uncertainty concerning [the] child's HIV status is hampering foster placement and if it is clearly demonstrable that testing will be beneficial to the child, even if the child is seropositive."[71]

Many public agencies do not follow the CDC guidelines, some fearing that disclosure of a child's HIV status will jeopardize foster care placements. On the other hand, some child advocates argue that prospective foster or adoptive parents have a right to know that a child in their care is infected. These advocates also argue that agencies need this information to assess the fitness of parents to handle HIV-positive children and determine eligibility for special financial subsidies.[72]

The right to know may be more important for prospective adoptive parents. Otherwise, adoptive parents may attempt to return HIV-infected children to the state, claiming that they were misled or not fully informed at the time of adoption. Some states already allow abrogation of adoptions, despite opposition by many courts and the drafters of the Uniform Adoption Act.[73]

However, there are several arguments against disclosure under these circumstances. First, reporting children's HIV status almost inevitably discloses the parents' status or at least the mother's, if she is still living. Once more there is the question of who should balance the competing interests here, and how they should be balanced. It may be difficult for the mother to decide whether her interest or her children's is paramount, and the law provides little guidance in this area. Second, departments of social services may not be able to maintain adequate confidentiality and deal appropriately with this information. The very difficult question is whether the benefits of disclosing children's antibody status outweigh the detriments. Given the continued public hysteria toward people with HIV, it may be best for infected children to be adopted by people who are fully aware of their status. This reasoning may not apply to foster parents, however, since placement is temporary and the virus is not transmitted through casual contact. Even then, disclosure may be warranted where there is some showing of a clear danger to the foster parents or their immediate family; where special monthly allowances are given to foster parents of HIV-positive children; or where the foster children are eligible for special medical benefits because of their HIV status. (For a detailed discussion of privacy law, see chapter 7.)

Treatment. The state has an affirmative obligation to insure the safety and general welfare of children in its custody.[74] Children in foster care also have a right to treatment or medical care.[75] In fact, federal law provides children with a private right of action against state foster care agencies for failure to provide adequate health care[76] or adequate services. Of course, having a right does not always ensure that it will be respected, and better monitoring of state foster care agencies is needed.

When HIV-infected children are in foster care, serious medical treatment issues may arise, such as whether they should be given AZT. Since infants and young children are not legally competent to consent to medical treatment, in the absence of parental involvement the state must petition the court for authority to consent to even routine medical treatment.[77]

Much HIV treatment, especially for infants and young children, is experimental, and special procedures are warranted. Clinical drug trials are now more widely available to children, but some children in foster care may be denied access to these opportunities. For example, some states refuse to allow children in foster care to participate in AZT protocols when there is no active parental involvement, because they do not want to be responsible for giving consent. Other states may claim that some AIDS-related protocols, because they are experimental, do not constitute medical treatment, and may deny access on that basis. In New Jersey, a local child-protection agency refused on those grounds to let infants under its care participate in then-experimental AZT treatment clinical trials.[78] States may also refuse to let HIV-positive children in their custody enroll in clinical drug trials using a placebo control,[79] but there are stronger arguments for this position since the children receiving the placebo obtain no possible benefit from their participation. In some instances court-appointed special advocates will review and monitor special treatment for the children,[80] but to date there is no uniform policy for handling treatment issues.

At present, seven states have policies specifying the conditions under which the state may consent to experimental treatment for children in foster care.[81] Four states do not allow foster children to enroll in clinical trials without parental consent, the consent of some designated committee, or a court order if the natural parent is unavailable.[82] Other states have created central boards that review treatment protocols and make decisions on a case-by-case basis.[83] Although approximately 26 percent of HIV-positive children are in foster care, a 1989 study found that only 16 percent of children participating in NIH-funded clinical trials were in foster care. The researchers speculated that many other children in foster care are denied access because proper consent cannot be obtained.[84]

When parental rights have not been terminated, it is often difficult to determine who has the authority to consent to experimental treatment of children in foster care. It also is important to remember that children's health may not necessarily require that they participate in research, and their use in experimental HIV clinical trials is still controversial. In addition, because a disproportionate number of infected children are Black and Latino, there are potential racial overtones to either decision, allowing or denying participation.

It is difficult to adopt a single approach to the participation of children in foster care in clinical trials. Admission to these trials may be the only means by which they can obtain free medical care. Therefore, no children who can benefit from experimental treatment should be denied access simply because they are in foster care. Nevertheless, no children in foster care should be enrolled in an experimental treatment protocol without the informed consent of their biological parents. When the biological parent is unavailable, there must be some review and monitoring of the treatment protocols, coupled with a determination that the child can benefit from participation. This determination should be made by either a neutral multidisciplinary committee (which includes an ethicist, pediatrician, social worker, and community member or parent of an HIV-infected child), or a court of law.

These precautions may not be sufficient to prevent abuse of HIV-positive children in clinical trials. Meaningful constraints on human experimentation by medical researchers are fairly recent, and they were influenced by the history of abuses directed at various groups including people of color, poor people, and children. There are sound reasons for excluding children from some clinical trials, and when the children most likely to be participating are members of economic, racial, or ethnic groups who historically have been exploited by medical researchers, there is even more reason for concern.

Increased participation of children in clinical trials, justified by the fact that participation may be the only way these children can receive medical care, is a harsh indictment of the United States' health care system. It is hoped that public outrage at these shortcomings will stimulate action to restructure the entire health care system or, at the very least, make health care more readily available for women and children.

CONCLUSION

The AIDS pandemic could provide the United States with the opportunity to seriously reassess both its health care and its social support systems for families, especially poor women, women of color, and their children. Since any strategy directed toward HIV-positive women carries with it the legacies of sexism and racism in medicine coupled with class biases, models must be developed for planning effective health care strategies that take all of these factors into account. We must be more willing to draw distinctions between individuals, rather than allowing our biases about the parenting abilities of poor HIV-infected mothers to control our decisions about their children.

It is also important that our legal and social services systems be able to provide for hospital "boarder babies" and children who are abandoned; to attend to the needs of dysfunctional mothers and give them a second chance once their lives are stabilized; to acknowledge and support mothers and other family members or close friends who are eager to serve as full-time caregivers; and to make allowances for, and provide support to ease, any temporary periods when HIV-positive mothers are disabled. Our health care policies for women and their children will remain ineffective so long as race, sex, and class biases influence who gets care and the quality of that care.

NOTES

1 *Update: Acquired Immunodeficiency Syndrome—United States, 1981–1990,* 265 J.A.M.A. 3226, 3226 (1991). In 1981 women made up only 3 percent of the total cases reported to the CDC. Weissman, *Working with Pregnant Women at High Risk for HIV Infection: Outreach and Intervention,* 67 Bull. N.Y. Acad. Med. 291, 292 (1991). Today, AIDS is fifth in the leading causes of death among women of childbearing age. Gayle, Selik & Chu, *Surveillance for AIDS & HIV Infection among Black & Hispanic Women of Childbearing Age, 1981–1989,* 39 MMWR 23, 24 (1990).

2 *Update: Acquired Immunodeficiency Syndrome—United States, 1981–1990,* note 1 above at 3226; Gayle, Selik & Chu, note 1 at 24.

3 Zylke, *Another Consequence of Uncontrolled Spread of HIV among Adults: Vertical Transmission,* 265 J.A.M.A. 1798, 1798 (1991).

4 *HIV Prevalence Estimates and AIDS Case Projections for the United States,* 39 13

(1990); Zylke, note 3 above at 1798 (1,800 to 2,000).

5 Pizzo & Butler, *In the Vertical Transmission of HIV, Timing May Be Everything,* 325 New Eng. J. Med. 652, (1991) (noting maternal-fetal transmission average of about 25 to 30 percent).

6 As Antonia C. Novello, the Surgeon General of the United States, said recently: "The issue of infected women and AIDS is much broader than the actual numbers of infected women. It goes to the heart of how we as women are going to live our lives. Too many women take care of their families and not themselves. We must do both." Novello, *Women and HIV Infection,* 265 J.A.M.A. 1805, 1805 (1991).

7 Amaro, *Women's Reproductive Rights in the Age of AIDS: New Threats to Informed Choice,* 5 The Genetic Resource 39, 40 (1990); *accord* Weissman, note 1 above, at 293.

8 *See* Anastos & Marte, *Women—Missing Persons in the AIDS Epidemic* in The AIDS Reader: Social, Political, Ethical Issues 190 (N. McKenzie ed. 1991). A recent study by Georgetown University Hospital found that 75 percent of urban women had T-cell counts under 500 at the time they discovered their seropositive status. Pfeiffer, *Highlights from the National Conference on Women and HIV Infection, Part One: Early Care and Policy Issues,* 5 AIDS Patient Care 67, 68 (1991); *see also* White, *Highlights from the National Conference on Women and HIV Infection, Part Two: Case Definition and Clinical Trials,* 5 AIDS Patient Care 70, 72 (1991) (women are sicker at the time of diagnosis and die sooner after diagnosis than men).

9 Gwinn, *et al., Prevalence of HIV Infection in Childbearing Women in the United States,* 265 J.A.M.A. 1704, (1991); CDC, *Characteristics of and HIV Infection among Women Served by Publicly Funded HIV Counseling and Testing Services—United States, 1989–1990,* 265 J.A.M.A. 2051 (1991). Black and Latino women also comprise a disproportion-

ate percentage of the women who die from AIDS. CDC, *AIDS in Women—United States,* 265 J.A.M.A. 23, 23 (1991) (Black and Hispanic women, only 19 percent of all U.S. women, comprise 72 percent of all U.S. women diagnosed with AIDS).

I capitalize "Black" because I use the term as proper noun to refer to a specific cultural group rather than merely skin color. I use "Latina" rather than "Hispanic" to emphasize that most of the Hispanic HIV-positive women are from the Americas. When referring to both groups of women and other non-White women in America (Asians and Native Americans), I use the term "women of color." The term "people of color" refers to the collective non-White communities in America.

10 House Committee On Government Operations, 101st Cong. 2d Sess., AIDS Treatment and Care: Who Cares? 36–41 (1990) (noting the disproportionate impact of AIDS on poor residents of the larger urban inner cities).

11 Gwinn, *et al.,* note 9 above at 1706; CDC *Characteristics of and HIV Infection among Women Served by Publicly Funded HIV Counseling and Testing Services,* note 9 above, at 2051.

12 *See, e.g.,* Nsiah-Jefferson, *Reproductive Laws, Women of Color, and Low-Income Women,* 11 Women's Rts. L. Rep. 15, 20–23, 30–32 (1989); Asaro, *The Judicial Portrayal of the Physician in Abortion and Sterilization Decisions: The Use and Abuse of Medical Discretion,* 6 Harv. Women's L. J. 51, 93–101 (1983); Grosboll, *Sterilization Abuse: Current State of the Law and Remedies for Abuse,* 10 Golden Gate L. Rev. 1147, 1153–56 (1980).

13 *See* Minkoff, *Care of Pregnant Women Infected with Human Immunodeficiency Virus,* 258 J.A.M.A. 2714, 2714 (1987). The CDC is currently revising this guideline.

14 Hilts, *Many Hospitals Found to Ignore Rights of Patients in AIDS Testing,* N.Y. Times, Feb. 17, 1990, at A1; *see also* Henry, Willenbring & Crossley, *Human Immunodefi-*

ciency Virus: Analysis of the Use of HIV Anti-body Testing, 295 J.A.M.A. 1819, 1820 (1988) (34 percent of 183 United States hospitals that conduct infectious disease training and 57 percent of 103 Minnesota hospitals rarely obtained patient consent to HIV antibody tests).

15 Hilts, note 14 above.

16 *See, e.g., Doe v. Jamaica Hospital,* N.Y. L. J., May 16, 1991 at 21; Angell, *AIDS Babies Remain a Puzzle,* Gannet News Service, May 21, 1991 (LEXIS) ("The prevalent recommendation is that [HIV] infected women should consider postponing pregnancy and should have an abortion if they do become pregnant."); Flannery, *Whose Rights Come First—Victim or Her Endangered Baby?,* Chicago Tribune, Nov. 18, 1990, at C3 (HIV-infected women are told to be sterilized).

17 Mays & Cochran, *Issues in the Perception of AIDS Risk and Risk Reduction Activities by Black and Hispanic/Latina Women,* 43 Am. Psychologist 949, 953 (1988).

18 For a more detailed discussion of these issues, see Banks, *Women and AIDS—Racism, Sexism, and Classism,* 17 Rev. L. & Soc. Change 351 (1989–1990).

19 Angell, *A Dual Approach to the AIDS Epidemic,* 324 New Eng. J. Med. 1498, 1499 (1991); *see* Zylke, note 3 above, at 1798. Two states appear to require prenatal HIV tests: Del. Code Ann. Rev. tit. 16, § 708 (1988); Tenn. Code Ann. §§ 68–5–102, 68–5–602 (1987). Florida requires prenatal screening for all sexually transmitted diseases, including HIV. 14A Fla. Stat. Ann. §§ 384.31, 384.23(3) (defining sexually transmissible disease). However, it is reported that Florida is applying the HIV prenatal screening requirement only to "high-risk" women. I AIDS: A Public Health Challenge 2–28 (M. Rowe & C. Ryan eds. 1987).

20 Minkoff, note 13 above, at 2714–15.

21 *Compare* Allen & Curran, *Prevention of AIDS and HIV Infections: Needs and Priorities for Epidemiologic Research,* 78 Am J.

Pub. Health 381, 383 (1988) *with* Minkoff & DeHovitz, *Care of Women Infected With the Human Immunodeficiency Virus,* 266 J.A.M.A. 2253, 2256 (1991).

22 Minkoff & DeHovitz, note 21 above, at 2257.

23 Pizzo & Butler, note 5 above, at 652.

24 Zylke, note 3 above, at 1798.

25 The protocol was subsequently modified so that HIV-positive mothers would continue receiving AZT after their child's birth. But even under the modified protocol, the trial is focused on preventing transmission to the fetus, and the mother is viewed simply as the vector who is, at best, a secondary beneficiary.

26 Kolder, Gallagher & Parsons, *Court-Ordered Obstetrical Interventions,* 316 New Eng. J. Med. 1192 (1987); *see* Gallagher, *Prenatal Invasions & Interventions: What's Wrong with Fetal Rights,* 10 Harv. Women's L. J. 9, 48 n.203 (1987).

27 *See, e.g.,* Goldberg, *Medical Choices during Pregnancy: Whose Decision Is It Anyway,* 41 Rutgers L. Rev. 591 (1989); Johnsen, *From Driving to Drugs: Government Regulation of Pregnant Women's Lives After Webster,* 138 U. Pa. L. Rev. 179 (1989); Johnsen, *The Creation of Fetal Rights: Conflicts with Women's Constitutional Rights to Liberty, Privacy, and Equal Protection,* 95 Yale L. J. 599 (1986); Litchtenberg, *Gestational Substance Abuse: A Call for a Thoughtful Legislative Response,* 65 Wash. L. Rev. 377 (1990).

28 *See, e.g.,* Rehabilitation Act of 1973, 29 U.S.C. § 794 (1982 & Supp. V 1987); Civil Rights Restoration Act of 1987, Pub. L. No. 100–259, 102 Stat. 31 (*codified at* 29 U.S.C. § 706 (Supp. V. 1987); Americans with Disabilities Act of 1990, Pub. L. 101–336, 104 Stat. 327 (1990); *see also,* N.Y. Exec. Law, §§ 291 *et seq.* (McKinney 1992).

29 *But see* Rust v. Sullivan, 111 S. Ct. 1759 (1991) (prohibition of abortion counseling by recipeints of federal family planning funds does not violate the Constitution).

30 President's Commission for the Study of Ethical Problems in Medicine and Biomedical and Behavioral Research, Screening and Counseling For Genetic Conditions: A Report on the Ethical, Social and Legal Implications of Genetic Screening, Counseling and Education Programs 47–52 (1983).

31 Selwyn, *et al., Knowledge of HIV Antibody Status and Decisions to Continue or Terminate Pregnancy among Intravenous Drug Users,* 261 J.A.M.A. 3567, 3568 (1989).

32 Twenty-nine states have legislated the equivalent of the Hyde Amendment and restrict Medicaid funds to women in life-threatening situations. Ten states pay for abortion in which rape and incest are involved; twelve states, including Washington, New York, and California, still fund all abortions. Carlson, *Abortion's Hardest Cases,* Time. July 9, 1990, at 22.

33 Donovan, *AIDS and Family Planning Clinics: Confronting the Crisis,* 19 Fam. Plan. Persp. 111, 113 (1987). A more recent study of abortion clinics in New York City found that two-thirds refuse to treat HIV-positive women. Zarembka & Franke, *Women in the AIDS Epidemic: A Portrait of Unmet Needs,* 9 St. Louis U. Pub. L. Rev. 519, 525 (1990).

34 *See* Elias & Annas, Reproductive Genetics and the Law 43, 243 (1987).

35 *Health Data Show Wide Gap between Whites & Blacks,* N.Y. Times, Mar. 23, 1990, at A17. In addition, the number of pregnant women who received either no prenatal care or care late in their pregnancy increased dramatically. *Infant Deaths,* Wash. Post, Mar. 13, 1990, at A24 (editorial); Council on Ethical & Judicial Affairs, Am. Med. Ass'n, *Black-White Disparities in Health Care,* 263 J.A.M.A. 2344 (1990) (noting persistent and often substantial differences in health between Blacks and Whites

and citing obstetrics as one of the areas studied). For a discussion of the general lack of access to health care for Blacks and Latinos, see Blendon, Aiken, Freeman & Corey, *Access to Medical Care for Black and White Americans: A Matter of Continuing Concern,* 261 J.A.M.A. 278 (1989); Munoz, *Care for the Hispanic Poor: A Growing Segment of American Society,* 260 J.A.M.A. 2711 (1988).

36 *See, e.g.,* Working Group on HIV Testing of Pregnant Women and Newborns, *HIV Infection, Pregnant Women, and Newborns,* 264 J.A.M.A. 2416 (1990) (setting out a ten-point program for pregnant women and newborns).

37 For a more detailed discussion of this point, see Nolan, *Ethical Issues in Caring for Pregnant Women and Newborns at Risk for Human Immunodeficiency Virus Infection,* 13 Seminars in Perinatology 55, 56–57 (1989).

38 Levine & Bayer, *The Ethics of Screening for Early Intervention in HIV Disease,* 79 Am. J. Pub. Health 1661, 1662 (1989).

39 Connor, *Advances in Early Diagnosis of Perinatal HIV Infection,* 266 J.A.M.A. 3474, 3475 (1991); Quinn, *Early Diagnosis of Perinatal HIV Infection by Detection of Viral-Specific IgA Antibodies,* 266 J.A.M.A. 3439 (1991); Lindesman, *Clinical Utility of HIV-IgA Immunoblot Assay in the Early Diagnosis of Perinatal HIV Infection,* 266 J.A.M.A. 3443 (1991).

40 In State v. Johnson, No. 89–890-CFA (Fla. Cir. Ct. 1989) a woman was criminally prosecuted for delivering drugs to her newborn through the umbilical cord moments after birth.

41 *In re* Baby X, 293 N.W.2d 736 (Mich. App. 1980), a state court allowed evidence of a mother's drug use during pregnancy to be used a proof of neglect or abuse in a state-initiated proceeding to deprive the woman of her newborn child.

42 Stewart v. Stewart, 521 N.E.2d 956 (Ind. App. 1988); Doe v. Roe, 139 Misc. 2d 209

(N.Y. Sup. Ct. 1988); *In re* Marriage of Lena Roe v. Leslie Roe, Chicago Daily L. Bull., May 16, 1988, at 3 (Cir. Ct. Ill.); Jane W. v. John W., 519 N.Y.S.2d 603 (Sup. Ct. 1987); *In re* Marriage of Grein, 491 N.E.2d 1382 (Ill. App. 1984). *See generally*, Note, *Public Hysteria, Private Conflict: Child Custody and Visitation Disputes Involving an HIV Infected Parent*, 63 N.Y.U. L. Rev. 1092 (1988).

43 Drucker, *Drug Users with AIDS in the City of New York: A Study of Dependent Children, Housing, and Drug Addiction Treatment* in The AIDS Reader: Social, Political, Ethical Issues, note 8 above, at 147.

44 V. B. v. Department of Social Services (on file at Maryland AIDS Law Clinic).

45 Drucker, note 43 above, at 154.

46 *See, e.g.*, Mo. Rev. Stat. § 475.024 (1986); *In re* Marriage of Criqui, 798 P.2d 69 (Kan. Ct. App. 1990).

47 For a discussion of the inadequacy of law in this area, see Zarembka & Franke, note 33 above, at 539–41.

48 *See* Greene, *D.C. Children in Crisis, New Report Declares*, Wash. Post, Sept. 1, 1991, at A1, (citing $3,000 annual cost per child of intensive family preservation programs compared to $10,000 annual cost per child for foster care). For an example of a support program geared to HIV-infected women, see Rierden, *Yale Center Helps Families Learn to Live with AIDS*, N.Y. Times, Sept. 29, 1991, § 12CN, at 1.

49 More than half of children in foster care remain in that status for six years or more, and long-term foster care often results in severe emotional and behavioral problems. Besharov, *The Misuse of Foster Care: When the Desire to Help Children Outruns the Ability to Improve Parental Functioning*, 22 Family L. Q. 213, 220 (1986).

50 D. Duquette, Advocating for the Child in Protection Proceedings 95 (1990).

51 42 U.S.C. §§ 620, 671(a)(15) (1988). Recently the Foster Care Review Board in

Maryland issued a report recommending increased expenditures for its model Intensive Family Services program which is designed to prevent foster care placements. The Board concluded that early preventive action with troubled families not only reduces the number of children placed in foster care, but also reduces costs to the extent of $30,000 for every child not placed into foster care. Maryland Department of Human Resources, Foster Care Review Board, 1990 Annual Report 5–7 (1991).

52 *See* Grant v. Cuomo, 509 N.Y.S.2d 685 (N.Y. Sup. Ct. 1986), *modified*, 518 N.Y.S.2d 105 (App. Div. 1987). For example, a recent study by the Children's Legal Defense Fund found that virtually nothing was spent on intensive family preservation programs in the District of Columbia, and as a result, the number of children (overwhelmingly Black) in foster care is almost twice the national average. Greene, note 48 above, at A8.

53 *See* Suter v. Artist M., 112 S.Ct. 1360 (1992).

54 *See e.g.*, Vosburg v. Department of Social Services, 884 F.2d 133 (4th Cir. 1989); Jenkins v. County of Orange, 260 Cal. Rptr. 645 (Cal. Ct. App. 1989); Myers v. Contra Costa County Department of Social Services, 812 F.2d 1154 (9th Cir.), *cert. denied*, 484 U.S. 829 (1984); Kurzawa v. Miller, 732 F.2d 1456 (6th Cir. 1984).

55 Weissman, note 1 above at 293; *see also* Henderson, *Care: What's in It for Her?* in AIDS: Responses, Interventions and Care 266 (P. Aggleton, G. Hart & P. Davies eds. 1991) (study of women in Britain, Ireland and Italy).

56 For a discussion of this point in the context of drug-addicted Black mothers, see Roberts, *Punishing Drug Addicts Who Have Babies: Women of Color, Equality, and the Right of Privacy*, 104 Harv. L. Rev. 1419, 1423–4, 1436–1444 (1991).

57 *Id.*

58 *Id.* at 1448.

59 Karan, *AIDS Prevention and Chemical Dependence Treatment Needs of Women and Their Children,* 21 J. Psychoactive Drugs 395, 396 (1989).

60 Hogan & Sui, *Minority Children and the Child Welfare System: An Historical Perspective,* 33 Social Work 493 (1988).

61 *See, e.g., In re* Danielle Smith, 128 Misc.2d 976 (Fam. Ct. N.Y. 1985); *In re* Gloria C. & William C.*,* 124 Misc.2d 313 (Fam. Ct. N.Y. 1984). Recently a New York State appeals court upheld a New York City policy of seeking neglect hearings whenever a hospital informs it that a child has been born with cocaine in her/his system. Three-fourths of the newborns reported are taken from their mothers and one-half enter foster homes. Baquet, *Hearings on Neglect Upheld in Newborn Cocaine Cases,* N. Y. Times, May 30, 1990, at B3.

62 *In re* Sharon Fletcher & Lisa Flynn, 141 Misc.2d 333 (Fam. Ct. N.Y. 1988).

63 Black children are more likely to be in foster homes and stay in those homes, longer than White children. They are also less likely to be adopted if their parents die or parental rights are terminated. Jenkins, *et al., Ethnic Differences in Foster Care Placements,* 19 Social Work Research & Abstracts 41 (1983). A recent American Civil Liberties Union (ACLU) study of the foster care system in Washington, D.C., found numerous violations of regulations adopted under the Federal Adoption Assistance and Child Welfare Act of 1980. Similar violations were found in seven of the twenty-three state foster care systems studies. Barden, *A.C.L.U. Says Violations Pervading Foster Care System in Capital,* N.Y. Times, Oct. 28, 1990, at A22. Subsequently, the ACLU filed suit in New York City, the District of Columbia, Philadelphia, Kansas City, Missouri, and against the states of Connecticut, Kansas, Louisiana, New Mexico, and Pennsylvania, challenging the adequacy of existing foster care systems. In December 1990 Connecticut settled its suit

by agreeing to have an outside panel direct its child welfare system. In April 1991 a federal district judge ruled that the District of Columbia's foster care system violated the constitutional rights of children in the system and violated federal laws by not regularly reviewing foster care placements. Barden, *Washington Cedes Control of Foster Care System to Private Agency,* N.Y. Times, July 14, 1991 at A11.

64 Hogan & Siu, note 60 above, at 493.

65 For example, Dr. James Oleske, who works with HIV infected children at Children's Hospital in Newark, New Jersey, reported that approximately 40 percent of his patients are wards of child protective services departments. Staff of the Select Committee On Children, Youth, And Families, 100th Cong., 2d sess., Continuing Jeopardy: Children and AIDS, 7 (1988).

66 Lambert, *AIDS Abandoning Growing Generation of Needy Orphans,* N.Y. Times, July 17, 1989, at A1. (citing M. Boland, Management of the Child With HIV Infection: Implications for Service Delivery, Report of the Surgeon General's Workshop on Children with HIV Infection and their Families (1987)); Shaw & Paleo, *Women and AIDS,* in What to Do about AIDS (L. McKusick ed. 1986).

67 Weimer, *Beyond Parens Patriae: Assuring Timely, Informed, Compassionate Decision Making for HIV-Positive Children in Foster Care,* 46 U. Miami L. Rev. 379 (1991).

68 *Education and Foster Care of Children Infected with Human T-Lymphotropic Virus— Type III—Lymphadenopathy Associated Virus,* 34 MMWR 517 (1985).

69 *Research Involving Greater than Minimal Risk and No Prospect of Direct Benefit to Individual Subjects, but Likely to Yield General Knowledge about the Subject; Disorder of Condition* 45 C.F.R. §§ 46.406-.409 (1989).

70 Hankins, *Issues Involving Women, Children, and AIDS Primarily in the Developed World,* 3 J. AIDS 443, 446 (1990).

71 Field, *Testing for AIDS: Uses and Abuses,* 16 Am. J. L. & Med. 33, 100 (1990).

72 The Abandoned Infants Act of 1988, 42 U.S.C. § 670 (1988), provides funds for demonstration grants for the care of HIV-infected infants in foster families, as well as their own families; *see also* the Federal Adoption Assistance & Child Welfare Act, 42 U.S.C. §§ 602–628 (1988).

73 Uniform Adoption Act, § 15 9 U.L.A. 11, 477 (1979); *see, e.g.,* Cal. Civil Code § 227b (1982); Allen v. Allen, 330 P.2d 151 (Or. 1958). *See generally* Annot., *Annulment or Vacation of Adoption Decree by Adopting Parent or Natural Parent Consenting to Adoption,* 2 A.L.R.2d 887 (1948); Annot. *Action for Wrongful Adoption Based on Misrepresentation of Child's Mental or Physical Condition or Parentage and Uniform Adoption Act,* 56 A.L.R.4th 375 (1987).

74 *See* Escamilla v. City of Santa Ana, 796 F.2d 266, 269–70 (9th Cir. 1986) (state has an affirmative duty to protect when there is a custodial relationship with an individual); Taylor *ex rel.* Walker v. Ledbetter, 818 F.2d 791, 797–98 (11th Cir. 1987) (1983 action will lie where foster child was beaten in home due to special relation between child and the state); L. J. *ex rel.* Darr v. Massinga, 838 F.2d 118, 122 (4th Cir. 1988) (civil rights action permitted for physical and medical abuse in foster home because of state's special relation to foster child), *cert denied,* 488 U.S. 1018 (1989).

75 Doe v. N.Y. City Department of Social Services, 709 F.2d 782 (2nd Cir. 1983); Lynch v. Dukakis, 719 F.2d 504 (1st Cir. 1983).

76 *Massinga,* 838 F.2d 118; G. L. v. Zumwalt, 564 F. Supp. 1030 (W.D. Mo. 1983); Lynch v. King, 550 F. Supp. 325 (D. Mass. 1982), *aff'd sub nom,* Lynch v. Dukakis, 719 F.2d 504 (1st Cir. 1983).

77 Martin & Sacks, *Do HIV-Infected Children in Foster Care Have Access to Clinical Trials of New Treatments?* 5 AIDS & Pub. Pol'y J., Winter 1990, at 3 (citing four methods of obtaining consent, including parental consent and court order).

78 Staff of the Select Committee on Children, Youth and Families, note 65 above, at 8 (testimony of Dr. Oleske about the Division of Youth and Family Services in New Jersey). This policy is currently under review and is expected to change shortly. Martin & Sacks, note 77 above, at 3.

79 Prentice, *et al., Can Children Be Enrolled in a Placebo Controlled Randomized Clinical Trial of Synthetic Growth Hormone?* IRB: A Review of Human Subject Research, Jan.-Feb. 1989 at 6.

80 45 C.F.R. § 46.409.

81 Martin & Sacks, note 77 above, at 3 (Connecticut, Georgia, Illinois, Massachusetts, New Jersey, Texas & Wyoming).

82 *Id.* (Illinois, New York, Pennsylvania & Wyoming).

83 *Id.* (New York City, Georgia & Massachusetts). Although Martin & Sacks include Maryland among the states that grants foster parents a medical guardianship which enables them to consent for the child, lawyers in that state question this interpretation of the law. *Id.* (citing Md. Est. & Trust Code Ann. 13–708(b)(8) (1990)).

84 Martin & Sacks, note 77 above, at 4.

11 Criminal Law

Harlon L. Dalton

Increasingly over the course of the AIDS epidemic, the criminal law has been brought into play as a mechanism for both deterring and punishing behavior thought to put others at risk of HIV transmission. In particular, people who know that they are HIV-positive run the risk of criminal prosecution if they conduct themselves in ways that threaten the larger society's sense of safety. In addition, once they are caught up in the criminal justice system, for whatever reason, people living with HIV run the risk that their status will have a negative impact at virtually every stage of the proceedings, from arraignment through sentencing.

THE CRIMINALIZATION OF RISKY BEHAVIOR

According to a study commissioned by the federal government, by the end of 1991 more than three hundred people had been prosecuted for allegedly putting others at risk of HIV transmission. Approximately one-sixth of those cases—fifty or so—had resulted in convictions. Somewhat surprisingly, about half of the convictions involved armed services personnel prosecuted in military courts under military law.[1]

Most of the civilian cases involve courtroom, jailhouse, or arrest-scene skirmishes in which a prisoner or detainee allegedly spit at or bit a law enforcement officer. More often than not, the detainee punctuated the hostilities by announcing that he or she was infected with HIV. In some cases, the detainee reportedly expressed the desire to transmit the virus to the officer. Not surprisingly, the officers in these cases reacted with alarm, anger, and fear, especially if they were poorly informed about the ways in which HIV is and is not transmitted. Seeking retribution, they turned to a criminal justice system that, at least at the margin, could be expected to respond sympathetically to those who serve it day in and day out.

The high water mark of such cases is *Texas v. Weeks*, in which an inmate was

242

convicted of attempted murder and sentenced to ninety-nine years in prison for spitting at a correctional officer.[2] Similar is *State v. Smith*, in which a New Jersey inmate was sentenced to twenty years in prison for attempted murder plus an additional five years for aggravated assault, for allegedly biting an officer and shouting "now die."[3] (As of April 1992, both convictions were being vigorously challenged on appeal).

It is still too early to tell whether cases like *Weeks* and *Smith* constitute the rule or the exception, since it is difficult to determine how frequently and on what terms prosecutions are "disposed of" prior to trial. When biting and spitting cases do go to trial, however, convictions and stiff sentences appear to be the norm, notwithstanding the many "proof problems" described later.

When the scene shifts to the appellate courts, the experience has been mixed. On one side are cases like *Scroggins v. State*, in which the Georgia Court of Appeals upheld an "assault with intent to kill" conviction for biting a police officer.[4] On the other is *Brock v. State*, in which the Alabama Court of Criminal Appeals overturned a first degree assault conviction, concluding that the prosecution had failed to "prove that the [HIV-positive] defendant used his mouth and teeth under circumstances highly capable of causing death or serious physical injury."[5] In between these extremes is *United States v. Moore*, in which a federal appellate court sought to finesse the issue of the defendant's HIV status, despite its prominent mention at trial. The court upheld an aggravated assault conviction by resting on the dubious proposition that the defendant's teeth constituted a deadly weapon wholly apart from his HIV infection.[6] In so doing, the court failed to treat seriously the probability that absent the defendant's HIV infection, an assault with a deadly weapon charge would not have been lodged, the case would not have gone to trial, and in any event the jury would not have convicted on that count.

Some civilian prosecutions, and the vast majority of military ones, involve allegations of sexual irresponsibility. In these cases, defendants are charged with failing to tell their sex partners about their HIV infection. Until the late 1980s, most such prosecutions were brought under traditional penal statutes, such as those punishing assault and attempted murder.[7] Some military cases also charged the defendant with disobeying a direct order to refrain from engaging in sex with uninformed partners.[8] Increasingly, however, civilian prosecutions proceed under newly enacted HIV-specific statutes, which make sex without notice of infection a crime, whether or not anyone is harmed and regardless of the defendant's "state of mind."

Some HIV-specific statutes single out commercial sex by making it a crime for infected prostitutes to continue doing business once they have been informed of their HIV status. Usually these statutes do not take account of whether the particular sex acts at issue involve a significant risk of HIV transmission.[9] This omission is especially noteworthy in commercial settings, where the most commonly purchased sex acts pose relatively little risk, and where the use of condoms is the norm.[10]

The "sex without notice" cases differ from the biting and spitting ones in several important respects. First, HIV transmission is a real possibility in the sex cases, at least to the extent that safer sex precautions are not taken. In contrast, when biting and spitting constitutes the relevant behavior, the likelihood of transmission approaches zero. However, in the sex cases the defendants rarely can be said to have acted out of malice. Their failure to inform their sexual partners of their HIV status is, in most cases, attributable to the pursuit of pleasure or, at worst, profit. Notwithstanding the awkwardness with which we as a nation approach the subject, consensual sex can be a socially, as well as personally, rewarding activity. In contrast, there is little to be said for spitting at or maliciously biting one another.

Finally, there is a different "impulse to criminalize" at work in the two sets of cases. The sex cases tap into an incredibly deep and murky reservoir of worry, fear, excitement and dread. Quite apart from AIDS, sex (especially, but not exclusively, casual sex) embodies, for many of us, an unsettling mix of reward and risk, pleasure and danger.[11] The thought that, unbeknownst to us, a lover might be infected with HIV serves to remind us of how vulnerable we truly are, emotionally as well as physically, when it comes to sex. The fact that we cannot tell whether a lover has HIV is scary, both in its own right and because it reminds us that so much else of importance is also beyond our immediate powers of observation. Will Mr. or Ms. Right prove sensitive to our needs, we wonder? Will she or he find us wanting? Will he turn out to be a jerk? Has she been completely forthcoming about her sexual past? About the present? Given our unease surrounding sex, together with its near universality as a human pastime (or at least aspiration), it is not surprising that we would look for ways to *compel* others to behave responsibly. We want to feel safe, to be made safe, to be protected from bad choices, to avoid having to fully reckon with the risks of carnal knowledge.

By contrast, the biting and spitting cases do not tap into anything so elemental or widespread, apart from our generalized, culturally reinforced fear of disease and death. Indeed, our impulse to criminalize seems to arise not so much from an engaged sense of vulnerability as from a kind of institutional sympathy for those who are the usual targets of spittle. Then, too, there is a more troublesome explanation for the prominence of these cases and for the draconian punishments imposed in the most well-publicized ones. These cases represent a new phase in an ongoing struggle for control and respect between keepers of the peace and those who are kept. In a sense, HIV represents a new weapon possessed by HIV-positive detainees (at least to the extent that law enforcement personnel fear transmission via saliva), and major prosecutions for minor assaults represent a new weapon in the arsenal of the men and women in blue.

Arguably, rash prosecutions, unsupported convictions and harsh sentences constitute the functional equivalent of the jury verdict in the police-brutality trial arising out of the savage beating of Rodney King. That case reminds us that when presented with a forced choice between the keepers and the kept, society's surrogates will often favor order at the expense of law. This is especially true when those in detention are objectified or treated as other than human. During the police-brutality trial, King was frequently described in animalistic and monster-like terms (for example, "like a bull''; "Hulk-like''). Similarly, the defendants in biting and spitting cases often are casually dismissed as "ticking time bombs," "deadly weapons," and the like.

In addition to biting, spitting, and engaging in sex, other behaviors have, on occasion, been deemed criminal when engaged in by people who are HIV-positive. Examples include selling blood,[12] intentionally splashing blood,[13] and throwing feces at a prison guard.[14] In addition, prosecutions could easily be brought, especially in states that specifically make it a crime, against people who know they are HIV-positive and nevertheless share drug injection equipment.[15] To date, however, no such cases have been reported, perhaps because would-be complainants fear self-incrimination, because proving that a given individual's act caused a recognizable harm is not easy, and because the general public feels little empathy for substance users whose illegal behavior puts them at risk for HIV.

Traditional Crimes

Many of the criminal charges lodged in HIV exposure cases have a familiar ring: assault, aggravated assault, assault with a deadly weapon, attempted manslaughter, and attempted murder. Most of these charges are quite serious, reflecting (in addition to routine overcharging to offset plea bargaining) the fact that some prosecutors are highly phobic when it comes to AIDS; that some prosecutors are overly attentive to the publicity value of high-profile AIDS cases; and that some victims, especially in biting and spitting cases, are highly adept at making the system work for them.

Unlike the sex cases, which increasingly are brought under HIV-specific penal statutes, the biting and spitting cases continue to be squeezed into traditional criminal categories. In order to prove that a traditional crime has taken place, certain requisites or "elements" must be established. Typically, the prosecution must prove at least three elements beyond a reasonable doubt: that a socially unacceptable "harm" has been suffered; that the accused's actions "caused" that harm to occur; and that the accused acted with a blameworthy "state of mind." Although the requisite state of mind varies from crime to crime, usually we require that the accused acted *purposefully* in that she intended to cause harm, or that she acted *knowingly*, fully aware that harm would ensue. Sometimes, we punish those who act *recklessly* or *negligently*, by grossly deviating from ordinary regard for others, thereby putting them at grave risk of harm. Usually, however, we leave it to the tort law system to deter, as well as compensate for, negligent behavior. (For more on torts, see chapter 15).

As spelled out below, these elements are difficult to prove in HIV transmission cases. Moreover, these traditional elements do not correspond very well to many of the real world encounters that prompt police and prosecutors to act, since they envision a very different kind of criminal and crime.

Harm. Obviously, death constitutes a "legally cognizable" harm. So, too, does having to live with a debilitating disease. However, in few of the cases prosecuted to date has there been proof that HIV actually was transmitted.[16] In the biting and spitting cases, this is not surprising, since the likelihood of transmission is practically nil. (For more on transmission, see chapter 2). Similarly, in the blood sale cases, the risk of transmission is minimal, thanks to universal blood screening. By contrast, where risky unprotected sex forms the basis of the criminal charge, transmission is a distinct possibility.

Where risky encounters do not result in the transmission of HIV, the harm question is more complex. The criminal law applies most straightforwardly where physical injuries (including death) have been sustained. Similarly, when the accused intends to cause physical injury or exhibits gross indifference to the probability that such injuries will be sustained, if she takes a step in that direction she may not escape criminal liability just because, through fortuity, no injury occurs. What makes the HIV cases difficult, however, is that the injury inflicted is mostly psychic. Indeed, in the biting and spitting cases, that is often the point: to instill fear and express loathing. True, a bite in and of itself constitutes a physical assault, but the additional fact of the assailant's HIV status produces mental, not physical, anguish.

Conduct amounting to the intentional infliction of psychic pain is punishable under the criminal law, as disorderly conduct, menacing, and the like. By and large, however, offenses against the psyche occupy the lower rungs of the penal ladder. More serious crimes—aggravated assault and attempted murder, for example— usually require proof of actual physical harm, of an intent to inflict physical harm, or of a conscious indifference to the real prospect of physical harm. The crime of simple assault stands somewhere in the middle. Although the Model Penal Code (which most states have adopted) defines assault as causing or "attempt[ing] to cause . . . *bodily injury* to another'' (emphasis added),[17] the line between bodily pain and mental anguish is routinely fuzzed over in practice.

Causation. Even where a legally cognizable harm has been established, the prosecution must prove beyond a reasonable doubt that the accused's conduct ''caused'' the harm. Thus, even if an infected person knowingly engages in high-risk behavior with someone who subsequently is diagnosed as HIV-positive, he cannot be held to account for transmitting the virus absent proof that the accuser's infection is traceable to that behavior.

In the biting and spitting cases, this hurdle will rarely if ever be cleared, because HIV generally is not transmitted in that fashion. Even in the sex cases, proof of ''causation'' is difficult, so long as other possible sources of infection cannot be discounted. The proof problem is especially acute where considerable time has elapsed between the act in question and the accuser's HIV diagnosis. In effect, the ''causation'' element extends to defendants an open invitation to explore the accuser's sex life and drug use history, in search of other possible causes of HIV infection. If the prosecution cannot establish that the accuser was HIV negative prior to his encounter with the defendant, and that all of the accuser's other sex partners (if any) were also negative, the defendant may be able to argue that reasonable doubt exists.

In cases where actual harm is not claimed, but instead the accused is charged with intending to cause harm, ''causation'' becomes irrelevant. Nevertheless, logic would seem to suggest that in such cases the state would be obligated to prove that the evil intent, if carried out fully, *would have caused* harm. Similarly, where recklessness is claimed, logic would seem to dictate that there be proof that a ''substantial and unjustifiable risk'' at least existed. Surprisingly, in most states no such proof is required.

That is because of the evisceration of the ''impossibility doctrine.'' At common law, that doctrine specified that when the facts are such that the intended harm could not have been produced by the means employed, a jury may not convict. The issue is often put in question form: can a person be convicted for attempted murder if the gun she used lacked a firing pin, or was a water pistol? The ''impossibility doctrine'' answered the question in the negative. However, despite the doctrine's impressive lineage, most states have, in modern times, abrogated it. Thus, it is sufficient for conviction that a defendant *believes* that his or her act can cause harm, even if that belief is mistaken.[18]

Presumably, most defendants in biting and spitting cases, at least those who were properly counseled at the time they received their HIV test results, understand cognitively that transmission of the virus by means of saliva is extremely unlikely. Yet, many of them reportedly express the wish to infect their antagonists. How should we understand this? Are such expressions the equivalent of a "belief" in the efficacy of transmission by biting or spitting, or are they more properly viewed as futile attempts at wish fulfillment? Consider, alternatively, defendants who do not themselves believe that transmission via saliva is possible, but who correctly anticipate the fears of law enforcement personnel. Unfortunately, we have barely begun to grapple with the true mind-set of the defendants in these cases. Quite possibly, our conceptual apparatus is not up to the task. After all, our working tools—concepts like "intent" and "belief"—are much cruder than is actual human thought and feeling.

State of Mind. As is by now apparent, in AIDS criminal cases much turns on the accused's "mens rea," or "state of mind." We have already seen how this mental element substitutes for "causation" when the crime charged does not involve actual physical harm. But even in cases where physical injury has been sustained, a criminal state of mind must also be proved.

Specifying the precise state of mind is never easy. In most biting and spitting cases, there is ample evidence that the defendant harbored ill will toward the victim. But that is a far cry from a murderous intent or a desire to inflict severe bodily harm. And given the extreme unlikeliness of transmission, it is hard to say that such defendants acted "knowingly" or "recklessly," there being no "substantial and unjustifiable risk of harm" for them to disregard. Even where the defendant has expressed the wish that the victim become infected or die, skepticism regarding state of mind is in order.

Consider, for example, the story of Donald Haines. Following a jury trial he was found guilty of attempted murder for splashing emergency medical technicians and a police officer with HIV-infected blood. The circumstances that gave rise to the prosecution are revealing. The complaining witnesses had been summoned to Haines's home to stop him from committing suicide. Haines had slit his wrists and was determined to see the attempt through to completion. In an effort to keep his unwanted rescuers at bay, he told them his blood was infected with HIV. When they approached him anyway, he began flinging blood at them. He reportedly bit and spit on them as well.[19]

How should we characterize Haines's state of mind? Did he wish to scare his rescuers? Apparently so. Did he intend to harm them? Not really. In truth, he lashed out in a kind of inverted self-defense. Although the people he fought off were seeking to save his life, his goal was the same as if they were attackers—to assert autonomy over his own person.

To be sure, the Haines case may be more sympathetic than the average biting and spitting scenario, but it serves as a cautionary lesson in the importance of looking beneath the surface. As noted above, in the more typical case, aggressive behavior and angry rhetoric are part of a power struggle between jailers and the jailed. The scary words, much more than spittle or incisors, are the real weapon, as the defendant seeks to inflict *psychic* pain by promoting an irrational but nonetheless real fear of infection.

It is not a good idea to permit inmates and detainees to threaten law enforcement personnel at will. Ideally, however, we should treat microaggressions like biting and spitting in the same way we did before AIDS. To the extent that we invoke the criminal law, the appropriate charge in most cases would be disorderly conduct, menacing, simple assault, and, where warranted, resisting arrest or interfering with a peace officer.

At the same time, we should redouble our efforts to educate both law enforcement officers and those they seek to control about how HIV is and is not transmitted. To the extent that detainees recognize that their mouths are *not* lethal weapons, and appreciate that they can no longer induce apoplexy in officers by mounting a salivary attack, the incentive to confront in this way will be greatly reduced.

Properly characterizing the defendant's state of mind is no easier in cases where sexual transmission is feared. It is, however, a gross distortion to suggest that people living with HIV who fail to reveal their status to sex partners ordinarily do so out of a desire to cause harm. More commonly, their goal is to avert isolation, savor intimacy, affirm life, and confirm that they remain sexually desirable.[20] It is especially ludicrous to charge them with attempted murder. Given the low probability of HIV transmission even under "ideal" circumstances (such as anal sex without a condom) and the increasingly long period between infection and death, it is hard to imagine that sexual intercourse would be anyone's weapon of choice.

A decent argument can be made, however, that people who engage in sex without disclosing their HIV infection act "knowingly," fully conscious that transmission may occur. Thus, prosecution may be appropriate under statutes that apply to defendants who act with knowledge of the natural consequences of their acts. However, a key question in such cases would be whether, under the relevant statute, it is sufficient that harm *can* occur, or whether instead it must be probable, or even highly likely. The more certain harm must be, the less suitable is a claim that the accused acted with knowledge.

It is sometimes suggested that the best way to respond to sexual irresponsibility is to invoke penal laws that target reckless behavior. Under the Model Penal Code, many crimes, ranging from aggravated assault to murder, can be committed with a reckless state of mind. The higher one climbs up the ladder, the more "recklessness" must be accompanied by an ever more unattractive mind-set, such as "extreme indifference to the value of human life."[21]

There is, however, a significant risk that bias and arbitrariness will infect the process whenever "recklessness" is the applicable mental element in AIDS cases. In effect, the prosecutor and jury are invited to draw lines: between what is normal and abnormal; between ordinary care and "gross deviations" from the regard we owe one another; between an acceptable risk and an "unjustifiable" one; between foolhardiness and "extreme indifference to the value of human life." In drawing these distinctions, who or what is the standard, the template, the reference point? A reasonably prudent person living with HIV? A person who cannot in a million years imagine becoming infected herself? A person who finds the prospect of HIV infection terrifying? A person who has had only one sex partner his entire life?

Concepts like "recklessness" and "negligence" assume a common psychology, a common set of concerns, a common way of viewing the world. However, one of the realities spotlighted by the HIV epidemic is that we don't always identify successfully with one another, or comprehend the lived experience of people very different from ourselves. Especially when sexual risk-taking is at issue, there is palpable risk that jurors will bring to the evaluative process pre-existing images of and attitudes toward the groups most closely identified with AIDS: gay men, intravenous drug users, African Americans, and Latinos. There is a risk that jurors will be predisposed to see HIV-positive defendants as "abnormal," "deviant," and "reckless."

HIV-Specific Penal Statutes

Needless to say, traditional penal statutes were not drafted with HIV, or any other communicable disease, in mind. They provide little guidance to prosecutors regarding what constitutes HIV-related criminal behavior, and little for judges and juries to go on in determining when behavior can be excused. Their use in the HIV context imperils the accused's due process right to fair notice of what the law commands. For this reason, as well as because of the manifest proof problems outlined above, many states have enacted carefully tailored, HIV-specific statutes in recent years.

Typically, these statutes are composed of three elements: "knowledge" (the accused knew that she was HIV positive); a "prohibited act" (usually a sex act, but some statutes also include other conduct, such as sharing drug injection equipment and donating blood, sperm, tissue, or organs); and an "omission" (the accused failed to inform the sex or needle sharing partner of her HIV-status). Some statutes treat the latter element as an "affirmative defense," that is, an issue on which the defendant must take the initiative and bear the burden of proof.[22]

Unlike traditional penal laws, HIV-specific statutes do not require proof of either "harm," "causation," or "state of mind." It is sufficient that the accused engaged in the forbidden behavior. At the same time, the explicit inclusion of the "omission" element makes it clear that people living with HIV are not expected to be celibate— just responsible. Thus, sex with consenting partners does not violate the law. In contrast, many state courts have ruled that one may not consent to what would otherwise be deemed an assault. The net effect, then, is that under traditional penal law, even sex with a fully informed and fully willing partner may constitute a crime.

HIV-specific statutes have several additional advantages over traditional laws. They provide much clearer warning of what constitutes a crime. They focus on real risks (as distinct from, say, biting and spitting) and place the responsibility for defining crime in the hands of legislatures rather than individual prosecutors.

To be sure, these statutes are not without their drawbacks. A few focus narrowly on prostitutes,[23] without any basis for believing that they are disproportionately likely to transmit HIV.[24] Many are underinclusive, in that they reach unsafe sex but not unsafe drug use.[25] Others are overinclusive, in that they fail to distinguish between sexual conduct likely to transmit HIV, and conduct that poses little risk.[26] Most do not make allowances for defendants who fail to inform their partners but nevertheless take appropriate precautions to minimize the risk of transmission.

The single greatest failing, however, is that few of these statutes require proof that the accused was even aware that the conduct he engaged in posed a significant risk of HIV transmission. Unfortunately, the bare fact that a person has been informed of his HIV-status does not mean that he received adequate risk-reduction counseling, or any counseling at all. Absent such counsel, provided at a time and in a manner well calculated to promote understanding, we cannot be confident that the accused even knew, for example, which sex acts are risky and which are relatively safe.

More fundamentally, it is far from certain that HIV-specific laws, any more than traditional penal statutes, truly advance the purposes that criminal law is generally thought to serve.

Justifications for Invoking the Criminal Law

Although the possible justifications for invoking the criminal law are many, four have emerged over time as paramount: general deterrence (that is, punishing the accused so as to deter others from engaging in similar conduct); incapacitation (keeping the particular offender from victimizing others for a period of time); rehabilitation; and retribution. When measured against each of these, the case for criminalizing risky behavior is highly dubious.

At first glance, the biting and spitting prosecutions would seem easily justifiable on grounds of general deterrence. After all, the conduct at issue, although often spontaneous, is volitional, noncompulsive, and at least fleetingly calculated. Faced with the right incentive (imprisonment, for example), would-be assailants could exercise a degree of self-control, and channel their anger in another way.

However, general deterrence breaks down when potential wrongdoers have little to lose by risking the available sanctions. In many biting and spitting cases, the defendant is already incarcerated at the time of the incident. In such cases, especially where the defendant already expects to remain in prison for the rest of his foreshortened life, the marginal pain of an additional sentence is rather small. Even the threat of segregation from the general prison population is not very effective if the inmate is already separately housed because of HIV, or if he or she would rather live apart for safety reasons.

By contrast, the defendants in sexual transmission cases typically have much to lose should they go to prison. Therefore, the prospect of prosecution would seem to be a powerful deterrent—but only if the message can be received without a lot of psychic interference. The notion that we can deter Paul from engaging in risky sex by punishing Peter assumes a great deal that may not be true. It assumes that Paul engages in rational risk calculation; that he is future oriented; that he will focus on what happens to Peter; that he has come to grips with his HIV status and the fact that he might pose a transmission risk to others; and that he has fully accepted the fact that for the rest of his life he will face more than occasional rejection by potential sex partners.

However, the Pauls of the world, especially those who are newly diagnosed, are not always at their rationally calculating best. They tend not to take the long view; the future seems so bleak. At times, they engage in self-denial regarding their illness and the risk they pose to others. When they do face the specter of death from AIDS, the threat of prosecution for having sex or sharing a needle looms small. At the same time, people who are infected are acutely aware of the risks that attend disclosure of their HIV status—rejection by friends and family, and a life stripped of physical intimacy.

Putting general deterrence to the side, criminalization at least can be counted on (assuming incarceration and ignoring the fact that HIV transmission may occur in prison) to incapacitate known wrongdoers for a period of time. But as always with incapacitation, a larger question arises: is incarceration the best way to accomplish the goal?

Conceivably, there are alternative, less costly ways to neutralize individuals who threaten the public. For example, in dealing with infected people who have sold their bodies or their blood out of financial need, we might well alter their behavior at a fraction of the cost of imprisonment by addressing their economic plight. We might, for example, keep HIV-positive people in the work force through vigorous enforcement of antidiscrimination and confidentiality laws, provide alternative employment to those (including sex workers) who cannot or ought not continue in their regular professions, and provide adequate levels of public assistance to those who are unemployed or unemployable. Similarly, in cases in which the defendants have displayed extreme manifestations of mental disorder, we might reduce the risk they pose to the public by attending to their psychiatric and spiritual needs. In extreme cases, involuntary psychiatric commitment might be appropriate. More commonly, interventions ranging in intrusiveness from peer counseling to voluntary placement in a structured living setting might be attempted.

Rehabilitation has gone out of fashion as a penological goal, insofar as it connotes altering inmates' basic characters. However, we do hang onto the belief that by educating inmates and by imparting to them useful habits and skills, we can help them return successfully to the outside world. Unfortunately, correctional facilities are by and large poorly suited to provide the kinds of education and skills needed by persons with AIDS (PWAS). Mostly, HIV-infected people need help in negotiating a largely hostile world, in adjusting to the cascade of losses they will experience, and in bolstering their self-esteem. Although the best prisons struggle to provide such support to HIV-positive inmates, such efforts are peripheral to the institutions' central mandate.

Which brings us to retribution. The retributive impulse is greatest when great harm has been inflicted. Where transmission occurs, the horror of the harm is clear. But transmission is close to impossible in the biting and spitting cases, and not very common even in the sex cases. Absent transmission, are we as a society entitled to vent our spleen? Perhaps yes, in the biting and spitting cases, at least where the defendant deliberately seeks to inflict emotional harm on the officer. But what about the sex cases? Is payback justified for the psychosexual turmoil inflicted on the victim, and derivatively on the rest of us?

In assessing whether retribution is called for, we also consider whether the transgressor is blameworthy. Is he or she callous, hardened, truly indifferent to the welfare of others? We try to enter the person's head. What was he or she thinking, feeling, and going through at the time of the crime?

Unfortunately, in trying to understand the mind-set of those who fail to disclose their HIV infection to potential sex partners, our vision is clouded by sensationalized media accounts of individuals who appear bent on infecting the world. Consider, for example, Fabian Bridges, a Black gay man whose sexual irresponsibility was showcased in a nationally televised PBS documentary first broadcast in 1986.[27] While filming a contemporaneous account of Bridges' struggle with HIV, the filmmakers learned that he occasionally engaged in sex with others, notwithstanding his HIV status. They then decided to make that fact—and the failure of various public agencies to intervene effectively—a central theme of the documentary.[28] Thus, millions of Americans watched transfixed as Bridges promised his doctor that he would not put others at risk, and then later admitted breaking the promise by picking up, and having sex with, a young man. When asked by the voice behind the camera whether it bothered him to think that he might have transmitted the virus, Bridges answered, without affect, ''I'm just to the point where I just don't give a damn. I really don't.''

At first glance, Bridges appears to be ''a miserable, wretched, uncaring victim-turned-victimizer who used his body as a lethal weapon.''[29] But upon closer inspection, the documentary revealed something else: a man who was lonely, adrift, broke and broken. His voice betrayed resignation and despair, not anger or revenge. Bridges was perhaps most revealing when he described a particular sexual encounter in detail. ''We talked mostly. I liked him. What I liked most was how tender he was. After we cleaned each other up and stuff, he just held me in his arms. I like it when they hold me.'' For Bridges, as for many people, sex served as a sometimes poor proxy for intimacy, and as a temporary escape from life's miseries. Although he may have put his partners at risk (no one bothered to inquire whether Bridges used a condom or otherwise engaged in safer sex), it was not out of malice or evil intent.

This reading of the story is born out by its ending. Disturbed by what he read in the local newspapers, a leader of Houston's gay community tracked Bridges down and offered him the one thing no one else thought to provide: a place to stay and a network of support. Thus sheltered and protected, Bridges no longer was tempted to put others at risk.

Fabian Bridges was never prosecuted for his antisocial behavior. However, the bad press generated by story and by others of similar notoriety[30] set the stage for a wave of prosecutions. Among the most widely publicized was that of Joseph Edward Markowski, a homeless male prostitute charged with attempted murder for selling his blood and for soliciting sex while knowingly infected with HIV.[31]

Was Markowski a proper target for retribution? Consider his long and well-documented history of mental illness. Five times in the five months immediately preceding his arrest, he had been picked up by Los Angeles police for behavior suggestive of psychiatric disorder. On one occasion he was found walking directly into the flow of traffic on Sunset Boulevard. On another, he was found "crying, breaking down emotionally and stating that he would kill himself." On another, he had walked into a bank, sought to remove the security guard's revolver, and pleaded: "Kill me, kill me, I have AIDS." Following each of these encounters, the police sought to have Markowski committed for psychiatric evaluation and treatment.[32]

As even this brief history makes plain, the government knew from the outset that Markowski—a diagnosed psychotic maintained on psychotropic drugs—was more troubled than trouble. In addition, he was in desperate financial straits. The district attorney nevertheless charged Markowski with attempted murder, punishable by life imprisonment. Moreover, despite his belief that Markowski would not survive for more than a year, he nursed the case along for eight months until the jury finally brought it to a merciful end.

Doubtless cases will arise in which retribution is fully justified. The world is full of evil people, some of whom are HIV-positive. But we should not be quick to demonize those whose lives have been turned upside down by this disease. For if we look at them as people rather than as "vectors" or "walking time bombs," we may discover that societal scorn is misplaced.

Criminalization and Public Health

Even if one or more penological or social goals were served by prosecuting the likes of Markowski, Bridges, and Haines, and even if money were no object, a wise nation would consider whether in so doing we advance the public health. If the answer is neutral or positive, we are well ahead of the game. If, on the other hand, criminalization serves to undermine our overall public health response to the HIV epidemic, then we must seriously question whether the gains from criminalization are worth it.

Admittedly, there is great psychological comfort in identifying bad actors— evil people who intentionally or recklessly spread this dread disease—and isolating them from the rest of society. But engaging in purification rituals rarely leaves us safer in fact.[33] HIV is much too widespread to be so easily contained. In fact, the major risk we face is not from evil people who transmit the virus knowingly or callously, but from ordinary people who transmit it unwittingly.

But demonology is not just wrongheaded. It is downright dangerous from a public health perspective, for it lulls us into irresponsibility. We are most at risk, and least able to protect ourselves, when we conclude that we are safe so long as the bad guys are locked up. That is a mentality that inhibits us from exploring, openly and honestly, whether there is anything *in our own lives* that makes us vulnerable to this disease. To take a concrete example, statutes that target prostitutes for prosecution repeat an old and costly mistake. (For more on that subject, see chapter 3.) By falsely suggesting that prostitutes play a major role in HIV transmission in this country, they divert our attention from a much more significant problem: people who engage in sex for pleasure and think of themselves as facing no risk. Moreover, such statutes in effect absolve "johns" from taking responsibility for their own safety, in spite of the fact that it is usually they who insist on not using condoms.

A second, and even more worrisome, concern is that by prosecuting HIV-positive people for biting and spitting, we spread a false message about how HIV is transmitted. In effect, the scientifically unsound fears of law enforcement personnel are projected onto the criminal justice system writ large, and are thereby given a credence that no amount of expert testimony can dissipate. The public hears that an indictment has been handed down, and watches as a prosecutor grabs for headlines with talk of "assault with a deadly weapon" or "attempted murder." Even if calm reason subsequently prevails, and the charges are reduced or dismissed, the damage has been done. In such circumstances, the benefits, if any, that flow from the prosecution are more than outweighed by the harm done to the overall public health effort. After all, confusion and hysteria surrounding HIV transmission only frustrate efforts to develop a sensible, sane and workable public health response.

HIV AS A FACTOR IN CRIMINAL PROCEEDINGS

Given the stigma that still attaches to AIDS, once a criminal defendant's HIV status becomes broadly known, there is a significant risk that his right to a fair trial will be compromised. Therefore, discretion suggests taking appropriate steps to minimize disclosure. That is, however, more easily said than done. If the defendant is incarcerated pending trial, corrections authorities will often be apprised of his status and will pass that information along to the officers who transport him to and from court. Similarly, if the defendant is a repeat player, records from past incarcerations or criminal proceedings may reveal his status. The prosecutor may discover that the defendant is HIV positive, and think it appropriate to inform the court. Often the defendant's own counsel raises the issue, in pleading for release on bail so that medical care is not interrupted, in seeking leniency during plea negotiations, or for similar purposes thought to be in the client's best interest.

At every step of the process, a defendant's HIV status may be taken into account inappropriately. As noted earlier, in marginal cases (such as those involving biting and spitting) it may influence the prosecutor's decision regarding whether to bring charges in the first place, and if so, which. Typically, however, the first stage at which the defendant's HIV is likely to prove a problem is the bail hearing.

Although one hopes it is not common, there is considerable anecdotal evidence that some judges treat defendants' HIV infection as a justification for setting higher bail.[34] Absent proof that a particular defendant's infection makes it more likely that he or she would flee the jurisdiction, such determinations would seem to be wrongful in states where the sole permissible bail consideration is whether (and how large) a "bond" is needed to assure that the defendant will appear in court. Even in states that allow judges to consider whether the defendant poses a danger to the community, a blanket judgment that everyone with HIV constitutes a public health risk, without regard for whether a given individual is aware of and willing to abide by risk-reduction guidelines, would seem to be overly broad. For that reason, the American Bar Association has opposed the use of high bail as a means of isolating people who are HIV positive and has concluded that "a criminal bail hearing is not a proper substitute" for the full-scale civil hearing needed to determine whether an individual's liberty should be circumscribed on public health grounds.[35]

At and prior to trial, a number of things can go wrong. Among the most damaging are the exclusion of HIV-positive defendants from the courtroom, the taking of unnecessary safety precautions when someone with HIV is present in the courtroom, and the disclosure of the defendant's (or a witness's) HIV status to the jury.

When defendants are unable to make bail or are incarcerated for other reasons, they cannot appear in court without the cooperation of several actors including: jail personnel; transportation personnel (who may or may not be employed by the corrections department); security personnel in the courthouse holding pen (who may or may not be employed by the judicial system); and courtroom personnel. AIDS phobia on the part of any one of them can result in the de facto exclusion of defendants from the courtroom. A New York City Bar Association study uncovered evidence of corrections officers who refused to transport HIV-positive prisoners to court; officers who refused to escort them to the holding pen; court officers who falsely informed defense counsel that their clients were not present in the courthouse; prisoners who were held on the transportation van all day and not permitted to enter the courthouse; and court officers who simply refused to allow HIV-positive defendants to enter the courtroom. Sometimes judges are complicitous, choosing to convene court in holding pens or at a prison.[36] Sometimes judges are more than complicitous, and "have actively encouraged attorneys to waive their clients' presence in court."[37] In Birmingham, Alabama, three judges who refused to allow HIV-positive defendants to enter their courtrooms were reduced to taking pleas over the telephone.[38]

Quite apart from the needless aggravation these exclusions cause the defendants and their counsel, and the unnecessary costs they impose on the system, at some point such shenanigans deprive defendants of their concededly limited constitutional right to be present at critical stages of the proceedings, where their participation might be beneficial.[39]

The catalog of unnecessary safety precautions taken by corrections, transportation, and court personnel is lengthy, and includes both apparel (surgical gloves, masks, and gowns, for starters) and equipment (such as body-sized plastic shields and shackles of various sorts).[40] The use of such paraphernalia serves to undermine efforts to develop a thoughtful and coherent public health response to the HIV epidemic, because it, like felony prosecutions for biting or spitting, spreads a false message about how HIV is transmitted. In addition, such measures, when uncorrected, serve to reward and reinforce unwarranted and unproductive fears.

What is more, they sometimes signal the jury that the defendant is HIV positive. When this happens, or when the prosecutor, the judge, or some other court officer informs the jury of the defendant's status, his constitutional right to a fair trial may be severely compromised. Thus, in *Wiggins v. Maryland,* the Maryland Court of Appeals held that the defendant had been deprived of a fair trial when the trial court ordered the guards to wear rubber gloves and directed the jurors not to touch trial exhibits.[41] The concern in such cases is that the disclosure (even when implicit, as in *Wiggins*)[42] of the defendant's HIV status will tend to prejudice the jury. In this context, the term "prejudice" is a shorthand for the concern that the jury may deem the defendant "immoral," and convict him on that basis quite apart from whether he is guilty of the crime charged, or may decide that he should be locked up in the interests of public safety. In the words of the court in *Wiggins*, "in the public mind AIDS has yet to be demystified or destigmatized. AIDS prevails in a climate of fear."[43]

Not every "fair trial" challenge is decided in the defendant's favor. Thus, in *State v. Hudson,* a Tennessee appellate court upheld a murder conviction despite the fact that two sacks of evidence from another trial, on which the notation "CAUTION, AIDS" appeared, had been left on the prosecution table in full view of the jury. Although the defendant's attorney had objected at trial, and the court had order the sacks removed, somehow "if ever removed, [they] reappeared." Nevertheless, the appellate court concluded that the defendant had not been prejudiced because "the specter of AIDS hovered over this case from the start." Curiously, nowhere in the opinion does the court explain or support this assertion.[44] In between *Wiggins* and *Hudson* is *State v. Mercer*, in which the Connecticut Supreme Court ducked the issue by relying on the defense attorney's failure to object at trial to various steps taken by the judge to explore the jurors' attitudes toward the fact that the defendant was infected. The failure to object, reasoned the court, reflected the defendant's own assessment that the judge's efforts were not prejudicial.[45]

Ultimately, the best solution to in-court difficulties of the sort discussed here may lie not in sporadic litigation, but in concerted efforts to frame proper procedures and guidelines, and to educate judicial and criminal justice personnel. It is surely seemly and proper for bench and bar to get their collective act together, without the spur of lawsuits by people living in extremis. Some notable examples of what can be done are the AIDS Guidelines for the Connecticut Supreme Court, excerpted in *State v. Mercer*, and AIDS and the Criminal Justice System: A Final Report and Recommendations, prepared for the Association of the Bar of the City of New York.[46]

Even after the jury renders its verdict, the defendant's HIV status sometimes comes to haunt him or her. In particular, it is sometimes a factor at time of sentencing. For example, in *State v. Guayante*, the Oregon appellate court upheld a thirty-year cumulative sentence imposed on a sex offender by a judge who explicitly treated the defendant's HIV infection as an aggravating factor. The sentencing judge characterized AIDS as "one of the most deadly and dangerous diseases to hit the earth since the 13th Century," and castigated the defendant for causing the victim to "suffer for years, and die one of the most horrible deaths possible."[47] On the other hand, in *Brooks v. State*, a Florida appellate court struck down an enhanced sentence imposed on a prostitute who was convicted of grand theft.[48]

An obvious, but important, difference between the two cases is the relationship between the crimes for which the defendants stood convicted and HIV. In the Oregon case, the court emphasized that the aggravating factor was not the defendant's HIV status, per se, but the fact that he displayed callousness in sexually abusing a thirteen-year-old while fully aware of his infection. In the Florida case, the court stressed that the defendant had been convicted of theft, not prostitution. The other factor that seems to be key in sentencing cases is whether the enhanced sentence falls within the normal sentencing range for crimes of the sort at issue. Where a sentence falls outside the range, reversal is at least a possibility; where it falls within the range, affirmance on appeal is highly likely.

Much more common than the use of the defendant's HIV status as a basis for sentence enhancement is its attempted use to reduce sentences or to dismiss indictments altogether "in the interest of justice." While defendants have sometimes been successful in this regard, much more often they have not. And the likelihood of success on appeal is smaller still.

NOTES

1 Walt, *AIDS Exposure Laws Debated,* N.Y. Newsday, Sept. 23, 1991, at 27.

2 58 U.S.L.W. 2343 (Tex. Dist. Ct. Nov. 4, 1989) (No. 15–183).

3 *Inmate with AIDS Guilty of Trying to Kill by Biting,* N.Y. Times, Apr. 12, 1990, at B–4.

4 401 S.E.2d 13 (Ga. 1991).

5 555 So.2d 285 (Ala. Ct. App. 1989), *aff'd,* 580 So.2d 1390 (Ala. 1991).

6 846 F.2d 1163 (8th Cir. 1988).

7 *See, e.g.,* United States v. Johnson, 30 M.J. 53 (C.M.A. 1990); United States v. Stewart, 29 M.J. 92 (C.M.A. 1989).

8 *See, e.g.,* United States v. Womack, 29 M.J. 88 (C.M.A. 1989); *see also* Mississippi v. McIntyre, No. E–367(B) (Miss. Cir. Ct., April 13, 1989) (prosecution of civilian for failing to follow a public health order).

9 *See, e.g.,* Cal. Penal Code § 647f (West Supp. 1990); Ga. Code Ann. § 16–5–60(c) (Harrison Supp. 1989); Nev. Rev. Stat. Ann. § 201.358 (Michie Supp. 1989); *cf.* Fla. Stat. Ann. § 796.08(5) (West Supp. 1990) (limiting scope to prostitution performed "in a manner likely to transmit" HIV).

10 *See* Decker, *Prostitution as a Public Health Issue,* in AIDS and the Law: A Guide for the Public 81 (H. Dalton, S. Burris & the Yale AIDS Law Project eds. 1987); Rosenberg & Weiner, *Prostitutes and AIDS: A Health Department Priority?,* 78 Am. J. Pub. Health 418 (1988).

11 I borrow this latter opposition from Carol

Vance, who employed it as the conceptual umbrella for an extraordinary collection of essays, Pleasure and Danger: Exploring Female Sexuality, (C. Vance ed. 1984).

12 *See, e.g.,* Pristin, *AIDS-Tainted Blood Seller Ordered to Stand Trial,* Los Angeles Times, Sept. 4, 1987, pt. 2, at 1.

13 *See, e.g.,* Indiana v. Haines, 545 N.E.2d 834 (Ind. Ct. App. 1989).

14 Pennsylvania v. Brown, No. 1263 of 1988 (C.P. Pa. Dec. 13, 1989).

15 *See, e.g.,* Ga. Code Ann. § 16–5–60(c) (Harrison Supp. 1989). However, most HIV-specific criminal laws apply to sexual risk-taking only.

16 One possible exception is California v. Crother, 232 Cal. App. 3d 629 (1991), in which an HIV-positive man was charged with assault for having unprotected sex with a woman. The indictment alleged that she subsequently became pregnant and bore an HIV-positive child. *See also Man Sentenced to Abstinence for Knowingly Infecting Girlfriend,* AIDS Litig. Rep. (Andrews) 7,198 (Nov. 22, 1991) (Oregon v. Gonzalez, No. C91–0733392 (Or. Cir. Ct. Oct. 28, 1991)).

17 Model Penal Code §211.1(1)(a). The common law treated physical injury as "battery" and attempted battery as "assault." Most states, however, have adopted the Model Penal Code's approach, labeling as "assault" what the common law would have called "battery."

18 It some of these states, it may still be possible to distinguish between "factual impossibility'' (the case of the fortuitously defective firing pin) and ''inherent impossibility'' (the water pistol that could not, under any circumstances, constitute a dangerous weapon). Arguably, HIV transmission in biting and spitting cases is more like the latter than the former.

19 545 N.E.2d 834.

20 And, where commercial sex is involved, there is the financial motive.

21 Model Penal Code 210.2(1)(b).

22 *See, e.g.,* Ill. Ann. Stat. ch. 38, para. 12–16.2 (Smith-Hurd Supp. 1990).

23 *See, e.g.,* Ga. Code Ann. §16–5–60(c) (Harrison Supp. 1989).

24 *See* Decker, *Prostitution as a Public Health Issue,* in AIDS and the Law: A Guide for the Public 81 (H. Dalton, S. Burris & the Yale AIDS Law Project eds. 1987); Rosenberg & Weiner, *Prostitutes and AIDS: A Health Department Priority?,* 78 Am. J. Pub. Health 418 (1988).

25 For an example of a fully inclusive statute, *see* Ill. Ann. Stat. ch.38, para. 12–16.2 (Smith-Hurd Supp. 1990).

26 *See, e.g.,* Idaho Code §39–608 (Supp. 1989).

27 *AIDS—A Story* (PBS Frontline television broadcast, Mar. 25, 1986).

28 Howard Rosenberg, *Documentary Makers' Relentless Focus on the Lethal Life Style of a Dying Fabian Bridges Puts Minneapolis Station and PBS in the Spotlight,* Los Angeles Times, March 27, 1986, pt. 6, at 1.

29 *Id.*

30 For most Americans, the first time we ever confronted these issues was when we heard news reports about Gaetan Dugas, the Canadian airline flight attendant identified by the Centers for Disease Control as the sex partner, or partner once removed, of forty of the first 248 people diagnosed with AIDS in the United States. Dugas was widely reported as having declared: ''It's my right to do what I want with my own body. . . . I've got it [AIDS]. They can get it too.'' R. Schiltz, And

The Band Played On 147, 200 (1987). In fairness to Dugas, in the same conversation, he asserted that others have a ''duty to protect themselves. . . . They know what's going on there. They've heard about this disease.'' *Id.*

31 At the close of the preliminary hearing, the trial court dismissed the sex-based attempted murder counts when the alleged victim refused to testify. Pristin, note 12 above. Subsequently, the court dismissed the attempted murder counts arising out of the blood sale because of the prosecution's failure to establish specific intent, and dismissed the assault with a deadly weapon counts because of an absence of proof of injury. The court let the case proceed to trial on a charge of attempt to poison a pharmaceutical product. Pristin, *Charges of Attempted Murder Voided in Case of AIDS-Tainted Blood,* Los Angeles Times, Dec. 2, 1987, pt. 2, at 1. Eventually, the jury returned a verdict of not guilty. ''It was basically clear-cut,'' observed one juror. '' . . . He obviously was down there [at the blood bank] for no other reason than to just get money, so he didn't have that specific intent.'' Pristin, *Jury Frees AIDS Victim Who Sold Infected Blood,* Los Angeles Times, Mar. 3, 1988, pt. 2, at 1.

32 Pristin and Nelson, *AIDS Victim Faces Prosecution over Blood Donation,* Los Angeles Times, June 30, 1987, pt. 2, at 1; Cummings, *Charges Filed against Blood Donor in AIDS Case,* N. Y. Times, June 30, 1987, at A18; Pristin, *5 Attempts to Confine AIDS Patient Told,* Los Angeles Times, July 1, 1987, pt. 1, at 1. The bank incident led directly to the attempted murder prosecution when the police discovered in Markowski's pocket a receipt for the blood donation. *Id.*

33 *See generally* Mohr, *Policy, Ritual, Purity: Gays and Mandatory AIDS Testing,* 15 Law, Med. & Health Care 178 (Winter 1987).

34 *See, e.g.,* Hendricks, *Problems and Issues in Criminal Prosecutions,* in AIDS Practice Manual 13–4 (3d edition, Albert, Eisenberg, Hansell & Marcus, eds. 1991) at 13–4; Jt.

Subcomm. on AIDS in the Crim'l Justice
Sys., Ass'n of the Bar of the City of New
York, AIDS and the Criminal Justice System:
A Final Report and Recommendations 155–56
(July 1989).

35 *See* A.B.A. Policy on AIDS and the
Criminal Justice System 16 (adopted by the
House of Delegates, Feb. 7, 1989).

36 AIDS and the Criminal Justice System,
note 34 above, at 161–63.

37 *Id.* at 163.

38 Smothers, *3 Judges Exclude AIDS Defendants,* N.Y. Times, Dec. 14, 1988, at A–21.

39 *See* Kentucky v. Stincer, 482 U.S. 730,
745 (1987); *see generally* Hendricks, note 34
above, at 13–6 and 13–7.

40 Hendricks, note 34 above, at 13–17.

41 554 A.2d 356 (1989).

42 In fact, in *Wiggins* the trial court did not
even know for sure whether Wiggins was,
himself, HIV-positive. The precautions were
taken based on the fact that both the murder
victim and Wiggins's co-defendant were infected. Moreover, the judge may have been
influenced by the fact that Wiggins is gay.

43 *Id.*

44 1989 Tenn. Crim. App. Lexis 773 (Mar.
5, 1990).

45 544 A.2d 611 (1988).

46 *See* note 34, above.

47 783 P.2d 1030 (Ct. App. 1989).

48 519 So.2d 1156 (Dist. Ct. App. 1988).

12 HIV in Prison

Alexa Freeman

With over one million people in prisons and jails, the United States now has the unhappy distinction of incarcerating more of its population than any other country in the world, surpassing even the former Soviet Union and South Africa. There are three times as many people locked up in the United States as in all twenty-four European Council member countries combined, and there is no indication that this trend is reversing. In 1990, federal and state prison populations increased by over 8 percent, reaching a record high.[1]

A shocking percentage of those imprisoned are people of color. As a nation, we imprison African American males at a rate of 3,370 per 100,000, five times the rate of South Africa.[2] Latinos are also imprisoned in large numbers. In California and New York, Latinos compose nearly a third of all prisoners, and in New Mexico, they account for more than half. Similarly, Native Americans jam the prisons in Alaska, Montana, and the Dakotas. The high number of people of color in prison is not simply a problem in states with large minority populations. The figures for the federal prison system—where one would expect the statistical differences among the states' minority populations to flatten out in national averages—are consistently, strikingly high: one-third African American and one-fourth Hispanic. (No figures are available on Native Americans in federal prison.)[3]

Incarceration is also closely tied to drug use. The "war on drugs," which has targeted resources at the arrest, prosecution and incarceration of drug offenders, is the main cause of the dramatic rise in the prison population. One government study indicates that in some cities, 70 percent of all those arrested test positive for one or more drugs. Inevitably, many of those swept up in the criminal justice system for drug offenses are HIV-positive. In New York, for example, 95 percent of prisoners with AIDS are intravenous (IV) drug users. The National Commission on AIDS predicts that by 1995, 70 percent of federal prisoners will be drug offenders, concluding that "presently the United States maintains a de facto policy of incarcerating

263

more and more HIV infected individuals by choosing mass imprisonment as the . . . response to the use of drugs.''[4]

No prison is likely to remain free of HIV disease, and many prisons will have seroprevalence rates far higher than those in most "free world" communities. Prisons and jails are now populated with poor, drug-using people of color who are among those at highest risk of acquiring HIV. HIV disease thus presents a grave duty of care, and a significant opportunity for prevention, to prison authorities and public health officials.

HIV DISEASE IN PRISONS AND JAILS

Epidemiology and Demographics

According to a July 1991 report by the National Institute of Justice (NIJ), a cumulative total of almost seven thousand AIDS cases have been reported among prisoners in the United States in all regions of the country. This number is derived from reports by federal and state prisons and the larger city or county jails. It represents a minimum estimate of the actual number of cases because the sample included some estimates based on earlier figures and did not include all city or county systems. The estimate must also be discounted in light of the problems prisons have in identifying people with AIDS, both because of poor medical care and because many people will decline to seek care out of fear of the discrimination that would follow a diagnosis. NIJ researchers report that the chief medical officer for the New York State Department of Corrections estimates that there are eight thousand HIV-positive prisoners in New York, but only thirty-two hundred know their status. Fully one-third of the New York prison system's AIDS cases through 1987 were not diagnosed until autopsy.[5]

Information on HIV seropositivity is of uneven quality because of the variety of testing programs in different correctional systems, but it is likely that every state has infected prisoners. Most states conducting mass screening programs have seroprevalence rates of 1 percent or less in their correctional institutions. However, in prisons and jails that are located in high-prevalence areas, the problem is severe. For example, in a 1988 blind epidemiological study of a New York state prison, 17 percent of male, and nearly 19 percent of female, prisoners tested HIV-positive.[6] Also in 1988, close to 7 percent of Florida prisoners tested positive. Prison officials at the Rikers Island detention facility in New York City once estimated that a quarter of its population of fifty thousand was HIV-positive.[7] Officials in New Jersey estimate the infection rate among state prisoners to be 30 to 50 percent.[8] A blind study of new entrants to the Philadelphia jail found a rate of 5 percent,[9] and in the Fulton

County, Georgia, jail, the number topped 7 percent.[10] Most states do not conduct mass screening, but rather rely on blind studies to estimate prevalence, probably because identifying the infected would create an obligation to produce expensive medical care. Given the increasing rate of HIV infection among urban drug-users, it seems inevitable that the number of HIV-infected people in prison and jail can only grow.

While the data on characteristics of HIV-positive prisoners are sketchy, they reveal a high rate of infection among incarcerated African Americans and Hispanics. A study of over ten thousand prisoners entering ten prison systems, conducted by the Centers for Disease Control (CDC) and Johns Hopkins University, revealed overall seroprevalence rates to be almost twice as high for non-Whites as for Whites. North Carolina reports that 88 percent of infected prisoners admitted between November 1989 and April 1990 were African American. In New York, as of September 1990, 48 percent of infected prisoners were Hispanic and 38 percent were African American.[11]

The data are inconclusive on rates of infection among women prisoners. The NIJ reports more cases of HIV infection and AIDS in prison among men, but the CDC/Johns Hopkins study shows significantly higher rates among women in nine of the ten systems analyzed.[12] Two statistical trends are bound to increase the need for specialized care for women: women are becoming infected at a greater rate than are men, and their rate of incarceration over the last decade has surpassed that for men.[13]

Although there are many people with HIV in prison, the evidence suggests that transmission within prison walls accounts for only a small fraction of the total cases. Studies reveal that rates of HIV transmission are lower in prison than on the streets and that the great majority of HIV-positive prisoners come into the system infected. This fact surprises many people, because common perceptions of the extent to which prisoners engage in sex and drug activity are exaggerated. While these high-risk activities certainly occur, they are illegal, and opportunities are fewer than on the streets. Research also shows a correlation between the prevalence of AIDS cases and HIV positivity in prisons and jails and prevalence in the geographic areas from which their residents come.[14]

There is, however, one significant disease linked to HIV that is being transmitted in correctional institutions: tuberculosis.[15] TB is contagious, but not highly so, and then only in its active stage. Most people with TB are asymptomatic carriers who pose no threat of transmission. Normally, TB can be cured with antibiotics, although successful treatment can require several months. Tuberculosis has always been prevalent in prisons and jails because the environmental characteristics are conducive to transmission and because many of those incarcerated have received inadequate medical care for most of their lives. Many systems are now reporting TB rates of more than 10 percent.[16] The NIJ reported in its 1989 survey that those systems with the largest number of AIDS cases also generally had the largest number of TB cases.[17] In 1989, all seventy patients with active tuberculosis in the New York prison system were also HIV-positive.[18] Given this high correlation, it is extremely important that correctional systems identify and treat those who are TB positive. Although most systems routinely screen for TB upon intake, one out of five prisons and nearly one out of three jails reportedly does not know what percentage of its population is TB-positive.[19]

Recently, drug-resistant strains of TB have appeared in several concentrated outbreaks around the country, most notably in prisons and hospitals. Drug-resistant strains develop when patients do not complete the full course of treatment necessary for a cure. Thus prisons, where medical care and the dispensing of medicines are often sporadic, are potential breeding grounds of resistant strains. These new forms, although still rare, have alarmed health officials because drug-resistant TB can be fatal if not treated promptly and can still be deadly even when treated, particularly in patients with weakened immune systems.

Resistant TB and HIV are a particularly problematic combination. People with weak immune systems are more likely to contract TB and to move quickly to the active, contagious stage. Several of those who have died in the recent outbreaks of drug-resistant TB have had AIDS. Moreover, standard TB screening is unreliable in people with HIV, because the tests require a healthy immune system. This diagnostic gap has led some health officials to call for strict quarantining of HIV-infected people who exhibit active TB symptoms, and many prison doctors have advocated isolating any HIV-infected person with a cough. Some prison systems are beginning to take TB more seriously, but control will not be easy. Identifying and properly treating those who are infected will require substantial new resources. People with latent TB will need to be monitored during treatment to ensure that they do not become contagious. Many prisons will have to create new isolation facilities for prisoners with active TB.[20]

An Adequate Response

There is surprisingly little disagreement among public health experts on what to do about the HIV epidemic in correctional facilities. Even most corrections officials give lip service to the same principles. The problem is the enormous gap between what should be done and what is being done. Society has moral and public health reasons to close this gap.[21]

The starting point is to recognize that, despite the walls and barbed wire, these institutions remain part of the larger community. The National Commission on AIDS noted, in its report on HIV in correctional facilities: "Even though legal and architectural barriers have been erected between institutionalized populations and the community at large, such barriers are often illusory. Individuals move to and from institutions, return to their communities and loved ones, as new waves of entrants await confinement. We must learn that we cannot speak of the health of the nation without also addressing the health of individuals in prisons, jails and other institutions."[22] There are no legitimate reasons why interventions that are appropriate and effective in "free world" communities should not also be used in correctional institutions. Accordingly, we must carefully scrutinize the usual protestations about security that impede application of the same standards. As several systems have shown, genuine security concerns can be accommodated without sacrificing generally utilized medical and public health practices.

Prisoners should receive medical care that meets contemporary community standards pertaining both to treatment protocols and to the provision of services. Quality assurance programs are needed to evaluate prison medical care for compliance with these standards. Compulsory testing is counterproductive in correctional institutions for the same reasons that it is counterproductive in the free world. On the other hand, voluntary testing and counseling should be regarded as basic medical needs, because they are critical to controlling the spread of disease and identifying people who need treatment. Once identified as infected, imprisoned people should be assessed and plans developed for their treatment, including prophylaxis and regular monitoring. There should be no barriers to their contact with the medical department. They should be given the choice to take experimental drugs and participate in clinical trials. Drug addiction treatment services should be considered basic and made readily available. Adequate dental and mental health care should be provided. Finally, because the pressure to identify those with HIV is especially great, strict procedures protecting their confidentiality must be implemented, and confidential information must be kept from nontreating personnel.

Seropositive prisoners should be housed in nonsegregated units and permitted to participate in all programs for which they are otherwise qualified. Discriminatory and punitive treatment must be forthrightly condemned, and sanctions against these actions, as well as for breaches of confidentiality, should be clear and effective. Contrary policies create disincentives for prisoners to seek testing and medical care.

Prisons and jails should make HIV education a priority because, without it, prisoners and staff members are often consumed with fear, leading to panic and discriminatory policies. Education is also an essential public health tool in changing high-risk behavior, a tool that correctional institutions are uniquely positioned to employ. Programs must be specifically designed to address the varying concerns of different groups within the corrections community, including prisoners, corrections staff, medical personnel and other employees. These programs should be linguistically and culturally appropriate. Infection control measures, including universal precautions, should be taught, and condoms should be distributed freely. Prisoner peer education and support groups should be encouraged, as should cooperation with outside community-based AIDS service organizations.

Finally, imprisoned people with HIV disease must be helped to prepare for release. Their foremost need is ensuring that, on departure, they will be able to continue on prescribed medications and obtain referrals to appropriate health care providers. Continuity of care is also crucial for prisoners being transferred to other institutions. Pre-release counseling can help teach such life-saving skills as how to sterilize needles and practice safer sex. Families and employers should be offered HIV education to allay their fears. Early release procedures should be adopted for prisoners who are terminally ill, whose incarceration no longer serves any purpose.

THE BASIC LEGAL RIGHTS OF PRISONERS

The prisoners' rights movement, like so many other social change movements, grew out of the civil rights struggles of the 1950s through 1970s. Prison riots riveted the public's attention on the shocking conditions of incarceration. Institutional litigation, first directed at eliminating segregation in the schools, next sought to reform prisons and other social institutions. Over the past two decades, litigation has been remarkably effective in uncovering prison abuses that were previously shielded from scrutiny by a long-standing "hands off" judicial stance. Unhappily, there is powerful evidence that the courts are again turning away from their constitutional role of protecting basic human rights.

The Eighth Amendment to the United States Constitution, which prohibits cruel and unusual punishment, has been the primary source of protection for prisoners. Under it, the United States Supreme Court held during its enlightened era that prisoners may not be subjected to unsanitary and hazardous physical facilities or unreasonable violence, or deprived of basic medical, dental, and mental health care. In addition, under the Constitution prisoners are entitled to marry, to observe their religion, to communicate with their lawyers and have access to the courts, and to receive limited due process in disciplinary procedures.

But numerous barriers stand in the way of prisoners who seek to exercise even these minimal rights. Legal doctrine provides that their constitutional rights must be balanced against the security concerns of prison officials, giving courts a ready excuse for rejecting prisoners' claims. Legislatures, quick to pass mandatory sentencing laws, resist appropriating the funds necessary to run prisons and jails in a constitutional manner, even when under court order. The worst problem of all is overcrowding, which strains every aspect of prison administration and threatens to undo what progress has been made over the last twenty years. Forty-one states are operating their prisons under court order because they house prisoners in overcrowded and unconstitutional conditions.[23]

Challenges to prison policies have become more daunting in recent years, as the federal courts have become dominated by Reagan and Bush appointees. The federal judiciary as a whole now takes a less expansive view of what is due prisoners in all areas of the law, and an even broader view of the deference to be accorded prison officials. Indeed, deferring to government judgment has become a substitute for coherent constitutional analysis. Prevailing under these circumstances has become a matter of both chance and of resources: chance will determine whether the judge who is drawn will be receptive to prisoners' claims and ready to scrutinize prison officials' justifications; and resources will determine whether enough evidence can be found and presented to convince a court to intervene.[24]

Another factor affecting the development of the law involving HIV in prison is that many of the cases have been brought *pro se*—that is, by prisoners representing themselves without a lawyer. This phenomenon is not unusual in prison law, but it has been a particular problem in the HIV area. It is hardly surprising that nearly all of the early HIV-related prison cases were lost by pro se litigants unequipped to present complicated factual and health policy arguments. Because these cases are continually cited as adverse precedent, they constitute yet another obstacle that prisoners must struggle to overcome.

MEDICAL CARE

Testing and Counseling

As of 1991, eighteen prison systems, including the Federal Bureau of Prisons, mandate HIV antibody testing of all prisoners in order to identify those who are positive.[25] The number of systems opting for this procedure has grown only slightly over the past several years.[26] In contrast, twenty-two systems rely exclusively on voluntary testing.[27] This division reflects a lack of clarity among corrections officials as to the purpose of testing. Moreover, the number of systems offering voluntary testing at all, whether alone or in combination with mandatory testing, is down to thirty-three from thirty-seven in 1989. As a consequence, prisoners in nearly a third of the prison systems in the United States are denied a basic medical necessity.[28]

When antibody tests became widely available in 1985, prisoner advocates opposed involuntary testing in correctional institutions for the same reasons that AIDS activists struggled against such testing in the free world. The cogency of their arguments was bolstered by the unavailability of effective treatment for HIV. However, due to developments in early treatment of HIV in the past three years, testing has become the key to obtaining effective medical care. Now voluntary and confidential testing, when coupled with appropriate pre- and post-test counseling, have become the accepted medical and public health protocol.

The fact that HIV testing can benefit prisoners does not make forced testing a better idea. As on the outside, the behavioral and educational purposes of HIV testing are not well served by compulsion. Moreover, mass prison screening programs send misleading and dangerous messages. Screening can lull people into a false sense of security, suggesting that testing can accurately classify everyone as either HIV-positive or HIV-negative. It shifts the emphasis from self-protection to reliance on a testing program that is inherently unreliable. Prison staff may find it easier to act according to what they think they know about a prisoner's HIV status than to employ universal precautions. Similarly, prisoners may believe that it is possible to prevent infection by avoiding risky behavior with only those they have reason to believe are HIV-positive.

These problems are compounded by inadequate counseling for those who are tested. Pre- and post-test counseling standards are frequently compromised or ignored in prison. Although all prison systems and many jails claim to provide pre- and post-test counseling, the quality of that counseling remains a question, particularly in light of many prisoners' ignorance about HIV. One encouraging development is the use of trained HIV counselors in correctional facilities. The 1989 NIJ survey reported that seventy-eight systems claim to use trained counselors. When the counselors come from outside agencies, such as AIDS service organizations or public health departments, rather than from within the prison system, prisoners may have greater confidence that their confidences will not be divulged.[29]

The barriers to an effective program of voluntary testing and counseling in prison are substantial. Foremost among these is the fact that prisoners are reluctant to come forward if they cannot be assured that the results will be kept private. Confidentiality in the small prison community is difficult to maintain under the best of conditions, and only now are some prisons beginning to recognize the need to keep HIV information private. Typically, news of a positive test result travels through the grapevine, setting off hysteria and causing ostracism. In systems where staff and prisoners are poorly educated about HIV, knowing who is positive is perceived as a matter of life-saving importance, further fostering the information's dissemination.

Prisoners' fears of disclosure are magnified in systems where social discrimination is formalized by institutional policies. Some systems have opted for segregated housing and the exclusion of all HIV-positive prisoners from some or all prison programs. In others, those who test positive are forced to disclose their status to parole boards, family members, former sexual partners, and potential employers. Finally, it is evident that voluntary testing will never be effective if it does not lead to good medical care. There is little point in encouraging prisoners to be tested if the medical department is incapable of treating those who are infected.[30]

Prisoners' Legal Rights Regarding Testing

Prisoners have brought suits both seeking and opposing mandatory testing, and, in the most recent trend, seeking voluntary testing. The common denominator of these suits is that the prisoners have usually lost as the courts have deferred to the decisions of prison officials.

Prisoners have employed various theories to try to block compulsory HIV testing, including the Fourth Amendment's ban on unreasonable searches and seizures, the right to privacy, the due process clause of the Fifth and Fourteenth Amendments, the First Amendment, and the Eighth Amendment, which prohibits cruel and unusual punishment. With a single exception—a bizarre case involving correctional officers who forced a prisoner who had already had one test to submit to another by threatening to shoot him with taser guns[31]—prisoners have never won. Indeed, the courts have often decided the cases without ever critically evaluating the evidence.

A good example of uncritical deference is *Dunn v. White,* in which the court dismissed the complaint without any fact-finding whatsoever. The plaintiff prisoner alleged that various of his constitutional rights were violated when he was forced to submit to an HIV antibody test. His claims, under the Fourth and First Amendments, were considered on the prison's preliminary motion to dismiss his complaint. Applying traditional analysis to the Fourth Amendment claim, the court balanced the prisoner's rights against the state's interest and concluded that the testing was justified in order to prevent the spread of AIDS. The court made this finding even though the plaintiff was denied the opportunity to make a factual record about the ramifications of the test, and even though the defendants presented no evidence to prove their interests in mandatory testing or the relationship of these interests to the testing. The dismissal in *Dunn* was particularly harsh because the prisoner was forced to litigate major constitutional issues involving important public policy without an attorney.[32]

Judicial deference to prison officials regarding compulsory testing is also evident in cases in which prisoners have sought to compel corrections departments to undertake such testing. While the results of these cases are consistent with the general public health consensus opposing involuntary testing, the consistency may be mere coincidence because the courts have again simply deferred, without serious examination of the facts and issues, to the views of prison officials. The fact that prisoners continue to bring actions to compel testing, in the belief that compulsory testing will protect them, is a sorry reflection on the inadequacy of HIV education in most institutions.[33]

The refusal of correctional institutions to offer voluntary testing is also a growing source of litigation. Policies denying access to HIV antibody testing are at odds with the position of the public health community that education and voluntary testing, coupled with counseling, are the most effective means of reducing transmission of the virus. The National Commission on AIDS has recommended that confidential voluntary testing, with pre- and post-test counseling, be made available to all prisoners who wish it. With the new emphasis on early identification and treatment of HIV, a denial of voluntary testing is a denial of basic, necessary medical care in contravention of the Eighth Amendment. This legal theory is being tested in a couple of current lawsuits attacking the unavailability of testing.[34]

The only case decided to date is *Feigley v. Fulcomer*. While the court in this case refused to impose compulsory intake testing, it also denied the prison's motion for summary judgment upholding its refusal to provide voluntary testing. The court suggested that the plaintiff's Eighth Amendment rights would be violated if he requested an HIV antibody test and the test was not administered because refusal to test a prisoner upon request " 'involve[s] the unnecessary and wanton infliction of pain' by failing to relieve the anxiety which might accompany a prisoner's uncertainty as to whether he or she has a fatal disease.''[35] It is an encouraging sign that voluntary testing programs have been instituted as part of court-approved settlements in a number of cases.[36]

Medical Care after Diagnosis

Because there are few data on the medical treatment of HIV-positive prisoners, it is a difficult area to evaluate comprehensively. The NIJ reports that AZT is available in 94 percent of prison systems, and aerosolized pentamidine in 80 percent.[37] One can also assume that virtually all prison and jail systems have developed, on paper, policies and procedures for providing medical care to prisoners, including, in many cases, specific protocols for HIV disease. Moreover, many systems have obtained accreditation by the National Commission on Correctional Health Care for their health care delivery procedures.[38]

None of this means, however, that seropositive prisoners are receiving adequate care. One shocking statistic is that prisoners with AIDS in the state of New York live only half as long as people with AIDS in the free world.[39] The fact is that medical care for all prisoners is too often abysmal. Prison officials are more concerned about security than about medical care and treatment, and they direct their limited funds to that purpose. The practical and financial pressures of overcrowding exacerbate the competition for scarce resources.

Prisoners with HIV are particularly likely to encounter obstacles to adequate care. There are often not enough physicians for the number of prisoners who need attention, and few are trained in the treatment of HIV disease. Many systems lack effective programs either for early diagnosis and intervention or for ongoing case management. Opportunistic infections and cancers in women are frequently overlooked because poorly trained health care staff may be unaware of the ways in which HIV disease manifests itself in women. Other typical problems include lack of acute care and emergency capacity, meager infirmary space, poor record-keeping, restricted prisoner access to the medical department, failure to make specialty referrals, inadequate dental care, lack of special diets, and poor or no discharge planning.

Systems with large numbers of HIV-infected prisoners are experiencing enormous budgetary pressure because prisoners are ineligible for Medicaid. According to a study by the George Washington University Intergovernmental Health Policy Project, the growing number of HIV-positive prisoners has made even more severe the already-heavy financial burden on correctional systems. In some states, the largest share of their total AIDS budget is spent on prisoners. In Georgia, for example, the prisoner share of state funds for AIDS is 80 percent, and in New York, prisoners receive three-fourths of the state's non-Medicaid patient care funds.[40]

Although virtually all prison systems claim to make AZT and pentamidine available, prisoners from around the country report problems in receiving these drugs in conformity with Food and Drug Administration (FDA) and other expert recommendations. Likewise, many systems fail to monitor these potentially toxic drugs. In Alabama, the problem was so severe that prisoners not taking AZT were afraid to begin because they saw others who were on the drug develop debilitating anemia, a common side effect, without being treated.[41]

People who have been diagnosed as HIV-positive face the emotional strain of coping with a terminal illness, and some may ultimately experience AIDS dementia. Testing positive has been found to increase levels of anxiety, depression and suicidal thinking.[42] Given the extent of formal and informal discrimination, and the general inadequacy of mental health care in prison, it is likely that the special mental health needs of HIV-positive prisoners are being neglected.

Another medical issue is prisoner access to experimental drug trials. Because of historic abuse, most states and local jurisdictions are reluctant to use prisoners in medical research; indeed, many impose bans. Federal regulations also impose difficult requirements on researchers who want to open clinical trials to prisoners. Prisoner advocates have long supported these measures. In the context of the HIV epidemic, however, these protective rules have had the paradoxical effect of denying prisoners access (or providing an excuse for prisons to deny them access) to the most advanced drugs, such as ddI, that are being used in the larger community. These drugs may offer the only hope of survival or easing of symptoms. The National Commission on AIDS and other experts have urged that prisoners be given access to clinical trials as long as certain safeguards are in place.[43]

Finally, correctional systems have massively failed to offer sufficient drug-abuse treatment. One study found that only 11 percent of addicted prisoners were enrolled in drug treatment programs, counting general drug education and self-help programs.[44] In the context of the AIDS epidemic, it is a public health disaster not to view drug treatment as a necessary part of medical care in correctional institutions.

A state is constitutionally obligated to provide medical and mental health care to incarcerated people. In *Estelle v. Gamble,* the Supreme Court held that "deliberate indifference to serious medical needs" of prisoners violates the Eighth Amendment. The denial of medical care need not be so severe as to cause death or amount to deliberate torture. The Court in *Estelle* held that "less serious cases" in which denials of medical care result in pain and suffering without penological purpose also violate the Eighth Amendment.[45]

Prisoners with HIV often have to live with the knowledge that there are state-of-the-art treatments for HIV available in the community that they cannot obtain in prison. This issue first reached the courts as AZT became a standard treatment—except in prisons. In several cases, however, courts were reluctant "to delve into the particulars and intricacies of modern medicine or to make narrow distinctions on debatable interpretations of what should be acceptable in the medical community."[46] The FDA's approval of AZT for prophylactic use has made it harder for prisons to refuse to provide it on medical grounds, but, in *Harris v. Thigpen,* a federal judge justified the denial of that and other drugs on a more novel and distressing ground: the Constitution does not require prisons to pay for expensive drugs. Indeed, the judge cynically predicted that to do so "would inevitably lead" to poor sick people's committing crimes just to get medical care. *Harris* is also the only reported decision that has specifically confronted the issue of the mental health needs of HIV-positive prisoners, finding no constitutional violation—without discussion and consistent with its holding on medical care—despite numerous deficiencies.[47]

Unfortunately, the Eleventh Circuit affirmed *Harris* on the medical care issue, although it disagreed with the district court's rationale that "poor states" may deny prisoners adequate medical treatment. Thus, the truly appalling horror stories that bad HIV care in prison can produce, while not totally unnoticed, have gone unanswered.[48] Another serious issue is whether the courts will make themselves available to deal with the chronic deficits in HIV care, deficiencies that merge with larger problems of high populations and small staffs. Courts are more and more reluctant to micromanage prisons themselves, but in several instances the threat of judicial action has led to settlements setting forth detailed medical care requirements. Two in particular stand out.

Doe v. Meachum was a class action that challenged the Connecticut Department of Correction's policies on HIV. As part of a settlement, the Department agreed to a comprehensive program of care for HIV-infected prisoners. The settlement mandated infectious disease specialist services for each prison. It also set forth detailed treatment plans for intake and assessment; routine and acute care; drug therapies (including experimental drugs under investigation); diet; mental health, dental and eye care; special care for women; discharge planning; housing; staffing; staff education; confidentiality; and quality assurance. The agreement also established an "agreement monitoring panel" to oversee implementation.[49]

In *Starkey v. Matty,* the parties settled a suit challenging a county prison's administrative and medical practices and protocols regarding HIV disease. The prison officials agreed to provide medical care at a level comparable to that available in the community and to conduct HIV antibody testing whenever medically indicated or when a prisoner requested it. All prisoners were to be advised within twelve weeks of their arrival of the availability of pre-test counseling and testing, and all HIV-related information was to be kept confidential, available only to medical staff and to those for whom the prisoner had given consent.[50]

Some systems may be improving even without the threat of litigation. The 1991 NIJ study favorably describes Rhode Island's medical program for HIV-positive prisoners. Its services are provided cooperatively by the state health department, the corrections department, and Brown University. Among its constructive features is a discharge-planning program that provides for continuity of care. It includes pre-release counseling, referrals to outside physicians (often the treating physician in prison), and post-release clinical follow-up.[51]

SOCIAL MEASURES

Prisoners with HIV, like people in the free world, face discrimination based purely on fear and misinformation. The effects are the same, stigmatizing the infected and driving them away from care. In prison, as on the outside, some efforts have been made to identify, isolate, and exclude the infected, despite the lack of a medical basis for such measures. Unlike the situation on the outside, however, some courts have countenanced these practices.

Housing Policies

Segregated housing is an area in which correctional institutions have recently taken a more rational approach than they have in the past. States are shifting from blanket segregation of infected prisoners to case-by-case determinations. Three-quarters of the prison systems currently "mainstream" HIV-positive prisoners, while another 14 percent make individualized decisions regarding housing. Only four states continue to segregate all HIV-positive prisoners.[52] Even housing policies for prisoners with AIDS have undergone a dramatic shift from 1988, when no prison system housed them in the general population without restriction, to 1990, when fifteen do so and less than a fifth automatically segregate them. In spite of these changes, only a third of the prisons and a quarter of the jails surveyed completely prohibit segregation.[53]

There are several reasons for rejecting segregation. First, it is impossible to preserve the confidentiality of test results when prisoners with HIV disease are housed separately. People inside and outside quickly learn that a particular block is the "AIDS block." Second, segregation—like mass testing—undermines prevention messages. It gives the false impression that unsegregated prisoners need not change their sexual or needle-sharing behavior. It also implies that HIV can be transmitted through casual contact by telling prisoners and staff members that living, going to school, or working with an HIV-positive person is dangerous. Finally, and of most practical importance, the sheer administrative cost and logistical burden of maintaining separate housing make it unfeasible, except in places with few infected prisoners or policies discouraging testing.[54]

Management problems are compounded if, as is true in many cases, infected prisoners are not only housed separately but are also barred from participating in prison programs. Idle prisoners are generally acknowledged to be bad correctional policy, yet the cost of providing wholly separate education, work, recreation, religious and other programs is formidable. The result is that segregated prisoners often are idle, unable to use the law library, to earn money to send home or pay for basic canteen items, to study for a high school diploma, or to learn a trade.

Prison officials commonly justify segregation policies as a means of preventing HIV transmission, as a means of preventing violence against HIV-positive prisoners, and as a means of facilitating medical care for those who are sick with HIV-related diseases. None of these justifications withstands scrutiny.

Public health and corrections experts are virtually unanimous in their belief that segregation is a poor way to protect seronegative prisoners from the possibility of infection through sexual contact and IV drug use. In a system that does not test and retest everyone at regular intervals, segregation of the few prisoners known to be HIV-infected is obviously pointless and even dangerous. As on the outside, education to induce voluntary behavior change is the better way.[55] Prison officials possess many effective tools to control HIV transmission through coerced sex. With rape, the problem is sexual violence, not HIV, and the solution is to identify and control the sexually violent regardless of whether or not they are HIV-infected. Any prisoner who officials fear may harm another person should be administratively segregated. Another effective way of protecting prisoners is the classification process, during which new prisoners are assessed based on a variety of factors used to predict behavior. Most assaultive prisoners are well-known to prison officials through classification procedures and can be managed accordingly.

The argument that HIV-positive prisoners must be segregated to protect them from AIDS-phobic violence is circular. No action by prison officials could more completely disclose to the prison population that certain people are seropositive, and validate the fear and hatred directed at them, than to segregate them in an HIV unit. It is worth noting that systems that have desegregated have not reported serious problems of violence against the newly integrated seropositive prisoners.

The argument that segregation may facilitate better medical care, while seriously flawed, cannot be so easily dismissed. Both large and small systems may be tempted to house seropositive prisoners together to improve medical care delivery. Small systems with few sick prisoners are likely to be in low-prevalence states where there are not many specialists in the treatment of HIV disease, and fewer still who are willing to care for prisoners. Systems with large numbers of sick prisoners are likely to be in states where there are many medical professionals experienced in treating HIV disease, but these systems, such as New York and California, are also apt to be severely overcrowded and overwhelmed by the number of infected prisoners. In both situations, centralizing infected prisoners in one location, and concentrating skilled medical staff there, may be a less expensive way to provide prisoners with better care.

The trade-off is the loss of confidentiality and the potential for discrimination in access to prison programs. The prison may also not keep its side of the bargain: care may not be better or may, after an early period of improvement, revert to lower quality as the number of prisoners in the unit rises. In at least two cases, HIV-positive plaintiffs have alleged that segregation served to *deny* them adequate medical care. One case has not yet been tried,[56] but in *Harris v. Thigpen,* the prisoners presented voluminous evidence that once they were diagnosed as HIV positive, they were presumed to be untreatable and were left to die.[57]

Program Exclusion

The government does not collect data on systems that exclude HIV-positive prisoners from various institutional programs and jobs. Prisoner complaints and a reading of the cases indicate that many prisons and jails discriminate against infected prisoners by denying them the right to participate in various activities that they are otherwise qualified to undertake. The consequences of segregated housing and program denial endure beyond life in prison. A major factor weighed by parole boards is the prisoner's institutional record, including whether he or she has participated in programs. The failure to learn a marketable skill in prison can mean not getting a job upon release, and a prisoner who has been denied family visits may find these important ties difficult to rebuild. This treatment is usually justified as a way of allaying the fears of other prisoners and staff members.

Prisoners' Legal Rights Concerning Segregation and Program Exclusion

Just as in the area of testing, there is a long line of cases in which prisoners have sought to require prison officials to segregate those who are seropositive. As in the testing cases (in many of which both issues are raised), courts are deferring to the judgment of officials.[58] Likewise, in many cases challenging segregation, courts are declining to interfere with prison decisions that segregation or other forms of discrimination are necessary.[59]

Unlike the testing cases, however, there have been several decisions ending discriminatory practices. In some of them, legal theories not heretofore deemed very important in prison law have been successfully asserted. In *Doe v. Coughlin,* plaintiffs challenged the New York Department of Corrections' plan to force them into a special dormitory for HIV-positive prisoners. They did not challenge the Department's purpose—to facilitate better services—but alleged that putting them in a special dorm would effectively announce their status to other prisoners, family members, and anyone who subsequently became aware of the nature of the unit. The court enjoined the program as a violation of the right to privacy, reasoning that the benefits of such a program could also be obtained by allowing individual prisoners to choose separate housing.[60]

Recent cases have also raised the claim that discrimination against seropositive prisoners is prohibited by Section 504 of the Rehabilitation Act of 1973,[61] the same law that prohibits discrimination against people with HIV in employment and school settings. The statute forbids discrimination against handicapped individuals by agencies that receive federal funds and applies to people with contagious diseases, including HIV. Most state prison systems fall within its reach because they receive federal funding. Assuming that a prisoner is otherwise eligible for the program or housing in question, the important legal issue is whether he or she presents a significant risk of HIV transmission, a determination that must be based on a rational, medically supported evaluation of the individual prisoner. (For more on HIV and antidiscrimination law, see chapter 13.)

Prisoners are just beginning to utilize the Rehabilitation Act in HIV litigation. The early results are encouraging. In *Harris v. Thigpen,* the court of appeals reversed the district court's flat rejection of the prisoners' Section 504 claim and remanded the issue for a particularized inquiry into the risks posed in each program and activity from which prisoners were excluded.[62] In another case, HIV-positive prisoners in Arizona successfully challenged their exclusion from kitchen jobs. Interestingly, a group of federal prisoners had lost a similar case, brought under the Constitution rather than Section 504.[63] Finally, the Department of Health and Human Services Office of Civil Rights found, in 1989, that a Pennsylvania Department of Corrections policy of segregating HIV-positive prisoners and denying them programming violated Section 504. While the policy was voluntarily rescinded before court proceedings became necessary, this official interpretation of Section 504 by an enforcement agency is encouraging.[64]

There have also been important settlements to end segregation and program exclusion. In *Smith v. Meachum,* for example, the parties agreed that Connecticut prisoners with HIV could not be segregated from the general prison population.[65] In Colorado, although the federal district court rejected a proposed settlement, prison officials have stopped segregating HIV-positive prisoners on intake and have reintegrated segregated prisoners into prison programs, separating them only at night.[66] In Arizona, prison officials voluntarily desegregated seropositive prisoners even though no litigation was pending.

It seems clear that the trend away from general segregation and program exclusion will continue. Both the 1990 NIJ study and the National Commission on

AIDS advise against segregation policies. At least in the short term, however, segregation for the purpose of providing centralized medical care and job restrictions based on others' fears will continue to be subjects of legal and policy disputes. Excessive isolation in response to TB may also become a problem. If a system of centralized medical care is needed, HIV-positive prisoners could be housed in centers where expert medical staff and support programs are available without being made to live in special housing units within the centers. If the program is administered carefully, the medical status of the HIV-positive prisoners need not be revealed. As the *Coughlin* case suggests, prisoners ought to be given a choice when the promise of better care comes with a threat of exposure.

In the area of discrimination generally, it is noteworthy that the Americans with Disabilities Act (ADA), signed into law on July 26, 1990, should apply to prisoners with HIV disease. Title II of this far-reaching civil rights legislation extends the protection of Section 504 to all state or local government programs, whether or not they receive federal assistance. The ADA contains no exclusions for prisons and jails.[67]

PRIVACY

Policies

According to the 1990 NIJ study, the attending physician or health care worker is notified of HIV test results in all prison and jail systems. The state public health department is also notified in the majority of systems. A little less than two-thirds notify the rest of the medical staff or correctional management in the institution and the central office. Seven prison systems directly notify correctional officers as a matter of policy. Others, like the Federal Bureau of Prisons, allow disclosure on a "need to know" basis, but this vague term is not defined. In most systems, prisoners' HIV status is released to nonmedical staff one way or another.[68]

Over a third of all prison systems notify parole agencies, with the predictable result that HIV-positive prisoners appear on average to serve more time against the same sentences than seronegative prisoners. In some cases, this result reflects an explicit policy against granting parole to infected prisoners, but more often it is the indirect result of prisoners' inability to secure home and job placements.[69]

Sixteen percent of prison systems require disclosure of HIV infection to a spouse or outside sexual partner, down from 24 percent in 1989. It is not clear from the data whether this disclosure takes place at the time of release or as soon as infection is known, or whether the prison system or the health department is responsible for making the disclosure. There are no cases on point, but a legal and moral argument could be made that the state has a duty to disclose this information to people who are indisputably within the zone of risk. However, each state faces this same dilemma regarding people in the free world, and there is no basis for reporting and disclosure laws that distinguish between prison and nonprison populations.[70]

In 1989 the Federal Bureau of Prisons proposed regulations that would have required prisoners to disclose their HIV status to their outside sexual partners prior to release, but would have allowed them to choose how to do it. These regulations were not adopted, even though all prisoners under the Bureau's jurisdiction are still tested before they are released. The health department of the state in which the prisoner is released, and the United States Probation Office, are informed of positive test results, as is the Immigration and Naturalization Service for prisoners released on an INS detainer. It is not clear how any of these agencies use this information.[71]

Some systems have taken important steps to prevent disclosure, including such obvious measures as making it clear that wrongful disclosure will result in the firing of culpable staff members or the disciplining of culpable prisoners. For example, Nevada brings a disciplinary action, pursuant to its employee discipline code, against any employee who wrongfully discloses a prisoner's HIV test result.[72] At least one state allows prisoners to self-administer their AZT dosages, which eliminates their tell-tale trip to the infirmary every four hours.[73]

Confidentiality is closely linked to education. Prison is a small world where information is hard to conceal. As long as prisoners and staff members believe that their lives depend on knowing who is infected, such information will be at a premium. To deflate their fears, correctional officers must be taught the universal precautions and the reasoning behind them, as well as the basic facts about HIV and its transmission. Also, prisons and jails should develop precise guidelines on when disclosure is authorized. They should limit disclosure to the health care provider, the public health department (if required by state law), and those who have a written release from the prisoner. If other recipients are included, the disclosure policy should specify the circumstances justifying their inclusion.[74]

Prisoners' Right to Privacy Regarding HIV Status

The principal source of protection for prisoners' medical privacy is the constitutional right to privacy. While the cases are divided, it is clear that prisoners do not entirely lose right upon incarceration. In *Turner v. Safely,* the Supreme Court relied on privacy to strike down a restriction on the right of prisoners to marry, holding that a regulation that impinges on prisoners' constitutional rights must be "reasonably related to legitimate penological interests." This test is deferential to the judgments of prison officials, but it is not one that they automatically pass.[75] Among the interests protected under the mantle of privacy are the interests in avoiding disclosure of personal matters and in exercising autonomy in making certain important decisions.

It is hard to imagine more sensitive medical information than a prisoner's HIV status, or a more basic decision than whether to release the information to others. As the court in *Doe v. Coughlin* observed:

> There are few matters of a more personal nature, and there are few decisions over which a person could have a greater desire to exercise control, than the manner in which he reveals the diagnosis to others. An individual's decision to tell family members as well as the general community that he is suffering from an incurable disease, particularly one such as AIDS, is clearly an emotional and sensitive one fraught with serious implications for that individual. Certain family members may abandon the AIDS victim while others may be emotionally unprepared to handle such news. Within the confines of the prison the infected prisoner is likely to suffer from harassment and psychological pressures. Beyond the prison's walls the person suffering from AIDS is often subject to discrimination.[76]

Woods v. White was the first reported decision to find that an HIV-positive prisoner had a claim under the right to privacy. In that case, the medical service personnel at the prison's health care unit disclosed the prisoner's HIV status to nonmedical staff and other prisoners. The court did not find it necessary to balance the prisoner's right to avoid disclosure against any governmental interest, because the government did not claim that any important public interest has been served.[77] The *Woods* decision was followed by *Doe v. Coughlin,* which barred the New York Department of Corrections from involuntarily transferring HIV-positive prisoners to a separate housing unit. And in *Rodriguez v. Coughlin,* the district court held that an HIV-positive prisoner stated a valid claim under the right of privacy when the staff had told other prisoners he was infected and had transferred him from one facility to another dressed in a "hygiene suit," thereby effectively identifying him as a "health hazard."[78]

Once again, *Harris v. Thigpen* provides a striking counterexample. In Alabama, the identities of seropositive prisoners were disseminated throughout the entire prison system and beyond. The prisoners were housed in special HIV units and for a period of time were required to wear masks and gloves outside their cells, even during visits. Officers, arriving prisoners, and institutional visitors were told about the units, and officials disclosed this information to prisoners' individual visitors, to the parole board, and, on occasion, to local courts and law enforcement agencies. Despite the lack of specific justification for these practices, the court found that the need to protect others from infection outweighed the privacy rights of HIV-positive prisoners; indeed, said the court, prisoners had no privacy interest to protect because their infection was a matter of "public interest."[79]

Many states have enacted laws governing the disclosure of medical information and records about prisoners infected with HIV. Some of them deal not only with HIV but with all sexually transmitted diseases.[80] In addition, prison systems regulate who may receive information of this sort. Many states now also have HIV-specific confidentiality laws that apply both in prison and on the outside. New York's confidentiality law has now been applied to prisoners in several cases. In the most important one, a federal court ruled against a county prison's policy of placing red stickers on the "intake card, cash record index card, clothing bag, court papers, cell card and other items" of HIV-infected prisoners. The court rejected the prison's argument that the stickers did not reveal the prisoners' infection because various other diseases were also subject to the policy. Like many other states, New York forbids the release of information that "reasonably could identify" a person as having HIV, as well as information that unmistakably does so.[81] (For more on the constitutional right of privacy and state HIV-confidentiality laws, see chapter 7.)

HIV EDUCATION

Intensive education is the only method of preventing transmission that has so far proven successful in stemming the tide of the HIV epidemic. Incarceration settings offer an ideal opportunity to reach people at high risk for contracting HIV, such as IV drug users, because prisoners are, literally, a captive audience. According to Dr. Charles Braslow, former Director of Medical Services at New York's Rikers Island:

> Correctional facilities provide a particularly auspicious location for such [educational] efforts since they contain a concentration of drug users who are removed from states of drug intoxication and drug-seeking behavior and so are likely to benefit from educational efforts. Equally important, lessons learned inside are not forgotten outside, resulting in an increased level of knowledge "in the streets" after discharge. These "street" drug abusers have so far been a difficult population for AIDS educators to reach, and correctional facilities can be a major focal point in targeting them for risk reduction.

HIV education is also crucial in addressing irrational fears and quieting panic among both prisoners and staff members. Yet most prison HIV education programs are sadly lacking.[82]

The National Commission on AIDS found that "almost a decade into the epidemic, in many jurisdictions prisoners and staff remain substantially misinformed about HIV disease.'' It quoted a prisoner who wrote, ''[i]gnorance is the norm in a place like this . . . [and] you can be hurt or killed if your confidentiality is breached and other prisoners find out.'' A 1988 survey by the Federal Bureau of Prisons of its staff showed that close to 40 percent were ''bothered a great deal'' by the presence of HIV-positive prisoners.[83]

Surveys conducted by numerous state prison systems have also uncovered vast ignorance about the virus and irrational concerns about its transmission. A survey of incoming Virginia prisoners revealed the ignorance and fear prisoners have about AIDS. One-third of the men and one-fifth of the women either were not sure or thought it was unsafe to live or work with an HIV-positive prisoner. Almost all thought it was unsafe to have a blood transfusion. Nearly half thought that donating blood was dangerous, and that HIV could be transmitted via eating or drinking utensils, mosquito bites, and contact with sweat, tears, saliva, or urine. They were also poorly informed about methods of sexual transmission.[84]

The 1990 NIJ study shows that 96 percent of prisons and 74 percent of reporting jails provide some sort of live HIV education, but all of the evidence indicates it is not being done properly. One expert identified a series of obstacles hindering effective HIV education in prison: the authoritarian atmosphere, the restrictions imposed for the sake of security, the fear of violence from other prisoners and correctional officers if one is identified with the program, the negative attitudes of prison officials, and the opposition of public officials. One way around the problem of violence is to require HIV education of all prisoners and staff members, yet only a little over half of prison systems do so.[85]

Perhaps the greatest barrier to effective education is a lack of well-trained, credible educators in corrections. Public health authorities can and should be brought in to provide HIV education for both staff members and prisoners. In Philadelphia, for example, the city health department employs a full-time HIV educator in the county prison. Correctional institutions should also take advantage of community-based AIDS service organizations by bringing them in to provide education and support for prisoners who are infected or at risk. In the past, these organizations have often ignored the prisons and jails in their areas, but this is beginning to change. A growing number of educators are working with prisons to reach incarcerated populations. One of the most important developments in prison HIV education is the use of peer groups, in which prisoners are trained (or train themselves) to lead workshops. Because prisoners are more likely to trust a fellow prisoner, this approach can be very effective. Only eleven prison systems report having such programs.[86] One of the oldest and best is a program at Bedford Hills, a women's prison in the state of New York. It was initiated by prisoners and involves peer education as well as counseling and support groups for the HIV-infected.[87]

Education, no matter who provides it, must deal with the reality of voluntary sex and drug use in prison. The great majority of prisons and jails surveyed convey information about safer sex practices, including the use of condoms, but only Mississippi, Vermont, New York City, Philadelphia, and San Francisco County actually provide condoms to prisoners. Officials in these five jurisdictions characterize condom distribution as highly successful, with no resulting serious security breaches.[88] Approximately two-thirds of the prisons and jails surveyed cover methods of cleaning needles in their education programs, but none provides bleach for this purpose, in part because of fear that it could be used as a weapon. Also, as with condoms, prison officials do not want to be perceived as condoning illegal activity.[89]

Ultimately, the responsibility for education must fall on public officials, including public health departments and prison and jail administrators. Although there have been few legal challenges to the lack of adequate HIV education in correctional systems, the Connecticut settlement in *Doe v. Meachum* may portend a change. Relying on the Eighth Amendment and the *Estelle* standard, prisoners claimed that failure to educate in the face of a life-threatening epidemic amounted to deliberate indifference to a serious medical need. In a partial consent judgment, the defendants agreed routinely to provide newly admitted prisoners with HIV education consisting of written materials, a videotape, and a live question-and-answer period. Regular sessions dispensing additional information are to be held in the prisons and jails, and discharged prisoners are to be given a packet containing referral numbers for AIDS programs, more written information, and condoms. Requirements for counseling were also included in the settlement. In *Starkey v. Matty*, the settlement included both HIV education for all prisoners and an official role for a community-based health clinic in providing education, testing, counseling and general support services. Prisons in other jurisdictions are presently altering their practices to meet the demands of prisoners who have sued for better HIV education.[90]

EARLY RELEASE OF PRISONERS WITH AIDS

Prisoners who are near death or whose serious medical needs are not being met in prison should be entitled to an early release into a more appropriate setting. There are several procedures under existing law to accomplish this humane result, but none deal with a disease like AIDS, and all have major drawbacks.

The most common form of early release is parole. The rules for parole eligibility vary from jurisdiction to jurisdiction, but typically a prisoner must serve some portion of the imposed sentence. One of the problems with parole as a form of early release for prisoners with AIDS is that parole eligibility guidelines typically require that the prisoner have a job. If the prisoner is too sick to work, this option is foreclosed. Moreover, some parole boards may hesitate to release a prisoner with AIDS into the community, or may require disclosure to prospective home and job placements. Another problem is that the process itself is prolonged—the parole officer must determine eligibility, investigate the prisoner's home and job plans, and make a recommendation to the parole board, which must meet and make a decision. And if the prisoner has not yet served the requisite minimum time, parole is usually not a possibility.

Prisoners may seek some form of medical furlough or ''compassionate release'' before they are eligible for parole. According to the 1990 NIJ study, 39 percent of prison systems have such a program.[91] New York City actively pursues the release of terminally ill prisoners, and some 125 prisoners have been released.[92] The California legislature recently passed a bill to allow the release of prisoners who were not sentenced to life without parole and who either are disabled or have a terminal illness with a life expectancy of a year or less. Unfortunately, California's Governor Wilson vetoed the legislation.[93]

Prisoners in need of early release may also request a pardon from the chief executive officer of the governing jurisdiction (the president of the United States for federal prisoners and the governor for state prisoners). Traditionally, the exercise of the clemency power is not guided by precedent and is not subject to judicial review. The procedure for petitioning varies among the states, and while all states give the governor this power, few prisoners benefit from it. As is true of parole, applicants are faced with a catch–22 situation: they are not likely to be eligible for a pardon until death is near, but the process takes so long that they may well be dead before it is completed.[94]

Prisoners may also seek modification of their sentences from the sentencing court. This alternative may be the best choice if a state has not adopted a special early-release program. As with all post-conviction procedures, however, the prospects for success are greatly enhanced if the prisoner is represented by counsel, a luxury most cannot afford. The rules under which a court may grant relief, and the procedures to be followed, vary from state to state. Among federal prisoners, sixteen out of twenty-three applications were approved between 1987 and August 1990.[95]

Prisoners can also file a habeas corpus petition, which is a special pleading in federal court to challenge unconstitutional imprisonment. In the one reported case in which the procedure has been tried, the prisoner, who was seriously ill with AIDS, challenged the legality of his confinement because of the prison's inability to provide him with adequate medical care. The trial court released him to get outside medical care pending trial on his petition, but the Eleventh Circuit reversed. The Eighth Amendment, it said, protects prisoners from deliberately indifferent medical care, but does not allow prisoners to be released just because they are not getting adequate medical care. The court suggested that the proper remedy would be an order requiring prison authorities to bring the treatment in prison up to constitutional standards.[96]

The arguments in favor of early release for prisoners in end-stage AIDS are compelling: it allows them to be with their families as the end approaches; it may enable them to obtain better medical and psychological services than are available in prison; and it permits prison systems to save money. Indeed, there is a danger that early release will be misused to save prisons the expense of treatment. Such a result would be the ultimate irony: as prison medical care improves, the extremely ill may find themselves on the streets. In one case, a ninety-five pound AIDS patient in a wheelchair was released from the Pittsburgh County Jail because he became too sick to handle and was dumped at a county hospital emergency room without any provision for his care or housing.[97] This prisoner's fate illustrates the need for discharge planning to ensure that people released from correctional institutions will have adequate care and support on the outside.

CONCLUSION

Looking back over the first decade of the HIV epidemic as it has affected those in prison, two trends have emerged. The first is that, in most respects, corrections departments are beginning to shape their HIV policies in accordance with public health principles. It is equally clear, however, that implementation has a long way to go. The task for prisoner advocates is to reinforce this trend by continuing to press for reform and to further prison officials' education about HIV. At the same time, legislatures must be made to recognize the public health value of addressing the crisis in prisons instead of reacting with ineffective and even harmful measures. Correctional institutions desperately need funds to provide necessary and appropriate HIV care for their charges, including medical and mental health care, voluntary testing and counseling, and drug treatment. Legislation is also needed to remedy problems in a variety of other areas. Laws must be passed to protect the confidentiality of medical information, to facilitate prisoner participation in experimental drug trials, to allow condom distribution, and to establish streamlined compassionate-release mechanisms. Measures calling for mandatory testing and reporting and discriminatory treatment of the HIV-infected are counterproductive and should be defeated.

The second trend is that relying on litigation alone to improve conditions for HIV-infected prisoners has turned out to be a gamble at best. Prisoners should stay out of court whenever possible and attempt to resolve their concerns by negotiating with prison administrators, by educating themselves when apparent conflicts among them arise, and by enlisting the support of public health advocates. In HIV prison litigation, the best results have been achieved through negotiated settlements based on sound public health policy. To a large extent, a good settlement depends on the involvement of a sensitive judge who foresees that settlement is in the best interest of both sides. Unfortunately, due to our random system of dispensing justice, HIV-infected prisoners in Alabama continue to suffer, while those in Connecticut have obtained substantial relief.

NOTES

1 M. Mauer, Americans Behind Bars: A Comparison of International Rates of Incarceration (1991); European Common Council, Prison Information Bulletin (June 1990); Bureau of Justice Statistics, U.S. Dep't of Justice, Bulletin: Prisoners in 1990 (1991).

2 M. Mauer, note 1 above; see also Butterfield, U.S. Expands Its Lead in the Rate of Imprisonment, N.Y. Times, Feb. 11, 1992, at A16 (reporting 1992 Mauer study results).

3 G. Camp & C. Camp, The Corrections Yearbook 1991 at 4–5; Correctional Association of New York & New York Coalition for Criminal Justice, Imprisoned Generation (1990); National Center on Institutions & Alternatives, Young African American Men and the Criminal Justice System in California (1990); Norris, Study: Black Men Pack State Courts, Prisons, Reno Gazette-Journal, Feb. 2, 1991, at 1A.

4 National Commission on Acquired Immunodeficiency Syndrome, Report on HIV Disease in Correctional Facilities 15 (1991);

Hammett & Daugherty, 1991 Update: AIDS in Correctional Facilities 15.

5 Hammett & Daugherty, note 4 above, at 12, 20; New York State Commission on Corrections, Update: Acquired Immune Deficiency Syndrome, A Demographic Profile of New York State Inmate Mortalities (1987).

6 New York State Commission on Corrections, note 5 above, at 19; Hammett & Daugherty, note 4 above, at 17, fig. 6 at 18, 19–20.

7 N. Freudenberg, Preventing AIDS: A Guide to Effective Education for the Prevention of HIV Infection 188 (1989).

8 C. Hannssens, AIDS Issues for New Jersey's Incarcerated, Testimony before the National Commission on AIDS, Hearings on HIV Infection and AIDS in Correctional Facilities (Aug. 17, 1990).

9 Davidson, et al., Retrovirus Seroprevalence in the Short-Term Incarcerated: The Philadelphia Prison Seroprevalence Study, Abstract

No. M.A.O.39, Fifth International Conference on AIDS, Montreal (June 5, 1989).

10 Hammett & Daugherty, note 4 above, fig. 7 at 20.

11 Hammett & Daugherty, note 4 above, at 15; Vlahov, *et al., Prevalence of Antibody to HIV-1 among Entrants to U.S. Correctional Facilities,* 265 J.A.M.A. 1129 (1991).

12 Hammett & Daugherty, note 4 above, at 15; Vlahov, *et al.,* note 11 above.

13 *AIDS in Women—United States,* 39 MMWR 845 (1990); Bureau of Justice Statistics, U.S. Dep't of Justice, Prisons in 1990 (1991).

14 Brewer, *et al., Transmission of HIV-1 within a Statewide Prison System,* 2 AIDS 263 (1988); Horsburgh, *et al., Seroconversion to Human Immunodeficiency Virus in Prison Inmates,* 80 Am. J. Pub. Health 209 (1990); *see also AIDS Spreading More Slowly Than in General Population,* 3 AIDS Pol'y & L. (BNA), June 1, 1988, at 4 (spread of disease slower among prisoners than in population at large). The mid-Atlantic region, including New York, New Jersey & Pennsylvania, accounts for over 55 percent of the AIDS cases in prisons nationally. Hammett & Daugherty, note 4 above, fig. 4 at 16. In prisons and jails, however, the percentage of people with AIDS is higher than it is in the surrounding geographic area, mostly due to the high concentration of IV drug users behind prison walls. *Id.* at 15.

15 The CDC has surveyed the states for prevalence of tuberculosis in general and found that its incidence is on the rise. Even in states where the prevalence of HIV is low, the prevalence of tuberculosis is high. Presentation by Mary Hutton (CDC), American Public Health Association Conference, Chicago, Ill. (Oct. 1989). The data from the survey are unpublished. At the same workshop, Dr. Charles Braslow, then Director of Medical Services, Rikers Island Detention Center, New York City, reported that the number of tuberculosis

cases there had doubled in two years. *See also* Skolnick, *Government Issues Guidelines to Stem Rising Tuberculosis Rates in Prisons,* 262 J.A.M.A. 3253 (1989).

16 Hammett & Daugherty, note 4 above, at 25, fig. 9 at 26.

17 Moini & Hammett, 1990 Update: AIDS in Correctional Facilities 27.

18 National Commission on Acquired Immunodeficiency Syndrome, note 4 above, at 14.

19 Hammett & Daugherty, note 4 above, at 25, fig. 9 at 26.

20 *See* Altman, *Deadly Strain of Tuberculosis Is Spreading Fast, U.S. Finds,* N.Y. Times, Jan. 24, 1992, at A1; Altman, *For Most, Risk of Contracting Tuberculosis Is Seen as Small,* N.Y. Times, Jan. 20, 1992 at A1; Navarro, *New York Asks U.S. Help in Tracking New TB Cases,* N.Y. Times, Jan. 24, 1992, at B6; Rosenthal, *HIV Infection Foiling Tests That Detect Deadly TB Germ,* N.Y. Times, Dec. 10, 1991, at A1.

21 This discussion relies generally upon the recommendation set forth in National Commission on Acquired Immunodeficiency Syndrome, note 4 above.

22 *Id.* at 36.

23 National Prison Project, Status Report: The Courts and the Prisons (1990).

24 The Supreme Court in the 1991 term confronted prisoners with a new hurdle. In Wilson v. Seiter, 111 S.Ct. 2321 (1991), the Court held that plaintiffs in cases alleging cruel and unusual punishment must prove not only objective conditions resulting in unconstitutional deprivations, but also a ''subjective component'' or ''culpable state of mind.'' *Id.* at 2324.

25 The Federal Bureau of Prisons and Alabama, Arkansas, Colorado, Georgia, Idaho, Iowa, Michigan, Missouri, Mississippi, Nebraska, Nevada, New Hampshire, North Dakota, Oklahoma, Rhode Island, Utah and Wyoming conduct mandatory mass screening of prisoners. Statistics on city and county jails are not available. Hammett & Daugherty, note 4 above, fig. 14 at 44. The Federal Bureau of Prisons is included on this list because it requires testing prior to release. The Bureau's policy also prescribes testing in a number of other circumstances. Federal Bureau of Prisons, U.S. Dep't of Justice, Operations Memorandum 179–89 (Nov. 30, 1989) [hereinafter Operations Memorandum].

26 The seventeen systems doing mass screening represent a net increase of one since the 1989 survey, and four since the 1988 survey. Hammett & Daugherty, note 4 above, at 43, fig. 14 at 44; Moini & Hammett, note 17 above, at 45, fig. 14 at 46; T. Hammett, AIDS in Correctional Facilities: Issues and Options 59, fig. 4.1 at 60 (3d ed. 1988).

27 Hammett & Daugherty, note 4 above, fig. 16 at 47. Some systems do both. According to the NIJ study, thirty-three prison systems test upon a prisoner's request. Eleven of the systems that impose testing also make it available when a prisoner requests it. *Id.*, figs. 15 at 46, 16 at 47.

28 Moini & Hammett, note 17 above, fig. 15 at 47. Corrections officials also experience intense pressure from politicians and the public to institute testing in the prisons. T. Hammett, note 26 above, at 59. For example, in 1990 Congress passed the Ryan White Comprehensive AIDS Resources Emergency Act to provide emergency assistance to communities disproportionately affected by the HIV epidemic. This otherwise useful legislation includes a section that requires states seeking funds to provide early treatment for prisoners, and to test all prisoners on intake and thirty days prior to release from the system. 42 U.S.C.A. § 300ff–48(c)(1) (West 1991).

29 Hammett & Daugherty, note 4 above, at 30; Langston, Workshop on HIV/AIDS Education and Health Concerns for Incarcerated Populations, Washington, D.C. (July 18, 1990); Moini & Hammett, note 17 above, at 49.

30 Hammett & Daugherty, note 4 above, fig. 17 at 48.

31 Walker v. Sumner, 917 F.2d 382 (9th Cir. 1990). A "taser gun" fires an electrically charged dart, which temporarily incapacitates the prisoner.

32 Dunn v. White, 880 F.2d 1188 (10th Cir. 1989) (per curiam), cert. denied, 493 U.S. 1059 (1990); see also Harris v. Thigpen, 727 F. Supp. 1564 (M.D. Ala. 1990), *aff'd in part, vacated in part,* 941 F.2d 1495 (11th Cir. 1991).

33 *See, e.g.,* Portee v. Tollison, 753 F. Supp. 184 (D.S.C. 1990), *aff'd,* 929 F.2d 694 (4th Cir. 1991); Jarrett v. Faulkner, 662 F. Supp. 928 (S.D. Ind. 1987); Feigley v. Fulcomer, 720 F. Supp. 475 (M.D. Pa. 1989).

34 *See, e.g.,* Austin v. Pennsylvania Department of Corrections, No. Civ. A. 90–7497 (E.D. Pa. filed Nov. 27, 1990); Inmates of New York State with Human Immune Deficiency Virus v. Cuomo, No. 90-CV–252 (N.D.N.Y. filed Mar. 6, 1990).

35 *Feigley,* 720 F. Supp. at 481 (quoting Estelle v. Gamble, 429 U.S. 97, 102–03 (1976)).

36 *See, e.g.,* Doe v. Meachum, No. 88–562, 1990 WL 261348 (D. Conn. Dec. 6, 1990) (order entering consent judgment); Starkey v. Matty, No. CIV. A. 89–9011 (E.D. Pa. May 24, 1991) (order entering consent decree).

37 Hammett & Daugherty, note 4 above, figs. 20 at 58, 21 at 59.

38 National Commission Acquired Immunodeficiency Syndrome, note 4 above.

39 New York State Commission on Corrections, note 5 above.

40 Rowe & Keintz, *National Survey of State Spending for AIDS,* Intergovernmental AIDS Reports, Sept.-Oct. 1989, at 1.

41 The National Prison Project AIDS Project almost daily receives reports from prisoners complaining of problems getting AZT. However, the 1990 NIJ survey indicates improvement in this area. According to information reported by the systems themselves, 78 percent have protocols adhering to the FDA's eligibility criterion for AZT (T-cell count of five hundred or below), and 90 percent of these systems claim success in compliance. Hammett & Daugherty, note 4 above, at 58.

42 *See* Frierson & Lippmann, *Management and Treatment of AIDS-Related Depression,* Clinical Advances in the Treatment of Psychiatric Disorders, Mar.-Apr. 1988, at 1; Marzuk, *et al., Increased Risk of Suicide in Persons with AIDS,* 259 J.A.M.A. 133 (1988).

43 *See* 45 C.F.R. § 46.306(a)(2)(D) (1990); National Commission on Acquired Immunodeficiency Syndrome, note 4 above, at 14–15, 37; Dubler & Sidel, *On Research on HIV Infection and AIDS in Correctional Institutions,* 67 Milbank Q. 171 (1989); Hammett & Dubler, *Clinical and Epidemiologic Research on HIV Infection and AIDS among Correctional Inmates,* Evaluation Rev., Oct. 1990, at 482–501; Levine, *et al., Building a New Consensus: Ethical Principles and Policies for Clinical Research on HIV/AIDS,* IRB, A Review of Human Subjects Research, Jan./Apr. 1991, at 1.

44 M. Chaiken, In-Prison Programs for Drug Involved Offenders 5 (1989) (available from the National Criminal Justice Reference Service, Document Number NCJ 117999).

45 429 U.S. 97, 103 (1976).

46 Hawley v. Evans, 716 F. Supp. 601, 603 (N.D. Ga. 1989); *accord* Wilson v. Franceschi, 730 F. Supp. 420, *amended,* 735 F. Supp. 396 (M.D. Fla. 1990).

47 727 F. Supp. at 1578, 1583 (M.D. Ala. 1990), *aff'd in part, vacated in part,* 941 F.2d 1495 (11th Cir. 1991).

48 941 F.2d at 1509; *see also* Maynard v. New Jersey, 719 F. Supp. 292 (D.N.J. 1989).

49 Doe v. Meachum, No. 88–562, 1990 WL 261348 (D. Conn. Dec. 6, 1990) (order entering consent judgment).

50 Starkey v. Matty, No. CIV. A. 80–9011 (E.D. Pa. May 24, 1991) (order entering consent decree).

51 Hammett & Daugherty, note 4 above, at 60.

52 *Id.,* fig. 18 at 52. Alabama, California, Colorado, and Mississippi segregate all categories of HIV-infected prisoners, but Colorado and California are in the process of altering their housing policies. *Id.* at 51.

53 Moini & Hammett, note 17 above, at 53; Hammett & Daugherty, note 4 above, fig. 18 at 52, fig. 19 at 53.

54 Hammett and Daugherty, note 4 above, at 56.

55 American Bar Association, Policy on AIDS and the Criminal Justice System (Feb. 7, 1989); American Correctional Association, Resolution on AIDS (Aug. 17, 1988); American Correctional Health Services Association, Correctional Information Bulletin, Acquired Immune Deficiency Syndrome (Jan. 1988); Joint Subcommittee on AIDS in the Criminal Justice System of the Committee on Corrections and the Committee on Criminal Justice Operations and Budget of the Association of the Bar of the City of New York, AIDS and the Criminal Justice System: A Final Report and Recommendations (July 1989) [hereinafter AIDS and the Criminal Justice System]; National Commission on Acquired Immunodeficiency Syndrome, note 4 above, at 23; National Commission on Correctional Health Care, Policy Statement Regarding the Administrative Management of Inmates with HIV Positive Test Results, ARC or AIDS (adopted Nov. 8, 1987 and amended Apr. 30, 1989).

56 Roe v. Fauver, No. CIV. A. 88–1225, 1988 WL 106316 (D.N.J. Oct. 11, 1988) (order denying defendant's motion for summary judgment).

57 727 F. Supp. 1564 (M.D. Ala. 1990), *aff'd in part, vacated in part,* 941 F.2d 1495 (11th Cir. 1991).

58 *See e.g.,* Holt v. Norris, No. 88–5979. (6th Cir. Feb. 24, 1989); Glick v. Henderson, 855 F.2d 536, 539 (8th Cir. 1988).

59 *See, e.g., Harris,* 727 F. Supp. at 1575; Muhammad v. Carlson, 845 F.2d 175 (8th Cir. 1988), *cert. denied,* 489 U.S. 1068 (1989); Judd v. Packard, 669 F. Supp. 741 (D. Md. 1987); Powell v. Department of Corrections, 647 F. Supp. 968 (N.D. Okla. 1986); Brickus v. Frame, Civ. No. CIV. A. 89–2490, 1989 WL 83608 (E.D. Pa. July 24, 1989); Lewis v. Prison Health Services, No. CIV. A. 88–1247, 1988 WL 95082 (E.D. Pa. Sept 13, 1988); Cordero v. Coughlin, 607 F. Supp. 9 (S.D.N.Y. 1984); *see also* Farmer v. Moritsugu, 742 F. Supp. 525 (W.D. Wis. 1990) (food service jobs); Doe v. Coughlin, 518 N.E.2d 536 (N.Y. 1987) (family visits), *cert. denied,* 488 U.S. 879 (1988).

60 697 F. Supp. 1234 (N.D.N.Y. 1988).

61 29 U.S.C. § 794 (1988).

62 941 F.2d 1495, 1527 (11th Cir. 1991).

63 *Compare* Casey v. Lewis, 773 F. Supp. 1365 (D. Ariz. 1991) *with* Farmer v. Moritsugu, 742 F. Supp. 525 (W.D. Wis. 1990).

64 Letter from Paul Cushing, regional manager, Region III, Dep't of Health and Human Services, Office of Civil Rights, to David Owens, Jr., commissioner, Pennsylvania Department of Corrections (Sept. 19, 1989).

65 Smith v. Meachum, No. 87–221 (D. Conn. Mar. 14, 1990) (order entering consent judgment); *see also* Gates v. Deukmejian, No. CIV. S. 87–1636 (E.D. Cal. Mar. 8, 1990) (order entering consent decree); Starkey v. Matty, No. CIV. A. 89–9011 (E.D. Pa. May 24, 1991) (same).

66 Ramos v. Lamm, No. 77-K–1093 (D. Colo. Mar. 7, 1990) (bench order rejecting settlement); Personal Communication, David Miller, Legal Director of the ACLU of Colo-

rado and counsel to the plaintiffs (Mar. 7, 1990).

67 42 U.S.C. § 12101 *et. seq.* (1991).

68 Hammett & Daugherty, note 4 above, fig. 17 at 48; Operations Memorandum, note 25 above.

69 Hammett & Dougherty, note 4 above, fig. 17 at 48. The estimate that HIV-positive prisoners serve longer sentences is based upon numerous reports to the National Prison Project's AIDS Project, rather than on a formal survey. However, the plaintiffs in *Harris* were able to document that HIV-positive prisoners in Alabama, where their status was disclosed to parole boards, potential employers *and* home placements, on average served more time than other prisoners. 727 F. Supp. 1564.

70 Hammett & Daugherty, note 4 above, fig. 17 at 48; Moini & Hammett, note 17 above, fig. 17 at 51.

71 Operations Memorandum, note 25 above.

72 Nevada Department of Corrections Administrative Regulation 344.

73 Hammett & Daugherty, note 4 above, at 58.

74 New York state has a fairly good policy on disclosure. New York State Dep't of Correctional Services, Policies, Procedures and Guidelines Manual, Records Section, Item 71: Release of AIDS/HIV Information (May 23, 1990).

75 482 U.S. 78 (1987).

76 697 F. Supp. 1234, 1237 (N.D.N.Y. 1988).

77 689 F. Supp. 874 (W.D. Wis. 1988), *aff'd,* 889 F.2d 17 (7th Cir. 1990).

78 No. CIV–87–1577E, 1989 WL 59607 (W.D.N.Y. June 5, 1989); *accord* Nolley v. County of Erie, 776 F. Supp. 715 (W.D.N.Y. 1991).

79 *Harris,* 727 F. Supp. at 1576. On appeal, the circuit court held that HIV-positive prisoners retain some privacy interests, but that their interests in this case were outweighed by those of the general prison population. 941 F.2d 1495 (11th Cir. 1991).

80 For example, 1989 Conn. Acts 246 (Reg. Sess.) authorizes disclosure only to employees with a direct need to receive the information to achieve an authorized purpose. Other statutes are broader still, authorizing disclosure to correctional, probation, and parole officers and other law enforcement personnel. *See* Colo. Rev. Stat. § 25–4–1404 (West Supp. 1990); Wash. Rev. Code § 70.24.105 (1988); Wis. Stat. § 146.025 (5) (1987–88). State statutes governing disclosure of medical records of the population at large generally do not protect prisoners. L. Bowleg, Confidentiality/Disclosure Provisions for Prisoners' Medical Information (Aug. 27, 1990) (available from AIDS Policy Center, Intergovernmental Health Policy Project, George Washington Univ.); Personal Communication, L. Bowleg (Aug. 27, 1990).

81 Nolley v. Erie County, 776 F. Supp. 715 (W.D.N.Y. 1991); *see* Inmates of New York State with Human Immune Deficiency Virus v. Cuomo, No. 90-CV–252, 1991 WL 16032 (N.D.N.Y. Feb. 7, 1991) (applying state law in discovery decision); V. v. State, 556 N.Y.S. 2d 987 (Ct. Cl. 1991).

82 N. Freudenberg, note 7 above, at 188; *see also* AIDS and the Criminal Justice System, note 55 above, at 62; Vlahov & Polk, *Intravenous Drug Use and Human Immunodeficiency Virus (HIV) Infection in Prison,* 3 AIDS & Pub. Pol'y J. 42 (1988).

83 National Commission on Acquired Immunodeficiency Syndrome, note 4 above, at 16; Federal Bureau of Prisons, U.S. Dep't of Justice, Research Bulletin: HIV Infection Among Bureau of Prisons Inmates (1988).

84 Virginia Department of Corrections & Virginia Department of Health, HIV Seropositivity Study (1989).

85 Hammett & Daugherty, note 4 above, figs. 11 at 31, 12 at 32; N. Freudenberg, note 7 above, at 189.

86 N. Freudenberg, note 7 above, at 192; Gilbert & Rivera, *Views from the Inside: Prisoners Offer Perspectives about AIDS,* 4 Focus 3 (1989); Hammett & Daugherty, note 4 above, fig. 11 at 31; M. Farid, The Social Dimensions of AIDS in the Prisons (1989).

87 Lown, AIDS Prevention Programs in the New York State Prisons, PWA Support, May 1989; M. Rivers, Incarcerated HIV-Positive Women, Testimony before the National Commission on Acquired Immunodeficiency Syndrome, Hearings on HIV Infection and AIDS in Correctional Facilities (Aug. 17, 1990).

88 Hammett & Daugherty, note 4 above, fig. 13 at 33, 40–41; Fornaci, Condom Distribution Policies in State and Local Jails and Prisons (May 1, 1991) (unpublished memorandum on file with author).

89 Hammett & Daugherty, note 4 above, fig. 13 at 33, 40–41.

90 Doe v. Meachum, No. 88–563, 1990 WL 261348 (D. Conn. Dec. 6, 1990) (order entering partial consent decree); Starkey v. Matty, No. CIV. A. 89–9011 (E.D. Pa. May 24, 1991) (order entering consent decree); *see also* Crutchfield v. Wright, No. 88–2308 (D. Md. filed Aug. 3, 1988) (settlement on July 18, 1990 required AIDS counseling and education programs at the Montgomery County Detention facility). *But see* Harris v. Thigpen, 727 F. Supp. 1564 (M.D. Ala. 1990), *aff'd in part,* 941 F.2d 1495 (11th Cir. 1991).

91 Hammett & Daugherty, note 4 above, at 55.

92 Potler, Testimony on Early Release for Inmates with AIDS, National Commission on AIDS, Hearings on HIV Infection and AIDS in Correctional Facilities (Aug. 17, 1990).

93 S. 414, 1991–92 Reg. Sess. Cal. Leg.

94 In a survey conducted by the Correctional Association of New York of five states with large numbers of prisoners with AIDS (California, Florida, New Jersey, New York & Texas), only California's governor has failed to grant executive clemency to terminally ill prisoners. However, New Jersey's governor receives nine to ten applications a year from prisoners dying of AIDS, and grants three to four. In Texas, approximately 40 percent, or fifty-eight, of the medical applications received by the governor in recent years have been approved, of which 10 percent were AIDS cases. Potler, note 92 above.

95 *Id.*

96 Gomez v. United States, 899 F.2d 1124 (11th Cir. 1990).

97 *See AIDS Patient Dies at Godspeed House,* Propriety to the United Press International, Regional News, Oct. 14, 1990.

IV   Private Sector Responses to HIV

13 Discrimination

Arthur S. Leonard

From the earliest reports of a serious new illness spread through an infectious agent, a secondary epidemic of fear has accompanied the epidemic of illness and death, generating a wave of discrimination against those identified with the disease. In addition, the serious expenses of dealing with AIDS have generated their own wave of discrimination by government agencies and private businesses. This discrimination has not focused narrowly on those diagnosed with AIDS, but has reached out to touch asymptomatic people infected with HIV and even uninfected people suspected of being infected because of their membership in so-called high-risk groups or their association with people who have AIDS.

A 1990 survey of state and local civil rights agencies showed that approximately thirteen thousand complaints of HIV-related discrimination had been received by those agencies from 1983 to 1988, with 30 percent involving people who experienced discrimination because of the perception that they were HIV-infected or because they cared for somebody with HIV disease. These complaints ran the gamut from discrimination in access to health care, insurance, housing, or public benefits to workplace discrimination against employees or customers.[1]

DISABILITY DISCRIMINATION LAW AS THE FOUNDATION

In the early days of the epidemic, businesses seeking information about their legal obligations and individuals encountering discrimination both turned to lawyers, hoping that the legal system would be able to respond in a rational way to a new challenge. At that time, in the early 1980s, there was no existing body of ready-made precedents to deal with discrimination due to a contagious condition. Lawyers looking for answers settled upon the growing body of law dealing with discrimination against people with disabilities as a possible source. As the epidemic progressed

297

through the 1980s, lawyers, judges and legislators responded to the need for answers by adapting disability discrimination law (which had rarely been used in cases involving contagious disease) to this new problem.

This process culminated in 1990 with the federal government's enactment of the Americans with Disabilities Act (ADA),[2] which will become the basic law governing HIV-related discrimination in employment, public services, and public accommodations as its various provisions go into effect during the 1990s. The Act will apply broadly to businesses and individuals providing goods and services to the public, employers of fifteen or more employees,[3] and most federal and state agencies. Congress enacted the ADA "to provide a clear and comprehensive national mandate for the elimination of discrimination against individuals with disabilities."[4] Many political forces came together to support the passage of the ADA. It is likely, however, that the AIDS epidemic, and the strong recommendations of respected public bodies that action be taken on a national level to help counter HIV-related discrimination, played a significant part in moving Congress to pass the law and the president to sign it.

Congress was not writing on a clean slate when it passed the ADA. The federal government had prohibited discrimination in many of its own activities and the activities of federal contractors and funding recipients in the Rehabilitation Act of 1973,[5] and in 1988 Congress had adopted the Fair Housing Amendments Act to add disabilities to the list of prohibited bases for discrimination in the rental, sale and financing of residential housing.[6] During the 1970s and early 1980s, most of the states passed laws prohibiting disability discrimination in employment, housing, and public accommodations. (A "public accommodation" is generally defined as a business offering goods or services to the public.) These laws differ widely in their interpretation and application.[7] One of the key differences in the application of public accommodations laws, for example, is whether the laws apply to the practices of insurance companies or to the offices of individual professional practitioners, such as lawyers, doctors, dentists, or psychiatrists. In a few states and localities, discrimination laws focusing specifically on AIDS and HIV were also passed, adopting the general methodology of disability discrimination law.[8]

In order to understand the legal issues surrounding HIV-related discrimination, one must understand this intricate body of laws, many of which will continue to play an important role because the application of the ADA in the private sector is limited. Most important, the ADA does not supplant the operation of other federal, state or local laws which provide the same or greater protection from discrimination.[9]

The Legal Concept of Handicap or Disability

When Congress passed the Rehabilitation Act of 1973, it specified protection for "otherwise qualified individual[s] with handicaps."[10] (Responding to the preferences of the people affected, the vocabulary of the law has changed in the intervening years to "disability" rather than "handicap.") The original, narrow definition of the term "individual with handicaps" in the Rehabilitation Act as enacted in 1973 was modified by Congress as experience under the law showed that the original definition, which limited protection to people with actual impairments, was too limited to achieve the goal of preventing unjustified discrimination. The Fair Housing Act Amendments of 1988 adopted the same broad definition of handicaps then contained in the Rehabilitation Act.[11] By the time the ADA was passed, the Rehabilitation Act's definition had been broadened sufficiently to ensure that people with contagious diseases would be protected (and the United States Supreme Court so held in 1987),[12] but the legislative history of the ADA makes this coverage clearer by specifying contagious conditions among the examples of covered disabilities.

The legal concept of "handicap" or "disability" differs from everyday usage, because the goal of the law is to prevent unjustified discrimination. One commonly thinks of a disability as a catastrophic loss of a body part or a fundamental body function making it extremely difficult or impossible to see, hear, move, or communicate. (Indeed, some state and local "handicap" ordinances have been interpreted to provide protection only for such severe impairments.[13]) Common examples would include blindness, deafness, loss or paralysis of limbs, or loss of memory or analytical ability due to a head injury. The federal law casts its net wider, recognizing that many other impairments of function may lead to unjustified discrimination.

Under the Rehabilitation Act, an "individual with handicaps" is "any person who (i) has a physical or mental impairment which substantially limits one or more of such person's major life activities, (ii) has a record of such an impairment, or (iii) is regarded as having such an impairment."[14] People who in fact suffer no impairments at all would be considered "individual[s] with handicaps" if they encountered discrimination because of former impairment, or if they were mistakenly believed to be impaired and suffered discrimination as a result of the mistaken perception. Even if an actual impairment does not limit a "major life activity" such as talking, hearing, or walking, people who suffer discrimination because others incorrectly believe their impairments will have such an effect may also find protection in this law.

The Supreme Court endorsed this broad understanding of the statutory concept of "handicap" in *School Board of Nassau County v. Arline,* a case involving an elementary school teacher with tuberculosis infection.[15] Gene Arline had suffered from tuberculosis as a child, but medical treatment had suppressed the infection. She was discharged by the school district in 1979 when her tuberculosis infection became active three times over a two-year period. At the time of her discharge, Mrs. Arline was receiving medication which had rendered her tuberculosis infection inactive and noncontagious, and she was not suffering from any physical impairment. The school board discharged her because it feared that she might infect schoolchildren if her tuberculosis again became active.

Mrs. Arline filed a discrimination complaint with Florida civil rights officials, but they dismissed her complaint, ruling that it was not covered by the state's civil rights law. Then she filed a lawsuit under the Rehabilitation Act. The federal district judge dismissed her case, stating that Arline was not a "handicapped person under the terms of the statute" because it was "difficult . . . to conceive that Congress intended contagious diseases to be included within the definition of a handicapped person." Arline's appeal to the court of appeals was successful, and the decision was upheld by the Supreme Court. Since Arline had been so severely affected by her tuberculosis in the past that she had to be hospitalized, the Court concluded that she qualified as a person with a "record of an impairment" who was suffering discrimination on account of that record, even though at the time of her discharge she did not suffer from any actual impairment. That her condition might become contagious in the future did not make her any less an "individual with handicaps" under the statute. In a subsequent trial, the district court found that Mrs. Arline was entitled to reinstatement to her job.[16]

HIV infection and AIDS have come to be considered handicaps or disabilities by most of the administrative agencies and courts considering discrimination claims. It is easy to conceptualize AIDS—that is, the full-blown syndrome meeting the surveillance definition of the Centers for Disease Control (CDC)—as a handicap. AIDS is a condition in which organs of the body (the hemic and lymphatic systems) are impaired from performing their normal function of cell-mediated immunity, due to the subversion and destruction of a class of cells by the infecting virus. The symptoms and opportunistic infections associated with AIDS are themselves handicapping conditions, since they may affect seeing, breathing, walking, and other normal activities and may certainly impair the ability to work.

HIV infection without other symptoms, or with symptoms falling short of a diagnosis of AIDS, may also be described as a physical impairment affecting major life activities. There is evidence that as soon as HIV infection occurs there may be some immune impairment, and body systems of infected people may be impaired in varying degrees during the course of infection short of full-blown AIDS. However,

HIV infection is more easily classified as a handicap or disability under the broader concept of disability that includes conditions regarded by others as disabling or handicapping.

This expansive definition of an "individual with handicaps" has been crucial to the protection of people affected by the HIV epidemic, because much of the discriminatory treatment affects people who do not have AIDS. While the earliest reported court cases addressing HIV-related discrimination did involve persons with AIDS or AIDS-related complex (ARC), the problem of discrimination rapidly spread to people suspected of being infected, despite the lack of physical symptoms, once the virus was identified and a test for antibodies was licensed. Because the public identified AIDS with those groups of people public officials loosely called "risk groups," many uninfected people who belonged to those groups (such as gay men, Haitians, and intravenous drug users) also encountered HIV-related discrimination. Once again, the category comprising people regarded by others as having an impairment was crucial to protecting uninfected risk group members.

Although the Supreme Court has not directly addressed the issue of discrimination on the basis of HIV infection, lower federal courts have concluded that HIV infection is a handicapping condition under the rationale of the *Arline* case. Thus, people who encounter discrimination either because they have AIDS or HIV infection, or because they are regarded as having or being at risk for having HIV infection, are covered by the Rehabilitation Act's concept of "individual[s] with handicaps."[17]

The ADA defines a "disability" as "(A) a physical or mental impairment that substantially limits one or more . . . major life activities . . . ; (B) a record of such an impairment; or (C) being regarded as having such an impairment."[18] Because this definition is virtually identical to the definition under the Rehabilitation Act, the rationale of the *Arline* case and lower court rulings on HIV infection under that Act will apply in cases under the ADA.

Although the ADA provides that homosexuality, bisexuality, transsexualism, and a variety of other statuses or conditions are not to be considered disabilities,[19] homosexual or bisexual men would clearly be covered if they encountered HIV-related discrimination because as members of a "risk group" they were regarded as having the impairment of HIV infection or a high possibility of contracting it in the future.

A good example of this analysis under a state discrimination law is the New Jersey case of *Poff v. Caro*. Three gay men attempted to rent an apartment. The landlord initially offered them the apartment, then rescinded the offer because he feared they might develop AIDS. They claimed unlawful disability discrimination. The state superior court agreed, ruling that although there was no evidence that any of the men was infected with HIV or suffering from AIDS, they were discriminated against because of the landlord's belief that they might be infected or become infected. Consequently, this was disability discrimination under the broad understanding of disability.[20]

Scope of Protection

Although most disability discrimination laws define disabilities expansively to protect a wide range of people, the actual scope of that protection varies significantly with the context and the particular statute. For example, if an individual with a disability were to go into a doctor's office seeking medical treatment for a condition that the doctor was qualified and prepared to treat, the doctor would probably violate the ADA and most state disability laws by denying treatment because of the individual's disability, unless the doctor could show that the disability somehow disqualified the individual. It would normally be very difficult for a doctor to prove that an HIV-infected person was not qualified to receive medical treatment, regardless of whether the infection had induced dementia, caused blindness, or given rise to any of a number of gross physical impairments, although some doctors have argued strongly against being required to deal with HIV-infected patients.[21] (The ADA specifically provides that "the professional office of a health care provider" is a public accommodation required to comply with its nondiscrimination requirements. Whether such offices are covered by state laws may vary from place to place, and the question is being litigated in several states.[22])

By contrast, same people seeking protection from employment discrimination are clearly unprotected if dementia, blindness, or any other HIV-related condition actually makes it extremely difficult to perform essential job duties productively and safely. The Supreme Court has interpreted disability law as protecting from employment discrimination only those who can safely perform a job up to a reasonable standard of productivity. In *Southeastern Community College v. Davis,* a case in which a student with a significant hearing impairment challenged her exclusion from a nurse training program, the Court held that the college had met its burden of showing that the ability to hear was an essential qualification for being a nurse. Even though the student clearly had a disability, her inability to hear disqualified her from the training she sought because she would be unable adequately to perform the duties of a nurse.[23]

The Supreme Court's interpretation of the Rehabilitation Act has been adopted explicitly by Congress in the ADA, which provides protection from employment discrimination for any "qualified individual with a disability," defined as "an individual with a disability who, with or without reasonable accommodation, can perform the essential functions of the employment position that such individual holds or desires."[24] Similar descriptions of the scope of protection can be found in the sections of the ADA that mandate "reasonable accommodation" in public services and public accommodations offered by privately owned businesses. This concept will be described in the next section of the chapter.

An important new element in the ADA is the concept of "essential functions of the employment position," which takes an idea developed in the Rehabilitation Act case law and gives it more concrete form. The statute requires that courts consider "the employer's judgment as to what functions of a job are essential," and that written job descriptions prepared in advance of advertising or interviewing job applicants are to be considered "evidence of the essential functions of the job."[25] However, neither the employer's judgment nor the written job description would be controlling over evidence that a particular function was peripheral rather than essential. In its regulations administering the ADA, the Equal Employment Opportunity Commission (EEOC) adopts a rather strict definition of what is an essential function: "fundamental job duties . . . not includ[ing] the marginal functions of a position."[26] Marginal or peripheral functions that might be assigned to any of a number of jobs would not be considered essential, and the inability of people with disabilities to perform such functions would not disqualify them. However, the requirement that applicants or current employees be able to perform all essential job functions in order to be qualified remains a stringent test, and those who could not perform any essential function would be considered unqualified for the entire job.

Because of this understanding of the limited protection of disability discrimination law, people with HIV symptoms that actually impair their major bodily or mental functions may find themselves without significant protection from workplace discrimination. Only so long as they can work productively on all essential job functions without presenting a significant threat to the health and safety of other employees or members of the public will they be protected. Once they become physically or mentally unable to work, they will be entitled to the same treatment that their employer extends to people with other disabling conditions. If the employer routinely discharges such people, those with HIV disease could similarly be discharged unless they could show that their discharge violated some other law or public policy or was inconsistent with the employer's general policy for dealing with employees who become disabled.

Some employers might take the position that they should be able to discharge people with HIV infection or actual symptoms because there is a high probability that the disease will eventually incapacitate them, rendering them unable to perform their duties and imposing significant costs on the employer's benefit plan. Furthermore, they may create morale problems in the workplace, and other employees may suffer productivity loss, or even refuse to work, due to fear of transmission. Some employers might also argue that customers would refuse to patronize their businesses if it became known that they had such employees. None of these arguments should carry weight in court, because these defenses have normally been rejected under discrimination law. Courts normally restrict their consideration to the ability of employees to perform essential job functions safely at the time of discharge, and find a violation of the law if employers base their decisions on the presumed preferences of customers or co-workers or speculation about future disability or expense.[27] Of course, if an illegally discharged employee is no longer able to perform job functions at the time the employee wins a discrimination case, the remedy cannot include job reinstatement but could include back pay from the date of discharge to the date when the employee's condition made it impossible to perform essential job functions. The argument that employing people with disabilities will generate extra employee benefit expenses runs afoul of public policies protecting employee benefits rights, discussed later in this chapter.

In addition to its lack of protection for people whose impairments actually render them unable to perform essential job functions, disability discrimination law will not protect those whose contagious condition presents a significant risk of transmission. This is not a major factor for most claims of HIV-related discrimination: because HIV is not easily transmissible under normal conditions, and no significant expense or inconvenience need be incurred in preventing transmission if infected employees suffer minor cuts or scrapes, the contagious nature of HIV will not normally justify discriminatory treatment.

There may be circumstances, however, in which legal protections will be diminished because of the possibility of HIV transmission. The most serious questions arise in the context of emergency service workers (police, ambulance attendants, firefighters) and health care workers, where it is possible that those providing or receiving services may be exposed to a more-than-minimal risk of becoming infected through exposure to the blood of an infected person. The problem for emergency workers can be largely, although not completely, surmounted by providing them with protective clothing and equipment and requiring them to observe blood precautions regardless of the known or unknown HIV status of the people they assist. The problem may be more significant in health care, especially when providers perform medical procedures that will likely lead to significant blood exposure for themselves or their patients. On the other hand, if the risk of HIV transmission is truly insignificant, refusal to treat HIV-infected patients is a form of discrimination that would appear to violate the ADA. Similar arguments have arisen from surgeons in other specialties and from dentists.

The problem of HIV-infected health care providers also generates considerable debate, despite the paucity of solid evidence that HIV is transmitted to patients during the performance of invasive procedures. The CDC reported during 1990 that five patients of a dentist who had died from AIDS appeared to have been infected while receiving treatment from the dentist but was unable to provide any firm explanation of how the transmission occurred, apart from speculating about inadequately sterilized instruments. Although several surgeons and dentists are known to have died from AIDS, and it is reliably estimated that several hundred HIV-infected surgeons and dentists have continued to work over the first decade of the epidemic, these five patients stand as lonely examples of such possible transmission.

Infected health care workers have begun turning to the courts. In *Leckelt v. Board of Commissioners of Hospital District No. 1,* the federal Fifth Circuit Court of Appeals upheld a hospital's decision to discharge a licensed practical nurse who had refused to reveal his HIV status after his roommate died from AIDS. The court determined that some of the procedures the nurse would perform might expose a patient to his blood, and that the circumstances of his roommate's death gave the hospital a reasonable basis for demanding such information and excluding a person who refused to give it. (The nurse had gone to an anonymous testing center for an HIV test, but had decided not to go back for the results.[28]) Similarly, a New Jersey Superior Court judge ruled in 1991 that a medical center properly suspended a surgeon with AIDS from performing invasive procedures unless he would agree to inform his patients about his HIV status, although it also ruled that the surgeon's co-workers did not have the right to know about his HIV status.[29] (For more on HIV and health care, see chapter 17.)

The proper resolution of these cases depends upon what one conceives to be the fundamental policy of disability discrimination law, and the appropriate restrictions on the government's public health authority. In the *Arline* case, the Supreme Court said that an entity covered by the Rehabilitation Act has a legitimate interest in "avoiding exposing others to significant health and safety risks."[30] The legislative history suggests that the ADA's treatment of contagious conditions rests on the same principle: people presenting a "significant" risk of occupational transmission can be excluded from performing those tasks during which transmission might occur. The question whether employers or patients have a right to such information, at least under the principles of disability law, would then turn on whether the infected health care worker presents a significant risk of transmission. People differ over the meaning of "significant" in this context. The chance that HIV transmission will occur is very slight, but if it does occur, the recipient apparently is permanently infected with a virus that can cause serious illness and perhaps death in a significantly high proportion of cases. The most rational approach is probably to focus on the infection control mechanisms rather than to restrict infected health care workers from performing duties they are trained and competent to perform.

Another area where popular misconceptions about HIV transmission have resulted in unnecessary concern is food-handling. There is no evidence that HIV-infected food-handlers need be a source of concern to patrons of establishments where they work. Although HIV is present in the saliva of some infected people, there is no evidence that ingestion of the saliva with food will result in infection. There is also no evidence that transmission will occur if food-handlers cut themselves and bleed on food. The epidemic is far enough along, and there have been enough infected food-handlers, that it is highly unlikely that there would be no evidence if transmission were actually occurring in these circumstances.

Nonetheless, some politicians have seized upon public fears to suggest that infected people be removed from food-handling positions. (Indeed, some state public health laws specifically require that people with communicable conditions be barred from food-handling positions, among other jobs. This is one reason why public health officials who understand the issue of HIV transmission hesitate to classify HIV infection as a communicable or sexually transmitted disease under archaic public health laws.)[31] During consideration of the ADA, the House of Representatives initially accepted an amendment that could have barred anyone infected with a contagious condition from working as a food-handler. Eventually sanity prevailed, and the amendment was modified to reflect modern understandings of disease transmission. The secretary of health and human services is required to maintain a list of contagious conditions that present a risk of transmission through food-handling, and employees infected with such conditions are to be prevented from food-handling.[32] Since HIV is not transmitted in that way, the secretary has not placed it on such a list.

The Requirement of Reasonable Accommodation

Regulations issued by federal agencies to enforce the Rehabilitation Act require that federal funding recipients make reasonable accommodations for people with handicaps.[33] In *Davis* and *Arline,* the Supreme Court acknowledged these regulations but noted that their requirements were not particularly demanding, because an accommodation would not be considered reasonable if it imposed "undue financial or administrative burdens" on the funding recipient or required "a fundamental alteration in the nature" of the recipient's program. The Court also noted that employers "are not required to find another job for an employee who is not qualified for the job he or she was doing" but "cannot deny an employee alternative employment opportunities reasonably available under the employer's existing policies."[34] Although the regulations included some general guidelines for determining whether a particular accommodation presented "undue burdens," many of those providing legal advice to employers felt that the regulations were unduly vague and provided little real guidance.

Congress adopted the reasonable accommodation requirement for the ADA and provided statutory definitions and guidance as to its applicability and scope. The ADA protects people with disabilities who can perform their jobs "with or without reasonable accommodation." In other words, if an individual can perform the job only with the assistance of a reasonable accommodation, that individual is deemed qualified. The accommodation obligation has two basic components: either altering the physical environment to make it accessible to and usable by the individual with disabilities, or altering the job so that its essential functions can still be performed by that person. The statute spells out a variety of possible accommodations: "job restructuring, part-time or modified work schedules, reassignment to a vacant position, acquisition or modification of equipment or devices, appropriate adjustment or modifications of examinations, training materials or policies, the provision of qualified readers or interpreters, and other similar accommodations." The last phrase indicates that the list is merely suggestive, and other accommodations will not be ruled out unless they present an "undue hardship" for the employer.[35]

The ADA defines "undue hardship" as "an action requiring significant difficulty or expense" as judged by the following factors: the nature and cost of the accommodation; the overall financial resources of the facility or facilities involved in the provision of the accommodation; the number of persons employed at the facility; the effect on expenses and resources, or the impact otherwise of such accommodation upon the operation of the facility; the overall resources of the parent company, if a particular facility is one of several commonly owned operations; and the degree to which it is appropriate to require that a particular employing subunit call on the resources of the larger entity to effect a particular accommodation.[36]

The ADA adopts essentially the same approach as the Rehabilitation Act regulations. During Congressional consideration of the ADA, it was suggested that the Act specify some percentage of company revenues as the ceiling expense for required accommodations. Congress rejected this approach. Instead, the statute embraces case-by-case subjective decision-making, based on the view that the diversity of American workplaces makes it impossible to do more than state general principles on this subject. The EEOC's regulations also followed this subjective, case-by-case approach.[37] Although some employer groups had requested that the EEOC adopt a "rule of thumb" for determining whether a particular accommodation was reasonable by some mathematical calculation based on employer revenue, the agency refused to do so, arguing that Congress had rejected that approach and that it would be impossible to adopt any particular formula without compromising the policy of the statute.

The ADA requires accommodation not only with respect to job duties, but also with respect to employee selection and promotion procedures and accessibility of facilities. Under the public accommodation provisions, businesses that provide services to the public are supposed to render their facilities accessible to people with disabilities and to refrain from using eligibility criteria that tend unjustifiably to screen out people with disabilities. Under the employment provisions, even those areas of an employer's facilities not open to the general public should be made accessible for employees. Tests and physical examinations used to screen job applicants or to select employees for assignment and promotion must be modified to meet the needs of people with disabilities unless, of course, the relevant aspect of the test is necessary to measure a skill for an essential job function.

The accommodation requirements are likely to be most helpful to people with HIV infection who require time off for medical treatment or modified schedules to cope with reduced energy. One of the most characteristic symptoms of HIV illness is reduced stamina; those affected can continue to perform the same job functions, but may lack the energy to perform them over the length of a normal workday. Depending upon the size and scope of the employer's business, a modified work schedule may be the most suitable accommodation. Many people with HIV infection take prophylactic medications (to prevent opportunistic infections) that require periodic time off for in-hospital administration. Once again, employer flexibility in scheduling may be an appropriate accommodation. Finally, some people with HIV infection may experience neurological difficulties which affect locomotion. The accessibility requirements imposed by the ADA may make it possible for such people to continue to perform their job functions with slight modifications of workplace facilities.

The regulations issued by the EEOC state that employers should consult with their affected employees to determine appropriate accommodations, and that the statute imposes no obligation on the employees to accept any particular accommodation.[38] Of course, if they reject all possible reasonable accommodations, they will forfeit the right to continue working if they are unable to perform the essential functions of their jobs. Because of uncertainty as to what might be deemed an essential job function should the matter come to litigation, it is important for employers to maintain a flexible approach to this issue in deciding how to accommodate an employee.

Testing for and Inquiring about HIV Infection

Disability law forbids employers, landlords and other housing providers, and furnishers of public accommodations from discriminating on the basis of disability. Whether it forbids these actors from requiring HIV testing is another matter. As with the issue of scope of protection, the degree to which the law may restrict testing varies with the context.

HIV testing remains controversial for many reasons. Since the tests available for screening purposes detect antibodies formed in response to HIV infection, they will show a negative result if the test subject is infected but has not developed antibodies. Although most of those infected develop antibodies within a few months of infection, some take longer. In addition, because the screening tests were developed to protect the blood supply from HIV contamination, they were made extremely sensitive and may generate a significant number of false-positive results when used to screen large populations of people among whom only a small percentage is truly infected. Consequently, even though the HIV screening tests now in use are highly sensitive and specific, they require careful confirmation and confidential handling when used for routine screening because of the emotional impact of receiving a positive result, the likelihood that some number of results will be inaccurate, and the severe social consequences that may befall people who test positive. Because the false positive problem is most significant in a population where the likely rate of infection is low, accuracy problems are most severe when the test is used by employers and insurance companies, and probably least severe when it is used to screen IV drug users or hospital patients in areas with a high incidence of IV drug use. (For more on HIV testing, see chapters 2 and 7.)

Beyond the question of accuracy, HIV testing is controversial because it is seen by some as an inappropriate invasion of privacy. The tests now in use require the extraction of blood (rather than the less intrusive urinalysis widely used in government and industry to detect drug and alcohol use), and a positive result will give rise to certain assumptions about the sexual lifestyle or drug-using habits of the test subject. (Constitutional protection of privacy and its impact on testing are discussed in chapter 7.)

In the employment context, the Rehabilitation Act makes no mention of pre- or post-employment physical examinations, but regulations promulgated under the Act prohibit pre-employment testing that cannot be shown to be job-related.[39] The regulations impose no restrictions on post-employment testing, so long as test results are not used to engage in discrimination forbidden by the Act. Some states have specifically restricted the use of HIV testing for employment purposes or imposed more general testing restrictions that also apply to employment, either forbidding testing for particular purposes or requiring informed consent and mandating confidentiality of test results.

The ADA goes beyond the Rehabilitation Act, stating that "the prohibition against discrimination . . . shall include medical examinations and inquiries."[40] Pre-employment medical examinations or inquiries about disabilities are strictly prohibited, although employers may ask applicants whether they have the ability to perform job-related functions. Employers may make an offer of employment conditional upon the applicant's passing a medical examination if (1) all entering employees are subject to the same examination, (2) the resulting information is treated as a confidential medical record and disclosed only under limited, need-to-know circumstances, and (3) the information is not used to discriminate unlawfully. Employers may not subsequently require medical examinations unless they are shown to be job-related and consistent with business necessity, although employers may offer employees voluntary medical examinations. If employers do offer such examinations, they must observe the same confidentiality requirements that pertain to pre-employment examinations.[41] Unless employers can show that knowledge of HIV status is job-related and necessary for the conduct of business, the ADA appears to forbid mandatory HIV testing, although there will undoubtedly be disagreement about when such knowledge is necessary. As noted above, for example, some have argued that the HIV status of certain health care workers is relevant to employers and to patients.[42]

The ADA is less specific in dealing with the possibility of HIV testing in the context of public accommodations. It labels as discriminatory "the imposition or application of eligibility criteria that screen out or tend to screen out an individual with a disability or any class of individuals with disabilities from fully and equally enjoying any goods, services, facilities, privileges, advantages, or accommodations, unless such criteria can be shown to be necessary for the provision of the goods, services, facilities, privileges, advantages, or accommodations being offered." On its face, this provision would appear to forbid using HIV test results to exclude people from public accommodations unless being uninfected is a necessary qualification, but it leaves open the question of whether service providers may require tests for informational purposes (provided, always, that no state law imposes stricter requirements).[43]

An example of this phenomenon under existing state disability laws is the Hawaii

Supreme Court's decision in *Doe v. Kahala Dental Group*. The Court decided that a dentist had a right to refuse to treat a patient who would not reveal his HIV status. The dentist argued that he would take different precautions when performing procedures involving exposure to blood if he knew that a patient was infected with HIV. The court concluded that the dentist's refusal was justified in the circumstances, since it was not an absolute refusal to treat but rather a refusal due to the patient's unwillingness to provide information that the dentist needed in order to treat him.[44]

The Continuing Importance of State and Local Laws

Despite the broad sweep of the ADA and the Fair Housing Act Amendments of 1988, state and local laws remain very important in combating HIV-related discrimination. The federal laws do not cover all private-sector activities. The ADA will not cover workplaces with fewer than fifteen employees and will cover only public accommodations that "affect commerce." Even though the Supreme Court has taken a broad view of the range of activities that affect commerce, it is conceivable that some very small, purely local operations might escape federal regulation. Moreover, because many state and local civil rights agencies have been dealing with HIV-related discrimination under state law for many years without a comprehensive federal regulatory scheme, many have developed expertise and procedural efficiency that it may take federal agencies years to achieve. Although existing case law under the Rehabilitation Act and analogous state and local laws should be persuasive for federal agencies and courts applying the ADA to HIV-related discrimination charges, the acceptance of basic principles under a new statute may take time.

Stronger remedies may also be available under state law. The Civil Rights Act of 1991 substantially increased the range of damages available to victims of intentional discrimination in violation of the Rehabilitation Act and the ADA. Instead of being limited to actual monetary damages, such as back pay, winning plaintiffs can recover "compensatory damages" (covering such intangibles as emotional pain and loss of enjoyment of life) and, if the defendant acted "with malice or reckless indifference to the . . . rights of an aggrieved individual," the plaintiff may even be awarded "punitive damages" (an additional sum, beyond any loss suffered by the plaintiff, designed to punish the defendant).[45] But the Civil Rights Act, unlike some state laws, includes fixed caps on punitive damages. In egregious cases, where high punitive damages are a possibility, a plaintiff may be better off using state law.[46]

Finally, state and local law may address variations on HIV-related discrimination not covered by handicap-discrimination statutes. Five states (Connecticut, Hawaii, Massachusetts, New Jersey, and Wisconsin) and almost one hundred municipalities forbid discrimination on the basis of sexual orientation. Since some HIV-related discrimination may be entwined with discrimination based on sexual orientation, people in these jurisdictions might better resort to state and local laws.

EMPLOYEE BENEFITS LAW

In addition to laws regulating discrimination against people with disabilities, a separate body of law governs employee benefits entitlements and may also protect employees with HIV infection. The Employee Retirement Income Security Act of 1974 (ERISA) specifically forbids discharging, suspending, expelling, or discriminating against participants or beneficiaries under an employee benefit plan for exercising their rights to benefits under the plan or "for the purpose of interfering with the attainment of any right to which such participants may become entitled under the plan."[47] This means that employees who are discharged because they apply for benefits to which they are entitled, or to prevent them from getting benefits to which they might become entitled, can sue their employers in federal court. The normal remedy in such a case is compensation, including restoration of benefit rights.[48]

The high medical costs accompanying HIV infection and AIDS have been well publicized, and it would be reasonable to conclude that some HIV-related employment discrimination is due to employers' fears of such costs. Several employers have reduced the level of benefits for HIV-related symptoms under their self-insured health plans. In some cases employers have cancelled policies purchased from insurance companies and self-insured their employee benefit plans in order to impose such restrictions without violating state insurance regulations. Court challenges have been filed against these actions, but they have not been notably successful because the courts have concluded that ERISA does not prohibit such action and that it preempts state and local government regulation of such action.[49]

ERISA does not, however, preempt federal laws. Some have argued that employers subject to the nondiscrimination requirements of the Rehabilitation Act or the ADA would be prohibited from imposing HIV-related limits or exclusions in their self-insured employee benefit plans. So far this claim has not been tested in the courts. Section 501(c) of the ADA says that the Act should not be interpreted to prevent employers from maintaining "bona fide benefit plans" that "are based on underwriting risks, classifying risks, or administering such risks that are based on or not inconsistent with State law" or that are "not subject to State laws that regulate insurance," so long as there is no "subterfuge to evade the purposes" of the ADA.[50]

The regulations issued by the EEOC provided no insight into whether limits on or exclusions of HIV claims under self-insured benefit plans would be subject to ADA nondiscrimination requirements, and a final answer awaits possible litigation after the ADA employment provisions go into effect in July 1992. (For more on ERISA and discrimination, see chapter 18.)

WORKPLACE HEALTH AND SAFETY

One of the most important HIV-related issues in the minds of many workers and employers is workplace health and safety. Although fears of HIV transmission under normal working conditions have been largely dispelled as the public has become better informed about the nature of HIV, people are still genuinely concerned about transmission through blood exposure resulting from accidents, emergency assistance, or health care.

Early in the epidemic, unions representing health care workers asked the Occupational Safety and Health Administration (OSHA) to specify workplace safety measures to prevent occupational transmission of HIV. OSHA at first took the position that employers would be expected, as part of their "general duty" to provide "a place of employment" that is "free from recognized hazards that are causing or are likely to cause death or serious physical harm to [their] employees,"[51] to comply with the CDC's guidelines for preventing HIV transmission in the workplace. This would involve training employees about avoiding HIV infection in circumstances where it might be transmitted on the job and providing necessary equipment to clean up blood spills with minimal exposure to infection. OSHA eventually adopted a more specific standard governing occupational exposure to blood-borne contagious conditions, including both HIV and hepatitis, and issued its long-awaited final regulations in late 1991.[52]

In some cases, unions have demanded HIV-related information directly from employers, or have asserted demands based on collective bargaining agreements relating to employer safety policies and AIDS. For example, one union representing prison guards in Delaware demanded to know which prisoners had HIV infection, under a collective bargaining provision requiring the prison to inform guards about inmates with contagious conditions. The arbitrator, applying clear language from the collective bargaining agreement, ruled in favor of the union, and the decision was upheld in an appeal to the state courts.[53]

Perhaps the most complex workplace health and safety issues have to do with the rights, if any, of health care and emergency service workers to know the HIV status of their fellow employees or clients, and the rights, if any, of their clients to know the same information about them. Some states have passed confidentiality laws regarding HIV status that sharply circumscribe the availability of such information,[54] and others already have general privacy statutes that penalize unauthorized disclosure of such information.[55] (For more information on these developments, see chapter 7.)

OTHER SOURCES OF PROTECTION AGAINST DISCRIMINATION

HIV-infected employees who have been discriminated against may have legal arguments other than those available under disability law or AIDS-specific discrimination laws. For example, in many states the courts now recognize common law actions for intentional or negligent infliction of emotional distress, wrongful discharge in violation of public policy, breach of confidentiality or invasion of privacy, and discipline or discharge in violation of procedures specified in employee or personnel manuals. Some of these claims may be limited or preempted by statutory claims in particular cases, but lawyers should consider them all when representing people with HIV infection who have suffered discrimination at the hands of employers, businesses or housing operators.

In addition, employees represented by labor unions may have protection from unjust discharge under their collective bargaining agreements. Disputes about unjust discharges are typically resolved through a grievance procedure culminating in final and binding arbitration by a neutral third party selected jointly by the employer and the union. Arbitrators normally insist that companies accord full due process protection to employees, and they place the burden on the employer to show that a discharge is objectively justified by the employee's inability to do the work. Most labor arbitrators take the view that their jurisdiction is limited to interpreting and applying the collective bargaining agreement, and will not consider arguments based on state or federal disability discrimination laws or other statutes. However, some collective bargaining agreements incorporate federal and state civil rights laws by reference, and arbitrators deciding cases under such agreements may consider and give weight to court precedents.

An example of an arbitrator's approach to an AIDS-related discharge is found in *Local 517-S Production, Services and Sales District Council v. The Bucklers, Inc.*[56] Although the collective bargaining agreement expressly incorporated state and federal discrimination laws, the arbitrator based his decision primarily on due process concerns. An employee who had missed work because of AIDS-related symptoms had presented to the company a series of notes from treating physicians concerning his medical condition, and the company, disbelieving one of the notes, discharged him. The arbitrator ruled that the company had an obligation to contact the physician about the note before taking action against the employee. The arbitrator also ruled that the employee was entitled to unpaid medical leave and reinstatement if a physician specializing in AIDS and informed of the employee's "regular duties" certified him as fit. The arbitrator's decision is typical of the informal, process-oriented approach in labor arbitration, which emphasizes problem-solving in the interest of both parties rather than a legalistic determination.

Finally, employees and members of the public may find that many businesses have voluntarily adopted HIV-related nondiscrimination policies or more general policies protective of the rights of people with physical disabilities. In some states, an employer's voluntary policy may be considered part of an employee's contract, giving rise to an action for breach of contract and damages if the policy is not followed.[57] Even where such voluntary policies do not have the force of law, they may provide a basis for invoking internal dispute-resolution systems.

A RESPONSIBLE APPROACH TO AIDS

Discrimination laws provide a legal foundation for the rights of people with HIV infection and AIDS, but this foundation is not really adequate to ensure that they receive the humane treatment to which everyone is entitled as a basic human right. The statutes provide limited remedies, and their administration frequently takes more time than people with HIV infection or AIDS can afford to wait. Although many discrimination charges have been settled expeditiously, litigation in contested cases has become quite protracted, and it is not unusual in reading published appellate decisions to learn that the plaintiff died well before the final opinion was issued.

This means that the ethical issues posed by HIV in the workplace and the marketplace must take precedence if true justice is to be done.[58] It is clearly beyond the bounds of ethical behavior for an employer or other business person to engage in unjustified discrimination on the basis of HIV infection or its perception, knowing that the applicant, employee, or potential client or customer is unlikely to survive litigation. The legal foundation can buttress moral obligation, but in a regime of due process and appellate review the law can do little more than compensate for ethical failure well after the fact. Employers and businesses must focus on the obligations of citizenship in a civilized society, and conform their behavior to the policies expressed in the law, if those policies are to be effective in protecting the human rights of people with HIV.

NOTES

1 *See* American Civil Liberties Union, AIDS and Civil Liberties Project, Epidemic of Fear (1990).

2 Pub. L. No. 101–336, 104 Stat. 327 (1990) (codified at 42 U.S.C.A. §§ 12101 *et seq.* (West Supp. 1991)).

3 The employment discrimination provisions of the ADA are effective July 26, 1992, but from then until July 26, 1994 only employers of twenty-five or more employees will be covered. 42 U.S.C.A. §§ 12111 note, 12111(5)(A) (West Supp. 1991).

4 42 U.S.C.A. § 12101(b)(1) (West Supp. 1991).

5 29 U.S.C. §§ 701 *et seq.* (1988).

6 Pub. L. No. 100–430, 102 Stat. 1619 (1988) (codified at 42 U.S.C. §§ 3601 *et seq.* (1988).

7 For a detailed analysis of state laws and their applicability to HIV-related discrimination in employment, see Leonard, *Employment Discrimination against Persons with AIDS,* 10 U. Dayton L. Rev. 681 (1985).

8 In California, many cities passed HIV-specific discrimination ordinances when it appeared uncertain that state discrimination laws would cover the issue. This uncertainty was resolved in 1989 in Raytheon Co. v. Fair Employment & Hous. Comm'n, 261 Cal. Rptr. 197 (Cal. Ct. App. 1989).

9 *See* 42 U.S.C.A. § 12201(b) (West Supp. 1991).

10 Section 504, 29 U.S.C. § 794(a) (1988).

11 42 U.S.C. § 3602(h) (1988).

12 School Bd. of Nassau County v. Arline, 480 U.S. 273 (1987). Congress subsequently enacted 29 U.S.C. § 706(8)(C) to incorporate the Supreme Court's "significant risk" analysis of the issue of contagious diseases into the Rehabilitation Act. Pub. L. No. 100–259, 102 Stat. 31 (1988).

13 *E.g.,* Chevron Corp. v. Redmon, 745 S.W.2d 314 (Tex. 1987).

14 29 U.S.C. § 706(8)(B) (1988). The Fair Housing Act definition is essentially the same. 42 U.S.C. § 3602(h) (1988).

15 480 U.S. 273 (1987).

16 Arline v. School Bd. of Nassau County, 692 F. Supp. 1286 (M.D. Fla. 1988).

17 The leading case under the Rehabilitation Act is Chalk v. United States Dist. Court, 840 F.2d 701 (9th Cir. 1988). The leading case under the Fair Housing Act is Baxter v. City of Belleville, 720 F. Supp. 720 (S.D. Ill. 1989).

18 42 U.S.C.A. § 12102(2) (West Supp. 1991).

19 *Id.* §§ 12208, 12211.

20 549 A.2d 900 (N.J. Super. Ct. Law Div. 1987).

21 *See* Glanz v. Vernick, 756 F. Supp. 632 (D. Mass. 1991); *see also* Doe v. Centinela Hosp., 1988 WL 81776, 57 U.S.L.W. 2034 (C.D. Cal., June 30, 1988) (California hospital that excluded HIV-infected people from its clinical program for drug and alcohol abuse violated Rehabilitation Act because there was no medical or other justification for exclusion).

22 *See, e.g.,* Elstein v. State Div. of Human Rights, 555 N.Y.S.2d 516 (App. Div.), *appeal denied,* 564 N.E.2d 671 (N.Y. 1990); Doe v. Jamaica Hosp., N.Y.L.J., May 6, 1991, at 27 (N.Y. Sup. Ct., Kings Cty. May 6, 1991).

23 442 U.S. 397 (1979).

24 42 U.S.C.A. § 12111(8) (West Supp. 1991).

25 *Id.*

26 *Equal Employment Opportunity for Individuals with Disabilities,* 56 Fed. Reg. 35726, at 35728–29 (1991) (to be codified at 29 C.F.R. § 1630).

27 State Div. of Human Rights v. Xerox Corp., 480 N.E.2d 695 (N.Y. 1985), is a prime example of this approach.

28 909 F.2d 820 (5th Cir. 1990); *cf.* Anonymous Fireman v. City of Willoughby, 779 F. Supp. 402 (N.D. Ohio 1991) (firefighter with HIV poses risk to others). *But cf.* Doe v. District of Columbia, No. 91–1642, 1992 U.S. Dist. LEXIS 9168, (D.D.C. 1991) (firefighter with HIV does not post significant risk to others).

29 Estate of Behringer v. Medical Ctr. at Princeton, 592 A.2d 1251 (N.J. Super. 1991).

30 *Arline,* 480 U.S. at 287.

31 *See* New York State Soc'y of Surgeons v. Axelrod, 572 N.E.2d 605 (N.Y. 1991).

32 42 U.S.C.A. § 12113(d) (West Supp. 1991).

33 *See, e.g.,* 45 C.F.R. § 84.12 (1990).

34 *Arline,* 480 U.S. at 287 n.17, 289 n.19.

35 *See* 42 U.S.C.A. § 12111(9) (West Supp. 1991).

36 *See* 42 U.S.C.A. § 12111(10) (West Supp. 1991); *Equal Employment Opportunity for Individuals with Disabilities,* note 26 above, at 35744–45.

37 *Equal Employment Opportunity for Individuals with Disabilities,* note 26 above.

38 *Id.* at 35736.

39 45 C.F.R. §§ 84.13, 84.14(c) (1990).

40 42 U.S.C.A. § 12112(c) (West Supp. 1991).

41 42 U.S.C.A. § 12112(c)(2)-(4) (West Supp. 1991).

42 Leckelt v. Board of Comm'rs of Hosp. Dist. No. 1, 909 F.2d 820 (5th Cir. 1990); Estate of Behringer v. Medical Ctr. at Princeton, 592 A.2d 1251 (N.J. Super. 1991).

43 42 U.S.C.A. § 12182(b)(2)(A) (West Supp. 1991). Like the ADA public accommodations provisions, the Fair Housing Act does not specifically mention tests or inquiries about disabilities.

44 808 P.2d 1276 (Haw. 1991).

45 The Civil Rights Act of 1991, Pub. L. No. 102–166, § 102(b)(1), 105 Stat. 1071 (1991).

46 *See, e.g.,* N.Y. Exec. Law §§ 296, 297 (McKinney 1991).

47 29 U.S.C. § 1140 (1988).

48 Folz v. Marriott Corp., 594 F. Supp. 1007 (W.D. Mo. 1984).

49 *See, e.g.,* McGann v. H & H Music Co., 742 F. Supp. 392 (S.D. Tex. 1990) (employer did not violate ERISA § 510 by placing $5,000 lifetime cap on HIV-related health benefits after learning of employee's diagnosis), *aff'd,* 946 F.2d 401 (5th Cir. 1991).

50 42 U.S.C.A. § 12201(c) (West Supp. 1991).

51 29 U.S.C. § 654 (1988).

52 *Occupational Exposure to Bloodborne Pathogens,* 56 Fed. Reg. 64004 (Dec. 6, 1991).

53 Delaware Dep't of Corrections, No. 14–390–1407–85-J (1986) (Gill, Arb.) (unpublished decision), *enforced sub nom.* State of Delaware Dep't of Corrections v. Delaware Pub. Emp., Council 81 (Del. Ch. 1986) (unpublished disposition).

54 *E.g.*, N.Y. Pub. Health Law § 2782 (McKinney 1992).

55 *See, e.g.*, Cronan v. New England Tel., 11 Fair Empl. Prac. Cases (BNA) 1273, 1 Indiv. Empl. Rts. Cas. (BNA) 658 (Mass. Super. Ct. 1986) (relying on Mass. Gen. Laws Ann. ch. 214, § 1B (West 1987)); Zinda v. Louisiana Pac. Corp., 440 N.W.2d 548 (Wis. 1989) (relying on Wis. Stat. Ann. § 895.50(2)(c) (West 1983)).

56 90 Lab. Arb. (BNA) 937, 88–1 Lab. Arb. Awards (CCH) ¶ 8238 (1986) (N.Y. Mediation Bd., Braufman, Arb.).

57 *E.g.*, Woolley v. Hoffmann-La Roche, Inc., 491 A.2d 1257, *modified*, 499 A.2d 515 (N.J. 1985).

58 The ideas in this section are developed at greater length in Leonard, *Ethical Challenges of HIV Infection in the Workplace*, 5 Notre Dame J. L. Ethics & Pub. Pol'y 53 (1990).

14 Housing Issues

Daniel R. Mandelker

People with HIV face difficulties in obtaining and keeping housing. They may have difficulty renting or buying housing and may be evicted from rental housing they occupy. Individuals and organizations providing services for people with HIV have been denied office space. Group homes and other special facilities for people with HIV have been opposed under local zoning ordinances. As the number of homeless people with HIV grows (one study estimated that almost 10 percent of New York's homeless had AIDS-related conditions), some are warning of a crisis in housing for the infected.[1] In this chapter, I consider the legal protections available to assist people with HIV in securing and keeping housing.

In the first section, I consider the legal problems that arise in the purchase and rental of private housing by people with HIV, explaining the legal protections against discrimination in the federal Fair Housing Act and state and local antidiscrimination laws. I also review the disclosure obligations of real estate brokers in the sale of housing formerly occupied by people with HIV. In the second section, I discuss legal problems that arise in the provision of special facilities for people with HIV, such as group homes, and the application of the Act to zoning ordinances that exclude or restrict the location of these facilities.

DISCRIMINATION IN THE SALE AND RENTAL OF INDIVIDUAL DWELLINGS

People with HIV often face discrimination in the private market for the sale and rental of individual dwellings. Traditionally, legal rules gave little protection to tenants of rental housing.[2] People who were denied rental housing had no cause of action, and tenants had no protection against eviction at the end of their leases.[3] Similarly, property owners were free to refuse to sell housing for any reason.

319

Recent developments in general landlord and tenant law have substantially increased landlords' obligations to their rental tenants.[4] Courts have relied on consumer protection law to infer clauses in leases and tenancies that protect tenants ("implied clauses"), rather than on the property law principles that favor landlords. One implied clause the courts have read into leases is a requirement that landlords must ensure that the premises are in a habitable condition when they are rented.[5] Although no appellate court has yet found an implied clause limiting a landlord to eviction for "good cause"—a provision that would not allow the eviction of people solely because of their HIV status—a few states have adopted legislation limiting eviction to good cause in all housing or in mobile homes.[6] By far the most important development in this area of law, however, has been the extension of the federal Fair Housing Act to protect people affected by HIV.

Discrimination Prohibited by the Fair Housing Act

The Fair Housing Act, adopted by Congress in 1968, prohibits discrimination in the sale or rental of housing and in advertising, financing, and the provision of brokerage services. Congress amended the law in 1988 to prohibit discrimination because of "handicap."[7]

The Fair Housing Act defines "handicap" as a "physical or mental impairment which substantially limits . . . major life activities."[8] People are also protected if they are perceived as having a handicap, even if they do not. This definition was taken from Section 504 of the Rehabilitation Act of 1973,[9] which courts have unanimously interpreted to include HIV. (See chapter 13). The Department of Housing and Urban Development (HUD), which drafted the regulations for administering the Act, has concluded that Congress chose the Section 504 definition with the intention of including people with HIV as handicapped people protected by the Fair Housing Act, a conclusion with which two federal courts have so far agreed.[10] People subjected to discrimination in violation of the Fair Housing Act may file a complaint with HUD and may bring a lawsuit in federal court. The Attorney General may also bring actions in court to prohibit "a pattern or practice" that violates the Fair Housing Act.[11] The Act applies to all housing with minor exceptions that do not affect the availability of housing for people with HIV.

While discrimination in housing on the basis of HIV infection is illegal, proving that a refusal to sell or rent property was rooted in discrimination can be very difficult indeed. Defendants will rarely admit that animus toward people with HIV was the basis for discriminatory action, leaving it to plaintiffs to prove that supposedly legitimate justifications for adverse housing decisions are actually pretextual or based on unfounded fears of HIV transmission. In practice, then, judicial rules prescribing how violations of the Act may be proved are crucial to a lawsuit's outcome.

A violation of the Act occurs when an individual seeking housing is subjected to "disparate treatment" based on racial prejudice, and courts will probably apply the same principles to cases charging discrimination based on disability. The United States Supreme Court requires proof of a racially discriminatory intent in disparate treatment cases brought under the Fourteenth Amendment,[12] but it has not yet decided whether such proof is necessary under the Fair Housing Act. The lower federal courts, however, have virtually all decided that proof of a discriminatory intent is not necessary to establish a violation of the Act, and that only a discriminatory effect is necessary.[13] These holdings make proof of discrimination much easier, because the courts have adopted a "prima facie case" rule to assist plaintiffs who claim housing discrimination. Under this rule, as stated by a leading decision,[14] a prima facie (that is, presumptively sufficient) case can be established by a person who shows that he has HIV, that he applied for and was qualified to rent or purchase a dwelling, that he was rejected, and that the dwelling is still available. Once a plaintiff establishes a prima facie case, the burden shifts to the defendant to articulate some legitimate, nondiscriminatory reason for the housing denial.[15]

State and Local Antidiscrimination Laws

Thirty-seven states have their own laws prohibiting discrimination in housing on the basis of handicap, some including HIV infection.[16] Several cities have also adopted ordinances prohibiting discrimination in housing against people with HIV.[17] State and local laws have also been used to oppose discrimination by landlords against agencies and professionals providing services to people with HIV. In a case brought under the New York Human Rights Law, for example, two doctors won punitive damages from a property owner who refused to execute a contract to sell a medical office after learning that one of the doctors treated people with AIDS.[18] AIDS service agencies in Virginia and Philadelphia have also brought suits after rental agreements were broken because of their clients' disabilities.[19]

The Fair Housing Act recognizes the validity of state and local antidiscrimination laws if the substantive rights, procedures, and remedies they offer are substantially equivalent to those in the federal law.[20] If a complaint is made to HUD in a place where a local law applies, HUD must refer the complaint to the local enforcement agency and can take no further action if the local agency proceeds with reasonable promptness.[21] Local antidiscrimination laws that protect people with HIV are also important because local agencies may provide quicker and more effective relief than HUD or the courts.[22]

Disclosure Problems in the Sale of Housing

The value of a dwelling may be lowered if the seller is required to disclose that it was previously occupied by people with HIV. Such a requirement might, in turn, affect the future availability of housing to people who are, or are suspected of being, infected. If the seller has a duty to inform prospective buyers that the residence has been previously occupied by someone with HIV, the purchaser could sue to rescind the sales contract and ask for damages if this disclosure is not made. Owners will then be discouraged from renting to people with HIV, and the marketability of residences used as group homes for such people will also be affected.

The maxim *caveat emptor* (let the buyer beware) has historically been applied to contracts for the sale of real estate, but exceptions have recently been made to this general rule. Sellers in some jurisdictions are now under a duty to disclose conditions that physically or legally impair the use of residential property, such as conditions that make the use of the property unsafe.[23] The California courts have extended this duty to include disclosure of material facts that significantly affect the value of property. In one case, for example, a California court held that a seller had a duty to disclose that multiple murders had occurred in a residence because this fact could significantly affect the value of the property.[24]

This duty to disclose could be read to require sellers to inform buyers that people with HIV have resided on the premises, but courts should not adopt this view. The test should be whether a *reasonable* purchaser would find the fact withheld so material that it affects the value of the property. Occupation by people with HIV does not create risks for subsequent purchasers and so does not affect the value of the property. Perhaps to prevent courts from applying the multiple murder precedent to HIV, California has now adopted legislation providing that a legal cause of action against the seller of a property or his agent is not created by failure to disclose that "an occupant of that property was afflicted with, or died from," HIV.[25]

The duty of real estate brokers to disclose that dwellings have been occupied by people with HIV is also affected by the Fair Housing Act. The Texas attorney general has ruled, for example, that the Act invalidated a Texas law requiring brokers to disclose that previous residents had HIV. The attorney general noted that the courts had forbidden practices that violated the purpose of the Act, even though they were not expressly prohibited by the Act.[26]

SPECIAL FACILITIES: HOSPICES, GROUP HOMES, RESIDENTIAL CARE FACILITIES, AND HOMELESS SHELTERS

State and federal law now provides considerable protection against discrimination in the sale or rental of individual housing. Unfortunately, people with HIV may lose their homes because of inability to make rent or mortgage payments and may grow too ill to live alone. Some people with full-blown AIDS need specialized care facilities or group housing. Many people with HIV become homeless and require housing assistance.[27]

The law provides very little support for general claims that the government must provide shelter to those who need it.[28] But people with HIV have redress under the Fair Housing Act and local antidiscrimination laws when they are refused admission to or are evicted from group housing, such as homeless shelters and publicly owned housing, because of their condition. Discrimination on the basis of HIV status may also violate Section 504 of the Rehabilitation Act and the 1990 Americans with Disabilities Act, both of which are discussed in detail in chapter 13.

In the long run, most litigation is likely to concern special-care facilities and group homes for people with HIV. Organized community opposition to group homes or care facilities—whether for people with HIV, the developmentally disabled, or recovering drug addicts—is a common barrier. Even people who believe such facilities are needed may support their construction somewhere else, but "not in my back yard." These facilities generally must meet state and local health and fire codes, and sometimes political opposition to the opening of a home can influence the approval process. Usually, however, efforts to prevent homes from opening focus on zoning restrictions. Discriminatory use of zoning restrictions is subject to challenge under both the United States Constitution and the Fair Housing Act.

Zoning Restrictions

Zoning ordinances may restrict housing opportunities for people with HIV who wish to live together as an unrelated family in a family residence, in a hospice, or in a group home or similar facility. For convenience, I will refer to any formal group living arrangement as a group home and to unrelated people who live together, without organizing or designating their arrangement as a "group home," as an unrelated family. Zoning ordinances, which divide a community into districts and designate land uses appropriate to each, always include districts limited solely to residential uses. Single family and multifamily residences are usually assigned separate districts. The ordinances define the type of family permitted in residential districts and may limit the number of unrelated people who may live together. This may effectively prohibit informal group living arrangements for people with HIV, because the number of such unrelated people in the group home usually exceeds the number permitted by the zoning ordinance.

Zoning ordinances may provide specifically for group homes by allowing them as a "special use" or "special exception" in residential districts.[29] The purpose of a special-use provision is to allow approval of a use that is presumptively compatible with the neighborhood but requires individualized review because it may present special problems. A special use is allowed in a zoning district only after it has been approved by a local zoning agency or by the municipal governing body. Although special-use provisions do not on their face present a serious obstacle to group homes for people with HIV, opponents of such homes may use these provisions to block their establishment in locations where they are needed.

Some zoning ordinances specifically allow group homes as permitted uses in residential districts but limit the number of such homes or the extent to which they can be concentrated. The ordinances do this by placing a quota on the group homes allowed in particular residential use districts or by adopting dispersal ordinances that require a minimum distance between group homes. State legislation that prohibits the exclusion of group homes from residential districts may contain similar restrictions. Requirements of this type are intended to integrate group homes into residential neighborhoods.

Constitutional Questions Raised by Zoning Restrictions

Zoning restrictions on group homes and unrelated families may not serve a constitutionally acceptable zoning purpose. They may also deny people the equal protection of the laws guaranteed by the Fourteenth Amendment. A few words on what equal protection means will explain why courts divide on its application to zoning.

Not all laws that treat people unequally violate the equal protection clause, so the Supreme Court has struggled to develop a test to determine how rigorously it will review a disputed law. Normally, a state may justify a challenged law by showing that the law has a "rational relationship" to the fulfillment of a legitimate state goal. If a law impairs a fundamental right (such as the right to vote) or uses an inherently "suspect" classification (such as race, religion, or alienage), the Court will apply "strict scrutiny," requiring the state to demonstrate that the law is necessary to meet a "compelling" need. If the classification may sometimes be legitimate but has historically been associated with discrimination—examples include gender and illegitimacy—the Court treats it as "quasi-suspect" and uses an "intermediate scrutiny," generally requiring the law to be "substantially related" to an "important" governmental interest. There is general agreement on the proposition that the level of scrutiny tends to determine the outcome of the case: it is considerably easier for a state to show a law's *rational* relationship to a *legitimate* goal than its *necessary* relationship to a *compelling* one.[30]

Constitutionality of Zoning Restrictions on Unrelated Families

People with HIV living together informally will often be subject to restrictions on the sharing of homes by unrelated people. The case law in this area is dominated by a Supreme Court decision, *Village of Belle Terre v. Boraas*.[31] This case upheld a suburban zoning ordinance that allowed no more than two unrelated people to live together in a single-family residence. The Court applied the "rational relationship" test because the ordinance was not directed at a minority group and did not infringe upon a fundamental constitutional right. The Court held that the numerical limitation on unrelated family members served the legitimate governmental objective of protecting the integrity of single-family areas.

Although state courts must follow the Supreme Court's reading of the federal Constitution, they are free to interpret their own constitutions more strictly. A number of state courts have followed *Belle Terre* by upholding zoning ordinances restricting the number of unrelated people who may live together,[32] but other state courts have invalidated such restrictions. These courts have accepted the rationale of the dissenting opinion in *Belle Terre*, which argued that a zoning restriction on unrelated families invades fundamental constitutional rights to privacy and freedom of association and therefore should be subject to "strict scrutiny."

The California Supreme Court decision in *City of Santa Barbara v. Adamson*[33] is a leading state case holding a zoning restriction on unrelated families unconstitutional under the dissent's rationale in *Belle Terre*. The court found that the ordinance infringed upon the right of privacy guaranteed by the state constitution. An invasion of this right must be justified by a "compelling public need," which the court did not find. The restriction on unrelated families did not protect residential areas because it was not sufficiently related to noise, parking, and other neighborhood problems. Less restrictive alternatives were available to remedy these land-use problems, including regulations limiting population density and parking. Other state courts have also invalidated this type of regulation.[34] These courts, applying similar reasoning, should also invalidate the use of family restrictions in zoning ordinances to limit the number of people with HIV who may live together.

Constitutionality of Zoning Restrictions on Group Homes

State courts have adopted a variety of views on zoning ordinances that restrict the location of formally established group homes or special-care facilities. Some courts avoid constitutional problems by holding that group homes are a permitted use in residential districts.[35] Several states followed the reasoning of *Belle Terre* and held that the exclusion of group homes from residential districts is constitutional.[36]

The federal constitutional law governing zoning restrictions on group homes is dominated by a highly unusual 1985 Supreme Court decision, *City of Cleburne v. Cleburne Living Center.*[37] The zoning ordinance in that case required a special-use permit for a group home for the mentally retarded in an area zoned for "apartment houses." It did not require a special-use permit for similar facilities, such as nursing homes. A special permit for a group home for the mentally retarded was denied. Because similar group homes were treated differently, the special permit denial raised an equal protection problem.

The Court rejected the group home's claim that the denial should be subjected to intermediate scrutiny because of the history of discrimination against the developmentally disabled. For the Court, the political muscle of the retarded—evidenced in the passage of laws protecting their rights—and their heterogeneity precluded a finding that they were in need of special judicial protection as a class. The Court therefore applied the rational relationship test. Normally this would have meant that the permit denial would be upheld, because in most minimum scrutiny cases the Court accepts virtually any coherent justification for a government action, without itself questioning the factual basis for the action. In *Cleburne,* however, the Court looked closely at the record and concluded that the permit denial had been based on "mere negative attitudes" and "vague, undifferentiated fears" about retarded people. The Court therefore found the denial unconstitutional.

Cleburne's significance is not entirely clear. While some courts have found in the decision a possible basis for special protection of the disabled,[38] only a few cases have applied *Cleburne* to strike down similar zoning restrictions as violations of the equal protection clause.[39] *Cleburne* also raises constitutional questions concerning legislation adopted in several states that is intended to *protect* group homes from discrimination in zoning ordinances.[40] Although this legislation may require municipalities to allow group homes in all residential districts, some statutes allow municipalities to require special-use permits for group homes and to limit the total number and proximity of group homes in the community. It is clear, however, that under *Cleburne,* any discriminatory treatment of group homes in zoning ordinances may violate the equal protection clause.[41]

Validity of Zoning Restrictions on Group Homes under the Fair Housing Act

Given the uncertainty of constitutional protection, advocates are relying on the Fair Housing Act to oppose discriminatory zoning practices. Although the Act does not expressly prohibit zoning discrimination, it does prohibit acts that "otherwise make unavailable or deny" housing because of a handicap, such as HIV or race. The courts have held that this language applies to discrimination that occurs through zoning ordinances.[42] Two cases under the amended Act have already rejected zoning restrictions on AIDS group homes.

Baxter v. City of Belleville indicates how courts applying the Fair Housing Act are likely to handle claims of discrimination in the zoning process against group homes for people with HIV. Baxter applied to the city for a special-use permit to use a home as a hospice for people who were terminally ill with AIDS. The city denied the permit. He then filed an action against the city under the Act to have the denial overturned. The court held that he had shown evidence of discriminatory intent sufficient to indicate a probable violation of the Act. The evidence established that "irrational fear of AIDS was at least a motivating factor in the City's refusal to grant Baxter's special use permit," and that the city's actions were "specifically and intentionally" designed to prevent people with AIDS from living in the hospice.[43]

The court also found that the city's action had a discriminatory impact on people with AIDS as compared with people who did not have this handicap,[44] and that the city's claimed zoning interests in denying the special permit were a pretext: "the City's actions were based on fear of HIV, and not a legitimate zoning interest." The court found, finally, that the permit denial was not validated by an exception in the Act providing "that a dwelling [need not] be made available to an individual whose tenancy would constitute a direct threat to the health or safety of other individuals."[45]

As another judge put it in a very similar case:

No one can blame the residents of any town for making a priority of the health and safety of their families and community. But when legitimate concern is fanned by a profound misunderstanding of the causes of AIDS, the rush to panic can easily result in illegal and unjustifiable discrimination against not only the disease's victims but also against the laudable efforts of individuals working to contain the flames. [The zoning authority], by misguidedly succumbing to community pressure, has itself become a party to such discrimination. This the Fair Housing Act does not allow.[46]

The Fair Housing Act invalidates any conflicting state or local laws or regulations. This provision can invalidate many practices that discriminate against group homes for people with AIDS.[47] It has, for example, been held to invalidate a provision in a zoning ordinance that defined the term *family* in a way that excluded group homes for the handicapped from residential districts.[48] Similarly, several state attorneys general have found that state laws imposing dispersal and other restrictions on community residences for the disabled were invalidated by the Act. (Federal courts have split on this issue.)[49]

HOUSING STRATEGIES

The 1988 amendments to the Fair Housing Act have considerably improved the legal remedies available to prevent discrimination in housing against people with HIV. Discrimination in the sale or rental of housing is prohibited. Interpretation of the Act is also making it clear that discriminatory restrictions in zoning ordinances and discriminatory zoning actions, such as special-use permit denials, are violations of the Act. Some cases have also applied the equal protection clause of the federal Constitution to invalidate zoning restrictions and decisions that discriminate against group homes for special populations, such as people with HIV.

Although the Fair Housing Act is the principal legal tool to prevent discrimination against people with HIV in the housing market, other measures can also be useful. State and local nondiscrimination laws can supplement the remedies available under the Act. Judicial recognition in leases of an implied clause limiting eviction to good cause would supplement the Act's prohibitions on discrimination in rental housing. States should also adopt the California law that protects residential sellers from being sued for failure to disclose that a previous occupant had HIV.

Much has been done for people with HIV, through legislation at the federal, state, and local levels, to eliminate discrimination in housing. People with HIV now have a more effective array of legal measures to combat discrimination in the housing market. Much remains to be done, however, in meeting their housing needs. Funding for housing is crucial, a fact Congress recognized in the 1990 Cranston-Gonzalez National Affordable Housing Act, which includes a block grant program designed to encourage state and local governments to provide housing for people with HIV.[50] It is also important that the Department of Housing and Urban Development, either on its own or under Congressional pressure, becomes more supportive of housing initiatives for people with HIV.[51]

NOTES

1 *See* Schulman, *AIDS and Homelessness: Thousands May Die in the Streets,* The Nation, Apr. 10, 1989, at 480; Bernstein, *From Pesthouses to AIDS Hospices: Neighbors' Irrational Fears of Treatment Facilities for Contagious Diseases,* 22 Colum. Hum. Rts. L. Rev. 1, 7–11 (1990); National Commission on AIDS, Housing and the HIV/AIDS Epidemic: Recommendations for Action (1992).*see also* note 27 below.

2 *See generally* R. Schoshinski, American Law of Landlord and Tenant § 13 (1980); Cunningham, *The New Implied and Statutory Warranty of Habitability in Residential Leases: From Contract to Status,* 16 Urb. L. Ann. 3 (1979); Glendon, *The Transformation of American Landlord-Tenant Law,* 23 B.C. L. Rev. 503, 539–40 (1982); Rabin, *The Revolution in Residential Landlord Tenant Law: Causes and Consequences,* 69 Cornell L. Rev. 517 (1984).

3 Glendon, note 2 above, at 539–50.

4 *See generally* Salzberg & Zibelman, *Good Cause Eviction,* 21 Willamette L. Rev. 61 (1985).

5 The leading case is Javins v. First Nat'l Realty Corp., 428 F.2d 1071 (D.C. Cir.), *cert. denied,* 400 U.S. 925 (1970).

6 For all housing, *see, e.g.,* D.C. Code Ann. § 45–2551 (1990 & Supp. 1991); N.J. Stat. Ann. § 2A:18–61.1 (West Supp. 1990) (upheld in Stamboulos v. McKee, 342 A.2d 529 (N.J. Super. Ct. App. Div. 1975)). For mobile homes, *see, e.g.,* Fla. Stat. Ann. § 723.061 (West 1988 & Supp. 1990) (upheld in Palm Beach Mobile Homes Inc. v. Strong, 300 So. 2d 881 (Fla. 1974)).

7 42 U.S.C. §§ 3604–3606 (1988); *see* Kushner, *The Fair Housing Amendments Act of 1988: The Second Generation of Fair Housing,* 42 Vand. L. Rev. 1049 (1989).

8 42 U.S.C. § 3602(h) (1988).

9 29 U.S.C. § 794 (1988).

10 24 C.F.R. § 100.200 *et seq.*(1990); Baxter v. City of Belleville, 720 F. Supp. 720 (S.D. Ill. 1989); Association of Relatives and Friends of AIDS Patients v. Regulation and Permits Admin., 740 F. Supp. 95 (D.P.R. 1990) (*"Relatives and Friends"*); *see* 54 Fed. Reg. 3232, 3245 (1989) (HUD stated in regulatory preamble that definition of "handicap" to be interpreted consistent with regulations under Rehabilitation Act); *see also* H.R. Rep. No. 711, 100th Cong., 2d Sess. 18 (1988) ("People with Acquired Immune Deficiency Syndrome (AIDS) and people who test positive for the AIDS virus have been evicted because of an erroneous belief that they pose a health risk to others.").

11 42 U.S.C. §§ 3610–3614 (1988).

12 Washington v. Davis, 426 U.S. 229 (1976).

13 Schwartz, *The Fair Housing Act and "Discriminatory Effect": A New Perspective,* 11 Nova L. Rev. 71 (1987).

14 Robinson v. 12 Lofts Realty, 610 F.2d 1032 (2d Cir. 1979).

15 This burden-shifting rule is derived from cases decided under the federal Equal Employment Opportunity Act, which the courts apply to the Fair Housing Act. *See* Huntington Branch, NAACP v. Town of Huntington, 844 F.2d 926 (2d Cir.) (adopting as controlling in Fair Housing Act cases the standard of McDonnell Douglas Corp. v. Green, 411 U.S. 792 (1973)), *aff'd,* 488 U.S. 15 (1988). *See* Stick, *Justifying a Discriminatory Effect Under the Fair Housing Act: A Search for the Proper Standard,* 27 UCLA L. Rev. 398 (1979).

16 Ala. Code § 21–7–9 (1990); Alaska Stat. § 18.80.240; (1991); Cal. Civ. Code § 54.1(b) (West 1982); Colo. Rev. Stat. § 24–34–502 (1988 & Supp. 1990). Conn. Gen. Stat. § 46a–64 (Supp. 1991); Del. Code. Ann. tit. 6, § 4603 (1975 & Supp. 1990);

Fla. Stat. Ann. § 413.08 (West 1986 & Supp. 1991); Haw. Rev. Stat. § 515–3 (1988 & Supp. 1990); Ill. Rev. Stat. ch. 68, para. 3–102.1 (1989) and Ill. Const. art. I, § 19; Iowa Code § 601A.8 (1991); Ky. Rev. Stat. Ann. § 207.180 (Baldwin 1991); La. Rev. Stat. Ann. § 46: 2254 (West 1982); Me. Rev. Stat. Ann. tit. 5, § 4582 (West 1989 & Supp. 1990); Md. Ann. Code art. 49B, § 20 (1990 & Supp. 1991); Mass. Ann. Laws ch. 151B, § 4 (Law Co-op. 1989 & Supp. 1991); Mich. Comp. Laws § 37.1502 (West 1985); Minn. Stat. § 363.03 (1990); Mo. Rev. Stat. §§ 191.665, 209.190 (Supp. 1990); Neb. Rev. Stat. § 20:131.01 *et. seq* (1987); N.J. Stat. Ann. § 10:5–29.2 (West Supp. 1991); N.M. Stat. Ann. § 28–1–7 (Michie 1991); N.Y. Exec. Law § 296 (McKinney 1982 & Supp. 1991); N.C. Gen. Stat. § 41A–4 (1990); Ohio Rev. Code Ann. § 4112.02 (Anderson 1991); Okla. Stat. Ann. tit. 25, § 1452 (West 1987); Or. Rev. Stat. § 659.430 (1989); Pa. Stat. Ann. tit. 43, § 955 (1991); R.I. Gen. Laws § 34–37–4 (1984 & Supp. 1990); S.D. Codified Laws Ann. § 20–13–20 (1987 & Supp. 1991); Tenn. Code Ann. § 4–21–601 (Supp. 1990); Tex. Hum. Res. Code Ann. § 121.003 (1990); Utah Code Ann. § 57–21–5 (1990); Va. Code Ann. § 36–96.3 (Michie 1991); Wash. Rev. Code Ann. § 49.60.222 (West 1990); W. Va. Code § 5–11–9 (1990); Wis. Stat. Ann. § 101.22 (West 1988 & Supp. 1990); Wyo. Stat. § 35–13–201 (1988).

17 San Francisco, Los Angeles, West Hollywood, and Berkeley, California, as well as Austin, Texas, also have ordinances banning AIDS-based discrimination in housing. 1 AIDS Pol'y & L. (BNA) Dec. 31, 1986 at 1; *id.* Mar. 26, 1986 at 6. Local ordinances provide first for the mediation of complaints by the agency charged with administering the law. The ordinances also authorize actions for injunctive relief. Court actions to remedy violations of the ordinance may be necessary because administrative agencies do not always enforce the law effectively.

18 Seitzman v. Hudson River Assoc., 542 N.Y.S.2d 104 (Sup. Ct. 1989).

19 Whitman Walker Clinic v. Mounzer Sibay, M.D., Ch. No. 88–957 (Va. Cir. Ct., Arlington County, filed Nov. 7, 1988); Action AIDS v. Dirot Delaware Inc. (Philadelphia Commn. on Human Relations, filed Sept. 9, 1988), AIDS Litig. Rep. (Andrews) Sept. 23, 1988 at 1,499.

20 42 U.S.C. § 3615 (1988).

21 42 U.S.C. § 3610(f) (1988).

22 The authority of a city to pass an antidiscrimination ordinance may be challenged, and some ordinances may be preempted by state law, although at least one has been upheld. Citizens for Uniform Laws v. County of Contra Costa, No. A051054, 1991 Cal. App. LEXIS 1060 (Sept. 10, 1991). For discussion of statutory powers, home rule and preemption see D. Mandelker, D. Netsch, P. Salsich & J. Wegner, State and Local Government in a Federal System ch. 3 (3d ed. 1990); *see also* Note, *Municipal Civil Rights Legislation—Is the Power Conferred by the Grant of Home Rule?* 53 Minn. L. Rev. 342 (1968); Note, *Conflicts Between State Statutes and Local Ordinances,* 72 Harv. L. Rev. 737 (1959).

23 *See generally* Basso, *Reed v. King: Fraudulent Nondisclosure of a Multiple Murder in a Real Estate Transaction,* 45 U. Pitt. L. Rev. 877 (1984).

24 Reed v. King, 193 Cal. Rptr. 130 (Ct. App. 1983).

25 Cal. Civ. Code § 1710.2 (West Supp. 1990).

26 Texas Attorney General Opinion No. JM–1093 (1989), 1989 Tex. AG LEXIS 95.

27 M. Burt & B. Cohen, America's Homeless (1989); Rossi, *The Family, Welfare and Homelessness,* 4 Notre Dame J. L. Ethics & Pub. Pol'y 281 (1989). Studies have shown rates of HIV infection among homeless populations in ranges between 2 and 7 percent. *See* Sugarman, *et al., AIDS and Adolescents;*

Knowledge, Attitudes and Behavior of Runaways and Homeless Youths, 145 Am. J. Dis. Child. 431 (1991) (citing studies showing seropositivity among adolescents in homeless youth shelters: Houston, 2 percent; Vancouver, 5.4 percent; New York City, 7 percent). More recent studies suggest that this number may be sharply increasing. Torres, *et al.,* *HIV Infection among Homeless Men in a New York City Shelter,* 150 Arch. Intern. Med. 2030 (1990) (62 percent of 169 high-risk homeless men); Dahl, *Up to 20% of Homeless People Carry AIDS Virus, Says New Report by CDC,* Wall St. J., Nov. 12, 1991, at B4 (HIV infection rate among homeless two to forty times higher than in average population); Fitterman, *Homeless Run High AIDS Risk, Study Finds,* Montreal Gazette, Aug. 27, 1991, at A3 (13 percent at Montreal homeless shelter).

28 Coates, *The Legal Rights of Homeless Americans,* 24 U.S.F. L. Rev. 297 (1990); Morawetz, *Welfare Litigation to Prevent Homelessness,* 16 N.Y.U. Rev. L. & Soc. Change 5656 (1987–88); Malaesta, *Finding a Right to Shelter for Homeless Families,* 22 Suffolk U.L. Rev. 719 (1988); Hirsch, *Making Shelter Work: Placing Conditions on an Employable Person's Right to Shelter,* 100 Yale L.J. 491 (1990); Sherburne, *The Judiciary and the Ad Hoc Development of a Legal Right to Shelter,* 12 Harv. J.L. & Pub. Pol'y 193 (1989).

29 D. Mandelker, Land Use Law §§ 6.49–6.57 (2d ed. 1988).

30 D. Mandelker, J. Gerard & T. Sullivan, Federal Land Use Law § 1.03; L. Tribe, American Constitutional Law § 16 (2d ed. 1988).

31 416 U.S. 1 (1974).

32 *E.g.,* Town of Durham v. White Enters., 348 A.2d 706 (N.H. 1975).

33 610 P.2d 436 (Cal. 1980).

34 *E.g.,* Charter Township of Delta v. Dinolfo, 351 N.W.2d 831 Mich. (1984); State v. Baker, 405 A.2d 368 (N.J. 1979).

35 *E.g.,* Linn County v. City of Hiawatha, 311 N.W.2d 95 (Iowa 1981); *see also* D. Mandelker, note 29 above, § 5.05.

36 *E.g.,* Hawyard v. Gaston, 542 A.2d 760 (Del. 1988); Macon Ass'n for Retarded Citizens v. Macon-Bibb County Planning & Zoning Comm'n, 314 S.E.2d 218 (Ga. 1984), *appeal dismissed,* 469 U.S. 802 (1984).

37 473 U.S. 432 (1985). For discussion of *Cleburne,* see Mandelker, *Group Homes: The Supreme Court Revives the Equal Protection Clause in Land Use Cases,* in 1986 Inst. on Plan. Zoning & Eminent Domain § 3.

38 *E.g.,* Brennan v. Stewart, 834 F.2d 1248 (5th cir. 1988).

39 *See, e.g., In re* Millcreek Township Zoning Ordinance, Fair Housing-Fair Lending Rptr. (P-H) ¶ 18,071 (Pa. C.P. 1989) (exclusion of group homes for mentally retarded, dependent children, physically handicapped and people over sixty-two years of age from all residential districts); Burstyn v. City of Miami Beach, 663 F. Supp. 528 (S.D. Fla. 1987) (zoning restrictions on housing for elderly).

40 *See, e.g.,* Cal. Welf. & Inst. Code §§ 5115–5116 (West 1984) (designated group homes to be considered residential use for zoning purposes); N.J. Stat. Ann. § 30:4C–26(d) (West 1981) (prohibiting discrimination against homes for foster children). For a table describing a number of these statutes, see Am. Plan. Ass'n, *Homes for the Developmentally Disabled,* Zoning News, Jan. 1986, at 1, 2. For discussion of the state legislation and the text of a model law, see Hopperton, *A State Legislation Strategy for Ending Exclusionary Zoning of Community Homes,* 19 Urb. L. Ann. 47 (1980).

41 See Jaffe, *Coping with Cleburne,* 38 Land Use L. & Zoning Dig., Feb. 1986, at 5.

42 42 U.S.C. § 3604(f)(1) (1988). The 1988 amendments also prohibit discrimination against households with children, and this provision may invalidate restrictions on group homes for people with HIV when children are part of the household group. *See* Doe v. City of Butler, 892 F.2d 315, 323 (3d Cir. 1989) (suggesting but not deciding whether there would be a violation); *see also, e.g.,* Huntington Branch, NAACP v. Town of Huntington, 844 F.2d 926 (2d Cir.) (racial discrimination), *aff'd,* 488 U.S. 15 (1988). The House Judiciary Committee Report on the 1988 amendments affirmed that ''[t]he Act is intended to prohibit the application of special requirements through land-use regulations . . . and conditional or special use permits that have the effect of limiting the ability of such individuals to live in the residence of their choice in the community.'' H.R. Rep. No. 711, note 10 above, at 24. The legislative history also indicates that courts are to apply a discriminatory effect, rather than a stricter discriminatory intent, test to claims of zoning discrimination against group homes for the handicapped. *See id.* at 89 (additional views of Congressmen who proposed amendment, rejected by the Committee, requiring intent).

43 720 F. Supp. 720 (S.D. Ill. 1989); *accord* Association of Relatives and Friends of AIDS Patients v. Regulations and Permits Admin., 740 F. Supp. 95 (D.P.R. 1990); McKinney v. Town Plan, 790 F. Supp. 1197 (1992). *See also,* Maryland Attorney General Opinion No. 90–014, 1990 Md. AG LEXIS 12 (''community acceptance'' may not be factor in licensing decision on group homes). *Compare* Project B.A.S.I.C. v. City of Providence, Fair Housing-Fair Lending Rptr. (P-H) ¶ 15,634 (D.R.I. 1990) (claim that opposition to homeless shelter was influenced by race states claim under Fair Housing Act).

44 The court relied on a leading case that had adopted rules to determine when a racially discriminatory effect occurs under the Fair Housing Act. Metropolitan Housing Dev. Corp. v. Village of Arlington Heights, 558 F.2d 1283 (7th Cir. 1977), *cert. denied,* 434 U.S. 1025 (1978).

45 42 U.S.C. § 3604(f)(9) (1988).

46 *Relatives and Friends,* 740 F. Supp. at 107.

47 42 U.S.C. § 3615 (1988); *see* Opinion of the California Attorney General No. 89–902, 73 Op. Att'y Gen. Cal. 58 (1990) (licensed real estate agent is neither required nor permitted to disclose the location of a licensed care facility serving six or fewer people to prospective buyers of residential property).

48 United States v. Schuylkill Township, 1990 U.S. Dist. LEXIS 7202 (E.D. Pa. 1990); *see also In re* Millcreek Township, Fair Housing–Fair Lending Rptr. (P-H) ¶ 18,071; Kansas Attorney General Opinion No. 89–99, 1989 Kan. AG LEXIS 100 (special use provision for group homes invalid).

49 *E.g.,* Maryland Attorney General Opinion No. 89–126, 1989 Md. AG LEXIS 22, Fair Housing-Fair Lending Rptr. (P-H) ¶ 23,005 (1989). The Attorney General also found a violation of HUD regulations, including 24 C.F.R. § 100.70(c)(4) (1991) (''[a]ssigning any person to a particular section of a community, neighborhood or development . . . because of . . . handicap'' violates Act). *See also* Delaware Attorney General Opinion No. 90–1001 (1990), Fair Housing-Fair Lending Rptr. (P-H) ¶ 23,007 (1990); Kansas Attorney General Opinion No. 89–99, 1989 Kan. AG LEXIS 100.

One federal district court upheld a separation provision, finding the interest of a city and state in the deinstitutionalization and integration of the mentally ill into the community ''mainstream'' to be compelling. The court found that the separation requirement implemented this interest by preventing the overconcentration of group homes in areas of the community and that a less restrictive measure for accomplishing this purpose was not available. Familystyle of St. Paul v. City of St. Paul, 728 F. Supp. 1396, 1404 (D. Minn. 1990), *aff'd,* 923 F.2d 91 (8th Cir. 1991). *But see* United States v. Village of Marshall, No. 90-C–524-S (W.D. Wis. Apr. 22, 1991). The *Familystyle* decision is incorrect. It is hard to believe that Congress intended, when it amended the Fair Housing Act in 1988, to authorize any land use requirements for group homes for the handicapped that differ from those imposed on similar groups. This interpretation has been legislated into law in Massachusetts, which states that any special land use requirements of this type constitute discrimination: "Imposition of health and safety laws or land-use requirements on congregate living arrangements among non-related persons with disabilities that are not imposed on families and groups of similar size or other unrelated persons shall constitute discrimination." Mass. Ann. Laws ch. 40A, § 3 (Law. Co-op. Supp. 1991).

50 42 U.S.C.A. §§ 12901 *et seq.* (West Supp. 1992).

51 National Commission on AIDS, note 1 above, at 11–12.

15 Torts: Private Lawsuits about HIV

Donald H. J. Hermann and
Scott Burris

Tort law is the mechanism this society uses to discourage people from subjecting others to unreasonable risks of harm, and to compensate those who have been injured by unreasonably risky behavior. It has its impact not only through the rules handed down by courts and legislatures, but also through the legal advice concerning those rules given by lawyers for hospitals, insurance companies, and other powerful institutions and individuals. A single decision in a single state court—which in theory decides only the issue raised by the party in that case and makes law only for other courts in that state—can have enormous impact on the advice lawyers give and on the way people behave throughout the nation. The impact of the tort system can be particularly powerful where, as in many areas of the HIV epidemic, primary policymakers in legislatures and executive agencies have failed to establish clear rules. In the first decade of the HIV epidemic, the tort system has had a strong influence on medical practice issues, most recently on the obligations of HIV-infected health care providers.

Notwithstanding the public-policy impact of tort law, individuals are usually moved to file tort suits by a desire to be compensated for injury. As one might expect, HIV-related tort litigation in the first decade of the epidemic has been aimed at defendants who have liability insurance, or other forms of wealth with which to pay compensation to an injured plaintiff. Thus, while there is a sound legal basis for a wide variety of suits against people with HIV who endanger or infect others through sex or needle sharing, most lawsuits have been brought against doctors, hospitals, and blood banks by people infected by blood or blood products in a health care setting.

Detailed discussion of every type of tort claim is beyond the scope of this chapter. Instead, we will focus on four areas in which actual HIV-related tort litigation has arisen: exposure of another to a risk of being infected with HIV; actual transmission of HIV through sex or infected medical equipment; transmission through blood or blood products; and medical malpractice in the diagnosis or treatment of HIV disease. (Tort suits for defamation and invasion of privacy are discussed in chapter 7.) We begin with a description of tort law generally.

INTRODUCTION TO THE LAW OF TORTS

The subject of torts covers a variety of harms that one person can inflict upon another. In everyday life, it is impossible for anyone to avoid being harmed or offended by others. Tort law, however, recognizes that not every injury should be tolerated, and that everyone owes to other people a "duty of care" to avoid unreasonably harming or offending others. That is, at some point everyone is obligated to act in such a way as to avoid either intentionally or carelessly inflicting certain harms on others. Tort law defines the obligations that courts or legislatures have determined should be legally enforceable.

There are several reasons that certain obligations are made enforceable through law. Foremost is the desire to see that those who are wronged are compensated. In addition, making wrongdoers liable for their torts discourages behavior that puts others at risk of harm. Tort law can also allocate to injuring parties those costs of doing business that otherwise would be placed on injured parties or upon those—including society in general—that would otherwise have to provide care or treatment to the injured. Finally, tort law is seen as a mechanism for assigning the costs of unavoidable risks to those who can best pay them, or who can spread them as broadly as possible (although there is always concern that if the losses resulting from unavoidable risks are assigned to those involved in an important activity, such as blood collection, the activity may become too expensive to continue).

Although tort law is something of a miscellaneous collection of legal causes of action, most torts have a common structure that rests on the concept of "negligence"—a person's unreasonable decision to expose another to a foreseeabcommon structure that rests on the concept of "negligence"—a person's unreasonable decision to expose another to a foreseeable risk of harm. To prevail, the plaintiff must demonstrate at least that the defendant owed her a duty to exercise "due care" to avoid causing harm; that the defendant "breached" that duty; that the breach "caused" the plaintiff injury; and that the injury resulted in losses compensable by money "damages." Breach of duty, causation, injury, and the extent of damages must be proved by a "preponderance of the evidence." That is to say, the plaintiff must prove that it is "more probable than not" that each of these "elements" occurred.

"Due care" is a variable concept. Generally, the care that is due is that which would be exercised by a reasonably prudent adult under similar circumstances. As situations, surroundings, and hazards vary, so do the specific requirements of due care. Moreover, the care that is due depends upon such factors as the relationship between the parties, the likelihood that a given standard will deter undesirable behavior, and the ease with which the risk of injury can be reduced. The precise conduct that duty demands is determined by considering the particulars of each case in the light of prior cases of a similar character.

Once the appropriate standard has been identified, it is possible to determine whether a breach has occurred—that is, whether the defendant has failed to act in conformity with that standard. Then it must be shown that the breach caused the injury in question. For some HIV-related torts, proving causation may be extremely difficult. This is especially true with respect to suits seeking compensation for the sexual transmission of HIV.

Once a breach of a duty of care has been established and its link to the plaintiff's injury shown, the plaintiff may recover damages for injuries that will become manifest in the future as well as those that are immediately apparent. However, an injured party ordinarily may maintain only one lawsuit for damages resulting from a single incident, whether the injuries are present or prospective. Plaintiffs who fail to sue for future damages will usually be prohibited from suing again when later injuries develop.

Anyone considering suing in tort must also evaluate his or her chances of actually collecting any damages that may be awarded by a court. A plaintiff who could win a case on the facts but would recover nothing, because the defendant lacks the means to pay, does not have a suit economically worth filing. Attorneys usually accept personal injury cases on a contingency basis, which means that the attorney collects a predetermined portion of any damage award or settlement—generally one-third—rather than payment on an hourly basis. If there is no damage award or settlement, the plaintiff must pay certain expenses, but no fee, to the attorney. Not surprisingly, few attorneys will take on a personal injury case unless they stand to collect enough to pay a reasonable return on the time they spend on the case. And experience indicates that very few injured people are willing to pay an attorney out of their own pockets to file a suit simply to gain the satisfaction of a judicial ruling placing blame on someone who is financially judgment-proof.

The defendant's ability to pay damages may be a crucial consideration in an HIV-related tort suit. Physicians, blood banks, or hospitals sued by recipients of infected blood generally have "deep pockets," in the form of assets and insurance. By contrast, in a suit for sexual transmission of HIV, where the potential defendant has AIDS or may develop AIDS and lacks great wealth or does not have insurance coverage that might provide a source of recovery, medical expenses may deplete any assets out of which damages could be paid. A defendant who is an intravenous drug user is even less likely to have sufficient financial resources to justify a suit.

Unlike human beings, lawsuits enjoy a certain measure of immortality, and may even go on after both the plaintiff and the defendant are no more. Virtually every state has a "survival" statute, which permits a personal lawsuit to continue after the death of either the plaintiff or the defendant. Most of these statutes permit plaintiffs' estates to recover from defendants' estates for negligent or intentional injuries. Under most statutes, the cause of death is not the determining factor; a lawsuit will survive whether or not death resulted from the defendant's tort.

If death results from a tort, the victim's survivors will usually be able to bring their own "wrongful-death" action against the person who caused the injury. Unlike a survival right of action, which is based on the injured party's damages (such as pain and suffering between the injury and death), a wrongful-death suit allows family members and others to recover for damage to them (such as loss of financial or psychological support) caused by the death of the originally injured party.

Even if a plaintiff establishes each of the elements of the tort, the defendant can still avoid liability by establishing (again by a preponderance of the evidence) a legally recognized defense. For example, if the suit is based on transmission through sex or needle sharing, and the plaintiff was or should have been aware of the risks of such behavior, the defendant may raise the defenses of contributory or comparative negligence, arguing that the plaintiff's own negligence should prevent or reduce the plaintiff's recovery. The most effective defense so far, however, is that the plaintiff has filed the suit too late.

A "statute of limitations" defines a period of time after which a suit cannot be brought. The rationale for such statutes is that potentially disruptive states of affairs should not be allowed to continue indefinitely; that potential defendants have a right to know, at a certain point, that they no longer are exposed to liability; and that unless suits are commenced reasonably soon after operative events occur, witnesses' memories grow stale, evidence disappears, and proof one way or the other becomes difficult.

Often, a crucial question is when the limitations period begins. Typically, the statute begins to run when the injury occurs or when the cause of action (the facts that give a person the right to seek a judicial remedy) becomes available.[1] In an HIV-related suit, neither standard is unambiguous. To take the simpler one, what is the relevant "injury" when HIV is transmitted through a blood transfusion? Is it the causing of the medical condition necessitating the transfusion, the decision to give the transfusion, the transfusion itself, the discovery by medical professionals or blood banks that the transfused blood was infected, a positive HIV test of the patient to whom the blood was transfused, the first signs of a suppressed immune system, the development of an opportunistic infection or condition, or a diagnosis of AIDS?

When infection with HIV triggers the statute, potential plaintiffs face a serious dilemma. If they file suit a year (or two or three years) after exposure, they might not yet know what the full consequences of their infection will be. They may develop serious long-term debilitating conditions requiring extensive treatment; they may experience an acute episode of a fatal opportunistic condition; or they may not develop the immune suppression on which an AIDS diagnosis is based in the foreseeable future. They may lose their jobs or find themselves uninsurable, but perhaps not. By filing suit prematurely, a person runs the risk that an attempt to recover for possible future costs will be rejected by the court as too speculative. Yet, if filing suit is delayed, a person risks letting the statutory limitations period run out.

The position of the potential plaintiff is made all the more complicated if we assume what is probably true in most cases, that the plaintiff does not even know that he or she is infected until well after exposure to the virus. Many, indeed most, people infected with the virus are asymptomatic. Without taking an HIV antibody test, they have no way of knowing whether they are seropositive. A statute of limitations that is interpreted as running from the date of exposure rather than from the date of the plaintiff's discovery of infection would work substantial unfairness.

Some courts have determined that where an injury or disease is inherently latent, the statute of limitations does not begin to run until the injured person becomes aware, or should have become aware, of his or her exposure.[2] Moreover, courts that have addressed the statute of limitations problem in HIV-related cases have recognized the unique timeliness problem resulting from the indefinite and protracted incubation period between initial infection and the manifestation of symptoms. The courts have noted that people testing positive may delay bringing an action because they have not shown symptoms. Further, these courts have noted that an action prematurely initiated before a person has symptoms may result in under-compensation.[3] In a significant New York case, a court ruled that a physician's workplace exposure to HIV should be treated not as a negligence claim subject to a one-year, ninety-day statute of limitations running from the date of injury, but rather as a claim of exposure to a toxic substance, for which one can sue within three years of the discovery of the latent effects of exposure.[4]

Of course, a court or legislature might view some event other than exposure to HIV (or discovery of the fact that one has been exposed) as the event that starts the statute running. For example, some jurisdictions "toll" (stop the running of) the statute in medical malpractice cases until the end of the plaintiff's patient treatment relationship with the defendant doctor. However, if the treatment relationship ends long enough before the date of discovery of infection, some courts have held that the statute of limitations continues to run from the termination date, and HIV-infected plaintiffs in such cases are barred from recovery.[5]

Statutes of limitations vary not only from state to state, but also from tort to tort within a state. The same injury as alleged against separate defendants may constitute separate torts with varying statutes of limitations. For example, patients who received tainted blood during surgery may sue their doctors for medical malpractice and their hospitals for negligence, and each of these claims may have a different limitation period.[6] Blood banks are also liable for HIV transmission, but it is not always clear from the statutes if their liability is more analogous to that of professionals, and thus governed by the statute of limitations for professional malpractice, or to that of providers of products or services, and thus subject to the limitations period for simple negligence. Courts have split on this issue when deciding if suits against blood banks are time-barred.[7] Until all these questions are resolved by the courts, the cautious tort plaintiff will consult a lawyer early and file suit within the shortest possible limitations period. Wrestling with the thorny problem of proving future damages is preferable to being shut out altogether.

Finally, a tort action for sexual transmission of HIV must overcome the assertion that it violates the constitutional right to privacy. This hurdle is not so much a defense designed to avoid a finding of fault as a claim that public policy forbids the state to intervene—through its court system—in intimate private affairs. Courts traditionally have been reluctant to sanction state intrusion into private relationships. The question that must be answered in such a case, however, is whether such intrusion is warranted under the particular circumstances at issue.

The California Court of Appeals found in 1984 that the constitutional right of privacy did not preclude an unmarried woman from suing a man in tort for sexually transmitting herpes to her. The defendant maintained that it was not the business of the judiciary to supervise promises or claims made between consenting adults concerning the circumstances of their private sexual conduct. The court acknowledged that courts have recognized that the right of privacy precludes unwarranted governmental intrusion in matters relating to marriage, family, and sex, but decided that the right of privacy must be subordinated to the state's fundamental right to enact laws that promote public health and welfare and the safety of its citizens.[8]

The fact that several jurisdictions have enacted legislation that imposes criminal penalties for engaging in sexual activity, knowing one is HIV-infected, suggests that this is an area of significant state concern.[9] This concern should provide an adequate basis for the courts to justify subordinating the privacy rights of people who knowingly transmit AIDS, endanger the health of the community, and inflict physical injury and suffering on their sexual partners, to the right of people harmed by such conduct to seek a legal remedy.

LIABILITY FOR EXPOSING ANOTHER TO HIV

The injuries that flow from being infected with HIV are apparent, and later in this chapter we will discuss the cases arising from the actual transmission of HIV through one means or another. But the awful consequences of infection, combined with the hysteria HIV often evokes, have resulted in a significant number of lawsuits by people who have been exposed to (but not infected with) HIV through another's lack of care.

Liability for Sexual Exposure

In general, each of us has a legally enforceable duty to protect our sexual partners against exposure to or transmission of venereal and contagious diseases. Even before HIV became a major issue, court decisions had found defendants liable for failing to live up to this duty in cases involving other sexually transmitted diseases. In the leading herpes case, the California Court of Appeals upheld the plaintiff's right to sue the defendant for "having sexual intercourse with her at a time when he knew, or in the exercise of reasonable care should have known, that he was a carrier of venereal disease."[10]

The most widely reported case involving sexual activity and HIV is *Christian v. Sheft*, in which the plaintiff convinced a jury that Rock Hudson and his personal secretary withheld the fact that Hudson suffered from AIDS while the plaintiff and Hudson continued to have sexual relations.[11] As the Hudson case shows, there are several legal theories under which such a suit may be brought. A single lawsuit may assert more than one cause of action, and usually does, because one can never be certain which theory will be best supported by the facts as they are developed in court.

Fraudulent Misrepresentation. One who deliberately lies about his or her HIV infection to a sex partner may be liable in fraud, just as Rock Hudson and his secretary were. A successful case of fraudulent misrepresentation must prove six elements: (1) the representation by the defendant was false; (2) the defendant knew the representation was false; (3) there existed no reason for the defendant to believe that the misrepresentation was true; (4) the defendant intended and expected the plaintiff to rely upon the misrepresentation; (5) the plaintiff did rely upon the representation and was justified in doing so; and (6) damage to the plaintiff resulted from this reliance.[12]

Marc Christian established the fraud and reliance elements of his case by showing that his former lover Rock Hudson knew he had AIDS in June 1984 but concealed this from Christian and continued to have unprotected sexual intercourse with him until February 1985. In addition, Hudson informed his personal secretary, Mark Miller, of his disease at the time of his diagnosis and instructed Miller to conceal it from Christian. For thirteen months, both Hudson and Miller explained Hudson's AIDS-related symptoms (skin tumors, severe weight loss, and profuse sweating) as the result of excessive drinking, anorexia, and a persistent flu. As the film star's weight loss became apparent to the media, he repeatedly denied that he had AIDS, both privately and publicly. Christian eventually discovered the truth in July 1985 from a television broadcast, after which Miller admitted both that the broadcast was true and that he and Hudson had concealed the fact from Christian for thirteen months.

Christian, who as of March 1992 has continually tested HIV negative, also managed to establish that he was damaged by this reliance in that he suffered from what is now loosely referred to as "AIDS phobia," or the fear of contracting AIDS, for at least several years after his exposure to the virus. After learning of his exposure, Christian suffered depression, chills, insomnia, nightmares, vomiting, weight loss, and irritability. Christian's damages resulted not from the biological effects of HIV exposure, but from its psychological ones. For that suffering, he eventually recovered about $5 million.[13]

Fraudulent misrepresentation may also occur through silence that is meant to lead another person to place himself or herself in a position involving risk or injury: "It has commonly been stated as a general rule, particularly in the older cases, that ... [a tort claim cannot be based on] tacit nondisclosure. ... To this general rule, if such it be, the courts have developed a number of exceptions, some of which are as yet very ill defined, and have no very definite boundaries. ... [One exception] is found where the parties stand in some fiduciary or confidential relationship to each other."[14]

Such a relationship exists legally between a husband and wife; whether the relationship between unmarried sexual partners would also be considered "confidential" in this sense is unclear. It has been cogently argued that "partners to the sexual intercourse, if only for a brief time, share a trust and intimacy that elevates their relationship from the level of mere friend or acquaintance. Their confidential relationship should invoke a heightened duty, requiring disclosure of specific facts as circumstances dictate: the risk of contracting an incurable disease demands disclosure even to one with whom intimacy has only briefly been shared.''[15]

An HIV-positive woman in Nevada successfully used this theory to win a $2.1 million award against the estate of her former husband who, during the marriage and the divorce proceedings, failed to disclose that he had AIDS. During the marriage, she presumably continued to have sexual intercourse with him, and at the divorce settlement she signed a blanket release of all her rights to his assets, including her right to sue for exposure to HIV. The husband died of AIDS three months after the divorce.[16]

Battery and Intentional Infliction of Emotional Distress. Battery is defined as an intentional, harmful or offensive, and unjustifiable contact with the body of another, made without that person's consent.[17] Unlike negligence, which is aimed at careless behavior, intentional torts like battery are aimed at deliberate, or at least reckless, bad acts. To prove the first element of an HIV-related battery—that the defendant acted intentionally—the plaintiff need not show that the defendant sought purposely to transmit the infection. Rather, it is enough to show that the defendant, knowing that he or she was infected, intended to cause the sexual contact that led to transmission, or went ahead with the contact in reckless disregard of the high risk of transmission. If, on the other hand, the defendant lacked actual knowledge of his or her infected state, the intent element cannot be satisfied. As for the second element, there can be little doubt that a sexual contact that could transmit a deadly infection is "harmful or offensive." Even if the sex act, in and of itself, is not offensive, the knowing exposure of one's partner to HIV certainly is.[18]

Battery also requires that the contact between the plaintiff and the defendant be unjustifiable or, in legal jargon, "unprivileged." In some states, a wife may still be deemed to consent to sexual relations with her husband by virtue of having entered into the marital relationship, thus making intramarital sex, in general, "privileged conduct." Nevertheless, even in those states a wife will not be deemed to have consented to exposure to a sexually transmitted disease.[19] Therefore, where HIV transmission is at issue, lack of consent and lack of privilege will be presumed.

Sexual activity satisfies the contact requirement.[20] Moreover, that contact is sufficient to allow recovery for intentional infliction of emotional or psychological distress. Since recovery for negligently induced emotional distress may be limited to the distress that accompanies demonstrable physical injury, a plaintiff may have a better chance of success with a suit based on battery if the injury flowing from exposure to HIV is primarily psychological and the defendant acted knowingly. This was one basis of Marc Christian's successful suit against Rock Hudson.

Negligence. Because he could prove that Hudson deliberately pursued a course of conduct that put him at risk, Marc Christian did not allege the most common form of tort, negligence. To prevail on a negligence theory, a plaintiff must establish four elements: (1) the defendant had a legal duty to act prudently so as to protect others from the unreasonable risk of harm; (2) the defendant breached that duty; (3) there is an adequate causal connection between the defendant's conduct and the plaintiff's injury; and (4) the plaintiff suffered damage or loss.[21]

The first element is satisfied only if a court or legislature has decided that a duty of care should be imposed in situations of the type at issue. Courts will impose such a duty with respect to sexual exposure to HIV, not simply because the precedent has been set in the herpes cases, but more important because requiring infected sexual partners to take reasonable precautions constitutes sound social policy. The state has an undeniable interest in checking the spread of HIV and in seeing to it that people who are unwittingly endangered are adequately compensated. Moreover, one who negligently endangers an unwitting sexual partner is morally culpable. Finally, using the tort system to place an obligation of caution on the infected does not necessarily undermine the public health message that all citizens should be careful and take responsibility for their own safety. Through doctrines like comparative negligence, discussed later, courts can adjust the amounts awarded to plaintiffs to reflect their own failure to exercise due care, while not entirely absolving defendants.

Once the plaintiff has established that a duty of care has been or ought to be imposed, the next question is whether the defendant has breached that duty by failing to conform to the standard of conduct it entails. In a sexual exposure case, the determination of whether a breach has occurred is fairly straightforward, once the requirements of reasonable prudence have been spelled out. If, for example, a reasonably prudent person infected with HIV would inform sex partners of that fact and would also follow safe-sex guidelines, then the issue of breach reduces to the question: Did the defendant make the proper disclosure and take the proper precautions? In the California herpes case, the plaintiff apparently alleged that the defendant was negligent both in engaging in intercourse while knowingly infectious and in failing to warn her of his condition.[22]

Statutory Violation. The position of most courts is that conduct violating a statute created for the protection of the public is "negligent per se," which means that it is treated as being conclusively negligent, and the plaintiff must prove only that it caused damage.[23] A minority of courts, however, consider violation of such a statute to be only *evidence* of negligence, leaving defendants free to present evidence that they in fact exercised due care under the circumstances.[24]

Several states have enacted statutes making it a crime for an HIV-infected person to knowingly engage in activity likely to result in transmission. For example, a Louisiana statute provides: "No person shall intentionally expose another to any acquired immune deficiency syndrome (AIDS) virus through sexual contact without the knowing and lawful consent of the victim."[25] These HIV- or AIDS-specific criminal statutes are analogous to other state statutes that make the communication of a venereal disease a crime.[26] Some courts have construed statutes of this kind to establish negligence per se in cases involving the transmission of venereal diseases, and may well do so in HIV transmission cases.[27]

Liability for Exposure through Careless Use of Needles or Other Medical Equipment

There have been a number of cases brought by people who were stuck with needles which, they claim, were carelessly discarded, stored, or used. People have brought suit after being stuck with needles during hospital procedures,[28] while disposing of trash that contained used needles,[29] and when the needle had apparently been left by an earlier guest in a hotel room and not removed by the cleaning staff.[30] In an Illinois case, a patient has sued a doctor and hospital alleging that the physician reused a disposable swab in performing her Pap smear.[31]

Needles and other sharp medical devices that are contaminated with HIV can and do transmit the virus, so society has an interest in encouraging those who use such instruments to use and dispose of them carefully. Moreover, a person who is stuck with an object that is or may be contaminated has every reason to be upset and will have to endure the expense and uncertainty of HIV testing and retesting for several months. And yet, an uncontaminated instrument obviously cannot transmit HIV, and even contact with an infected instrument presents a statistically low risk of infection. There is a line beyond which prudent concern about possible exposure becomes sheer AIDS phobia.

So far, courts are split on whether and to what extent they should award damages purely for anxiety arising from possible exposure to HIV, whether it happens in bed, in a hospital, or at work. Although one needle exposure case settled for a six-figure sum, and the Rock Hudson case was a major plaintiff victory, other courts have refused to recognize that AIDS phobia constitutes any injury at all, at least in the absence of proof that the plaintiff actually suffered contact with infected blood in a manner actually capable of transmitting HIV. One court, rejecting the plaintiff's claim, noted that it had been "unable to locate a single case, from any jurisdiction, which has permitted recovery for emotional distress arising out of fear of contracting disease when the plaintiff cannot prove exposure to the agent which has the potential to cause the disease."[32] This approach, we suggest, is wise for at least two reasons. An individual's level of fear of HIV is highly subjective and difficult to measure, particularly if the plaintiff stands to make money from his or her phobia. It is, furthermore, a questionable use of the tort system to punish defendants who did not actually place anyone in a position of real danger. With courts going both ways, this will certainly be an area of considerable legal ferment over the next several years.

Liability for Exposure by an Infected Health Care Worker

The fear of transmission by a health care worker has turned a number of patients into plaintiffs alleging they were harmed by exposure to HIV during medical treatment. Even before the publication of the mysterious case of the Florida dentist who may have infected five patients, a patient in Maryland had sued the estate of her surgeon, who had died of AIDS, claiming that learning of his infection had caused her severe emotional harm even in the absence of transmission. The court refused to accept the suggestion that the surgeon's being HIV-infected was enough to constitute an "exposure": "Because there are no reported cases of transmission of AIDS from a surgeon to a patient, such transmission is only a theoretical possibility when proper barrier techniques are employed. . . . Plaintiff has not alleged that Dr. Almaraz failed to use proper barrier techniques . . . [or] that any incident . . . occurred during surgery that would have caused Dr. Almaraz's blood to enter her body." The fact that the plaintiff had not tested positive for HIV years after the surgery added to the court's conviction that she had not been exposed in the first place. Dismissing the case, the court expressed its sensible reluctance to allow recovery based on only the fear of a disease.[33]

Whereas cases of sexual and needle exposure are likely to be rooted in a real possibility of transmission, treatment by an infected health care worker, even in the operating room, presents very little risk of HIV transmission to a patient. Hospitals and doctors, however, have traditionally been held to a higher standard of care based on their professional status and the serious consequences of their lapses, and in any event the public appears to be convinced either that the risk is high or that any risk of transmission from a doctor is unacceptable. Courts right now are torn between concerns about rewarding plaintiffs for irrational fears and defending patients' right to avoid exposure to a frightening disease, neither of which necessarily involves an intelligent consideration of the important public health issues.[34] At stake are not only the careers of thousands of health care workers and the integrity of the health care and public health establishments, but also the basic principle that the lives of people with diseases should not be restricted when those people do not pose a real risk of harm.

Given the widespread public fear of health care providers with HIV, suits based on fear of contracting the virus will continue to arise as long as some courts will indulge them. As hospitals and health departments increasingly trace the patients of providers they learn are infected, more and more people are finding out that they have received care from an HIV-positive doctor or dentist.[35] (For more on this issue, see chapter 17.)

LIABILITY FOR TRANSMISSION OF HIV

Tort cases based on actual transmission of HIV have arisen in the same settings as cases based on mere exposure, but also in the one area in which exposure is virtually tantamount to infection: the transfusion of contaminated blood and blood products.

Liability for Sexual Transmission

A person who actually transmits HIV to a sexual partner is open to suit for resulting harm under the same theories available to one who has merely been exposed— negligence, battery, misrepresentation, and statutory violation.[36] Cases based on negligence, however, are likely to be more difficult to prove where the damage at issue is actual infection. While the case is obviously more compelling, the plaintiff faces the difficult task of proving that the defendant was the source of infection, and the defendant may have more useful defenses.

Negligence liability may arise not only when people know facts that would cause a reasonable person to recognize the existence of an unreasonable risk of harm, but also when they should have known such facts. How might this standard be applied in the HIV context? When is it fair to say that a person should have known that he or she was infectious? Some cases are fairly easy. For example, the steady sexual partner of someone who has AIDS probably could not escape liability for transmitting the virus to a third party by claiming that he or she was unaware of his or her seropositivity. Similarly, a frequenter of bath houses with a penchant for unprotected anal sex is likely to be found to possess constructive knowledge of his seropositivity in any suit for negligent sexual transmission. At the other end of the scale is the infected, but asymptomatic, female sex partner of a male she does not know is bisexual. In between these extremes are a host of most troublesome cases.

Consider, for example, "R. L.," who infected his fiancée with HIV sometime in 1984 or 1985. At the time, he had had one high-risk homosexual experience and had never heard of AIDS until Rock Hudson's diagnosis became public in July 1985. In April 1985, the couple broke off sexual relations when R. L. suffered the first serious symptoms of what would later be diagnosed as AIDS. The antibody test was not available to people in his area until three months later. In rejecting his fiancée's claim for negligence, a Minnesota court found insufficient evidence that R. L. should have known about his risk based on the information available to the general public, or that his homosexual activity was so extensive that he should have been more aware of the risks than the average person.[37] In such circumstances, although the goal of compensating unwitting victims could be met by presuming knowledge, it is not obvious that the unwitting victimizers are especially blameworthy, or that they are in a markedly better position than their partners to assay the risks of unprotected sexual activity. To be sure, some courts may decide to hold people like R. L. liable, in the belief that an incentive will be created for people in similar situations to take the HIV antibody test. This, of course, assumes that the distant threat of tort liability will create a significantly greater incentive for antibody testing than is already created by fear of AIDS itself or by knowledge of the availability of early medical intervention for HIV infection.

For reasons of both privacy and practicality, courts are unlikely to define the prudent person's duty of care as a blanket duty not to have sex, at least with respect to people who do not know they are infected. Instead, courts are likely to impose a duty of candor and cooperation in safe behavior. For example, a court could conclude that a reasonably prudent person would inform potential sex partners about behavior that makes infection a possibility (for example, "I used to shoot drugs, but I stopped four years ago") and would not resist reasonable precautions suggested by the partner in response to that information. As long as a low-risk person acted prudently, the costs of infection would remain where they fall. Such an approach would have the virtue of creating an incentive for both partners to take steps to avoid transmission.

Once a duty and breach of duty are established, the plaintiff in any tort case must convince the judge or jury that his or her injury was caused by the defendant's conduct. In the case of HIV infection, even where other possible means of transmission (such as contaminated blood or dirty needles) can be ruled out, serious problems of proof remain. The virus may lay dormant in a person for years. It is therefore often difficult, if not impossible, to determine how long someone has been infected prior to the discovery of positive antibody status or the onset of AIDS.

In the ideal case (from the plaintiff's perspective), the plaintiff would be able to prove that he or she was seronegative before engaging in sex with the defendant and that he or she did not engage in high-risk sex with anyone else between that encounter and the point that infection became manifest. Few people could clear even the first hurdle; it requires the fortuity of either having had an antibody test close to the time of the encounter (and no intervening high-risk sex) or having had blood drawn during that same period that somehow remains available for testing. Without this kind of hard data, the plaintiff must rely on evidence of long-term chastity or, at a minimum, low-risk sex, prior to engaging in sex with the defendant. (DNA testing to match identical viral strains, which received considerable publicity when it was used in the investigation of the Florida dentist case, is a controversial and expensive process that is not likely to be widely available to litigants in the near future.)

Alternatively, the plaintiff could offer proof that all of his or her other sex partners (going back perhaps as far as the late 1970s) are seronegative. A single unaccounted-for partner, however, would cloud the issue and might even raise the question of who transmitted HIV to whom. Similarly, a single unaccounted-for partner *following* the plaintiff's encounter with the defendant could break the chain of causation between the defendant's conduct and the plaintiff's present plight. Remember, though, that the plaintiff need not disprove every other possible cause of infection but need only show that it is "more probable than not" that the defendant was the source of the virus.[38]

Even where causation is established, proof of damages may be problematic in some cases. In suits brought by people who have been diagnosed with AIDS or serious opportunistic diseases, determination of damages will be fairly straightforward; they will include compensation for pain and suffering, as well as for medical expenses, lost wages, necessary support services (such as psychotherapy, nursing care, child care, and the like) and other expenses incurred as a consequence of having AIDS. Damage awards in suits brought by asymptomatic plaintiffs, by contrast, will be based largely on compensation for emotional trauma—including trauma caused by adjustments in lifestyle undertaken to reduce the risk of transmitting the virus to others, and by the fear of developing AIDS in the future.[39] Still, uncertainty about the specific medical conditions that will result from HIV infection, and the timing of any ultimate AIDS diagnosis, renders considerations of future damages rather speculative. To the extent that suppression of the immune system can be shown to be "more likely than not," an award of damages for that likely consequence is appropriate. As medical understanding of AIDS improves, it is becoming easier to make a reasonably reliable prognosis of the course of a given person's HIV infection. Even now, many states allow arguments for damages based on reduced life expectancy.

One concrete loss experienced by everyone who is seropositive is a drastic reduction in insurability. Most insurance companies exclude applicants on the basis of HIV antibody status. Damages for being rendered uninsurable or for the increased cost of insurance would be an appropriate element of any damages award. In particular cases, other nonmedical costs or losses may be compensable as well.

Even if the plaintiff has proved every element of a negligence claim, the defendant may still avoid liability by establishing a recognized defense. The negligence defenses most likely to be used in sexual transmission cases are contributory (and comparative) negligence and assumption of the risk, all of which implicate the plaintiff's own conduct as a significant cause of the harm.

"Contributory negligence" and "comparative negligence" refer to conduct on the part of the plaintiff that is judged to fall below the standard of care that one is required to exercise to protect oneself.[40] Traditionally, a finding of plaintiff negligence completely precluded recovery. In theory at least, even the most blatant negligence of the defendant was excused if the plaintiff was negligent in even a small way. In recent decades, however, this doctrine of contributory negligence has largely been replaced by a system of comparative negligence. Under this system, the plaintiff's lack of care does not totally bar recovery; it simply diminishes the awardable damages in proportion to the amount of negligence attributable to the plaintiff.[41]

From a public health point of view, HIV prevention will best be achieved when every sexually active person assumes that his or her partner may be infected, and therefore engages only in safer sex. Courts may well use comparative negligence as a device to encourage this behavior by limiting or denying recovery to plaintiffs who fail to behave with reasonable prudence. A plaintiff engaging in sex with a partner with whom a relationship of trust has not been established might be deemed partially negligent for failing to wear a condom (or to ask the partner to wear one) or for engaging in sexual practices that the plaintiff knows, or should know, have been determined by health officials to be unsafe. Whether such a rule would be fair, or effective for that matter, depends in part on the extent to which useful safe-sex information has been disseminated to the plaintiff's community.

The defense of "assumption of risk . . . has been a subject of much controversy, and has been surrounded by much confusion, because [it] has been used by the courts in several different senses.''[42] The thread common to all these uses is that the plaintiffs recognized the particular risk at issue, understood its nature and consequences, and voluntarily chose to expose themselves to it.[43] When proved, the defense completely precludes recovery in a suit claiming negligence. Thus, when a person infected with HIV informs a sexual partner of his or her condition, and the sexual partner truly understands the risk and voluntarily consents to high-risk sexual activity, that partner has expressly assumed the risk of contracting the virus and cannot prevail in a negligent transmission suit.

As comparative negligence, with its flexible approach to plaintiff misconduct, has replaced the strict rule of contributory negligence, assumption of risk has also been passing from the legal scene. Most instances of assumption of risk can be equally well analyzed under the heading of comparative fault, so assumption of risk would probably be applied, if at all, only to a scenario as unlikely as the one just described.[44]

Whenever circumstances are such that the plaintiff should know that the defendant is infected, it is probable that the defendant is even more aware (actually or constructively) of that grim reality. At the same time, for the plaintiff to proceed with unsafe sex is scarcely prudent. Recognizing a defense of comparative negligence seems to be the optimal way to achieve the goals of compensating victims, discouraging unreasonable risk-taking, expressing societal disapproval of advantage-taking, and slowing the spread of AIDS.

Liability for Transmission through Needles or Other Medical Equipment

A person who is actually infected through contact with a carelessly used medical instrument is even more entitled to recovery than one who is merely exposed, although proving that the plaintiff was not infected in some other way and at some other time may again be difficult. In the most publicized case to date, a New York medical resident reached a substantial settlement with the hospital she worked for and through whose negligence, she alleged, she contracted HIV from an infected needle carelessly left on a patient's bed by another doctor. Several similar cases are working their way through the system.[45] Generally, however, workers who are infected in the course of their employment will find themselves confined to the worker's compensation system for relief.[46] (For more on the problem of occupational exposure to HIV, see chapter 17.)

Liability for Transmission from a Health Care Provider to a Patient

No one yet knows how five patients of Florida dentist David Acer became infected with HIV while under his care. Although speculation about how it happened includes the possibility that Acer deliberately injected patients with his own blood, there is little doubt that something went wrong and that Acer was responsible. Acer's insurance carriers, evidently recognizing that a jury would resolve any doubts about how the transmission occurred in favor of the plaintiffs, settled quickly with three of the patients, exhausting Acer's $3 million coverage and leaving the two other patients with strong claims but no one to pay them.[47]

The extremely low risk of transmission from health care provider to patient makes it unlikely that a case like Acer's will present itself again soon. It is quite possible, however, that people who have been infected through sex or drug use may bring claims if they have been treated by a doctor whom they later learn was HIV infected. It is even possible that patients who infected their doctors may claim that transmission happened the other way around. Such cases will present the same problems of proving (or disproving) causation as do sexual transmission cases, but insurance companies may settle rather than risk putting a possible case of transmission by a health care worker before a jury.

Liability Related to the Provision of Blood and Blood Products

Transmission of HIV through blood and blood products, including cases related to transfusions and to use by hemophiliacs of the clotting product Factor VIII, has accounted for approximately 2 to 3 percent of the reported cases of AIDS. Despite their small numbers, recipients of HIV-contaminated blood constitute a disproportionately high percentage of HIV-related tort plaintiffs. Since there is little that transfusion patients and hemophiliacs can do to reduce the risk of infection, a powerful argument can be made that the cost of occasional accidental transfusions of HIV-contaminated blood or blood products should be borne by the blood supplier (and then spread across all people who receive blood through slightly higher fees to cover the blood supplier's increased insurance) rather than by the unlucky individual who becomes infected with HIV through receipt of blood or a blood product.

Suits brought by people contracting HIV infection from contaminated blood or blood products have used several legal theories including breach of implied warranty, strict liability, medical malpractice, and negligence. Suits have been brought against hospitals at which HIV-infected blood or blood products were received, against blood banks and manufacturers of blood products that supplied the blood, and against the physicians who ordered the transfusion or negligently created the medical condition that required it. Claims have come from not only the recipients of contaminated blood, but also their spouses who attribute their sexually transmitted infection to the blood supplier's original misconduct. (A few suits have even been brought against donors of blood, so far without success.[48]) While hemophiliacs who have used large amounts of clotting factor made by many different manufacturers may have serious difficulties proving that any particular defendant caused their infection, many transfusion recipients have no lifestyle risk factors and can point to the exact unit of blood that infected them.[49]

Breach of Implied Warranty and Strict Liability. An initial wave of blood-related suits included claims of implied warranty and strict liability. For the most part, however, these theories have foundered on a technical issue regarding the nature of the blood and blood product industries. Under the implied warranty theory, the plaintiff claims that the provision of blood is the sale of a product, and that the contract for that sale should be read by the court to include an unwritten guarantee that the blood product is fit for transfusion. Under the strict liability theory, plaintiffs claim that manufacturers and distributors of blood and blood products, like manufacturers and distributors of other goods, should be responsible, even without proof of negligence, for defects and dangers in the product. Courts have virtually all rejected both theories, relying on statutes in almost every state that legally characterize the supplying of blood and blood products as a service rather than the sale of a product.[50]

Negligence in the Preparation of the Blood Product. Negligence appears to be the only theory under which a plaintiff can recover against a supplier of blood or blood products contaminated with HIV. The most common claim is that the blood bank failed to take reasonable steps to insure the safety of the blood they collected, although plaintiffs may also claim that the blood bank gave false or misleading information about donation practices or risks.[51] To prevail in a suit for negligence, a plaintiff must show that the blood supplier failed to perform a duty of care owed to him or her, and that this failure caused the plaintiff injury.

The first, and frequently the decisive, issue in such cases is what standard of care is due from blood bankers and blood product manufacturers. Nearly all courts that have considered the issue have decided that the provision of blood and blood products is a *professional* service, and that those who engage in the service should be held to a professional, rather than general, standard of care. Instead of asking what a reasonably prudent person would do under similar circumstances, a court applying a professional standard of care looks to the customs and practices in the profession. Specifically, a recipient of HIV-infected blood needs to establish that donor-screening and blood-screening measures recommended by relevant public health agencies and industry groups were not employed or, if employed, were carried out in a manner below the general standard of the blood product industry. A defendant blood supplier will be protected from negligence suits under this standard as long as it can show that it performed the questioned procedure—testing for HIV or screening donors, for example—no more negligently than other blood banks did at the same time, even if plaintiffs can show that the general practice of the industry was a questionable response to the risk of HIV transmission.[52]

In considering the potential liability of hospitals, blood banks, and blood products manufacturers for negligently supplying contaminated blood, we must distinguish between cases involving blood and blood products administered before the availability of screening tests for HIV antibodies and cases involving blood and blood products administered thereafter. Since the test became available in March 1985, the blood industry has used it as the main way of screening blood for HIV. Failure to use the test is obviously likely to be found to be negligent. In fact, in one case a blood bank was found negligent for failing to use the test the very first day it became available.[53]

The question of liability for injury caused by HIV-infected blood or plasma administered prior to the development of the antibody test is more complex. By the end of 1982, evidence had developed associating AIDS with blood transfusions and with Factor VIII. In March 1983, the Food and Drug Administration issued to all blood- and plasma-collecting facilities in the United States specific guidelines for preventing the transmission of AIDS through blood products.[54] These guidelines call upon collection centers to provide information about AIDS to donors so that they can recognize whether they are members of groups at increased risk, to revise standard operating procedures to include specific questions regarding signs and symptoms of AIDS, and to advise donors that members of high-risk groups should voluntarily forego donating blood. Failure to follow applicable government guidelines might well leave a collection facility open to liability for negligence. Some courts have permitted plaintiffs to argue that the 1983 guidelines were insufficient and that collection facilities should have been required to inquire affirmatively into whether donors were at risk for AIDS or, alternatively, to argue that surrogate testing should have been used to test for some other blood contaminant, such as hepatitis B, which could have served as a marker for the substance that was the causative agent of AIDS.[55]

Malpractice by Hospitals and Physicians. People infected through blood transfusions have been most successful in suits against their physicians for medical malpractice. A breach of the duty of care physicians owe to their patients is called malpractice. As a general rule, physicians and other health care providers are held to a professional standard of care, which requires them to act with the level of skill and learning commonly possessed by members of the profession in good standing.

In the area of transmission through blood and blood products, physicians (and the hospitals they work for) have been sued for two basic sorts of malpractice: failure to obtain the patient's proper informed consent for the transfusion that resulted in infection, and failure to act with proper skill by causing the medical crisis that required the transfusion. In both sorts of cases, the doctors did not have any role in the contamination of the blood that was used; rather, they were held legally responsible for the HIV infection because they made an earlier mistake without which the transfusion would not have occurred. Under these circumstances, courts have found the physician's misconduct to be the "proximate" (or legal) cause of the infection.

Failure to obtain any consent at all for a procedure is usually treated as an unprivileged, intentional touching (that is, battery). This claim has been raised, for example, where a physician ordered a blood transfusion for a child without obtaining the parents' permission, and where the patient conditioned consent for transfusion (or the underlying surgery) on the use of her own or a designated donor's blood and blood from the general supply was used instead. As with any other battery claim, the plaintiff must show that the defendant acted intentionally or in reckless disregard of the plaintiff's well-being.[56]

A physician's failure to provide a patient an opportunity to give *informed* consent—by not giving the patient all the information needed to make an intelligent treatment choice—is usually treated as a breach of professional duty (that is, medical malpractice). In a California case, for example, a jury awarded over $3 million to a child who claimed that her hospital and surgeons failed to properly inform her parents about the risks of blood transfusions or about the option of obtaining blood for her surgery from friends and family.[57] By contrast, a Texas court ruled that a hospital and its physicians did not have a duty to warn a patient about HIV in February 1983, because at that time "AIDS was not a known inherent or material risk associated with transfusion of blood."[58] Informed consent may be especially important in relation to HIV infection, inasmuch as some risk remains that blood producing a negative test result may nevertheless carry the virus. There can be no doubt that any physician today has a duty to fully warn a transfusion patient or hemophiliac about the small but real risk of infection through contaminated blood.

A number of infected patients have placed the primary blame for their injury on a physician whose substandard care led to their needing a transfusion in the first place. These have led to sizable damage awards. A classically horrible example of this sort of case is *Gaffney v. United States*. Doctors at a U.S. Navy hospital botched Mrs. Gaffney's obstetric care, causing her to need a cesarean section. The cesarean section also went badly, and she needed blood transfusions, which infected her with

HIV. Unaware of her infection, she passed HIV on to her husband and a later child. All of the HIV infections, and the resulting suffering and death, were found to have been legally caused by the hospital's medical malpractice, and the United States paid Mr. Gaffney, shortly before his death, $3.5 million in damages for the care of his one surviving, uninfected child.[59]

LIABILITY FOR MEDICAL MALPRACTICE

Like other patients, people with HIV are entitled to sue their physicians when the care they receive does not measure up to professional standards. Chief among the failings likely to lead to malpractice suits by HIV-infected patients are failure to diagnose or misdiagnosis of HIV infection and failure to inform patients of the diagnosis. (The physician's duty to warn sexual partners and other third parties at risk is discussed in chapters 7 and 17.)

Errors in Diagnosis

Tort law holds a physician liable for mistakes only when they are caused by failure to comply with the standards of the profession. In other words, a faulty diagnosis arising from unusual circumstances that would have caused any reasonable physician to err does not give rise to liability for malpractice. Because AIDS is a syndrome involving multiple symptoms and even other diseases, diagnosis is not a simple matter. Physicians may be liable for failing to identify HIV infection or for misidentifying another condition as HIV disease.

Doctors and medical researchers agree that prompt, aggressive treatments may hold the virus in check and substantially improve and lengthen a patient's life. This makes timely diagnosis of HIV infection crucial. Failing to order an HIV test when it is indicated by the patient's condition or history or misreading a test result may lead to a delay in, or failure to obtain, necessary treatment, which may in turn result in an aggravated condition, the hastening of the disease, or premature death. A failure to diagnose properly may also lead to the erroneous prescription of a course of treatment harmful to the patient or others, including the omission of necessary warnings regarding safe sexual practices.

Each of these harms may be compensated for in a suit for malpractice.[60] Thus, the fact that AIDS would eventually have resulted in the plaintiff's death, even if an accurate diagnosis had been made earlier, does not preclude a sizable award of damages. A patient whose AIDS or HIV-related disease has been misdiagnosed or gone undiagnosed may also recover for emotional distress resulting from the delay in getting treatment and the possible loss of a chance to remain healthy.[61] It is even possible that a spouse or sexual partner, infected by unsafe sex practices after the misdiagnosis, could successfully sue the physician if a correct diagnosis and proper warnings would have forestalled the infection.[62]

A false diagnosis of HIV infection can be damaging, too. Being told one has a fatal disease is obviously a shock, and plaintiffs have successfully recovered damages for their emotional distress arising from a negligent failure to conduct the alternate and confirmatory tests necessary to properly make a diagnosis of HIV disease or AIDS.[63] Similarly, people diagnosed erroneously as being HIV-infected or as having AIDS would have a malpractice claim if their employment interests were compromised by the false test results.[64]

Failure to Inform Patients of HIV or AIDS Diagnosis

Some physicians may not wish to inform a patient that he or she has HIV disease, falsely reasoning that a patient with an untreatable, fatal disease does not benefit by knowing about it. Professional ethics and public policy suggest that a failure to inform a patient of an HIV diagnosis, like failure to make an accurate diagnosis, will create liability if knowledge of the diagnosis would have enabled the patient to take measures or obtain treatment that might have prolonged life, or to change behavior in order to protect a sexual or needle partner.[65]

In a similar situation, a federal court recognized liability based on negligence when a physician failed to inform a patient of the discovery of a suspected tumor during a preemployment examination, even though the plaintiff failed to show that the tumor would have been operable at the time it was discovered. The court found that the plaintiff was entitled to damages for being deprived of the benefit of earlier treatment, which might have arrested the tumor's growth or slowed its development and possibly prolonged the patient's life and decreased his suffering.[66]

WHAT TORT LAW CAN AND CANNOT DO

Exposure to HIV has the potential for producing great psychological stress and anxiety. AIDS, with its associated opportunistic infections, most often involves pain, suffering, incapacitation, and death. Some people are likely to seek compensation for at least some of these harms through tort litigation. There are well-established causes of action that may be pursued in various HIV-related contexts. Nevertheless, many practical problems beset the tort plaintiff. Some of these relate to the difficulty of proving certain of the elements of the various causes of action. Others stem from uncertainty regarding which defenses are available. Finally, there are procedural obstacles (such as satisfying the statute of limitations) and evidentiary problems (such as proving future damages) to overcome. In any case, there is the fact that HIV disease often proceeds more quickly than do the courts, depriving an injured party of the fruits of legal victory.

Nevertheless, recognition of tort liability for HIV transmission and for HIV-related medical malpractice will make it possible for some people to obtain compensation. Furthermore, tort suits will provide at least a small incentive to use proper diagnostic techniques and to alter behaviors and procedures to limit the likelihood of HIV transmission. But tort suits, especially those directed at the sexual transmission of HIV, are not a very satisfactory means of achieving a third, critically important goal: spreading the cost associated with this dreadful, and dreadfully expensive, disease. That is perhaps best done by society as a whole, using a combination of private-sector insurance and public-sector funding.

We must also be concerned that the tort system is serving as a policymaker in public health matters. A lawsuit by one injured person is often a poor vehicle for gathering facts and weighing the social costs and benefits of a particular standard of conduct. For example, courts that find that the tort law of informed consent requires an HIV-infected physician to inform patients of his or her infection may not deal with the social costs of enforcing the patient's "right to know." Issues of mandatory screening, retraining physicians whose practices are ruined, and deciding who pays for it all are not squarely presented in the case of a single frightened patient suing a single doctor. Yet even if health officials eventually conclude that forcing doctors to disclose HIV infection to their patients is counterproductive, and indeed even if legislatures decline to pass laws requiring disclosure, medical institutions may impose it as standard practice out of fear of tort liability. In that way, tort law can become as much of a problem as an answer in the social struggle with HIV.

NOTES

1 *Compare, e.g.,* Cal. Civ. Proc. Code § 340 (Deering 1973) (injury) *with* Ill. Rev. Stat. ch. 110 § 13–202 (1966) (cause of action).

2 Prosser & Keeton, The Law of Torts § 30, at 165–68 (1984).

3 *See, e.g.,* Roe v. Miles Labs., AIDS Litig. Rep. (Andrews) 6033 (D. Alaska Mar. 1,

1991) (Alaska's two-year statute of limitations for medical malpractice runs from date of discovery of possible HIV infection); Matter of Saun Miller (New York City Health and Hosps. Corp.), N.Y.L.J., Apr. 24, 1989, at 22 (N.Y. Sup. Ct. Apr. 24, 1989) (ninety-day statute of limitations for negligence claims

against New York City tolled for more than
four years after negligent unauthorized transfusion of infant because of delay of discovery
that infant had AIDS); Seitzinger v. American
Red Cross, Nos. 90–0046, 90–3890, 1991
U.S. Dist. LEXIS 6860 (E.D. Pa. May 21,
1991) (Pennsylvania's two-year statute of limitations for personal injury and four-year statute of limitations for breach of warranty run
from date of discovery of seriousness of
infection).

4 Prego v. City of New York 541 N.Y.S. 2d
995 (App. Div. 1989).

5 *See, e.g.,* Sweeney v. Presbyterian/Colum-
bia Medical Ctr., 738 F. Supp. 802
(S.D.N.Y. 1990) (medical malpractice claims
against surgeon time-barred under two-year
statute of limitations running from last treatment); Hoemke v. New York Blood Ctr., 720
F. Supp. 45 (S.D.N.Y. 1989) (same), *aff'd,*
912 F.2d 550 (2d Cir. 1990).

6 *Compare Sweeney,* 738 F. Supp. 802
(medical malpractice claims against surgeon
barred) *with id.,* 763 F. Supp. 50 (S.D.N.Y.
1991) (negligence claims against hospital not
time-barred for same injury).

7 *Compare* Kaiser v. Memorial Blood Ctr. of
Minneapolis, 721 F. Supp. 1073 (D. Minn.
1989) (two-year statute for medical malpractice applied to blood banks, running from last
date of treatment) *with* DiMarco v. Hudson
Valley Blood Servs., 532 N.Y.S.2d 488
(Sup. Ct. 1988) (blood bank's liability sounds
in negligence, covered by longer statute of
limitations), *rev'd on other grounds,* 542
N.Y.S.2d 521 (App. Div. 1989); Silva v.
Southwest Florida Blood Bank, 1992 Fla.
LEXIS 986 (May 28, 1992) (suits against
blood banks governed by four-year general
negligence statue of limitations).

8 Kathleen K. v. Robert B., 198 Cal. Rptr.
273 (Ct. App. 1984).

9 *See, e.g.,* Ill. Rev. Stat. ch. 38, para. 12–
16.2 (1989) (a person commits criminal transmission of HIV when he or she, knowing that
he or she is infected with HIV . . . engages in

intimate contact with another); *see also* chapters 11 (discussing criminal law) and 9 (discussing military cases involving sexual
behavior by infected people) in this volume.

10 *Kathleen K.,* 198 Cal. Rptr. at 274; *accord, e.g.,* R.A.P. v. B.J.P., 428 N.W.2d
103, 106–07 (Minn. Ct. App. 1988).

11 Christian v. Sheft, No. C574153, AIDS
Litig. Rep. (Andrews) 2281 (Cal. Super. Ct.
filed Jan. 29, 1985); *California Jury Awards
Rock Hudson's Lover $21 Million in AIDS
Cover Up,* AIDS Litig. Rep. (Andrews) 2267
(1989); *Christian,* AIDS Litig. Rep. (Andrews) 2599 (Cal. Super. Ct. Apr. 21, 1989)
(damages awards cut to $5 million compensa-
tory and $500 thousand punitive), *aff'd,* No.
S022074, AIDS Litig. Rep. (Andrews) 6528
(Cal. Ct. App. June 13, 1991); *Private Settlement Reached in Suit Against Rock Hudson's
Estate,* AIDS Litig. Rep. (Andrews) 6906
(1991) (settlement amount undisclosed).

12 Restatement (Second) of Torts § 525
(1965); *see, e.g.,* Barbara A. v. John G., 193
Cal. Rptr. 422 (Ct. App. 1983).

13 Christian v. Sheft, No. S022074, AIDS
Litig. Rep. (Andrews) 6528 (Cal. Ct. App.
June 13, 1991).

14 Prosser & Keeton, note 2 above, § 106, at
737–38.

15 Note, Kathleen K. v. Robert B.: *A Cause
of Action for Genital Herpes Transmission,*
34 Case W. Res. L. Rev. 488, 522 (1984).

16 *Nevada Woman Gets Award From Husband's Estate for AIDS Infection,* AIDS Litig.
Rep. (Andrews) 2112 (1989) (Doe v. Estate
of Silva, No. 88–637 (Nev. Dist. Ct.)).

17 Restatement (Second) of Torts §§ 13, 18
(1965).

18 *See, e.g.,* Hill v. Miller, No. 90–5455,
AIDS Litig. Rep. (Andrews) 5001 (Fla. Cir.
Ct. filed Aug. 20, 1990).

19 *See* State v. Lankford, 102 A. 63, 64
(Del. 1917).

20 Note, *Liability in Tort for the Sexual
Transmission of Disease: Genital Herpes and*

the Law, 70 Cornell L. Rev. 101, 125 (1984). *But see* United States v. Perez, 1991 CMR LEXIS 1423 (Nov. 27, 1991) (no criminal battery where vasectomy precluded defendant from transmitting infectious body fluid).

21 Restatement (Second) of Torts § 4 (1965).

22 Kathleen K. v. Robert B., 198 Cal. Rptr. 273, 274 (Ct. App. 1984); *cf.* C.A.U. v. R.L., 438 N.W.2d 441 (Minn. Ct. App. 1989) (assuming that knowledge of HIV infection would give rise to duty).

23 *See, e.g.,* Azure v. City of Billings, 596 P.2d 460, 464 (Mont. 1979); Bayne v. Todd Shipyards Corp., 568 P.2d 771, 772 (Wash. 1977).

24 *See, e.g.,* Gill v. Whiteside-Hemby Drug Co., 122 S.W.2d 597, 601 (Ark. 1938) (violation of state law merely evidence of negligence).

25 La. Rev. Stat. Ann. § 14:43.5 (West Supp. 1992); *accord, e.g.,* Ark. Code Ann. § 5–14–123 (Michie 1991); Fla. Stat. Ann. § 384.24 (West Supp. 1992); Idaho Code § 39–608 (Supp. 1991); Ill. Rev. Stat. ch. 38, para. 12–16.2 (1989). *See generally* Gostin, *Public Health Strategies For Confronting AIDS,* 261 J.A.M.A. 11 (1989).

26 *See, e.g.,* Ala. Code § 22–16–17 (1977) (misdemeanor); Colo. Rev. Stat. §§ 25–4–401(2), 25–4–407 (1982) (misdemeanor); Idaho Code §§ 39–601, –607 (1977) (misdemeanor); Nev. Rev. Stat. §§ 441.220, 44.290 (1981) (misdemeanor); N.Y. Pub. Health Law § 2307 (McKinney 1977) (misdemeanor); Okla. Stat. Ann. tit. 63, § 1–519 (West 1984) (felony); Utah Code Ann. § 26–6–5 (Supp. 1983) (misdemeanor).

27 *See, e.g.,* Panther v. McKnight, 256 P. 916 (Okla. 1926) (court recognized limited private right of action for money damages for conduct in violation of criminal statute proscribing transmission of venereal disease).

28 *E.g., New York Court Voids Nurse's Needle Stick Suit in Lieu of Workers' Comp,* AIDS Litig. Rep. (Andrews) 4609 (1990)

(Peters v. New York City Health & Hosps. Corp., No. 22907–89 (N.Y. Sup. Ct. filed Mar. 29, 1990)) (dismissing emotional damages suit brought by nurse who was stuck by another nurse with used needle as covered by nurse's pending workmen's compensation suit); Burk v. Sage Prods., 747 F. Supp. 285 (E.D. Pa. 1990) (paramedic stuck with needle as he tried to dispose of it properly; emotional damages suit dismissed without evidence either paramedic or needle infected with HIV).

29 *E.g.,* Castro v. New York Life Ins. Co., No. 01941/90, AIDS Litig. Rep. (Andrews) 6816 (N.Y. Sup. Ct. July 29, 1991) (refusing to dismiss AIDS phobia suit by janitor in office building stuck by needle in trash bag).

30 *E.g.,* Doe (Bressler) v. Hyatt Hotels Corp., No. 90–1071, AIDS Litig. Rep. (Andrews) 4528 (D. Md. filed Apr. 17, 1990) (hotel guest stuck by dirty needle left in bed by previous guest); *Hotel Chain Settles Suit by Man Stuck with Dirty Needle,* AIDS Litig. Rep. (Andrews) 6394 (1991) (plaintiff in above case eventually settled for $120 thousand despite no evidence of HIV transmission, nor evidence of HIV on needle).

31 *Chicago Internist Accused of Reusing Possibly HIV-Infected Swab,* AIDS Litig. Rep. (Andrews) 6398 (1991) (Doe v. Illinois Masonic Hosp., No. 91L06294 (Ill. Cir. Ct. filed Apr. 23, 1991)).

32 Burk v. Sage Prods., 747 F. Supp. 285, 287 (E.D. Pa. 1990). *Compare id.* (no suit for emotional distress without evidence of actual exposure to HIV) *and* Petri v. Bank of New York, No. 12357/91, AIDS Litig. Rep. (Andrews) 7788 (N.Y.Sup. Ct. July 29, 1991) (emotional distress from mere HIV exposure is too speculative and remote a harm to be compensated) *and* Ordway v. Suffolk County, 583 N.Y.S. 2d 1014, (Sup. Ct. 1992) (in absence of actual exposure, physicians' fear of AIDS from HIV-infected patient not actionable as negligent infliction of emotional distress); *and* Transamerica Insurance Company v. John and Jane Doe, No. 1 CA-CV-90456, AIDS Litig. Rep. (Andrews) 8205 (Ariz. Ct. April 28,

1992) (motorists' exposure to accident victim's HIV-infected blood not compensable bodily harm absent competent evidence of impairment from mere exposure) *and* Hare v. State, 570 N.Y.S.2d 125 (App. Div.) (no suit for emotional distress of hospital employee bitten by suicidal inmate without showing that inmate had HIV), *appeal denied*, 580 N.E.2d 1058 (N.Y. 1991) *and* Rossi v. Estate of Almaraz, No. 90344028, 1991 WL 166924 (Md. Cir. Ct. May 23, 1991) (no suit for emotional distress by patient operated on by HIV-infected surgeon without showing of transmission) *and* Funeral Servs. by Gregory v. Bluefield Community Hosp., No. 19778, 1991 W. Va. LEXIS 217 (Dec. 5, 1991) (mortician's AIDS phobia suit dismissed without evidence of actual exposure to HIV in course of embalming remains of person with AIDS) *with* Johnson v. West Virginia Univ. Hosps., No. 19678, AIDS Litig. Rep. (Andrews) 7535 (W. Va. Nov. 21, 1991) (upholding $1.9 million award to hospital security guards bitten by HIV-infected patient) *and* Castro v. New York Life Ins. Co., No. 01941/90, AIDS Litig. Rep. (Andrews) 6816 (N.Y. Sup. Ct. July 29, 1991) (refusing to dismiss "AIDS phobia" suit by office building janitor stuck by needle in trash can) and *California Policeman Awarded $250,000 Over Blood Splash From HIV Corpse*, AIDS Litig. Rep. (Andrews) 4951 (1990) (police officer and wife recover for employer's failure to provide protective garments needed to protect policeman from blood splash during autopsy of HIV-infected corpse).

33 Rossi v. Estate of Almaraz, No. 90344028, 1991 WL 166924 (Md. Cir. Ct. May 23, 1991).

34 *Compare* Estate of Behringer v. Medical Ctr. at Princeton, 592 A.2d 1251 (N.J. Super. Ct. 1991) (patients should be informed of doctor's infection) *and In re* Application of Milton S. Hershey Med. Ctr., 595 A.2d 1290 (Pa. Super. Ct. 1991)(same) *with Burk*, 747 F. Supp. 285 (fear of HIV alone does not ground lawsuit) *and Rossi*, 1991 WL 166924

(being operated on by infected surgeon does not constitute "exposure").

35 *See, e.g.*, Wolgemuth v. Milton S. Hershey Med. Ctr., No. 2694-S-1991 (Pa. C.P. Jan. 30, 1992) (denying defendant's motion to dismiss suit by patients treated by HIV-infected obstetrical resident); *see also id.*, AIDS Litig. Rep. (Andrews) 6595 (1991) (complaint).

36 *See, e.g.*, Hill v. Miller, No. 90–5455, AIDS Litig. Rep. (Andrews) 5001 (Fla. Cir. Ct. filed Aug. 20, 1990) (alleging battery, negligence and fraud in sexual transmission case).

37 C.A.U. v. R.L., 438 N.W.2d 441 (Minn. Ct. App. 1989).

38 *Cf.* Christian v. Sheft, No. S022074, AIDS Litig. Rep. (Andrews) 6528 (Cal. Ct. App. Jun. 13, 1991) (upholding trial court's denial of discovery of names of Christian's other sex partners prior to his relationship with Hudson).

39 *See* Prosser & Keeton, note 2 above, § 54, at 361–65. *See generally* Note, *Tort Liability for the Transmission of the AIDS Virus: Damages for Fear of AIDS and Prospective AIDS*, 45 Wash. & Lee *Tort Liability for the Transmission of the AIDS Virus: Damages for Fear of AIDS and Prospective AIDS*, 45 Wash. & Lee L. Rev. 185 (1988).

40 Restatement (Second) of Torts § 463 (1965).

41 *See, e.g.*, Li v. Yellow Cab Co., 532 P.2d 1226 (Cal. 1975).

42 Prosser & Keeton, note 2 above, § 68, at 480.

43 Restatement (Second) of Torts §§ 496B, 496C (1965).

44 *See, e.g.*, Murry v. Ramada Inns, 521 So. 2d 1123 (La. 1988); Rutter v. Northeastern Beaver County Sch. Dist., 437 A.2d 1198 (Pa. 1981); McGrath v. American Cyanamid Co., 196 A.2d 238 (N.J. 1963).

45 *Infected Doctor and New York City Settle Before Deliberations,* AIDS Litig. Rep. (Andrews) 4147 (1990) (Prego v. City of New York); *see* Verhovek, *Infected Nurse Wins $5.4 Million from New York State in AIDS Suit,* N.Y.Times, July 15, 1992, at A1; Jose Doe v. Cedars Med. Ctr., No. 90–08190, AIDS Litig. Rep. (Andrews) 4190 (Fla. Cir. Ct. filed Feb. 8, 1990) (janitor claims infection contracted from needle carelessly discarded in patient's room); *see also* Hamley v. Becton Dickinson & Co., 886 F.2d 804 (6th Cir. 1989) (medical assistant infected with HIV entitled to jury determination of whether needle manufacturer should be strictly liable for failure to warn of danger of needle stick injuries). *But see* Burk v. Sage Prods., 747 F. Supp. 285 (E.D. Pa. 1990).

46 *See, e.g., New York Court Voids Nurse's Needle Stick Suit in Lieu of Workers' Comp,* AIDS Litig. Rep. (Andrews) 4609 (1990) (Peters v. New York City Health & Hosps. Corp., No. 22907–89 (N.Y. Sup. Ct. Mar. 29, 1990)).

47 *Patient of Florida Dentist Settles Suit Against Insurer,* AIDS Litig. Rep. (Andrews) 7689 (1992); *Driskill and Webb Settle, Leave $2 for Two Other Acer Patients,* AIDS Litig. Rep. (Andrews) 6830 (1991).

48 *See, e.g.,* Howell v. Spokane & Inland Empire Blood Bank, 117 Wash. 2d 619, 818 P. 2d 1056 (Wash. Oct. 31, 1991) (suit against infected donor dismissed because donor had no reason to know, in 1984, that he might be infected).

49 *See* Ray v. Cutter Labs., 744 F. Supp. 1124 (M.D. Fla. 1990) (judgment in defendants' favor because plaintiff unable to prove causation), *modified in part,* 754 F. Supp. 193 (M.D. Fla. 1991) (allowing plaintiffs to proceed on market share liability theory); Smith v. Cutter Biological, 60 U.S.L.W. 2399 (Haw. Nov. 29, 1991) (allowing plaintiffs to proceed on market share liability theory).

50 *See, e.g.,* Ariz. Rev. Stat. Ann. § 32–1481 (1974); McKee v. Cutter Labs., 866 F.2d 219 (6th Cir. 1989); Kozup v. Georgetown Univ., 663 F. Supp. 1048 (D.D.C. 1987), *aff'd in part and vacated in part,* 851 F.2d 437 (D.C. Cir. 1988); Doe v. Travenol Labs., 698 F. Supp. 780 (D. Minn. 1988); Gibson v. Methodist Hosp., No. 01–89–00645-CV, AIDS Litig. Rep. (Andrews) 7130, 7134–34 (Tex. Ct. App. Oct. 17, 1991); Ray v. Cutter Labs., 744 F. Supp. 1124 (M.D. Fla. 1990); Dale v. Irwin Memorial Blood Bank, No. 884160, AIDS Litig. Rep. (Andrews) 2760 (Cal. Super. Ct. S.F. County May 2, 1989); *see also* Hyland Therapeutics v. Superior Ct., 220 Cal. Rptr. 590 (Ct. App. 1985). *But see* Doe v. Miles Labs., 927 F.2d 187 (4th Cir. 1991) (under Maryland law, blood clotting factor concentrate is product but not an "unreasonably dangerous" product subject to strict liability). *See generally* Comment, *Hospital and Blood Bank Liability to Patients Who Contract AIDS through Blood Transfusions,* 23 San Diego L. Rev. 875 (1986); Annot., *Liability of Blood Supplier or Donor for Injury or Death Resulting from Blood Transfusion,* 24 A.L.R.4th 508 (1983 & Supp. 1991); Annotation, *Liability of Hospital, Physician or Other Individual Medical Practitioner for Injury or Death Resulting from Blood Transfusion,* 20 A.L.R.4th 136 (1983 & Supp. 1991); Comment, *Strict Liability for Blood Derivative Manufacturers: Statutory Shield Incompatible with Public Health Responsibilities,* 28 St. Louis U. L.J. 443 (1984).

51 Matthews & Neslund, *The Initial Impact of AIDS on Public Health Law in the United States–1983,* 257 J.A.M.A. 344, 346 (1986); Rabkin & Rabkin, *Individual and Institutional Liability for Transfusion Acquired Diseases,* 256 J.A.M.A. 2242, 2243 (1986); *see* Osborn v. Irwin Memorial Blood Bank, 5 Cal. App. 4th 234, *rev. denied,* 1992 Cal. LEXIS 3512 (July 9, 1992).

52 *See, e.g.,* Shelby v. St. Luke's Episcopal

Hosp., No. H–86–3780 (consolidated with No. H–87–901), slip. op. (S.D. Tex. Mar. 17, 1988); Valdiviez v. United States, 884 F.2d 196 (5th Cir. 1989); McKee v. Miles Labs., 675 F. Supp. 1060 (E.D. Ky. 1987), aff'd sub nom. McKee v. Cutter Labs., 866 F.2d 219 (6th Cir. 1989); Kozup v. Georgetown Univ., 663 F. Supp. 1048, 1051 (D.D.C. 1986), aff'd in part and vacated in part, 851 F.2d 437 (D.C. Cir. 1988); Kirkendall v. Harbor Ins. Co., 698 F. Supp. 768 (W.D. Ark. 1988), aff'd, 887 F.2d 857 (8th Cir. 1989); Doe v. American Red Cross Blood Serv., 377 S.E.2d 323 (S.C. 1989); Jackson v. Tarrant County Hosp. Dist., No. 48–95022–86, AIDS Litig. Rep. (Andrews) 4923 (Tex. Dist. Ct. Tarrant County July 9, 1990). For a strong criticism of applying the professional standard of care in these cases, see Quintana v. United Blood Servs., 811 P.2d 424 (Colo. App. 1991), aff'd, 827 P. 2d 509 (Colo. 1992).

53 *Ohio Common Pleas Court Rejects Retrial in Tainted Blood Case,* AIDS Litig. Rep. (Andrews) 4458 (May 11, 1990) (Jeanne v. Hawkes Hosp. of Mt. Carmel, No. 87–03–1669 (Ohio C.P.)) (infected plaintiff was infused with blood collected on first day test was available, but blood was not tested before transfusion; plaintiff awarded $12 million); *see, e.g.,* Sicuranza v. Northwest Florida Blood Ctr., No. 90–3130, AIDS Litig. Rep. (Andrews) 6729 (Fla. Dist. Ct. App. June 13, 1991) (allowing negligence claims to go forward against a blood bank for blood drawn in late 1986 and transfused in early 1987, which was allegedly not tested for HIV); *HIV-Infected Maine Man Reaches Settlement with Red Cross,* AIDS Litig. Rep. (Andrews) 3489 (Oct. 27, 1989) (Brown v. American Red Cross, No. 89–1244 (D. Md.)) (blood was donated one day before test became available, was not tested as it waited to be used, and transmitted HIV to patient). Moreover, even if a blood bank properly tested all donated blood, it conceivably could be found negligent for failing to screen out high-risk donors as well, in accordance with Food and Drug

Administration guidelines dating back to 1983. Once the principal means of protecting the blood supply, donor screening could be viewed by courts today as a prudent adjunct to antibody testing. *See generally* Office of Biologics, National Center for Drugs and Biologics, Food and Drug Administration, Recommendations to Decrease the Risk of Transmitting Acquired Immune Deficiency Syndrome (AIDS) from the Plasma Donors (1983); *Possible Transfusion-associated Acquired Immune Deficiency Syndrome (AIDS),* 31 MMWR 652 (1982); *Update on Acquired Immune Deficiency Syndrome (AIDS) Among Patients with Hemophilia A,* 31 MMWR 664 (1982).

54 *Prevention of Acquired Immune Deficiency Syndrome (AIDS): Report of Interagency Recommendations,* 32 MMWR 103 (1983).

55 *See, e.g., Texas Jury Awards Infected Widow $800,000 in Negligence Suit,* AIDS Litig. Rep. (Andrews) 6460 (1991) (Beeson v. Wadley, No. 89–04827-E (Tex. Dist. Ct.)); *Washington Blood Bank Denied Retrial After $1.8 Million Plaintiff Award,* AIDS Litig. Rep. (Andrews) 5619 (1991) (Doe v. Puget Sound Blood Ctr., No. 88–2–10861-7 (Wash. Super. Ct.)); *see also Private Agreement Announced in Suit Over Tainted '84 Transfusion,* AIDS Litig. Rep. (Andrews) 5845 (1991) (Crawford v. United Blood Servs., No. 98164 (Cal. Super. Ct.)) (woman infected in May 1984 transfusion sues blood bank, alleges it should have done surrogate testing; blood bank settles); *California Jury Awards $3 Million in Tainted-Transfusion Suit,* AIDS Litig. Rep. (Andrews) 5024 (1990) (Katz v. Children's Hosp., No. C683049 (Cal. Super. Ct.)) (family of child transfused with tainted blood in 1984, before availability of HIV test, sued Red Cross on theory that it should have used surrogate tests on blood supply; Red Cross settles despite argument that in 1984, standard of care did not include surrogate testing); Osborn v. Irwin Memorial Blood Bank, 5 Cal. App. 4th 234, *rev. denied,* 1992 Cal. LEXIS 3512 (July 9,

1992) (blood bank not negligent for employing HIV-screening procedures then in common use but which resulted in transfusion of HIV-contaminated blood). *But see* Okoro v. American Red Cross, No. 5325–87, AIDS Litig. Rep. (Andrews) 4007 (D.C. Super. Ct. Jan. 17, 1990) (vacating as moot a previous ruling that Red Cross may have been negligent in not using surrogate tests in July 1984; Red Cross had settled with family of infected child); *California Superior Court Jury Finds for Hospital in 1984 Transfusion Suit,* AIDS Litig. Rep. (Andrews) 5482 (1990) (Polikoff v. Regents of Univ. of Cal., No. 590154 (Cal. Super. Ct.)); Anonymous Blood Recipient v. William Beaumont Hosp., No. 89–3673705, AIDS Litig. Rep. (Andrews) 5942 (Mich. Cir. Ct. Feb. 7, 1991) (dismissing suit against blood bank for 1983 transfusion, where only two out of six thousand blood collectors were at the time doing surrogate testing); O'Rourke v. Irwin Mem. Blood Bank, No. A047081, AIDS Litig. Rep. (Andrews) 6413 (Cal. Ct. App. May 30, 1991).

56 *See, e.g., Kozup,* 851 F.2d 437 (dismissing all other claims, but remanding to trial court question whether hospital obtained parental consent before transfusing infant who later developed AIDS from HIV-tainted blood); *Illinois Family Sues over Son's "Medically Unnecessary" Transfusion,* AIDS Litig. Rep. (Andrews) 4082 (1990) (Doe v. Little Corp. of Mary Hosp., No. 90-L–1459 (Ill. Cir. Ct.)) (complaint alleges that physician unnecessarily and without consent performed transfusion on one of newborn twins, who later developed AIDS from HIV-tainted blood); *Arizona Blood Plaintiffs Settle for $6 Million of $28.7 Million Award,* AIDS Litig. Rep. (Andrews) 4951 (1990) (Edwards v. Kuruvilla, No. CV–87–35695 (Ariz. Super. Ct.)) (physician diluted red blood cells with HIV-infected plasma and injected mixture into infant without parental consent; post-verdict settlement for $6 million); Ashcraft v. King, 278 Cal. Rptr. 900 (Ct. App. 1991) (battery claim valid against physician who transferred non-family HIV-positive blood to patient despite

her insistence that she receive only family-donated blood).

57 *California Jury Awards $3 Million in Tainted Transfusion Suit,* AIDS Litig. Rep. (Andrews) 5024 (1990) (Katz v. Children's Hosp. of L.A., No. C683049 (Cal. Super. Ct.)); *see also* Valdiviez v. United States, 884 F.2d 196 (5th Cir. 1989) (jury question whether, given information, plaintiff would have had transfusion); *New Jersey Woman Files $10 Million Suit over Infection by Husband,* AIDS Litig. Rep. (Andrews) 7201 (1991) (Jones v. Frader, No. 91-CV–6790 (E.D. Pa.)) (alleging that doctor and hospital transfused plaintiff's husband in 1986 without either obtaining his consent or informing him that procedure could be done without transfused blood; plaintiff later allegedly was infected through intercourse).

58 Gibson v. Methodist Hosp., No. 01–89–00645-CV, AIDS Litig. Rep. (Andrews) 7130, 7134 (Tex. Ct. App. Oct. 17, 1991).

59 Gaffney v. United States, No. CIV. A. 88–1457, 1990 WL 57625 (D. Mass. Apr. 26, 1990); *id.,* No. Civ. A. 88–147, 1990 WL 167492 (D. Mass. Oct. 26, 1990); *see, e.g., Chicago Couple Awarded $2.4 Million for Husband's HIV Contraction,* AIDS Litig. Rep. (Andrews) 4742 (1990) (Doe v. Massaysay, No. 85-L–13319 (Ill. Cir. Ct.)) (jury awards damages to patient who contracted HIV through transfusions made necessary by doctor-caused pancreatitis); Doe v. United States, No. 86–0179-T, AIDS Litig. Rep. (Andrews) 4554 (D.R.I. May 9, 1990) (awarding $1 million to family of boy infected with HIV after transfusions necessitated by misperformed tonsillectomy).

60 *See, e.g.,* Chester v. United States, 403 F. Supp. 458 (W.D. Pa. 1975) (physician's negligence in failure to order cancer tests permitted metastasis and death), *aff'd,* 546 F.2d 415 (3d Cir. 1976); Trapp v. Metz, 271 N.E.2d 697 (N.Y. 1971) (negligent diagnosis caused two-year delay in surgery for cancer); Kaplan v. Haines, 232 A.2d 840 (N.J. Super. Ct. 1967) (alleged erroneous diagnosis of spinal problem resulted in unnecessary operation), *aff'd*, 241 A.2d 235 (N.J. 1968); Willard v. Hutson, 378 P.2d 966 (Or. 1963) (misdiagnosis caused erroneous treatment of child known to be suffering from hemophilia).

61 *See, e.g.*, MacMahon v. Nelson, 568 P.2d 90 (Colo. App. 1977) (emotional distress of cancer victim upon learning that removal of growth had been delayed for eight months due to misdiagnosis actionable).

62 *See* DiMarco v. Lynch Homes, 583 A.2d 422 (Pa. 1990) (physician owes a duty of care to third parties to provide correct information to patient exposed to communicable disease); *see also* McIlwain v. Prince William Hosp., 774 F. Supp. 986, 991 n.6 (E.D. Va. 1991) (wife allegedly infected with HIV after prison doctor failed to inform husband of positive test results could have cause of action under civil rights law); *cf.* Funeral Servs. by Gregory v. Bluefield Community Hosp., No. 19778, 1991 W. Va. LEXIS 217 at *8–10 (Dec. 5, 1991) (mortician's battery suit dismissed for failure to allege that hospital, which hired him to embalm HIV-positive corpse, intended to cause him injury).

63 *See, e.g.*, *San Francisco Man Awarded $202,800 for False ARC Diagnosis*, AIDS Litig. Rep. (Andrews) 6518 (1991) (Welenken v. Smith Kline Bio-Science Labs., No. 881107 (Cal. Super. Ct.)); *see also Punitive Damages Will Be Unavailable in California False-Positive Suit*, AIDS Litig. Rep. (Andrews) 4955 (1990) (Brogan v. Kimberly Servs., No. 893414 (Cal. Super Ct.)) (plain-

tiff allowed to pursue compensatory damages claims); Hayes v. Humana, No. A300868, AIDS Litig. Rep. (Andrews) 7180 (Nev. Dist. Ct. filed Oct. 9, 1991) (hospital allegedly negligent for plaintiff's false positive HIV test as well as for treating plaintiff unnecessarily with AZT); Kraus v. Spielberg, 236 N.Y.S.2d 143 (Sup. Ct. 1962) (doctor liable for misinforming patient that she had tuberculosis, thus causing her to develop "tuberculosis phobia"). On fear of HIV among the uninfected, see *AIDS Anxiety in the "Worried Well,"* in Psychiatric Implications of Acquired Immune Deficiency Syndrome 49–60 (S. Nichols & D. Ostrow eds. 1984).

64 *See* Beadling v. Sirotta, 176 A.2d 546 (N.J. Super. Ct. 1961) (plaintiff denied employment because his preemployment physical examination produced a diagnosis of active tuberculosis brought successful malpractice suit after other tests established that he had never had tuberculosis).

65 *See, e.g.*, Dowling v. Mutual Life Ins. Co., 168 So. 2d 107 (La. App. 1964) (liability for failure to notify plaintiff that he had tuberculosis), *writ refused*, 170 So. 2d 508 (La. 1965); Hoover v. Williamson, 203 A.2d 861 (Md. 1964) (failure to notify patient that he had silicosis).

66 James v. United States, 483 F. Supp. 581 (N.D. Cal. 1980); *cf.* McIlwain v. Prince William Hosp., 774 F. Supp. 986 (E.D. Va. 1991) (prison physician may be liable under civil rights law for failure to notify inmate of positive test result).

V   HIV in the Health Care and Insurance Systems

16 Physicians versus Lawyers: A Conflict of Cultures

Daniel M. Fox

The HIV epidemic raises problems of public health policy that should require physicians and lawyers to work together as never before. They should collaborate, for example, in safeguarding the rights of people with HIV infection and AIDS while protecting the broader interests of society. They should also collaborate in proposing policies that are consistent with the best scientific knowledge and current due process protections.

During the first decade of the epidemic, physicians and lawyers have collaborated to what seems to be, in a broad historical view, an unprecedented extent. They have also fought with and talked past each other, as they have been doing for at least two centuries. Moreover, recent controversy about the obligations of infected health care workers to their patients has created new grounds for estrangement between physicians and lawyers.[1]

If we are to move in the direction of cooperation rather than conflict, we must understand the roots of the antagonism between these professions and the contemporary forces that threaten to deepen it. But understanding history, I caution, hardly ever has practical consequences.

I observed the antagonism of physicians toward lawyers during fourteen years as a faculty member and senior manager of an academic health center—a teaching hospital and five professional schools—that is a unit of a large state university. This experience no doubt provided a limited view of both professions. The lawyers I observed were either public employees or private counsel retained to assist them. The physicians were clinicians and scientists who were full-time faculty members at a medical school. I also observed physicians and lawyers concerned about AIDS while doing research on issues of public policy raised by the disease and coediting a special issue of a journal addressing the public context of the epidemic.

In this chapter, the relationship between physicians and lawyers is oversimplified in order to examine the conflict between them. In particular, physicians' antagonism to lawyers is emphasized more than lawyers' role in the conflict, in part because I have little first-hand knowledge of lawyers' unguarded opinions about physicians. But it is also because experience suggests that most lawyers are not normally antagonistic toward physicians, the negligence bar aside. Many physicians, however, strongly believe they are frequently taken advantage of by lawyers who do not understand medicine or value it properly. They are, moreover, mortified because the conflict is usually displayed in public settings controlled by lawyers—court proceedings and legislative hearings.

Not all physicians fall within the terms of this analysis, however. Some of them enjoy a role analogous to that of barracks or jailhouse lawyers. A few even study the law and enjoy legal reasoning. Others relish it: I know an eminent physician, for example, who is fond of quoting in his administrative and political activities aphorisms about the law he learned from his late father.

The conflict between physicians and lawyers, though it is rooted in the modern history of the two professions, has become more intense in recent years as the authority most people accord physicians has diminished. Some physicians accuse lawyers of helping to undermine public confidence in them by mindlessly pursuing malpractice litigation. Many attribute their rising premiums for malpractice insurance to the work of greedy and unscrupulous lawyers. Others assert that so-called defensive medicine, ordering marginally useful tests and therapies to avoid being sued, has helped to increase the cost of medical care. Physicians often blame lawyers for the mass of regulations that burden and, they say, often demean them. In an astonishing display of professional bigotry, the president of the Association of American Medical Colleges told a medical school graduating class in 1986, ''We're swimming in shark-infested waters where the sharks are lawyers.''[2]

Events during the HIV epidemic have reinforced physicians' irritation with lawyers. Many physicians were offended that decisions about whether particular children with HIV infection or AIDS could attend school were made by judges after argument by lawyers. They were dismayed when an official of the U.S. Department of Justice issued a ruling about discrimination against people with AIDS in the workplace that ignored medical opinion. They raged in 1991 when Congress considered passing a law that would have inflicted criminal penalties on health professionals who infected their patients with HIV. Even though physicians disagree among themselves about precisely who is at what risk of infection, many of them condemn lawyers who argue on behalf of their clients that any conceivable risk is intolerable. (But some of them also have been distressed by lawyers who argue that small risks do not justify mandating the testing of either patients or health workers.)

To some extent these complaints by physicians are part of their routine cursing of politicians and even public health officials who debate laws or issue regulations that, in their view, interfere with the practice of medicine. Some physicians, that is, regard most of the regulations issued by public agencies and third-party payers as interference with medical autonomy.

Physicians are, in contrast, often grateful to the lawyers who defend them against lay intruders into the practice of medicine. For instance, no one complained about the lawyers who defended the State University of New York, my employer at the time, against the Right-to-Life movement and the federal government in the Baby Jane Doe case in 1983 and 1984. Occasionally, however, physician colleagues would recall, in vexed tones, that lawyers had caused the problem in the first place— notably several free-lance Right-to-Life activists and the attorneys who advised the Department of Health and Human Services (HHS) that Section 504 of the Rehabilitation Act of 1973 applied to newborns with disabling conditions.

The antagonism many physicians feel toward lawyers is the result of fundamental disagreement about five issues: the nature of authority; how conflict should be resolved; the relative importance of procedure and substance; the nature and significance of risk; and the legitimacy of politics as a method of solving problems. This disagreement began in the early nineteenth century, when physicians and lawyers began to make very different assumptions about the sources of useful knowledge and the nature of authority. Until then, elite lawyers, physicians, and clergy shared knowledge and values derived from a common education in classical languages and history and in moral and natural philosophy. As knowledge became more specialized in the nineteenth century, the basis of physicians' expertise became the experimental sciences that had emerged from *natural* philosophy: anatomy, biochemistry, microbiology, pharmacology, physiology, and experimental pathology. Lawyers, in contrast, derived their expertise from the disciplines that emerged from the old *moral* philosophy—notably history, philosophy, economics, and politics—as well as from the traditions of the law itself.[3]

This difference in the sources of knowledge of the two professions became, by the middle of the nineteenth century, the basis of divergent views of authority. Lawyers held that authority derived from the law and its institutions; that is, from texts and how opposing counsel and judges interpreted them. Authority, like knowledge, was, for lawyers, as cumulative and contingent on the interplay of people and events as it was constrained by logic, precedent, and values. Lawyers *made* law, as litigators, judges, and legislators. The law was what lawyers, following the rules of their profession and conscious of the dominant values of their society, said it was.

Physicians, on the other hand, derived authority from their command of increasingly effective technologies for diagnosis and treatment that were based on science. Unlike lawyers, who made law, scientists *discovered* the laws that, they presumed, governed nature. To most scientists, arguments about the relations between laws of nature and social arrangements interfered with experiment and observation. For them, the persistence of adherence to discredited science was an impediment to progress. Although some aspects of physicians' clinical acumen were cumulative, their command of science and the technology derived from it was the antithesis of reliance on precedent. Authority reposed in individual physicians, when they were armed with the latest knowledge, and not in precedent or in institutions.

Lawyers were, moreover, officers of the court. Their public obligations as officers of the court took precedence over their autonomy as members of a self-governing profession. In sharp contrast, Anglo-American physicians were formally aloof from hospitals, which became the dominant institutions within which they practiced by the early twentieth century. Lay trustees accorded them the privilege of practicing in hospitals.

These contrasting views of authority have persisted to the present. Where lawyers value cumulative knowledge and textual analysis, physicians embrace the latest knowledge and experimental or at least statistical methods of proof. Where physicians have remained privileged practitioners in institutions they dominate but do not govern, lawyers have been agents of the public institutions that administer justice.

To most physicians, moreover, adversarial proceedings are an ineffective and irrational method for resolving conflict. Where Anglo-American lawyers presume that a person accused of a crime is innocent until proven guilty in a court of law, physicians believe it is dangerous to make any presumptions before examining evidence. Similarly, most physicians do not understand the history or the logic of lawyers' claim that formalized conflict between plaintiffs and defendants in a courtroom or around a table resolves disagreements with reasonable equity and preserves social peace. To physicians, the claim that lay jurors can find fact is aberrant nonsense.

Physicians are trained to rely on two methods for resolving conflicts about data and their interpretation that are very different from adversarial proceedings. The first method is the assertion of authority from the top of a hierarchy in which power is, in theory, derived from knowledge. The second method is peer review—discussion to consensus among experts of roughly equal standing and attainment. Both methods, the hierarchical and the consensual, rest on the assumption that truth is best determined by experts.

Hierarchical authority characterizes medical education, clinical decision-making in teaching hospitals, and the presumed relationship between authors of papers in the most prestigious journals and their readers. A principal goal of medical education is to inculcate lifelong habits of deference to hierarchically superior knowledge and experience. Most academic physicians, by contrast, use consensus to resolve conflicts about scientific findings and the appropriateness of particular methods of diagnosis and treatment. Moreover, outside academic medicine, consensus is more important than deference to authority. According to many studies, for example, physicians' decisions about the indications for particular surgical procedures and appropriate lengths of hospital stays can vary widely from one geographic area to another.[4]

Courtroom procedure violates what most physicians believe about how conflicts ought to be resolved. The role of juries particularly appalls them. It is difficult for anyone trained in medicine to comprehend how people without explicit training and substantive expertise can determine guilt or innocence, fault or liability—especially when a professional is accused of negligence. Physicians are also bewildered by the behavior of judges. They are amazed that the person with the authority to interpret the law asks questions of witnesses and makes comments that sometimes seem to reveal personal opinions, and they are confused when apparently personal opinions (say, irritation with a lawyer or a witness) and the result do not match. In addition, the notion that one set of rules governs the character and admissibility of evidence and another the interpretation of law is foreign to people who are unfamiliar with legal institutions.

Least comprehensible of all to physicians is the role of counsel. Most physicians do not believe that people's interests (except perhaps their own) can be served by making the best possible legal case on their behalf. Like lawyers, physicians have a privileged, confidential relationship with the people who engage their services. Unlike lawyers, however, they diagnose and treat, rather than defend, these people, whom they call patients. Most physicians dislike the use of the word *client* by lawyers or social workers, or by some nurse practitioners, because it connotes advocacy rather than an obligation to act honorably. Many physicians assert that lawyers are often too willing to distort evidence, or just take it out of context, to make the best case for their clients. Moreover, they accuse lawyers of being too willing to meddle in physicians' areas of expertise for the sake of a fee.

I have observed this aspect of conflict between physicians and lawyers whenever allegations are made of cheating by medical students or of erratic or unethical behavior by physicians. Those who are accused almost always retain a lawyer, which incenses the members of the faculty or the medical staff of the hospital who are obligated to address the incident. To them, peer review is the proper way to determine facts and remedy errors. Moreover, the only really justifiable remedies are, they believe, either exoneration, expulsion from the institution, or medical treatment. The concept of a settlement violates their values. As one of my medical colleagues once said with disgust, "This is not a legal case; it is the case of an impaired physician."

Efforts to explain the purpose of adversarial proceedings to physicians rarely succeed. Yet physicians are no more ignorant of the law than most other Americans. They may even know more about legal institutions than most people as a result of their general education and personal experience. Like most nonlawyers, however, they do not truly comprehend what the rules of evidence are meant to accomplish. Nor do physicians understand the role of such central legal ideas as precedent, procedure, and legislative intent.

The convention that law, like history, is written in words rather than in unfamiliar symbols or diagrams sometimes creates an illusion of communicability, even though the law is just as difficult for outsiders to comprehend as medical science. That is because the words—the letter of the law—represent only a segment of what lawyers mean by "the law." The words derive much of their meaning from such considerations as what those who enacted the provision, choosing a particular set of words, meant to convey; what they were seeking to accomplish; the presence or absence of conflicting goals that need to be harmonized; how the words to be interpreted fit within the overall structure of the enactment; lessons drawn from earlier attempts to interpret the same or similar language used in the same or a similar context; the doctrinal consequences that flow from each plausible interpretation; the practical consequences; the existence or nonexistence of stable business or social arrangements based on a particular interpretation; and the imperatives of the institutions through which the law operates.

Even more incomprehensible to physicians than the vagaries of textual interpretation is the fact that law, lawyers, and legal institutions are as committed to employing the right process as to arriving at the right outcome. Lawyers' attachment to procedure, sometimes to the seeming detriment of substance, is the third issue that fundamentally divides the medical and legal professions.

Physicians find it difficult to appreciate, even after detailed explanation, why a case has been dismissed because a defendant's rights were violated or why a verdict was overturned because of a violation of procedural rules. Physicians value results over process—or, more accurately, over any processes other than those used by the medical profession. Examples of processes that are highly valued by physicians include the rituals of clinical education and training. Until recently, however, most physicians believed that the proper process almost always led to the optimal outcome. Thus outcome was what really mattered.

Even physicians who are admirably attentive to their patients as people are often irritated by fervent advocates of patients' rights. For many of them the central question is not whether a patient's autonomy is respected but whether the best possible medical care is provided. Due process is, at best, a vague memory from high school about the Fourteenth Amendment to the Constitution. Physicians usually associate the phrase "due process" with legal interference in matters of medical judgment: with, for instance, cases in which consent must be obtained for blood transfusions for minor children of Jehovah's Witnesses or for surgery on long-term patients in state mental hospitals.

Equally incomprehensible to physicians is the approach lawyers sometimes take to risk assessment. Physicians often contrast their own sophisticated view of risk with what they consider the simplistic notions of lawyers. For physicians, risk is inherent in every activity, including every medical procedure. Their primary concern is relative risk; that is, the balancing of risk and benefit in the best interests of patients or (in environmental cases) of people who come into contact with toxic substances. Physicians have often accused lawyers—who, they insist, should know better—of advocating, on behalf of clients, concepts of risk held by the most frightened or uneducated members of the lay public. Just as physicians generally uphold the law, many of them argue, lawyers have an obligation to insist that because risks are inherent in life they must always be compared to other risks, not to the impossible ideal of certainty.

There are, of course, competing views of risk within medicine. Some medical experts endorse an epidemiological view of risk, others one that is based on the assumptions of laboratory medicine, still others one that is grounded in clinical experience. The epidemiological view has become familiar in many court cases and legislative committee hearings during the HIV epidemic: a low level of risk is not sufficient cause to exclude a child from school, or a physician from practice. Indeed children on the way to school (or patients to a medical encounter) have a greater risk of accidents than of infection with HIV after they arrive at their destination. Many laboratory scientists testify to a different view: a risk that has not been ruled out by scientific analysis cannot be dismissed; whatever is not impossible, that is, should be considered possible. The views of most clinicians fall in between: patients should guard against any demonstrated risk (though many have recently made an exception for risks from infected physicians).

Physicians and lawyers have different views about conflicts between their personal anxieties and professional opinions about risk. Physicians are troubled by such conflicts. For example, after the New York City trial to determine whether a child with HIV infection should attend school, two medical witnesses for the city told reporters that, as parents, they would worry about sending their children to a classroom attended by a child with HIV infection. Lawyers regard their role as advocates as separate from their personal opinions. For instance, counsel for the plaintiffs in the same trial cheerfully admitted to a conference of mostly appalled health professionals that he did not know which definition of risk he personally supported.

Lawyers' personal opinions about risk may be influential in settings where the lawyers do not represent clients in litigation—when, for example, they work in regulatory agencies or legislatures, or when they are advocates for interest groups whose views they share. In 1991, for instance, most civil rights lawyers argued against federal guidelines or legislation that would require health workers to be tested for HIV and to disclose positive status to patients. As one of them told me, he "oppose[s] restrictive policies on a cost benefit basis alone"; that is, the high probability of non-infection is more important than the rare chance of infection.[5] Such lawyers appropriated scientific analysis to serve the individual members of the groups of people on whose behalf they were advocating. As one of them wrote, justifying voluntary reporting of HIV-positive status to employers and patients, policy should draw a "rational line before an irrational line is imposed by the courts and/or public opinion."[6]

Lawyers representing hospitals, in contrast, used probabilistic reasoning to reach a different conclusion. Since any risk of HIV transmission from a physician or hospital employee to a patient could be an occasion for a lawsuit, mandatory testing and disclosure would limit the potential liability of their institutional clients.

The controversy about the testing of health workers and disclosure of HIV-positive status also made plain that physicians, like many other people, can rationalize away the implications of their expert knowledge when their self-interest is at stake. Thus some physicians advocated mandatory testing of all or some patients, despite the probabilities, while others defended their right to decide as professionals when they themselves should be tested and what to disclose to patients, despite evidence of the ineffectiveness of self-policing.

It is tempting to explain as ideologically motivated or self-interested such behavior by physicians and lawyers. But that is outside the scope of this chapter, which is about professional perceptions and roles, not about human nature.

The final area of profound disagreement between physicians and lawyers is the purpose and uses of politics. For lawyers, politics is a normal and essential aspect of professional life. Most physicians, in contrast, regard politics as intrusive, a distraction from more important matters. Lawyers write or seek to influence laws and regulations as an extension of their other professional roles. Most physicians consider these activities to be so distasteful that, when they are unavoidably caught up in them, they behave petulantly. Even virtuosi of medical politics often claim to be apolitical.

Most physicians I have encountered are actually ambivalent about politics. On the one hand, they regard political activities as wasteful and undignified. On the other, they use politics, often successfully, to press their collective interests. This ambivalence has made them difficult allies in most of the public debates about health policy in this country. There is no reason to expect most of them to behave differently in issues relating to HIV infection and AIDS, even if what is at stake is protecting their patients' rights to jobs, insurance, or housing.

The AIDS epidemic has to date reinforced physicians' antagonism to lawyers, because it is rooted in fundamentally different assumptions about knowledge and authority. Antagonism has been reinforced by countless anecdotes and sour jokes and often by personal experience. Most physicians will probably continue to growl and grumble about lawyers while they rely on them for defense against intrusions into medical practice.

But there is also evidence during this epidemic that some physicians and some lawyers have devised a different relationship. An unusual number of physicians have been working collegially with lawyers. Physicians who treat substantial numbers of people with AIDS occasionally say they are impressed by lawyers' efforts to keep them in school or at work and to protect their entitlement to employee benefits and public funds. Many physicians understand that, for most of the last decade, AIDS was the only epidemic in this century in which lawyers could do as much for patients as doctors, and often considerably more until the end stages of the disease.

Another reason for collaboration—and one that emphasizes the central argument of this essay—is that many of the physicians who are deeply involved in the AIDS epidemic were not particularly hostile to lawyers in the past. In order to describe the dominant medical attitude of antagonism to lawyers, the attitudes of the medical profession have been necessarily oversimplified. However, within medicine there have always been people who understood perfectly well the purposes and practices of lawyers. Many of these physicians have been, in some significant way, marginal within medicine. These marginal physicians include those who have chosen careers in public health but also clinicians who pride themselves on being liberally educated intellectuals and, of course, those who are openly gay. Sadly, the collaboration of these physicians with lawyers on issues raised by the HIV epidemic will most likely increase their marginality.

For most physicians, encounters with lawyers remain occasions for impatience or anger. Individuals and their rights continue to be more important to most lawyers than the distribution of unfortunate events in populations. Physicians continue to express their dedication to their individual patients almost entirely within the context of biological and epidemiological science.

There are few signs of change. Only a few lawyers regard good science as a guide to the making of good law in the broad area of public health. Even fewer physicians regard good law as essential for regulating the medical encounter in the interests of patients, physicians and society. The numbers of scientifically sensitive lawyers and legally aware physicians may increase; but to predict an increase would, in 1992, be wishful thinking.

NOTES

1 For examples of collaboration and misunderstanding, *see* Gostin, *The AIDS Litigation Project: A National Review of Court and Human Rights Commission Decisions on Discrimination*, in AIDS: The Making of a Chronic Disease (E. Fee & D. Fox eds. 1992).

2 *196 New Doctors Are Told of Problems Awaiting Solutions*, N.Y. Times, June 3, 1986, at A2 (quoting Dr. Robert G. Petersdorf).

3 For sources about the impact of the divergence between natural and moral philosophy on medicine and the social sciences, *see* D. Fox, Economists and Health Care (1979).

4 For physicians' views of hierarchy and peers and their relationship to public policy, *see* D. Fox, Health Policies, Health Politics: The Experience of Britain and America, 1911–1965 (1986). For small area variation in medical practice, *see, e.g.*, Wennberg, *Unwanted Variations in the Rules of Practice*, 265 J.A.M.A. 1306 (1991); Wennberg, *The Paradox of Appropriate Care*, 258 J.A.M.A. 2568 (1987).

5 Personal communication, Professor Scott Burris (August 21, 1991).

6 Gostin, *The HIV-Infected Health Care Professional: Public Policy, Discrimination, and Patient Safety*, 18 L. Med. & Health Care 303, 308 (1990).

17 Patients and Health Care Workers

Troyen A. Brennan, M.D.

As the human immunodeficiency virus (HIV) epidemic enters its second decade, it has begun to create tensions within the relationship between health care workers and patients. These tensions center on the transmission of the virus: from the patient to other patients; from the patient to the health care provider; and from the health care provider to the patient. This chapter traces the manner in which each of these vectors, or paths of transmission, generates regulation and litigation and also addresses ways in which both statutory and common law can prevent or minimize such vectors and the irrational fears that accompany them.

At the beginning of the epidemic, there was little attention paid to occupational infection with HIV, likely because the risk of such transmission was thought to be nearly zero.[1] In the summer of 1987, however, the Centers for Disease Control (CDC) reported three cases of HIV infection in health care workers who were splashed with HIV-seropositive blood.[2] Since that time, concern has grown with the appearance of more cases, more highly publicized lawsuits, and the increasing number of HIV-positive patients.[3]

Although there is great variation in the prevalence of HIV at various hospitals in the United States, the highest rates approach 10 percent.[4] Thus, in many institutions in the United States, health care workers regularly come into contact with large numbers of HIV-infected patients. The risk of acquiring HIV from patients is a function of several factors, including the nature of the exposure (for example, blood splash or needle stick); the likelihood that the patient is infected and, if so, the level of virus in the patient's blood; and the efficiency of the virus in infecting an exposed person. The risk of infection from a stick with a hollow needle carrying the blood of a patient in the advanced stages of HIV disease has been quantified at between 0.3 and 0.4 percent, but such estimates are based on limited, retrospective data and are not generalizable to other sorts of exposures. Whatever the precise level of the risk, the possibility of transmission is real and accumulates as exposures continue over the course of a medical career. One study estimated that surgical personnel at San Francisco General Hospital, where the prevalence of infected patients is quite high, faced a cumulative risk of 0.125 per year, or one infection among the staff every eight years.[5]

There is little that a health care provider can do to influence the biological transmissibility of the virus, although the use of AZT after exposures to prevent seroconversion has been tried for several years.[6] Practitioners can try to avoid treating people with HIV, but, as I will discuss, this is legally, ethically, and practically problematic. Thus, efforts to control occupational transmission of HIV have increasingly focused on reducing exposure to patient blood.

Occupational exposure to patient blood is common. Pioneering studies observing medical professionals at work indicate that surgical personnel are cut or stuck with a sharp instrument in 1.7 to about 5 percent of operations. Their skin or mucous membranes are exposed to patient blood in up to one-third of procedures.[7] The degree of exposure is as variable as the kinds of surgery and the individual technique of surgeons and their teams. Important factors heightening the risk of exposure include the length of the operation (more than one hour), patient blood loss exceeding 250–300 milliliters, and procedures involving burns, orthopedic surgery, and trauma.[8] Thus, all health care workers do not face the same level of risk, and even people performing the same tasks may perform them at significantly different levels of safety.

The same studies suggest that the majority of exposures of all kinds are preventable, through barrier precautions and changes in technique. (There is, by the way, no evidence that screening patients for HIV would enhance worker safety.[9]) Skin and mucous membrane exposures from blood-soaked garments or splashes on unprotected parts of the body are, for example, far more common than necessary. Indeed, one review of the studies estimated that 93 percent of exposures could be prevented by the use of such barrier precautions as face masks, a second pair of gloves, shoe covers or rubber boots, and gowns or aprons that are impermeable to blood.[10]

The increased focus on surgical technique has also produced recommendations for safer surgical methods and equipment. Several studies have found that the surgeon's nondominant hand, used in many procedures to hold back tissue or guide a sharp instrument, is particularly at risk to be cut. Adjustments in technique have been suggested to avoid exposure-prone uses, as has the provision of extra protective equipment, such as a thimble to protect the index finger. Such specific suggestions arise from the growing recognition that risks of injury depend very much on the particular procedure being performed.[11]

In both its extent and importance, the development of safer medical practices has been analogized to the introduction of antiseptic practices to medicine in the nineteenth century.[12] Much more research into the specific mechanisms of exposure in various sorts of activity, and considerable education for practitioners, will be required to successfully systematize so ambitious a norm of behavior. But even full compliance with safer techniques would not prevent all exposures, and, in some percentage of those exposures, transmission of HIV.[13] Occupational transmission of HIV is, and will remain, a reality, both physiologically and psychologically, for health care workers.

Although the risk of transmission is still thought to be exceedingly low, the fact of occupational transmission haunts health care workers, particularly in high-prevalence hospitals.[14] A sense of disquiet is becoming especially pronounced in residency training programs, where younger, relatively less experienced physicians are in much more frequent intimate contact with patients' body fluids.[15] The demands for greater efforts to curb occupational exposure[16] and to provide emotional and financial support for resident physicians (the so-called house staff) and other health care workers caring for people with AIDS[17] represent a rational commitment to avoiding accidents and defraying their costs without obstructing care to those who need it.

The reactions of many other health care workers has not been so rational or humane. Even though most physicians recognize a duty to treat HIV-infected patients, it is not clear that this translates into a willingness to care for such patients.[18] Some astute observers have noted profound changes in physicians' attitudes toward patients, and attribute these to fear of transmission.[19] In light of this, the leading medical journals frequently remind doctors and other health care workers of the need for compassion, especially to people living with AIDS.[20] Nonetheless, there appears to be a growing number of decidedly mean-spirited refusals to care for sick HIV-infected patients. For instance, a high proportion of surgeons advocate testing and then curtailment of surgery for those infected with HIV.[21] Few dentists will care for AIDS patients.[22] Such actions unfairly leave the burden of caring for HIV-infected patients on a subset of health care providers, and can inhumanely limit care for HIV-infected patients.

The story of transmission in the other direction—from health care worker to patient—is at an earlier stage. As of this writing, the only documented instances of such transmission involve a cluster of patients who appear to have been infected during their treatment by an HIV-positive dentist. Although speculation about the mechanism of transmission ranges from accidental lapses in infection control to deliberate injection, epidemiologists have been unable to discover how the five patients acquired HIV.[23] "Look-back" studies of thousands of past patients of surgeons and other providers with HIV or AIDS have found no similar cases of transmission.[24]

In theory, patients can be infected by providers in the same ways that providers can be infected by patients. In practice, however, the risks are not at all symmetrical. A patient stands virtually no chance of being splashed with large amounts of a provider's blood. A provider who is cut will spill far less blood than a patient undergoing invasive surgery, and a provider who feels a cut may step away from the patient before any blood is spilled. There is never an occasion to use a needle on a patient after it has pricked a provider. It follows that the risk of transmission from provider to patient is thought to be much lower than the risk a patient poses to a provider. The CDC has estimated the probability of transmission from surgeon to patient through a cut or stick at between 1 in 41,667 and 1 in 416,667. Other commentators have offered a "best estimate" of one chance of infection per 83,000 hours of surgery.[25]

The development of a policy response to the risk posed by infected health care workers has had much less to do with the numerical likelihood of transmission than with its exceptional unacceptablity. The public's over-estimation of the likelihood of being infected by a health care provider may be better understood as a belief that any risk is too high. The lay view has been shared by several leading medical organizations. The American Medical Association, for example, has taken the position that doctors with HIV "have an ethical obligation not to engage in any professional practice which has an identifiable risk of transmission," regardless of how low.[26] The fear of transmission in the health care setting is creating suspicions on both sides of the doctor-patient relationship, making occupational transmission of HIV an ever more complicated social problem.

To organize a discussion of legal issues raised in this chapter, I will use the paradigm of the natural history of the care provider-patient relationship: from the initiation of treatment, to the period in which therapy is underway, to the problems that can arise after occupational transmission of the virus has occurred, and finally to the end of the relationship. The kinds of legal problems that occur will depend, to a certain extent, on whether or not the patient or the health care worker is known to be infected with HIV at the time the relationship begins. If HIV status is unknown, concerns about testing usually dominate, since everyone is a potential carrier. When one party is known to carry HIV, legal issues center on fear of transmission.

At each stage of the discussion, I will examine the rights and obligations of each party to the other. Throughout I will assume that both patients and health care workers are bearers of rights that are protected by the law. Some might argue this is inappropriate, in that medical ethics should produce virtuous behavior regardless of whether "the law" commands it. I have proposed elsewhere that such reliance on professional conduct is misplaced, and that medical ethics and the law of the liberal state have complementary roles.[27] Moreover, even those who believe that professional ethics should be the sole answer to professional conduct in the HIV epidemic must realize there are many health care workers who are not subject to a well-developed ethical code. While doctors and nurses are members of professions that have traditions of ethical behavior, other health care workers such as orderlies, transport personnel, maintenance people, and a variety of others, do not envision special moral duties in their work and yet are at risk for accidents that could lead to HIV transmission. Thus, in this chapter, I will leave ethics aside and discuss the law.

PROBLEMS IN INITIATING TREATMENT

The HIV-Infected Patient or Provider

One of the problems we now face as part of the HIV epidemic is the fear that health care workers will refuse to treat patients who are infected.[28] This would not be so important if there were a thoroughgoing right to health care in our country. Unfortunately, there is not. The doctor-patient relationship has traditionally centered on notions of contract.[29] The common law allowed physicians to refuse care for patients who were not acutely ill. In addition, health care workers have always been allowed to limit their care to particular kinds of medical problems, or to particular subspecialties.[30]

However, many AIDS advocates recognized early on that HIV-positive patients might be subject to discrimination by health care workers who would wish to avoid the social issues that arise in the context of care for such patients. Fear of occupational transmission from patients was seen as another reason physicians in particular might try to avoid caring for HIV-infected people. In light of these concerns, several states have promulgated regulations prohibiting health care workers' discrimination against HIV-positive patients. For example, the state of Washington specifically defines HIV-positive people as handicapped, and therefore protected by the general antidiscrimination statute. More important, facilities offering medical care are defined as places of accommodation, increasing the breadth of the antidiscrimination statute.[31] Maine, Vermont, and West Virginia also specifically prohibit discrimination by health care workers.[32] Missouri has prohibitions that are specific to health maintenance organizations (HMOs).[33] Florida forbids AIDS-related discrimination at any hospital that receives state financial assistance.[34]

General antidiscrimination law is also being brought to bear by patients alleging HIV discrimination. Courts have found that a doctor or dentist's refusal to treat a person purely because of HIV infection is illegal under the federal Rehabilitation Act of 1973, state handicap-discrimination laws, and the Americans with Disabilities Act, which explicitly includes medical and dental offices in the list of public services that are prohibited from discriminating on the basis of handicap. Application of antidiscrimination law to medical care providers will put upon courts the difficult job of distinguishing between legitimate professional judgments about whom a provider is competent to treat, and invidious personal decisions about whom a provider is willing to treat.[35]

Other states have used licensing authorities to set forth regulations for physician and nurse behavior, including rules that curb physician discrimination against HIV-positive patients. New Jersey's law is an excellent example.[36] Yet states have hesitated to require physicians to treat diseases that they do not understand or have not been trained to address. Thus, licensure regulations like New Jersey's will prohibit the surgeon who is capable of removing spleens from refusing to remove the spleen of a patient infected with HIV, but it may not prevent the general practitioner or internist who does not wish to provide primary care for an HIV-infected patient from citing inadequate knowledge and refusing to care for such a patient.

Perhaps in light of this, some progressive physicians have argued that all primary care practitioners should be required to receive training in the treatment of AIDS.[37] At least one state has now set forth regulations mandating, for example, that internists learn how to care for HIV-related disease.[38] Nonetheless, the use of licensure powers will not create a thoroughgoing right to health care for HIV-positive patients.

Indeed, these statutes present a rather difficult problem for well-meaning general practitioners. Many of them will be accustomed to dealing with hypertension and diabetes, diseases which in many ways are more complicated than the initial stages of HIV disease. The majority, however, will refer to specialists such illness as chronic leukemia or breast cancer in an early state, both diseases that are also relatively uncomplicated. The difference between the diseases they treat, and those they refer, seems to center on the potential for the disease process to suddenly accelerate into life-threatening circumstances that are treated with drugs infrequently used elsewhere. AIDS, and increasingly asymptomatic HIV infection, is like this, and so often falls into the referred category. Primary care practitioners are uncomfortable with it on the disease's own terms, not only because of social issues or fear of transmission.

One must ask, is it good public health policy to overcome this impulse to refer? Certainly, a requirement that unwilling primary care providers must care for HIV-positive patients would not seem to be in the best interest of the patient. Thus, control of individual practitioners' clinical care must be exercised delicately.

States have traditionally maintained more oversight over hospitals (and their employees) than over individual practitioners. First, antidiscrimination laws apply generally to public institutions, as well as to workers.[39] Second, institutions that offer emergency care must, at the common law, treat all acutely ill patients who present themselves there.[40] This means that patients with AIDS or infected with HIV cannot be turned away from emergency rooms. It does not, however, mean that the hospital must continue to care for them once the acute illness has been stabilized. In addition, to enforce this right, patients must be willing to bring suits if they are refused care. Unfortunately, many ill people are not aware of their rights. The federal government has attempted to address the problem by creating more stringent penalties for the dumping of patients from one emergency room to another,[41] but problems likely still exist. Moreover, even the federal law requires only stabilization and safe transfer.

Another potential source of a limited right to health care is the Hill-Burton Reconstruction Act.[42] The Hill-Burton Act provided grants for hospital construction grants with an implicit quid pro quo that services be provided by the recipients to poor patients.[43] After litigation in the 1970s on behalf of the rights of poor people, the Department of Health and Human Services created a so-called community service requirement that prohibited Hill-Burton hospitals from discriminating on the basis of race, color, natural origin, or other grounds unrelated to individual need for care.[44] Presumably an individual infected with HIV could make a case that failure of a Hill-Burton-funded hospital to offer treatment is a matter of discrimination. But this is certainly less than a full-blown right to health care. In summary, neither individual practitioners nor hospitals are required in all situations to care for the HIV-infected; to the contrary, large gaps exist.

There has been, overall, much less thought given to patient discrimination against infected providers. Presumably, we would wish to maintain patients' prerogatives regarding selection of a physician. Thus an HIV-infected provider can expect little relief if patients do not seek his care.

HIV Status of Patient or Provider Unknown

When an individual whose HIV status is unknown chooses a health care provider, a series of new questions will arise if individual workers or institutions request that patients be screened for the presence of HIV. In addition, patients may now begin to make similar demands on health care workers. These screening requests are, and will likely remain, one of the most sensitive policy issues generated by the HIV epidemic.

Let us turn first to the screening of patients. Physicians often request a "panel" of laboratory tests on patients. Consent to these tests is part of the general consent to treatment. Testing for HIV is, however, quite different than other sorts of laboratory tests.[45] Thus, patients should perform an explicit cost-benefit analysis before undergoing testing. The major benefit to being tested is that therapy is now available for asymptomatic individuals who carry the human immunodeficiency virus.[46] There are also potential benefits of testing to the public health, as transmission of the virus may decrease when an infected individual takes special precautions before engaging in sexual relations or other high-risk behavior.[47]

In contrast, there are many negative features associated with testing, including breach of confidentiality and discrimination. Thus, undergoing HIV testing in a non-anonymous setting is a difficult decision for most people, and, in light of this, many states have required explicit counseling before administration of the test. Nevertheless, some believe that hospitals are quietly engaging in routine screening of patients without their consent.[48]

The law generally prohibits such screening. First, many states by statute prohibit screening without informed consent.[49] Some of these statutes, however, have exceptions. For example, Colorado condones involuntary testing if a patient is undergoing a procedure that may expose health care workers to HIV.[50] Several states allow emergency response personnel to have access to a patient's HIV test data if they are exposed to body fluids, presumably even without patient consent.[51] In any case, state statutory provisions, while quite supportive of patient's rights, are not completely protective, and, more important, are not present in all fifty states.

The second line of protection against nonconsensual testing is the common-law principle of informed consent. Informed consent doctrine, based on patient autonomy, requires that patients understand and approve of the therapy they are to undergo. This applies equally to therapy and diagnostic testing.[52] While in some states the level of information necessary for consent is set by the physician, in most states a doctor is required to provide the information a "prudent patient" would need to make a reasonable decision. Even in those states where the standard is provider-based, most would recognize that a test having the impact that an HIV test has should be a matter of patient consent. Therefore, a patient tested against his or her will or without his or her knowledge would likely be able to bring a successful informed-consent claim in most jurisdictions.[53]

Another common-law basis for discouraging involuntary testing is a battery action. Unconsented touching, such as involuntary testing, is prohibited by the common law. The only way in which such suits might not succeed are those situations in which the court unreasonably focuses on the biological facts of drawing blood, or when the standard of care in a jurisdiction is to test for HIV without consent.[54]

There are also constitutional bases for prohibition of involuntary testing by public agencies and institutions. The federal Constitution and many state constitutions recognize a right to privacy, which several courts have found to protect the confidentiality of HIV-related information.[55] Mandatory testing has also been found, under some circumstances, to violate the Fourth Amendment's prohibition of unreasonable searches and seizures.[56] (For more on constitutional rights, privacy, and testing, see chapter 7.) Given all these common-law, statutory, and constitutional provisions, hospitals are best advised to avoid any sort of uniformed HIV testing of patients.

The correct policy for hospitals is to redouble their efforts to bring about compliance with occupational health standards to protect workers. In 1991, the Occupational Safety and Health Administration issued final rules requiring health care employers to train and equip their personnel to use barrier precautions against blood-borne diseases such as HIV.[57] Although these are quite laudable, they are not self-enforcing. Health care workers need more information about methods for controlling infection,[58] and effective strategies must be designed for increasing compliance with such guidelines.[59] The experience of the staff at the emergency ward at the Johns Hopkins Medical Center is revealing. There, the administration threatened discharge for those who failed to follow a specific standard and, not surprisingly, rates of compliance rose immediately.[60]

Most of the same arguments apply to individual providers who desire to test their patients. Given the sensitive risk/benefit ratio associated with an HIV test, a health care worker can hardly be justified in testing the patient without the patient's knowledge. (An ethical analysis by doctors or nurses reaches the same conclusion.[61]) A more difficult question is raised when a fully informed patient declines to be tested. May health care workers or institutions refuse to provide care in such circumstances? As discussed at length above, various state and federal laws prohibit providers from discriminating based on a particular disease or disability. Arguably, these same laws prohibit refusals to treat based not so much on the patient's HIV status, but rather on the patient's unwillingness to let the provider make a determination one way or the other. This is, however, an uncharted area.[62]

When presented with a case of this sort, courts will have to consider whether conditioning care on testing fatally undermines the idea of patient autonomy upon which the doctrine of informed consent rests; whether the provider is able to provide competent care without knowing the patient's HIV status; whether compromises in care that flow from not knowing have been properly explained to the patient as part of the informed consent process; whether the patient incorporated these limitations into his or her decision; and the extent to which the provider's refusal to treat appears to be driven by safety concerns rather than by concerns over providing quality care. More globally, courts will have to consider the consequences that would flow from a decision either way, both from the standpoint of patients (for example, would patients denied treatment because of their refusal to consent suffer harm?) and of providers (for example, would being obligated to provide care to patients whose HIV status is unknown put them at risk?).[63]

Like the question of mandatory patient testing, the question of whether care can be denied to those who decline voluntary testing will propel courts into an ongoing debate over whether provider safety is more enhanced by knowing which patients are HIV positive, or by treating all patients as if they were. A strong public health consensus has formed behind the latter position, but there remain powerful voices within the medical establishment contending that physicians need to know patients' HIV status in order to protect themselves.

Requests by patients that health care workers be tested are relatively new. We have witnessed only one cluster of documented cases of transmission to patients in a health care setting, and, as previously described, the available studies suggest that the risk of transmission to patients is extraordinarily small. Nonetheless, patients are increasingly concerned about the fact that their providers may carry the virus, and many would like to know the HIV status of a physician who undertakes invasive procedures.[64] There may be some reasons to think that the risk-benefit ratio of testing would be different for health care providers than it is for patients. For example, a single infected health care provider who practices invasive procedures may have the capacity to infect more people than does an HIV-positive patient. Nonetheless, given the small risk of transmission, it appears that the balancing between utility and risk does not warrant mandatory testing of health care workers. Moreover, the risk of transmission to patients pales in comparison to the overall risks of being hospitalized. I extrapolate from a recent study[65] to estimate that there are 100,000 deaths due to medical negligence in United States hospitals per year.

During 1991, concerns over provider-to-patient transmission took center stage in the aftermath of the CDC's reports that first one, then three, then a total of five patients had been infected with HIV while undergoing treatment by the same Florida dentist. Moreover, one of the patients engaged in a high-profile campaign, during the waning months of her life, for mandatory testing of health care workers and practice restrictions on those who are infected.[66]

In July 1991, in an effort to get out front on the issue, the CDC issued a set of guidelines for protecting patients from HIV transmission in the health care setting. The guidelines stressed that the true risk of such transmission is quite small, that the most effective safety measure continues to be strict adherence to barrier precautions and sterilization techniques, and that mandatory testing of health care workers is unwarranted. Paradoxically, the guidelines also called upon workers who perform "invasive procedures" to be tested voluntarily for HIV and, if infected, to seek the approval of a local medical panel before resuming the performance of "exposure-prone" procedures. In no event were infected providers to perform any "exposure-prone" procedures without informing their patients of their HIV status.[67]

Despite this effort on the part of the CDC to restore some measure of calm to what was, by then, a wildly careening debate, several ill-conceived measures were introduced into Congress. The worst, which handily passed in the Senate, would have made it a crime punishable by ten years in prison for an HIV-positive health care worker to continue to practice after being apprised of his or her infection. Eventually, the Senate leadership took control, and in the fall of 1991 a bipartisan compromise bill passed both houses and was signed into law. The law directed state governments, on pain of losing Medicaid and Medicare funding, to adopt the CDC's guidelines, or their equivalent, within one year (or two years in states with legislatures that meet biennially).[68]

At the end of 1991, the CDC circulated a draft of new, significantly different guidelines, reflecting the medical community's unanimous view that the agency's classification of procedures into "invasive" and "exposure-prone" was practically unworkable and medically insupportable. Moving closer to the position of leading state health departments, such as New York's, the CDC made universal precautions, rather than practice restrictions, the mainstay of prevention. The agency calls for providers who learn they are infected to submit to local panels for an evaluation of their ability to comply with barrier precautions and avoid exposing patients to their blood. The draft backs off from requiring disclosure to patients in all cases, but leaves local panels the option to require it "in circumstances where the panel is uncertain about whether the procedures may pose a small risk." In June 1992, the CDC abruptly abandoned its efforts to fashion a national policy, calling upon the states to issue their own guidelines instead.[69]

As of this writing, the states are in the midst of fashioning their responses to the Congressional mandate. The CDC has said that it will be guided by the states and other interested parties in deciding whether a given state's scheme is equivalent to its own guidelines as finally adopted. The first half-dozen states to act have echoed the CDC's emphasis on universal precautions and opposition to mandatory testing.

They have divided, however, over precisely which health care workers should be encouraged to undergo voluntary testing, and over whether infected workers can continue performing invasive practices without medical panel approval, given the absence of evidence that infected workers pose a significant risk to patients. These states have also divided over when, if at all, HIV-positive providers who opt to continue working should be required to inform their patients of their status. Even if a national consensus is achieved on the terms of a policy, reliance on the discretion of local review panels will assure that very different rules are developed and applied to similarly situated providers.[70]

It appears that courts will be willing to allow health care institution screening of employees. In the case of *Glover v. Eastern Nebraska Community Office of Retardation,* a federal district court ruled that the agency's policy of requiring employees to undergo testing for tuberculosis, hepatitis B, and HIV was inappropriate, based largely on the fact that such policies would have little effect in "preventing the spread of HIV or in protecting their clients."[71] On the other hand, in *Leckelt v. Board of Commissioners of Hospital District 1,*[72] the court held that requiring a health care worker to be tested was not a matter of discrimination because patient welfare outweighed the privacy right. Recent cases such as *In Re: Application of Hershey Medical Center*[73] and *Behringer v. Medical Center at Princeton*[74] support the AMA view that patients have a right to know a provider's HIV status and that hospitals can reveal this information without an infected provider's approval. Therefore, if screening of hospital employees is completed, it is unlikely this information will remain confidential.

ISSUES ONCE TREATMENT IS UNDERWAY

Infected Patient's Confidentiality and Provider's Common-Law Duty to Warn

It is a fact of life that physicians and other health care workers will be providing care for some patients who they know are HIV-positive, and for many whose HIV status they do not know. Patients will be unaware of providers' infection with HIV unless it is voluntarily disclosed by the health care worker. When the provider is aware of a patient's HIV infection, the legal issue in the therapeutic relationship shifts to confidentiality of HIV diagnosis and care. In particular, the tension between the duty of a health care provider to warn third-party contacts of HIV-positive patients and the confidentiality of the provider-patient relationship comes to the fore.

Confidentiality of doctor-patient communications has a relatively long ethical tradition, even though the common law did not always recognize it.[75] Legislatures have tended to reinforce the ethics of confidentiality with state laws.[76] The protection provided by these statutes, the so-called doctor-patient privilege, is now in place in all but two states. The privilege was intended to protect doctors and patients from compulsion to testify at the behest of third parties, but it also resonated with the ethical commitment to confidence and trust between doctor and patient.[77] Typically, legislators have made explicit exceptions to confidentiality for reporting venereal diseases, evaluating worker's compensation claims, and protecting battered children. In addition, several courts have interpreted confidentiality statutes to allow providers to warn third parties who may be endangered by a patient.[78] All this means that provider-patient communications are not tightly sealed; a number of exceptions exist to protect third parties.

In the case of highly contagious diseases, courts have clearly signaled that health care professionals have a duty to warn people who would foreseeably come into contact with an infectious patient.[79] By the mid–1920s, several courts had established that, for instance, physicians were to warn people who were exposed to patients with scarlet fever.[80] These opinions also allowed that the duty to warn potential victims extended beyond the physician's requirement to comply with state health reporting law. Common-law duties to warn are in turn reinforced by statutory public health requirements for warnings of close contacts.[81] The applicability of these precedents to HIV would, however, hardly be automatic: because HIV is not casually transmitted, general warning of casual contacts would be pointless and, indeed, destructive.

Of greater relevance are the few, but widely known, cases concerning a health care professional's duty to warn third parties of a behavioral risk posed by a patient. In the influential case of *Tarasoff v. Board of Regents of the University of California*,[82] the California Supreme Court ruled that a psychotherapist must advise a third party who had been threatened by the psychotherapist's patient during treatment sessions. This patient eventually carried through on his threat of murder, and the victim's family sued the provider and his employer, the state of California. The supreme court noted that once "a therapist determines . . . that his patient presents a serious danger of violence to another, he incurs an obligation to use reasonable care to protect the intended victim against such danger. The discharge of this duty . . . may call for him to warn the intended victim."[83]

Although the *Tarasoff* decision has actually been adopted as law by only a few lower courts in other states, it has had a significant impact on health care workers' perception of their duty to protect third parties. It has, for example, influenced therapists caring for outpatients: they are now more likely to break confidentiality and warn potential victims.[84] Hospital psychiatrists now seek judicial input before discharging patients who may potentially be dangerous.[85] Dr. Alan Stone makes the important point that, rather than increasing the safety of those threatened by psychiatric patients, *Tarasoff* may have the opposite effect in that psychiatrists may refuse to care for dangerously ill patients.[86]

Undeterred by such cautionary advice, a few courts have even extended the reach of the *Tarasoff* decision. The original opinion relied heavily on the fact that the dangerous mental patient had identified a particular individual as the target of his rage. It was predictable that this one individual might be harmed.[87] This requirement of "foreseeability" has been diluted by courts considering other sorts of tort claims based on a duty to warn.[88] Moreover, there is no indication that the *Tarasoff* rationale does not clearly apply to all areas of medical therapy, not just psychiatry.[89] One court has now held that physicians owe a duty to third parties to provide accurate safe-sex information for a patient with hepatitis B.[90]

The contagious disease cases, *Tarasoff* and its progeny, have created more questions than answers with respect to a health care worker's obligation to warn third-party contacts of HIV-positive patients. The common-law duty to warn would appear to be strongest in cases where a patient has made clear to a health care provider his or her intention to engage in dangerous behavior with a third party known to the provider. There is little legal support, however, for a general duty to warn third parties every time a patient is diagnosed as having HIV. An HIV-positive person who does not engage in unsafe sex or drug use does not pose a risk to anyone, even under the loosest standard of foreseeability. Finally, as I discuss next, most states have passed specific laws governing HIV confidentiality, laws which supersede any inconsistent duties imposed by common-law courts.

State HIV-Specific Laws

The standard, common law analysis of confidentiality and duty to warn is not dispositive because most states have passed special HIV testing legislation.[91] In particular, the right to privacy and the doctor-patient privilege have been reinforced with statutory requirements that HIV-related information be held confidential. For example, until recently, California law punished unauthorized disclosure of HIV antibody test results to a third party with a year's imprisonment or a fine of $10,000.[92] Massachusetts's law provides that disclosure of antibody test results can occur only with the written consent of the patient.[93] In light of such provisions, hospital lawyers recommend that health care workers be very careful about disclosing results, and indeed have routinely advised against third-party warnings.[94] In effect, these confidentiality laws appear to have insulated health care workers in some states from tort litigation by third parties premised on a common-law duty to warn.[95]

Although confidentiality of HIV test results is of utmost importance, some legislators have thought it unjust to prohibit a physician from warning in cases where a particular person, whom the health care worker could easily contact, is placed at risk of contracting HIV by unreasonable behavior on the part of the patient. In recognition of this, California, for example, has changed its provisions regarding HIV testing to allow physicians to warn spouses of HIV-positive patients.[96] Texas statutes create a general rule of confidentiality, but allow spousal disclosure.[97] Finally, New York and several other states have passed comprehensive legislation that strengthens the confidentiality of HIV-related information, but contains an exception for disclosure to a readily identifiable third-party contact.[98] Most of these statutes are physician specific, and are not applicable to all health care workers. (For a detailed discussion of state confidentiality and testing laws, see chapter 7.)

These exceptions to the general rule of confidentiality have rather broad support. Many clinicians and service providers feel morally obligated to warn readily identified third parties who are at risk, yet they feel legally constrained from doing so. Perhaps more tellingly, a broad array of public health figures, legislators, civil libertarians, and AIDS activists view third-party warnings as a preferable alternative to aggressive contact tracing. Although the two approaches have different goals and underlying rationales (namely, protecting known partners from infection versus identifying people who may already be infected), practically and politically they are often juxtaposed.[99] (For more on contact tracing, see chapter 5.)

Of course, the virtues of warning third parties must be balanced against a number of drawbacks. There is an appreciable risk that some patients will forego being tested or seeking care, out of fear that partner notification will jeopardize their safety or support. Likewise, there is a risk that many providers will issue warnings prematurely, without first determining whether patients in fact pose a danger to others (they may, for example, be practicing safe sex), and without first counseling patients, over an appropriate interval of time, in ways that enable them to warn their partners themselves. Concerns have been raised that providers' own prejudices and stereotypes, including those rooted in gender, may influence whom they feel duty-bound to warn. Often the sole object of concern is the heterosexual spouse, in particular the ''innocent wife.''

Finally, a perceived duty to warn third parties might undermine health care professionals' willingness to take care of patients with HIV. In many cases, the process will severely strain the provider-patient relationship, making it harder to render quality care. Moreover, a broad duty to warn would obviously be unworkable in a country where more than a million people have HIV. Simply identifying third parties may be difficult. Even when it is not, proper notification requires the provider not simply to locate, but also to counsel and provide testing to the third party. Health care providers are generally neither trained nor willing to do this sort of public health work.[100] Providers also fear being sued for failing to properly identify third parties, or for failing to warn and properly counsel them all. This fear may be sufficient by itself to drive providers away from patients with HIV. In recognition of this, several states, including New York and Texas, have insulated health care workers from suit for failure to warn. Moreover, some states have set forth in detail the people who must be warned, including spouses, emergency personnel, and health care workers.[101]

Other Confidentiality Issues

There are several other slightly more tractable issues that arise regarding confidentiality and the care of patients infected with HIV. First, confidentiality laws generally give way to state or federal laws mandating that the names of people with particular diseases be reported to public health authorities. In every state, the names of patients with CDC-defined AIDS are reportable upon diagnosis. In half the states, the names of people who test positive for HIV antibodies must be reported, although in all but seven states (as of this writing) individuals have the option of being tested anonymously and thus circumventing the reporting system.

Another set of confidentiality concerns arises when care of a patient with HIV is transferred from one health care worker to another. Generally, such transfers can be handled by obtaining informed consent, in writing, for release of results, a process now required by law in many states.[102] For instance, when a patient is discharged from a hospital, but still needs care at home, the visiting nurse often will need information on the patient's HIV status. In such circumstances, most patients will be willing to release the information.

Of course, fire fighters, police officers, emergency medical technicians, paramedics and others outside health care institutions may all like to have access to test results. State laws governing releases of this kind are discussed in more detail in chapter 7.

PROBLEMS AFTER OCCUPATIONAL TRANSMISSION HAS OCCURRED

Compensating Infected Providers

When a health care worker is exposed to HIV as a result of a needle stick or other workplace mishap, complex questions of compensation arise. Like other people living with HIV disease, he or she will likely experience extreme mental anguish, economic hardship, a foreshortened life, extended periods of disability, uninsurability, and diminished professional opportunities and satisfaction. Rather than leaving individuals to shoulder the burden alone, we in the United States have traditionally relied on insurance and, when necessary, tort litigation to shift the costs of accidents from injured individuals to a broader pool of others.[103]

We are in the midst of a full-scale public debate about health care finance. The inadequacies of health insurance are, however, only part of the problem. Although more than 75 percent of Americans have some form of health insurance, many fewer have disability insurance. The latter would be especially important for individuals infected with HIV who develop neurological syndromes or other problems that prevent return to their usual jobs at the health work place.[104] Some segments of the health care work force have advocated much broader availability of disability and life insurance for health care workers, an option that will be expensive for hospitals. Indeed, given the rather large risks faced, for instance, by physicians in training, actuaries may be unwilling to write such premiums.[105] Hospitals have not yet hurried to address these proposals.[106] Without such insurance, however, divisive litigation over occupational transmission will no doubt continue.[107]

Not that it will be easy for infected health care workers to bring suits against hospitals. First, it will be somewhat difficult to define the standard of care that was violated. Infected health care workers will likely allege that the hospital should have enforced occupational safety parameters set forth by the CDC and OSHA. Hospitals will counter that the prevailing standard of care is clearly not that specified by these national safety standards, because most hospitals have been unable to actually get their personnel to comply. Since the duty of care is not easily defined, it will likely be difficult to prove negligence.[108] (For more on the elements and proof of negligence, see chapter 15.)

Even more important, infected health care workers must prove that their infection occurred at the work place. While most providers should, given the greater attention paid to these issues today, recall and report needle stick injuries that occur, these accidents usually will not be witnessed. Since transmission of HIV occurs much more commonly through sexual or parenteral transmission outside the work place, infected health care workers will face the prospect of proving that this more common form of transmission is not the cause of their HIV infection. Hospitals will resist establishment of a legal presumption that infected health care workers contracted the virus at work. Indeed, health care institutions facing suits by their workers will likely make every effort to investigate the private lives of litigants, which may in turn deter further suits. Thus, the causation question represents a significant threshold to successful suits.

In light of this, some health care workers may choose to sue manufacturers of needles or other equipment if they contract HIV at the work place. These suits would sound in product liability and would be based on a claim that the equipment was designed in a substandard fashion, increasing the risk of injury. While no such cases have been reported, third-party product liability claims have played a major role in personal injury litigation over the past twenty years and likely will soon occur in this setting.

Presumably, however, tort litigation will not play an important role in compensation of injured health care workers, even though quite a few cases have been filed. Indeed, many health care workers may be unable to sue employers because of the availability of workers' compensation benefits and the attendant exclusivity doctrine that prohibits suits against employers who provide such benefits. Workers' compensation is a no-fault system of injury compensation that requires only that an injured party show that the accident occurred in the work place. Once the causation threshold is met, administrative compensation is available in an expedited fashion for economic costs. Many health care workers, and especially support staff, nurses, and physicians employed by hospitals will be eligible for workers' compensation benefits. In the past, workers' compensation boards have provided benefits for workers' infections with hepatitis B, and indeed have developed presumptions regarding infectious causation.[109] This relaxation of causation standards makes workers' compensation a much more attractive alternative for shifting the costs of accidents.

This is not to say that it is a panacea for the costs associated with occupational infection with HIV. First, one must recall that workers' compensation has generally done a very poor job of compensating occupational disease.[110] Moreover, benefits will be quite small in general, and especially so for nurses and physicians in training who will have their compensation pegged to the salary they are earning at the hospital and not to the much larger salary they can expect once their training is completed.

Finally, self-employed physicians and nurses will not be eligible for benefits and likely will have to seek other alternatives.

All the foregoing assumes that the health care worker has information regarding the HIV status of the patient. This is not the case in many needle-stick or other types of accidents that occur. In these situations, health care workers will want to know the HIV status of the patient, and most would advocate the testing of a patient. Such testing is generally prohibited without the patient's consent. A constitutional analysis also favors nontesting because it is simple enough to perform serial antibody testing on the potentially infected health care worker, although these arguments are complicated somewhat by the fact that some individuals do not immediately develop antibodies. Some state legislatures, however, including Delaware, Maine, Rhode Island, South Carolina, and Texas, have balanced trade-offs and required testing of patients who may have exposed emergency, or "first response," health care workers.[111] Moreover, some courts have characterized exposed parties' interests as superior to privacy rights in cases of rape or other exposures to body fluids.[112] The law here, as elsewhere, is unsettled.

Compensating Infected Patients

Patients potentially infected in the health care setting face many of the same problems. Certainly they will have to rely on either insurance or tort litigation to receive compensation. Their tort claims will be even more greatly hampered by causation threshold issues in that, in most cases, patients will have no knowledge of the health care workers' HIV status. Yet, if they can make a colorable claim, at least some courts will be willing to force testing of health care workers to determine HIV status for purposes of assessing the infected patient's claim. The precedent in this regard is definitely shifting toward testing of providers, and in litigation arising out of a transmission from blood donations.[113] In a number of these cases, plaintiffs have attempted to gain access to donors who may have been the source of the infection.[114] Courts had rather consistently refused access of plaintiffs to donors, but in a case illustrative of the new trend, the Texas Supreme Court ruled that a plaintiff had the right to identification of a donor.[115] Given these kinds of decisions, it is unclear whether a court would allow nonconsensual testing of a health care worker at the behest of a patient who alleged that transmission occurred in the health care setting.

Failure to disclose an identity could be an insuperable obstacle to successful negligence litigation on the part of the injured plaintiff. It stands to reason that if the patient could make a good case that he or she had been cared for in a negligent fashion, perhaps by health care workers not observing appropriate safety precautions, a court may be willing to overturn the privacy right and order testing. More important, a court could fashion an order that required testing, but involved confidential examination of results and no further disclosure.[116] These issues will no doubt be defined by further litigation. (For more on lawsuits arising from exposure to or transmission of HIV, see chapter 15.)

ENDING THE RELATIONSHIP

When a health care provider learns that a patient is infected with HIV, he or she may often wish to terminate the relationship and transfer the patient to another provider. This desire may be born of fear, ignorance, or pure prejudice. It may also reflect legitimate doubts about the provider's professional capacity to stay on top of the situation as the disease process unfolds, especially in so rapidly changing an area of medicine.

May the provider terminate the relationship because of the patient's HIV status? The issues here are the same as in the forming of the relationship. At common law, a physician is not permitted to simply break off a therapeutic relationship during the course of an acute illness.[117] Of course, once the emergency has passed, a physician is free to end the relationship with the patient.[118] The matter of the acuity of care is central; if a particular illness is ongoing, there is an implied contract to continue to care, and an offending physician may be found to have abandoned the patient.[119] As discussed above, modern antidiscrimination laws have created additional limits on physicians' discretion to pick and choose whom they treat. If it can be clearly established that the basis for the termination is the patient's HIV status—by, for example, showing that the treatment sought by the patient is of a type normally offered by the provider and is not clinically complicated by the HIV infection—a lawsuit on behalf of the patient might well prove successful.

There remains the question of what remedy the law can offer. Courts and human rights commissions have the authority to order a physician or dentist to provide treatment, but there is likely to be little basis for a good provider-patient relationship between a plaintiff and a defendant. Individual providers can be ordered to undertake special training in the treatment of people with HIV and to abstain from future discrimination against other people with HIV. A large damages award to the individual plaintiff may also induce other providers to abandon discriminatory practices.[120]

As is true at the initiation stage, the difficult questions revolve around how to deal with assertions of lack of competence, how to separate the pretextual from the real reasons for refusing treatment, and whether to place on providers, especially in areas of high HIV prevalence, a duty to learn more about treating the infected.

Attorneys involved in health care discrimination cases have found that economic issues often are far more important to providers than medical ones. For example, many dentists who refuse to treat people with HIV are apparently not as afraid of the disease as of what would happen to their practices if other patients learned they were treating HIV-positive people.[121] Professional associations and licensing agencies can play a particularly important role in setting a standard of nondiscrimination. The public needs to be assured that all providers may have HIV-positive patients, and reassured that this poses no dangers. With optimal leadership from the professions, courts could become agencies of last resort rather than major players in the development of health care policy.

Finally, it is important to recognize that the issue of termination, like that of initiation, takes place in the context of a health care system that really is not much of a system at all. Access to health care is far from assured for many Americans, especially those most likely to be exposed to HIV. Therefore, providers cannot blithely assume that if they do not provide care, someone else will. People living with HIV disease usually have embarrassingly few health care options, and that reality is likely to shape the way courts approach many of these issues. The medical profession would be wise to take heed as well.

SUMMARY

Relationships between patients and health care workers present a number of challenging legal issues in the HIV epidemic. In particular, we must recognize and address the heightened concern that transmission can occur in either direction in the health care setting. This is not a set of issues that health care administrators, workers, or patient advocates have moved quickly to address with rational policies. Therefore, we can expect court-made law to continue to play a primary role and for precedent to be unsettled for some time to come.

NOTES

1 *See* Henderson, *et al., Risk of Nosocomial Infection with Human T-Cell Lymphotrophic Virus Type III/Lymphocyte Associated Virus in a Large Cohort of Intensively Exposed Health Care Workers,* 104 Annals Internal Med. 633 (1986); Jason, *et al., HTLV-III/*

LAV Antibody and Immune Status of Household Contacts, 255 J.A.M.A. 212 (1986); Friedland, *et al., Lack of Transmission of HTLV-II/LAV Infection to Household Contacts of Patients with AIDS or AIDS-Related Complex with Oral Candidiasis,* 314 New Eng. J.

Med. 344 (1986); Lifson, *et al.*, *National Surveillance of AIDS in Health Care Workers*, 256 J.A.M.A. 3231–4 (1986).

2 *Update: Human Immunodeficiency Virus Infections in Health Care Workers Exposed to Blood of Infected Patients*, 36 MMWR 285 (1987).

3 *See* Prego v. City of New York, 141 Misc. 2d 709 (N.Y.S. 1988), *aff'd*, 147 A.D.2d 165 (N.Y. App. Div. 1989); *see also* Brennan, *AIDS as an Occupational Disease*, 107 Annals Internal Med. 581 (1987).

4 St. Louis, *et al.*, *Sero-Prevalence of Human Immunodeficiency Virus Infection at Sentinel Hospitals in the United States*, 323 New Eng. J. Med. 213 (1990).

5 Gerberding & Schecter, *Surgery and AIDS: Reducing the Risk*, 265 J.A.M.A. 1572 (1991); Gerberding, *et al.*, *Risk of Exposure to Patients' Blood During Surgery at San Francisco General Hospital*, 322 New Eng. J. Med. 1788 (1990); Mangione, *et al.*, *Occupational Exposure to HIV Infection: Frequency and Rates of Under-Reporting of Percutaneous and Mucocutaneous Exposures by Medical House Staff*, 90 Am. J. Med. 85 (1991). *See generally* Chamberland, *et al.*, *Health Care Workers with AIDS: National Surveillance Update*, 266 J.A.M.A. 3459 (1991) (vast majority of 5,425 health care workers with AIDS probably acquired disease through non-occupational behavior).

6 *See, e.g.*, Henderson & Gerberding, *Prophylactic Zidovudine after Occupational Exposure to Human Immunodeficiency Virus: An Interim Analysis*, 160 J. Infectious Diseases 321 (1989).

7 *See* Gerberding, *et al.*, note 5 above; Jagger, *et al.*, *Rates of Needle Stick Injuries Caused by Various Devices in the University Hospital*, 319 New Eng. J. Med. 284 (1988); Panlilio, *et al.*, *Blood Contacts during Surgical Procedures*, 265 J.A.M.A. 1533 (1991); Wright, *et al.*, *Mechanisms of Glove Tears and Sharp Injuries Among Surgical Personnel*, 266 J.A.M.A. 1668 (1991); *see also*

Mangione, *et al.*, note 5 above (reporting that most needle sticks are not reported by health care workers). *See generally* Gerberding & Schecter, note 5 above (editorial review of the leading studies).

8 Gerberding, *et al.*, note 5 above; Panlilio, *et al.*, note 7 above.

9 *See* Gerberding, *et al.*, note 5 above; Panlilio, *et al.*, note 7 above.

10 Gerberding & Schechter, note 5 above; *see* Wright, *et al.*, note 7 above; Beesinger, *Preventing Transmission of Human Immunodeficiency Virus during Operations*, 167 Surgery, Gynecology & Obstetrics 287 (1988); Wong, *et al.*, *Are Universal Precautions Effective in Reducing the Number of Occupational Exposures among Health Care Workers: A Prospective Study of Physicians on a Medical Service*, 265 J.A.M.A. 1123 (1991).

11 *See, e.g.*, Lowenfels, *et al.*, *Frequency of Puncture Injuries in Surgeons and Estimated Risk of HIV Infection*, 124 Archives Surgery 1284 (1989); Wright, *et al.*, note 7 above; *see also* Beesinger, note 10 above (suggesting changes in "choreography" of surgery to reduce exposures).

12 Gerberding & Schechter, note 5 above.

13 *See* Reingold, *et al.*, *Failure of Gloves and Other Protective Devices to Prevent Transmission of Hepatitis B Virus to Oral Surgeons*, 259 J.A.M.A. 2558 (1988).

14 *See* Gerbert, *et al.*, *Primary Care Physicians and AIDS: Attitudinal and Structural Barriers to Care*, 266 J.A.M.A. 2837 (1991); Goldsmith, *Even in Perspective, HIV Specter Haunts Health Care Workers Most*, 263 J.A.M.A. 2413 (1990); Gerbert, *et al.*, *Why Fear Persists: Health Care Professionals and AIDS*, 260 J.A.M.A. 3481 (1988) [hereinafter *Why Fear Persists*].

15 *See* Cooke & Sande, *The HIV Epidemic in Training in Internal Medicine: Challenge and Recommendations*, 321 New Eng. J. Med. 1334 (1989); Mangione, *et al.*, note 5 above; Ness, *et al.*, *House Staff Recruitment to Mu-*

nicipal and Voluntary New York City Residency Programs during the AIDS Epidemic, 266 J.A.M.A. 2843 (1991).

16 *See Physicians in Training and HIV,* 322 New Eng. J. Med. 1392, 1393 (1990) (anonymous letter).

17 *See* Volberding, *Supporting the Health Care Team and Caring for Patients with AIDS,* 261 J.A.M.A. 747 (1989).

18 *Why Fear Persists,* note 14 above; Rizzo, *et al., Physician Contact with and Attitudes toward HIV-Seropositive Patients,* 28 Med. Care 251 (1990).

19 *See* Rogers, *Caring for the Patient with AIDS,* 259 J.A.M.A. 1368 (1988).

20 *See* Freedland, *AIDS and Compassion,* 259 J.A.M.A. 2989 (1988).

21 *AIDS in the Operating Room,* Surgical Practice News, Aug. 1987, at 5.

22 *AIDS Clinic Being Weighed by Chicago Dental Society,* N.Y. Times, July 21, 1987, at B4.

23 *See Possible Transmission of Human Immunodeficiency Virus to a Patient during an Invasive Dental Procedure,* 39 MMWR 489 (1990); *Update: Transmission of HIV Infection during an Invasive Dental Procedure—Florida,* 40 MMWR 21 (1991); *Update: Transmission of HIV Infection during Invasive Dental Procedure—Florida,* 40 MMWR 377 (1991); *Unreported Findings Shed New Light on HIV Dental Case,* 6 AIDS Alert 121 (1991). *See generally* Lo & Steinbrook, *Health Care Workers Infected with the Human Immunodeficiency Virus: The Next Steps,* 267 J.A.M.A. 1100 (1992).

24 *See, e.g.,* Armstrong, *et al., Investigation of a Health Care Worker with Symptomatic Human Immunodeficiency Virus Infection: An Epidemiologic Approach,* 152 Military Med. 414 (1987); Comer, *et al., Management Considerations for an HIV Positive Dental Student,* 55 J. Dental Educ. 187 (1991); Mishu, *et al., A Surgeon with AIDS: Lack of Evidence of Transmission to Patients,* 264 J.A.M.A. 467 (1990); Porter, *et al., Management of Patients Treated by a Surgeon with HIV Infection,* 335 Lancet 113 (1990).

25 *See* CDC, Estimates of the Risk of Endemic Transmission of Hepatitis B Virus and Human Immunodeficiency Virus to Patients by the Percutaneous Route During Invasive Surgical and Dental Procedures 6 (draft Jan. 30, 1991); Lowenfels & Wormser, *Risk of Transmission of HIV from Surgeon to Patient,* 325 New Eng. J. Med. 888 (1991); Lo & Steinbrook, note 23 above; Gostin, *The HIV-Infected Health Care Professional: Public Policy, Discrimination, and Patient Safety,* 18 Am. J. L. & Med. 303 (1990); *see also* Rhame, *The HIV Infected Surgeon,* 264 J.A.M.A. 507 (1990).

26 *See* Blendon, *et al., Public Opinion and AIDS: Lessons for the Second Decade,* 267 J.A.M.A. 981 (1992); Marshall, *et al., Patients' Fear of Contracting the Acquired Immunodeficiency Syndrome from Physicians,* 150 Archives Internal Med. 1501 (1990). *Compare* American Medical Association, Statement on HIV Infected Physicians (Jan. 17, 1991) *with* Daniels, *HIV-Infected Professionals, Patient Choice, and the 'Switching Dilemma,'* 267 J.A.M.A. 1368 (1992) (ethical argument against AMA position.

27 T. Brennan, Just Doctoring: Medical Ethics in the Liberal State (1991).

28 *See* Brennan, *Ensuring Adequate Health Care For the Sick: The Challenge of the Acquired Immunodeficiency Syndrome as an Occupational Disease,* 1988 Duke L.J. 293 (1988).

29 *See* McCoid, *The Care Required of Medical Practitioners,* 12 Vand. L. Rev. 549 (1959).

30 A. Southwick, The Law of Hospital and Health Care Administration 97 (1978).

31 *See* Wash. Rev. Code § 49.60.040 (1987).

32 *See* Edgar & Sandomine, *Medical Privacy Issues in the Age of AIDS: Legislative Options,* 16 Am. J. L. & Med. 155, 213 (1990).

33 *Id.* at 214.

34 Fla. Stat. Ann. § 395.0142(2)(d) (West 1989).

35 *See* Glanz v. Vernick, 756 F. Supp. 632 (D. Mass. 1991); Campanella v. Hurwitz, No. GA–00021030487 (N.Y.C. Commission on Human Rights July 31, 1991) (recommended decision and order); *cf.* Doe v. Kahala Dental Group, 808 P.2d 1276 (Haw. 1991) (no discrimination in requiring patient to disclose HIV-related medical information as condition of treatment). *But see* Sattler v. New York Comm'n on Human Rights, 147 Misc. 2d 189, 554 N.Y.S.2d 763 (Sup. Ct. 1990) (defendant's dental office not place of public accommodation), *aff'd,* 580 N.Y.S.2d 35 (App. Div. 1992).

36 *See* Annas, *Legal Risks and Responsibilities of Physicians in the AIDS Epidemic,* 18 Hastings Cent. Rep. 26 (1988).

37 *See* Northfeld, *et al., The Acquired Immunodeficiency Syndrome Is a Primary Care Disease,* 110 Annals Internal Med. 773 (1988).

38 *See* Gostin, *Public Health Strategies for Confronting AIDS: Legislative and Regulatory Policy in the United States,* 261 J.A.M.A. 1621, 1624 (1989); Clark, *AIDS Prevention: Legislative Options,* 16 Am. J. L. & Med. 107, 125 (1990).

39 *See* Glanz v. Vernick, 756 F. Supp. 632 (D. Mass. 1991).

40 *See* Hiser v. Randolph, 617 P.2d 774 (Ariz. 1980).

41 *See* Treiger, *Preventing Patient Dumping: Sharpening the COBRA's Fangs,* 61 N.Y.U. L. Rev. 1186 (1986).

42 *See* Hospital Survey and Construction Act, Pub. L. No. 79–725, 60 Stat. 1040 (1946) (codified as amended at 42 U.S.C. § 291–291(o) (1976)).

43 *Compare* Rose, *Federal Regulation of Services to the Poor Under the Hill-Burton Act: Realities and Pitfalls,* 70 Nw. U. L. Rev. 168 (1975) *with* Blumstein, *Court Ac-*

tion, Agency Reaction: The Hill-Burton Act as a Case Study, 69 Iowa L. Rev. 1227 (1984).

44 *See Medical Facility Construction and Modernization,* 42 C.F.R. 124.603(c)(ii) (1983); *see also* Wing, *The Community Service Obligation of Hill-Burton Health Facilities,* 23 B.C. L. Rev. 577 (1982).

45 *See* Swartz, *AIDS Testing and Informed Consent,* 13 J. Health Pol., Pol'y & L. 607 (1988).

46 *See* Lo, *et al., Voluntary Screening for Human Immunodeficiency Virus Infection Total and Weighing the Benefits,* 110 Annals Internal Med. 727 (1989).

47 *See* Rhame & Maki, *The Case for Wider Use of Testing of HIV Infection,* 320 New Eng. J. Med. 1248 (1989).

48 *See* Gostin, *Hospitals, Health Care Professionals, and AIDS: The Right to Know the Health Status of Professionals and Patients,* 48 Md. L. Rev. 12, 13 (1989).

49 *See* Field, *Testing for AIDS: Uses and Abuses,* 16 Am. J. L. & Med. 34, 47 (1990) (listing California, Colorado, Hawaii, Illinois, Indiana, Maine, Massachusetts, New York, North Carolina, Oregon, Rhode Island & Wisconsin).

50 Colo. Rev. Stat. § 25–4–1405(8) (1987). Texas has a similar statute. Tex. Rev. Civ. Stat. Ann. art. 44196–1, 9.02(g) (West 1987).

51 *See* Gostin, note 38 above, at 1627–28.

52 *See* T. Brennan, note 27 above, at ch. 5 (1991).

53 *See* Gostin, *The AIDS Litigation Project, A National Review of Court and Human Rights Commission Decisions, Part I: The Social Impact of AIDS,* 263 J.A.M.A. 1961, 1962 (1990).

54 *See* Doe v. Dyer-Goode, 566 A.2d 889 (Pa. Super. 1989), *appeal denied,* 588 A.2d 509 (Pa. 1990).

55 Furrow, *AIDS and the Health Care Provider: The Argument for Voluntary HIV Test-*

ing, 34 Vill. L. Rev. 823, 848 (1989); *see, e.g.,* Doe v. Coughlin, 697 F. Supp. 1234 (N.D.N.Y. 1988).

56 *See* Glover v. Eastern Neb. Community Office of Retardation, 686 F. Supp. 243 (D. Neb. 1988), *aff'd,* 867 F.2d 461 (8th Cir.), *cert. denied,* 493 U.S. 932 (1989). *Contra* Leckelt v. Board of Comm'rs, 714 F. Supp. 1377 (E.D. La. 1989), *aff'd,* 909 F. 2d 820 (5th Cir. 1990).

57 *Occupational Exposure to Bloodborne Pathogens,* 56 Fed. Reg. 64004 (Dec. 6, 1991); *see* Occupational Safety and Health Act, 29 U.S.C. §§ 651, 654(a)(1) (1982).

58 *See* Foy, *et al., HIV and Measures to Control Infection in General Practice,* 300 Brit. Med. J. 1048 (1990); Becker, *et al., Occupational Infection with Human Immunodeficiency Virus: Risks and Risk Reduction,* 110 Annals Internal Med. 653 (1989).

59 *See* Gostin, note 48 above, at 26–27.

60 *See* Kelen, *et al., Adherence to Universal (Barrier) Precautions during Interventions on Critically Ill and Injured Emergency Department Patients,* 3 J. AIDS 987 (1990); Personal Communication, Dr. David Celentano (Oct. 10, 1990).

61 *See* Peterson, *AIDS: The Ethical Dilemma for Surgeons,* 17 L. Med. & Health Care 139 (1989).

62 *See, e.g.,* 42 U.S.C.A. § 12201(c) (West Supp. 1991); *see also Nondiscrimination on the Basis of Disability by Public Accommodations and in Commercial Facilities,* 28 C.F.R. § 36 (1991).

63 These questions were given short shrift in the one case to directly consider whether conditioning treatment upon submission to HIV testing violated civil rights law. *See* Doe v. Kahala Dental Group, 808 P.2d 1276 (Haw. 1991).

64 *See* Marshall, *et al., Patients' Fear of Contracting the Acquired Immunodeficiency Syndrome from Physicians,* 150 Archives Internal Med. 1501 (1990).

65 Brennan, *et al., Incidence of Adverse Events and Negligence in Hospitalized Patients,* 324 New Eng. J. Med. 370 (1991).

66 For a concise account of the debate, see Lo & Steinbrook, note 23 above.

67 *Recommendations for Preventing Transmission of Human Immunodeficiency Virus, Hepatitis B Virus to Patients during Exposure-Prone Invasive Procedures,* 40 MMWR 1 (1991).

68 Treasury, Postal Service and General Government Appropriations Act, 1992, Pub. L. No. 102–141, § 633, 105 Stat. 834, 876.

69 Revised Recommendations for Preventing Transmission of Human Immunodeficiency Virus and Hepatitis B to Patients by the Percutaneous Route during Invasive Procedures (draft 1991).

70 *See* Lo & Steinbrook, note 23 above.

71 *Glover,* 686 F. Supp. at 249.

72 714 F. Supp. 1377 (E.D. La. 1989), *aff'd,* 909 F.2d 820 (5th Cir. 1990). *See* Doe v. Washington University, 780 F.Supp. 628 (E.D. Mo. 1991). *But see In re* Westchester County Medical Center, No. 91–504–2 (H.H.S. Appeals Brd. Apr. 20, 1992) (hospital violated Rehabilitation Act by restricting duties of HIV-infected pharmacist).

73 595 A.2d 1290 (Pa. Super. 1991).

74 592 A.2d 1251 (N.J. Super. 1991).

75 *See* Brennan, *Research Records, Litigation and Confidentiality: A Case of Research on Toxic Substances,* 4 I.R.B., A Review of Human Subjects Research 6 (1983).

76 *See* Winslade, *Confidentiality of Medical Records,* 3 J. Legal Med. 497 (1982).

77 *See* Brennan, note 75 above, at 9.

78 *See* McIntosh v. Milano, 403 A.2d 500 (N.J. Super. 1979).

79 *See* Davis v. Rodman, 227 S.W. 612 (1921).

80 *See* Skillings v. Allen, 173 N.W. 663 (1919).

81 *See, e.g.,* Cal. Code Regs. title 17, § 2514 (1986).

82 551 P.2d 334 (Cal. 1976).

83 *Id.* at 346.

84 *See* Givelber, *et al.,* Tarasoff, *Myth and Reality: An Empirical Study of Private Law in Action,* 1984 Wis. L. Rev. 443 (1984).

85 Personal Communication, Dr. Alan Stone (Feb. 15, 1988).

86 *See* Stone, *The Tarasoff Decisions: Suing Psychotherapists to Safeguard Society,* 90 Harv. L. Rev. 358 (1976).

87 *See* Beck, *The Psychotherapist's Duty to Protect Third Parties from Harm,* 11 MPDLR 141 (1987).

88 *See* Brennan, *AIDS and the Limits of Confidentiality: The Physician's Duty to Warn Contacted Seropositive Individuals,* 4 J. Gen. Internal Med. 242 (1989).

89 Nelke v. Kuzilla, 375 N.W.2d 403 (Mich. App. 1985).

90 DiMarco v. Lynch Homes Chester County, Inc., 583 A.2d 422 (Pa. 1990).

91 *See* Piorkowski, Jr., *Between a Rock and a Hard Place: AIDS and the Conflicting Physician's Duties of Preventing Disease Transmission and Safeguarding Confidentiality,* 76 Geo. L.J. 169, 180 n.63 (1987); *see also* North & Rothenberg, *The Duty to Warn Dilemma: A Framework for Resolution,* 4 AIDS & Pub. Pol'y 61 (1988); Turkington, *Confidentiality Policy for HIV-Related Information: An Analytical Framework for Sorting Out Hard and Easy Cases,* 34 Vill. L. Rev. 871 (1989); Price, *Between Scylla and Charybdis: Charting a Course to Reconcile the Duty of Confidentiality and the Duty to Warn in the AIDS Context,* 94 Dick. L. Rev. 435 (1990).

92 Cal. Health & Safety Code § 199.21(c) (West Supp. 1992).

93 *See* Mass. Gen. L. ch. 111, § 70(f) (1986).

94 *See Nurse's Exposure; An Incubation Period at Issue,* 2 AIDS Pol'y & Law 6 (1987).

95 *See* Urbaniak v. Newton, 226 Cal. App. 3d 1128 (1991) (oral release of HIV information by subject to doctor does not bring doctor within coverage of state confidentiality law); State v. Farmer, 805 P.2d 200 (Wash. 1991) (state HIV testing law noted by court weighing constitutional privacy claim); *see also* Snyder v. Mekhjian, 593 A.2d 318 (N.J. 1991) (Pollock, J., concurring) (discussion of respective roles of courts and legislatures in setting privacy policy).

96 *See* Cal. Health & Safety Code § 199.25 (West 1988).

97 *See* Tex. Rev. Civ. Stat. Ann. art. 4419(b)-(1), § 9.03 (West 1989).

98 *See* N.Y. Pub. Health Law § 2782(4)(a) (McKinney 1989).

99 The efficacy and methodology of partner notification are discussed, *e.g.,* in Munday, *et al., Contact Tracing in Hepatitis B,* 59 Brit. J. Venereal Disease 314 (1983); Wikoff, *et al., Contact Tracing to Identify Human Immunodeficiency Virus Infection in a Rural Community,* 259 J.A.M.A. 3563 (1988).

100 *See* Landis, *et al., Results of a Randomized Trial of Partner Notification in Cases of HIV Infection in North Carolina,* 326 New Eng. J. Med. 101 (1992) (describing burdens of partner notification); Marks, *et al., HIV-Infected Men's Practices in Notifying Past Sexual Partners of Infection Risk,* 107 Pub. Health Rep. 100 (1992) (patient's inability to identify past partners major reason for failure of patient to notify).

101 *See* Gostin, note 38 above (cataloging the reporting laws in the fifty states).

102 *See* Turkington, note 91 above, at 891.

103 *See generally* G. Calabresi, The Costs of Accidents (1970).

104 *See* K. Abraham, Distributing Risk 227 (1986).

105 *See* Mangione, *et al.,* note 5 above.

106 *See* Brennan, note 28 above.

107 *See* T. Brennan, note 27 above.

108 Although some cases will present a sympathetic enough factual situation to form the basis for successful suit. *See* Halverson v. Brand, 520 A.2d 67 (Pa. Super 1986).

109 *See* Booker v. Duke Medical Ctr., 256 S.E.2d 189 (N.C. 1979). There has been some litigation regarding the eligibility of professionals, such as physicians, for employee compensation benefits. Most courts have ruled that such benefits are available. *See* Higgins v. State Dept. of Health & Human Resources, 460 So. 2d 607 (La. 1984). *See generally* J. Chelius, Work Place Safety and Health: The Role of Worker's Compensation (1977).

110 Several studies have demonstrated that traumatic accident cases are much better compensated than are disease cases. *See* P. Barth & H. Hunt, Workers' Compensation and Work-Related Illnesses and Diseases (1980).

111 *See* Gostin, note 38 above, at 1625.

112 *See, e.g.,* Virgin Islands v. Roberts, 756 F. Supp. 898 (D.V.I. 1991).

113 *See* Doe v. Miles Laboratory, Inc., 675 F. Supp. 1466 (D. Md. 1987), aff'd, 927 F.2d 187 (4th Cir. 1991); Hyland Therapeutics, Div. of Travenol Laboratories, Inc. v. Superior Court, 175 Cal. App. 3d 509, 220 Cal. Rptr. 590 (1985).

114 *See* Doe v. American Red Cross Blood Servs, 125 F.R.D. 646 (D.S.C. 1989).

115 Tarrant County Hosp. Dist. v. Hughes, 734 S.W.2d 675 (Tex. App. 1987).

116 *See* Turkington, note 91 above, at 900–02.

117 *See* Hammonds v. Aetna Casualty & Sur. Co., 237 F. Supp. 96, 98–99 (N.D. Ohio 1965).

118 *See* Payton v. Weaver, 131 Cal. App. 3d 38, 182 Cal. Rptr. 225, 229 (Cal. App. 1982).

119 *See* McGulpin v. Bessmer, 43 N.W.2d 121 (Iowa 1950).

120 *See, e.g.,* Lyall v. Balshi, No. P–3422, AIDS Litig. Rep. (Andrews) 7501 (Pa. Human Relations Comm. Oct. 17, 1991) (dental discrimination).

121 Personal Communication, Scott Burris (March 22, 1992).

18 Private Insurance

Mark Scherzer

The public understands the relationship of the insurance industry to the HIV epidemic through the experiences of people like Thomas J. Bradley, a suburban New York public school teacher whose very private battle with AIDS became a highly public battle with his insurer to obtain funding for a sophisticated medical procedure. In 1990, his doctors told Bradley that his life might be prolonged by whole body radiation to wipe out his diseased blood cells, followed by a bone marrow transplant from his HIV-negative identical twin brother to reconstitute his immune system. The hospital offering the expensive treatment required authorization from Bradley's insurance company before his admission. Yet when he sought that authorization, the insurer refused, saying the treatment was experimental and not covered under his policy.

Bradley sued Empire Blue Cross and Blue Shield. He obtained an injunction in New York Supreme Court ordering the payment,[1] but in the eight weeks between Blue Cross's refusal to authorize his admission and the court's decision he developed an eye infection which the doctors said precluded him from receiving the treatment. He never received it, and died, as his doctors predicted, about a year after the court proceeding.

To many observers, the confrontation between Bradley and his insurer distilled into a single dramatic event the experience all people with AIDS have with insurers, in small daily battles waged without lawyers or TV cameras. After paying premiums for years, a person faced with a health crisis could find that his apparently heartless insurance company, its eye on the bottom line, would rely on a technicality to deny him benefits.

Like many symbolic dramas, the Bradley story crystallizes some moral truths while it obscures considerable moral ambiguities. On the one hand, it is understandable that people should resent large, impersonal, and bureaucratic financial institutions empowered to take their money and yet able to deny them medical treatment or other benefits for which the money has ostensibly been reserved. Their resentment reflects a more general and justifiable unease that access to health care, which we have by and large come to recognize as a fundamental entitlement, should depend on a person's access to financial resources.

On the other hand, the reality of the insurance system, and even of Mr. Bradley's case, is far more complex than the media images would suggest. While claims for some benefits are denied, insurers nonetheless pay billions annually in health, disability, and death benefits, including an estimated $1.2 billion in AIDS-related claims in 1990.[2] People who obtain the best care for illness are able to obtain it primarily because they have insurance coverage. Further, some insurance companies, including the defendant in the *Bradley* case, are not commercial enterprises at all, but are rather nonprofit cooperative organizations with a social mission of insuring as many people as possible, so that their contributed funds will be sufficient for the treatment of all those subscribers who need it. Even some "commercial" insurers are in fact mutual companies, whose profits accrue to their policyholders in the form of reduced premiums, rather than to investors.

As custodians of the funds contributed by all of their policyholders, insurers argue that they have a responsibility to act conservatively with those funds. If they were to pay for every creative treatment invented by every doctor, for example, they might quickly bankrupt themselves, leaving money unavailable for the well-established treatments for which policyholders routinely expect payment. In Mr. Bradley's case, Blue Cross argued that even if the scientific theory underlying the treatment appeared to have merit, it would be irresponsible to pay nearly $150,000 for a treatment that had been tried less than half a dozen times, and never to a demonstrably successful conclusion. As long as the treatment's effectiveness was still unproven, the cost, in Blue Cross's view, should more logically have been borne by medical research institutions or the government.

Thus, for an affected individual like Mr. Bradley, an insurance dispute may present a clear moral choice between permitting or denying an important personal benefit. From the broader social perspective of a policymaker, the same dispute may present a morally much more ambiguous choice: which among many potential sources should pay for that benefit? Both concerns are always present. Courts and legislatures may be called upon to answer the question "Who should pay?" but we as a society must always keep in mind the underlying concern of the insured person: "Will anyone pay?"

The determination of these questions in individual disputes between insurers and their insureds is part of a larger process, in which we as a society decide whether we should develop a different system to collect and disburse health care and welfare money (who should pay?) and whether, in devoting 12 percent of our gross national product to the purpose, we spend too much on health care (will anyone pay?). It is the purpose of this chapter to examine the issues confronted by those who regulate insurance in the age of AIDS. I will discuss how certain characteristics of the HIV epidemic (particularly the low social status of the gay men, drug users, and poor people of color who have been disproportionately devastated by the epidemic) have affected the resolution of disputes over who, if anyone, should pay for benefits, and how the disputes over HIV and AIDS relate to the larger national debate over the role of the insurance industry in delivery of health benefits.

HOW INSURANCE OPERATES

Private versus Public Insurance

This chapter primarily addresses the legal issues associated with private insurance, that is, insurance which is not provided through government agencies. Millions of Americans are unable to obtain private insurance because it is too expensive or because they have been rejected for coverage due to a medical condition such as HIV. Health insurance has traditionally been offered as a benefit of employment, so people who are unemployed, self-employed, or employed by a company that does not subsidize health benefits are particularly hard hit by the rising price of private insurance. People who are excluded from the private insurance market must depend on an assortment of government insurance and assistance programs, such as Medicaid, but not everyone who lacks private insurance can qualify for public coverage. For a comprehensive guide to public health insurance and assistance programs, the reader is directed to *The AIDS Benefits Handbook: Everything You Need to Know to Get Social Security, Welfare, Medicaid, Medicare, Food Stamps, Housing, Drugs, and Other Benefits*, by Thomas P. McCormack.

The Business of Insurance

Insurance involves a contract (embodied in an insurance policy) in which one party, the policyholder, makes periodic payments (premiums) to another party, the insurer, in return for a promise by the insurer to make payments when certain contingencies occur. The party who is protected by the contract, and to whom or on whose behalf the payments are to be made, is called the insured. The insured is usually, but not always, the owner of the policy and payer of premiums.

Among the major types of insurance of concern to people with HIV are: *medical insurance*, an agreement to pay or reimburse the paid medical expenses incurred by the insured under certain defined conditions; *disability insurance,* an agreement to make payments to the insured, usually in set monthly amounts, when the insured is unable to work; and *life insurance,* an agreement to pay money to a person or designated entity upon the death of the insured.

The premium payments made to the insurance company are generally periodic ones. These premiums and the money earned by investing them make up the funds used to make payments when the contingency covered by the insurance contract comes to pass. Although every insurance contract requires the payment of premiums by the policy owner, the insurer may or may not incur an obligation to pay benefits to the insured or to his or her beneficiary. For example, an insured may pay premiums throughout his or her life, and yet never become sick or disabled. Although death is inevitable, payment of life insurance proceeds may be contingent upon death coming in a specified manner (for instance, not by suicide) or within a specified time (such as, before expiration of a term policy).

The insurance contract thus bears some resemblance to a gambling contract, in which the bettor must pay money in order to participate in the game, but has no assurance of a return. However, the insured may collect benefits well in excess of the premiums he or she has paid. Consequently, the insurer—the person running the game—is successful to the degree that it establishes rules favorable to the house. If, in the aggregate, more money is placed in bets (insurance premiums) than is paid out in winnings (policy proceeds), the insurer will profit. Thus, insurers try to strike a favorable balance between broadening the number of people insured (to attract as wide a premium-paying base as possible) and limiting the exposure to claims arising from assumption of those extra risks. The more successful insurance companies have made better judgments about which risks, medical and otherwise, they can profitably assume.

The resemblance between insurance and gambling has at times worried those who regulate the industry. Public officials, including courts called upon to review statutes and regulations, have developed rules that remove insurance contracts from the realm of gambling contracts. An example is the statutory requirement that the purchaser of life insurance have an insurable interest (that is, an economic interest) in the life of the insured, a rule developed to discourage sales of insurance contracts that would amount to no more than sporting bets on the lives of the insureds.

If insurance were merely a matter of gambling, in which insureds sought to outsmart the insurance companies to reap an undeserved bonanza for themselves or their heirs, it would hardly be the focus of the intense political battle that appears to be occurring with respect to HIV. Insurance, however, is an important social institution, serving essential public functions.

In a society that places an extraordinarily high value on the cure of disease but makes provision of that cure a private business, medical treatment for many conditions costs more than most people can afford. They can obtain adequate treatment for serious illness or injury only through funds provided by others. The others could be family, neighbors, or friends. But when dealing with chronic illnesses like AIDS, even these affinity groups would in many instances have great difficulty in providing the required money. Larger aggregations of resources are required, and insurance companies constitute one of the primary means of creating such aggregated funds.

Disability and life insurance, too, must be treated as more than mere gambling contracts. Disability benefits enable sick people to maintain some of the spending power they had when they could work, and they diminish the need to rely upon public funds for nonmedical expenses like food and shelter. Life insurance maintains the financial security of people who depend upon a deceased person for support or for fulfillment of mutual financial or business obligations. Those whose assets are severely depleted by caring for a terminally ill person may be made whole to a degree through the proceeds of such insurance. Life insurance thereby may reinforce the stability of "family" units. As with medical insurance, people who are unable to set aside sufficient funds to cover needs associated with disability or death must rely on the sorts of aggregations of funds provided by insurance companies.

That aggregations of funds for these important social purposes be accomplished through insurance companies is not the only possible solution. Indeed, in the United States today there are two other principal means by which funds are so pooled: through monies reserved by employers or unions for workers and their dependents under "self insurance" plans; and through the tax revenues that fund government benefit programs like Medicare, Medicaid, and Social Security.

The degree to which each type of fund is used varies according to the type of benefit. Government medical benefits are available only to certain categories of people: the indigent, the long-term disabled, people over sixty-five, some people with specific needs arising out of particular catastrophic illnesses, veterans, and those who work for the government (civilians or military personnel) or are in its custody (prisoners). Most Americans have access to medical benefits through group plans tied to their private-sector employment.[3] In contrast, basic disability benefits are provided to most employed Americans through the government-sponsored Social Security disability system, although many obtain necessary supplemental benefits through employer-funded disability plans or personally purchased disability insurance policies. With respect to life insurance, relatively minimal benefits are provided through government programs. The bulk are obtained through individually purchased, as opposed to group, insurance policies.[4]

Although not the sole payer, therefore, the insurance industry is an important component in the system. Indeed, many employers and unions actually purchase insurance policies to provide some or all of their employee benefits. Still other self-insuring employers and even government agencies purchase the services of insurance companies to administer their benefit plans or programs. A healthy, functioning insurance industry is obviously in the public interest.

Underwriting

Underwriting is the process by which insurance companies decide whom they will insure and on what terms they will insure them. Underwriters are the gatekeepers, judging just how risky it may be to admit the gambler knocking on the casino door. In making those judgments, they rely on statistical analyses of risk provided by specialists known as actuaries. Actuaries examine historical claims experience and other information to develop profiles of risk and projections of benefits. They are the odds-makers of the business.

The assessment of risk in the insurance business has a long history. According to the American Academy of Actuaries, insurers began asking crude questions about health history to prospective purchasers of life insurance as early as the sixteenth century and were using family health history, occupation, and medical examinations to determine insurability by the 1800s.[5] Over time, the means to predict risk and to assess the health of the prospective insurance purchaser have become much more sophisticated and refined, and insurers have taken advantage of improved techniques to expand the numbers of people from whom they can accept premiums, set a fair price for their risk, and still limit exposure to large claims. Life insurers, for example, may distinguish among diabetics controlled by diet (insurable at a "standard" price), diabetics controlled by insulin (insurable but at a higher rate), and diabetics who developed the disease as children (because of greatly increased mortality, uninsurable at any price). Actuarial underwriting is so powerful a method of managing risks that its use has come to be known, along with the diametrically opposed concept of spreading risks among many people, as a fundamental tenet of the insurance system.

Indeed, underwriting is so embedded now in the concept of insurance that most American jurisdictions require that insurers set their premiums for individually underwritten policies on the basis of actuarial calculations: that is, the premium charged to an individual must be determined by the expenses which that individual is likely to incur (as determined by statistical evidence regarding individuals who share the identifying characteristics of the prospective buyer). An individual's projected health care costs (in the case of health insurance) or life expectancy (in the case of life insurance) will thus be used in determining insurance rates.

The requirement that insurance rates be based upon actuarial principles has been defended on grounds of fairness: an insurance buyer who seems likely to incur heavy expenses is purchasing a more valuable product, and thus should pay a higher premium, than a customer in a lower-risk group. The practice has also been defended as a means of creating economic incentives for efficient behavior. If individuals are charged premiums based upon the degrees of risk they represent, they may be induced to alter the characteristics which placed them at high risk.[6] For example, discounted premiums for nonsmokers might induce some smokers to give up the habit.

Even if insurers were not required by law to base their rates on actuarial principles, the mechanics of an unregulated competitive insurance market would force companies to rely on such principles in setting rates. A company that charged each customer the same premium simply could not compete with a company that differentiated among customers. Lower-risk consumers would shift their coverage to companies that set rates on an actuarial basis. As these low-risk consumers removed themselves from the nondiscriminating company's pool, it would be forced to raise its rates for the remaining customers. Those who could would react by dropping their insurance or switching to other carriers, leaving behind only those who most desperately needed benefits. Fewer and fewer people would be sharing ever higher average costs. This is the process described by the American Academy of Actuaries as the "spiral of adverse selection."[7]

The same forces are at work in the insurance of groups, although underwriting methods change in that context. Most people get their health and life insurance under group plans tied to their jobs. Traditionally, insurers have felt safe in assuming that the people who are able to work are the healthiest people in society, and have found it inefficient to expend money individually evaluating each member of an employee group before issuing insurance. By automatically taking all members of a large employee group they take enough premium payers to have ample reserves for the potentially high costs of the minority who become actively or chronically ill.

By taking very large groups, insurers could in theory ignore the state of health of all individual applicants (accepting everyone on an "open enrollment" basis) and charge a single per capita premium rate based on the anticipated claims experience of the entire community. In this way, the risk of loss is spread evenly to every member of the community. But to charge all large groups a single "community" rate ignores that some groups composed of younger people or those in less dangerous occupations, for example, will have better claims experience than others.

Employers of these groups, acting as consumers in the insurance marketplace, try to lower their costs by seeking out insurers willing to offer them a lower price based on their better-than-average health. Their health can be assessed not just by abstract estimates or actuarial predictions but by actual experience of the employee group. Today, groups of fifty or more people are quite often "experience rated"; that is, the employer agrees to pay sufficient sums in each year to cover any difference between the premiums paid and total group costs in the previous year. Such experience-rated groups are a small step away from being self-insured. Whereas forty years ago community rating for medical insurance was the norm in the United States, the introduction of commercial competition in the business quickly led to the exodus of many better risk groups from the community-rated pool, and eventually to the disappearance of community rating from the large group insurance market in all but a few communities.[8]

The small group market has undergone similar change. Commercial insurers have searched for better small-group risks by looking at the claims experience of small groups or the industries to which they belong, the demographics of the group (age, sex, and so forth), or even, in groups of fewer than ten or fifteen employees, by evaluating the health of each member as would be done for individual insurance applicants. As in the large-group market, community rating has been largely replaced by actuarial underwriting. The predictable result has been spiraling costs in the pools which do not underwrite, to the point at which the costs of providing benefits to the high-risk people in the non-underwritten pool has become prohibitive. In New York, one of the few remaining states where Blue Cross companies will insure all members of the community at the community rate, regardless of health, the largest insurer, Empire Blue Cross and Blue Shield, has blamed commercial "cherry picking" (that is, luring away of the better risks) for causing the loss of 400,000 subscribers and massive operating losses. The company sought permission in 1991 to begin to discriminate in the premiums charged its own sick and healthy subscribers in order to compete with commercial insurers for the better risks.[9]

The Blue Cross request was denied,[10] in large part because of the opposition of an unprecedented coalition of HIV advocacy groups and those with other chronic diseases. But the structural tension between the community-rated system and the actuarially underwritten system remained. Consumers and state regulators therefore joined in arguing that if the two systems could not coexist in the same market, the state should opt for the more inclusive model and abolish the discriminatory one. The New York legislature heeded these arguments and, in July 1992, took the radical step of prohibiting all underwriting and mandating community rating for the entire small group market. It simultaneously adopted a series of other reforms of particular benefit to those with chronic health conditions (discussed below) and took temporary control over commercial insurance prices. Although the reforms were precipitated by the crisis in the open enrollment community-rated market, their specific shape was in part attributable to the emergence of the chronic disease community as a mobilized, unified, and seemingly powerful interest group.

In many other states, however, where open enrollment and community rating are now just historical memories, the only way coverage has been made available to the medically uninsurable has been through state-subsidized "high-risk" pools which, even with subsidies, must charge members significantly more than the cost of regular insurance policies. By mid–1990, half the states had enabling laws for high-risk pools, and twenty-one were operational. Most lost money, and few had provisions to subsidize participants who could not afford the pool premiums.[11] Such is the power of the underwriting principle that it forces all to conform to its ways and results in the isolation, through one mechanism or another, of those at high risk who simply cannot support their own medical costs.

Those who view health care as a commodity have asserted that the competitive marketplace as epitomized by the actuarial underwriting system is the most efficient way to deliver the services; the shortcomings of the marketplace in making services generally available, in their view, can be addressed through safety nets like Medicaid for the poor and high-risk pools for the medically uninsurable. Those who in contrast view access to health care as a fundamental right have pointed out the absurdity of a system in which commercial imperatives render those most in need of top-quality medical benefits ineligible to obtain them. They have suggested that the underwriting process is in fact wasteful, requiring substantial resources to identify risk when those resources could better be devoted to providing medical benefits for those currently uninsured. As we shall see, HIV cast a new light on this already-existing debate, first by showing how crude and unfair the underwriting system could be when based on ignorance, and then by showing how powerful and far-reaching the system could be when based on sophisticated medical information.

How Insurance Companies Are Regulated

As the discussion of underwriting suggests, insurance companies' desires to promote their own financial well-being may conflict with the public interest in providing the broadest insurance coverage possible. While insurance companies maintain that they are private businesses whose decisions cannot solely reflect the public interest, there can be no doubt that they deal in a particularly crucial commodity. One might argue, indeed, that the availability of the insurance companies' aggregated funds in itself has a significant effect on health care. On the one hand, those without access to insurance may be reluctant or unable to obtain routine medical care and may be in poorer health generally. On the other hand, doctors treating such patients may be reluctant to order necessary medical tests and procedures.[12] Insurance companies, accordingly, are properly subject to extensive government intervention for the public welfare. The regulators' task is to maintain an environment in which insurers can operate profitably while restraining insurers on those occasions when the profit motive threatens important public values.

Under the terms of a 1923 federal law, the McCarran-Ferguson Regulation Act, the regulation of insurance companies has been a matter reserved to the individual states.[13] Thus, more than fifty jurisdictions have for some time fixed their own sets of rules. They have done so both through passing specific legislation and through creating specialized agencies with broad regulatory and rule-making authority.

One result of the continuing battles between insurance companies and HIV advocates has been to focus attention on the powers and limitations of the state insurance regulators. Early in the epidemic, advocates tried to limit the use of HIV antibody tests for judging insurability. In states where they could not induce the legislatures to act, they sometimes turned to the state insurance departments to regulate against the practice. Insurance industry organizations in New York and Massachusetts blocked those regulations in court, successfully arguing that only the legislature, not the administrative agencies, could interfere with underwriting practices, even though the agencies had exercised their authority in that way in the past without challenge.[14] Where, however, the legislature itself limited the use of antibody tests, its authority to do so was clearly upheld.[15]

Regulation of insurance is pervasive, extending to the very terms on which insurance may be offered or purchased. The operations of insurance companies and agents are also highly regulated, through licensing and other schemes, to make certain that they are financially and ethically responsible. For example, states have developed special mechanisms for dealing with insolvent insurers and have restricted trade practices deemed deceptive or unfair to consumers.[16] In recent years, regulation has focused on mandating insurance coverage for more people and on expanding the insurance benefits available to them. By 1984, twenty-five jurisdictions had legislation addressed to insurance discrimination based upon specific physical disabilities.[17]

Although the authority of state legislatures and insurance departments over insurers is extensive, there are important limitations on their authority, both legal and practical. In legal terms, the insurance industry is entitled to the same constitutional protections as other businesses from confiscatory action and from interference with its rights to speech and association. It is entitled to protection from arbitrary and capricious administrative actions. It has also, through a recent series of court interpretations of a federal statute, gained a measure of immunity from the state laws that were traditionally supposed to be the exclusive means of insurance regulation.

The Employee Retirement Income Security Act of 1974 (ERISA) was adopted by Congress primarily to stem fiduciary abuses in union pension funds.[18] It evolved to include antidiscrimination rules for pension plans and some rules regarding procedures in other "welfare benefit plans," including life, medical, and disability benefits. It thus appeared to provide a system of federal regulation of all the employer-provided plans that people commonly understand to compose their insurance benefits. ERISA provided that it would "preempt," that is supersede, any state laws governing employee benefit plans. Although the law stated that it would not preempt state laws specifically regulating insurance, it was careful to prohibit states from treating self-funded employee benefit plans as insurance policies, thereby removing them completely from the scope of state insurance regulation. Further, when the courts applied ERISA to group insurance policies purchased by employers, they broadened federal preemption by interpreting very narrowly what constituted a state law specifically regulating insurance. All sorts of state rules, from rules providing "bad faith" damages when insurers engage in unfair claim settlement, to rules requiring notices to employees about their insurance rights when they leave their jobs, have been held not to be "state laws regulating insurance" and have therefore been determined not to apply to employee benefit plans.[19]

Thus, an employer's self-funded plan (even when administered by an insurance company) is not considered to be insurance at all and is totally exempt from state regulation. Even when an insurer issues an insurance policy to an employer-sponsored group, that policy becomes for many purposes governed solely by ERISA and immune from regulation by the state. But while ERISA frees employee benefit plans from obeying most state rules, ERISA itself has few substantive rules about how benefit plans should be operated. While it requires disclosure to employees about benefit plans and affords participants some procedural rights, it does not regulate the content of benefit plans. In setting aside detailed state laws regarding insurance, ERISA has created a chaotic regulatory void.

Perhaps even more important than ERISA's legal limitations on state regulations are practical limitations that must be taken into account in formulating public policy. These practical limitations derive from the position of the insurance system, as discussed above, as just one band on the spectrum of payment systems subject to very different kinds of regulation and market incentives. Suppose, for example, that a state legislature were to enact a law requiring all medical insurance plans to pay for long-term, full-time home nursing service to all insured people whose doctors ordered it. The law, which might be highly desirable from the standpoint of public health and particularly to people with AIDS, might well increase the cost of insurance premiums. Insurance companies might reduce other policy benefits, just as socially desirable, in order to keep premium levels down. Equally likely, increased premiums might drive a large employer to determine that it could save money by cancelling its insurance policy and adopting a self-insured plan, in which it would be freed from providing the benefits mandated by the then-preempted state insurance law. Avoiding state-mandated benefits is thought to be one of the primary motives prompting the employers of a majority of the American work force to move to self insurance.[20]

Small employers facing higher premiums would not have the same option of establishing self-insured plans (they cannot usually aggregate sufficient sums on their own to cover employees' catastrophic health costs) but they do have the option of ceasing to offer insurance altogether. Rather than moving from the category of insured to self-insured, employees of such small employers might move to the category of the uninsured. A disproportionate number of the 37 million Americans who are said to be uninsured are employed by small employers.[21] If hit with catastrophic illness, the uninsured are likely to become impoverished and dependent upon government programs to pay for their needs.

That insurance is a voluntary arrangement and that there are much less stringently regulated alternative funding mechanisms ties the hands of state regulators to a significant degree. They cannot treat the insurance system as a self-contained entity, the manipulation of which will achieve social goals. They must regulate with an eye to keeping the insurance system as a whole in equilibrium with the alternatives, and different components of the insurance system competitive with each other.

With these regulatory limitations in mind, we can turn to our examination of the particular disputes that have been most vigorously and repeatedly fought between insurers and their HIV-infected customers.

UNDERWRITING: THE FIRST BATTLEGROUND

Underwriting was the first arena of political battle between insurers and HIV advocates. AIDS appeared from nowhere in 1981. If there were deaths from it before that year, they were presumably small in number and buried among statistics for deaths resulting from pneumonia or cancer. Obviously, assessments of risk and premium charges had been computed without AIDS medical or death claims in mind. An unanticipated condition like AIDS was a threat to the underwriting system.

In the period immediately following the initial identification of the disease, however, the insurance industry did not react with great alarm. The numbers of people affected were then quite small (if growing exponentially), and they appeared to be almost exclusively gay men in a few metropolitan areas. It may be that the industry was complacent because it assumed that it did not insure many such people. Some insurers still had restrictions in the "habits and morals" sections of their underwriting manuals against issuing policies to lesbians and gay men whom they presumed they could identify.[22] As was soon to become evident, many insurers also assumed that gay men were confined to certain stereotypical occupations. Not re-alizing that gay men were everywhere, insurance underwriters were medically so-phisticated but socially blind.

When, in 1984, significant numbers of new AIDS cases received a great deal of publicity and scientific consensus emerged that the disease had a viral cause, insurers mirrored the panic of the general public. There were even reports that some claims examiners were afraid to handle claim forms submitted by AIDS patients. Insurers scrambled to eliminate the risk of AIDS from their business.

Some insurers acted in crude ways that would have been inconceivable if those primarily affected by AIDS had been, for example, socially acceptable young het-erosexuals. They tried to eliminate high-risk groups from their policyholding pop-ulations altogether. Intravenous drug users, who by 1984 had already been identified as a high-risk group for AIDS, had long been considered uninsurable. But the epi-demic's main effect was to put an even greater—and more legally and politically explosive—emphasis on gay men.

A survey by the Congressional Office of Technology Assessment in 1988 showed that nearly one-third of responding health insurers admitted taking sexual orientation into account in underwriting.[23] While this might suggest the availability of routine procedures for identifying gay men, in fact their identification was not a finely honed skill among insurers. Most direct ways of ascertaining sexual orientation were simply not feasible. To request specific information about sexual activity in an application would require inquiries that many applicants, no matter what their sexual orientation, would find offensive. Moreover, an individual's statement that he was not gay (or was not sexually active) would be almost impossible to verify, and a subsequent attempt to prove misrepresentation would be difficult. Attempts to exclude gay applicants, therefore, had to be indirect.

The alternative many selected was a reliance on social stereotypes entirely at odds with the scientific basis on which insurers generally operate. Several insurance companies (notably major reinsurance companies whose guidelines tended to become public once distributed to the companies whose policies they reinsure) developed underwriting guidelines based upon detecting an apparently "gay lifestyle." The Great Republic Life Insurance Company, in guidelines challenged in a California suit, instructed underwriters to segregate the applications of single males without dependents in professions not requiring physical exertion. Explicitly included in this occupational category were florists, interior designers, and people in the fashion business. If an applicant in the segregated group had gained or lost more than ten pounds in the year prior to application, or had any sexually transmitted disease, his application would be declined.[24] Similarly, Munich American Reassurance Company, which eventually revised its guidelines under pressure from both National Gay Rights Advocates and the California Department of Insurance, instructed underwriters to be wary of single people in certain cities who named parents or siblings as beneficiaries or who had been exposed to a person capable of transmitting the HIV virus (though the guidelines did not specify what sort of exposure would cause refusal of the application).[25] Lincoln National Life Insurance Company focused on marital status and geographical location as well as "lifestyle" and "habits."[26]

If underwriting by excluding gay people was irrational (many gay men are not at risk for AIDS; many straight men are), underwriting by use of surrogate markers for homosexuality was doubly so. Hairdressers, dancers, and others in stereotypically gay occupations have repeatedly experienced difficulties in obtaining insurance, and have from time to time filed complaints with state insurance regulators under fair trade laws, asserting that occupational exclusions impermissibly treated people of similar risk differently. Even where insurers have suggested nondiscriminatory reasons for their occupational exclusions, public perception that the exclusions are targeted at gay people has run deep.

In late 1986, the National Association of Insurance Commissioners published recommended guidelines with respect to underwriting for AIDS. They suggested prohibiting both sexual orientation discrimination and the use of demographic factors such as occupation, marital status, living arrangements, and zip code to establish sexual orientation.[27] A small number of states adopted the guidelines through statute or regulation.[28] Continuing problems of apparent abuse (in 1988, for instance, a heterosexual man in New York sued an insurance company, alleging that it discriminated against him in not offering a life insurance policy because it mistakenly perceived him to be gay[29]) together with the general crisis of coverage among small employer groups (most uninsured people work for small employers, and stereotypically gay occupations are often carried out in the small business setting) have now led even the commercial insurance industry to acknowledge the legitimacy of reforms in which both occupational and sexual-orientation underwriting would be banned.[30]

To renounce publicly the crude and irrational use of criteria like occupation and sexual orientation in underwriting has been, in a sense, easy for the insurance industry. It now has a better means of avoiding risk, the HIV antibody test. Since the test became commercially available in 1985, those with antibodies have come to be considered uninsurable.

If we return to the analogy of the gambling casino, we can understand immediately the reluctance of insurance companies to insure people who are HIV-positive. People infected by HIV are far more likely than their seronegative counterparts to incur large health costs, disability claims, and premature death claims. They are, in gambling parlance, the possessors of stacked decks of cards or loaded dice, much more likely than the average person to emerge from the insurance casino with significant ''winnings.''

When insurers began trying to detect these loaded dice through antibody testing, advocates for people with HIV immediately disputed their right to do so. They argued that it was unfair to use a test which merely demonstrated exposure to HIV, rather than active illness. Relying on the preliminary findings of a retrospective study of gay men in San Francisco,[31] they pointed to the small percentages of HIV-infected people in each year who became ill and claimed, based on that data, that insurers could not predict who among the HIV-infected would become ill or when. They likened HIV antibody testing to testing for genetic traits that predispose one to certain diseases, something insurers had never before done.

Insurers responded by asserting that even the San Francisco data showed HIV-infected people to face unacceptable levels of risk of disease and death under traditional insurance company standards, and that they had for many years used similar tests, such as blood tests showing hepatitis exposure and blood pressure tests indicating heart disease, in underwriting. They argued that underwriting was not only fair but also necessary to keep insurance affordable for most Americans.

The insurers unquestionably had the better of the statistical arguments about degrees of risk, but that in itself did not dictate the ultimate outcome of the debate. Insurers have frequently been directed to provide coverage on terms which they would not have done if applying solely their judgments of actuarial risk (as when directed not to discriminate according to race, sex, or national origin), and they have accommodated the directives by adjusting the premiums for all other policyholders. The outcome of the political battle was probably influenced more by the relative ability of each side to demonstrate the social equities of its position.

As health policy scholar Deborah Stone has pointed out in her brilliant analysis of the politics of the HIV testing debate, the opponents of antibody testing concentrated on demonstrating the unfairness to gay men of being excluded from the insurance system. The insurance industry, in contrast, made a case that it would be unfair to grant people with HIV a privilege, access to insurance, which people with other serious conditions, like cancer or heart disease, were denied. Stone concludes that by framing the debate primarily in terms of discrimination (whether against gay men on the one hand or against people with cancer or heart disease on the other) the advocates obscured other potential policy choices, such as using the insurance system as a mechanism for broad cost-sharing in which access to benefits is determined by a person's medical needs.[32]

In any event, the industry's effort to frame the debate in terms of fairness to the broad mass of insurance policyholders succeeded. One indicator of that success was the surprising endorsement of HIV antibody testing by the National Insurance Consumers Organization, whose leaders declared that increased premium costs to the majority of consumers arising out of AIDS treatment should be avoided, even if it meant excluding HIV-positive people from the insurance system.[33] The more important measure of success was that no jurisdiction ultimately agreed to ban HIV antibody testing. The few jurisdictions that initially legislated bans or limits on the use of the test—California, Wisconsin, Maine, and Washington, D.C.—all scaled back or repealed those limitations within a short time. California, with the broadest remaining ban, now prohibits use of the antibody test, but not surrogate tests like T-cell tests or other medical underwriting, for health insurance purposes, and permits antibody testing for disability and life insurance.[34] Wisconsin retains only a nearly meaningless ban on antibody testing for *group* health policies where medical tests are rarely used anyway, a gesture in which it has been now joined by Florida and Rhode Island.[35] In most states, antibody testing is generally available to insurers so long as certain standards of informed consent and confidentiality are maintained. Although the possession of sensitive information like antibody test results subjects insurers to some risks—they may be sued if they disclose the results to the wrong parties on the one hand or if they fail to disclose the results to the insurance applicant on the other[36]—they find the risks worth taking.

One might in hindsight criticize those (like this author) who approached antibody testing as a gay rights issue in the mid–1980s. To have insisted upon achieving social equity for gay men in the inherently discriminatory commercial insurance context, when discrimination against them in numerous other realms like employment and housing was still not generally prohibited, may well have been to jump too far too fast. But such arguments were in political context actually the least radical ones available. In the mid–1980s the achievement of an insurance system, like a national health plan, that emphasized the cost-sharing function of insurance over the risk-selection function, was but a distant dream. Obtaining dispensation for a relatively small and traditionally oppressed minority at a time of catastrophic epidemic seemed a considerably more modest and achievable goal.

It does not seem, moreover, that the arguments advanced by HIV advocates were entirely futile. They may have shaped in important ways the current debate over national health plans. HIV advocates not only showed how irrational the underwriting system could be, but were also the first to question in a politically forceful way the exclusion from insurance of people with chronic medical conditions. Merely to raise the question opened the door for others with chronic illnesses to question their exclusion as well. It provided a model for disease group advocacy. It has helped make coverage of the actuarially uninsurable a fundamental aspect of *every* proposal for health insurance reform.

BENEFITS: THE ONGOING BATTLE

Winning the right to test blood for antibodies did not fully resolve for insurers the problems of AIDS; it only restricted HIV-positive people from obtaining new small group and individual insurance coverage. The industry still had to deal with the unanticipated claims that were bound to be presented by people already insured or by people who would, by virtue of their membership in large employee groups, become insured without satisfying any health requirements. To limit these latter risks, insurers have invoked with exceptional vigor their traditional repertoire of claim reduction techniques. Just as gambling casinos may try to establish rules of the game favoring the house, insurers set rules by which they can avoid paying out what they believe to be excessive benefits.

Rescission of Policies

Insurance is a contract, and the law requires that parties to a contract deal honestly with each other. From early in the epidemic, insurers have sought to rescind health, life, and disability policies issued to people who were alleged to have obtained their policies through misrepresentations about their health or lifestyle. The insurers were convinced that people at high risk had been knowingly and deliberately purchasing policies to which they were not entitled.

Insurance applications had no specific questions about AIDS or HIV in the early 1980s, and applicants from that era could therefore not usually be said to have misrepresented their HIV-related histories. Insurers, however, looked for other undisclosed facts on application forms, and asserted that knowledge of those facts would have materially changed their willingness to issue the policies. In one case, an insurer succeeded in its claim that, although none of the applicant's undisclosed sexually transmitted diseases would individually have been considered significant, in the aggregate his history of several sexually transmitted diseases showed him to be a promiscuous person who would therefore never have been offered insurance.[37] In another case, which the insurance company lost after trial, the designation of a proposed beneficiary as a "business partner" instead of as a "roommate" was said to have been a material misrepresentation justifying rescission.[38]

Although the advent of testing has diminished the need to rely on health representations to detect people actually infected with HIV, questioning applicants about their health and habits continues to be used as a way to attempt to identify people at higher risk of HIV. Because in most states any failure to disclose a material fact may be grounds for cancelling an insurance contract, insurers have a strong financial incentive to allege misrepresentation when faced with an expensive claim.

"Pre-Existing Condition" Limitations

Under "pre-existing condition" clauses, typically found in both medical and disability policies, insurers do not have to pay for claims arising during a stated period of time after the inception of the policy if those claims result from a condition the insured person had before coverage became effective. Such limitations may place new employees with chronic illnesses at substantial risk if they incur claims. Thirty percent of Americans in a recent survey said they or someone in their families have at some time stayed in a job in order to maintain health benefits.[39]

This has not yet been a major area of litigation in the HIV context. If litigation does occur, insured people are likely to rely on legal precedents fifty or more years old regarding conditions like tuberculosis, in which courts found that mere infection, if not causing active illness or certain to cause illness at a definite time, was insufficiently manifest and life-affecting to be considered a pre-existing condition.[40] Insurers are likely to, and are beginning to, rely upon a concept of AIDS as an inevitable manifestation of an HIV disease that runs a fully predictable course. If their view of the disease prevails for insurance purposes, and reimbursement early during insurance coverage is restricted, HIV infection will continue to present a formidable barrier to employee job mobility.

Pre-existing condition limitations may be justified as encouraging people to obtain and maintain insurance. If such limitations did not exist, consumers would in theory wait until they became sick to buy insurance. The rationale for the limitation as an incentive to participation in the insurance system breaks down, however, when insurance is obtained through employment. People do not usually change employment primarily because they need insurance benefits. There is no social benefit to making insurance coverage a primary motivation for either maintaining or changing employment.

Recognizing how pre-existing condition limitations could skew employment decisions, Congress in 1989 changed COBRA, the law regarding continuation of participation in larger group health plans, to permit people in new jobs to pay for and keep their former employer's medical benefits simultaneously with their new coverage if they were subject to a pre-existing condition limitation on their new employer's health plan. According to the office of Congresswoman Pelosi, who sponsored the legislation, the new benefits would extend coverage for about forty thousand disabled people per year, a significant portion of whom would have AIDS or symptomatic HIV infection.[41] Similarly, many proposals for reform in the small group market today (including the reforms actually adopted in New York in 1992) include "one time only" pre-existing condition limitations. After satisfying their first limitation period, employees could switch jobs without having to wait again to qualify for benefits.[42]

Experimental Treatment Exclusions

Most medical plans exclude reimbursement for experimental treatments. Yet there is very little about HIV or its treatments that is well established. Reimbursement difficulties have not been restricted to the realm of exotic procedures like those for which Tom Bradley sought coverage. Patients who have sought coverage for far more mundane treatments, like AZT, have also encountered barriers.

Courts generally will determine that treatments are no longer experimental when there is a consensus among a relevant group of doctors that the treatment is safe and effective. Thus, when the Missouri Medicaid program decided not to pay for AZT for patients with T cell counts over two hundred, on the grounds that the Food and Drug Administration had approved its use only for those with counts under two hundred, Medicaid's determination was overturned by the courts. When physicians, who were legally free to prescribe the drug, agreed that the drug should be used in a broader way than the Food and Drug Administration recommended, the use was considered medically necessary and reimbursable.[43]

Notwithstanding the well-publicized successes of people with HIV in court battles to obtain reimbursement for what insurers deemed experimental treatments, the frustratingly slow process by which government agencies and research facilities establish the efficacy of new treatments guarantees that experimental treatment disputes will remain a staple of AIDS litigation for some time to come.

Other Limitations

Not every reimbursement problem experienced by people with HIV is in an unsettled area of the law or unlike the mundane problems faced by other insured people. People with HIV face rather routine problems with clauses in insurance policies, for example, that restrict reimbursement to claims for "medically necessary" treatment, excluding check-ups (at the preventive-care end of the spectrum) or custodial care (at the stage when long-term care is needed). Similarly, most policies will cover only the "reasonable and customary" costs of treatment. Patients who go to the most expensive doctors in an area will find their reimbursement reduced to what the insurer considers a more typical fee.

One cost containment device, however, may have a particular impact on people with AIDS. Insurance policies may require that people with serious conditions enter into a "case management" arrangement. Case managers review the recommendations of physicians and sometimes suggest alternative, less costly or less burdensome treatments. Case management is a further elaboration of traditional pre-treatment review mechanisms, such as requirements that patients obtain second opinions before surgery or that they notify the insurer prior to elective hospitalizations, and has been promoted as a means of reducing the costs of serious illnesses. The obligations of case managers to patients remain in some ways ill defined, however, and, in a context of significant medical uncertainty about the best course of treatment, the arrangement seems likely to become the subject of contention among doctors, patients, and insurers.

Termination of Insurance

Insurers retain the right to terminate coverage under certain conditions. Loss of employment is the event that perhaps most frequently leads to termination of an individual's insurance, but high claims may lead an insurer to terminate an entire group or raise its premiums so high that the group is forced to drop the policy. In both of these contexts, the experiences of people with AIDS have driven reform movements. The federal COBRA law, which provides continuations of coverage for those who leave jobs with employers who have twenty or more employees, was amended in 1989 to extend the continuation for those who were disabled when they left their jobs. The COBRA continuation coverage period is now long enough to protect people disabled by HIV until they qualify for Medicare.[44] Efforts in New

York to extend continuation rights in small groups not covered by the COBRA law—efforts which bore fruit when the 1992 reforms conformed state rules to federal COBRA—have similarly been spearheaded by HIV advocates.[45]

The dreadful experiences of some small groups who found themselves subject to astronomical rate increases after members made AIDS claims, in effect terminating their coverage, have also had an effect on public policy. Kentucky, for example, has prohibited the dropping of policies because group members developed AIDS.[46] In New York, recent regulations restrict the use of small-group claims experience for setting rates or for selective nonrenewal of policies.[47] Restrictions on sudden and dramatic small-group rate rises are now, too, a part of many insurance reform packages.

The effects of termination of insurance and of the other claims reduction mechanisms described above are, of course, felt with equal strength by those with other serious chronic diseases. In some cases, like Tom Bradley's, the legal ground for people with AIDS was broken by people with conditions like breast cancer and multiple myeloma, who while severely ill fought for and won coverage for high-dose chemotherapy and bone marrow rescue.[48] In other cases, like the Missouri Medicaid case, the victory of people with AIDS became an important precedent for others, like cancer patients, to whom reimbursement for drugs used in ways not originally contemplated by the Food and Drug Administration has been a constant concern.[49]

Reforms benefitting people with AIDS ultimately benefit everyone with chronic illnesses. As their common interests become clear, the chronically ill will form effective coalitions advocating comprehensive health coverage. Concomitantly, if employers and insurers interested in rationing health benefits wish to diminish opposition to their schemes, they will find that they must narrow benefits in ways that appear to affect only a narrow spectrum of people—not the broad mass of the chronically ill.

They have begun to do so. As we shall now see, the AIDS battle has in a sense come full circle. Benefit planners are again isolating AIDS and treating it as exceptional. They may hope that if they appear to restrict the effects of their actions to those with AIDS, the continuing low status of the AIDS-affected community will deter concerted opposition by others who could potentially feel their interests to be at risk. This strategy reveals much about the regulatory environment of the insurance system; its likelihood of success will depend on the ability of the entire polity to realize that even AIDS-specific restrictions can ultimately hurt everyone.

ERISA: THE COMING BATTLE

The resurgence of especially discriminatory treatment of people with HIV is best illustrated by another story every bit as tragic as the story of Thomas Bradley. Houston resident John McGann was employed by H & H Music Company for five years before he was hospitalized for pneumonia and diagnosed with AIDS in late 1987. When he became ill, he was covered by a group health insurance policy that provided lifetime maximum benefits of $1 million per employee. Mr. McGann submitted claims for his treatment and informed his employer that he had AIDS. Company officials met with him to discuss his illness. Within months after that meeting, H & H Music decided to cancel its insurance policy and institute a self-insured plan in its place. Under the self-insured plan, the million dollar maximum benefit continued to be available for all serious illnesses, with a single exception: AIDS. For AIDS, there was a lifetime benefit cap of $5,000. Mr. McGann quickly exhausted his benefits.

McGann sued his employer for damages under Section 510 of ERISA, which prohibits discrimination against plan participants for exercising any rights under the plan, or for the purpose of interfering with the attainment of rights they might have under the plan. He lost his case before a federal district court. A federal circuit court of appeals upheld the decision, even though his employer conceded, for purposes of the court's decision, that it was motivated by a desire not to pay benefits for his AIDS treatment; even though the court assumed that there was a connection between McGann's filing of claims and the change in the plan; and even though the court acknowledged that the employer may have been motivated in part by prejudice against people with AIDS. The court held that such motivations would not constitute discrimination as long as the desire to eliminate payment for AIDS claims arose out of a desire to save money rather than a particularized, personally directed desire to deprive Mr. McGann of his benefits.[50]

The reasoning of the *McGann* case borders on the ludicrous. At one level, it would be hard to imagine a more particularized, personally directed act than the change of the plan to eliminate the very benefits a particular employee had just claimed. The plan changes were conceded to be responsive to, and specifically targeted at, the prospective claims of John McGann. The right to medical reimbursement for his disease was clearly a right that McGann might have had under the plan, but for his employer's actions. To suggest that McGann was not deprived of rights because the rights were being modified out of existence is to descend into a realm where language has no meaning. The court's decision leaves the door open to employers to eliminate benefits for the needs of any particular employee as soon as those needs are demonstrated, subject only to the constraint that the changes must affect any other similarly situated employees as well. Moreover, it seems perfectly apparent that the deprivation of McGann's rights was discriminatory in nature. Although most people think of discrimination as treating individuals differently because they belong to a particular disfavored class, the court in *McGann* took the opposite view. It pointed out that the benefit limit applied not just to McGann but also to "any other present or future plan beneficiary who might suffer from AIDS."[51] That it affected an entire class was, in the court's view, evidence that the change was not discriminatory.

The legal concept of discrimination does not mean that an individual is treated unfairly as a result of characteristics unique to him or her. It means, rather, that an individual has been treated unfairly as a result of membership in a class (racial, sexual, or religious, for example) that should not legitimately be used as the basis for differential treatment. People with AIDS are not just a group of people who happen to share the need for particular sorts of medical treatment. They constitute a class against which prejudice has been expressed through imposition of every imaginable form of social disadvantage and exclusion. Their disease is no more expensive to treat than many other serious conditions, and in fact may cost less.[52] AIDS accounts for less than 2 percent of all medical claims, while heart disease and cancers incur much higher total expense.[53] Yet the *McGann* court, faced with an employer that maintained a highly generous million dollar lifetime medical benefit for almost all its employees and selected AIDS as the only disease for which treatment would not be meaningfully reimbursed, still accepted at face value H & H Music's assertion that its motivation was to control medical costs and that Mr. McGann was not even entitled to a trial on the issue of whether there was a discriminatory motive at work as well.

Of course, H & H Music need not necessarily have been motivated solely by gross bigotry in doing what it did to Mr. McGann. But its effort to cut costs could not have succeeded without manipulating bigotry in an ugly way. In electing to deal with health costs by selectively cutting benefits for a person with AIDS and others like him, H & H Music was isolating a socially disfavored group. Other employees, not perceiving themselves to be at risk for AIDS, probably would not imagine that if they developed a serious condition, like heart disease or cancer, they might also lose all their benefits within months thereafter. Although the court's decision left the door open for employees with other diseases to suffer a similar fate, H & H

Music has not faced employee protests or even consumer boycotts over the issue. This suggests that its tactic of isolating HIV has succeeded.

Whether the *McGann* decision will lead to a common practice of excluding HIV treatment from employee benefit plans is difficult to predict. Sporadic attempts to exclude or cap HIV treatment earlier in the epidemic were in several instances suppressed by state insurance regulators.[54] H & H Music, however, moved from the world of insurance to the world of self-insurance. In the process, it left all vestiges of state insurance regulation behind,[55] and the Fifth Circuit's decision in *McGann* confirmed that federal regulation of the substance of benefit plans is an empty shell. There is now a road map for large employers and unions who wish to exclude HIV treatment from coverage in self-insurance plans. That such exclusions are now being disputed in several lawsuits around the country, and that numerous union plans now impose caps on differential HIV treatments, suggest that many others will indeed follow that road.

Some analysts have speculated that *McGann*-style discrimination might be invalidated by a new federal law, the Americans with Disabilities Act (ADA), which prohibits discrimination against the disabled. This outcome is by no means certain, however, since the statute specifically permits plans to be underwritten according to actuarial risk unless such underwriting is being used as a subterfuge to evade the ADA.[56] A court following the simplistic reasoning of the Fifth Circuit's *McGann* decision would be likely to find a refusal to cover AIDS actuarially justified under the ADA because AIDS is so likely to be a relatively expensive disease. If *McGann* is not reversed by the Supreme Court, the current regulatory environment suggests that groups considered socially expendable may continue to find their illnesses excluded from coverage without any recourse. Congress has not required that employers provide any health plans at all, and it seems reluctant therefore to mandate significant benefits or to prohibit discrimination in the plans employers do provide.

If nothing else, *McGann* has demonstrated the absurdity of a system in which health benefits are tied to employment. In a real insurance system, one can expand the risk-sharing aspect of insurance at the expense of the actuarial underwriting aspects and still fulfill the institutional purpose of the insurance company. In contrast, when the central purpose of the business enterprise is making money, regardless of the cost to employee health, the institutional purpose may not seem to be advanced by equitable provision of health benefits.

Thus, whereas the primary defects of our employment-linked health insurance system have in the past seemed to be the exclusion of so many by reason of unemployment, age, or failure of their employers to provide insurance, other defects affecting more influential segments of society have now become prominent. Employers who do provide benefits have begun to resent the negative effect of high health costs on profitability. Insured employees who find that their employers are willing to cancel important benefits in the interest of profits, and that their government is unwilling to step in to protect them, are now beginning to question the system as well.

Perhaps it is true that we must ration health care because we, as a society, cannot afford the medical establishment we have created. If so, the decision of how to ration should be a matter of reasoned policymaking and should not be ceded by the government to the whims, financial desires, or prejudices of individual employers. Once again, the gross unfairness suffered by people with HIV has highlighted significant defects in the insurance system as a whole. Once again, the positive outcome may be that as the debate over national health policy intensifies, this powerful example will help produce meaningful reform.

NOTES

1 Bradley v. Empire Blue Cross and Blue Shield, 149 Misc. 2d 20, 562 N.Y.S.2d 908 (Sup. Ct. 1990).

2 American Council of Life Insurance and Health Insurance Association of America, AIDS-related Claims Survey; Claims Paid in 1990.

3 U.S. Department of Health and Human Services, Public Health Services National Center for Health Services Research and Health Cancer Technology Assessment, Employer Based Health Insurance (1989).

4 American Council of Life Insurance, 1991 Life Insurance Fact Book Update 4.

5 Committee on Risk Classification, American Academy of Actuaries, Statement: Risk Classification and AIDS 2–3 (1986).

6 K. Abraham, Distributing Risk 71–74 (1986).

7 Committee on Risk Classification, note 5 above, at 1–2.

8 Padgug, *Looking Backward: Empire Blue Cross and Blue Shield as an Object of Histor-*ical Analysis, 16 J. Health Pol. Pol'y & L. 793 (1992).

9 Empire Blue Cross and Blue Shield, Proposal for New Rates and Rate Structure Affecting Certain Small Group and Direct Payment Customers (July 26, 1991).

10 S. Curiale, Superintendent of Insurance, Statement: Empire Blue Cross/Blue Shield Decision (Oct. 1, 1991); *Albany Denies Rate Increase for Leading Health Insurer*, N.Y. Times, Oct. 2, 1991, at 1; *Bill to Overhaul Health Insurance Passes in Albany*, N.Y. Times, July 2, 1992, at A1.

11 A. Trippler, Comprehensive Health Insurance for High-risk Individuals: A State-by-State Analysis (5th ed. 1991).

12 *Babies of Uninsured Parents Found to Be at Risk*, N.Y. Times, Aug. 24, 1989, at B13; *Uninsured Patients in Hospitals Are Found Far More Likely to Die*, N.Y. Times, Jan. 16, 1991, at A20.

13 15 U.S.C. §§ 1011–1015 (1988).

14 Health Ins. Ass'n v. Corcoran, 76 N.Y.2d 995, 564 N.Y.S.2d 713 (1990); Life Ins. Ass'n v. Singer, 403 Mass. Super. Ct. 410 (1988).

15 American Council of Life Ins. & Health Ins. Ass'n of Am. v. District of Columbia, 645 F. Supp. 84 (D.D.C. 1986).

16 *See, e.g.,* Conn. Gen. Stat. § 38a–816 (1991) (listing proscribed unfair trade practices).

17 Congressional Research Service, State Statutes Prohibiting Discrimination in Insurance on the Basis of Handicapping Conditions (1984); *see, e.g.,* Conn. Gen. Stat. § 38a–816 (1991) (defining as unfair insurance practice refusal of coverage or charging of different premiums to the blind, physically disabled, or mentally retarded except where based on sound actuarial principles or related to actual or reasonable anticipated experience); *id.* § 38a–493 (extending coverage by mandating home health care coverage in hospital or medical expense insurance policies); *id.* § 38a–538 (requiring extensions of coverage, at group insurance rates, to members of health insurance groups who become ineligible for continued participation in plan). Short-term extensions of group coverage at relatively low premiums are particularly important for people with AIDS and became broadly available to employees at companies with twenty or more employees as a result of the 1986 COBRA law. Pub. L. No. 99–272, 100 Stat. 223 (1986).

18 29 U.S.C. § 1001 *et seq.* (1988).

19 *See* Pilot Life Ins. Co. v. Dedeaux, 481 U.S. 41 (1987); Howard v. Gleason Corp., 901 F.2d 1154 (2d Cir. 1990).

20 Tolchin, *More Companies Choosing to Self-Insure Benefits,* N.Y. Times, Aug. 3, 1990, at D10. A majority of employees with medical coverage now work for self-insured companies, up from 5 percent in 1974. *See also* Greely, *AIDS and the American Health Care Financing System,* 51 U. Pitt. L. Rev. 73, 104–111 (1989).

21 Fewer than 40 percent of employees of firms with twenty-five or fewer employees have group health coverage, as opposed to more than 85 percent of those employed by firms with one thousand or more employees. M. Baily, Private Insurance and the HIV Epidemic (unpublished report, The George Washington University, HCFA Cooperative Agreement No. 18-C–99141/3–01, 1989). According to a 1987 survey, two-thirds of workers without employer-based coverage work for employers with fewer than twenty-five employees. Health Insurance Association of America, Health Care Financing for All Americans: Private Market Reform & Public Responsibility (1991).

22 In one reported 1986 episode, the persistence of the concept that homosexuality constitutes "immorality" for insurance purposes was demonstrated when an insurance investigator reported a gay applicant to be immoral, and the applicant was then asked to take an antibody test for life insurance. The request, by North American Life and Casualty Company, was revoked after a complaint to the California Insurance Department. *Insurance Company Reverses Anti-Gay Decision,* N.Y. Native, Aug. 11, 1986, at 6.

23 Office of Technology Assessment, AIDS and Health Insurance (1988).

24 National Gay Rights Advocates v. Great Republic Life Ins. Co., No. 857323 (Cal. Super. Ct., San Francisco), in which the court denied a motion by the insurer to dismiss the case in 1986, was finally settled in 1990, with an agreement not to use the questionnaire, a small damage payment to the individual plaintiff, and payment of eighty thousand dollars to the public interest lawyers who prosecuted the claim against Great Republic. 1990 Lesbian & Gay Law Notes at 43 (available from the Lesbian & Gay Law Association of Greater New York, P.O. Box 1899, Grand Central Station, N.Y., NY 10163).

25 *Gay Legal Organization Fights AIDS Insurance Bias,* N.Y. Native, May 19, 1986, at 12.

26 *Insurer Screening Unmarried Males,* N.Y. Times, Oct. 7, 1985, at 28.

27 National Association of Insurance Commissioners, Guidelines on Underwriting for AIDS (1986).

28 According to M. Baily, note 21 above, at 19, by 1989 eight states had adopted the guidelines and six others had adopted regulations with similar objectives.

29 Doe v. United Serv. Life Ins. Co., 88 Civ. 5630 (S.D.N.Y. Dec. 13, 1988). The case was settled without an admission by the defendant that it had discriminated against Doe, but with an agreement that it would nonetheless express its adherence to the National Association of Insurance Commissioners' guidelines. *See also* Doe v. United Servs. Life Ins. Co., 123 F.R.D. 437 (S.D.N.Y. 1988), granting the plaintiff's motion to prosecute this case under a pseudonym.

30 The industry's primary trade organizations, the American Council of Life Insurance (ACLI) and the Health Insurance Association of America (HIAA), officially endorsed the guidelines of the National Association of Insurance Commissioners (NAIC) and touted that endorsement as an affirmation that sexual orientation has no place in the underwriting process. Clifford & Iuculano, *AIDS and Insurance: The Rationale for AIDS-Related Testing,* 100 Harv. L. Rev. 1806, 1816 (1986). A spokesperson for the HIAA restated its opposition to the use of sexual orientation in underwriting when the Office of Technology Assessment reported that a large proportion of insurers were violating the NAIC guidelines in 1988. *Study Finds Most Health Insurers Screen Applicants for AIDS Virus,* N.Y. Times, Feb. 18, 1988, at 1. With respect to occupation, the industry's proposals for health insurance reform include issuance of small group policies to *all* small employers, regardless of their health risk. Health Insurance Association of America, Health Care Financing for All Americans: Private Market Reform and Public Responsibility (1991).

31 Jaffe, *et al.*, *The Acquired Immunodeficiency Syndrome in a Cohort of Homosexual Men, A Six-Year Follow Up Study,* 103 Annals Internal Med. 210 (1985).

32 Stone, *The Rhetoric of Insurance Law: The Debate over AIDS Testing,* 15 L. & Soc. Inquiry 385 (1990). Stone was analyzing principally the Clifford & Iuculano article referred to at note 30 above, and the counterpart commentary on behalf of the AIDS-affected communities, Schatz, *The AIDS Insurance Crisis: Underwriting or Overreaching?* 100 Harv. L. Rev. 1782 (1986).

33 Hunter & Angoff, *Insurers Are Right on AIDS Testing,* N.Y. Times, Sept. 18, 1987, at A39.

34 Cal. Health & Safety Code §§ 199.20-.23 (West 1990).

35 Wis. Stat. Ann. § 631.90 (West Supp. 1989) (legislation prohibiting HIV antibody testing generally for insurance purposes amended to terminate ban for insurance other than health insurance if state epidemiologist determined that test was reliable and insurance commissioner determined it was actuarially sound); Fla. Stat. Ann. § 627.429(5) (West Supp. 1990); R.I. Gen. Laws § 23–6–24 (1989). The Florida and Rhode Island statutes are quite weak. Rhode Island explicitly permits testing for small group (under twenty-five person) health insurance policies. Florida permits testing for any group policy for which individual underwriting is allowed by law.

36 One of the earliest suits alleging breach of confidentiality was Doe v. Prudential Life Ins. Co. of Am., 87 Civ. 2040 (S.D.N.Y. March 26, 1987), brought by Lambda Legal Defense and Education Fund in 1987. The case included an allegation that Prudential violated its obligations to keep plaintiff's test results confidential when an underwriter disclosed the results to a non-employee of Prudential. As part of a settlement, in which Prudential emphasized that its willingness to settle did not signify it admitted any of Doe's allegations, Prudential agreed to reinforce among its employees its existing policy on confidentiality with an emphasis on the sensitivity of AIDS-related information, and made a financial settlement with Doe. In Urbaniak v. Newton, 226 Cal. App. 3d 1128, 277 Cal. Rptr. 354 (1991), a California appellate court recently ruled that a person could sue a doctor who disclosed his positive HIV status to his employer, but not the workers compensation insurance company for which the doctor was working.

On the other end of the spectrum, the failure to disclose test results can have disastrous consequences as well. Although there has been much commentary on the rights of those unsuspecting people who become infected because the physician treating their infected spouse or sex partner did not disclose the infection, see Closen & Isaacman, *The Duty to Notify Private Third Parties of the Risks of HIV Infection,* 21 J. Health & Hosp. L. 295 (1988), the more novel cases (and, in the insurance context, the more likely ones) will be those brought by infected people who are not made aware of their own infection. One author has predicted that statutes which require that those tested for HIV be informed and counseled regarding the results will create tort liability for failure to inform or counsel. Closen, *Mandatory Disclosure of HIV Blood Test Results to the Individuals Tested: A Matter of Personal Choice Neglected,* 22 Loy. U. Chi. L.J. 445 (1991). Indeed, a physician who failed to disclose such results has been sued by a man who says he unintentionally infected several sex partners as the result of not being informed. Long v. Cutter, No. 89000525 (Cir. Ct., Roanoke, Va., May 25, 1989). Claims against insurers for negligent failure to disclose are also being litigated in New York and Washington, D.C.

37 Slevin v. Amex Life Ins. Co., 695 F. Supp. 712 (E.D.N.Y. 1988).

38 New England Mut. Life Ins. Co. v. Duke, No. 28359/87 (Sup. Ct. N.Y. Nov. 10, 1987).

39 Eckholm, *Health Benefits Found to Deter Switches in Jobs,* N.Y. Times, Sept. 26, 1991, at A1.

40 Mutual Benefit Health Accident Ass'n v. Ramage, 293 Ky. 586, 169 S.W.2d 624 (1943); Smith v. Benefit Ass'n of R. Employees, 187 Minn. 202, 244 N.W. 817 (1932).

41 Omnibus Budget Reconciliation Act of 1989, Pub. L. No. 101–239, § 6701, 103 Stat 2296, 2432–2433, 2435 (codified at 29 U.S.C. § 1162 (D)(i)) (1991).

42 *See* Health Insurance Association of America, Health Care Financing for all Americans: Private Market Reform & Public Responsibility (1991).

43 Weaver v. Reagan, 886 F.2d 194 (8th Cir. 1989).

44 29 U.S.C.A. § 1162(a) (1991).

45 A bill drafted by Gay Men's Health Crisis, an AIDS service organization, was introduced in 1992 to conform state continuation rules to federal COBRA rules.

46 Ky. Rev. Stat. Ann. § 304.12–230(7)(5)(b) (Michie/Bobbs-Merrill 1986).

47 N.Y. Comp. Code R. & Regs. tit. 11, § 52.40(f) (1991).

48 *See, e.g.,* Pirozzi v. Blue Cross-Blue Shield of Va., 741 F. Supp. 586 (E.D. Va. 1990) (breast cancer); Dosza v. Crum & Forster Ins. Co., 716 F. Supp. 131 (D.N.J. 1989) (multiple myeloma).

49 The issue is so important to cancer patients that they fought for and obtained special legislation in New York guaranteeing their reimbursement for off-label drugs when the prescription was supported by any peer-reviewed medical literature or medical compendia. N.Y. Ins. Law § 3221(1)(12) (McKinney 1992).

50 McGann v. H. & H. Music Co. & General Life Ins. Co., 946 F.2d 401 (5th Cir. 1991).

51 *Id.* at 404.

52 One recent study estimated that the average annual treatment cost for a person diagnosed with AIDS is $32 thousand, with a lifetime cost of about $85 thousand, while a person with HIV infection prior to an AIDS diagnosis has annual treatment costs averaging just over $5 thousand. Altman, *Outlay for AIDS Care in '91 Is Estimated at $5.8 Billion,* N.Y. Times, June 20, 1991, at A16. The average annual treatment cost for a person with hemophilia is double that of someone with AIDS—between $60 and $80 thousand, according to the National Hemophilias Foundation's testimony before the Prospective Payments Assessment Commission of the Health Care Financing Administration in the summer of 1991.

53 American Council of Life Insurance and Health Insurance Association of America, AIDS-Related Claims Survey, Claims Paid in 1990, at 8. According to Altman, note 52 above, national cancer treatment costs are more than six times greater than AIDS treatment costs; cardiovascular diseases cost more than sixteen times as much as AIDS.

54 State insurance departments in Indiana and California rejected requests by their local Blue Cross organizations to exclude AIDS coverage in the mid–1980s. *Indiana Blues Studying Cuts in AIDS Cover,* Business Ins., Feb. 24, 1986, at 4. According to National Gay Rights Advocates, eighteen state insurance departments responding to a survey said they

would not permit AIDS treatment exclusions or severe limitations in health policies. Florida and Washington, D.C., have statutorily prohibited AIDS exclusions, Fla. Stat. Ann. § 627.429(5) (West 1990); D.C. Code Ann. § 35–223(c) (1991), although Florida has a rather bizarre provision permitting an exclusion when an insured who was not asked health questions on a policy that could have been individually underwritten becomes sick in the first year, provided the insurer follows certain cumbersome procedures.

55 Ironically, Texas is not one of those states with regulations prohibiting AIDS exclusions, and its state insurance commission approved some policies with such exclusions in the mid–1980s. Texas does, however, now have specific bans on renegotiation of group medical insurance contracts to exclude particular illnesses for which benefits have been provided and on cancellations of policies because of diagnoses of HIV infection or AIDS. *See* Tex. Rev. Civ. Stat. Ann. art. 3.51–6c-d (West 1992).

56 42 U.S.C.A. § 12201(c) (West Supp. 1991); *see* Furfaro & Josephson, *Health Benefits of Employees with AIDS,* N.Y.L.J., May 3, 1991, at 3.

Contributors

Taunya Lovell Banks is professor of law at the University of Maryland School of Law. Professor Banks is the author of several articles on HIV-related legal issues and contributed a chapter on access to health care for *AIDS and the Law: A Guide for the Public*.

Allan M. Brandt is the Amalie Moses Kass Professor of the History of Medicine at Harvard Medical School's department of social medicine and professor of the history of science at Harvard University. Professor Brandt served on the National Academy of Sciences Committee on Monitoring the Social Impact of AIDS. He is author of *No Magic Bullet: A Social History of Venereal Disease in the United States since 1880*.

Troyen A. Brennan, M.D., a graduate of Yale University School of Medicine and Yale Law School, is an associate professor of medicine at Harvard Medical School and a physician at Brigham and Women's Hospital in Boston.

Helena Brett-Smith received her B.A. from Yale College and worked as a health educator in West Africa with the Peace Corps before obtaining her M.D. degree at Stanford University. She completed her residency and infectious disease training at Yale-New Haven Hospital. Since 1989 she has been a member of the Yale-New Haven AIDS Care Program and is director of AIDS Services at the Hospital of St. Raphael in New Haven.

Scott Burris is assistant professor of law at Temple Law School and counsel of the AIDS and Civil Liberties Project of the ACLU of Pennsylvania. Professor Burris has written extensively about HIV and the law and has litigated significant HIV-related cases involving access to health care, employment discrimination, and management of HIV in prisons.

Harlon L. Dalton is a professor of law at Yale Law School. He is a member of the National Commission on AIDS and of the New Haven Mayor's Task Force on AIDS. He serves on the editorial boards of AIDS Alert and of the Archives of Sexual Behavior, on the board of visitors of the CUNY Law School at Queens College, on the board of governors of the Society of American Law Teachers, and on the boards of directors of the Legal Action Center and of New Haven's AIDS Interfaith Network, Inc. (chairperson). He is the author of, inter alia, *AIDS in Blackface*.

Donna I. Dennis graduated from Yale Law School in 1987 and also holds an M.A. and a B.A. degree in history from Yale. Ms. Dennis was executive editor of *AIDS and the Law: A Guide for the Public*. She currently serves as an assistant attorney general with the Civil Rights Bureau of the Office of the New York Attorney General.

Daniel M. Fox became president of the Milbank Medical Fund in 1990. Before that he was professor of social sciences and humanities in medicine and director of the Center for Assessing Health Services at the State University of New York at Stony Brook. He holds A.B., A.M., and Ph.D. degrees in history from Harvard University, where he taught before going to Stony Brook in 1971. He has also served in state government in Massachusetts and on the staff of several federal agencies. He has written numerous articles on public policy, the history of medicine, health affairs and photography and several books which include the prize-winning *The Discovery of Abundance* (1967), *Economists and Health Care* (1979), *Health Politics, Health Policies: The Experience of Britain and America 1911–1965* (1986), and *Photographing Medicine: Images and Power in Britain and America since 1840* (1988). He recently co-edited and contributed to *AIDS: The Burdens of History* (1988), *Financing Care for Persons with AIDS: The First Studies, 1985–88* (1989), *Disability Policy: Restoring Social and Economic Independence* (1989), and the forthcoming *AIDS: The Making of a Chronic Disease* (1992).

Alexa Freeman is a senior staff attorney with the National Prison Project of the American Civil Liberties Union where she litigates class action cases challenging conditions of confinement for prisoners and juvenile offenders and directs its AIDS Project.

Gerald H. Friedland, M.D., is a professor of medicine, epidemiology, and public health at the Yale University School of Medicine and is the director of the Yale

AIDS Program. Formerly, he was a professor at the Albert Einstein College of Medicine and a co-director of the Montefiore Medical Center's AIDS Center. He is a fellow of the American College of Physicians. Dr. Friedland is the co-editor of *AIDS Clinical Care* and serves on the editorial board of *AIDS*. He serves on numerous boards and advisory committees, including the Drug and Vaccine Development Roundtable, Institute of Medicine, National Academy of Sciences. He has authored and co-authored many articles, including the watershed "Lack of Transmission of HTLV-III/LAV Infection to Household Contacts of Patients with AIDS or AIDS-Related Complex with Oral Candidiasis."

Larry Gostin is executive director of the American Society of Law and Medicine; adjunct professor of health law, Harvard School of Public Health; and lecturer on law, Harvard Law School. Mr. Gostin also sits on policy steering committees for the World Health Organization (WHO), the Council for International Organizations of Medical Sciences (CIOMS), and the U.S. Centers for Disease Control (CDC). He was consulting legislative counsel for the U.S. Senate Labor and Human Relations Committee and conducted a bi-partisan briefing of U.S. senators in the Senate. Mr. Gostin is director of the AIDS Litigation Project, supported by the National AIDS Program Office, Department of Health and Human Services. He was also co-chair for the law and policy track of the Eighth International Conference on AIDS, sponsored by Harvard University and held in the Netherlands, July 1992. Mr. Gostin is editor of *AIDS in the Health Care System*.

Donald H. J. Hermann holds a doctorate in philosophy as well as a graduate degree in law. He is professor of law and philosophy and director of the Health Law Institute at the DePaul University College of Law. Professor Hermann is a member of the American Academy of Hospital Attorneys, serving as editor of its monthly publication, *The Journal of Health and Hospital Law*. He is co-author of the treatise *Legal Aspect of AIDS* and *AIDS Law in a Nutshell*. He is currently working on a book on AIDS and art.

Arthur S. Leonard is professor of law at New York Law School, co-chair of the Committee on Lesbians and Gay Men in the Legal Profession, and a member of the Special Committee on AIDS of the Association of the Bar of the City of New York. He is a member of the Legal Advisory Committee and a former member of the board of directors of Lambda Legal Defense and Education Fund and is newsletter editor and past chair of the Section on Gay and Lesbian Legal Issues of the Association of American Law Schools. A frequent lecturer on issues involving AIDS at legal seminars for practicing attorneys, Professor Leonard is co-author of *AIDS Law in a Nutshell* and *AIDS: Cases and Materials*. He authored the first law journal article to be published on AIDS discrimination (in 1985).

Daniel R. Mandelker, holder of two graduate degrees in law, is Stamper Professor of Law at Washington University Law School, as well as a frequent consultant on municipal planning and zoning issues to cities across the United States. He is a member of the Development Regulations Council of the Urban Land Institute and has consulted with the Advisory Commission on Intergovernmental Relations on environmental regulation. Professor Mandelker is author or co-author of nearly twenty books and dozens of articles and book chapters on housing, zoning, and land use.

Belinda Ann Mason, a journalist and fiction writer, lived in rural Kentucky until her death in September 1991. In 1987 she was diagnosed with HIV and, thereafter, with AIDS. In 1988 she founded the Kentuckiana People with AIDS Coalition, the first organization of its kind in either Kentucky or Indiana. In 1989–90 she served as the president of the National Association of People with AIDS, and later as its chair emeritus. From 1990 to 1991, she served on the board of the AIDS Action Council in Washington, D.C. From 1989 to 1991, she was a member of the National Commission on AIDS. She was the recipient of numerous honors and awards including a distinguished leadership award from the Kentucky legislature.

Judith Leonie Miller is associate director for development at Yale Law School and a freelance editor. Before coming to Yale, she practiced law and taught legal writing for a number of years in Portland, Oregon.

Mark Scherzer is an attorney in private practice in New York City, concentrating on insurance and employee benefit law. Mr. Scherzer is a cooperating attorney for Gay Men's Health Crisis and Lambda Legal Defense and Education Fund. He has written practice guides for attorneys representing people with HIV and has been active at the state level with New Yorkers for Accessible Health Coverage, advocating for insurance reform.

Index